Signature

ADVANCED
MICROSOFT® WORD 2003
Desktop Publishing

Joanne Arford

College of DuPage • Glen Ellyn, Illinois

Judy Burnside

College of DuPage • Glen Ellyn, Illinois
Wheaton Warrenville South High School • Wheaton, Illinois

EMCParadigm
PUBLISHING

Developmental Editor	Desiree Faulkner
Cover and Text Designer	Leslie Anderson
Desktop Production	Desktop Solutions
Copyeditor	Susan Capecchi
Proofreader	Sharon O'Donnell
Indexer	Nancy Fulton

Publishing Team: George Provol, Publisher; Janice Johnson, Director of Product Development; Tony Galvin, Acquisitions Editor; Lori Landwer, Marketing Manager; Shelley Clubb, Electronic Design and Production Manager.

Acknowledgments: The authors and publisher wish to thank the following individuals for their academic and technical contributions:
- Nita Rutkosky, Pierce College at Puyallup, Puyallup, Washington
- Janet Blum, Fanshawe College, London, Ontario, Canada
- Nancy Stanko, College of DuPage, Glen Ellyn, Illinois

Permissions: The following have generously given permission for use of their materials: Edward Cardiovascular Institute, Naperville, Illinois; Floyd Rogers, Butterfield Gardens, Warrenville, Illinois; Naperville Chamber of Commerce, Naperville, Illinois; Dr. Bradley Kampschroeder, Naper Grove Vision Care, Naperville, Illinois; Bernadette and Roger Budny, The Summer Place, Inc., Naperville, Illinois; Wendy Felder, Assistant Professor, College of DuPage, Glen Ellyn, Illinois; Crowe Chizek & Company LLC, Oak Brook, Illinois; Jennifer Heyer, Student, College of DuPage, Glen Ellyn, Illinois; Entella Papajani, Student, College of DuPage, Glen Ellyn, Illinois.

Text: ISBN 0-7638-2182-9
Order number: 05649

© 2005 by Paradigm Publishing Inc.
  Published by **EMC**Paradigm
  875 Montreal Way
  St. Paul, MN 55102

  (800) 535-6865
  E-mail: educate@emcp.com
  Web Site: www.emcp.com

Contents

Contents

Introduction

Advanced Microsoft® Word 2003: Desktop Publishing by Joanne Arford and Judy Dwyer Burnside addresses the expanded desktop publishing features of Microsoft Word 2003. This textbook focuses primarily on advanced Word 2003 features with an emphasis on desktop publishing terminology and concepts. Word 2003 and other Office 2003 integrated applications, such as Excel, Access, PowerPoint, and Microsoft Publisher, allow the desktop publisher to create professional-looking documents in an efficient manner. In addition, Word's hyperlinks to the Microsoft Office Online Template Web page and the Microsoft Office Online Clip Art and Media Web site provide opportunities for students to customize templates and add graphical elements. Desktop publishing greatly reduces the cost of publishing documents, combines the roles of page designer and typesetter, offers immediate results, and allows control of production from start to finish.

Text Pedagogy

Advanced Microsoft Word 2003: Desktop Publishing is designed for students who are proficient in word processing. This textbook assumes that students are using a custom or full installation of Microsoft Word 2003, as part of the Office 2003 Professional Edition, in a computer lab or home study setting.

Most of the key desktop publishing concepts addressed in this textbook are presented in Chapter 1. Reinforcement and application of these key concepts are presented in the subsequent chapters. The applications are designed to develop skills in critical thinking, decision making, and creativity. Many applications in this textbook are designed to reinforce collaborative learning in planning, designing, and evaluating business and personal documents. In numerous applications, basic information is given for a task just as it may be given in a real-life situation.

If the student wishes to build a portfolio of documents for course requirements or job applications, particular exercises are identified for this purpose with a portfolio icon.

Emphasis on Visual Learning

In keeping with the Windows graphical environment, figures that illustrate numerous steps done at the computer are labeled with visual callouts corresponding to the steps. Students can easily follow the steps by seeing the exact spot on the computer screen where a certain action is required on their part.

Structure of the Text

The textbook contains three units with a total of 12 chapters. Each chapter contains the following elements:

- Performance Objectives
- List of desktop publishing terms with definitions in the margins
- List of Word 2003 features used
- Introductory overview of chapter concepts and features
- DTP Pointers in the margin to reinforce concepts
- Hands-on exercises within each chapter to reinforce concepts
- Chapter Summary
- Commands Review
- Reviewing Key Points (multiple choice, true/false, completion, or short answer review)
- Applying Your Skills (skill assessment exercises)

Design
and Create

The Applying Your Skills section includes Integrated assessments (except Chapter 1) and a Design and Create assessment. In the Integrated assessments students use the skills learned in the chapter and incorporate elements from other applications. These exercises are identified with an Integrated icon. The Design and Create assessment promotes collaborative learning, critical thinking, and individual creativity and is identified with a Design and Create icon.

Each unit ends with Performance Assessments that evaluate students' mastery of both the desktop publishing concepts and software skills presented in the unit.

Primary Program Outcomes

Students who successfully complete this course will have mastered the following competencies:

- Use and apply the design concepts of focus, balance, proportion, contrast, directional flow, consistency, and color.
- Evaluate documents for the use of basic design concepts.
- Integrate basic layout and design concepts, using desktop publishing features of Microsoft Word 2003, to enhance the readability of multiple-page, portrait or landscape documents such as letterheads, merged postcards, business cards, personal documents, certificates, labels, name tags, flyers, brochures, promotional documents, business forms, online forms, presentational materials, and newsletters.
- Produce and enhance business and personal documents with variable page layouts using standardized type and graphic design techniques while incorporating new Word 2003 features such as watermarks, varying letter and word spacing, styles, drawing canvas, AutoFormat, and smart tags along with Microsoft Office Online Template Web page and Word document templates.
- Manage Word 2003 document files and folders using a Windows operating system.
- Publish Word documents in a variety of formats, including PowerPoint presentations and Web pages.

- Become familiar with the basic features and capabilities of Microsoft Publisher 2003 to produce professional-looking flyers, brochures, and newsletters.

The authors would like to encourage the use of predesigned papers and label sheets for some documents, and the introduction of scanners and digital cameras if available.

Completing Computer Exercises

Some computer exercises in this textbook require that you open an existing file. Exercise files are saved on the CD that accompanies this textbook. The files you need for each chapter are saved in individual folders. Before beginning a chapter, copy the necessary folder from the CD to a preformatted data disk. After completing exercises in a chapter, delete the chapter folder before copying the next chapter folder. (Check with your instructor before deleting a folder.)

The Student CD also contains model answers in PDF format for the exercises within (but not at the end of) each chapter so you can check your work. To access the PDF files, you will need to have Adobe Acrobat Reader installed on your computer's hard drive. The program and installation instructions are included on the Student CD in the AdobeAcrobatReader folder.

For more information on copying a folder, deleting a folder, and viewing or print the exercise model answers see the inside back cover of this textbook.

Points to Remember

As you work through the desktop publishing information and exercises, you need to be aware of the following important points:

- All default formatting settings, such as fonts, margin settings, line spacing, and justification; toolbars; templates; and folders used in this textbook are based on the assumption that none of the original defaults have been customized after installation.
- Instructions for all features and exercises emphasize using the mouse. Where appropriate, keyboard or function key presses are added as an alternative.
- As you complete the exercises, view the completed figure that follows each exercise to see what the document should look like.
- Be aware that the final appearance of your printed documents depends on the printer you use to complete the exercises. Your printer driver may be different from the printer driver used for the exercises in this textbook. For example, not all printer drivers interpret line height the same, nor do they offer the same font selections. Consequently, you may have to make some minor adjustments when completing the exercises in this book. For instance, if you have to select an alternative font from the one called for in the instructions, you may need to change the type size to complete the exercise in the space allotted. You may also need to adjust the spacing between paragraphs or specific blocks of text. As a result, your documents will look slightly different from what you see in this text. As you will find in the chapters that follow, creating desktop published documents is a constant process of making small adjustments to fine-tune the layout and design.

Learning Components Available with This Text

Signature Internet Resource Center at www.emcp.com

The Signature Internet Resource Center provides a wealth of Web-based resources for students and teachers, including course syllabi, study aids, vital Web links, numerous tests and quizzes, a wide variety of performance tests, and PowerPoint presentations. The Student data files necessary for completion of exercises are available to be downloaded.

Instructor's Guide

The Instructor's Guide is available on CD and on the Internet Resource Center and contains suggested course syllabi, grade sheets, and assignment sheets; comprehensive unit tests and answers for use as final exams; Supplemental Performance Assessments; and model answers for all exercises, and for all end-of-chapter and end-of-unit assessments. For each chapter, the Instructor's Guide also provides a summary of chapter content, Teaching Hints, and Reviewing Key Points answers.

UNIT one

CREATING BUSINESS AND PERSONAL DOCUMENTS

CHAPTER 1

Understanding the Desktop Publishing Process

PERFORMANCE OBJECTIVES

Upon successful completion of Chapter 1, you will be able to evaluate design elements in a desktop published document for the appropriate use of focus, balance, proportion, contrast, directional flow, consistency, color, and page layout.

CHAPTER01

DESKTOP PUBLISHING TERMS

Alignment	Contrast	Symmetrical design
Asymmetrical design	Directional flow	Thumbnail sketch
Balance	Focus	White space
Color	Legibility	Z pattern
Consistency	Proportion	

WORD FEATURES USED

Getting Started task pane	Microsoft Office Online Templates
Microsoft Office Document Imaging	Microsoft Office Picture Manager
Microsoft Office Online Assistance	New Document task pane
Microsoft Office Online Clip Art and Media	Open as Read-Only
	Page Setup

Defining Desktop Publishing

Since the 1970s, computers have been an integral part of the business environment. Businesses use computers and software packages to perform a variety of tasks. For many years, the three most popular types of software purchased for computers were word processing, spreadsheet, and database. The introduction of the laser printer and the inkjet printer, with their ability to produce high-quality documents, in black and white as well as in color, led to the growing popularity of another kind of software called desktop publishing.

Desktop publishing involves using desktop publishing software, such as Microsoft Publisher 2003, or word processing software with desktop publishing capabilities, such as Microsoft Word 2003. Desktop publishing allows the user to produce professional-looking documents for both office and home use. The phrase "desktop publishing," coined by Aldus Corporation president Paul Brainard, means that publishing can now literally take place at your desk.

Until the mid-1980s, graphic design depended almost exclusively on design professionals. However, desktop publishing software changed all that by bringing graphic design into the office and home. Faster microprocessors, larger storage capacity, improved printer capabilities, an increased supply of clip art, CD-ROMs, and access to the Internet continue to expand the role of desktop publishing. Imagine everything from a flyer to a newsletter to a Web page designed, created, and produced at your own computer.

In traditional publishing, several people may be involved in completing a publication project, thus increasing the costs and the time needed to complete the project. With the use of desktop publishing software, one person may be performing all of the tasks necessary to complete a project, greatly reducing the costs of publishing documents. The two approaches, however, do have a great deal in common. Both approaches involve planning the project, organizing content, analyzing layout and design, arranging design elements, typesetting, printing, and distributing the project.

Desktop publishing can be an individual or a combined effort. As an individual effort, desktop publishing produces immediate results and offers you the ability to control the production from beginning layout and design to the end result—printing and distribution. However, desktop publishing and traditional publishing work well together. A project may begin on a desktop, where the document is designed and created, but an illustrator may be commissioned to create some artwork, and the piece may be sent to a commercial printer for printing and binding.

This book is designed to help those who possess an advanced skill level with Microsoft Word but who have little or no design experience. Today's office support staff are increasingly being required to create more sophisticated documents with little or no background on how to design a visually appealing document that still gets the message across to the reader. Home users are also finding the need to create similar professional-looking documents, whether it is for a home business, an organization, or personal use.

Initiating the Desktop Publishing Process

DTP POINTERS
Consider the demographics of your target audience.

The process of creating a publication begins with two steps—planning the publication and creating the content. During the planning process, the desktop publisher must decide on the purpose of the publication and identify the intended audience. When creating the content, the desktop publisher must make sure that the reader understands the publication's intended message.

Planning the Publication

Initial planning is probably one of the most important steps in the desktop publishing process. During this stage, consider the following:

- **Clearly identify the purpose of your communication.** The more definite you are about your purpose, the easier it will be for you to organize your material into an effective communication. Are you trying to provide information? Are you trying to sell a product? Are you announcing an event?

- **Assess your target audience.** Who will read your publication? Are they employees, coworkers, clients, friends, or family? What will your target audience expect from your publication? Do they expect a serious, more conservative approach, or an informal, humorous approach?

- **Determine in what form your intended audience will be exposed to your message.** Will your message be in a brochure as part of a packet of presentation materials for a company seminar? Or will your message take the form of a newspaper advertisement, surrounded by other advertisements? Will your message be in the form of a business card distributed when making sales calls? Or will your message be tacked on a bulletin board?

- **Decide what you want your readers to do after reading your message.** Do you want your readers to ask for more information? Do you want some kind of a response? Do you want your readers to be able to contact you in person or over the telephone?

- **Collect examples of effective designs.** Keep a design idea folder. Put copies of any designs that impress you into your idea folder. These designs may include flyers, promotional documents, newsletters, graphic images, interesting type arrangements, and the like. Look through your idea folder every time you begin a new project. Let favorite designs serve as a catalyst for developing your own ideas.

Creating the Content

The most important goal in desktop publishing is to get the message across. Design is important because it increases the visual appeal of your document, but content is still the most important consideration. Create a document that communicates the message clearly to your intended audience.

In analyzing your message, identify your purpose and start organizing your material. Establish a hierarchy of importance among the items in your communication. Consider what items will be the most important to the reader, what will attract the reader's attention, and what will spark enough interest for the reader to go on. Begin to think about the format or layout you want to follow. (Check your idea folder!) Clear and organized content combined with an attractive layout and design contributes to the effectiveness of your message.

DTP POINTERS
Pick up design ideas from the works of others.

Designing the Document

If the message is the most significant part of a communication, why bother with design? A well-planned and relevant design sets your work apart from others, and it gets people to read your message. Just as people may be judged by their appearance, a publication may be judged by its design. Design also helps organize ideas so the reader can find information quickly and easily. Whether you are creating a business flyer, letterhead, or newsletter, anything you create will look more attractive, more professional, and more convincing if you take a little extra time to design it. As in the planning stages, consider the purpose of the document, the target audience, and the method of distribution. In addition, think about the following factors:

DTP POINTERS
Take the time to design!

- What feeling does the document elicit?
- What is the most important information and how can it be emphasized so that the reader can easily identify the purpose of the document?
- What different types of information are presented and how can these elements be distinguished, yet kept internally consistent?
- How much space is available?

Answering these questions will help you determine the design and layout of your communication.

Thumbnail sketch
A rough sketch used in planning a layout and design.

An important first step in planning your design and layout is to prepare a thumbnail sketch. A *thumbnail sketch* is a miniature draft of the document you are attempting to create. As you can see in Figure 1.1, thumbnail sketches let you experiment with alternative locations for such elements as graphic images, ruled lines (horizontal or vertical lines), columns, and borders.

FIGURE 1.1 *Thumbnail Sketches*

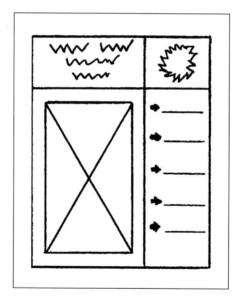
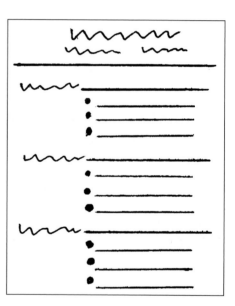

A good designer continually asks questions, pays attention to details, and makes well-thought-out decisions. Consider examples A and B in Figure 1.2. Which example attracts your attention, entices you to read on, looks convincing, and encourages you to take action?

FIGURE

1.2 *Before and After Documents*

A

ANNOUNCING
Ultra Fast Heart Scan

from the Edward
Cardiovascular Institute

15 minutes, start to finish…
Take it during your lunch hour.
(And be back in time for your 1 o'clock meeting.)

Ultra Fast Heart Scan is the simple, non-invasive heart test you've heard about—the one that uses powerful electron beam tomography to detect coronary artery calcification at an early, treatable state. It's the only test in the western suburbs with this technology.
To schedule your appointment, call Monday–Friday
8 a.m. to 5 p.m.
1-877-45-HEART

EDWARD
CARDIOVASCULAR INSTITUTE

B

ANNOUNCING

Ultra *Fast* Heart Scan

from the Edward
Cardiovascular Institute

15 minutes, start to finish…

Take it during your lunch hour…
(And be back in time for your 1 o'clock meeting.)

Ultra Fast Heart Scan is the simple, non-invasive heart test you've heard about—the one that uses powerful electron beam tomography to detect coronary artery calcification at an early, treatable state. It's the only test in the western suburbs with this technology.

To schedule your appointment, call Monday–Friday, 8 a.m. to 5 p.m.

1-877-45-HEART

EDWARD
CARDIOVASCULAR INSTITUTE

Overdesigning is one of the most common tendencies of beginning desktop publishers. The temptation to use as many of the desktop publishing features as possible in one document is often difficult to resist. Use design elements to communicate, not decorate. To create a visually attractive and appealing publication, start with the same classic design concepts professional designers use as guidelines. These concepts include focus, balance, proportion, contrast, directional flow, consistency, and color.

Creating Focus

The *focus* or focal point on a page is an element that draws the reader's eyes. Focus uses elements that are large, dense, unusual, and/or surrounded by white space. Two basic design elements used to create focus in a document are:

Focus
An element used to attract the reader's eyes.

- text created in larger, bolder, and often contrasting, typefaces;
- graphic elements such as ruled lines, clip art, photographs, illustrations, watermarks, logos, or images created with a draw program, scanned into the computer, or captured with a digital camera.

Creating Focus with Text

You will recognize focus instantly whether the focus is a graphic or text typed in strong, contrasting fonts. Text with weight, contrasting style, expanded letter-spacing, varying font sizes, reversed color, shape (WordArt), and even drop caps can effectively draw the reader's attention. To promote a clean-looking document, use the actual fonts from your computer, such as Arial Rounded MT Bold, rather than applying bold or italics to Arial. Organizing similar text, using a consistent strong alignment, and providing generous amounts of white space enhance the appeal of text as focus. ***White space*** is the background where no text or graphics are located. The amount of white space around a focal element can enhance its appearance and help to balance other design elements on the page.

White space
Background space with no text or graphics.

Notice the use of text as a focal point in Figure 1.3B. The title "Kids at College" is formatted in Whimsy ICG Heavy, which is a youthful, whimsical font. This formatted text along with a generous amount of white space generates focus in contrast to the unformatted text in document A. Also, notice the impact the reverse text has on the school name.

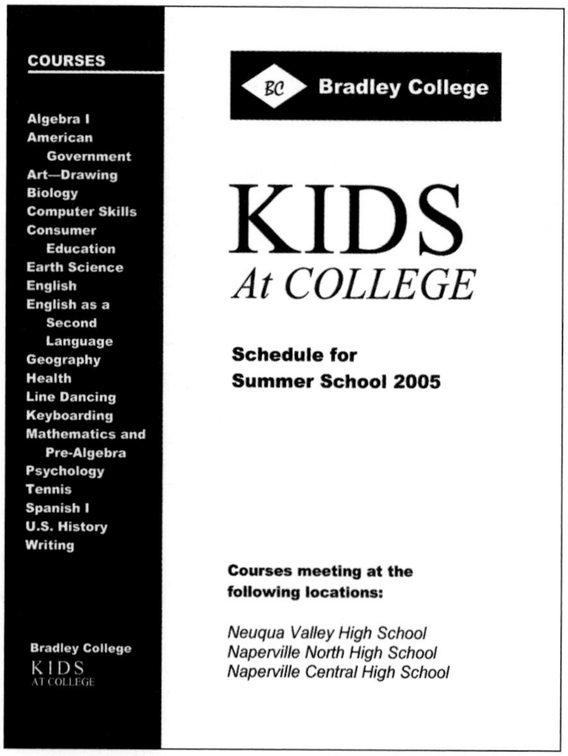

FIGURE 1.3 ***Creating Focus with Text***

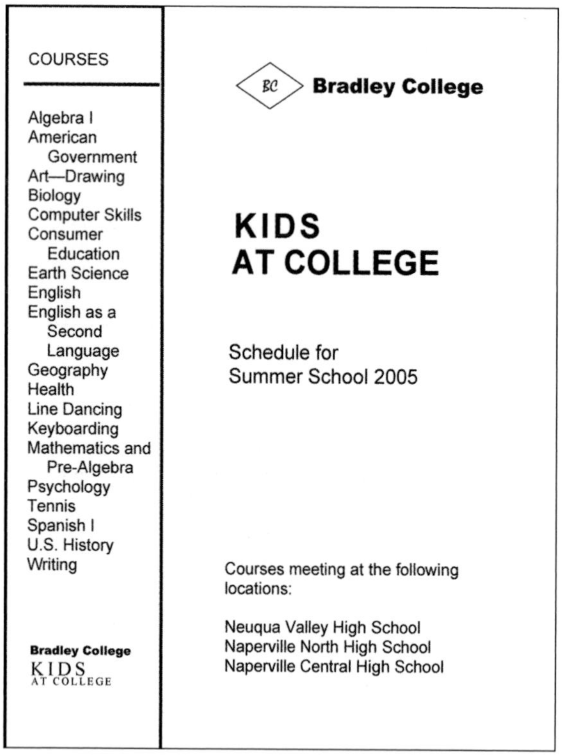

COURSES

Algebra I
American Government
Art—Drawing
Biology
Computer Skills
Consumer Education
Earth Science
English
English as a Second Language
Geography
Health
Line Dancing
Keyboarding
Mathematics and Pre-Algebra
Psychology
Tennis
Spanish I
U.S. History
Writing

Bradley College
KIDS
AT COLLEGE

BC Bradley College

KIDS
AT COLLEGE

Schedule for
Summer School 2005

Courses meeting at the following locations:

Neuqua Valley High School
Naperville North High School
Naperville Central High School

A

COURSES

Algebra I
American Government
Art—Drawing
Biology
Computer Skills
Consumer Education
Earth Science
English
English as a Second Language
Geography
Health
Line Dancing
Keyboarding
Mathematics and Pre-Algebra
Psychology
Tennis
Spanish I
U.S. History
Writing

Bradley College
KIDS
AT COLLEGE

BC Bradley College

KIDS
At COLLEGE

Schedule for
Summer School 2005

Courses meeting at the following locations:

Neuqua Valley High School
Naperville North High School
Naperville Central High School

B

Creating Focus with Titles, Headlines, and Subheadings

DTP POINTERS
A well-designed headline attracts the reader's attention.

In reports, procedure manuals, newsletters, term papers, and tables of contents, titles, headlines, and subheadings use large or bold type, surrounded by enough white space to contrast with the main text. When creating titles/headlines, keep the following points in mind:

Legibility
The ease with which individual characters are recognized.

- State your title or headline in a precise, yet easily understood manner.
- Select readable typefaces. ***Legibility*** is of utmost importance. Readers must be able to clearly see and read the individual letters in the title/headline.

- Size your title or headline in proportion to its importance relative to the surrounding text.
- Set your title or headline in a larger type size so the reader immediately knows the nature of the publication.

In any type of communication—a semiannual report, company newsletter, advertising flyer, or brochure—subheads may provide a secondary focal element. While headlines attract the reader's attention, the subheads may be the key to luring in the reader. Subheads provide order to your text and give the reader further clues about the content of your publication. Include appropriate fonts, line length, line spacing, and alignment.

Look at document A in Figure 1.4. Does any particular location on the page attract your attention? You might say the title attracts your attention slightly. Now look at document B in the same figure. Do you agree that the bolded text attracts your attention? Now look at document C. Do the title and subheads attract your attention more so than in documents A and B? The title is the primary focal point. The subheads, set in a type bolder and larger than the body text but smaller than the heading, provide secondary focal points on the page. Notice how the consistent font selection in all of the subheads makes the document's organization readily apparent to the reader. Also, notice that there is more white space before the subheads than after. This spacing connects the subhead to the text that follows.

DTP POINTERS
Subheads provide order to your text and give the reader further clues about the content of your publication.

FIGURE

1.4 *Evaluating the Use of Titles and Subheadings*

A

B

C

Creating Focus with Graphic Elements

Graphic elements provide focus on a page and can enhance the overall appearance of a publication. The following graphic elements establish focus in your document:

- ruled lines (horizontal or vertical lines of varying sizes and thickness; see Chapter 3)

- clip art (see Chapter 5)
- cropped images (to trim horizontal or vertical edges of an object; see Chapters 3, 5)
- watermarks (a lightened version of an image; see Chapter 2)
- AutoShapes (drawing objects; see Chapter 5)
- photographs (scanned, digital camera, online; see Chapter 5)
- charts, graphs, and diagrams (see Chapter 9)
- tables (AutoFormat; see Chapter 2)
- pull quotes (a direct phrase, summarizing statement, or important point associated with the body text; see Chapter 11)
- sidebars (a block of information or a related story that is set off from the body text in some type of a graphics box; see Chapter 11)
- preprinted papers (see Chapter 1)

When considering a graphic element as a focal point, remember the following points:

- Legibility is just as important with graphic elements as it is with titles and subheads. Graphic elements should support the message in your text and not interfere with its readability in any way.
- Communicate, do not decorate. Let your message dictate the use of graphic elements. Does the graphic element enhance your message or does it overshadow your message? Is it relevant, meaningful, and appropriate? Do not use it just for the sake of using it.
- Less is best; keep it simple. One simple, large, and effective graphic image provides more impact than using several smaller images. Too many images create visual confusion for the reader.
- Crop an image if necessary to increase impact. Crop to eliminate unnecessary elements and zoom in on the key parts of an image or crop in unexpected ways to draw attention to the image.
- Position the graphic to face the text. Graphics or photographs facing away from the text draw the reader's eyes away from the most important part of the document—the content. Compare documents A and B in Figure 1.5. The graphic in document B is a focal point positioned appropriately in the document.

DTP POINTERS
Graphic images should be relevant to your intended message.

DTP POINTERS
Keep your design simple.

DTP POINTERS
Graphics should face the text.

1.5 *Graphic Positioned in a Document*

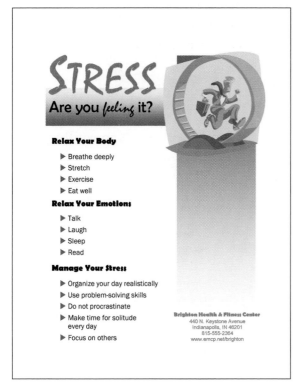

A

B

If all other factors are equal, publications containing graphic elements are noticed and perused before text-only publications. The chamber of commerce announcement A shown in Figure 1.6 is not as effective as announcement B. The sun graphic/watermark creates a major focal point. "Good Morning Naperville" stands out as a focal point, but not as strongly as the image. Varying the type size and typestyle helps to organize the remaining information and to provide minor focal points on the page.

Good Morning Naperville

If daytime luncheons and meetings don't work for you,
mark your calendar now for the second in a series of
General Membership Breakfast Meetings.
Start your day off with a breakfast full of
networking that will surely
get you on the right track.
Monday, September 19, 2005
7 a.m. – 8:30 a.m.
Holiday Inn Select
1801 N. Naper Blvd.
Naperville, IL
Topic: *Mergers & Acquisitions—How Do They Impact Our
Community?*
$15 for Members, $20 for Non-Members
RSVP to the Naperville Chamber of Commerce
by Thursday, September 15, 2005
(630) 555-4141 or chamber@emcp.net

A

Good Morning Naperville

If daytime luncheons and meetings don't work for you,
mark your calendar now for the second in a series of
General Membership Breakfast Meetings.

Start your day off with a breakfast full of
networking that will surely get you on the right track.

Monday, September 19, 2005
7 a.m. – 8:30 a.m.
Holiday Inn Select, 1801 N. Naper Blvd.
Naperville, IL

Topic: *Mergers & Acquisitions—How
Do They Impact Our Community?*
$15 for Members, $20 for Non-Members

RSVP to the Naperville Chamber of Commerce
by Thursday, September 15, 2005
(630) 555-4141 or chamber@emcp.net

B

Creating Balance

Balance

The equal distribution of design elements on a page.

Attain *balance* by equally distributing the visual weight of various elements, such as blocks of text, graphic images, headings, ruled lines, and white space on the page. Balance is either symmetrical or asymmetrical.

Symmetrical Balance

Symmetrical design

Balancing similar elements equally on a page (centered alignment).

A *symmetrical design* contains similar elements of equal proportion or weight on the left and right sides and top and bottom of the page. Symmetrical balance is easy to achieve because all elements are centered on the page. If you were to fold a symmetrically designed document in half vertically (in other words, along its vertical line of symmetry), you would see that both halves of the document contain the same elements.

To better visualize the concept of symmetrical balance, look at the shapes in the top half of Figure 1.7. The squares, representing identical graphic elements, are positioned on the left and right sides of the page. The rectangle, representing a block of text, is centered in between the two squares. Notice the dotted line, representing a vertical line of symmetry, splitting the design in half. It is easy to see that the elements on both sides of the dotted line are equal in weight and proportion because they are the same. Now look at the example of a symmetrically designed letterhead in the bottom half of Figure 1.7. If you were to extend that same line of symmetry down through the sample letterhead, you would see equally distributed design elements on both sides of the page.

1.7 *Symmetrical Balance*

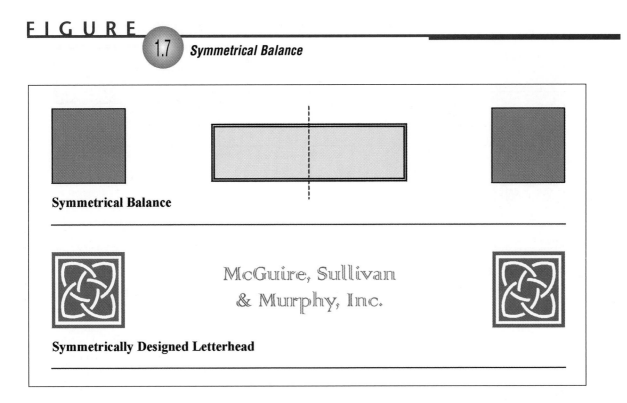

Symmetrical Balance

Symmetrical Balance

McGuire, Sullivan
& Murphy, Inc.

Symmetrically Designed Letterhead

Asymmetrical Balance

Symmetrical balance is easy to identify and to create. However, contemporary design favors asymmetrical balance. An ***asymmetrical design*** uses different design elements of varying weights and/or proportions to achieve balance on a page. Asymmetrical design is more flexible and visually stimulating than symmetrical design. Look at the shapes in the top half of Figure 1.8. Notice the dotted line (the line of vertical symmetry) that divides the page in half. Do both sides match? Are there similar or identical elements on both sides? Even without the dotted line, you can easily see that both sides do not match. Therefore, you know immediately that this is not a symmetrical design. However, just because the design is not symmetrical does not automatically mean that it is not visually balanced.

Remember, the key to asymmetrical design is achieving a visual balance on the page using dissimilar or contrasting elements. Look again at the shapes and the white space surrounding the shapes in Figure 1.8. Even though they differ and are not centered, would you agree that a visual balance is achieved on the page? The darker, denser square and its surrounding white space on the left half of the page are balanced by the longer, less dense rectangle and its surrounding white space on the right half of the page. Now look at how those same shapes are converted into the design elements used in the sample letterhead in the bottom half of Figure 1.8. Here, balance is achieved with dissimilar design elements resulting in an effective asymmetrical design.

Asymmetrical design
Balancing contrasting elements on a page.

FIGURE

1.8 *Asymmetrical Balance*

Asymmetrical Balance

McGuire, Sullivan
& Murphy, Inc.

Asymmetrically Designed Letterhead

Multiple-paged documents add another dimension to the challenge of achieving balance. Since balance must be achieved among the elements on more than one page, it is essential that you look at type and graphics in terms of each two-page unit, or spread, which is a set of pages facing each other as shown in Figure 1.9. Also, notice that the layout of document A is symmetrical and the layout of document B is asymmetrical.

FIGURE

1.9 *Symmetrical and Asymmetrical Newsletters*

A

Symmetrical Balance

B

Asymmetrical Balance
(Two-page Spread)

Providing Proportion

When designing a communication, think about all of the individual parts as they relate to the document as a whole. Readers tend to view larger elements as more important. Readers also are more likely to read a page where all of the elements are in *proportion* to one another. When incorporating the concept of proportion into your documents, consider the following points:

- Size design elements, whether text or graphics, in proportion to their relative importance to the message.

- Size design elements so they are in proportion to each other. However, try not to have everything the same size.

- When a page is split horizontally or vertically, try to divide the design elements at a 60/40 ratio or ⅓ to ⅔ proportions. These proportions have proved to be visually appealing. Text, graphics, and other design elements should take up two-thirds of the document and at least one-third of the document should be left for white space.

Decide which elements in your document are the most important in conveying your message. Decide which elements are the second most important, and so on. Then proportionally size the visual elements in your publication according to their priority. This way you can make sure your readers see the most important information first. Appropriate typeface and type size for headlines, subheads, and body text can set the proportional standards for a document.

Proportion

Sizing elements in relation to their relative importance and to each other.

Evaluating Proportion

When viewing the documents in Figure 1.10, look at the headline size in proportion to the body text. Think about this relationship when selecting the type size for titles/headlines and body text. When selecting the type size for subheads, consider how the subhead relates proportionally to the headline and to the body text.

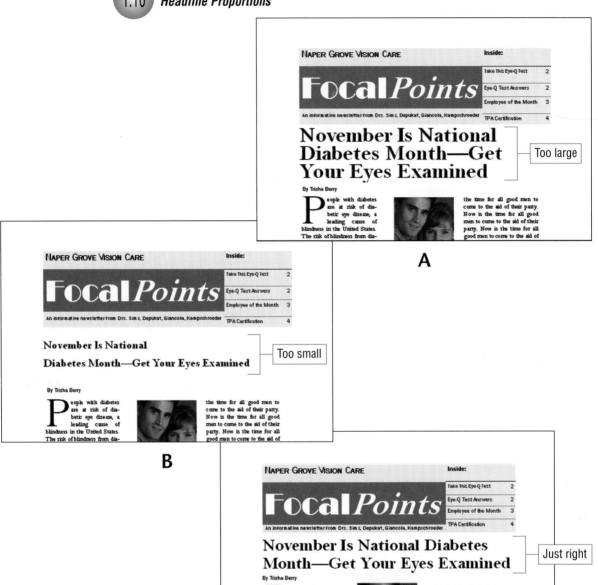

Sizing Graphic Elements to Achieve Proportion

Sizing of graphic elements is also important in maintaining proportion among all of the design elements on a page. For instance, look at illustration A in Figure 1.11. The size of the musical graphic image visually tells the reader that it is the most important item on the page. But should it be? As discussed earlier in this chapter, the message that you want to get across to the reader always takes top priority. The graphic image in illustration A may be relevant, but it is overpowering the message rather than supporting it. The image is definitely out of proportion to its relative importance in the message.

Now look at Figure 1.11B. The musical image is too small to be effective. Looking at the document as a whole, the image is out of proportion to the surrounding elements. What is your reaction to Figure 1.11C? Look at the individual elements as they relate to the whole document. All of the design elements appear to be in proportion to each other and to their ranking of importance in the intended message.

F I G U R E

1.11 *Sizing Graphics*

A

Private
Music
Lessons

Contact Kim Diehl at:
The Music Store
(708) 555-7867
210 S. Main Street, Lisle

B

Private
Music
Lessons

Contact Kim Diehl at:
The Music Store
(708) 555-7867
210 S. Main Street, Lisle

C

Using White Space to Achieve Proportion

White space is also important in sizing design elements proportionately on your page. Keep the following points in mind:

- Narrow margins create a typed line that looks long in relation to the surrounding white space.
- Too much white space between columns makes the line length look short.
- Too little white space between columns makes the text harder to read.
- Excess white space between lines of text creates gaps that look out of proportion to the type size.
- Not enough white space between lines of text makes the text hard to read. Achieve proportion consistently throughout your whole project. A whole, integrated, unified look is established when elements are in proportion to one another.

> **Contrast**
> The difference in the degrees of lightness and darkness on a page.

Creating Contrast

Contrast is the difference between different degrees of lightness and darkness on the page. Text with a low level of contrast gives an overall appearance of gray. Consider using strong contrast to achieve some emphasis or focus on your page. A high level of contrast is more visually stimulating and helps to draw your target

DTP POINTERS
Make contrasting elements strong enough to be noticed.

DTP POINTERS
Add contrast by setting headings and subheads in larger, denser type.

audience into the document. Use contrast as an organizational aid so that the reader can distinctly identify the organization of the document and easily follow the logical flow of information. Headlines and subheads set in larger and denser type help to create contrast on an otherwise "gray" page as shown in Figure 1.12.

FIGURE 1.12 *Using Contrast in Headlines and Text*

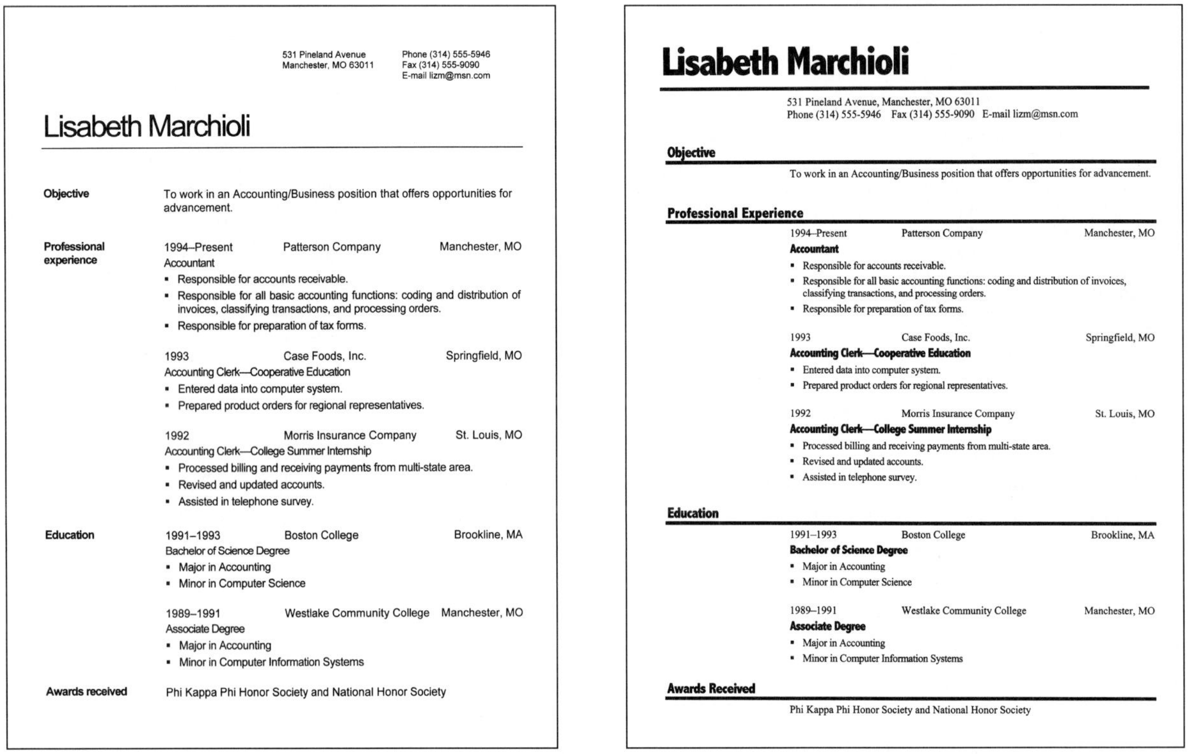

531 Pineland Avenue
Manchester, MO 63011
Phone (314) 555-5946
Fax (314) 555-9090
E-mail lizm@msn.com

Lisabeth Marchioli

Objective
To work in an Accounting/Business position that offers opportunities for advancement.

Professional experience
1994–Present Patterson Company Manchester, MO
Accountant
- Responsible for accounts receivable.
- Responsible for all basic accounting functions: coding and distribution of invoices, classifying transactions, and processing orders.
- Responsible for preparation of tax forms.

1993 Case Foods, Inc. Springfield, MO
Accounting Clerk—Cooperative Education
- Entered data into computer system.
- Prepared product orders for regional representatives.

1992 Morris Insurance Company St. Louis, MO
Accounting Clerk—College Summer Internship
- Processed billing and receiving payments from multi-state area.
- Revised and updated accounts.
- Assisted in telephone survey.

Education
1991–1993 Boston College Brookline, MA
Bachelor of Science Degree
- Major in Accounting
- Minor in Computer Science

1989–1991 Westlake Community College Manchester, MO
Associate Degree
- Major in Accounting
- Minor in Computer Information Systems

Awards received
Phi Kappa Phi Honor Society and National Honor Society

Lisabeth Marchioli

531 Pineland Avenue, Manchester, MO 63011
Phone (314) 555-5946 Fax (314) 555-9090 E-mail lizm@msn.com

Objective
To work in an Accounting/Business position that offers opportunities for advancement.

Professional Experience
1994–Present Patterson Company Manchester, MO
Accountant
- Responsible for accounts receivable.
- Responsible for all basic accounting functions: coding and distribution of invoices, classifying transactions, and processing orders.
- Responsible for preparation of tax forms.

1993 Case Foods, Inc. Springfield, MO
Accounting Clerk—Cooperative Education
- Entered data into computer system.
- Prepared product orders for regional representatives.

1992 Morris Insurance Company St. Louis, MO
Accounting Clerk—College Summer Internship
- Processed billing and receiving payments from multi-state area.
- Revised and updated accounts.
- Assisted in telephone survey.

Education
1991–1993 Boston College Brookline, MA
Bachelor of Science Degree
- Major in Accounting
- Minor in Computer Science

1989–1991 Westlake Community College Manchester, MO
Associate Degree
- Major in Accounting
- Minor in Computer Information Systems

Awards Received
Phi Kappa Phi Honor Society and National Honor Society

A B

Look at Figure 1.13. Do the documents grab your attention? Why? Contrast was achieved by using a larger type size for "London," reversed text, and bolded text. A black image against a solid white background produces a sharp contrast, as illustrated by the English guard graphic in Figure 1.13A. In addition, look at the program cover for the Brooks University Music Department in Figure 1.13B. A sharp contrast exists between the black background and the white text and piano image, and a not-so-sharp contrast between the light gray text and the watermark notes in the background of the cover. ***(Note: The piano image with the notes background is a clip art in Office 2003. You may access this graphic by typing* piano *in the* Search for *text box at the Insert Clip Art task pane. The image was ungrouped and the original text was removed and replaced with text created in two text boxes with the fill and lines removed.)***

As shown in Figure 1.13 in documents A and B, a graphic image in varying shades of gray or a watermark can produce contrast on a lower level. However, depending on the colors used in the image, a color graphic can also provide great contrast. Warm colors come forward and cool colors appear to recede.

1.13 *Text and Graphic Contrast*

A   B

Text contrast can be accomplished by changing text direction and by using a serif typeface (a small stroke at the end of a character) and a sans serif typeface (without a small stroke); a larger font size and a smaller font size; caps and lowercase; roman (regular font attribute) and italics; thick fonts and thin fonts; and drop caps and normal. See Figure 1.14 for examples. Avoid pairing fonts that are only slightly different from one another, such as Times New Roman and Bell MT. Instead, choose fonts with obvious differences, such as Arial Black (sans serif) and Invitation (serif).

FIGURE

1.14 *Contrasting Text*

Special characters used as bullets to define a list of important points, such as, , not only serve as organizational tools, but also contribute visual contrast to your page. Placing these special characters in a bolder and larger type size provides a higher level of contrast. Notice the flag bullets used in Figure 1.19 on page 24.

DTP POINTERS
Use bullets to organize information and add visual contrast.

Achieving Contrast with White Space

White space is an important tool in achieving contrast. Use more white space on a page to project a more open, lighter feeling. When space is limited, a more closed, darker feeling is projected. Think of white space as the floor space in a room. The more furniture and accessories in the room, the more closed or crowded the room becomes. Rearranging or removing some of the furniture can provide more floor space, producing an open, lighter feeling. Your page design, like a room, may need to have some elements rearranged or removed to supply some visually contrasting white space. See how too many design elements (accessories) are crowding the white space (floor space) in Figure 1.15A. Notice in illustration 1.15B how eliminating and rearranging some of the design elements to create more white space makes for a more open and lighter design.

DTP POINTERS
Use plenty of white space to convey an open, lighter feeling.

FIGURE 1.15 *Adding White Space*

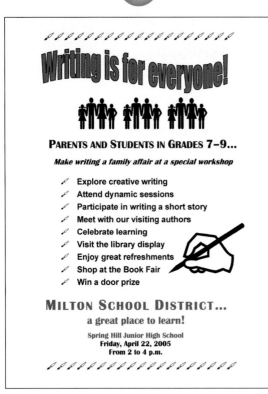

A

B

Achieving Contrast with Color

The use of color in a heading, a logo, a graphic image, a ruled line, or as a background can also add to the contrast level on a page. When using more than one color, select colors that provide a pleasing contrast, not colors that provide an unpleasant conflict. In addition, consider whether the color(s) used increases or decreases the legibility of your document. Color may look nice, but it will confuse the reader if there is not enough contrast in the text. Look at the examples in Figure 1.16. In illustration A, the color of the text and the color of the background are not different enough, making the text barely legible. As you can see in 1.16B, the stark contrast between the color of the text and the color of the background makes the text very easy to read. Use high contrast for the best legibility.

1.16 *Legibility*

Hard to read!	Easy to read!
Hard to read!	Easy to read!
A	**B**

Creating Directional Flow

Establish smooth *directional flow* in a document by organizing and positioning elements in such a way that the reader's eyes scan through the text and find particular words or images that the designer wishes to emphasize. By nature, graphics and display type (larger than 14 points) act as focal elements that attract the eye as it scans a page. Focal elements may include a well-designed headline, logo subheads, graphic images, ruled lines, boxes with text inside, charts, reverse text, or a shaded background. When trying to establish the directional flow of your document, you must:

- organize your information into groups of closely related items and then rank the groups in order of importance
- decide on how to emphasize the most important information
- place related items close to each other on the page
- use left or right alignment to establish a stronger visual connection between all of the elements on your page
- position elements so that the reader is drawn into the document and then directed through the document

Organizing Your Information Visually

Organize your information by grouping related items. Place the related items close to each other so the reader views the group as one unit rather than as separate pieces. For example, a subheading should be close to the paragraph that follows it so the reader recognizes the relationship between the two. Dates, times, and locations are frequently grouped close together because of the relationship of when? where? and at what time? Position titles and subtitles close to each other because of their obvious relationship.

What happens when there is little or no organization to the information in a document? Look at Figure 1.17A. Besides being very boring and uninviting to read, do you find it difficult to tell what this is really about, when it is going to take place, at what time, and so on? Now look at 1.17B. What has changed in 1.17B that did not exist in 1.17A? The AutoShapes filled with relevant graphics point toward the document content. Therefore, the directional flow directs the reader's eyes from the left side (focal point) to the right side where the grouped

Directional flow
Positioning elements to draw the reader's eyes through the document.

DTP POINTERS
Rank information according to its importance in conveying the intended message.

DTP POINTERS
Position related items close to each other on the page.

content is easily read. The italicized word "point" reinforces the right-pointing AutoShapes and the slant of the text gives a feeling of movement.

The colors you choose should reflect the nature of the business you represent. Someone in an artistic line of work may use bolder, splashier colors than someone creating documents for a business dealing with finance.

FIGURE

1.17 *Grouping Related Items and Using Good Directional Flow*

A

B

Headers and footers, text that appears repetitively at the top or bottom of each page, also contribute to directional flow in a publication. Chapter name, chapter number, report title, and page numbering are common items included in headers or footers. These page identifiers direct the reader to specific locations in a document.

Ranking Elements

Once you have organized your information into groups of related items, decide which information plays the most important role in conveying your message and then emphasize that information. For example, the purpose of the flyer in Figure 1.18 is to inform readers of the class schedules for the "Kids at College." The courses and the locations offered are important facts to the "kids." Reverse text and larger font sizes emphasize these facts. The gradient fill adds to the overall appeal of the flyer.

F I G U R E

1.18 *Emphasizing Important Information*

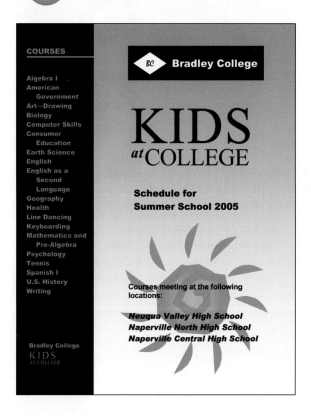

Recognizing the Z Pattern

Directional flow in a strictly symmetrical design (all elements centered) is limited to movement down the visual center of the page, producing a very static design. On the other hand, an asymmetrical design creates a dynamic directional flow. To accomplish this, think of how your eyes naturally scan a page. When scanning a page, the eyes tend to move in a *Z pattern*. The eyes begin at the upper left corner of the page, move to the right corner, then drop down to the lower left corner, and finally end up in the lower right corner of the page. In text-intensive publications such as magazines, newspapers, and books, visual landmarks are frequently set in these positions. In an advertisement, a company name, address, and phone number often appear in the lower right corner.

Z pattern
When scanning a page, the eyes tend to move in a Z pattern—upper left corner to bottom right corner.

Figure 1.19 helps you visualize the Z pattern in this document. Remember that the Z pattern is only a guideline. Some designs may contain modified versions of the Z pattern. However, since there are no hard-and-fast rules, not all designs fit exactly into this pattern.

F I G U R E

1.19 *Z Pattern Directional Flow*

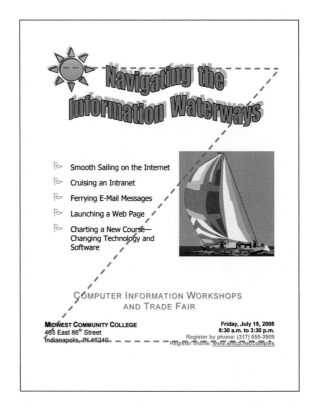

Choosing Visual Alignment

The way you choose to position and align text and/or graphics on a page greatly influences the directional flow in a document. One of the keys to creating dynamic directional flow and producing professional-looking documents is ***alignment***. Center alignment is fine when you are trying to achieve a more formal look, as in a wedding invitation, but tends to be dull and boring in other types of documents. Break away from the center alignment habit! Experiment with using a strong left or right alignment to connect different elements on your page.

Look at Figure 1.20. See what a dramatic difference it made to use a strong right alignment in 1.20B as opposed to 1.20A. The text in business card A is not connected and the reader's eyes tend to jump from one corner to another. Card B uses strong vertical alignment, grouped text, and bolded text to lead the eyes from the top to the bottom and back again.

Alignment
Aligning text and/or graphics on a page.

DTP POINTERS
Save center alignment for formal, conservative documents.

DTP POINTERS
Use a strong left or right alignment to visually connect elements on a page.

1.20 *Visual Alignment*

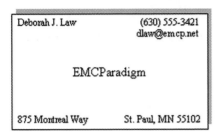

A

Weak Alignment

B

Strong Vertical Alignment

Establishing Consistency

Uniformity among specific design elements establishes a pattern of *consistency* in your document. Inconsistency can confuse and frustrate the reader and can lead to a reduction in your readership. To avoid this, design elements such as margins, columns, typefaces, type sizes, spacing, alignment, and color should remain consistent throughout a document to achieve a degree of unity. In any document, whether single-paged or multiple-paged, consistent elements help to integrate all of the individual parts into a whole unit. Additionally, in multiple-paged publications such as manuals, reports, or newsletters, consistency provides the connecting element between the pages. Repetitive, consistent elements can also lend identity to your documents and provide the reader with a sense of familiarity.

Consistent elements are evident in many of the figures in this chapter. Consider, for example, the flyer in Figure 1.19. Consistency is achieved by using the same color blue in the heading, the bullets, the sky in the sailboat clip art, the title of the event, and the phone number. Additional consistent elements in the flyer include the left alignment, the flag bullets, the spacing between the bullets, the typeface used for the text, and the margins.

Use consistent elements when designing separate business documents for the same company or person, such as a business card, a letterhead, and an envelope. Look at the documents in Figure 1.21. The consistent elements are obvious. You know immediately that all three documents are associated with the same company, which serves to reinforce the company's identity.

Consistency
Uniformity among design elements.

DTP POINTERS
Use of repetitive, consistent elements establishes unity within a document.

DTP POINTERS
Inconsistency confuses and frustrates the reader.

Evaluating Consistency

Consistency establishes unity not only *within* a section or chapter (or a newsletter, or an advertisement), but also *among* the sections or chapters (or a series of newsletters or advertisements). See how the consistent elements used in the manual pages displayed in Figure 1.22 contribute to the unified appearance of this document. Notice the green color scheme carried throughout the pages of the manual, including the cover page. The same typeface appears in the cover, the headers, the section headings, and the subheadings. A different typeface displays in the body text and remains consistent throughout the document. Additionally, a thin horizontal line appears in the header on every page except the cover.

FIGURE

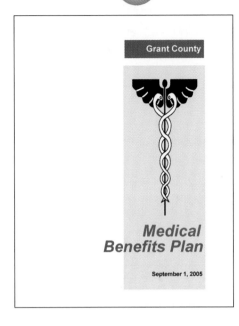

If you plan to insert a graphic image into your document, use the graphic to provide you with some ideas for consistency. For example, the globe/plane/mailbox graphic in the postcard in Figure 1.23 provided the idea for the consistent color scheme used in this document. The arrow pointing to the mailbox slot inspired the use of a dotted line and arrow pointing to the new address. To add consistency and create visual interest, the arrow was repeated in the return address box and in the delivery address section. Did you notice how three rectangles were cleverly arranged to resemble a mailbox in the return address section of the postcard? You, too, can be this creative, given time and lots and lots of practice! One word of advice—since consistent elements are repetitive elements, keep it simple and distinct. Too much of a good thing can be very distracting.

1.23 *Consistency in a Document*

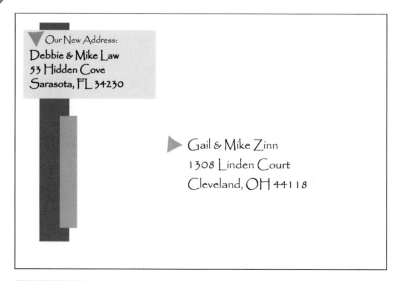

Using Color

As discussed earlier, *color* may create focus; however, it is also a powerful tool in communicating a message and portraying an image. The colors you choose should reflect the nature of the business you represent. Someone in an artistic line of work may use bolder, splashier colors than someone creating documents for a business dealing with finance. In addition, men and women often respond differently to the same color. Color can even elicit an emotional response from the reader; keep in mind cultural differences and how other cultures interpret the use of color. Always identify your target audience in planning your documents and think about the impact color will have on your audience. The colors in the fall leaves in Figure 1.24 reinforce the subject of the text, which is a list of courses offered during the fall quarter at a college. Color on a page can help organize ideas and highlight important facts. Publications that use color appropriately have a professional look. In Figure 1.22, you can see how the color green created focus, added emphasis, provided organization to the text, and served as a consistent element throughout the document.

FIGURE

1.24 *Using Color to Communicate*

Using Color Graphics and Text Elements

Word provides many ways of inserting color into your documents. You may use graphic pictures, borders, backgrounds, bullets, and lines of a specific design and color. You may also create your own color shapes, lines, borders, text boxes, and text. For instance, look at Figure 1.25A. This manual cover uses strong right alignment and grouping of related items. However, by putting the text in a text box and adding a gray fill as shown in 1.25B, the various text elements have a stronger visual connection and more appeal. Now look at 1.25C. The manual cover has evolved into a professional-looking document. The green reversed text box, green text, and the relevant graphic complete the look.

DTP POINTERS
Use color to create focus, organize ideas, and emphasize important elements.

FIGURE

1.25 *Color Graphics and Text Elements*

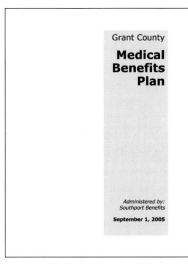

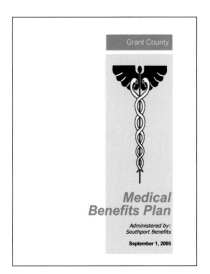

A   **B**   **C**

Using Colored Paper

If a color printer is not available, consider using colored paper to complement your publication. Colored paper can match the tone or mood you are creating in your document. Orange paper used for a Halloween flyer, as in Figure 1.26, is an inexpensive alternative to color graphics and text. Your audience will recognize the theme of the flyer by associating the paper color with the event. The colored paper provides contrast and adds vitality and life to the publication.

FIGURE

1.26 *Colored Paper*

A   **B**

Using Preprinted Stationery

You may also turn plain white documents into colorful, attention-grabbing documents by purchasing preprinted letterheads, envelopes, brochures, or presentation packets from paper supply companies or your local office supplies store. Achieve color, emphasis, and contrast through an assortment of colorful page borders, patterned and solid color papers, as well as gradient color, marbleized, and speckled papers. Many of these paper suppliers provide free catalogs and offer inexpensive sample paper packets.

Figure 1.27B illustrates a certificate printed on preprinted paper. Word 2003 was used to create the layout and text. The gray fill and green border reinforced the colors used in the paper. The Office 2003 handwriting interface was used to create the handwritten signature in the certificate (see Chapter 4). After carefully measuring and adjusting the text boxes, the document was printed on preprinted paper. (Experiment with plain paper first!)

FIGURE

1.27 *Using Preprinted Paper*

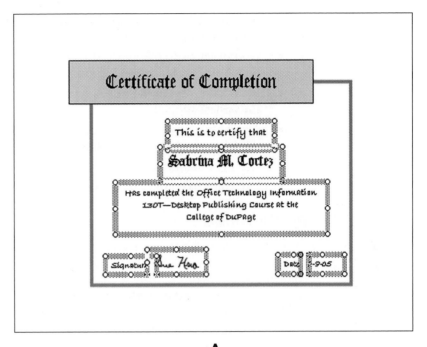

A

Layout and Text Created in Word

B

Printed on "Precision" by Paper Direct®

Guidelines for Using Color

Here are a few guidelines to follow when using color in documents:

DTP POINTERS
Use color
sparingly.

- Use color sparingly—less is best! Limit your use of colors to two or three, including the color of the paper.
- Color may identify a consistent element.
- Do not let color overpower the words. Color can add emphasis and style, but the message is most important!
- Do not set text in light colors—it is too difficult to read. Black text is still the easiest to read.
- Avoid changing all text to one color such as red. It is harder to read and the whole "color" of the document is changed.
- Use light colors for shaded backgrounds or watermarks.
- Use color to communicate, not decorate!

Printing Options

Even though laser printers have become more affordable, the color laser printer remains rather expensive. A less expensive, but very good, alternative is the inkjet color printer. The printer uses a color ink cartridge(s) to produce the color. The copy may be slightly damp when first removed from the printer. Improve the resolution using specially designed inkjet paper. Some inkjet printers are capable of achieving near-photographic quality with a resolution of 1440 dpi (dots per inch) or higher. Another option for color is to send your formatted copy to a commercial printer for color printing. You can get almost any color you want from a commercial printer, but it can add significantly to the cost of your project. Always check out the prices and your budget first!

Evaluating Documents Using the Document Analysis Guide

Up to this point, you have learned the importance of carefully planning and designing your publication according to the desktop publishing concepts of focus, balance, proportion, contrast, directional flow, consistency, and color. In Exercise 1, you will evaluate the document illustrated in Figure 1.28 using a Document Analysis Guide, which can be printed from your student data files. The Document Analysis Guide is a tool used to evaluate design concepts in selected documents. In addition, a Document Evaluation Checklist may be printed from your student data files. This tool serves as a way for you to evaluate your progress during the planning and creation stages of your document and is directed toward the finished product. The Document Evaluation Checklist will be used in Units 2 and 3. Both forms will be used to analyze your own documents, existing commercial publications, and/or other students' desktop publications.

Opening a Document as Read-Only

In Word, opening a document as "read-only" eliminates the risk of saving over the original copy of a document. A document opened as read-only may be read, printed, or edited. However, when a read-only document is saved with the Save command, Word displays the message, *This file is read-only*. Click OK for Word to lead you to the Save As dialog box so you can enter a new name for the document.

This option protects the original copy of a document from being saved with any changes. You will use this feature when you open the Document Analysis Guide and the Document Evaluation Checklist to complete exercises in this textbook.

Saving Documents

SAVE! SAVE! SAVE! AND SAVE SOME MORE! Creating desktop published documents involves many steps and, often, a lot of experimentation. Frequently save your work so you always have a recent version to fall back on and to avoid losing it if a power or system failure occurs. Word automatically makes a document recovery file every 10 minutes. You can change this setting by clicking Tools and then Options. Select the Save tab at the Options dialog box and then type 5 in the *minutes* text box if you prefer a shorter file recovery time. However, the AutoRecover should not replace the Save command—you must still save your document frequently.

(In several exercises in each chapter you will be opening documents from the CD that accompanies this textbook. The files you need for each chapter and for each set of unit assessments are saved in individual folders. Before beginning a chapter, copy the necessary folder from the CD to a formatted disk, zip disk, or CD-RW. After completing exercises in a chapter, delete the chapter folder before copying the next chapter folder. Check with your instructor before deleting a folder. Steps on creating a folder, making a folder active, and deleting a folder are presented in the Introduction to this textbook and on the inside of the back cover.)

Evaluating a Document

Evaluate the flyer illustrated in Figure 1.28 by completing the following steps:

1. Open **Document Analysis Guide** located in the Chapter01 folder.
2. Type your name and the exercise number at the top of the guide by completing the following steps:
   a. Click the Show/Hide ¶ button on the Standard toolbar to turn on this feature.
   b. Position the insertion point immediately to the right of the second space (dot) after *Name* in the upper right corner and then type your name on the line. (The text is in a text box.)
   c. Position the insertion point at the right of *Exercise #* and then type c01ex01.
3. Print one copy of **Document Analysis Guide**.
4. Turn to Figure 1.28 in your textbook.
5. Complete an analysis of the flyer in Figure 1.28 by writing or typing short answers to the questions in **Document Analysis Guide**. (If you prefer, you may type your answers on the guide, save it with another name such as **c01ex01, Document Analysis Guide**, and then print.)
6. Close **Document Analysis Guide** without saving your changes. (The read-only file will not save unless you rename the document.)

FIGURE

1.28 *Exercise 1*

Skyline Communications

305 East Wacker Drive, Chicago, IL 60654
Phone: (312) 555-5647 Fax: (312) 555-6521
Visit us at: www.emcp.net/skyline

For 2005, we are offering three different presentation formats to meet your learning and scheduling needs:

- ✔ One-day hands-on workshops
- ✔ One-day seminars
- ✔ Half-day distance learning seminars

Networking
Establishing Relationships

- ✔ **May 16, 2005**
- ✔ **9 a.m.–4 p.m.**
- ✔ One-day seminar
- ✔ Morris Inn, Rosemont

Presentations
Using PowerPoint

- ✔ **June 6, 2005**
- ✔ **9 a.m.–4 p.m.**
- ✔ One-day hands-on workshop
- ✔ Palmer House, Chicago

Team Building
Building Trust & Mutual Respect

- ✔ **June 20, 2005**
- ✔ **8:30 a.m.–3:30 p.m.**
- ✔ One-day hands-on workshop
- ✔ Holiday Inn, Lisle

Time Management
How to Increase Productivity

- ✔ **June 27, 2005**
- ✔ **8 a.m.–12 p.m.**
- ✔ Half-day distance learning
- ✔ Wheaton College, Wheaton

Read over the enclosed information for details and fees. Mail or fax the enclosed registration form to the address or fax number listed above or register on-line at www.emcp.net/skyline.

Using Word 2003 in Desktop Publishing

Word 2003 is a visual word processing program providing an efficient means of editing and manipulating text and graphics to produce professional-looking documents and Web pages. Word is linear in nature in that every character, picture, and object is part of a line of text. However, Word also contains many desktop publishing features and options that allow you to change linear objects to floating objects that can be moved easily on the document screen. Some of the desktop publishing features include a wide variety of fonts and special characters; drawing capabilities, text and graphics wrapping options, charting, and text design capabilities; graphics, graphics manipulation, and image editing tools; predesigned templates and template wizards; and even the capability of creating and designing Web pages on an intranet or the Internet.

Putting It All Together

Learn design by studying well-designed publications and by experimenting. Analyze what makes a specific design and layout visually appealing and unique and try using the same principles or variations in your publications. Take advantage of the special design and layout features that Word 2003 has to offer. Take time to design. Layout and design is a lengthy process of revising, refining, and making adjustments. Above all else, EXPERIMENT! View each document in terms of focus, balance, proportion, contrast, directional flow, consistency, and use of color. Ask the opinion of your peers, fellow workers, and others, and listen to their feedback. The final judge is the reader, so always look at your document from the reader's perspective.

DTP POINTERS

Experiment with different layouts and designs.

The rest of the chapters in this book will take you through the steps for creating specific business and personal desktop publishing applications, such as letterheads, business cards, flyers, brochures, postcards, Web pages, presentations, and newsletters. In addition to step-by-step directions for completing the applications using Word 2003, each project will introduce guidelines relevant to that document type as well as reinforce the design concepts introduced in this chapter.

Remember:

Take the time to design!

Communicate, do not decorate!

Less is always best!

Readability is the key!

Creating a Portfolio

Begin a "job-hunting" portfolio of the documents you will create in the exercises and assessments throughout this book. Exercises marked with the portfolio icon should be included in your portfolio. These documents have been chosen to show a prospective employer a wide range of your desktop publishing skills. You may also include any additional documents from the chapter and unit assessments. Since the assessments are less structured than the exercises, your creativity can really shine. You will create a title page for your portfolio in the Unit 3 Performance Assessments. As an optional assignment, you may create a table of contents after completing Unit 3. Your instructor will determine a due date and any other specific requirements for your portfolio. If possible, purchase plastic sheet protectors for your documents and a binder to hold them. See Figure 1.29 for sample portfolios.

FIGURE

1.29 *Sample Portfolios*

Using the Internet for Templates, Assistance Tips, and Clip Art and Media

The Internet can provide you with a wealth of information on desktop publishing as well as free Word templates, clip art, tips and tricks, articles, and assistance with new versions of software. For instance, through your preferred browser or search engine, you may type **desktop publishing** in the *Search* text box and access Web sites on various aspects of the desktop publishing field, which may include reviews on the newest books; definitions for common terms; discussions on graphics, layout, and design; and facts on career opportunities. You may find hyperlinks to free clip art, fonts, photos, and templates. Besides typing **desktop publishing** in your search, try other keywords such as *clip art, free clip art, fonts, graphics, graphic designers, Microsoft Word, word processing, Web design, logos, digital cameras,* and *scanning* to learn about different techniques and approaches to producing professional-looking documents.

Search engines that provide images and desktop information include www.altavista.com, www.askjeeves, www.google.com, www.hotbot.com, www.metacrawler.com, and www.yahoo.com. Be sure that you read the copyright information associated with each collection. Many images are free to use privately, but permission may be needed if the images are used for profit-making endeavors.

You can also download any graphic you may see on the Web by right-clicking on an image and, at the shortcut menu that displays, clicking the option Save Image As. A regular Save As dialog box displays where you may choose to name the file and save it to your hard drive or any other location. Again, be especially careful to make sure you have the rights to use the images. Most images are copyrighted!

Using Microsoft Resources

Besides the core applications in Office 2003, which may include Outlook, Word, Excel, PowerPoint, Access, and Publisher (availability is based on version type), Office 2003 also includes access to smaller utility programs and links to resources on the Microsoft.com Web site.

Using Microsoft Office Online Templates

If you have previously used Microsoft Word 2003, you may be familiar with the hundreds of Office templates that are available at the Microsoft Office Online Templates Web page. You may access this Web page by either clicking the <u>Connect to Microsoft Office Online</u> hyperlink at the Getting Started task pane or clicking the <u>Templates on Office Online</u> hyperlink at the New Document task pane. These hyperlinks take you to the Microsoft Office Online Templates Web page, shown in Figure 1.30, where Microsoft and content experts have collaborated to provide hundreds of professionally designed templates created in Word, Excel, Access, Publisher, and PowerPoint. You may browse by category or initiate a search to find the template you are looking for. When you find the desired template, click the Download Now button to send the document to the Office program where you can tailor the template to your exact needs. Many of the templates reinforce integration of the Office programs by using a common theme.

1.30 *Microsoft Office Online Templates Web Page*

Using Microsoft Office Online Assistance

You may access Microsoft Office Online Assistance for advice and answers to questions from formatting a party invitation to writing a persuasive cover letter. Figure 1.31 shows the Microsoft Office Online Assistance Web page, which includes the URL for this site, http://office.microsoft.com/assistance. Each category includes hyperlinks to related sites. You may also access this online assistance at the Word Help task pane by clicking the <u>Assistance</u> hyperlink or at the <u>H</u>elp menu by clicking Microsoft Office Online.

Using Microsoft Office Online Clip Art and Media

The Microsoft Office Online Clip Art and Media Web page shown in Figure 1.32 offers a gallery with hundreds of clip art, photos, and animated graphics you can download. To display the Microsoft Office Online Clip Art and Media Web page, you must have access to the Internet. While in Word 2003, you may access this site by clicking the <u>Clip art on Office Online</u> hyperlink in the Clip Art task pane.

FIGURE

1.32 *Microsoft Office Online Clip Art and Media Web Page*

Using Microsoft Office Tools

In addition to all of the Office 2003 components, every edition of Office 2003 also includes an assortment of office tools. Among the office tools, you may want to become familiar with Microsoft Office Document Imaging and the Microsoft Office Picture Manager. A brief description of each of these utilities is given below; however, applications of these tools will be presented in Chapter 5.

Using Microsoft Office Picture Manager

The Microsoft Office Picture Manager is a new tool introduced with Office 2003. With this utility, you will be able to organize large collections of image files, convert images to alternative formats, compress images, and edit images using the following tools: Brightness and Contrast, Color, Crop, Rotate and Flip, Red Eye Removal, Resize, Save, Save As, Save All, and Export. Many of these tools are also available on the Picture toolbar in Word. Figure 1.33 shows you the Picture Manager.

FIGURE

1.33 *Microsoft Office Picture Manager*

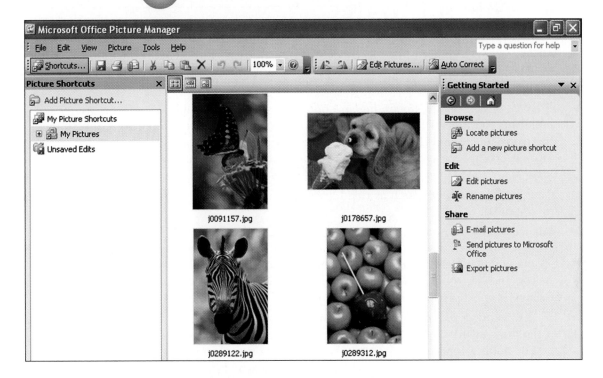

Using Microsoft Office Document Imaging

Microsoft Office Document Imaging may be used to scan single- and multiple-page documents and export scanned text and images to Microsoft Word. With this utility you may also search for text within scanned documents, reorganize scanned document pages, send scanned documents to others in e-mail or as a fax over the Internet, and annotate scanned documents and faxes as shown in Figure 1.34.

FIGURE

1.34 *Microsoft Office Document Imaging*

CHAPTER summary

➤ When creating a publication, clearly define your purpose, assess your target audience, decide the format in which your audience will see your message, and decide what outcome you are expecting.

➤ Effective design involves planning and organizing content. Decide what items are most important to the reader. Design concepts such as focus, balance, proportion, directional flow, consistency, and the use of color are essential to creating a visually attractive publication that presents information in a logical, organized manner.

➤ Focus can be created by using large and/or bold type, such as for titles and subheads; by using graphic elements, such as ruled lines, clip art, and photographs; and by using color for emphasis.

➤ Balance on a page is created by equally distributing the weight of elements on a page in either a symmetrical or asymmetrical manner. Symmetrical design (all elements centered) balances similar elements of equal weight and proportion on the left and right sides and the top and bottom of the page. Asymmetrical design balances contrasting elements of unequal proportion and weight on the page.

➤ In establishing a proportional relationship among the elements on a page, think about all of the parts as they relate to the total appearance. Proportionally size the visual elements in your publication according to their relative importance to the intended message.

➤ Contrast is the difference between varying degrees of lightness and darkness on the page. A high level of contrast is more visually stimulating and helps to draw your target audience into the document. Contrast is also used as an organizational aid so that the reader can distinctly identify the organization of the document and easily follow the logical flow of information.

➤ Directional flow can be produced by grouping related elements and placing them close to each other on the page, by using a consistent alignment to establish a visual connection between the elements on a page, and by positioning elements in such a way that the reader's eyes are drawn through the text and to particular words or images that the designer wishes to emphasize.

➤ Including consistent elements in a document such as margins, columns, typefaces, type sizes, spacing, alignment, and color helps to provide a sense of unity within a document or among a series of documents. Repetitive, consistent elements can also lend identity to your documents.

➤ Use color on a page to help organize ideas; emphasize important information; provide focus, contrast, directional flow, and consistency; and to establish or reinforce an identity.

➤ Use the Internet for free clip art, photographs, templates, and helpful newsletters.

➤ Access the Microsoft Office Online Web page by clicking the <u>Connect to Microsoft Office Online</u> hyperlink at the Getting Started task pane.

➤ Microsoft Office Online Templates includes hundreds of free office templates; access this site by clicking the <u>Templates on Office Online</u> hyperlink at the New Document task pane in Word 2003.

➤ Microsoft Office Online Assistance Web page provides helpful suggestions and tips on how to effectively integrate and use the Office components. Access this Web site by clicking the <u>Assistance</u> hyperlink at the Word Help task pane or by clicking <u>M</u>icrosoft Office Online at the <u>H</u>elp menu.

➤ The Microsoft Office Online Clip Art and Media Web site offers a gallery with hundreds of clip art, photos, and animated graphics you can download.

➤ Microsoft Office Document Imaging may be used to scan single and multiple-page documents and export scanned text and images to Microsoft Word.

COMMANDS review

Command	Mouse/Keyboard
Connect to Microsoft Office Online	View, Task Pane, Getting Started task pane, click Connect to Microsoft Office Online hyperlink; or Help, Microsoft Office Online, click hyperlinks to Home, Assistance, Training, Templates, Clip Art and Media, Downloads, Office Marketplace, or Product Information
Microsoft Office Online Clip Art and Media	View, Task Pane, Other Task Panes button, Clip Art, click Clip art on Office Online hyperlink; or Help, Microsoft Office Online, click Clip art on Office Online hyperlink
Microsoft Office Online Templates	View, Task Pane, New Document task pane, click Templates on Office Online hyperlink
Microsoft Office Document Imaging	Start, All Programs, Microsoft Office, Microsoft Office Tools, Microsoft Office Document Imaging
Microsoft Office Picture Manager	Start, All Programs, Microsoft Office, Microsoft Office Tools, Microsoft Office Picture Manager
Multiple pages options	File, Page Setup, Margins tab, Multiple pages down-pointing arrow; then choose *Normal, Mirror margins, 2 pages per sheet,* or *Book fold*
Task pane	View, Task Pane or Ctrl + F1

REVIEWING key points

Matching: On a blank sheet of paper, provide the correct letter or letters that match each definition.

Ⓐ Alignment
Ⓑ Asymmetrical
Ⓒ Balance
Ⓓ Color
Ⓔ Consistency

Ⓕ Contrast
Ⓖ Directional flow
Ⓗ Focal point
Ⓘ One-column
Ⓙ Proportion

Ⓚ Symmetrical
Ⓛ Thumbnail sketch
Ⓜ White space

1. Areas in a document where no text or graphics appear.
2. Type of balance achieved by evenly distributing similar elements of equal weight on a page.
3. A method used to establish a strong visual connection between elements on a page.
4. Use this design technique to help organize ideas, highlight important information, provide focus and consistency, and to reinforce an organization's identity.
5. Positioning elements in such a way that the reader's eyes are drawn through the text and to particular words or images that the designer wishes to emphasize.
6. An element that draws the reader's eye to a particular location in a document.
7. A preliminary rough draft of the layout and design of a document.
8. Uniformity among specific design elements in a publication.
9. The sizing of various elements so that all parts relate to the whole.
10. Contemporary design in which contrasting elements of unequal weight and proportion are positioned on a page to achieve balance.
11. The difference between varying degrees of lightness and darkness on the page.

APPLYING your skills

Assessment 1

In this assessment, you will begin a presentation project. The purpose of this assignment is to provide you with experience in planning, organizing, creating, and making a class presentation using Microsoft Word or PowerPoint. Specific instructions are provided for you in the document named **Presentation** located in your Chapter01 folder. To print this document, complete the following steps:

1. Open **Presentation** in your Chapter01 folder.
2. Print one copy and then close **Presentation**.

Begin researching a topic for your presentation. You may compose and create a presentation on a desktop publishing or Web publishing article or concept, a Word or PowerPoint desktop publishing or Web publishing feature(s) or process used to create a specific document, or an instructor-approved topic that you would like to share with your class. You may consider using any of the topics presented in this textbook. Include any Word or PowerPoint tips or techniques you may have discovered while creating your presentation. Use any one of the many desktop publishing, Word, and PowerPoint resources available online or at your local library or bookstore. Your instructor will notify you of a scheduled date for your presentation.

Assessment 2

The "information highway" is littered with many well-designed and poorly designed documents. Looking critically at as many publications as possible will give you a sense of what works and what does not. In this skill assessment, find three different examples of documents—flyers, newsletters, résumés, brochures, business cards, announcements, certificates, and so on. Evaluate these documents according to the desktop publishing concepts discussed in this chapter using Document Analysis Guide located in your Chapter01 folder. To do this, complete the following steps:

1. Open **Document Analysis Guide** from your Chapter01 folder.
2. Print three copies of this form and then close **Document Analysis Guide**.
3. Complete the evaluation forms and attach the corresponding form to the front of each example document. Write the exercise number as *c01sa02* on the front of each form.

Assessment 3

In this assessment, you will evaluate a poorly designed flyer according to the items listed in **Document Analysis Guide** located in your Chapter01 folder. On a separate piece of paper, list three suggestions to improve this flyer.

1. Open **Document Analysis Guide** in your Chapter01 folder.
2. Print one copy and then close **Document Analysis Guide**.
3. Open **Cleaning Flyer** in your Chapter01 folder.
4. Print one copy and then close **Cleaning Flyer**.
5. Complete the guide and name the exercise **c01sa03**. List your three suggestions for improvement on the back of the form.

Assessment 4

Create flyers for the situations described below. Draw two thumbnail sketches, using lines, boxes, and rough drawings to illustrate the placement of text and graphics on the page. You decide how to include focus, balance, proportion, contrast, white space, directional flow, and consistency in your thumbnail sketches. Be sure to consider the purpose and target audience for each situation. Designate areas in your sketches for such items as time, date, location, and response information. Label your sketches as **c01sa04**.

Design and Create

Situation 1: Annual office golf outing

Situation 2: Software training seminar

2

Preparing Internal Documents

PERFORMANCE OBJECTIVES

Upon successful completion of Chapter 2, you will be able to produce internal business documents such as a conference sign, handout cover sheet, fax cover sheet, memo, and agenda with a variety of typefaces, typestyles, type sizes, and special symbols.

CHAPTER02

DESKTOP PUBLISHING TERMS

Ascender	Kerning	Readability
Baseline	Legible	Sans serif
Cap height	Luminescence	Saturation
Cell	Monospaced	Serif
Descender	Normal.dot	Typeface (font)
Em dash	Pitch	Typestyle
En dash	Point size	Watermark
Hue	Proportional	x-height

WORD FEATURES USED

AutoFormat	Microsoft Office Online	Tables
Behind text	Templates	Task panes
Borders and Shading	Reveal Formatting task	Templates
Bullets and Numbering	pane	Text boxes
Clear Formatting	Smart Quote	Washout
Clip Art task pane	Special Characters	Watermark
Drawing canvas	Styles and Formatting	Wizards
Font color	task pane	
Header and Footer	Symbols	

Understanding Basic Typography

A document created on a typewriter generally contains uniform characters and spacing. A typeset document may contain characters that vary in typeface, typestyle, and size, and that are laid out on the page with variable spacing.

In this chapter, you will produce internal business documents using Word's Templates feature along with producing and formatting your own business documents. An important element in the creation of internal business documents is the font used to format the text. To choose a font for a document, you need to understand basic typography and the terms that apply.

As you learned in Chapter 1, when you plan your document, consider the intent of the document, the audience, the feeling the document is to elicit, and the emphasis on important information. Make sure the headlines, graphics, and the choice of typography work together to support the message.

Before selecting the desired type specifications in a document, a few terms used in desktop publishing need to be defined. Terms that identify the type specifications are typeface, type size, and typestyle.

Choosing a Typeface

Typeface (font)
A set of characters with a common design and shape.

A *typeface* is a set of characters with a common general design and shape (Word refers to typeface as font). One of the most important considerations in establishing a particular mood or feeling in a document is the typeface. For example, choose a decorative typeface for invitations or menus, but choose a simple block-style typeface for headlines or reports. Choose a typeface that reflects the content, your audience expectations, and the image you want to project.

Baseline
An imaginary horizontal line on which characters rest.

There are characteristics that distinguish one typeface from another. Type characters rest on an imaginary horizontal line called the *baseline*. Parts of type may extend above and/or below this baseline. Figure 2.1 illustrates the various parts of type.

FIGURE

2.1 *Parts of Type*

x-height
Height of the font's lowercase *x*.

Cap height
The distance between the baseline and the top of capital letters.

Ascender
The part of a lowercase character that rises above the x-height.

Descender
The part of a lowercase character that extends below the baseline.

The *x-height* is the height of the main body of the lowercase characters and is equivalent to the lowercase *x*. The *cap height* is the distance between the baseline and the top of capital letters. An *ascender* is the part of lowercase characters that rises above the x-height, and a *descender* is the part of characters that extends below the baseline. A *serif* is a small stroke at the end of characters.

Typefaces are either *monospaced* or *proportional*. A monospaced typeface allots the same amount of horizontal space for each character. Professional publications rarely use this typeface. Courier is an example of a monospaced typeface. Proportional typefaces allow a varying amount of space for each character. For example, the lowercase letter *i* takes up less space than an uppercase *M*. In addition, different proportional typefaces take up different amounts of horizontal space. The same sentence in Times New Roman, for example, takes up less horizontal space when set in the same size Century Gothic.

Proportional typefaces are divided into two main categories: serif and sans serif. Traditionally, a serif typeface is more readable (easier to read in blocks of text) and is used with documents that are text-intensive, such as business letters, manuals, or reports. Serifs help move the reader's eyes across the page.

A *sans serif* typeface does not have serifs (*sans* is French for *without*). Sans serif typefaces are generally more *legible* (higher character recognition), and are often used for headlines and advertisements. In modern designs, sans serif typefaces may also be used for body text, but avoid using more than seven or eight words per line; using bold, italics, outlining, or shadowing; or using a long line length. Figure 2.2 shows examples of serif and sans serif typefaces.

When using a proportional typeface, space once after end-of-sentence punctuation and after a colon. Proportional typeface is set closer together and extra white space is not needed at the end of a sentence or after a colon. Additionally, since proportional fonts take up varying amounts of horizontal space, you cannot use the spacebar to align objects on a page.

Serif
A small stroke at the end of a character.

Monospaced
Same amount of character spacing for each character in a typeface.

Proportional
Varying amount of space for each character in a typeface.

Sans serif
Without a small stroke at the end of a character.

Legible
Typefaces with higher character recognition.

DTP POINTERS
Use Word's Find and Replace feature to find ending punctuation with two spaces and replace with one.

FIGURE

2.2 *Serif and Sans Serif Typefaces*

Serif Typefaces	Sans Serif Typefaces
Bookman Old Style	Arial
Garamond	Eurostile
Goudy Old Style	Haettenschweiler
Modern No. 20	Impact
Rockwell	Lucida Sans
Times New Roman	Tahoma

Applying Desktop Publishing Guidelines

Desktop publishing includes general guidelines, or conventions, that provide a starting point for designing documents. Use moderation in choosing typefaces and type sizes—two fonts and three different font sizes are usually adequate for most publications. Too many typefaces and typestyles give the document a disorderly appearance, confuse the reader, and take away from the content of the document.

DTP POINTERS
Use a sans serif font for headings.

Serif fonts are more formal looking and are the standard for long text. Books, newspapers, and magazines typically use serif faces. Sans serif typefaces, for the most part, are clean and more contemporary in form. They are favored for large text or headlines. Line length and line spacing are also factors to consider in choosing the correct body type.

Font design may be harmonious, conflicting, or contrasting as shown in Figure 2.3. A harmonious design is calm and formal. This design is desirable, but not exciting. A formal invitation may be created using one font and include other design elements (borders, graphics, and symbols) that have the same qualities as the font. Apply italic, bold, and differing font sizes to add interest.

Conflicting font design exists when two or more typefaces are used on the same page, and they are too similar. The fonts are different, but not different enough to tell them apart easily. Avoid using conflicting fonts.

Contrasting fonts may create focus and attract the reader's eyes. Achieve contrasting design through varying the font size, weight, appearance, and color. For instance, if one typeface is light and airy, choose a thick black or dark gray font to go with it. If one typeface is small, make the other one large. Avoid creating weak contrasts, such as using a script font with an italic effect, or a large type size with a slightly larger font.

DTP POINTERS
Use a serif font for text-intensive documents.

FIGURE

2.3 *Harmonious, Conflicting, and Contrasting Font Designs*

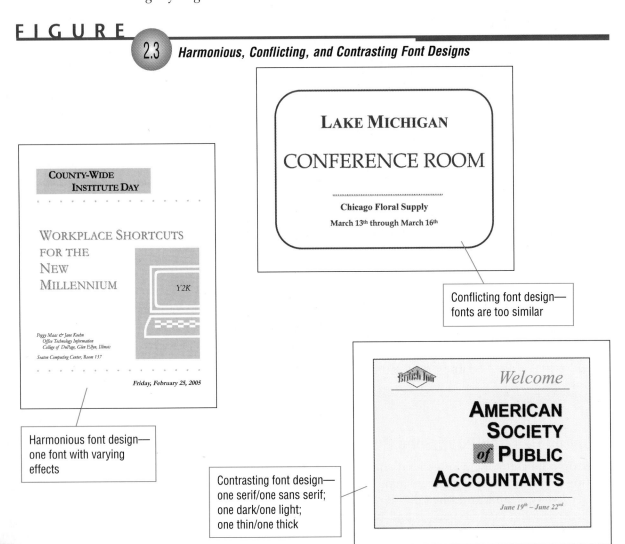

Conflicting font design—fonts are too similar

Harmonious font design—one font with varying effects

Contrasting font design—one serif/one sans serif; one dark/one light; one thin/one thick

Additionally, use fonts that complement the message of your document. Figure 2.4 displays fonts that match the mood and tone of your message.

FIGURE

2.4 *Matching Fonts to Your Message*

Alleycat Seafood Cafe   Papyrus

CARIBBEAN CRUISE   **BERMUDA SOLID**

ART DECO DESIGNS   TWENTIETH CENTURY POSTER

Wedding Invitation   Calligrapher

Casper the Ghost   Chiller

Kids at College   Curlz MT

Certificate of Completion   **Diploma**

COMPUTER SEMINAR   NEWTRON ICG

Line Dancing Class   Figaro MT

RED PAPERCLIPS   PAPERCLIP

Camp Sandy Feet   KidTYPEPaint

Four Corners Art Gallery   Matura MT Script Capitals

Choosing a Type Size

Type size (font size) is defined by two categories: *pitch* and *point size*. Pitch is a measurement used for monospaced typefaces; it reflects the number of characters that can be printed in 1 horizontal inch. (For some printers, the pitch is referred to as cpi, or characters per inch. For example, the font Courier 10 cpi is the same as 10-pitch Courier.)

Proportional typefaces can be set in different sizes. The size of proportional type is measured vertically in units called points (measured vertically from the top of the ascenders to the bottom of the descenders). A point is approximately 1/72 of an inch. The higher the point size selected, the larger the characters. Figure 2.5 shows Wide Latin and Arial Narrow typefaces in a variety of point sizes. Horizontally, the two fonts vary greatly, but vertically the point size remains the same.

Pitch
The number of characters that can be printed in 1 horizontal inch.

Point size
A vertical measurement; a point is approximately

DTP POINTERS
Sans serif typefaces are more readable than serif faces when set in very small point sizes.

DTP POINTERS
When using a proportional font, do not use the spacebar to align text; use a tab.

2.5   Varying Point Sizes in Wide Latin and Arial Narrow

8-point Wide Latin

10-point Wide Latin

12-point Wide Latin

18-point Wide Latin

24-point Wide Latin

8-point Arial Narrow

10-point Arial Narrow

12-point Arial Narrow

18-point Arial Narrow

24-point Arial Narrow

Choosing a Typestyle

Typestyle
Variations of the basic type design including regular or normal, bold, and italic.

At the Font dialog box, you can select a typestyle to apply regular, italic, bold, or bold italic formatting to a desired font. A *typestyle* is a variation of the basic font or typeface that causes the font to display thicker (bold) and/or slanted (italic). Within a typeface, characters may have a varying style. There are four main categories of typestyles: normal (or *light, black, regular, or roman*), bold, italic, and bold italic.

DTP POINTERS
Serif typefaces printed on textured paper or from 300 dpi or lower quality printers may lose detail in thin and delicate strokes.

DTP POINTERS
Substitute a different font if a particular font is not available.

DTP POINTERS
Unusual, bold, or distinctive fonts can distract the reader from the text.

Choosing Fonts

The types of fonts you have available with your printer depend on the type of printer you are using, the amount of memory installed with the printer, and the supplemental fonts you have. When software is loaded on your computer, any fonts associated with that software are loaded into the Fonts folder in Windows, possibly resulting in a list of fonts different from the ones in your school computer lab.

Soft fonts are available as software on a disk or CD. TrueType fonts are installed with Microsoft Office 2003. Additional fonts are available as a shared resource from other Windows-based software programs already installed on your hard drive. If your printer does not support a font or size you are using to format your text, Word may substitute the closest possible font and size. *(Hint: If the textbook calls for a particular font and you do not have this font, select a similar one.)*

Finding Similar Fonts

If you open a Word document that contains fonts that are not available on your computer, Word allows you to specify which fonts should be substituted. Choose Tools, Options, Compatibility, and then click the Font Substitution button. At the Missing Document Font dialog box, select the font change, and then select a font from the drop-down menu.

Similarity

In Windows XP, you may find similar fonts by double-clicking the *My Computer* icon on the Desktop, selecting the C drive, clicking the Windows folder, and then clicking the Fonts folder. At the Fonts folder, select the desired font and then click the Similarity button on the Fonts Standard toolbar. Scroll through the list of fonts, noting which of the fonts are Very similar, Fairly similar, or Not similar. Write down the names of the fonts you may want to substitute. To print a complete character set in varying point sizes and effects, click File and then Print.

Changing Fonts

Select fonts at the Font dialog box as shown in Figure 2.6, at the Formatting toolbar as shown in Figure 2.7, or at a shortcut menu that displays when right-clicking any text in a document. In Word 2003, the default font is 12-point Times New Roman. To change this default setting, click Format and then Font. At the Font dialog box, select the new defaults you want to use, then click the Default button located in the bottom left corner. At the dialog box stating that the change will affect all new documents based on the Normal template, click Yes. Font selections made within a document through the Font dialog box will override the default font settings for the current document only.

F I G U R E

2.6 *Font Dialog Box*

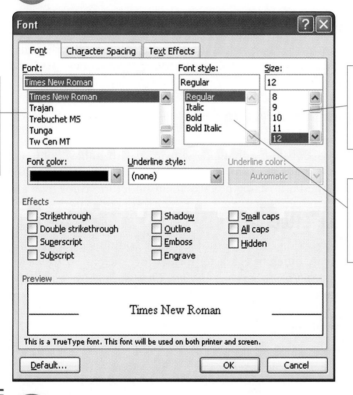

Choose a typeface in this list box. Use the scroll bar at the right side of the box to view various typefaces available.

Choose a type size in this list box; or, select the current measurement in the top box and then type the desired measurement.

Choose a typestyle in this list box. The options in the box may vary depending on the typeface selected.

F I G U R E

2.7 *Font Drop-Down List on the Formatting Toolbar*

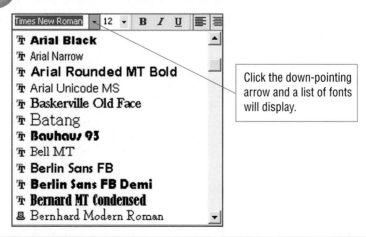

Click the down-pointing arrow and a list of fonts will display.

Changing Font Size

To change a font size at the Font dialog box, select a point size from the _Size_ option list box or type a specific point size in the _Size_ text box. The _Size_ option list box displays common increments ranging from 8 to 72 points. However, you may type a point size not listed. For instance, to create a font size at 250 points, position the arrow pointer on the number immediately below the _Size_ text box, double-click the left mouse button, and then type 250.

To change a font size on the Formatting toolbar, type or select a point size from the Font Size list box. **(Hint: Press the Tab key or press Enter after typing the point size in the Font Size list box**—the increment will remain when you move your insertion point back onto the document screen.) The point size of selected text can also be increased by 1 point by pressing Ctrl +]. The shortcut key combination to decrease the point size is Ctrl + [.

Changing Font Style

At the Font dialog box, select a font style from the list that displays below the _Font style_ option box. As you select different typefaces, the list of styles changes in the _Font style_ option box.

Selecting Underlining

In desktop publishing, underlining text has become somewhat dated. In place of underlining, consider enhancing your text with italics, bold, a different font size, all caps, or small caps. However, a list of lines is available at the _Underline style_ option at the Font dialog box where an underline color may also be applied.

Changing Effects

The _Effects_ section of the Font dialog box contains a variety of options that can be used to create different character formatting, such as _Strikethrough_, _Double strikethrough_, _Superscript_, _Subscript_, _Shadow_, _Outline_, _Emboss_, _Engrave_, _Small caps_, _All caps_, and _Hidden_. To choose an effect, click the desired option. The text in the _Preview_ box will illustrate the change. If the text already exists, select the text before applying these formatting options.

Consider using the following keyboard shortcuts for applying font formatting:

Boldface	Ctrl + B
Italicize	Ctrl + I
Underline	Ctrl + U
Underline words only	Ctrl + Shift + W
Double underline	Ctrl + Shift + D
All caps	Ctrl + Shift + A
Small caps	Ctrl + Shift + K
Toggle capitalization	Shift + F3
Subscript	Ctrl + =
Superscript	Ctrl + Shift + =
Hidden text	Ctrl + Shift + H
Apply Symbol font	Ctrl + Shift + Q
Clear font formatting	Ctrl + spacebar

Changing Font Color

You may change the color of a font by clicking the down-pointing arrow at the right of the Font Color button on the Formatting toolbar or the Drawing toolbar. In addition, you may change font colors by clicking the down-pointing arrow at the right of the *Font color* option at the Font dialog box with the Fo<u>n</u>t tab selected, as shown in Figure 2.8. If you are working with existing text, you must select the text first and then apply the font color change. From the color palette that displays in Figure 2.8, you may click a desired color and the color change will take effect or you may click More Colors to access the Standard and Custom tabs at the Color dialog box as shown in Figure 2.9 and Figure 2.10.

Font Color

FIGURE

2.8 *Font Color Palette at the Font Dialog Box*

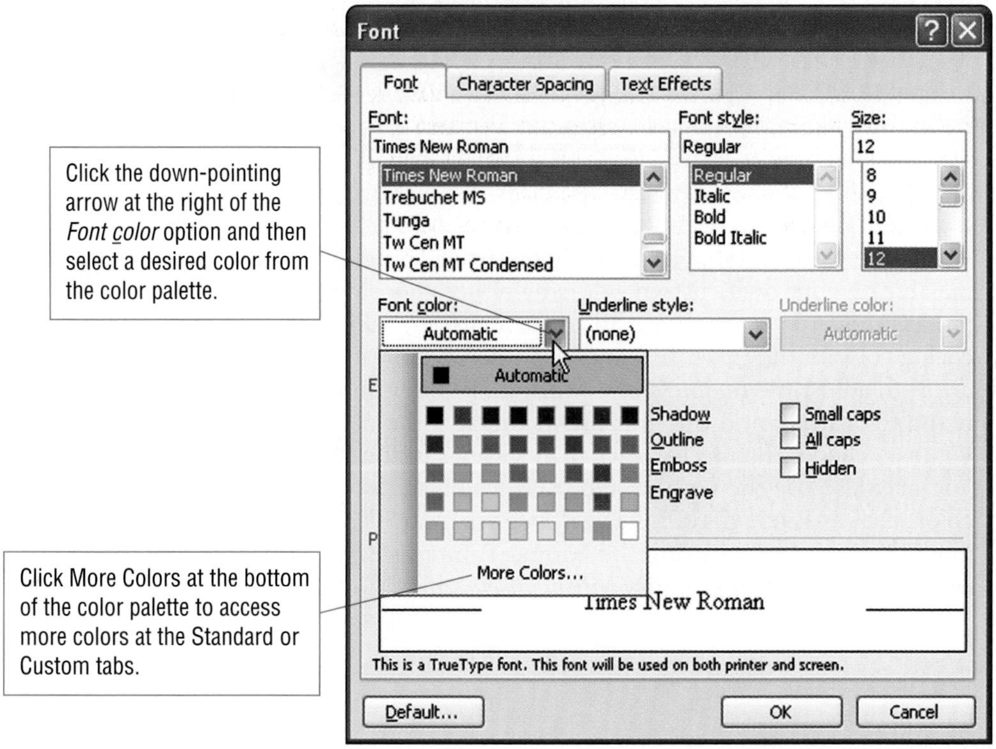

Click the down-pointing arrow at the right of the *Font color* option and then select a desired color from the color palette.

Click More Colors at the bottom of the color palette to access more colors at the Standard or Custom tabs.

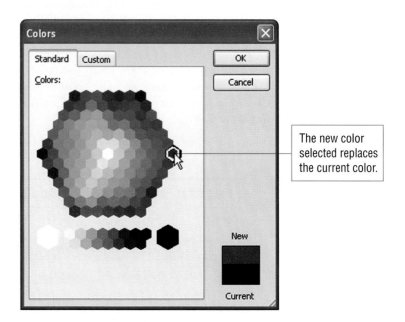

The new color selected replaces the current color.

Luminescence
The brightness of a color.

Hue
The color itself.

Saturation
The intensity of a color.

Format Painter

At the Custom tab, you may choose from 16 million colors. In addition, you may create your own custom colors by either choosing the RGB or HSL color models shown in Figure 2.10. To create a custom color using the HSL color model, click a color in the *Colors* box and click the up-pointing arrow or the down-pointing arrow to adjust the ***luminescence***, which is the brightness of the color; the ***hue***, which is the color itself; and the ***saturation***, which is the color's intensity. Alternatively, you may choose the precise three-digit settings in the *Hue, Sat,* and *Lum* text boxes. You may also use the Custom tab, RGB color model to approximately match a color, such as R:65, G:100, B:10 (*Red, Green,* and *Blue*). You may copy a color from one object to another using the Format Painter. *(Hint: Matching font colors to custom colors used in graphics will be discussed in Chapter 5.)*

2.10 *Customizing Colors Using Color Models*

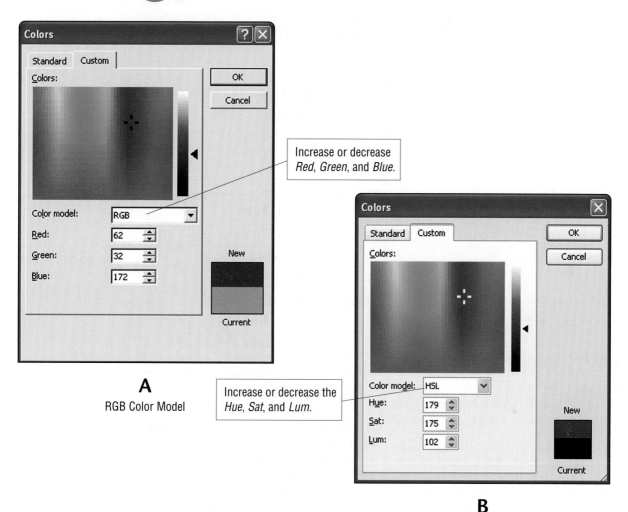

Increase or decrease
Red, *Green*, and *Blue*.

A

RGB Color Model

Increase or decrease the
Hue, *Sat*, and *Lum*.

B

HSL Color Model

Adjusting Character Spacing

Each typeface is designed with a specific amount of space between characters.
This character spacing may be changed with options at the Font dialog box with
the Character Spacing tab selected. Use options at the dialog box to scale, expand,
or condense character spacing. Options are also available to raise or lower selected
text and to adjust the spacing between certain characters pairs (referred to as
kerning). Kerned characters include *AV, Ta, Ty, Vi,* and *WA.*

Animating Text

Animation effects such as a blinking background, a shimmer, or sparkle may be
added to text for emphasis or drama. Animation text displays on the screen but
does not print. To add an animation effect, select the text, display the Font dialog
box with the Text Effects tab selected, click the desired effect, and then close the
Font dialog box.

Kerning

Decreasing or
increasing the
horizontal space
between specific
character pairs.

DTP POINTERS

Apply
animated text
effects to
documents that
will be viewed
online.

Using the Reveal Formatting Task Pane

Word's Reveal Formatting task pane lets you view detailed descriptions of the formatting in your document. You can use this task pane to modify or clear formatting, compare formatting of different selections, or find blocks of text with similar formatting. To access the Reveal Formatting task pane, complete the following steps:

1. Select the text you want to view or reformat.
2. Click Format and then Reveal Formatting.
3. Click one of the underlined commands in the description to modify the formatting as shown in Figure 2.11 (the related dialog box will display).

FIGURE

2.11 *Using the Reveal Formatting Task Pane*

Click a hyperlink in this section to display a dialog box with formatting options. Click a minus symbol preceding a heading to hide the display of items below. Click a plus symbol to display items below the heading.

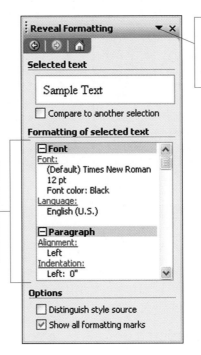

Click the down-pointing arrow (Other Task Panes button) to select another task pane.

Clear formatting by clicking the down-pointing arrow at the right of the *Selected text* list box and choose <u>C</u>lear Formatting from the drop-down list shown in Figure 2.12. The <u>C</u>lear Formatting command will then remove all character formatting or a character style, having the same effect as Ctrl + spacebar. The only formatting that <u>C</u>lear Formatting will not remove is the Highlight effect.

Using Clear Formatting

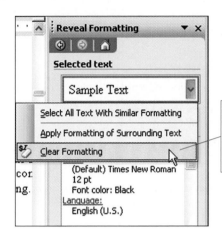

Select Clear Formatting to remove all character formatting from selected text.

The Clear Formatting command is also available at the Styles and Formatting task pane, where you can click this option at the top of the list to remove formatting and paragraph styles from selected text. The paragraph is converted to the Normal style. In addition, you may click the down-pointing arrow at the right of the Style button on the Formatting toolbar and select Clear Formatting from the drop-down list.

In Exercise 1, assume you are working at the British Inn and you are creating a sign welcoming the American Society of Public Accountants to your inn for a conference. Consider printing the sign on 24 lb. bond stock paper and placing it in an acrylic frame or sign stand in the lobby for the conference attendees to see.

Figure 2.13 displays the sign in Exercise 1 using two different methods for positioning the text. Both methods include a text box as the container of the text and a textured fill. A right tab aligned all of the text in the first example. Text boxes aligned the text in the second example. The text boxes provide an easy means of positioning text on the screen. The text box fill and line colors are changed to *No Fill* and *No Line* so that one box can overlap another. Click the Line button on the Drawing toolbar to create the horizontal lines. Otherwise, you may create lines using a graphic border, borderline, or a page border from the Borders and Shading dialog box.

2.13 *Using Tabs or Text Boxes to Create a Sign*

A

Using a Right Tab to Create a Sign

B

Using Text Boxes with No Fill to Create a Sign

DTP POINTERS

Use a logo for continuity and recognition.

Notice the font contrast—one thin serif font and one thick sans serif font. Text placed in text boxes facilitates easy movement. The logo, an AutoShape and WordArt combination, reinforces the British Inn's identity.

(Before completing computer exercises, delete the Chapter01 folder on your disk. Next, copy the Chapter02 folder from the CD that accompanies this textbook to your disk and then make Chapter02 the active folder.)

exercise

Formatting a Sign for a Conference

1. Open **Sign 01** from your Chapter02 folder.
2. Save the document with Save As to your hard drive, CD-RW, or a floppy disk and name it **c02ex01, Sign**.
3. Create a right tab by completing the following steps:
   a. Position the insertion point inside the text box and then display the Ruler by clicking <u>V</u>iew and then Ru<u>l</u>er.
   b. Click the Tab Alignment button until the Right Tab displays.
   c. Position the arrow pointer on 8.5 inches on the Ruler and then click the mouse to set a tab.
   d. Turn on the nonprinting characters by clicking the Show/Hide ¶ button on the Standard toolbar.
4. Create the sign text in Figure 2.14 by completing the following steps:
   a. With the insertion point in the upper left corner of the text box, press Enter three times.

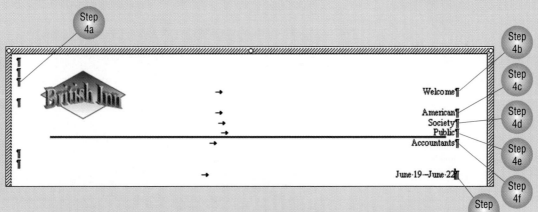

   b. Press Tab, type Welcome, and then press Enter twice. *(Hint: If pressing the Enter key twice turned on the AutoFormat feature that formatted* Welcome *with a heading style, simply press the Backspace key once to remove this heading style.)*
   c. Press Tab, type American, and then press Enter.
   d. Press Tab, type Society, and then press Enter.
   e. Press Tab, type Public, and then press Enter.
   f. Press Tab, type Accountants, and then press Enter three times.
   g. Press Tab and then type June 19 – June 22.
5. Format the sign text by completing the following steps:
   a. Select *Welcome* and change the font to 60-point Times New Roman bold, italic, and change the color to Gray-50%.

b. Select *American Society Public Accountants* and change the font to 65-point Arial, bold, shadow, small caps, and add the color Indigo (the second color from the right in the first row).

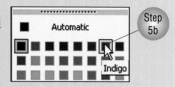

Step 5b

c. Select *June 19 – June 22* and change the font to 22-point Times New Roman bold, italic, and the color to Gray-50%.

6. Change the leading (line spacing) between *American...Accountants* by completing the following steps:

a. Select *AMERICAN SOCIETY PUBLIC ACCOUNTANTS*.

b. Click the down-pointing arrow at the right of the Line Spacing button on the Formatting toolbar and then click More.

c. At the Paragraph dialog box with the Indents and Spacing tab selected, click the down-pointing arrow at the right of the *Line spacing* option box and select *Exactly* from the drop-down list. Type **68** in the *At* text box and then click OK.

Step 6a

Step 6c

7. Select the red horizontal line below *Welcome* and while holding down the Ctrl key drag a copy of the line between *ACCOUNTANTS* and *June.... (Hint: Release the left mouse button and then the Ctrl key.)* You should now have a duplicate of the red line positioned below *ACCOUNTANTS*.

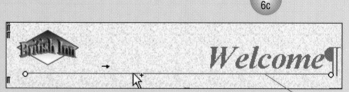

Step 7

8. Create the text box containing *of* by completing the following steps:

a. Display the Drawing toolbar by clicking the Drawing button on the Standard toolbar.

b. Click the Text Box button on the Drawing toolbar and draw a box approximately 0.5 inch square.

c. Create an exact measurement for the text box in Step 8b by completing the following steps:

   1) Double-click the border of the text box to open the Format Text Box dialog box.

   2) At the Format Text Box dialog box, select the Size tab. In the *Size and rotate* section, type **0.98** in the *Height* text box and **0.88** in the *Width* text box. Click OK.

9. Position the insertion point in the text box, change the font to 48-point Times New Roman, bold, italic, color Indigo, and then type *of*.

10. Change the shading in the text box containing *of* by completing the following steps:

   a. Double-click the border of the text box containing *of* to access the Format Text Box dialog box.

   b. Select the Colors and Lines tab, click the down-pointing arrow at the right of the *Color* option in the *Fill* section, and then click <u>F</u>ill Effects.

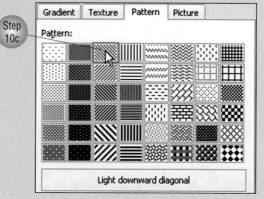
Step 10c

   c. At the Fill Effects dialog box, select the Pattern tab, and then click the third pattern from the left in the first row (Light downward diagonal). Click OK or press Enter.

   d. Click the down-pointing arrow at the right of the *Color* option in the *Line* section and click No Line. Click OK or press Enter.

   e. Click the border of the text box and when the arrow pointer displays as a four-headed arrow, drag the text box to the left of *Public* as shown in Figure 2.14.

11. Change the color of the border surrounding the sign text by completing the following steps:

   a. Double-click the border.

   b. At the Format Text Box dialog box, click the down-pointing arrow at the right of the *Color* option in the *Line* section and select Indigo. Click the down-pointing arrow at the right of the *Style* option box and select *3 pt*.

   c. Click OK or press Enter.

12. Add the textured fill by completing the following steps:

   a. Double-click the border.

   b. At the Format Text Box dialog box, click the down-pointing arrow at the right of the *Color* option in the *Fill* section and then click <u>F</u>ill Effects at the bottom of the color palette.

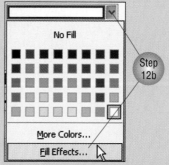
Step 12b

   c. At the Fill Effects dialog box, select the Texture tab and then select the first texture from the left in the first row (Newsprint).

   d. Click OK twice.

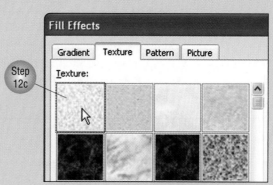
Step 12c

13. Save, print, and then close **c02ex01, Sign**. (Some printers do not print layered text boxes properly—the textured box containing *of* is positioned on top of the text box that contains all of the text for this sign.)

Welcome

AMERICAN
SOCIETY
of PUBLIC
ACCOUNTANTS

June 19 – June 22

Adding Symbols and Special Characters to a Document

DTP POINTERS
Special characters add visual interest to a document.

Symbols and special characters add interest and originality to documents. Sometimes it is the small touches that make a difference, such as adding a symbol (◈) at the end of an article in a newsletter, enlarging a symbol (Υ) and using it as a graphic element on a page, or adding a special character (©) to clarify text. Interesting symbols are found in such fonts as (normal text), Wingdings, Wingdings 2, Wingdings 3, and Webdings. Special characters may include an em dash (—), en dash (–), copyright character (©), registered trademark character (®), ellipses (…), or nonbreaking hyphens.

To insert a symbol as shown in Figure 2.15, click Insert and then Symbol from the Menu bar. At the Symbol dialog box, choose the Symbols tab, select a desired font, double-click the symbol or click Insert, and then click Close (or press Esc). To insert a special character, follow the same steps except choose the Special Characters tab and then select a desired character.

FIGURE

2.15 Inserting a Symbol

Click this down-pointing arrow to display a list of fonts. Choose the font that contains the desired symbol.

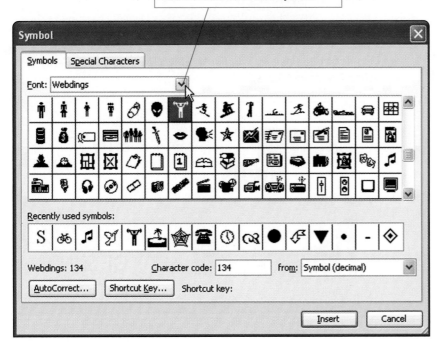

Creating Em and En Dashes

An *em dash* (—) is as long as the point size of the type used and indicates a pause in speech. An en dash (–) indicates a continuation, such as 116–133 or January–March, and is exactly one-half the width of an em dash. Besides inserting em and en dashes using the Symbol dialog box at the Special Characters tab, you may insert an em dash at the keyboard by pressing Alt + Ctrl + Num - or an en dash by pressing Ctrl + Num - . Additionally, the AutoCorrect feature includes an option that will automatically create an em and en dash.

Using Smart Quotes

In typesetting, the open quotation mark is curved upward (") and the close quotation mark is curved downward ("). In typesetting, the straight quotes are used to indicate inches (") or feet ('). The Smart Quote feature will automatically choose the quote style that is appropriate if it is typed in error. The Smart Quote option is turned on or off at the AutoFormat As You Type and AutoFormat tabs at the AutoCorrect dialog box.

In addition, symbols and special characters may be added to the AutoCorrect feature, which will automatically insert the desired symbol when using a specific keyboard command. Symbols may also be copied to the clipboard and pasted when needed.

Em dash
A dash that indicates a pause in speech; the dash is as wide as the point size of the font used.

En dash
A dash that indicates a continuation; the dash is exactly one-half the width of an em dash.

DTP POINTERS
Use straight quotation marks only to indicate measurements.

65

Using Special Characters and Contrasting Fonts in Design

DTP POINTERS

Contrasting fonts create interest in a document.

Consider the designs in Figure 2.16 and the effects these interesting fonts could have on a target audience. The designs incorporate many desktop publishing concepts, such as using contrasting fonts—thin and thick fonts, light and dark font color, serif and sans serif typefaces, ornate and plain appearance; using a variety of colors for focus; and using good directional flow.

FIGURE

2.16 *Creating Interesting Designs with Fonts (Thick/Thin, Serif/Sans Serif, Contrasting Colors and Sizes)*

In Exercise 2, assume you are working at Kendall Community College and creating a cover for a workshop handout as shown in Figure 2.17. Using text boxes makes it easier to position the text. However, some of the boxes overlap and it may be necessary for you to click in various locations to select the desired boxes. An alternative to multiple clicking is to click the Select Objects button on the Drawing toolbar. Pointing the Select Objects arrow near a text box or object allows you to grab the desired object. Click the Select Objects button to toggle it on or off.

Select Objects

DTP POINTERS
If you drag a text box to a wrong location, click the Undo button.

Creating a Cover for a Workshop Handout

1. Open **Cover 01** located in your Chapter02 folder.
2. Save the document with Save As and name it **c02ex02, Cover**. (Save to your Chapter02 folder.)
3. Format the text as shown in Figure 2.17 by completing the following steps:
    a. Select *Microsoft* and then change the font to 26-point Garamond bold.
    b. Add the registered trademark symbol (®) by completing the following steps:
        1) Position the insertion point after *Microsoft*.
        2) Click Insert and then click Symbol.
        3) At the Symbol dialog box, select the Special Characters tab.
        4) Select *Registered* from the *Character* list, click Insert, and then click Close or press Esc.
    c. Apply superscript to the ® symbol.
    d. Select *Word 2003* and then change the font to 48-point Garamond bold.
4. Create the gray dots shown in Figure 2.17 by completing the following steps:
    a. Position the insertion point in the area directly below *Word 2003* to access the text box that will contain the gray dots shown in Figure 2.17.
    b. Click Insert and then Symbol.
    c. At the Symbol dialog box, choose the Symbols tab and then select *Wingdings 2* from the *Font* list box.
    d. Click the dot (●) symbol (the eighth symbol from the left in the eighth row [Wingdings 2:151]).
    e. Click the Insert button and then press Esc.
    f. Press the F4 (Repeat) key 13 times.
    g. Position your insertion point between the first and second (●) and then press Tab. Continue pressing the Tab key between each symbol.
    h. Select all of the dots (Ctrl + A), click the down-pointing arrow at the right of the Font Color button, and then change the color to Gray-25%.
5. Format the text box containing the large mouse symbol by completing the following steps:

a.   Position the insertion point in the text box at the right of the *Microsoft Office Specialist...* text box (the insertion point will display about 1 inch from the top of the box). Insert the mouse (🖱) symbol found in the Wingdings font (the eighth symbol from the right in the second row [Wingdings: 56]).

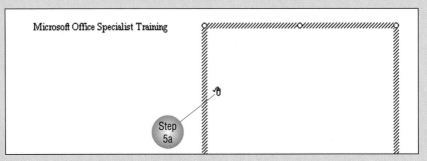

b.   Select the symbol and change the font size to 260 points. *(Hint: Hold down the Shift key and use the arrow keys to select text where text boxes overlap, or press Ctrl + A if all of the text in the text box is formatted similarly.)*

c.   Add shading to the text box containing the (🖱) symbol by completing the following steps:

   1)   Double-click the border of the text box.
   2)   At the Format Text Box dialog box, select the Colors and Lines tab, click the down-pointing arrow at the right of the *Color* option in the *Fill* section, and then click Fill Effects.
   3)   At the Fill Effects dialog box, choose the Pattern tab, and then select the third pattern from the left in the fourth row (Dark upward diagonal). (Make sure the *Foreground* option shows Gray-40% and the *Background* option shows White.) Click OK twice.

6.   Format the rest of the cover text by completing the following steps:

   a.   Select *Microsoft Office Specialist Training* and change the font to 34-point Wide Latin, shadow, and small caps. *(Hint: When using the Font Size button on the Formatting toolbar, press Tab after typing the measurement in the text box—this helps the number stay when you place the insertion back in your document.)*

   b.   Select *& Testing* (in another text box) and format as directed in Step 6a.

   c.   Select *Kendall Community College* and then change the font to 22-point Garamond bold italic.

   d.   Select *425 DeSoto Blvd., Des...* and *Academic Testing...* and change the font to 18-point Garamond italic. (If the *Smart Tag Actions* icon displays, click the down-pointing arrow and then click Remove this Smart Tag.)

   e.   Select *Authorized Testing Center* and change the font to 16-point Garamond bold italic.

7.   If necessary, drag to position any text boxes similar to Figure 2.17. *(Hint: Click the text box to select it and when the four-pointed arrow displays, drag the box(es) to the desired position on the page.)*

8.   Save, print, and then close **c02ex02, Cover**. (Some laser color printers do not print layered text boxes properly.)

FIGURE 2.17 ***Exercise 2***

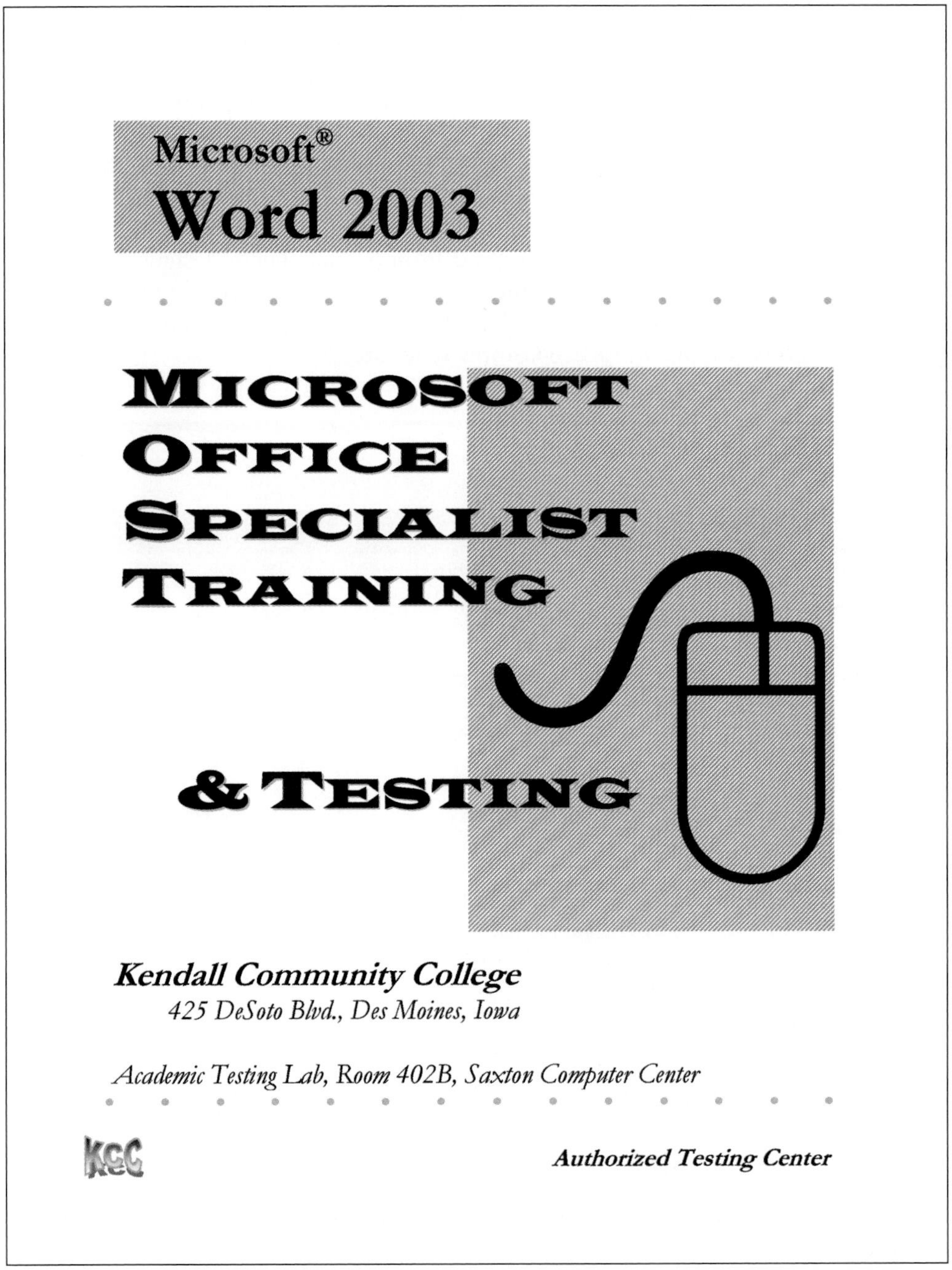
Microsoft®
Word 2003

MICROSOFT
OFFICE
SPECIALIST
TRAINING

& TESTING

Kendall Community College
425 DeSoto Blvd., Des Moines, Iowa

Academic Testing Lab, Room 402B, Saxton Computer Center

KCC

Authorized Testing Center

Creating Documents Using Templates and Wizards

Every document created in Word is based on a template. When you create a document at a clear document screen, you are using the default template. This default template, called the ***Normal.dot*** template, contains formatting instructions to use 12-point Times New Roman as the font, English (U.S.) as the language, left alignment, widow/orphan control, and single spacing. With Word templates,

Normal.dot
The default template in Word.

you can easily create a variety of documents, such as letters, memos, and brochures, with specialized formatting. Along with templates, Word also includes wizards. Wizards walk you through a series of steps in which you add or select information to set up formatting, content, and layout of your document.

Templates and wizards are available at the Templates dialog box. Display the dialog box, shown in Figure 2.18, by clicking the On my computer hyperlink in the New Document task pane. You can access the New Document task pane by clicking View and then Task Pane, or by clicking File and then New. If the Getting Started task pane displays, click the Other Task Panes button and then click New Document. The Templates dialog box contains several tabs for displaying a variety of templates and wizards. Many of the templates are formatted consistently using three designs—Contemporary, Elegant, and Professional. These designs make it easy to build a consistent set of documents. Notice the Templates on Office Online button in the lower left corner of the Templates dialog box. Click this button for easy access to the Microsoft Office Online Templates.

FIGURE

2.18 *Word Templates and Wizards*

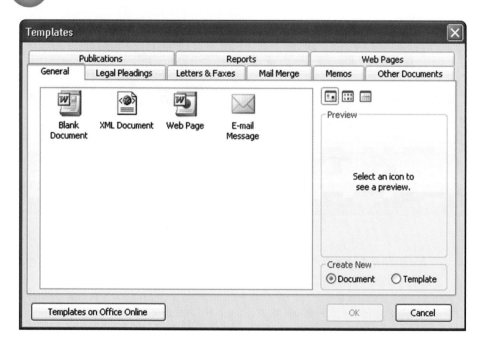

Accessing Microsoft Office Online Templates

The Microsoft Office Online Templates Web page provides hundreds of professionally authored templates. You may click the Templates on Office Online hyperlink at the New Document task pane or click the Connect to Microsoft Office Online hyperlink at the Getting Started task pane and then click the Templates hyperlink in the upper left corner of the Web page. In addition, at the New Document task pane, you may type a keyword for the template you want to locate in the *Search online for* text box and then click Go. You may have to access the Internet first through your Internet Service Provider before clicking these hyperlinks. Figure 2.19A illustrates the featured templates. All of the rest of the Office templates are located in various categories as shown in Figure 2.19B. Use the *Search* option at the top of the Templates Web page to narrow your search.

FIGURE

2.19 *Microsoft Office Online Templates*

Type a keyword in the *Search* text box to locate certain templates.

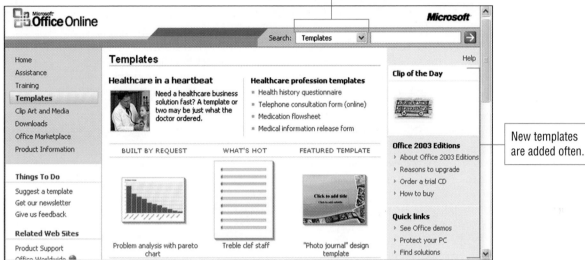

New templates are added often.

A

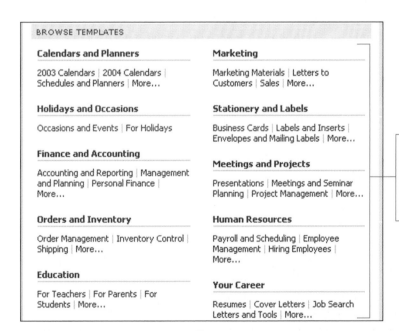

Template categories and locations may change with updates to the Microsoft Office Online Templates Web page.

B

Figure 2.20 displays the Preview screen where you can click the Download Now button to jump back to Word and then customize the Telephone Consultation Form shown in Figure 2.20. Visit this site often to view new templates. *(Note: Microsoft may periodically update the look of its Web pages so template locations may change. Remember to use the* Search *option to help in finding the desired template quickly.)*

2.20 **Sample Word Template**

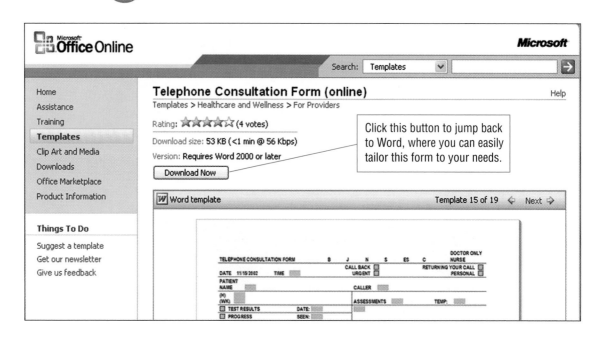

Customizing Templates

Readability

The ease with which a person can read and understand groups of words.

When customizing a template to meet your specific needs, remember to apply the basic design concepts discussed in Chapter 1. Always begin a document with the end in mind. Plan your text carefully to achieve your desired results without unnecessary wording or formatting. If you replace the existing fonts in a template, be sure the fonts increase the readability of the text. **Readability** is the ease with which a person can read and understand groups of words.

DTP POINTERS

Avoid "one size fits all" formatting by customizing to fit your needs.

Templates and wizards can help you create great-looking documents. However, if you do not want your documents to look like "one size fits all," consider the following suggestions:

- Change fonts, font styles, font sizes, font colors, and font effects
- Use expanded, condensed, lowered, or raised character spacing
- Use reverse text
- Add more or less leading (white space between the lines)
- Add fill color and fill effects—gradient, texture, pattern, or picture
- Add text box shading, shadows, or 3-D
- Insert special characters and symbols
- Create unique bullets
- Add borders and shading
- Add graphics, photos, drawing objects, or scanned images
- Use drop caps
- Add a company logo
- Create a watermark

- Use unique column layout and specialized tables
- Include links to other documents
- Add AutoText entries
- Include backgrounds and themes
- Add form fields that fit your needs

Creating a Document Based on a Template

To create a document based on a different template, double-click the desired template. If you click just once on the desired template, a sample template displays in the *Preview* box at the right of the dialog box. When you double-click a template, a template document opens with formatting already applied. Many times the placeholder text will provide instructions on how to use the template.

Basing a New Template on an Existing Document

If your existing document contains many of the features you want to add to a template, you can save time by basing your new template on that document. At the New Document task pane as shown in Figure 2.21, click the From existing document hyperlink in the *New* section and then select the document you want to use for your template. Click the Create New button and then make sure you save the document with the .dot extension.

FIGURE

2.21 **Template Based on a Document**

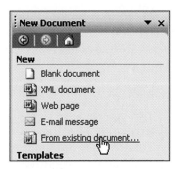

Saving and Deleting Templates

To save a document as a template based on an existing template:

1. At the New Document task pane, click the On my computer hyperlink.
2. At the Templates dialog box, select the tab containing the template you want to use.
3. Choose the *Template* option in the *Create New* section.
4. Double-click the template you want to use.
5. Name the template (Word will automatically assign the extension .dot).
6. Click Save. The template saves by default to C:\Documents and Settings\user\Application Data\Microsoft\Templates. To save the template so that it will appear on a tab other than General, switch to a corresponding subfolder within the Templates folder.

To save a document as a template:

1. Choose Save As from the File menu.
2. Name the template.
3. In the *Save as type* list box, select *Document Template (*.dot).*
4. Click the Save button.

To delete a template at the Templates dialog box, right-click on the template and then click Delete from the shortcut menu.

Changing File Locations

By default, Word saves a template document in the Templates folder on your hard drive. The templates you save in the Templates folder display in the General tab at the Templates dialog box. If you want to create a custom tab for your templates in the Templates dialog box, create a new subfolder in the Templates folder and save your templates in that subfolder. If you save your templates to a different location, the templates will not appear in the Templates dialog box.

In a setting where more than one person uses the same computer, such as a school or business, consider changing the location where Word saves template documents. (See your instructor about where to save your templates.) For example, in the next exercise, you will create a folder, DTP Templates, on your disk and save templates to this folder (your templates will not display in the Templates dialog box).

Alternatively, you may change the template file location permanently, until you change it again, by completing these steps (see Figure 2.22). (Consult your instructor before changing this setting.)

1. Click Tools and then Options.
2. At the Options dialog box, click the File Locations tab.
3. Click *User templates* in the *File types* list box.
4. Click the Modify button.
5. At the Modify Location dialog box, specify the desired folder in the *Look in* option box, and then click OK twice.

In Exercise 3, assume you are working for Butterfield Gardens, a nursery and gardening supply company. Frequently, you send and receive faxes directly from your computer. To reinforce your company's identity and save time, you are going to customize a fax cover sheet (include a logo), save it as a template, and reuse it as needed. The fax template provides the convenience of a "fill in the blanks" form, which makes it easy for the sender/recipient to enter data. To fill in areas containing the text "Click here and type," click and then key text between the brackets. Select any placeholder text in the template, and then type your desired text. **(Hint: Read the placeholder text first—sometimes it will provide helpful tips.)** In addition, you will create a folder on your designated drive (drive A, C, D, or E) and direct Word to save your templates there.

2.22 *Changing the Template File Location*

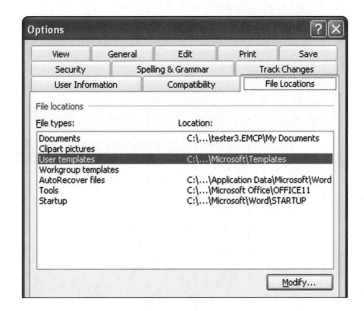

exercise 3

Customizing a Fax Cover Sheet Template

1. Use the Professional Fax template to create a customized fax cover template as shown in Figure 2.23 by completing the following steps:
   a. Display the New Document task pane.
   b. Click the <u>On my computer</u> hyperlink in the *Templates* section.
   c. At the Templates dialog box, choose the Letters & Faxes tab.
   d. Click *Template* in the *Create New* section.
   e. Double-click the *Professional Fax* icon.

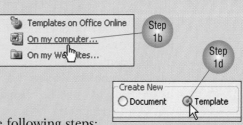

   f. Customize the fax design by completing the following steps:
      1) Position the I-beam pointer on the word *here* in the bracketed text in the return address area, click the left mouse button, and then type:

         29 W 036 Butterfield Road
         Warrenville, IL 60555
         Phone: 630-555-1062
         Fax: 630-555-3029
         www.emcp.net/grower2you

      2) Select *Company Name Here*, click the Center align button on the Formatting toolbar, and then type Butterfield Gardens.
   g. Add a logo by completing the following steps:
      1) Position the insertion point at the beginning of the first paragraph of the sample body text.

2) Change the zoom to *Whole Page*.
3) Click Insert, point to Picture, and then click From File.
4) At the Insert Picture dialog box, make sure the drive where the student data files are located displays in the *Look in* option box.
5) Double-click ***BGLogo.tif*** located in your Chapter02 folder.
6) Double-click the image to access the Format Picture dialog box.
7) At the Format Picture dialog box, select the Layout tab, and click *In front of text*. This permits you to move the image. ***(Hint: In Word 2003 a clip art image defaults to In line with text; however, this setting can be changed—see the "Using Word Layers in Documents" section of this textbook.)***

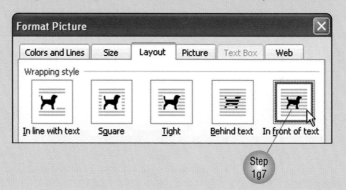

Step 1g7

8) Select the Size tab and change the height to 1.5 inches in the *Size and rotate* section. (If the *Lock aspect ratio* is turned on, the width will automatically display in proportion to the height.) Click OK.
9) Drag and drop the image to position it above the horizontal line at the bottom of the fax cover; see Figure 2.23. (The customized template could be saved at this point before any specific text is inserted, but for our textbook use, you will continue typing the text.)
h. Change the zoom to *75%*.
i. Type the text in the bracketed areas as shown in Figure 2.23.
j. Read the body placeholder text, select the text at the right of *Comments:*, and then replace it with the text in Figure 2.23. (Do not select and replace *Comments:*.)
2. Save your template by completing the following steps:
a. Click File and then Save As.
b. In the *File name* text box, type **c02ex03, BG Fax**.
c. Click the down-pointing arrow at the right of the *Save in* option and choose the drive where you want to save your template. (Did you notice that Word defaults to the Templates folder?)
d. Click the Create New Folder button on the Save As toolbar (third button from the right).
e. Type DTP Templates in the *Name* text box and then click OK.
f. Make sure *Document Template* displays in the *Save as type* option box and then click Save.
3. Print and then close **c02ex03, BG Fax.dot**.

29 W 036 Butterfield Road
Warrenville, IL 60555
Phone: 630-555-1062
Fax: 630-555-3029
www.emcp.net/grower2you

Butterfield Gardens

Fax

To:	P. Manich Floral Distribution	**From:**	Floyd Rogers
Fax:	616-555-7823	**Pages:**	2
Phone:	618-555-7720	**Date:**	7/8/05
Re:	Annual and perennial flowers	**CC:**	J. J. Whitman, Midwest Sales

☐ **Urgent**   ☐ **For Review**   ☐ **Please Comment**   x **Please Reply**   ☐ **Please Recycle**

● **Comments:** Please review the completed purchase order and confirm the availability of the flowers by return fax. The last shipment was beautiful.

Thank you for your prompt service.

Creating a Watermark

Watermark
A lightened graphic or text displayed behind text on a page.

A ***watermark*** is a lightened graphic or text that when printed appears either on top of or behind existing document text as shown in Figure 2.24. Watermarks are intended for printed documents. There are two different methods for creating watermarks in Word. One method involves using the Printed Watermark dialog box and the other uses the Picture toolbar. Word displays watermarks in Print Layout view and in Reading Layout view. Traditionally, a watermark is a design impressed in high-quality paper stock. This design can be seen more clearly when the paper is held up to the light.

FIGURE 2.24 ***Using Text and Graphics to Create Watermarks***

SAMPLE
This is an example of a text watermark. If you wanted to change the size or shape of this text watermark, you must access the Header and Footer pane and make the desired changes there. WordArt was used to create the text in this example.

Text Watermark

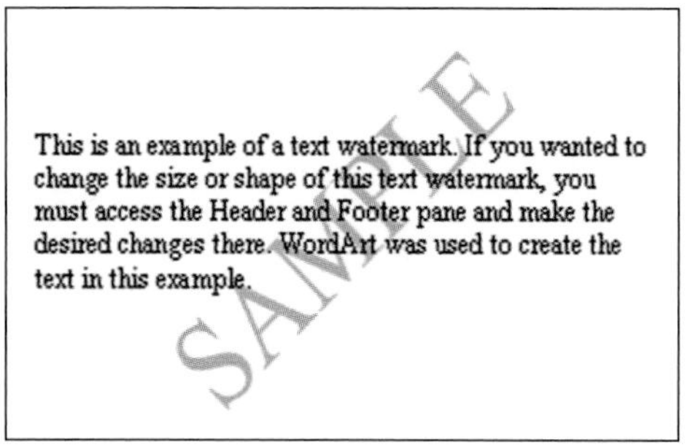

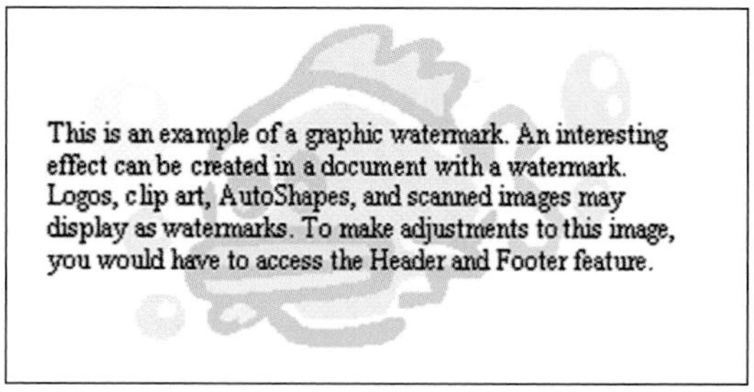

This is an example of a graphic watermark. An interesting effect can be created in a document with a watermark. Logos, clip art, AutoShapes, and scanned images may display as watermarks. To make adjustments to this image, you would have to access the Header and Footer feature.

Graphic Watermark

Creating a Watermark Using the Printed Watermark Dialog Box

With options at the Printed Watermark dialog box shown in Figure 2.25, you can create a picture watermark or a text watermark. Display the Printed Watermark dialog box by clicking Format, Background, and then Printed Watermark. If you are creating a picture watermark, click *Picture watermark*, and then click the Select Picture button. This displays the Insert Picture dialog box. At this dialog box, specify the drive or folder where the picture is located, and then double-click the desired picture image. Notice that the *Washout* option, which is checked by default, decreases the brightness and contrast of the image to improve the readability of the text. To create a text watermark, click the *Text watermark* option and then customize the watermark by choosing *Font, Size, Color,* and *Layout* options. Notice that the *Semitransparent* option, which is checked by default, lightens the color of the text.

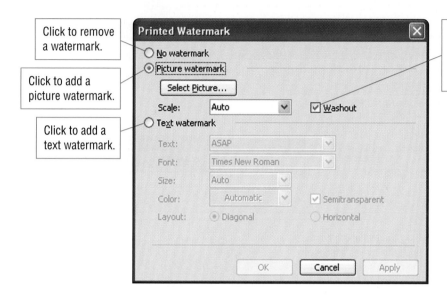

Click to remove a watermark.

Click to add a picture watermark.

Click to add a text watermark.

This option adjusts the brightness and contrast of an image to improve readability of text.

Word adds the watermark (graphic or text) to the document's header pane, which causes the watermark to appear on every page. If you divide your document into sections, you can remove the watermark from a particular section by deleting the picture or WordArt object from that section's header by selecting the *Different first page* option or the *Different odd and even* option on the Layout tab of the Page Setup dialog box. Otherwise, you may choose to create different headers and footers in different sections and deselect the *Link to previous* option on the Header and Footer toolbar.

To edit the watermark created with the method described above, you should click View and then Header and Footer. At the Header and Footer pane shown in Figure 2.26, select the WordArt text and edit it using the WordArt toolbar, or select the graphic and use the Picture toolbar to make desired changes to the image. When you are satisfied with the changes, click the Close button on the Header and Footer toolbar. To delete a watermark you added previously, select *No watermark* at the Printed Watermark dialog box.

FIGURE

2.26 *Editing a Watermark in a Header*

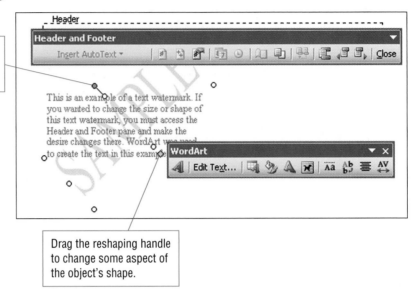

The rotation handle is used to rotate a graphic object.

Drag the reshaping handle to change some aspect of the object's shape.

Using Word Layers in Documents

Besides using the Header and Footer pane to create watermarks, you may also create a watermark by inserting an image or text at the document screen, altering the color of the object, and then sending it behind the text layer. The unique layering aspect of Word allows this to happen. A Word document contains three layers—foreground layer (or drawing layer), text layer, and background layer as illustrated in Figure 2.27.

FIGURE

2.27 *Word Document Layers*

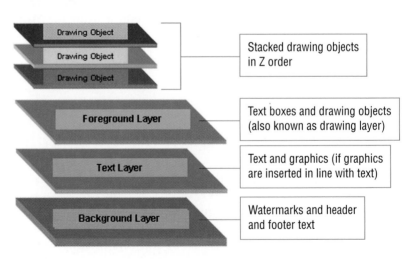

Stacked drawing objects in Z order

Text boxes and drawing objects (also known as drawing layer)

Text and graphics (if graphics are inserted in line with text)

Watermarks and header and footer text

The text layer is the one you may be most accustomed to working with in word processing. In Word 2003, graphics default to *In line with text* and anchor to a paragraph in the text layer. At times, you may find it helpful to change this setting to another setting where you can move the image freely about the screen. This is accomplished by clicking the Text Wrapping button on the Picture toolbar and then clicking one of the following options: *In Line With Text, Square, Tight, Behind Text, In Front of Text, Top and Bottom, Through*. **(Hint: To change this setting permanently, click Tools, Options, select the Edit tab, and then click the down-pointing arrow at the right of Insert/paste pictures as option and select one of the other settings, such as In front of text.)** Most drawing objects, which include AutoShapes, rectangles, ovals, WordArt, and lines, display in the foreground layer above the text layer and are easy to move. Text or graphics created in headers and footers display in the background layer where they display below the text layer. Additionally, objects may be sent behind text by accessing each respective dialog box or toolbar. Figure 2.28 illustrates objects and text in various layers in a document.

FIGURE

2.28 *Word Layers in a Document*

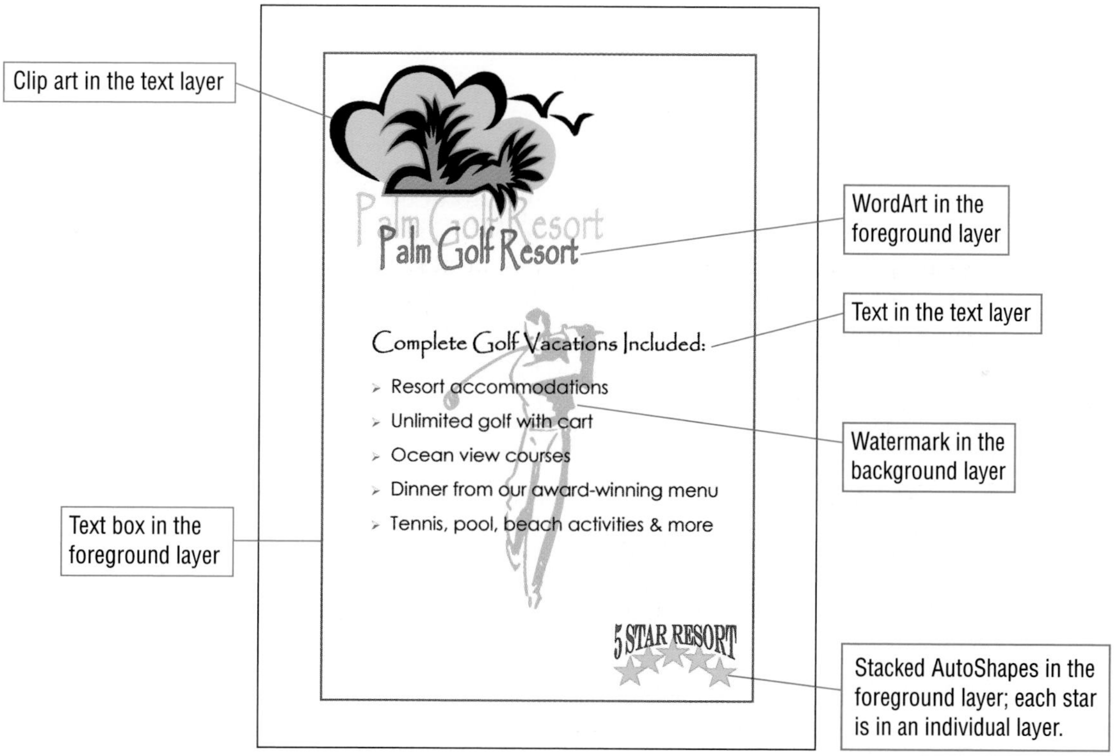

In addition to these basic layers, Word stacks drawing objects in individual layers in the foreground layer (also known as the Z order). Every time you add another object, it is drawn in the layer on top of the previous layer. The stacked objects are similar to the stack of cards in Figure 2.29. You can change the order of the drawing objects by clicking the Draw button on the Drawing toolbar, pointing to Order, and selecting options to Bring to Front, Send to Back, Bring Forward, Send Backward, Bring in Front of Text, and Send Behind Text.

Some laser printers are incapable of printing objects that are layered within text boxes in a document. Generally, most inkjet color printers can print all layers in a document without any difficulty. At times, you may need to use a table instead of a text box as the container for your text.

FIGURE 2.29 **Layered Objects Are Similar to a Stack of Cards**

Objects are stacked in layers like a deck of cards. The first object created is on the bottom, and the last object is at the top.

Inserting Images in a Document

Word 2003 includes a gallery of media images including clip art, photographs, and movie images, as well as sound clips. To insert an image into a document, click Insert, point to Picture, and then click Clip Art; From File; From Scanner or Camera (scanner and/or camera software needed); New Drawing; AutoShapes; WordArt; Organization Chart; or Chart. If you want to insert a clip art image, photo, movie, or sound clip, access the Clip Art task pane as shown in Figure 2.30.

FIGURE 2.30 **Clip Art Task Pane**

Type the search text here.

Click the down-pointing arrow to choose where you want to find your images.

Click the down-pointing arrow to choose which media type you want to use. If you want only photos, deselect all of the media types except *Photographs*.

Click here to organize your media clips.

Make sure you are connected to the Internet.

Another method for displaying the Clip Art task pane is to click the Insert Clip Art button on the Drawing toolbar. To display the Drawing toolbar, click the Drawing button on the Standard toolbar. You can also display the toolbar by right-clicking on any currently displayed toolbar and then clicking Drawing at the drop-down list, or by clicking View, pointing to Toolbars, and then clicking Drawing. To close the Insert Clip Art task pane, click the Close button *(X)* in the upper right corner. If the Picture toolbar does not display automatically when you insert a clip art image, right-click on the image and then click Show Picture Toolbar from the shortcut menu.

Insert Clip Art   Drawing

The first time you display the Clip Art task pane, you may see a dialog box with a message telling you that the Media Gallery can catalog picture, sound, and motion files found on your hard drive or in folders you specify, and it instructs you to click Now to catalog all media files, click Later to postpone the task, or click Options to specify folders. At this message, click the Now button and Media Gallery will catalog all of your picture, sound, and motion files. By default, the Clip Art task pane displays all media images and sound clips found in all locations. More information is provided on the Clip Organizer in Chapter 5.

Searching for Clip Art and Other Media

In this textbook, you will be instructed to insert an image as shown in the sample document at the end of each exercise. However, if the image is not available, you should replace the image with another similar one. The file name for each image, such as j0386361.jpg, is provided in each exercise. You may use the *Search for* text box at the Clip Art task pane to type the specific file name, j0386361.jpg, or to type a name for a category, such as beach, and then click Go. *All Collections* should display in the *Search in* option box and *All media file types* should display in the *Results should be* option box unless you wish to restrict your search to photographs only or sounds only, and so on, in which case you will need to click the down-pointing arrow at the right of the *Results should be* option box and select an option for a certain type of media file. Selecting a specific type of media file can save you a considerable amount of time when searching for photographs only. Be sure to return the option in the *Results should be* option box to *All media file types* after you have changed this setting. See Figure 2.30 for the options mentioned above.

Sizing and Moving Images

Once an image is inserted in a document, it can be sized using the sizing handles that display around a selected clip art image. To change the size of an image, select it and position the mouse pointer on a sizing handle until the pointer turns into a double-headed arrow as shown in Figure 2.31. Hold down the left mouse button, drag the sizing handle in or out to decrease or increase the size of the image, and then release the mouse button. Use the sizing handles in the corners to change the height and width at the same time and in proportion to each other.

To move a clip art image you must first select the image, make sure the Picture toolbar displays as shown in Figure 2.32, and then click the Text Wrapping button on the Picture toolbar. Choose a text wrapping style, such as In Front of Text, Square, Tight, Through, Top or Bottom, or Behind Text, and then position the mouse pointer inside the image until the pointer turns into a four-headed arrow shown in Figure 2.31. Hold down the left mouse button, drag the image to the desired position, and then release the mouse button. Rotate the image by positioning the mouse pointer on the green, round rotation handle.

2.31 **Sizing and Moving Images**

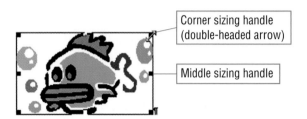

Corner sizing handle (double-headed arrow)

Middle sizing handle

Clip Art Positioned In Line With Text

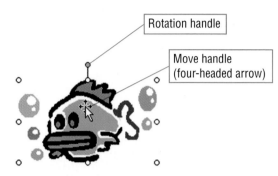

Rotation handle

Move handle (four-headed arrow)

Clip Art Positioned In Front of Text

F I G U R E

2.32 **Picture Toolbar**

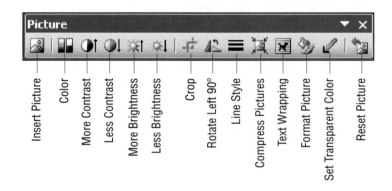

Insert Picture · Color · More Contrast · Less Contrast · More Brightness · Less Brightness · Crop · Rotate Left 90° · Line Style · Compress Pictures · Text Wrapping · Format Picture · Set Transparent Color · Reset Picture

Creating a Watermark with Buttons on the Picture Toolbar

Text Wrapping

By using the Text Wrapping button on the Picture toolbar, you can move an image to Behind Text. Next, click the Color button and, at the drop-down list that displays, select <u>W</u>ashout (see Figure 2.33). You will ultimately create a watermark effect. *(Hint: If you send an image behind the text layer and later decide to resize it or change a color, you may have difficulty selecting the image. Display the Drawing toolbar, click the Select Objects button, and then select the image. You should be able to "grab" it.)*

F I G U R E

2.33 **Using the <u>W</u>ashout Option**

Select the image and then click the Color button on the Picture toolbar.

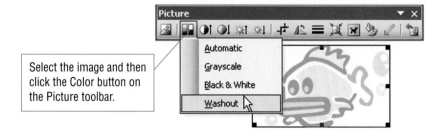

Troubleshooting Watermarks

If a document contains several text boxes, rectangles, or other AutoShape objects, the objects may obstruct the view of the watermark below them. If this should occur, click the down-pointing arrow at the right of the Fill Color button on the Drawing toolbar and select No Fill. Also, click the down-pointing arrow at the right of the Line Color button and select No Line.

Fill Color   Line Color

If you use a text box, rectangle, or other AutoShape as a container or border for a document, the graphics you select may fill the entire area of the text box or shape. When using graphics and watermarks in signs or other documents created with a border around them, you may find it helpful to use a page border or a border from the Borders and Shading dialog box to serve as the border around a document or place the image in a text box to control the size of the image.

If your watermark is a drawing object, select the Colors and Lines tab at the Format AutoShape dialog box, click the down-pointing arrow at the right of the *Color* option in the *Fill* section and choose a color at the color palette. Once the color is selected, drag the slider at the right of the *Transparency* option or type a percentage of the color to create a light fill. To use text as a watermark, use a light font color or create a WordArt object and adjust the *Transparency* option slider at the Format WordArt dialog box.

Using the Drawing Canvas

Before completing the following exercises, turn off the drawing canvas feature until you are specifically instructed to turn it back on. The drawing canvas enables you to draw several shapes or objects within its framelike boundary and then move or resize the objects as one unit as shown in Figure 2.34.

F I G U R E

2.34   *Using the Drawing Canvas*

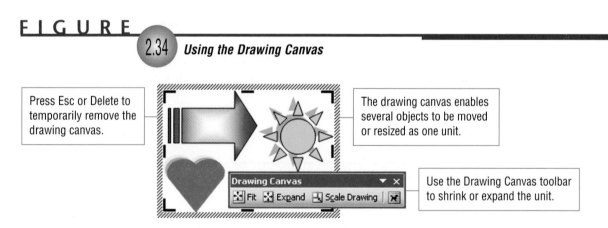

Press Esc or Delete to temporarily remove the drawing canvas.

The drawing canvas enables several objects to be moved or resized as one unit.

Drawing Canvas
Fit   Expand   Scale Drawing

Use the Drawing Canvas toolbar to shrink or expand the unit.

By default, the drawing canvas has no border or background, but you can apply formatting to the drawing canvas as you would any drawing object. You can shrink the drawing canvas to fit tightly around your drawing objects. You can also expand the drawing object and drawing canvas at the same time, or you can expand the drawing independently of the drawing canvas. If you want to add a picture to your drawing you can set the picture's wrapping style to floating, and then drag the picture onto the drawing canvas. If you do not want to use the drawing canvas, you can drag the drawing object off the drawing canvas, select the drawing canvas, and then delete it. To turn off the drawing canvas temporarily, press the Esc key or the Delete key as soon as it displays at the document screen. To turn off the drawing canvas permanently, complete the following steps:

1. Click Tools and then Options.
2. At the Options dialog box, select the General tab.
3. In the General options section, remove the check mark in the check box at the left of the *Automatically create drawing canvas when inserting AutoShapes* option.
4. Click OK or press Enter.

Inserting Bullets

Bullets

Bullets may be inserted in a document at the Bullets and Numbering dialog box or with the Bullets button on the Formatting toolbar. To display the Bullets and Numbering dialog box, click Format and then Bullets and Numbering. The Bullets and Numbering dialog box contains four tabs: Bulleted, Numbered, Outline Numbered, and List Styles. If you select a bullet and then click the Customize button at the bottom right corner of the dialog box, the Customize Bulleted List dialog box displays. At this dialog box, you can select a different font, character, or picture. The Picture option allows you to choose a decorative bullet for a Web page. The bullet and text positions may also be changed. For instance, to insert a different bullet character, click the Customize button, click the Character button, and then select a character at the Symbol dialog box. Change the size and color of the bullet by clicking the Font button.

You can create a bullet from a clip art image if the *Automatic bulleted list* option is selected on the AutoFormat tab at the AutoCorrect dialog box. Insert a clip art image and then resize it to approximately your font size, press the spacebar, type your text, and then press Enter. The next bullet displays and your text is formatted as a bulleted item as shown in Figure 2.35.

In Exercise 4, assume you are an employee at Chicago Mercy Hospital. In this exercise, you will customize a memo for the hospital using a watermark. You will also add bullets to help organize the text and add interest as well as white space to a text-intensive document.

FIGURE

2.35 *Creating a Graphic Bulleted List*

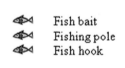

exercise 4

Creating a Memo with a Watermark

(Hint: Before completing this exercise, remember to turn off the drawing canvas feature.)

1. Open **Medical Memo** located in your Chapter02 folder.
2. Save the document with Save As and name it **c02ex04a, Watermark**.
3. Make the following changes to the document:
   a. Click the Show/Hide ¶ button on the Standard toolbar to turn on nonprintable characters.
   b. Select *Memorandum* and then type Chicago Mercy Hospital.
   c. Select *Chicago Mercy Hospital* and then change the font to 36-point Britannic Bold (or a similar font), in Pale Blue (the sixth color from the left in the last row), and apply the Shadow effect.
   d. Change the line style and color of the line above the memo text by completing the following steps:
      1) Position the insertion point anywhere in the subject line *(Re:),* click Format, and then click Borders and Shading.
      2) At the Borders tab, scroll downward in the *Style* option box and then select the three-line style.
      3) In the *Color* option box, select Pale Blue.
      4) Make sure the *Width* option box displays as *¾ pt.*
      5) Click the bottom line in the *Preview* box to apply the new line attributes and then click OK or press Enter.

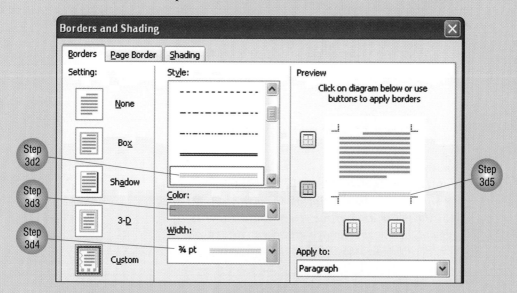

   e. Select the gray-shaded circle on the left side of the memo body text and press Delete.
   f. Add bullets to the listed text by completing the following steps:
      1) Select the text beginning with *Necessary operative forms...* and ending with *Anesthesiologist has reviewed....*
      2) Click Format and then Bullets and Numbering.
      3) At the Bullets and Numbering dialog box, select the Bulleted tab.

4) Choose any one of the bullets displayed, and then click Customize.

5) At the Customize Bulleted List dialog box, click the Character button.

6) At the Symbol dialog box, click the down-pointing arrow at the right of the *Font* option box and then choose *Wingdings*.

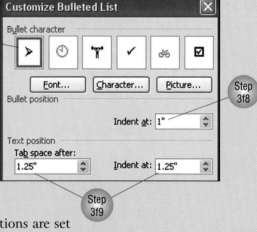

7) Click the arrow symbol (the ninth symbol from the left in the twelfth row [Wingdings: 216]) and then click OK. The arrow will appear in the Customize Bulleted List dialog box as the first item under *Bullet character*.

8) Make sure the bullet position is set at *1"*.

9) Make sure both the text position options are set at *1.25"*.

10) Click OK or press Enter. (If hollow bullets display, select the arrow symbol again.)

g. Create the medical watermark in Figure 2.36 by completing the following steps:

1) Click Format, point to Background, and then click Printed Watermark.

2) At the Printed Watermark dialog box, click *Picture watermark* and then click the Select Picture button. (Make sure *Washout* is selected.)

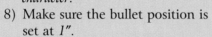

3) At the Insert Picture dialog box, click the down-pointing arrow at the right of the *Look in* option and select the following path:
C:\ProgramFiles\MicrosoftOffice\media\CntCD1\ClipArt1\j0205570.wmf. (Hint: If this image is not available, choose another similar image. Another alternative is to use the Clip Art task pane to find the desired image, right-click on the desired image at the Clip Art task pane, and then click Copy to send a copy of the image to the Office Clipboard. When you are at the Insert Picture dialog box, accessed from the Background command on the Format menu, you can right-click in the white area of the screen and then click Paste. Select your image and then click Insert.)

4) Select *j0205570.wmf*, click Insert, and then click OK.

5) Click View and then click Header and Footer.

6) At the Header and Footer pane, select the clip art image and drag a corner sizing handle outward to increase the size of the image similar to Figure 2.36. *(Hint: If you hold down Ctrl as you drag a corner sizing handle, the image will stay centered on the page.)*

7) Click to select the image and when the four-headed arrow displays, move the image similar to Figure 2.36.

8) Select the image and click the Less Brightness button on the Picture toolbar twice. (If the Picture toolbar does not display automatically when you select the image, right-click and then click Show Picture Toolbar.)

9) Click the Close button on the Header and Footer toolbar.

4. To demonstrate that the watermark created in the Header and Footer pane will automatically display on following pages, complete the following steps:

   a. Press Ctrl + End to move the insertion point to the end of the document.

   b. Press Ctrl + Enter to create an additional page. (The medical staff watermark should display on page 2.)

   c. Click the Undo button to delete the last command.

5. Save the memo with the same name **c02ex04a, Watermark**.

6. Print **c02ex04a, Watermark**.

7. Remove the watermark created in **c02ex04a, Watermark** and create another watermark using options on the Picture toolbar by completing the following steps:

   a. Click View and then Header and Footer.

   b. Select the watermark and then press the Delete key.

   c. Click Close on the Header and Footer toolbar.

   d. Position the insertion point at the beginning of the first paragraph of text.

   e. Display the Clip Art task pane by clicking Insert, pointing to Picture, and then clicking Clip Art.

   f. Click in the *Search for* text box, type j0229831.wmf or medical, and then click Go.

   g. Click the image as shown in Figure 2.37. (If this image is not available, choose another similar image.)

   h. Close the Clip Art task pane by clicking the *X* in the upper right corner.

   i. Click once on the image to select it.

   j. Click the Color button on the Picture toolbar and then click *Washout* at the drop-down list that displays. (If the Picture toolbar does not display automatically when you select the image, right-click and then click Show Picture Toolbar.)

   k. Click the Less Brightness button on the Picture toolbar three times.

   l. Click the Text Wrapping button on the Picture toolbar and then click *Behind Text* at the drop-down list.

   m. With the watermark image still selected, increase the size of the image and drag it so it is centered as shown in Figure 2.37.

   n. Click outside the image to deselect it.

8. Save the memo with Save As and name it **co2ex04b, Watermark**.

9. Print and then close **c02ex04b, Watermark**.

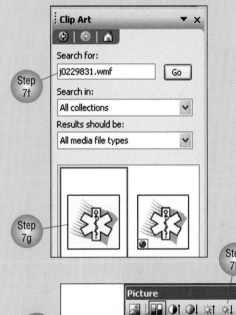

Step 7f

Step 7g

Step 7k

Step 7i

Step 7j

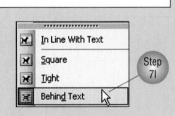

Step 7l

FIGURE

2.36 *Exercise 4, Steps 1–6*

Chicago Mercy Hospital

To: Fred Médard

From: Juliette Danner

Date: May 17, 2005

Re: PREOPERATIVE PROCEDURES

At the last meeting of the medical team, concern was raised about the structure of preoperative procedures. In light of recent nationwide occurrences in some city hospitals, members of the team decided to review written procedures to determine if additional steps should be added. A meeting of the surgical team has been set for Tuesday, May 22. Please try to arrange surgical schedules so a majority of the surgical team can attend this meeting.

Please review the following items to determine where each should be positioned in a preoperative surgical checklist:

> - Necessary operative forms are signed—admissions and consent for surgery.
> - Blood tests have been completed.
> - Blood type is noted in patient chart.
> - Surgical procedure has been triple-checked with patient and surgical team.
> - All allergies are noted in patient chart.
> - Anesthesiologist has reviewed and initialed patient chart.

I am confident that the medical team will discover that the preoperative checklist is one of the most thorough in the region. Any suggestions made by the medical team will only enhance a superior checklist.

xx:c02ex04a, Watermark

CONFIDENTIAL

2.37 *Exercise 4, Steps 7–9*

Chicago Mercy Hospital

To: Fred Médard

From: Juliette Danner

Date: May 17, 2005

Re: PREOPERATIVE PROCEDURES

At the last meeting of the medical team, concern was raised about the structure of preoperative procedures. In light of recent nationwide occurrences in some city hospitals, members of the team decided to review written procedures to determine if additional steps should be added. A meeting of the surgical team has been set for Tuesday, May 22. Please try to arrange surgical schedules so a majority of the surgical team can attend this meeting.

Please review the following items to determine where each should be positioned in a preoperative surgical checklist:

➢ Necessary operative forms are signed—admissions and consent for surgery.
➢ Blood tests have been completed.
➢ Blood type is noted in patient chart.
➢ Surgical procedure has been triple-checked with patient and surgical team.
➢ All allergies are noted in patient chart.
➢ Anesthesiologist has reviewed and initialed patient chart.

I am confident that the medical team will discover that the preoperative checklist is one of the most thorough in the region. Any suggestions made by the medical team will only enhance a superior checklist.

xx:c02ex04b, Watermark

CONFIDENTIAL

Preparing an Agenda

Before a business meeting, an agenda is generally prepared that includes such information as the name of the group or department holding the meeting; the date, time, and location of the meeting; and the topics to be discussed during the meeting. In Word 2003, you may create an agenda using the Agenda Wizard accessed by clicking the <u>On my computer</u> hyperlink at the New Document task pane and selecting the Other Documents tab. You may also create an agenda based on a template at the Microsoft Office Online Templates Web page by clicking the <u>Templates on Office Online</u> hyperlink or typing *agenda* in the *Search online for* option box shown in Figure 2.38. Otherwise, you may create a table as the underlying structure of an agenda and save it as a template. Figure 2.39 shows two customized agendas based on templates found on the Microsoft Office Online Templates Web site.

FIGURE 2.38 ***Templates on Office Online* Hyperlink**

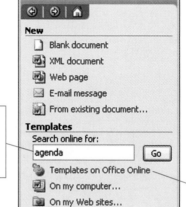

Type **agenda** in the *Search online for* option to access the Microsoft online agenda templates.

Click here to access the Microsoft Online Templates Web page.

FIGURE 2.39 *Customized Agendas from Microsoft Office Online Templates*

Agenda Template

Customized Template

Creating an Agenda Using a Table

Besides using the Agenda Wizard, an agenda may be prepared at a clear document screen with side-by-side columns, which are similar to parallel columns. Word does not include a parallel column feature where text displays across a page in rows. However, a table accomplishes the same results. To create a table, click the Insert Table button on the Standard toolbar or click Table from the Menu bar. To create the agenda in Figure 2.40, create a table with three columns and seven rows. The number of rows will depend on the number of entries in your agenda.

Insert Table

Entering Text in a Table

Information in a table is typed in cells. A *cell* is the intersection between a row and a column. With the insertion point positioned in a cell, type or edit text as you would normal text. Move the insertion point to other cells with the mouse by positioning the arrow pointer in the desired cell, then clicking the left mouse button. If you are using the keyboard, press Tab to move the insertion point to the next cell or press Shift + Tab to move the insertion point to the previous cell.

Cell
The intersection between a row and a column.

If you want to move the insertion point to a tab stop within a cell, press Ctrl + Tab. If the insertion point is located in the last cell of the table and you press the Tab key, Word adds another row to the table. When all of the information has been entered into the cells, move the insertion point below the table and, if necessary, continue typing the document, or save the document in the normal manner.

Assume you are an employee at Chicago Mercy Hospital and you are preparing an agenda for a project meeting. This agenda will be sent as an e-mail attachment to all of the project members. If your class has e-mail access, create the document in Exercise 5 and send it to a recipient in your class as an e-mail attachment.

exercise 5

Preparing an Agenda with a Table

1. Open **Agenda 01** located in your Chapter02 folder.
2. Save the document with Save As and name it **c02ex05, Agenda**.
3. Format the heading text displayed in Figure 2.40 by completing the following steps:
   a. Make sure the insertion point is positioned at the right margin (Align Right alignment).
   b. Change the font to 30-point Britannic Bold (or a similar font), small caps, shadow, font color Violet (second color from right in the third row of the color palette), type Chicago Mercy Hospital, and then press Enter.
   c. Change the font to 20-point Arial Black, the font color to Black, turn off small caps and shadow, type Quality Care Project, and then press Enter.
   d. Change the font to 18-point Arial Black, all caps, type Agenda, and then press Enter.
   e. Change the font to 12-point Arial.
   f. Change the alignment to Align Left and then press Enter two times.
4. Create a table for the agenda text by completing the following steps:
   a. Click Table, point to Insert, and then click Table.
   b. At the Insert Table dialog box, change the *Number of columns* to 3.
   c. Change the *Number of rows* to 7.
   d. Click the AutoFormat button.

e. At the Table AutoFormat dialog box, select the *Table Simple 1* style in the *Table Styles* section.

f. In the *Apply special formats to* section, remove the check mark from the *Last row* option. Click OK twice.

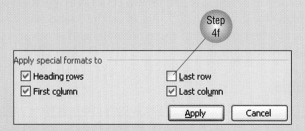

g. Click Table and then Show Gridlines if necessary.

5. Format the table by completing the following steps:

a. Position the insertion point in the table.

b. Click Table, point to Select, and then click Table.

c. Click Table and then Table Properties.

d. At the Table Properties dialog box, click the Options button.

e. At the Table Options dialog box, change the left and right margins to 0.2 inch. Click OK or press Enter.

f. Select the Table tab and then click *Center* in the *Alignment* section at the Table Properties dialog box.

g. Select the Row tab, click the check box at the left of *Specify height* option, and then type 0.75. Make sure the *Row height is* option shows *At least*.

h. Select the Cell tab and click Center in the *Vertical Alignment* section.

i. Select the Column tab, make sure a check mark displays at the left of the *Preferred width* option, and type 2.05 in the *Preferred width* option box.

j. Click the Next Column button and then make sure the *Preferred width* option for Column 2 displays *2.05*. Click the Next Column button.

k. Make sure the *Preferred width* of Column 3 is *2.05*.

l. Click OK or press Enter.

m. Select the first row and change the font to 12-point Arial, bold, all caps, and change the alignment to Center.

n. Position the insertion point inside the first cell and type Time; press Tab and type Topic; press Tab and type Discussion Leaders; and then press Tab.

o. Select all of the rows and columns below the header row, change the alignment to Align Left, change the font to 11-point Arial, turn off all caps if necessary, type 9 a.m. – 9:30 a.m. in the first cell, and then press Tab. (Insert an en dash between the times and add a space before and after the en dash.)

p. With the insertion point positioned in the second cell, type Call to order and introduction of new project members and then press Tab. Continue typing the text and pressing Tab until the agenda is completed as shown in Figure 2.40.

6. View the agenda using Print Preview.

7. Save, print, and then close c02ex05, Agenda.

CHICAGO MERCY HOSPITAL
Quality Care Project
AGENDA

TIME	TOPIC	DISCUSSION LEADERS
9 a.m. – 9:30 a.m.	Call to order and introduction of new project members	Becky Peterson, Chair
9:30 a.m. – 10 a.m.	Presentation of project mission statement	Charles-Etienne Visconti
10 a.m. – 11 a.m.	Determination of project goals and timelines	Katrina O'Dell, Geoffrey Benn, and Wendy Mitaki
11 a.m. – 11:45 a.m.	Brainstorming on public relations activities	Ellen Heitz and Hui Lenzi
11:45 a.m. – 12 Noon	Scheduling of next project meeting	Becky Peterson, Chair
12 Noon	Adjournment	Becky Peterson, Chair

CHAPTER summary

➤ A font consists of three characteristics: typeface, typestyle, and type size.

➤ The term *typeface* refers to the general design and shape of a set of characters.

➤ The typeface used in a document establishes a particular mood or feeling.

➤ Characteristics that distinguish one typeface from another include x-height, cap height, height of ascenders, depth of descenders, and serifs.

➤ A serif is a small stroke on the ends of characters. A sans serif typeface does not have serifs.

➤ Typefaces are either monospaced or proportional. Monospaced typefaces allot the same amount of horizontal space to each character, while proportional typefaces allot a varying amount to each character.

➤ Point size is a vertical measurement and is approximately 1/72 of an inch. The higher the point size chosen, the larger the characters.

➤ The Font color feature includes 40 colors on the color palette, 124 colors and 15 shades of gray at the Standard tab, and an option to mix your own colors at the Custom tab of the Colors dialog box.

➤ At the Custom tab of the Colors dialog box, you can change the *luminescence*, which is the brightness of the color; the *hue*, which is the color itself; and the *saturation*, which is the color's intensity. You can also change the values of Red, Green, and Blue.

➤ Readability is the ease with which a person can read and understand groups of words.

➤ For text set in a proportional typeface, space once after end-of-sentence punctuation.

➤ Special symbols may be inserted in a document at the Symbol dialog box with the Symbols tab or the Special Characters tab selected.

➤ The Fax Wizard helps you create and send a fax through your computer.

➤ The drawing canvas is an area where you can draw multiple shapes; because the shapes are contained within the drawing canvas, they can be moved and resized as a unit.

➤ An em dash (—) is as long as the point size of the type and is used in text to indicate a pause in speech.

➤ An en dash (–) indicates a continuation, such as 116–133 or January–March, and is exactly one-half the width of an em dash.

➤ Bullets may be inserted in a document at the Bullets and Numbering dialog box or with the Bullets button on the Formatting toolbar.

➤ In typesetting, the open quotation mark is curved upward (") and the close quotation mark is curved downward ("). In typesetting, straight quotes are used to indicate inches (") or feet (').

➤ Word's Reveal Formatting task pane lets you view detailed descriptions of the formatting in your document.

➤ The Clear Formatting command at the *Style* list box option or at the Styles and Formatting task pane will remove all character formatting or a character style. This command has the same effect as Ctrl + spacebar.

➤ Text boxes are often used to move and position text easily in a document. If text boxes overlap, select No Fill and No Line on the Colors and Lines tab at the Format Text Box dialog box.

- Word provides a number of templates and wizards used to produce a variety of documents. The default template document is Normal.dot.
- Wizards walk you through a series of steps in which you add or select information to set up formatting, content, and layout of your document.
- Click the down-pointing arrow at the right of the New Document task pane to access other task panes, such as Getting Started, Help, Search Results, Clip Art, Research, Clipboard, Shared Workspace, Document Updates, Protect Document, Styles and Formatting, Reveal Formatting, Mail Merge, and XML Structure task panes.
- Display the Clip Art task pane by clicking Insert, pointing to Picture, and then clicking Clip Art. You can also click the Insert Clip Art button on the Drawing toolbar.
- Drag the sizing handles around a selected image to size it.
- Move an image by selecting the image, changing the Text Wrapping style, and then using the mouse to drag the image to the desired position.
- Many of Word's templates are formatted consistently using three designs—Contemporary, Elegant, and Professional.
- You may access templates by clicking the On my computer hyperlink or the Templates on Office Online hyperlink at the New Document task pane.
- A watermark is a lightened image added to a document to add visual interest.
- Create a watermark with options from the Printed Watermark dialog box or the *Washout* option on the Picture toolbar.
- The *Washout* option adjusts the brightness and contrast of the image to make it less visible behind text.
- Word contains an agenda template used to prepare an agenda for a meeting.
- The agenda may be customized and saved as a separate template.
- Tables may be used when formatting an agenda into side-by-side columns.
- The Table Properties dialog box includes options to change table size, alignment, and text wrap; row height; column width; and cell size and vertical alignment.

COMMANDS review

Command	Mouse/Keyboard
Font dialog box	Format, Font; or press Ctrl + D
Header and Footer pane	View, Header and Footer
Borders and Shading dialog box	Format, Borders and Shading
New Document task pane	File, New; or View, Task Pane, Other Task Panes button, New Document
Clip Art task pane	Insert, Picture, Clip Art; or click Insert Clip Art button on Drawing toolbar
Watermark	Format, Background, Printed Watermark; Picture watermark or Text watermark
Symbol dialog box	Insert, Symbol
Word Templates	Display New Document task pane, click On my computer hyperlink

Microsoft Office Online Templates	Display New Document task pane, click <u>Templates on Office Online</u> hyperlink
Drawing canvas (on/off)	<u>T</u>ools, <u>O</u>ptions, General tab, Automati<u>c</u>ally create drawing canvas when inserting AutoShapes
Bullets and Numbering	F<u>o</u>rmat, Bullets and <u>N</u>umbering
Insert Table	Ta<u>b</u>le, <u>I</u>nsert, <u>T</u>able; or click Insert Table button on the Standard toolbar

REVIEWING key points

Matching: On a blank sheet of paper, provide the correct letter or letters that match each definition.

- **A** Ascenders
- **B** Baseline
- **C** Cap height
- **D** Descenders
- **E** Em dash
- **F** En dash
- **G** Monospaced
- **H** Point
- **I** Point size
- **J** Proportional
- **K** Sans serif
- **L** Serif
- **M** Typeface
- **N** Typestyle
- **O** x-height

1. A set of characters with a common design and shape.
2. Imaginary horizontal line on which text rests.
3. Height of the main body of the lowercase characters and equivalent to the lowercase *x*.
4. Distance between the baseline and the top of capital letters.
5. Parts of lowercase characters that rise above the x-height.
6. Parts of characters that extend below the baseline.
7. A special character that is used in a duration of time or continuation.
8. A small stroke at the edge of characters.
9. A typeface that does not contain serifs.
10. Approximately ½ of an inch.
11. Varying style of a typeface, including bold and italic.
12. A special symbol that is used to indicate a pause in speech.

True/False: On a blank sheet of paper, write *True* if the statement is true and *False* if the statement is false.

1. Proportional typefaces allot the same amount of horizontal space for each character in a typeface.
2. Text boxes may be used to position text in a document.
3. When text is set in a proportional typeface, space once after punctuation.
4. The default template document is the Main template.
5. Click the New Blank Document button on the Standard toolbar to display the New dialog box.

6. A watermark created with the *Background* option at the F̲ormat menu exists in the text layer of a document.

7. Display the New Document task pane to insert a clip art image.

8. The *Washout* option adjusts the brightness and contrast of the image to make it less visible behind text.

9. A watermark created in a header and footer pane will appear only on the page where it was created.

10. Press the Tab key to move the insertion point to the next cell in a table.

11. Word's New Document task pane lets you view detailed descriptions of the formatting in your document.

12. The Remove Format Style option clears formatting and styles from selected text.

APPLYING your skills

Assessment 1

1. Prepare a sign to be posted in the lobby and at the door of the Meade Conference Room informing committee members for the World Computing Consortium that their meeting location has been changed to the Fleetwood Conference Room on the sixth floor, room 608, of the Swiss International Hotel. *(Hint: Type Logo, Symbol, Computing, or World in the Search for option box at the Clip Art task pane and then click Go. You may also use a symbol from the Symbol dialog box and increase the point size of the symbol.)*
   a. Use at least one serif and one sans serif typeface.
   b. Use a font color.
   c. Insert a watermark or create a logo for the World Computing Consortium or for the hotel.
   d. Use two font attributes such as italics, bold, small caps, and so forth.
   e. Include one special character or symbol.
2. Save, print, and then close **c02sa01, Sign**.

Assessment 2

As an assistant to a committee member for the American Society of Public Accountants, you are responsible for creating an agenda for an upcoming meeting. Include a simple logo.

1. Create an agenda using the Agenda Wizard, an online agenda template, or a table and include the following specifications:

   Professional and Personal Liability Insurance Programs Committee
   August 1, 2005
   Executive Centre
   525 N. Michigan Avenue
   Chicago, IL 60601
   Continental Breakfast at the Executive Centre Cafe 7 a.m. to 8 a.m.; regular session 8 a.m. to 5 p.m.

8 a.m. – 9 a.m.	Overview of Program – YTD (J. Wisemann, K. Wolfe)
9 a.m. – 11 a.m.	Status of Member Awareness Initiative (K. Wolfe)

	Update on Marketing Efforts (S. Monroe)
	Overview of Rate Study for 2005 Pricing (J. Bossung)
11 a.m. – Noon	State Society Report (F. Collins)
Noon – 1 p.m.	Luncheon in Lake Michigan Room
1 p.m. – 2 p.m.	Technology Enhancements to Program (J. Wisemann)
2 p.m. – 3:30 p.m.	Investment Advisory Services (M. Reisser)
3:30 p.m. – 4:30 p.m.	Risk Management Issues (S. Monroe)
4:30 p.m. – 5 p.m.	Closing Remarks (F. B. Edwards)
	Future Meeting Date; November 7, 2005 – Dallas, TX

2. Save, print, and then close **c02sa02, Agenda**.

Assessment 3

As an employee at Chicago Mercy Hospital, prepare a memo to Audra Schöenbeck with an addition to next week's newsletter.

1. Choose one of the Memo templates in Word.
2. Save the memo as a template in your Chapter02 DTP Templates folder and name it **c02sa03, CMH Memo.dot**.
3. Type the heading text below. Use the (normal text) font for the character symbols.

> Date: March 17, 2005; To: Audra Schöenbeck; From: Marcus Cañete; Subject: Healthy Heart Week

4. Insert **Memo Text** located in your Chapter02 folder.
5. Customize the memo and include the following specifications:
   a. Use a sans serif font in the heading and a serif font in 12 points for the body text.
   b. Format the memo text appropriately.
   c. Use three font effects to emphasize text in the document.
   d. Insert appropriate bullets.
   e. Insert an appropriate watermark.
6. Save, print, and then close **c02sa03, CMH Memo.dot**.

Assessment 4

In this assessment you will customize a Word memo template and copy and paste a chart from an Excel worksheet into this memo as shown in the example in Figure 2.41. In addition, you will determine the average monthly cost of gas by inserting a formula into the Excel worksheet and record this amount in the text of the memo. Complete the following steps:

INTEGRATED

1. In Word, access the New Document task pane and then click the <u>On my computer</u> hyperlink.
2. Select the Contemporary Memo template at the Templates dialog box and open it as a Document (not a Template).
3. Select *Memorandum* and change the font color to Indigo.
4. Double-click the design element that resembles two halves of a circle and then change the color of the object to Light Yellow at the Format AutoShape dialog box at the Colors and Lines tab in the *Fill* section. Click OK.
5. Type the following text to replace the memo heading placeholder text:

> To: Susan Howard
> CC: Delete this line.
> From: Superior Gas
> Date: Insert the current date
> Re: Superior Gas Budget Plan

6. Select the heading text and change the font to 10-pt. Tahoma.
7. Select the body placeholder text and then insert **Budget Plan** from your Chapter02 folder. *(Hint: **Do not delete the placeholder text; select it and then insert the file text over it.**)*
8. Minimize Word and then Open Excel.
9. In Excel, open **Budget Plan Chart** from your Chapter02 folder.
10. Position your insertion point in Cell B14 and insert this formula to compute the average of the monthly bills: =Average(B2:B13).
11. Select the chart and then click the Copy button.
12. Minimize Excel and then maximize Word.
13. Position the insertion point a double space below the last line of the memo text and then click <u>E</u>dit, Paste <u>S</u>pecial.
14. At the Paste Special dialog box, make sure the *<u>P</u>aste* option is selected and then select *Microsoft Office Excel Chart Object* in the *<u>A</u>s* list box. Click OK.
15. Type the average amount that you computed in Excel in place of the text *(insert average cost here)*.
16. Save the document and name it **c02sa04, Budget Plan**.
17. Print and then close **c02sa04, Budget Plan**.
18. Close **Budget Plan Chart** without saving changes and then close Excel.

FIGURE

2.41 *Assessment 4 Sample Solution*

Memorandum

To: Susan Howard

From: Superior Gas

Date: Current Date

Re: Superior Gas Budget Plan

If your gas bills this winter are causing you undue concern, we would like to make you aware of a program that will take the surprise out of your monthly Superior Gas statement. We have a Budget Plan available for our customers. You can sign up to spread your natural gas bill payments over the next 12 months. Our program is quite simple. We will determine your individual Budget Plan amount for the next 12 months based on factors such as normal weather, gas prices, and prior gas usage at your home.

If you would like to sign up for your recommended minimum payment of **$123.68,** simply mark the line on your payment stub and send it in with your first payment for that amount. You will automatically be signed up for the program. If you would like more information about our Budget Plan, call us at 1.888.555.4890 or visit our Web site at www.emcp.net/superiorgas.

The chart below shows your monthly gas charges from January to December 2004.

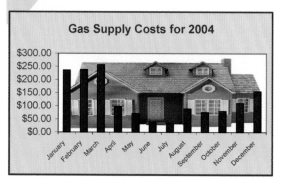

CONFIDENTIAL

1

Assessment 5

Create a cover for a Team Building Workshop handout in PowerPoint as shown in the example in Figure 2.42 by completing the following steps:

1. At a blank presentation screen, click File and then Page Setup.
2. At the Page Setup dialog box, change the slide orientation to *Portrait* and then click OK.
3. Click the Other Task Panes button at the top of the Getting Started task pane and then select Slide Design at the drop-down list.
4. Select the Eclipse.pot design template from the *Apply a design template* list box.
5. Click the placeholder text, *Click to add title,* type Team Building, press Enter, and then type Workshop 2005.
6. Click the placeholder text, *Click to add subtitle,* type Facilitated by:, press Enter, and then type your name. Press Enter three times and then insert the current date. Select the date and change it to 18-point Verdana.
7. Save the document and name it **c02sa05, Team**.
8. Print and then close **c02sa05, Team**.
9. Close PowerPoint.

FIGURE

2.42 **Assessment 5 Sample Solution**

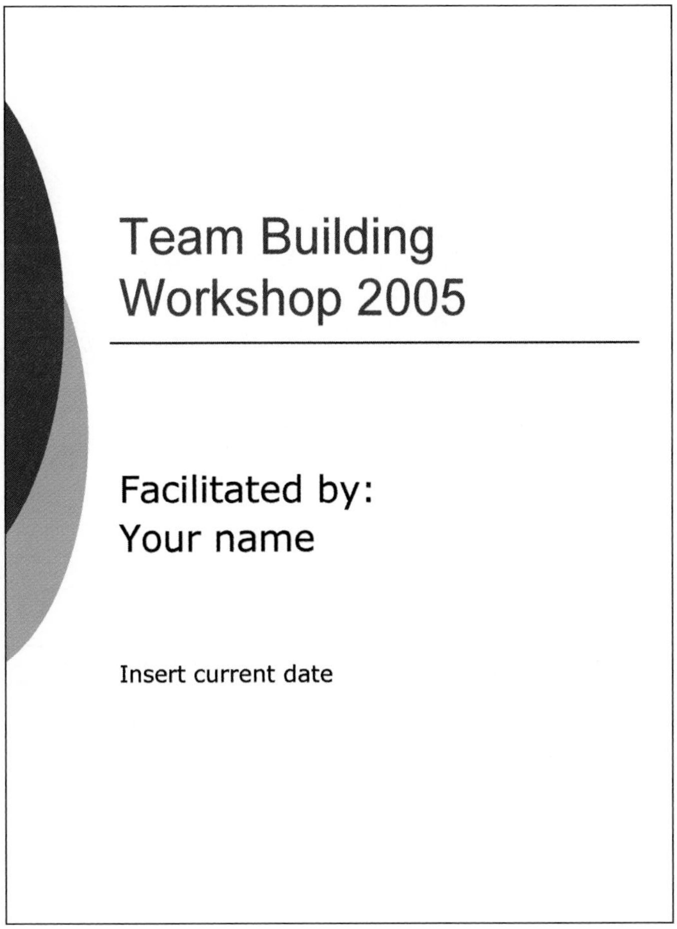

Team Building
Workshop 2005

Facilitated by:
Your name

Insert current date

Assessment 6

You work for a desktop publisher called Desktop Designs located at 4455 Jackson Drive, Raleigh, NC 27613. Create a press release describing the services performed by Desktop Designs. Include a simple logo and change the font and font sizes in the template. Use a press release template from the Microsoft Office Online Templates Web page and include the following information in your own words:

Design and Create

- Desktop Designs has been operating in the Raleigh area for over 12 years.
- The employees of Desktop Designs have over 30 years of combined graphics design and typesetting experience.
- The company provides a variety of services, including creating personal documents such as cover letters, résumés, invitations, programs, cards, envelopes and labels; creating business documents such as letterheads, envelopes, business cards, forms, logos, and slides; and creating promotional and marketing documents such as newsletters, flyers, and brochures.
- The company is open Monday through Saturday from 7 a.m. to 6 p.m.

After creating the press release, save it and name it **c02sa06, Press**. Print and then close **c02sa06, Press**.

CHAPTER 3

Creating Letterheads, Envelopes, and Business Cards

PERFORMANCE OBJECTIVES

Upon successful completion of Chapter 3, you will be able to produce letterheads, envelopes, and business cards using Word features such as text boxes, ruled lines, WordArt, and templates.

CHAPTER 03

DESKTOP PUBLISHING TERMS

Anchor	Nudging	Tracking
Exact placement	Ruled lines	Weight
Kerning	Template	

WORD FEATURES USED

Anchor	Envelopes and labels	Microsoft Office Online
Automatic kerning	Fonts	Templates Web
AutoText	Format Text Box dialog	page
Borders and shading	box	Templates folder
Business card label	Horizontal and vertical	Templates on Office
definition	lines	Online hyperlink
Character spacing	Letter templates	Text boxes
Click and Type	Letter Wizard	WordArt
Drawing toolbar	Manual kerning	

In this chapter, you will produce business letterheads, envelopes, and business cards using your own design and creative skills as well as Word's Templates feature and the Microsoft Office Online Templates Web page. Although Word and Office provide a variety of letter templates to choose from, they do not meet the needs of all situations. Information on how to customize an existing template and how to create your own design and layout from scratch are presented in this chapter.

Ruled lines, kerning (the spacing between pairs of letters), and tracking (character spacing) are discussed, along with text boxes and Word's Envelopes and Labels, and AutoText features.

Identifying the Purpose of Letterheads

In planning a letterhead design, think about its purpose. While the content of a letter may vary, the purpose of any letterhead is generally the same—to convey information, to establish an identity, and to project an image.

Conveying Information

Consider all of the necessary information you want to include in your letterhead. Also, consider what items your readers expect to find in your letterhead. Although the information provided may vary, letterheads commonly contain the following:

- Name of company or organization
- Logo
- Address
- Shipping or mailing address, if different from street address
- Telephone number, including area code (include actual numbers if your phone number incorporates a catchy word as part of the number; include extra phone numbers, such as a local number and/or an 800 number, if any)
- Fax number, including area code
- E-mail address
- Internet or Web address
- Marketing statement or company slogan

The information in a letterhead supplies the reader with a means of contacting you in person, by phone, by e-mail, or by regular mail. Leaving out an important component in your letterhead can affect your company's business and project a careless attitude.

Establishing an Identity

A business identity is often initiated through written communication. For example, a buyer from one company may write to another company inquiring about a certain product or asking for a price list; a real estate agent may send out a letter explaining his or her services to residents in surrounding communities; or, a volunteer organization may send letters to local businesses soliciting their support. Whatever the reason for the letter, a letterhead with a specific design and layout helps to establish an organization's identity. When readers are exposed to the same pattern of consistent elements in a letterhead over a period of time, they soon begin to establish a certain level of familiarity with the organization's name, logo, colors, and so forth. A letterhead is recognizable and identifiable.

You can further emphasize an organization's identity by using some of the design elements from a letterhead in other business documents. If you do not want to create your own design, many direct-mail paper suppliers offer a whole line of attractively designed color letterheads, along with coordinating envelopes, business cards, brochures, postcards, note cards, disk labels, and more. All you have to do is plan the layout of the letterhead text to complement the existing design and then print on the preprinted papers. Purchasing a coordinating line of preprinted

DTP POINTERS

A letterhead conveys information, establishes an identity, and projects an image.

papers can save on the high costs of professional designing and printing. It also provides a convenient way to establish your identity among your readers. Some paper suppliers offer a sample kit of their papers for purchase at a reasonable price. This is a great opportunity to see and feel the papers and to test some of them in your printer.

Projecting an Image

Along with establishing an identity, think about the image that identity projects to your readers. As mentioned in Chapter 1, assess your target audience. Who are they? What is their background, education, age, and so on? What image do you want your readers to form in their minds about your company, business, or organization? What does their experience tell them to expect?

Look at the two different letterheads in Figure 3.1. Without knowing any other supporting details, what image do you form in your mind about each of these hospitals? The top letterhead projects a fun, casual, somewhat juvenile, not-so-professional image while the bottom letterhead conveys a serious, businesslike attitude. Even though the projected image may not be an accurate representation of either hospital, it is the image presented to the reader and thus carries a lot of impact. On the other hand, giving your readers what they expect can sometimes lead to boredom. Your challenge is to create a design that gives readers what they expect and, at the same time, sets your letterhead apart from the rest.

FIGURE

3.1 *What Image Does Each of These Letterheads Project?*

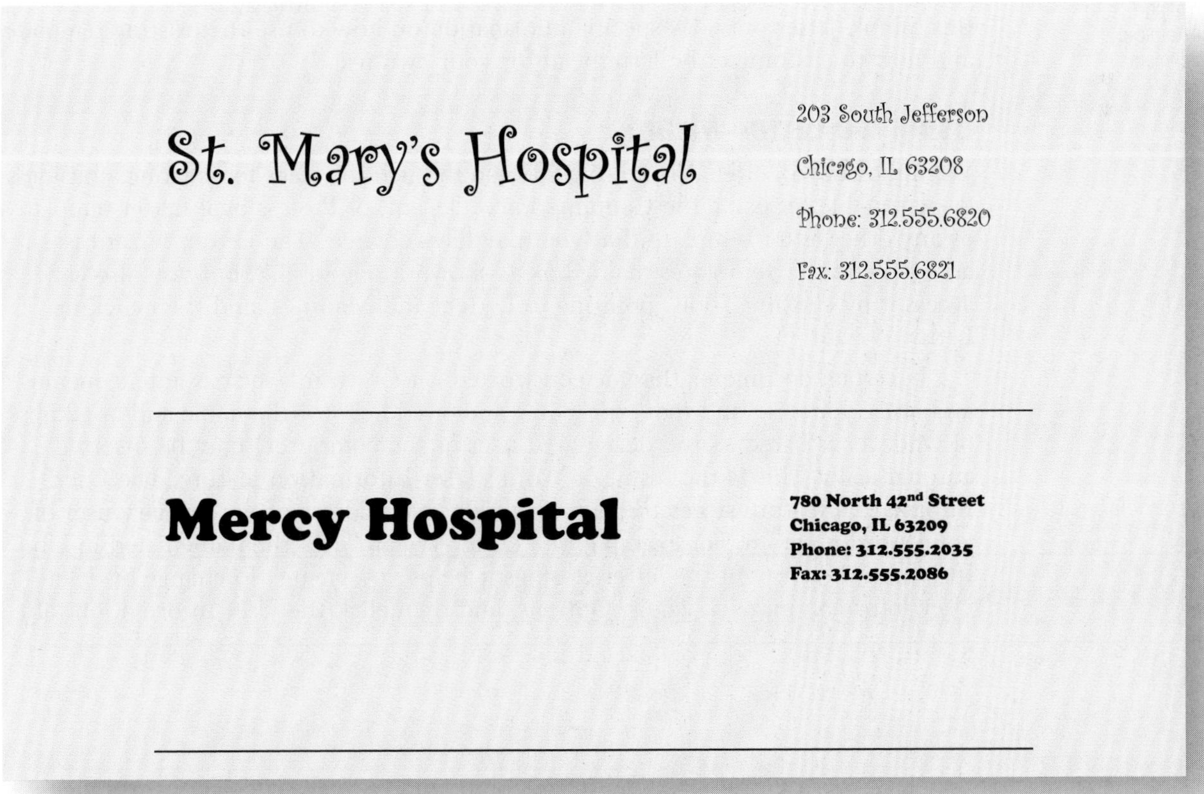

St. Mary's Hospital

203 South Jefferson

Chicago, IL 63208

Phone: 312.555.6820

Fax: 312.555.6821

Mercy Hospital

780 North 42ⁿᵈ Street
Chicago, IL 63209
Phone: 312.555.2035
Fax: 312.555.2086

DTP POINTERS
Printing on high-quality paper presents a professional image.

Printing your letterhead on high-quality paper may add to the cost, but it certainly presents a more professional image. An off-white, ivory, cream, or gray paper is a better choice than plain white. You may have to go to a commercial printer to purchase this kind of paper. Many print shops let you buy paper by the sheet, along with matching envelopes.

Using Word's Letterhead Templates

Template
A predesigned document used as a basis for other documents.

As discussed in Chapter 2, Word includes a variety of predesigned ***template*** documents, including letterheads. At the New Document task pane, click the On my computer hyperlink to open the Templates dialog box, and then select the Letters & Faxes tab to display the following Word letter templates:

- Letter Wizard (Helps you create a letter)
- Contemporary Letter
- Elegant Letter
- Professional Letter

DTP POINTERS
Establish identity and consistency among your internal and external business documents.

The descriptive names of the letterhead templates coordinate with the descriptive names for the memo, fax, report, and resume templates provided by Word. This is an easy way for you to establish identity and consistency between your internal and external business documents.

DTP POINTERS
Templates can provide the framework for creating customized documents.

The body of a template document may contain some valuable user information. For example, when you select the Contemporary Letter, the body of the letter contains a brief paragraph that includes the following sentence: *For more details on modifying this letter template, double-click this icon* ✉. When you double-click the *Envelope* icon, the letter is replaced with a completed sample letter. The body of this sample letter provides specific information on how to use the existing template and how to customize the letterhead for your own use.

Using the Letter Wizard

Word provides a Letter Wizard to guide you through the steps for creating a business or personal letter using the Contemporary, Elegant, or Professional Letter template or any other letter template that you may have created. The Letter Wizard is accessible at the Templates dialog box as shown in Figure 3.2, but you also can access it by clicking Tools, pointing to Letters and Mailings, and then clicking Letter Wizard.

In certain documents that are constructed with a wizard, such as letters, memos, and faxes, you may find that your name and/or address (or the name and/or address of whoever is listed as the designated user of the computer) may be inserted automatically. This is the result of Word's User Information feature. The User Information feature stores the name, initials, and address of the primary user of your Word program. For example, the Letter Wizard uses the name listed in User Information in any of the letter closings it helps you create. To change or delete User Information, click Tools, Options, and then click the User Information tab.

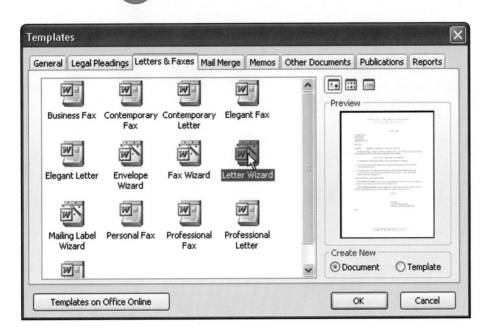

Customizing the Letter

After constructing a document with a wizard or template, the existing template document can be customized once it is displayed at the document screen. Any changes made affect only the document displayed on the screen, leaving the template available in its original format.

Using the Microsoft Office Online Templates Web Page

In addition to the Agenda templates that were used in Chapter 2, the Microsoft Office Online Templates Web page also includes Resume, Cover Letter, Resignation Letter, Request, Problem, Positive Feedback, Meeting, Event, Project, Stationery, Label, and Card templates, and many more. The different templates are categorized under headings such as Calendars and Planners, Holidays and Occasions, Human Resources, and so on. In Exercise 1, you will use the professionally designed letterhead template shown in Figure 3.3.

3.3 **Letterhead with Dots Theme Template**

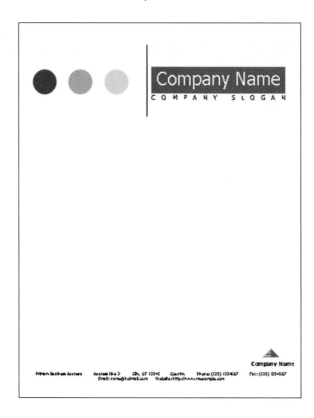

(Before completing computer exercises, delete the Chapter02 folder on your disk. Next, copy the Chapter03 folder from the CD that accompanies this textbook to your disk and then make Chapter03 the active folder.)

exercise

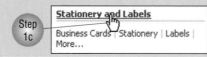

Creating a Letterhead Using a Template from the Microsoft Office Online Templates Web Page

1. At a clear document screen, create the letter in Figure 3.4 by completing the following steps:
   a. Click View, Task Pane, and then display the New Document task pane.
   b. Click the Templates on Office Online hyperlink. (If necessary, first access the Internet through your Internet Service Provider.)
   c. At the Microsoft Office Online Templates Web page, click the Stationery and Labels hyperlink located under the *Browse Templates* section of the page.

Step 1c

d. At the Stationery and Labels Web page, click the Stationery hyperlink.
e. At the Stationery Web page, scroll down the page and then click the Letterhead (Dots theme) hyperlink.
f. At the Letterhead with Dots theme Preview Web page, click the Download Now button. *(Note: Depending on your computer's configuration, you may see a message indicating that the ActiveX Control for Microsoft is automatically being downloaded to your computer. Click the Continue button when the download process is complete. Another message may appear letting you know that you can download links to additional assistance and resources from the template resources available at Microsoft Office Online. Click Yes to display the links, or No to close the dialog box without displaying the links.)*

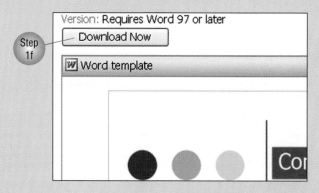

g. At the Word document screen, save the letterhead and name it **c03ex01, Graphic**.

2. Position the insertion point at the beginning of the document and insert a text file by completing the following steps:
a. Click Insert and then File.
b. Insert the **Graphic Text** file located in your Chapter03 folder.

3. Insert the company name at the top of the document and adjust the letter spacing in the slogan placeholder text by completing the following steps:
a. Select the company name placeholder text and then type Graphic Edge.
b. Select the slogan placeholder text and then type **Desktop Designs**. (The text will not fit properly in the text box. Adjustments will be made in the next few steps.)
c. Select *Desktop Designs* (press Ctrl + A), click Format, and then click Font.
d. At the Font dialog box, select the Character Spacing tab.
e. Change *Spacing* to *Expanded* and make sure the *By* list box displays *12 pt*.
f. Click OK or press Enter. (The text should fit squarely below the company name text box in the letterhead; make any necessary adjustments.)

4. Replace the placeholder text at the bottom of the letter with the text in Figure 3.4. *(Hint: If the e-mail address or Web site address displays as a hyperlink, select the address, right-click the mouse, and click Remove Hyperlink.)*

5. The date should display about a double space below the last line of the letterhead; make any necessary adjustments.

6. Save, print, and then close **c03ex01, Graphic**.

FIGURE

3.4   *Exercise 1*

Graphic Edge
DESKTOP   DESIGNS

August 5, 2005

Mr. Gregory Marshall
347 North Hillside Drive
Cincinnati, OH 45207

Dear Mr. Marshall:

It is with great pleasure that I am able to offer you a position at Graphic Edge as a graphic designer.

After reviewing your portfolio, considering your outstanding grades at Miami University, and discussing your creative contributions during your internship at CDP, I am excited about inviting you to join our team. In addition to the salary we discussed, you will receive two weeks' paid vacation every 12 months, a bonus equaling two weeks' salary payable the payday before Christmas, health benefits, and $75,000 of life insurance. This position is a two-year agreement, after which it may be renegotiated. Either party may terminate with a two-week notice.

I am very pleased to offer you the position and am sure that you will make a superb addition to our firm. If you have any questions, please call me at any time.

Sincerely,

Georgiana Forrester
Art Director

ka

Graphic Edge

27 Keystone Avenue   Indianapolis, IN 46204   Phone (317) 555-6011   Fax: (317) 555-6012
Email: GraphicEdge@emcp.net   Website: http://www.emcp.net/graphicedge

Designing Your Own Letterhead

Designing your own letterhead lets you create your own identity and image while cutting costs at the same time. In upcoming exercises, you will have the chance to create a letterhead from scratch and to convert the letterhead into a template.

Incorporating Design Concepts in a Letterhead

When creating thumbnail sketches and, ultimately, your letterhead, think of the following design concepts:

- Focus—create a focal point in the letterhead to draw your audience in.

- Balance—use a symmetrical layout where similar elements are distributed evenly on the page, or use an asymmetrical layout where dissimilar elements are distributed unevenly on the page in such a way as to balance one another.

- Proportion—design elements sized in proportion to their relative importance to the intended message. Your letterhead should not take up any more than 2 inches at the top of the page, preferably less.

- Contrast—use enough contrast to make it noticeable and make sure there is enough surrounding white space assigned to darker elements on the page.

- Directional flow—group related items close to each other and establish a visual connection between items on the page by using a strong alignment.

- Consistency—use a typeface consistently in your letterhead even though it may vary in type size, typestyle, or color. Repeat elements that tie the letterhead to subsequent pages, such as a ruled horizontal line that is repeated as a footer on each page.

- Color—use color sparingly to provide emphasis and contrast and use a color that meets your readers' expectations for the mood, tone, and image of your organization and your message.

Using the Click and Type Feature to Position Design Elements

Word's Click and Type feature can be used to quickly insert text, graphics, tables, or other items into a blank area of a document. Change to Print Layout View and then click in a blank area to view the Click and Type pointer as shown in Figure 3.5. The Click and Type pointer displays the alignment formatting that will be applied. Double-click the mouse button to apply the formatting necessary to position the insertion point where you double-clicked the mouse button. If the Click and Type feature does not work, check to see that it is enabled by clicking Tools and then Options to open the Options dialog box, then click the Edit tab to make sure that there is a check in the *Enable click and type* check box.

FIGURE

3.5 *Click and Type Alignment*

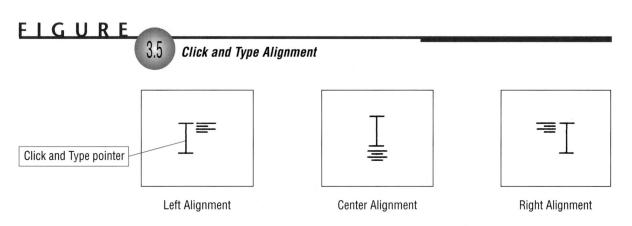

Click and Type pointer

Left Alignment   Center Alignment   Right Alignment

Using Text Boxes to Position Design Elements

DTP POINTERS

Use the text box feature to place design elements at exact locations on the page.

Text boxes are extremely useful in desktop publishing because text, tables, worksheets, pictures, or other objects can be enclosed in a text box and dragged to any position on the page using the mouse, or exact horizontal and vertical locations can be specified at the Format Text Box dialog box. (Exceptions include a page break, column break, section break, or text formatted into columns.)

Another important feature of a text box is that it is created in the drawing (foreground) layer and is considered a drawing object. Like any other object in Word, a text box may be placed above or below the text layer in a Word document. Text can be wrapped around a text box in a variety of ways, the direction of the text can be changed, and text boxes may also be linked.

Additionally, text boxes, as well as other Word objects, may be formatted by using options from the Drawing toolbar, such as applying 3-D effects, shadows, border styles and colors, fills, and backgrounds.

Turning on the Drawing Toolbar

Drawing

To turn on the display of the toolbar, choose one of the following methods:

- Click the Drawing button on the Standard toolbar.
- Choose View, point to Toolbars, and click Drawing (this inserts a check mark beside *Drawing*).
- Position the arrow pointer in any currently displayed toolbar, right-click, and then click *Drawing* from the pop-up list.

When you select the Drawing toolbar, the toolbar appears at the bottom of the screen above the Status bar. Figure 3.6 illustrates the Drawing toolbar and the names of each button.

F I G U R E

3.6 Drawing Toolbar

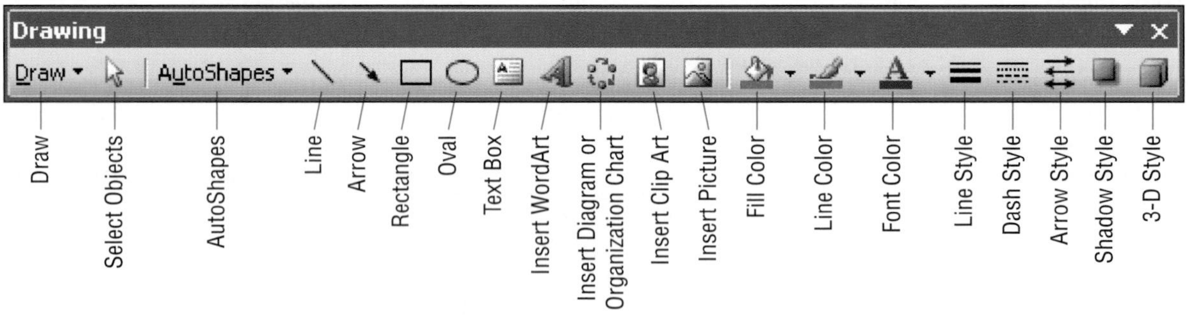

Setting Internal Margins in a Text Box

By default, a text box has left and right internal margins of 0.1 inch, and top and bottom internal margins of 0.05 inch. These margins can be adjusted to increase or decrease the distance between the contents of the text box and the text box borders. To do this, select the desired text box, click Format, Text Box, or double-click the text box border, and then select the Text Box tab. At the Text Box tab, as shown in Figure 3.7, change the left, right, top, and bottom internal margins as desired.

3.7 | *Text Box Internal Margins*

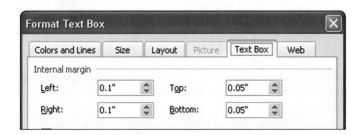

Sizing a Text Box

A text box (or object) must first be selected before the size can be changed. To do this, position the I-beam pointer within the text box, and then click the left mouse button. This selects the text box and adds sizing handles (white circles) to the text box borders. The following two methods may be used to size a text box:

- **Using the Mouse:** Select the text box (or object) and then position the mouse pointer on a sizing handle until it turns into a double-headed arrow as shown in Figure 3.8. Hold down the left mouse button, drag the outline of the text box toward or away from the center of the object until it is the desired size, and then release the mouse button. To maintain the proportions of the existing text box dimensions, use one of the corner sizing handles to change both the width and the height at the same time. Hold down the Ctrl key as you drag one of the corner sizing handles and the object will remain centered.

3.8 | *Resizing a Text Box Using Sizing Handles*

Sizing handle displays as a diagonal double-headed arrow; drag a corner sizing handle to resize.

Drag a corner sizing handle while holding down the Ctrl key to size from the center.

- **Using the Format Text Box Dialog Box:** The Format Text Box dialog box can be opened by selecting a text box (or object) and doing any of the following: double-clicking the text box border, right-clicking and then selecting Format Text Box from the shortcut menu that appears, or clicking Format at the Menu bar and then clicking Text Box. Once the Format Text Box dialog box is displayed, choose the Size tab. In the *Size and rotate* section, type the desired measurements for the width and height of the text box as shown in Figure 3.9.

As an alternative to putting in specific measurements in the *Size and rotate* section, you can enter width and height measurements as a percentage of the original size of the text box in the *Scale* section. If you want to change the height and width settings in relation to each other, select the *Lock aspect ratio* option in the *Scale* section. Using the Format Text Box dialog box for sizing allows you to adjust the size of the text box precisely.

F I G U R E

3.9 *Resizing a Text Box Using the Format Text Box Dialog Box*

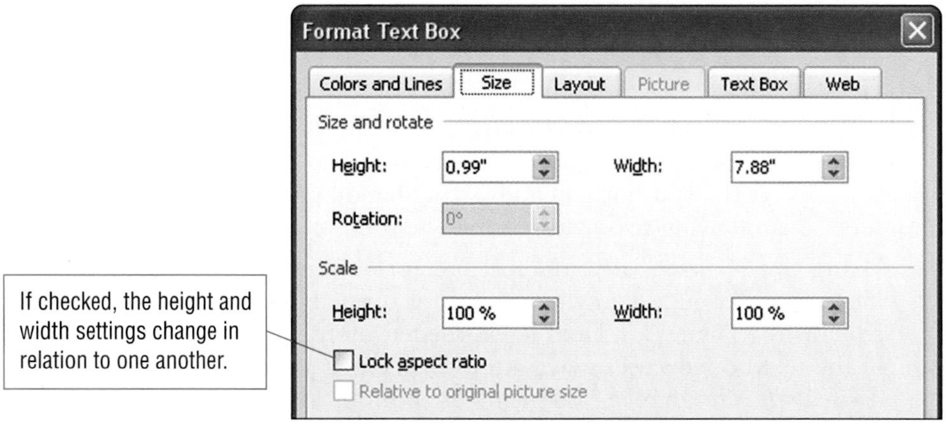

If checked, the height and width settings change in relation to one another.

Positioning a Text Box at an Exact Location on a Page

DTP POINTERS
Change the zoom by holding down the Ctrl key and scrolling with your mouse.

DTP POINTERS
Change the display to *Whole Page* when repositioning a text box.

One of the biggest advantages to using a text box is the ability to position the text box anywhere on the page. When positioning a text box on a page, change the zoom to *Whole Page* or, if working with multiple pages, change the zoom to accommodate several pages. You can use one of the following three methods (individually or in combination) to position a text box:

- **Using the Mouse:** Position the I-beam pointer on the text box border (or object) until it displays as an arrow with a four-headed arrow attached. Hold down the left mouse button, drag the outline of the object to the new location, and then release the mouse button.

Nudging
Moving an object in small increments using the arrow keys or Drawing toolbar Nudge command.

- **Using the Keyboard:** Select the text box (or object) and then press one of the arrow keys (left, right, up, or down). This method is very useful when you want to make slight adjustments to the position of the text box. *Nudging* is the term used to describe moving objects small increments (1 point) using the arrow keys or by clicking D̲raw, pointing to N̲udge, and then clicking an option at the pop-up menu. Also, remove the *Snap objects to grid* option by clicking D̲raw, Gri̲d, and then removing the check mark.

- **Using the Format Text Box Dialog Box:** Use one of the previously described methods to open the Format Text Box dialog box and then choose the Layout tab. In the *Horizontal alignment* section shown in Figure 3.10, you can choose *L̲eft, C̲enter,* or *R̲ight* alignment, or set your own specifications.

FIGURE
3.10 *Using Horizontal Alignment to Position a Text Box*

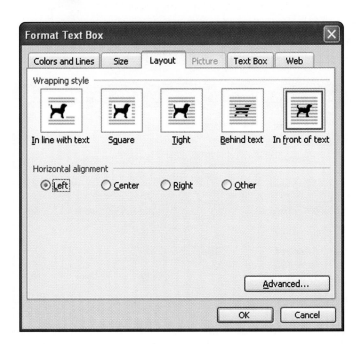

To set other exact placement specifications, make sure *Other* is selected and click the Advanced button. At the Advanced Layout dialog box in Figure 3.11, select the Picture Position tab. In the *Horizontal* section, make sure *Absolute position* is selected, and then type the desired measurement in the corresponding text box. In the *to the right of* list box, select the point *(Margin, Page, Column,* or *Character)* from which you want to horizontally position the selected line. Follow the same process with the *Vertical* section. This method allows precise control over the placement of an object. For example, the settings in Figure 3.11 indicate that the selected line will be positioned horizontally 2.5 inches from the left edge of the page and 1.2 inches below the top edge of the page.

Exact placement
Positioning text or graphics in exact horizontal and vertical locations.

FIGURE
3.11 *Advanced Layout Dialog Box*

Aligns the object to the left, center, or right relative to a margin, page, column, or character.

Aligns the object with the inside or outside of the margins or the page.

Aligns the object horizontally using the amount of space you specify relative to a margin, page, column, or character.

Aligns the object to the top, center, bottom, inside, or outside margin, page, or line.

Aligns to specified amount of space you specify relative to a margin, page, paragraph, or line.

Moves the selected object up or down on the page if you move the paragraph to which the object is anchored.

Advanced Layout

Picture Position | Text Wrapping

Horizontal
- ◯ Alignment — Left — relative to — Column
- ◯ Book layout — Inside — of — Margin
- ◉ Absolute position — 2.5" — to the right of — Page

Vertical
- ◯ Alignment — Top — relative to — Page
- ◉ Absolute position — 1.2" — below — Page

Options
- ☐ Move object with text
- ☐ Lock anchor
- ☑ Allow overlap
- ☐ Layout in table cell

OK   Cancel

Keeps the object anchored in the same place.

Allows objects with the same wrapping style to overlap.

Anchors an object or picture within a table cell.

Copying a Text Box

If you want to make an exact copy of a text box so you can place it in a different location, position the insertion point on the text box border until the I-beam turns into an arrow with a four-headed arrow attached. Hold down the left mouse button and press the Ctrl key while dragging a copy of the text box to a new location as shown in Figure 3.12.

FIGURE
3.12 *Copying a Text Box*

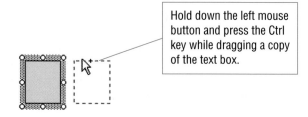

Hold down the left mouse button and press the Ctrl key while dragging a copy of the text box.

Anchoring a Text Box

All objects, including text boxes, are automatically anchored or attached to the paragraph closest to the object. With the object selected and nonprinting symbols displayed (click the Show/Hide ¶ button on the Standard toolbar), an *anchor* symbol will display to the left of the paragraph to which the object is anchored as shown in Figure 3.13.

Anchor
A symbol that represents the connection between a text box and the nearest paragraph.

FIGURE

3.13 *Text Box Anchored to Paragraph*

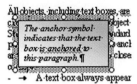

If a text box is repositioned, the anchor moves to the paragraph closest to the text box. The following points clarify the anchoring concept:

- A text box always appears on the same page as the paragraph to which it is anchored. By default, the text box moves with the paragraph to which it is anchored.

- If you do not want the text box (or object) to move with the paragraph to which it is anchored, double-click the text box border to access the Format Text Box dialog box. Select the Layout tab and then click *A*dvanced. At the Advanced Layout dialog box, make sure the Picture Position tab is selected, and then remove the check mark from the *M*ove object with text check box.

- To always keep the object on the same page as the paragraph to which it is anchored, access the Advanced Layout dialog box, make sure the Picture Position tab is selected, and click the *L*ock anchor check box to insert a check mark. This feature allows the object to be moved anyplace on the same page as the paragraph to which it is anchored, but not to another page. If the paragraph is moved to another page, the object will then be moved to that page also.

- For an object to remain stationary at a specific location on a page regardless of the text that surrounds it, access the Advanced Layout dialog box, make sure the Picture Position tab is selected, and enter specific measurements at the *Absolute position* (*Horizontal* section) and the *Absolute position* (*Vertical* section) options, and make corresponding selections at the *t*o the right of and *below* list boxes. Last, remove the check mark from the *M*ove object with text check box.

Wrapping Text around a Text Box

By default, a text box displays in the layer above or "in front of" text as illustrated in Figure 3.14. If you want text to wrap around a text box, first select the text box, display the Format Text Box dialog box, and then click the Layout tab. Several wrapping options are available as explained in Figure 3.15.

3.14 *Text Box Wrapping Style Examples*

The Wrapping styles offered at the Format dialog tab

| Square |

Text Box box Layout include:

- In line with text: The text box exists in the text layer in line with the document text.

| Through |

• Square: Text wraps around all the sides of the text box.

- Tight: Text wraps tightly around the shape of

| Tight |

an object or text box.

- Behind text: Text wrapping is removed and the text box or

| In front of text |

behind the text lay lect Objects bu wing toolbar to help you access

| In line with text |

the text box or object once it is send behind the document text.

- In front of text: Text wrapping is

| Top and bottom |

removed and the text box or object is placed in front of the document text. This is the default setting.

The Advanced Layout dialog box, accessed by clicking the Advanced button at the Layout tab and then selecting the Text Wrapping tab, offers additional wrapping options:

| Behind text |

- Through: This option is similar to

3.15 *Text Box Wrapping Style Options*

The wrapping styles offered at the Format Text Box dialog box Layout tab include:

- *In line with text:* The object is placed in the text layer at the insertion point in a line of text.
- *Square:* Text wraps around all four sides of the selected text box or object.
- *Tight:* Text wraps tightly around the shape of an object rather than the box holding the object. (This style is more apparent when applied to a shape other than a square or rectangle.) After you select *Tight,* you can adjust the dotted wrapping perimeter by clicking the Text Wrapping button on the Picture toolbar and then clicking Edit Wrap Points. Drag the dotted line or sizing handles to reshape the wrapping perimeter.
- *Behind text:* Text wrapping is removed and the text box (object) is placed behind the text layer in the document. To access an object behind text, click the Select Objects button on the Drawing toolbar, then position the mouse pointer over the object until it turns into an arrow with a four-headed arrow attached. Click the left mouse button to select the text box (object).
- *In front of text:* Text wrapping is removed and the text box (object) is placed in front of text. This is the default setting.

The Advanced Layout dialog box, accessed by clicking the Advanced button at the Layout tab and then selecting the Text Wrapping tab, offers additional wrapping styles and associated options:

- *Through*: This option is the same as *Tight*. Text not only wraps around the shape of an object, but it also flows through any open areas of the object box. This option may produce a visible change with certain graphic images, but no changes will occur when applied to a text box.

Continued on next page

- *Top and Bottom:* Text wraps around the top and bottom of the text box (object) but not on both sides. Text stops at the top of the text box (object) and restarts on the line below the object.

The *Wrap text* section at the Text Wrapping tab in the Advanced Layout dialog box operates in conjunction with the *Wrapping style* section and offers:
- *Both sides:* Text wraps on both sides of the text box.
- *Left only:* Text wraps along the left side of the text box but not on the right side.
- *Right only:* Text wraps along the right side of the text box but not on the left side.
- *Largest only:* Text wraps along the largest side of the object. This does not produce any changes when applied to a text box.

Customizing a Text Box

By default, a text box has a black single-line border around all sides and contains white background fill. However, a text box can be customized in a variety of ways, including changing border style and color, and changing the background fill color.

DTP POINTERS
Customize borders by changing the line style, thickness, color, and location.

Changing the Text Box Border

The following methods, along with your own imagination, can be used to customize the border of a text box (object) as shown in Figure 3.16:
- **To add, remove, or change the color of a text box border:** Select the text box and then click the down-pointing arrow to the right of the Line Color button on the Drawing toolbar to display the Line Color palette (or click Format, click Text Box, and then select the Colors and Lines tab). Select a color from the Line Color palette or select the More Line Colors command to pick from an extended selection of standard colors or to create your own custom colors. Select Patterned Lines to add a pattern to the text box border. Choose No Line to remove a border from a text box (object).

Line Color

- **To change the style and thickness of a text box border:** Select the text box (or object), then click the Line Style button on the Drawing toolbar to display the Line Style palette. Select the desired line style and thickness. To refine the line style and weight of your text box border, select More Lines to display the Colors and Lines tab of the Format Text Box dialog box. You may also choose from a selection of dashed lines by clicking the Dash Style button on the Drawing toolbar.

Line Style

Dash Style

- **To add shadow box effects to a text box border:** Select the text box (or object), then click the Shadow Style button on the Drawing toolbar. Select a shadow design from the Shadow palette that displays. Click the Shadow Settings command to display the Shadow Settings toolbar shown in Figure 3.17. Use the four Nudge Shadow buttons to move the shadow in small increments either closer to the shape or farther away. Use the Shadow Color button to change the color of the shadow, and use the Shadow On/Off button to add or remove the shadow effect.

Shadow Style

FIGURE
3.16 *Text Box Borders*

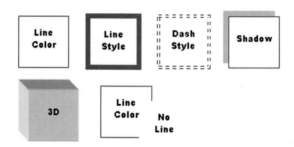

FIGURE
3.17 *Shadow Settings Toolbar*

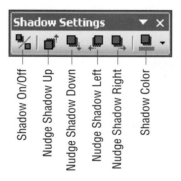

3-D Style

- **To add a three-dimensional look to a text box (or object):** Select the text box or object, and then click the 3-D Style button on the Drawing toolbar. Select from the choices offered on the 3-D options palette. To customize any of the 3-D options, click the 3-D Settings option to display the 3-D Settings toolbar shown in Figure 3.18. Use the buttons on this toolbar for turning 3-D on or off and changing the tilt, depth, direction, light source, and surface. The down-pointing arrow next to the 3-D Color button can be clicked to select a 3-D color from a color palette.

FIGURE
3.18 *3-D Settings Toolbar*

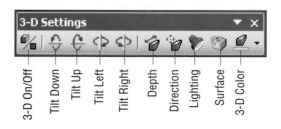

Changing the Fill

You can use the following methods to fill a text box or any drawing object with solid or gradient (shaded) colors, a pattern, a texture, or a picture as shown in Figure 3.19:

Fill Color

- **To add solid color background fill:** Select the desired text box, then check the color of the stripe on the Fill Color button on the Drawing toolbar. If the stripe is the fill color you want, simply click the Fill Color button. To select a different fill color, click the down-pointing arrow at the right of the Fill Color button to display the Fill Color palette and select the desired color. If you do not see the color you want, click More Fill Colors to display the Colors dialog box. Click a color on the Standard tab, or click the Custom tab to mix your own color. Click OK or press Enter. Word saves the custom color you select in the Standard tab or the Custom tab and places it in its own color block in the Fill Color palette in a new row above the More Fill Colors command. You can also find these same color options by selecting the Colors and Lines tab in the Format Text Box dialog box, and then clicking the *Color* list box in the *Fill* section. A transparent effect can be added to the fill color of a text box at either the Fill Color palette or at the Format Text Box dialog box. The *Transparency* option makes the selected color partially transparent. Drag the slider to the right to increase transparency. The result is displayed in the color drop-down box.

F I G U R E

3.19 *Text Box Fills*

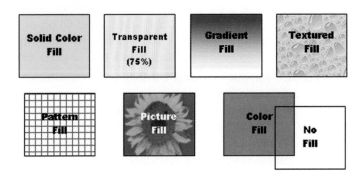

- **To add gradient (a color that fades gradually to another color) background fill:** Select the text box (or object) and then click the down-pointing arrow to the right of the Fill Color button on the Drawing toolbar. Select Fill Effects, and then select the Gradient tab at the Fill Effects dialog box. (Or you can click Format, click Text Box, click the Colors and Lines tab, click the *Color* list box in the *Fill* section, click Fill Effects, and then select the Gradient tab at the Fill Effects dialog box.) In the *Colors* section of the Gradient tab, select *One color* to produce a single color gradient that gradually fades to black or white; then choose the color you want from the *Color 1* list box. Drag the slider on the Dark/Light slider bar toward Dark to make the selected color fade to black or toward Light to make the color fade to white. Use the *Two colors* option to produce gradient shading that gradually fades from one color to another color. Use the *Preset* option to select from a list of predesigned gradient fills. In the *Shading styles* section, select the desired style of gradient shading, and then select the desired variation of the shading style in the *Variants* section. Click OK or press Enter. See examples of different gradient colors, shading styles, and variations in Figure 3.20.

3.20 **Examples of Gradient Color and Shading Styles**

| One Color Horizontal Gradient | One Color from Corner Gradient | Two Color Diagonal Up Gradient | Two Color from Center Gradient | Preset Horizontal Gradient |

- **To add textured background fill:** Select the text box (or object); then access the Fill Effects dialog box. Select the Texture tab and then click the desired texture sample in the *Texture* section. Click OK or press Enter. At the Texture tab, click the Other Texture button to be able to access other texture or background files you may have stored on disk.

- **To add a pattern to background fill:** Select the text box (or object), then access the Fill Effects dialog box. Select the Pattern tab and then click the desired pattern block in the *Pattern* section. Click the *Foreground* list box to select a color for the dots, dashes, lines, waves, and so on of the pattern. Click the *Background* list box to select a color for the spaces between the dots, dashes, lines, waves, and so forth. Click OK or press Enter.

- **To add a picture for background fill:** Select the text box (or object), then access the Fill Effects dialog box. Select the Picture tab and then click the desired picture in the *Picture* section. Click OK or press Enter. At the Picture tab, click the Select Picture button to be able to access other picture files you may have stored on disk. Click the *Lock picture aspect ratio* check box to turn on this feature. This prevents the picture from being distorted.

Using Linked Text Boxes

An additional characteristic of a text box is that two or more text boxes may be linked to each other and text that does not fit in one box may be poured into another linked box. This feature is particularly useful when formatting a newsletter. To link text boxes, you must first create two or more text boxes. To create a link between the two text boxes, complete the following steps:

1. Click the text box that is to be the first text box in the chain of linked boxes.
2. Display the Text Box toolbar as shown in Figure 3.21.
3. Click the Create Text Box Link button on the Text Box toolbar. The mouse displays as a small upright pitcher.

4. Position the pitcher in the text box to be linked. The pitcher appears tipped with letters spilling out of it. Click once to complete the task.

5. To create a link from the second text box to a third text box, click the second text box and then repeat Steps 3 and 4.

FIGURE

3.21 *Linked Text Boxes and the Text Box Toolbar*

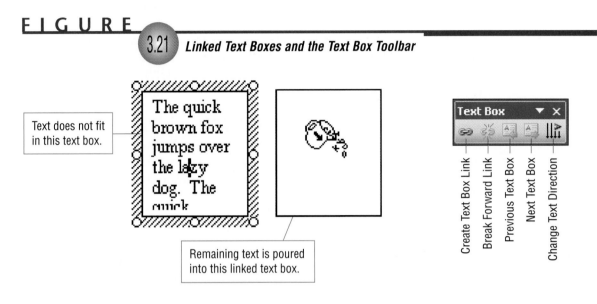

Text does not fit in this text box.

Remaining text is poured into this linked text box.

Create Text Box Link
Break Forward Link
Previous Text Box
Next Text Box
Change Text Direction

Creating Horizontal and Vertical Ruled Lines Using Word's Drawing Toolbar

In Word, you may create horizontal and/or vertical lines anywhere on a page using the Line feature on the Drawing toolbar. As with text boxes, you can adjust the size, position, color, and shading of lines drawn with the Drawing toolbar. In typesetting, these horizontal and vertical lines are called *ruled lines, rules,* or *ruling lines* to distinguish them from lines of type.

Horizontal and vertical ruled lines are used to guide a reader's eyes across and/or down the page, to separate one section of text from another, to separate columns of text, or to add visual interest. Remember that ruled lines act as boundaries to the surrounding text. A thicker line serves as more of a barrier than a thinner line. Place ruled lines above the heading rather than below the heading. This way, the reader definitely knows that the heading belongs to the text that follows it. In addition, when using ruled lines, be consistent in their purpose and their appearance.

Ruled lines
Horizontal or vertical lines.

DTP POINTERS
Ruled lines act as boundaries to surrounding text.

Drawing Horizontal and Vertical Lines

To insert a horizontal or vertical line using the Drawing toolbar, click the Line button and then position the crosshairs where you want the line to begin. To create a straight horizontal or vertical line, hold down the Shift key and the left mouse button, drag the mouse horizontally or vertically to the location where you want the line to end, and then release the mouse button and the Shift key. (Ragged or imperfect lines are created when the Shift key is not pressed during the drawing process.) To create horizontal or vertical arrow lines, follow the same basic procedure, but click the Arrow button. To display the crosshairs continuously to draw additional lines, double-click the Line (or Arrow) button, and then draw any number of lines. Click the Line (or Arrow) button again to discontinue line drawing.

Line

Arrow

Sizing Horizontal and Vertical Lines

Sizing a line created with the Drawing toolbar is similar to sizing a text box. Select the line to be sized, position the mouse pointer on either sizing handle until it turns into a double-headed arrow (hold down the Shift key if you want a straight line), drag the crosshairs in the appropriate direction until the line is the desired length, and then release the left mouse button. For precise measurements, select the line (or object) and then double-click the left mouse button (or select the line first, and then select Format, AutoShape). At the Format AutoShape dialog box, select the Size tab. In the *Size and rotate* section, type the desired length of the line in the *Width* list box.

Positioning Horizontal and Vertical Lines

Horizontal and vertical lines may be positioned in the same way a text box is positioned. Select the line, and then use the mouse, the arrow keys on the keyboard, or the options at the Format AutoShape dialog box Layout tab or the Advanced Layout dialog box.

Anchoring Horizontal and Vertical Lines

Lines created from the Drawing toolbar are automatically anchored or attached to the paragraph closest to the object. Refer to a previous section in this chapter, "Anchoring a Text Box," for clarification on the relationship between a line (or object) and the paragraph to which it is anchored.

Customizing Horizontal and Vertical Lines

The Drawing toolbar can be used to customize the weight (thickness), style, and color of a line, and to create shadow and 3-D effects.

Weight and Style

Weight
The thickness of a line.

Line Style

Dash Style

Arrow Style

In typesetting, the thickness of a line, called its **weight**, is measured in points. Word defaults to a line thickness of 0.75 point. To change the style or weight of a line, select the line first. You can then select different styles and weights of solid lines from the Line Style palette that displays when you click the Line Style button on the Drawing toolbar. Click the Dash Style button on the Drawing toolbar to choose from various styles of dashed lines, or click the Arrow Style button to choose from a variety of arrow lines that begin and/or end with arrows, circles, or diamond shapes.

To have more control over the style of your lines (solid, dashed, or arrow), you can select More Lines from the Line Style palette or More Arrows from the Arrow Style palette to display the Format AutoShape dialog box. (You may also double-click the line you want to edit or select the line first, and then click Format, AutoShape.) From this dialog box with the Colors and Lines tab chosen, you can increase or decrease the point measurement by 0.25 point by using the up or down arrows in the *Weight* list box, or you can type any desired measurement into the list box. Figure 3.22 shows several styles of horizontal ruled lines at varying point sizes (weights).

FIGURE

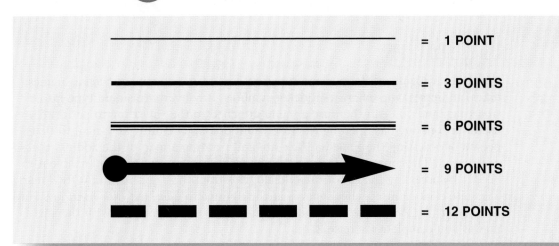

3.22 *Varying Weights and Styles of Lines*

= 1 POINT

= 3 POINTS

= 6 POINTS

= 9 POINTS

= 12 POINTS

Color

Changing the color of a horizontal or vertical line created from the Drawing toolbar is done the same way as changing the color of a text box border. Refer to the previous section in this chapter, "Changing the Text Box Border," under the heading *Customizing a Text Box.*

Shadow and 3-D Effects

Shadow and 3-D effects can be applied to lines just as they can with text boxes. Refer to a previous section in this chapter, "Customizing a Text Box."

Creating Horizontal Lines Using the Borders Toolbar

Word's Borders feature may be used to add horizontal or vertical lines in headers and/or footers, as well as to any other text. Every paragraph you create in Word contains an invisible frame. (Remember that a paragraph may contain text or it may consist of only a hard return.) To create a border on the top or sides of your paragraph, you may use the Border button on the Formatting toolbar. The Border button icon changes according to the most recent border position selected. To change the position of the border, click the down-pointing arrow at the right of the Border button, and then select the desired border location. You can further customize lines created with the Border button by choosing F̲ormat, then B̲orders and Shading. At the Borders and Shading dialog box, options exist to change the border settings, the border line style, the border line color, the border line width, the border location, and the distance between any border and text.

Border

In Exercise 2, you will create a letterhead using a text box inserted in the header and footer pane. Inserting it in this layer is a safeguard against users who might inadvertently make a change in the letterhead. Placing letterhead content in the header and footer layer will result in the content appearing on all subsequent pages, which is not appropriate for a multiple-paged letter. To eliminate the letterhead on subsequent pages, the header may be created as a different first page header by checking the *Different first page* check box in the Page Setup dialog box (Layout tab). This option tells Word that this header is to be used for the first page only. Subsequent pages may have a different header if desired.

Using Smart Tags

Word can recognize different data types entered into a document such as names, dates, addresses, and even stock ticker symbols. It converts this data type into a smart tag, and you can then use a menu attached to the smart tag to perform useful actions such as opening Microsoft Outlook and sending an e-mail to that person or accessing the Expedia Web site and printing a map of the address that was tagged. The Smart Tag feature is on by default; however, you can enable it if needed by accessing the AutoCorrect dialog box from the <u>T</u>ools menu. At the Smart Tags tab, click to insert check marks at the options to <u>L</u>abel text with smart tags and *Show Smart Tag Actions <u>b</u>uttons.* You will gain additional experience with the smart tags as you complete Exercise 2.

exercise 2

Creating a Letterhead Using a Customized Text Box in a Header and Footer Pane

1. At a clear document screen, create the letterhead shown in Figure 3.23 by completing the following steps:
   a. Change the left margin to 2.5 inches and the right margin to 1 inch.
   b. Insert a text box for the company letterhead by completing the following steps:

      1) Click <u>V</u>iew and then <u>H</u>eader and Footer to display the Header pane. (The letterhead text box is going to be inserted in the header and footer layer. This way you can prevent other users from inadvertently changing the letterhead.)

      Step 1b1

      2) Click the *Zoom* list box down-pointing arrow on the Standard toolbar and then select *Whole Page.*

      3) Display the Drawing toolbar and then click the Text Box button on the toolbar. Position the crosshairs in the upper left corner of the page and click and drag to draw a text box in the left margin approximately the same size as that shown in Figure 3.23. (The text box will be specifically sized and positioned in the next few steps.)

      Step 1b3

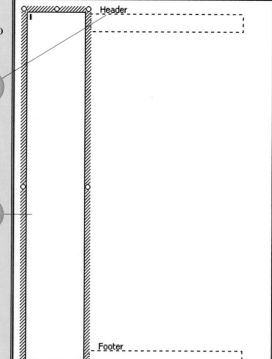

c. Size and position the text box by completing the following steps:
  1) Double-click the text box border to display the Format Text Box dialog box.
  2) Select the Size tab and then change the height of the text box to 9.75 inches and the width to 1.9 inches.
  3) Select the Layout tab, and then click the Advanced button to display the Advanced Layout dialog box. In the *Horizontal* section, change the *Absolute position* to *0.3″* and the *to the right of* option to *Page*. In the *Vertical* section, change the *Absolute position* to *0.6″* and the *below* option to *Page*.

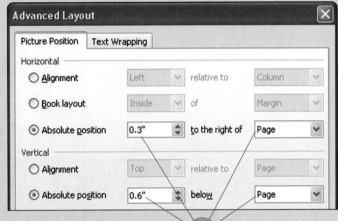

Step 1c3

  4) Click OK to close the Advanced Layout dialog box, but do not close the Format Text Box dialog box.
d. Insert a textured fill and remove the text box borders by completing the following steps:
  1) With the Format Text Box dialog box still displayed, click the Colors and Lines tab.
  2) In the *Fill* section, click the *Color* list box, click *Fill* Effects, and then click the Texture tab in the Fill Effects dialog box.
  3) In the *Texture* section, click the first texture block from the right in the first row. *Stationery* will display as the name of the texture below the texture selections. Click OK.

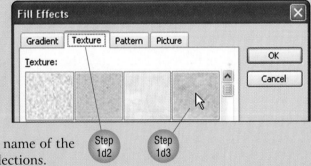

Step 1d2   Step 1d3

  4) In the *Line* section, click the *Color* list box, and then click No Line. Click OK to close the Format Text Box dialog box.
e. Insert and format the text box contents by completing the following steps:
  1) Change the zoom to *75%*.
  2) Click once inside the text box to position the insertion point and then type the following text. Press Enter at the end of every line except the last line and where indicated otherwise.

> Desktop
> Designs (press Enter twice)
> "Where Concepts Become a Reality" (let text wrap before pressing Enter)
> 568 Pine Street
> St. Louis, MO 63131
> Phone: (314) 555-8755
> Fax: (314) 555-8758
> E-mail: dtpd@emcp.net (press Enter twice)

If the e-mail address displays as a hyperlink, select the e-mail address, right-click the mouse, and then click <u>R</u>emove Hyperlink. If the Header and Footer toolbar gets in the way, click the Title bar and drag it to a new location.

3) Select all of the text just entered (Ctrl + A) and then change the font to 12-point Papyrus Bold and the text color to Teal.

4) Select *Desktop Designs*, display the Font dialog box, change the type size to 29-point, and then apply *Emboss* from the *Effects* section. Click OK to close the Font dialog box.

5) Position the insertion point within the word *Desktop*, click For<u>m</u>at and then <u>P</u>aragraph. At the Paragraph dialog box with the <u>I</u>ndents and Spacing tab selected, change the *Before* paragraph spacing to *28 pt*, the *Line spacing* option to *Exactly*, and then select *30 pt* in the *At* list box. Click OK to close the Paragraph dialog box.

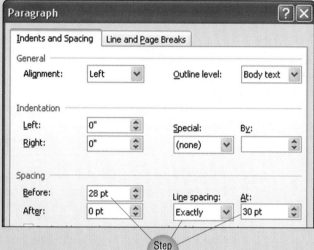

6) Turn on the nonprinting characters (Show/Hide ¶ button) and then position the insertion point just before the paragraph symbol below *Designs*.

7) Click <u>I</u>nsert and then <u>S</u>ymbol. At the Symbols tab, select *Wingdings 2* from the drop-down list of fonts and then click the symbol (the second symbol from the left in the tenth row, #177). Click <u>I</u>nsert and then Close.

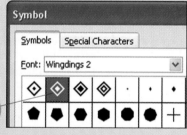

8) Press F4 (Repeat key) six times.

9) Select the line of symbols, change the font color to Dark Red, and then change the horizontal alignment to Center.

10) With the insertion point on the line of symbols, click For<u>m</u>at and then <u>P</u>aragraph. At the Paragraph dialog box, change the *Before* spacing to *3 pt* and the *After* spacing to *12 pt*. Click OK to close the Paragraph dialog box.

11) Select the slogan *"Where Concepts Become a Reality,"* display the Font dialog box, change the type size to 14 points, change the typestyle to Bold Italic, and then apply *Emboss* from the *Effects* section. Click OK to close the Font dialog box.

12) With the slogan still selected, access the Paragraph dialog box. Change the *After* spacing to *415 pt*, the *Line spacing* option to *Exactly*, and then select *17 pt* in the *At* list box. Click OK to close the Paragraph dialog box.

13) Select the address, phone number, fax number, and E-mail address. *(Hint: To select all of the text, including any text that is not visible, position the insertion point at the beginning of the address, and then press Ctrl + Shift + End.)*

14) Change the font size to 10.5 points.

15) At the Paragraph dialog box, change the *Line spacing* option to *Exactly* and then select *14 pt* in the *At* list box. Click the OK button to close the Paragraph dialog box.

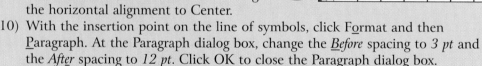

16) Position the insertion point just before the second paragraph symbol below the last line of text and then insert three symbols using steps similar to Steps 1e7, 8, and 9.

    f. Click Close on the Header and Footer toolbar. (Due to the wide left margin setting, the insertion point is located an appropriate distance to the right of the text box in the text layer so that letter text may be entered at a later date.)

    g. Turn off the nonprinting characters (Show/Hide ¶ button).

    h. Use Print Preview to view the entire document.

2. View the Smart Tag Actions associated with the address in this letterhead by completing the following steps:

    a. Click View and then Header and Footer.

    b. At the Header and Footer pane, move the mouse pointer over the street address in the letterhead (a red dotted line displays below the line). When the *Information* icon appears above and to the left of the text, click the Smart Tag button. (The Smart Tag option must be checked at the Smart Tags tab in the AutoCorrect dialog box.)

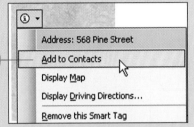

    c. From the drop-down list of commands, click Add to Contacts. View the Contact dialog box and then click the Close button *(X)*. At the Microsoft Outlook prompt to save changes, click No.

    d. Click the Smart Tag button again and then click Display Map. (You will need Internet access.) At the msn.com Web site, click the Get Map button to display the map, and then click the *Printer* icon to print a copy of the map. Close the site when you are finished. ***(Note: Initially you may be asked to choose from a list of similar addresses. Select the first address in the list and then click the Get Map button to proceed.)***

    e. Click the Smart Tag button and then click Display Driving Directions. At the Driving Directions dialog box, view the contents and then click Cancel. (Optional: Type your address in the Address 1 text boxes, click OK, click the Get Directions button at the MSN.com Web site, click the *Printer* icon to print the driving directions, and then close the site.)

    f. Click the Smart Tag button and then click Remove this Smart Tag.

    g. Click Close on the Header and Footer toolbar.

3. Save the letterhead and name it **c03ex02, ddltrhead**.

4. Print and then close **c03ex02, ddltrhead**.

Desktop
Designs
❖❖❖❖❖❖❖
*"Where Concepts
Become a Reality"*

568 Pine Street
St. Louis, MO 63131
Phone: (314) 555-8755
Fax: (314) 555-8758
E-mail: dtpd@emcp.net

❖❖❖

Refining Letter and Word Spacing

Certain refinements such as kerning and tracking make your letterhead or any other document look more professional.

Kerning Character Pairs

The process of decreasing or increasing the white space between specific character pairs is called **kerning**. Generally, the horizontal spacing of typefaces is designed to optimize body text sizes (9- to 13-point). At larger sizes, the same relative horizontal space appears "loose," especially when uppercase and lowercase letters are combined. Kerning visually equalizes the space between specific characters and generally is used only on headlines and other blocks of large type (14-point and larger). Figure 3.24 illustrates common character pairs that are affected by using the kerning feature.

Kerning
Decreasing or increasing the horizontal white space between specific character pairs.

DTP POINTERS
Kern when the type size exceeds 14 points.

FIGURE

3.24 **Examples of Character Pair Kerning**

WA (kerned)	Ta (kerned)
WA (not kerned)	Ta (not kerned)
Ty (kerned)	Vi (kerned)
Ty (not kerned)	Vi (not kerned)

Using Automatic or Manual Kerning

In Word, kerning can be accomplished automatically or character pairs may be selected and kerned manually.

Automatic Kerning

When automatic kerning is turned on, Word adjusts the space between certain pairs of letters above a specific point size. Not all character pairs are affected with automatic kerning. Some common character pairs that may be automatically kerned are *Ta, To, Ty, Vi,* and *WA.* The amount of space that is adjusted for specific character pairs is defined in a kerning table, which is part of the printer definition. The printer definition is a preprogrammed set of instructions that tells the printer how to perform various features.

To turn on automatic kerning, access the Font dialog box, then select the Character Spacing tab as displayed in Figure 3.25. Click the check box to the left of the *Kerning for fonts* option to insert a check mark. In the *Points and above* text box, use the up and down arrows to specify the minimum point size for kerning to take effect; or type the desired point size.

3.25 *Kerning at the Character Spacing Tab*

Adjust character spacing for manual kerning of specific pairs.

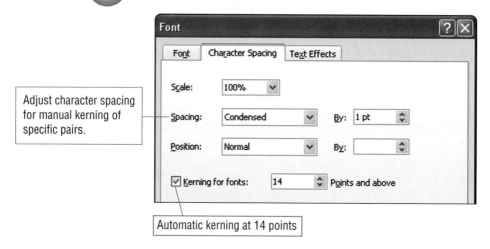

Automatic kerning at 14 points

Manual Kerning

If you choose to kern letters manually, you make the decision as to which letters to kern. Manual kerning is especially helpful if you need to increase or decrease space between letters to improve legibility, to create a special effect, or to fit text in a specific amount of space. As a word of caution, do not sacrifice legibility when making kerning adjustments. To manually kern a pair of letters, select the pair of characters you want to kern, then access the Font dialog box, Character Spacing tab. Click the *Spacing* list box; then select *Expanded* (if you want to increase the spacing between the selected character pair) or *Condensed* (if you want to decrease the spacing). In the *By* list box, click the up or down arrows to specify the amount of space the selected character pair is to be increased or decreased. Manual kerning can provide accurate results; however, it can be very tedious. For example, compare the normal text to the manually kerned text in Figure 3.26. The *S* and the *A* were selected and the character spacing was condensed. This then led to minor character spacing adjustments between some of the other letters and several printings to achieve the desired result.

3.26 *Normal Text and Manually Kerned Text*

RIDE SAFE, INC. (normal)

RIDE SAFE, INC. (manually kerned)

Tracking
Equally reducing or increasing the horizontal space between all characters in a selected block of text.

Tracking Text

In traditional typesetting, equally reducing or increasing the horizontal space between all characters in a block of text is called *tracking*. Tracking affects all characters, while automatic kerning affects only specific character pairs. The purpose of tracking is the same as kerning: to produce more attractive, easy-to-read type. In addition, you can use tracking to create unusual spacing for a specific design effect or to fit text into a certain amount of space.

In Word, tracking is virtually the same as manual kerning because both processes involve condensing or expanding character spacing at the Font dialog box. Whereas manually kerning involves adjusting the character spacing of selected character pairs, tracking involves adjusting the character spacing of a selected block of text, such as a heading, a subheading, a phrase, and so on.

Figure 3.27 provides examples of headings that have been tracked (expanded) to produce a special effect.

DTP POINTERS
Kern and track headings and subheadings.

F I G U R E

3.27 *Examples of Tracking (Condensed and Expanded Character Spacing)*

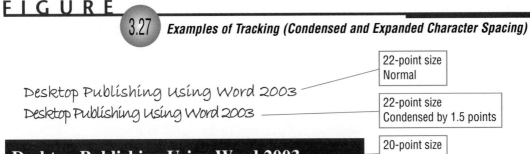

Desktop Publishing Using Word 2003
— 22-point size / Normal

Desktop Publishing Using Word 2003
— 22-point size / Condensed by 1.5 points

Desktop Publishing Using Word 2003
— 20-point size / Normal

DESKTOP PUBLISHING USING WORD 2003
— 20-point size / Expanded by 2 points

In Exercise 3, you will make tracking adjustments and also save the letterhead as a template. Since your letterhead helps to establish an identity for your organization, it will probably stay the same for quite a long period of time. Converting your letterhead into a template ensures that your letterhead is always available in its original form. If you mistakenly rearrange the letterhead while typing the letter content, you can open the original template to start again. For more efficiency, you can even include styles, AutoText entries, field codes, macros, and more in your template letterhead.

DTP POINTERS
Consider creating a template of your letterhead.

 *exercise* 3

Making Tracking Adjustments in a Letterhead and Saving It as a Template

1. Open **c03ex02, ddltrhead** and make the following changes:
   a. Click <u>V</u>iew and then <u>H</u>eader and Footer.
   b. In the letterhead text box in the Header and Footer pane, adjust the character spacing by completing the following steps:
      1) Select *Designs* and then display the Font dialog box.
      2) Select the Character Spacing tab. Change *Spacing* to *Expanded* and make sure the *By* list box displays *1 pt*. Click OK or press Enter.

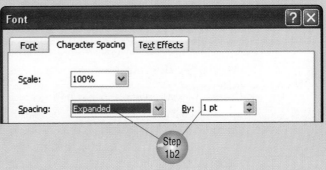

Font

| Font | Cha<u>r</u>acter Spacing | Te<u>x</u>t Effects |

S<u>c</u>ale: 100%

<u>S</u>pacing: Expanded   <u>B</u>y: 1 pt

Step 1b2

3) Select *"Where Concepts Become a Reality,"* display the Font dialog box again, and expand the character spacing to 0.5 pt. Click OK or press Enter.

c. Save the letterhead as **c03ex03, ddltrhead**.

d. Close the Header and Footer toolbar, and then print **c03ex03, ddltrhead**.

e. Before saving the letterhead as a template, select a font for the body of the letter and insert an automatically updated date field by completing the following steps:

   1) Turn on the nonprinting characters (Show/Hide ¶ button), and with the insertion point at the top of the document, select the paragraph symbol to the right of the insertion point and then change the font to 12-point Book Antiqua.

   2) Insert an automatically updated date field by completing the following steps:

     a) Press Enter five or six times so the insertion point is located approximately 2 inches from the top of the page.

     b) Click <u>I</u>nsert, then Date and <u>T</u>ime.

     c) At the Date and Time dialog box, select the appropriate date format for a business letter (third from the top in the <u>*Available formats*</u> list box).

     d) Click the <u>*Update automatically*</u> check box to turn on this feature.

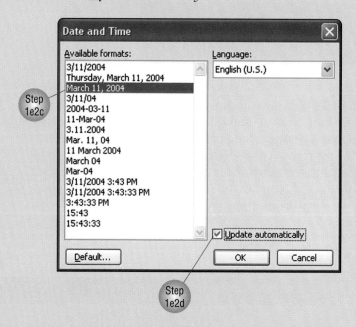

Step 1e2c

Step 1e2d

     e) Click OK or press Enter.

     f) Turn off the nonprinting characters (Show/Hide ¶ button).

     g) Press Enter four or five times so that the insertion point is positioned for the user to enter the inside address for the letter.

2. Save the letterhead as a template by completing the following steps:

a. Click <u>F</u>ile, Save <u>A</u>s, and then change the *Save as type* option to *Document Template*.

b. Change the folder location in the *Save <u>in</u>* list box to the template folder that you created in Chapter 2. (Most likely the location is A:\DTP Templates.)

c. Name the file **ddtemplate**.

3. Close **ddtemplate**.

Using WordArt for Interesting Text Effects

You can create compelling text effects with WordArt as illustrated in Figure 3.28. WordArt can distort or modify text to conform to a variety of shapes. This is useful for creating company logos and headings and can be easily incorporated into a company letterhead. It is also especially useful for headlines in flyers and announcements. The available shapes can exaggerate the text to create an interesting focal point. Using WordArt in a letterhead is one way to project a particular image and to establish an identity with your target audience. *(Hint: Type logos at the Search text box at the Microsoft Office Online Clip Art and Media Web page and view the predesigned logos that are available. Add your company name, formatted in WordArt, to any one of these images to create a simple logo. In addition, view the various Signs and Symbols clips that are available in the Office Collections category of the Microsoft Clip Organizer. Another idea is to type logos at a search engine and view the suggestions that are usually provided on the Web sites.)*

F I G U R E

3.28 *WordArt Text Effects*

Creating a WordArt Object

To create a WordArt object, click the Insert WordArt button on the Drawing toolbar; or click Insert, point to Picture, and then click WordArt; or click the Insert WordArt button on the WordArt toolbar. At the WordArt Gallery dialog box, double-click the desired WordArt style. At the Edit WordArt Text dialog box with the words *Your Text Here* selected, type the text to be included in your WordArt object in the *Text* box. Press the Enter key if your WordArt object is to include more than one line of text. The WordArt toolbar appears automatically whenever you select a WordArt object. Figure 3.29 illustrates the WordArt toolbar. You may also display the WordArt toolbar by right-clicking the mouse in any existing toolbar area and then clicking WordArt or clicking View on the Menu bar, pointing to Toolbars, and then clicking WordArt. The WordArt toolbar enables you to edit text; change the WordArt style and/or shape; and change alignment, color, color effects, size, position, wrapping style, rotation, vertical text position, letter height, and character spacing (kerning and tracking).

3.29 *WordArt Toolbar*

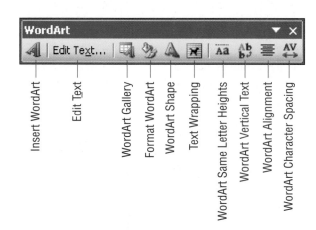

Changing the Shape of a WordArt Object

If you decide you want a different shape for your WordArt object, click the WordArt Shape button on the WordArt toolbar. The WordArt Shape button opens up a palette of 40 shapes. Some shapes produce different results depending on how many lines of text and spaces you type into the text entry box in WordArt. Experiment with several shapes to find the right effect. You may want to experiment with various fonts, font sizes, colors, and color effects to find the right combination for your text. As a cautionary note, make sure your WordArt object is readable.

Adding Enhancements

As with any other objects such as text boxes, lines, AutoShapes, and pictures, you can size, move, copy, add fill shading or color, add or remove a border, and add shadow or 3-D effects to a WordArt object by using options from the Drawing toolbar or the Format WordArt dialog box. The Format WordArt button on the WordArt toolbar opens the Format WordArt dialog box where you can change the fill color of the letters or add gradient, texture, pattern, or picture fill. You can change the color, style, and weight of the borders surrounding the letters depending on the options selected. Additionally, you can change the height, width, and rotation of the object depending on the options you select at the Format WordArt dialog box.

exercise

Using WordArt to Create a Letterhead

1. At a clear document screen, use WordArt to create the letterhead shown in Figure 3.30 by completing the following steps:
    a. Click <u>V</u>iew and then <u>H</u>eader and Footer.
    b. Click the Page Setup button on the Header and Footer toolbar.

c. Make sure the Layout tab is selected and then make sure there is a check mark in the *Different first page* check box.

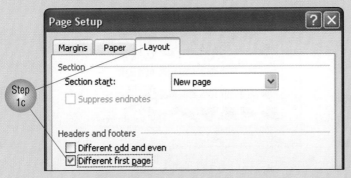

Step 1c

d. Select the Margins tab and change the left and right margins to 0.75″.
e. Click OK or press Enter.
2. Insert a WordArt object inside the header by completing the following steps:
   a. Click the Insert WordArt button on the Drawing toolbar, or click Insert, point to Picture, and then click WordArt to open the WordArt Gallery dialog box.
   b. Double-click the WordArt style located in the upper left-hand corner of the gallery to open the Edit WordArt Text dialog box.
   c. With the *Your Text Here* text selected, type Wildflower, press Enter, and then type Florists.
   d. Change the font to Elephant and then click the OK button to close the Edit WordArt Text dialog box.

WordArt Gallery

Select a WordArt style:

Step 2b

3. Insert a picture fill in the WordArt object by completing the following steps:
   a. With the WordArt object selected, click the Format WordArt button on the WordArt toolbar to open the Format WordArt dialog box.
   b. Click the Colors and Lines tab and then click the *Fill Color* list box.
   c. Click the Fill Effects command and then click the Picture tab.
   d. Click the Select Picture button to open the Select Picture dialog box. Use the dialog box to navigate and locate the **Flowers** file in your Chapter03 folder. Click the file to select it and then click the Insert button.
   e. Make sure there is a check mark in the *Lock picture aspect ratio* check box and then click OK twice.

Step 3d

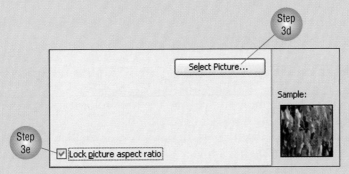

Select Picture...

Sample:

Step 3e

Lock picture aspect ratio

   f. Click the WordArt Shape button on the WordArt toolbar.

g. Select the Deflate Inflate shape in the fourth row.

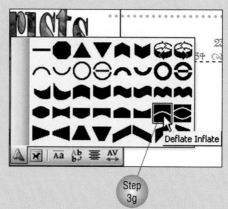

Step
3g

4. Create a line to the right of the WordArt object by completing the following steps:
   a. Click the Line button on the Drawing toolbar.
   b. Hold down the Shift key as you drag the crosshairs to create a straight line approximately 4.25 inches in length.
   c. With the line selected, click the down-pointing arrow at the right of the Line Color button on the Drawing toolbar and then click the fourth color in the third row (Sea Green).
   d. Click the Line Style button and then select *3 pt* from the drop-down list.
   e. Click the Dash Style button and then select the second line from the top of the drop-down list.
   f. Drag the line to a position similar to Figure 3.30.
5. Create a text box with the address by completing the following steps:
   a. Click the Text Box button on the Drawing toolbar.
   b. Drag the crosshairs to create a box that is approximately 0.5 inch in height and 4.25 inches in width. Double-click the border of the text box to access the Format Text Box dialog box. Select the Size tab and verify the height and width.
   c. Select the Colors and Lines tab and in the *Line* section, change the *Color* to *No Line*.
   d. Click OK or press Enter to close the Format Text Box dialog box.
6. Create the text inside the text box by completing the following steps:
   a. Position the insertion point inside the text box, change the alignment to Align Right, change the font to 11-point Harrington, and then type 232 Rice Lake Square.
   b. Press the spacebar two times, click Insert, and then Symbol.
   c. At the Symbols dialog box, select the Symbols tab and then select *Wingding 2* at the *Font* list box.
   d. Select the fifth symbol in the fifth row (#100). Click Insert and then Close.
   e. Press the spacebar two times.
   f. Type Wheaton, IL 60187, press Enter, type 630.555.1234, press the spacebar two times, insert the same symbol as in Step 6d, press the spacebar two times, and then type Online Ordering www.emcp.net/wildflower.
   g. Select each of the symbols and change the font color to Sea Green.
   h. Position the text box as shown in Figure 3.30.
   i. Click the Close button on the Header and Footer toolbar.
7. Save the document as **c03ex04, Flower Letterhead**, print it, and then close it.

Creating Envelopes

Let your company's letterhead be the starting point for the design of your other business documents. An envelope designed in coordination with a letterhead is another way of establishing your identity with your target audience. Using some of the same design elements in the envelope as in the letterhead contributes to continuity and consistency among your documents. These same elements can be carried over into memos, faxes, business cards, invoices, and brochures.

DTP POINTERS
Use your company's letterhead as the starting point for the design of your other business documents.

Designing Your Own Envelope

DTP POINTERS

Consider
the actual size of
the design area.

DTP POINTERS

Use
consistent
elements to
establish a visual
connection
between your
envelope and
letterhead.

When planning your design, remember that the envelope design does not have to be an exact replica of the letterhead. Select enough common elements to establish a visual link between the two documents. For example, using the same typeface and typestyles in a smaller type size and repeating a graphic element on a smaller scale may be just enough to establish that link.

Using Word's Envelope Feature

Word's envelope feature makes creating professional-looking envelopes easy and inexpensive. You can create a blank envelope that already contains appropriate formatting for margins and a text box in the mailing address position. First, you must add a blank envelope to a document, then add your own design and return address. To create a customized envelope, complete the following steps:

1. At a clear document screen, click Tools, point to Letters and Mailings, and then click Envelopes and Labels.
2. At the Envelopes and Labels dialog box, select the Envelopes tab.
3. Click the Options button.
4. At the Envelope Options dialog box, select the Envelope Options tab, and then make sure the desired envelope displays at the *Envelope size* list box. If not, change to the desired size. (If the size you want is not listed, click *Custom size* from the drop-down list, and then enter the dimensions of your envelope.) Click OK.
5. At the Envelopes and Labels dialog box, click Add to Document.

Word adds the envelope to the beginning of the current active document (which is usually a blank document). Word numbers the envelope as page 0 and the blank page as page 1. When you print your envelope, print the current page only to avoid sending a blank piece of paper through the printer.

Word's envelope feature also includes an option to add electronic postage to envelopes and labels. However, you need to install electronic postage software before you can use this feature. The Microsoft Office Web site provides information about this electronic postage add-on.

Checking Printing Options

Word determines the feed method for envelopes and the feed form that is best suited to your printer in the *Feed* section of the Envelopes and Labels dialog box (with the Envelopes tab selected). If this method does not work for your printer, choose the correct feed method and feed form at the Envelope Options dialog box with the Printing Options tab selected. Feed methods are visually displayed at this dialog box. You can also determine if the envelope is fed into the printer face up, as shown in Figure 3.31, or face down.

3.31 *Choosing Envelope Printing Options*

exercise 5

Designing and Creating an Envelope Template Using the Envelope Feature

1. At a clear document screen, create an envelope design, as shown in Figure 3.32, to coordinate with the Desktop Design letterhead created in Exercise 1, by completing the following steps:

   a. Click <u>T</u>ools, <u>L</u>etters and Mailings, <u>E</u>nvelopes and Labels, and then select the <u>E</u>nvelopes tab.

   b. Select and delete any text that displays in the *Delivery address* text box.

   c. If a default address appears in the *Return address* text box, click the *Omit* check box to insert a check mark, or select and delete the address.

   d. Make sure a business-sized envelope appears in the *Preview* box and then click <u>A</u>dd to Document

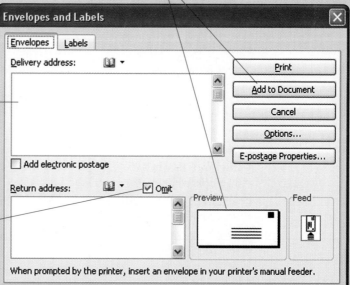

   to insert a blank envelope form in your document. The screen will display with the insertion point in the return address position. The page number in the status line will display as *Page 0*. A blank page will also be included following the envelope because the envelope was added to a clear document screen.

e. With the insertion point in the upper left corner, make sure the left margin is 0.4 inch. Click OK to close the dialog box. If Word prompts you that your printer will not accept this measurement, choose <u>F</u>ix to accept the minimum margin setting as determined by Word, and then click the OK button again.

f. Display the Drawing toolbar, click the Text Box button on the Drawing toolbar, and then draw a text box on the left side of the envelope that is approximately the same size and in the same location as that shown in Figure 3.32.

g. Customize the text box at the Format Text Box dialog box by completing the following steps:
   1) Display the Format Text Box dialog box by double-clicking one of the text box borders, or click F<u>o</u>rmat and Text B<u>o</u>x.
   2) Select the Colors and Lines tab and make the following changes:
      a) In the *Fill* section, click the <u>C</u>olor list box, <u>F</u>ill Effects, and then the Texture tab in the Fill Effects dialog box. In the *Texture* section, click the last texture block in the first row *(Stationery)*. Click OK or press Enter.
      b) In the *Line* section, click the C<u>o</u>lor list box and then *No Line*.
   3) Select the Size tab and change the height of the text box to 3.2 inches and the width to 1.45 inches.
   4) Select the Layout tab and change the horizontal alignment to left. Click the <u>A</u>dvanced button and change the vertical position to 0.45 inch below the page.
   5) Click OK twice.

h. Insert and format the text box contents by completing the following steps:
   1) Click inside the text box and then type the following text, pressing Enter as indicated. *(Hint: The longer lines will wrap.)*

      Desktop (press Enter)
      Designs (press Enter twice)
      568 Pine Street (press Enter)
      St. Louis, MO 63131 (press Enter)
      "Where Concepts Become a Reality"

   2) Select all of the text just entered and then change the font to 12-point Papyrus Bold and the text color to Teal.
   3) Select *Desktop Designs*, access the Font dialog box, change the type size to 22 points, and then apply *Emboss*. Click OK.
   4) With the company name still selected, click F<u>o</u>rmat and then <u>P</u>aragraph. At the Paragraph dialog box, change the line spacing to exactly 26 points.
   5) Change the paragraph *Before* and *After* spacing to *4 pt*. Click OK.
   6) Select the word *Designs* and then expand the character spacing by 1 point at the Font dialog box.

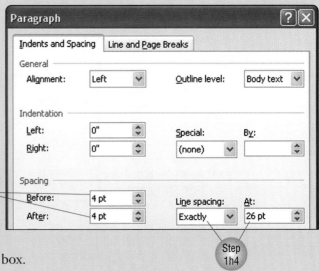

Paragraph

Indents and Spacing | Line and <u>P</u>age Breaks

General
Alig<u>n</u>ment: Left   <u>O</u>utline level: Body text

Indentation
<u>L</u>eft: 0"   <u>S</u>pecial: (none)   B<u>y</u>:
<u>R</u>ight: 0"

Spacing
<u>B</u>efore: 4 pt   Li<u>n</u>e spacing: <u>A</u>t:
A<u>f</u>ter: 4 pt   Exactly 26 pt

Step 1h5

Step 1h4

7) Select the address, change the type size to 9 points, then access the Paragraph dialog box and change the line spacing to exactly 10 points. Click OK.

8) Position the insertion point in the last line of the address, display the Paragraph dialog box, and then change the after spacing to 90 points. Click OK.

9) Select the slogan *"Where Concepts Become a Reality"* (press Ctrl + Shift + End) and change the type size to 11 points, change the font style to Bold Italic, and apply *Emboss*.

10) With the slogan still selected, access the Paragraph dialog box and then change the line spacing to exactly 12 points.

i. Insert the symbols shown in Figure 3.32 by completing the following steps:

1) Turn on the nonprinting characters (Show/Hide ¶), and then position the insertion point just before the paragraph symbol below *Designs*.

2) Click Insert and then Symbol.

3) At the Symbol dialog box, select the *Wingdings 2* font and then select ◈ (the second symbol from the left in the tenth row, #177). Click Insert and then Close.

4) Press F4 (Repeat key) four times.

5) Select the symbols and change the font color to Dark Red and change the horizontal alignment to Center.

6) With the symbols still selected, display the Paragraph dialog box and change the *Before* and *After* spacing to *6 pt*. Click OK.

j. Click File and then Print Preview to view the completed envelope. Click the Close button to close Print Preview and return to the document.

2. Save the envelope and name it **c03ex05, ddenvelope**.

3. Print **c03ex05, ddenvelope** (current page only).

4. Save your envelope as a template by completing the following steps:

a. Add placeholder text to indicate placement of the mailing address by completing the following steps:

1) Click the paragraph symbol located in the mailing address area to display a frame (similar to a text box) reserved for the mailing address. (This frame exists when an envelope is produced using the Envelopes and Label feature.)

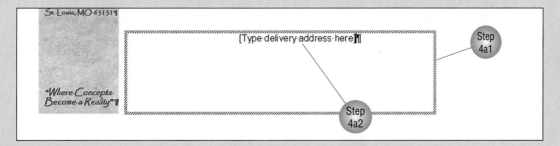

2) Type [Type delivery address here].

3) Turn off the nonprinting characters (Show/Hide ¶).

4) Use Print Preview to view the entire envelope.

b. Save your envelope as a template by completing the following steps:

1) Click File and Save As, and then change the *Save as type* option to *Document Template*.

2) Change the folder location in the *Save in* list box to the template folder that you created in Chapter 2. (Most likely the location is A:\DTP Templates.)

3) Name the envelope template **ddenvelope** and then click Save.

5. Close **ddenvelope**.

FIGURE
3.32 *Exercise 5*

Using AutoText to Store and Reuse Text and Graphics

AutoText lets you quickly and easily store and reuse commonly used text and/or graphics, including any associated formatting, and insert them into documents whenever you need them. The AutoText feature is useful for items such as a company logo, company name, addresses, lists, standard text, a closing to a letter, or any other text and/or graphics that you use on a frequent basis or that would take too much time to recreate as shown in Figure 3.33. By default, AutoText entries are saved as part of the Normal template and, therefore, are always available for future use in all documents based on the Normal template.

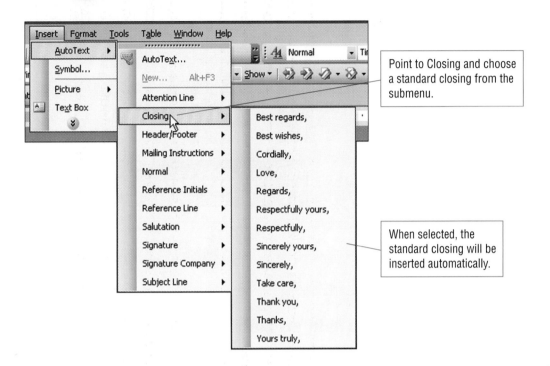

Point to Closing and choose a standard closing from the submenu.

When selected, the standard closing will be inserted automatically.

Creating an AutoText Entry

To create and save an AutoText entry, complete the following steps:

1. Type the desired text, apply any formatting, and/or insert any graphics or objects.
2. Select the text and/or graphics you want to store as an AutoText entry. If any paragraph formatting is applied to the text, make sure you include the paragraph mark with the selected text. Turn on the display of nonprinting characters to make sure the paragraph mark is included.
3. Click Insert, point to AutoText, and then click New.
4. At the Create AutoText dialog box, either accept the default name assigned to the AutoText entry or type a new short name. Click OK.

If you plan to create, insert, or edit several AutoText entries, display the AutoText toolbar shown in Figure 3.34 to save time. To display the AutoText toolbar, position the arrow pointer anywhere within a toolbar that is currently displayed on the screen and then right-click. Select *AutoText* from the toolbar drop-down list. After selecting the desired text and/or graphics, click New on the AutoText toolbar to access the Create AutoText dialog box.

3.34 *AutoText Toolbar*

Opens the AutoCorrect dialog box with the AutoText tab displayed.

Displays all AutoText entries. Normal option displays New AutoText entries.

Displays the Create AutoText dialog box.

AutoText

All Entries

Create AutoText

Inserting an AutoText Entry

An AutoText entry may be inserted into a document by using two different shortcut methods. To use the first shortcut method, type the name given to the AutoText entry and then press the shortcut key F3. The AutoText entry will appear immediately in your document at the location of the insertion point.

The second shortcut method works only if an AutoText entry name contains at least four characters. If the *Show AutoComplete suggestions* option is checked in the AutoText tab at the AutoCorrect dialog box as shown in Figure 3.35, as you begin typing an AutoText entry name into a document, Word displays the entry text (or at least part of it) in a box near the insertion point. The box appears after you have typed at least four characters. When the suggestion appears, press Enter or F3 to accept Word's suggestion or continue typing to ignore the suggestion.

An AutoText entry can also be inserted by choosing Insert, pointing to AutoText, and then clicking AutoText. At the AutoCorrect dialog box with the AutoText tab selected, click the name of the AutoText entry in the list box; then click Insert.

3.35 *Show AutoComplete Suggestions Option*

Editing an AutoText Entry

An AutoText entry may be edited by inserting the entry in a document, making any necessary changes, and then saving it again with the same AutoText entry name. When Word asks if you want to redefine the AutoText entry, choose Yes.

Deleting an AutoText Entry

An AutoText entry can be removed from the AutoCorrect dialog box. To do this, display the AutoText tab in the AutoCorrect dialog box, select the entry name from the *Enter AutoText entries here* list box, and then click the Delete button. In a classroom lab setting, check with your instructor about deleting AutoText entries after you are finished with them. Deleting them would allow other students the opportunity to create their own entries with the same names.

Creating Business Cards

A business card is one of your best marketing opportunities. A business card usually includes your name, title, company or organization name, address, telephone number, fax number, e-mail address, and if appropriate the URL of your Web site. You can also include a one-sentence description of your business, business philosophy, or slogan. To establish your identity and to stay consistent with other business documents such as letterheads, envelopes, and so on, include the same company logo or symbol in reduced size. Also, continue to use the same typefaces and colors used in your other business documents. Most business cards are created with sans serif typefaces because the characters are easier to read. The type sizes vary from 12 to 14 points for key words and 8 to 10 points for telephone and fax numbers. Vary the appearance by using bold, italics, or small caps. Figure 3.36 illustrates two similar business cards that include all of the necessary information, but are slightly different in design. The one on the right is the best choice as it reinforces a consistent strong right alignment. The photograph adds an updated professional feel over the clip art image used in the first example.

Business cards should be printed on high-quality cover stock paper. Specially designed full-color papers and forms for creating business cards more easily and professionally are available at office supply stores and paper companies. Printing your own business cards saves you the expense of having to place a large minimum order with an outside printer. This is especially helpful to a new small business. You may decide to design your own card and then take it to a professional printer to be printed in large quantities. Be sure to call the printer first to confirm that your Word file will be acceptable or if a hard copy will suffice.

DTP POINTERS
Using coordinating design elements in your business documents establishes identity and consistency.

Right Alignment   Left Alignment

Good

Right Alignment   Right Alignment

Better

Using Word's Labels Feature to Create Business Cards

Although Word does not include a template for creating business cards, you can use Word's business card label definition to design and create your own business cards. You can also use the business card label definition to create membership cards, name tags, coupons, placeholders, or friendly reminders. Most label definitions will produce 10 business cards—two columns of labels with five rows in each column. The columns and rows are set up automatically in a Word table. Each label is actually a cell in the table.

When creating business cards, use the label definition that matches the labels you have purchased. A common label is the Avery standard 5371 or 8371 Business Card label definition. The only difference between these two label product numbers occurs in the actual product when you purchase these brand-name items at an office supply store—the 5371 is made to be used in a laser printer and the 8371 is made to be used in an inkjet printer. In both cases, the business card will be 3½ by 2 inches and the sheet containing the business cards will be 8½ by 11 inches.

Using the Microsoft Office Online Templates Web Page for Business Cards

As an alternative to designing business cards, you may use an array of professionally designed business card templates at the Microsoft Office Online Templates Web page. To access these templates, complete the following steps:

1. Display the New Document task pane.
2. Click the Templates on Office Online hyperlink.
3. At the Templates Web page, click the Business Cards hyperlink located under the Stationery and Labels hyperlink in the *Browse Templates* section or type the keywords Business Cards in the *Search for* text box and then click Go.
4. At the Business Cards Web page you will find a number of hyperlinks to business card templates. Some of these templates are shown in Figure 3.37. Click the Download Now button to download the business card template you want into Word.

When the card templates are edited in Word, they will display as a full sheet of formatted labels. To customize this sheet of cards (labels), you may use one of the following two methods:

Using AutoText to Customize Business Cards Based on a Template:

1. Click the Download Now button to download the business card template you want from the Microsoft Office Online Templates Web page into Word. Make a note of the label definition or definitions listed as suitable for the card, such as Avery 5371, 8371, 8871, etc., as you will need to specify that later on.

2. Delete all of the cards in the template except for the card in the upper-left corner of the template, and then modify the remaining business card to meet your needs. *(Note: Do not delete the table cells containing the cards.)*

3. Select the text in the business card you modified and then click the Text Box button on the Drawing toolbar—a text box should display around the selected text.

4. Hold down the Shift key and select each text box, picture, or object in the formatted card. *(Note: The text box you inserted may obscure other objects or text boxes in the card. If that is the case, right-click the text box, point to O**r**der, and then click Send to Bac**k** so that other objects can be viewed and selected.)*

5. Click the **D**raw button on the Drawing toolbar and then click **G**roup to group all of the objects together.

6. With the grouped objects still selected, click **I**nsert, **A**utoText, and then **N**ew.

7. At the Create AutoText dialog box, give your entry a short name. Click the OK button to close the Create AutoText dialog box, and then close the business card template document.

8. At a clear document screen, click **T**ools, **L**etters and Mailings, and then Envelopes and Labels.

9. At the Envelopes and Labels dialog box with the **L**abels tab selected, click the **O**ptions button. At the Label Options dialog box, select a label definition that corresponds with the label definition you noted when you downloaded the business card template from the Microsoft Office Online Templates Web page (e.g., Avery 5371, 8371, etc.). Click the OK button.

10. Type your AutoText entry name in the *A**ddress** text box and then press F3 or Enter (depending on the length of the name).

11. Make sure that the *F**ull page of the same label* option is selected and then click the New **D**ocument button.

12. Your customized business cards should display in Print Preview as a full sheet of cards. (Complete Skill Assessment 4 for practice on using this method.)

Using Copy and Paste to Customize Business Cards:

1. Delete all of the business cards *except* the first row of formatted cards. (Do not delete the table structure.)

2. Customize the remaining two business cards.

3. Select the two business cards (select them as a row in a table).

4. Click <u>E</u>dit and then <u>C</u>opy.

5. Position the insertion point in the first cell of the second row of the table, click <u>E</u>dit, and then click <u>P</u>aste Rows. *(Note: If the table gridlines do not display, click T<u>a</u>ble and Show <u>G</u>ridlines.)*

6. Press F4 to repeat copying the rows.

7. Students should select and then delete any blank rows at the end of the copied rows.

F I G U R E

3.37 **Sample Business Card Templates Available on the Microsoft Office Online Templates Web Page**

 CJR CONSTRUCTION

CHRISTOPHER RODRIGUEZ
Owner

57 North Walnut Drive, Suite 120, New Orleans, LA 12329
Phone (800) 555-1212   Fax (800) 555-1414
License #M29857

Your Name

Street Address
City, State, ZIP Code
555.555.0198
555.555.0199 fax

Business Name | someone@example.com

Your Company Name

YOUR NAME
Street Address
City, State, ZIP
000.000.0000
000.000.0000 Fax
e-mail@yourserver.com

Humongous Insurance

Medical ♦ *Dental* ♦ *Long-Term Care*

ERIC ROTHENBERG
Owner

56 N Walnut Drive, Suite 120, New Orleans, LA 12329
Phone (409) 555-0112   Fax (409) 555-0114
License #M45678

exercise 6

Creating Business Cards Using Word's Envelopes and Labels Feature and AutoText Feature

1. At a clear document screen, create the AutoText entry used to produce the business cards shown in Figure 3.38 by completing the following steps:
    a. Create a blank sheet of labels by completing the following steps:
        1) Click <u>T</u>ools, <u>L</u>etters and Mailings, and then <u>E</u>nvelopes and Labels.
        2) At the Envelopes and Labels dialog box, select the <u>L</u>abels tab, and then click <u>O</u>ptions.

3) At the Label Options dialog box, select *Avery standard* in the *Label products* list box and then select *5371- Business Card* from the *Product number* list box. Click OK or press Enter.

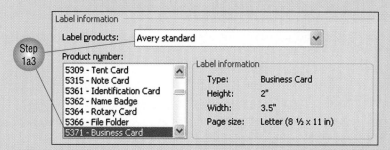

4) At the Envelopes and Labels dialog box, delete any text that may appear in the *Address* list box.
5) At the same dialog box, make sure *Full page of the same label* is selected and then click New Document.
b. If the table gridlines do not display, click Table and Show Gridlines.
c. Insert the text box that will contain the company name, slogan, and address by completing the following steps:
   1) Change the zoom to *Page Width*.
   2) Display the Drawing toolbar and click the Text Box button.
   3) Position the crosshairs in the upper left corner of the first label (or cell) and draw a text box that is approximately the same size and in the same location as the *Desktop Designs* text box shown in Figure 3.38.
d. Customize the text box by completing the following steps:
   1) Double-click the text box border to display the Format Text Box dialog box (or click Format and Text Box).
   2) Select the Colors and Lines tab. In the *Fill* section, click the *Color* list box and then click Fill Effects. Select the Texture tab in the Fill Effects dialog box. In the *Texture* section, click the last texture block from the left in the first row. The texture name, *Stationery*, will display below the texture selections. Click OK or press Enter.
   3) In the *Line* section, click the *Color* list box, and then click No Line.
   4) Select the Size tab and change the height of the text box to 1.8 inches and the width to 1.22 inches.
   5) Select the Layout tab and then click the *Advanced* button. Change the horizontal position to 0.15 inch to the right of the page and the vertical position to 0.1 inch below the page. Click OK.
   6) Select the Text Box tab and change the left and right margins to 0.05 inch. Click OK.
e. Insert and format the text box contents by completing the following steps:
   1) Position the insertion point in the text box and change the font to 9-point Papyrus and the color to Teal.
   2) Type the following text, pressing Enter as indicated:

   Desktop (press Enter)
   Designs (press Enter twice)
   "Where Concepts Become a Reality" (let text wrap and then press Enter)
   568 Pine Street (press Enter)
   St. Louis, MO 63131

3) Select *Desktop Designs* and change the font size to 20 points. Apply bold and apply *Emboss* at the Font dialog box. Click OK.

4) Position the insertion point within *Desktop* and change the spacing before the paragraph to 2 points and the line spacing to exactly 18 points at the Paragraph dialog box. Click OK.

5) Select *Designs* and use the Font dialog box to expand the character spacing by 0.5 point. Click OK.

6) Select *"Where Concepts Become a Reality"* and apply italics.

7) With the slogan still selected, change the spacing after the paragraph to 16 points and the line spacing to exactly 11 points at the Paragraph dialog box. Click OK.

8) Select the address, city, state, and ZIP Code, and change the font size to 7 points.

9) With the address, city, state, and ZIP Code still selected, use the Paragraph dialog box to change the line spacing to exactly 10 points. Click OK.

10) Position the insertion point just before the paragraph symbol after *Designs* and then change the horizontal alignment to Center. *(Note: If necessary, click the Show/Hide ¶ button on the Standard toolbar to display nonprinting symbols.)*

11) Click Insert and then Symbol.

12) At the Symbol dialog box, click the down-pointing arrow at the right of the Font list box and select *Wingdings 2*.

13) Click the symbol ◈ (the second symbol from the left in the tenth row, #177), click Insert, and then click Close.

14) Press F4 two times, select the symbols, and then change the font color to Dark Red.

f. Insert and customize the text box that will contain the business person's name, title, phone number, fax number, and e-mail address by completing the following steps:

1) Draw a text box to the right of the first text box that is approximately 1.5 inches by 2 inches.

2) Double-click one of the text box borders to display the Format Text Box dialog box and make the following changes:

   a) Select the Colors and Lines tab and change the line color to No Line.

   b) Select the Size tab and change the height of the text box to 1.57 inches and the width to 1.8 inches.

   c) Select the Layout tab and then click the Advanced button. At the Advanced Layout dialog box, with the Picture Position tab selected, change the horizontal position to 1.5 inches to the right of the page and the vertical position to 0.25 inch below the page.

   d) Click OK twice.

g. Insert and format the text box contents by completing the following steps:

1) Position the insertion point inside the text box and then type the following text, pressing Enter once after each line:

   Linda Urban
   Publications Designer
   Phone: (314) 555-8755
   Fax: (314) 555-8758
   E-mail: urban@emcp.net

2) Select all of the text just entered (Ctrl + A) and change the font to 12-point Papyrus and change the font color to Teal.

3) Select *Linda Urban*, change the type size to 17 point, turn on bold, and apply the *Emboss* effect from the Font dialog box. Click OK.

Step 1g3

Steps 1g4–6

Step 1g7

4) Select *Publications Designer*, change the type size to 10 point, and apply italics.

5) Select both the name and title and change the line spacing to exactly 15 points.

6) Position the insertion point within the title only and change the spacing after the paragraph to 34 points. Click OK.

7) Select the phone, fax, and e-mail address, change the type size to 10 point, and then change the line spacing to exactly 12 points. *(Hint: To select the text, position the insertion point to the left of* **Phone:***, then press Shift + Ctrl + End.)*

h. To save the business card as an AutoText entry, the objects in the business card must be grouped together so they can be treated as one unit. Group the objects by completing the following steps:

1) Select the text box that contains the company name.

2) Hold down the Shift key and select the remaining text box. (Both objects should be selected.)

3) Click <u>D</u>raw on the Drawing toolbar and then click <u>G</u>roup. (Sizing handles should display on all four sides of the business card.)

Step 1h3

i. Save the business card (now an object) as an AutoText entry by completing the following steps:

1) With the business card selected, click <u>I</u>nsert, point to AutoText, and then click <u>N</u>ew.

2) At the Create AutoText dialog box, type business card, and then click OK or press Enter.

j. Save the object (the business card) as a Word document so that you can always go back to this point if your AutoText entry is deleted. Name the document **ddbusiness card**.

k. Close **ddbusiness card**.

l. Create a full sheet of business cards using your business card AutoText entry by completing the following steps:

1) Click <u>T</u>ools, Le<u>t</u>ters and Mailings, and then <u>E</u>nvelopes and Labels. Make sure the <u>L</u>abels tab is selected and then click <u>O</u>ptions.

2) At the Label Options dialog box, select *Avery standard* in the *Label products* list box, and then choose *5371-Business Card* from the *Product number* list box. Click OK or press Enter.

Step 1i2

3) At the Envelopes and Labels dialog box with the Labels tab selected, delete any text that may appear in the *Address* list box, type **business card**, and then press F3. *(Note: Some versions of Word 2003 have a bug that prevents this from working. If this happens to you, try pressing F3 again, or type only the first three or four characters of the AutoText entry and then press F3. Alternatively, you can use the copy and paste method described earlier to create a sheet of business cards.)*

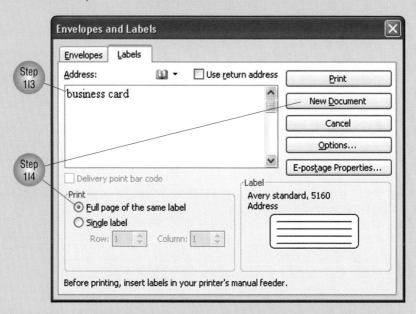

4) At the same dialog box, make sure *Full page of the same label* is selected, and then click New Document. A full sheet of business cards will display on your screen.

5) Use Print Preview to make sure your document will print correctly. Depending on your printer's unprintable zone and the margins set in the business card's label definition, the printing on the bottom row of the business cards may be cut off. One easy way to avoid this is to fool your printer into thinking your document is going to be printed on a longer piece of paper. To do this, complete the following steps:

a) Click File, click Page Setup, and then select the Paper tab.

b) In the *Paper size* list box, select *Legal* and click OK. Word may prompt you that *One or more margins are set outside the printable area of the page.* If so, click Ignore.

2. Save the full sheet of business cards with the name **c03ex06, Business Card**.

3. Print and then close **c03ex06, Business Card**. Printing the business cards on a sheet of business cards made especially for your type of printer is preferable. If you print the business cards on plain paper, you may want to print the table grid lines as shown in Figure 3.38. To print the grid lines, complete the following steps:

a. Click Table, point to Select, and then click Table.

b. Click Format, Borders and Shading, and then select the Borders tab.

c. In the *Setting* section, click All.

d. In the *Style* list box, click the fourth line choice (the dashed line) from the top. Click OK.

FIGURE 3.38 **Exercise 6**

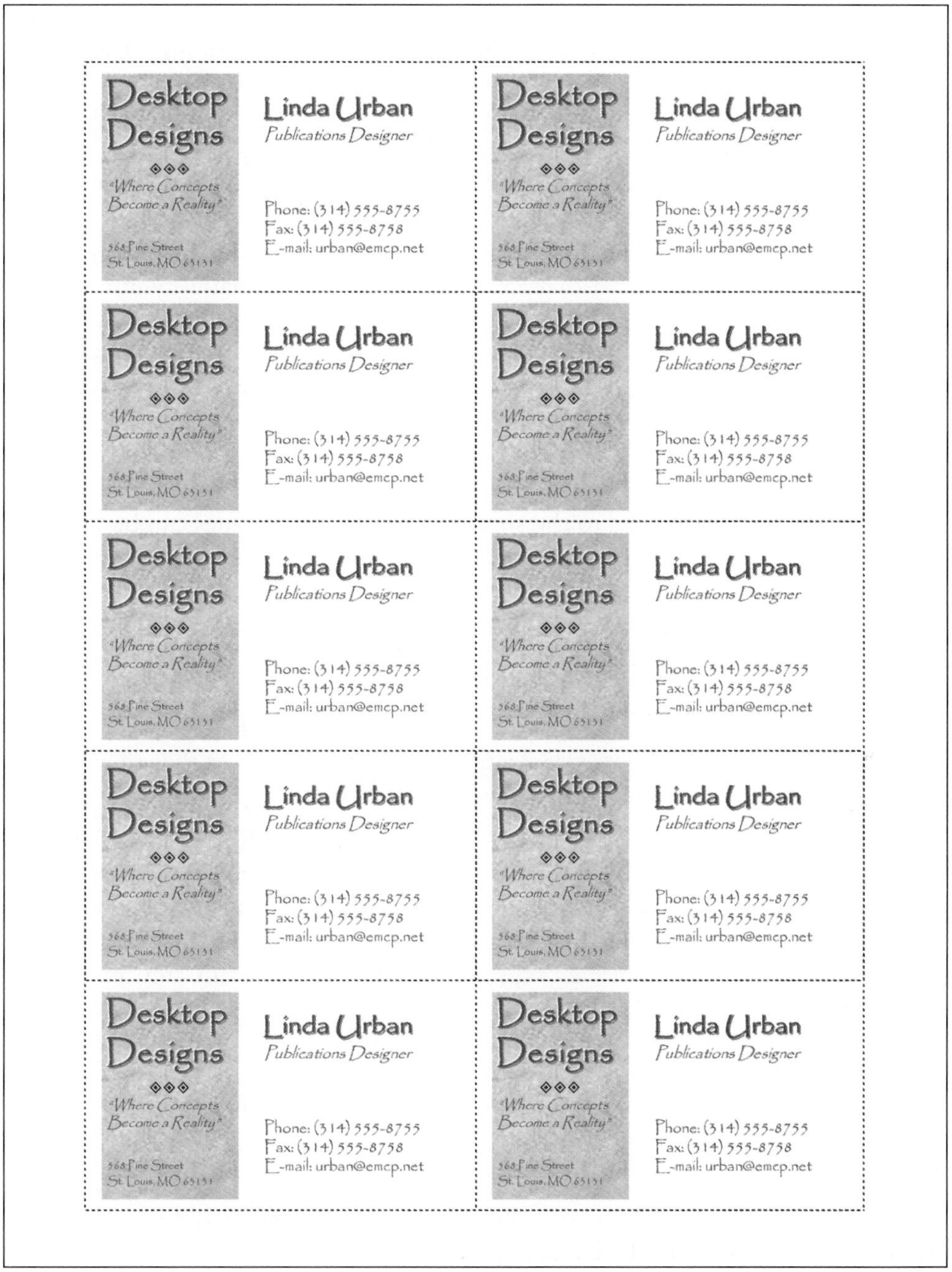

CHAPTER summary

➤ A letterhead contains a design and layout that helps establish an organization's identity with a target audience. Designing and producing your own letterhead can be a less costly alternative to having it designed and produced through a professional printer.

➤ A number of letter templates are available, including Contemporary, Elegant, and Professional. A Letter Wizard is also available that guides you through the creation of a business letter.

➤ The Click and Type feature allows you to click in any blank area of the screen and positions the insertion point at that location along with automatically inserting associated formatting such as tabs and paragraph returns. This feature also lets you position the insertion point so that text to be keyed will be left-, right-, or centered-aligned.

➤ A text box is used as a container for text and/or graphics. Text boxes are extremely useful in desktop publishing because text and/or graphics can be placed at exact horizontal and/or vertical locations on the page. They can also serve as placeholders for items such as illustrations and photos.

➤ Ruled lines act as boundaries to the surrounding text. Ruled lines can be used in a document to create a focal point, draw the eye across or down the page, separate columns and sections, or add visual appeal.

➤ An existing template document can be customized once it is displayed at the document screen. Any changes made affect only the document displayed on the screen, leaving the template available in its original format.

➤ A new template can be created from any existing Word document. Saving documents, such as letterheads or envelopes, as template documents ensures that they are always available to use over again and thus increases efficiency and productivity.

➤ Kerning is the process of decreasing or increasing the white space between specific character pairs and is used on headlines and other blocks of large type.

➤ Tracking is the equal reduction or enlargement of the horizontal space between all characters in a block of text.

➤ Word can recognize different data types entered into a document and convert the data types into smart tags which perform useful actions such as opening Microsoft Outlook and sending an e-mail or accessing a Web site to print a map of an address tag.

➤ When creating a design for an envelope, select enough common elements so that a link is established in the viewer's eyes between the letterhead and the envelope.

➤ Use the AutoText feature to save and insert frequently used text and/or graphics.

➤ Business cards are another way to establish identity among a target audience. Establish an identifying connection between a business card and a letterhead by repeating some of the design elements from the letterhead.

COMMANDS review

Command	Mouse/Keyboard
General Templates	View, Task Pane, New Document task pane, click the On my computer hyperlink
Microsoft Office Online Templates Web page	View, Task Pane, New Document task pane, click the Templates on Office Online hyperlink
Letter Wizard	View, Task Pane, New Document task pane, On my computer, Letters & Faxes tab, Letter Wizard; or Tools, Letters and Mailings, Letter Wizard
User Information	Tools, Options, User Information tab
Insert symbol	Insert, Symbol, Symbols tab
Change font	Format, Font; or click the Font list box or Size list box down-pointing arrows, and/or the character formatting buttons on Formatting toolbar
Display Drawing toolbar	Click the Drawing button on Standard toolbar; or right-click any existing toolbar, select Drawing; or View, Toolbars, and then Drawing
Format AutoShape dialog box	Select object, click Format and AutoShape; or double-click the object
Border a paragraph	Position insertion point, click Border button or arrow on Formatting toolbar; or click Format, Borders and Shading, and Borders tab
Create Header/Footer	View, Header and Footer
Insert a text box	Text Box button on Drawing toolbar, position crosshairs, click and drag to draw box; or Insert and then Text Box
Format Text Box dialog box	Select text box, click Format and Text Box; or double-click the text box border
Kerning (character spacing between specific pairs of characters)	Format, Font, Character Spacing tab, Kerning for fonts, and enter Points and above
Tracking (character/letter spacing)	Format, Font, Character Spacing tab, Spacing, enter By amount in point increments
Envelopes and Labels dialog box	Tools, Letters and Mailings, Envelopes and Labels, and select Envelopes or Labels tab
Create an AutoText entry	Insert, point to AutoText, and then click New
Insert an AutoText entry	Type AutoText entry name and press F3; or click Insert, point to AutoText, and then click AutoText

REVIEWING key points

Completion: On a blank sheet of paper, indicate the correct term, command, or number for each item.

1. This feature guides you through the steps for creating a business letter using any of the available letter templates.
2. This term refers to the decreasing or increasing of white space between specific character pairs.
3. In typesetting, the thickness of a line is called its weight and is measured in this.
4. A customized horizontal or vertical ruled line can be created using this feature.
5. This term refers to the equal reduction or enlargement of the horizontal space between all characters in a block of text.
6. Use this feature to position the insertion point in a blank area of the document or to change paragraph alignment for text to be typed.
7. Turn on kerning for specific point sizes and above at this dialog box.
8. This feature allows you to store commonly used text and/or graphics along with their formatting.
9. Use this type of paper size definition when designing and creating your own business cards.

Short Answer: On a blank sheet of paper, provide the correct answer for each question.

1. What is the purpose of a letterhead?
2. What information might be contained in a letterhead?
3. Define the User Information feature. What other Word features does it affect?
4. When creating your own letterhead, design concepts such as focus, balance, and proportion should be considered. What are some other design concepts that should be considered?
5. Name two methods of creating ruled lines in Word. Explain advantages or disadvantages of using one method over the other.
6. Explain the various ways a text box may be customized.

APPLYING your skills

Assessment 1

1. You have decided to open your own restaurant. Design a letterhead for your business that will be used for a mailing to introduce it to the community and for all of your future business correspondence. Include the following information:

Company Name:	You decide on the name depending on the picture/graphic that you incorporate into your design.
Name of Owner:	Use your own name and include *Owner* or *Proprietor* as your title.
Slogan:	You choose a slogan.
Address:	250 San Miguel Boulevard Mission Viejo, CA 92691
Phone:	714.555.8191
Fax:	714.555.8196

2. Create thumbnail sketches of your restaurant's letterhead by incorporating the following elements:
   a. Create an asymmetrically balanced design.
   b. Use appropriate and proportional typeface, type size, and typestyle selections.
   c. Turn on kerning and use tracking (condensing or expanding character spacing), if necessary, for a desired effect.
   d. Incorporate some of these suggestions for graphics and layout:

   1) Include a clip art image; possible search keywords may include: *food, coffee, dining,* or *restaurant*. Use the image to inspire a theme and a color scheme. (You may use any other relevant clip art that is available to you.)

   2) Create a restaurant logo using WordArt and/or AutoShapes.

   3) Include a ruled horizontal or vertical line.

   4) Include consistent elements such as typeface, color, alignment, repetitive symbol or graphic element, and so on.

   5) Group related items close to each other.

   6) Use color (sparingly) if a color printer is available.

   7) Make sure your letterhead is not too large.

   8) Use special characters, if appropriate.

3. Save the document and name it **c03sa01, Restaurant ltrhd**.
4. Print **c03sa01, Restaurant ltrhd**.
5. Save your letterhead as a document template in your Templates folder on your hard drive or a floppy disk and name it **Restaurant ltrhd**. Close **Restaurant ltrhd**.
6. As a self-check for your design, print a copy of **Document Analysis Guide.doc** located in your Chapter03 folder, name it **c03sa02, DAG Restaurant** (if typed), and then answer the questions on the form.
7. Attach the document analysis guide to the hard copy of the letterhead.

Assessment 2

1. Design an envelope to be used with the letterhead created in Assessment 1. Include some consistent elements that demonstrate continuity from the letterhead to the envelope. Include the following specifications:
   a. Create thumbnail sketches of your proposed envelope design.
   b. At a clear document screen, use the automatic envelope feature and add the envelope to the blank document.
   c. Use the same typeface(s) as in your letterhead. Pay attention to size and proportion.
   d. Turn on automatic kerning and adjust character spacing, if necessary.
   e. Use the same color scheme in the envelope as in your letterhead.
2. Save your envelope as a template and name it (**your name**) **restaurant env**.
3. Close (**your name**) **restaurant env**.
4. Access your envelope template and insert your own name and address in the mailing address area.
5. Save the document and name it **c03sa02, Restaurant env**.
6. Print and then close **c03sa02, Restaurant env**.

Assessment 3

1. Create a page of business cards to coordinate with the restaurant letterhead and envelope created in Assessments 1 and 2. Even though a business card does not have to be an exact replica of your letterhead, include some consistent identifying elements that link the two documents together. Include the following specifications when creating the business cards:
   a. Create thumbnail sketches of your proposed business card design and layout.
   b. Use the Labels feature and the Avery 5371 (or 8371) business card label definition.
   c. Create an AutoText entry that will work easily in the Envelopes and Labels feature. If you have difficulty using the AutoText entry in the Envelopes and Labels feature, you may have to add a blank sheet of label forms to a clear document screen, create the business card in the first label form, and then copy it to the rest of the labels.
2. Save and name the business cards as **c03sa03, Restaurant buscard**.
3. Print and then close **c03sa03, Restaurant buscard**.

Assessment 4

1. Create a sheet of business cards for an art supply company and use one of the business card templates from the Microsoft Office Online Templates Web page. Include the information below and follow steps similar to the ones given. You may create the sample business card shown in Figure 3.39, or create cards using a different template and incorporating your own design. Be creative and have fun. Include the following information:

> Art-fordable Arts
> Supplies you can afford
> Rachel Arford, Manager
> 231 Marietta Avenue
> Atlanta, GA 30312
> Phone: (800) 555-5665
> Fax: (800) 555-5667
> www.emcp.net/artfordable

2. Your customized business cards should display as a full sheet of cards.
3. Save and name the business cards as **c03sa04, Art Cards**.
4. Print and then close **c03sa04, Art Cards**.

FIGURE

3.39 **Sample Business Card**

ART-FORDABLE ARTS

...supplies you can afford

RACHEL ARFORD
Manager

231 Marietta Avenue, Atlanta, GA 30312
Phone (800) 555-5665   Fax (800) 555-5667
www.emcp.net/artfordable

Assessment 5

Download and modify a Microsoft Office Online Templates
Web page thank-you note, modify the design, type a letter,
and then use Microsoft Access to merge contact details for a friend into the letter.

INTEGRATED

1. Locate the Thank-you note stationery template on the Microsoft Office Online
   Template Web page. The template is located in the <u>Browse Templates</u> section by
   clicking <u>Stationery and Labels</u>, <u>Personal Correspondence</u> and then <u>Thank-you note
   Stationery</u> hyperlink.
2. Download and save the template as a Word document named **c03sa05, Thank You
   Letter**.
3. Click <u>V</u>iew and then <u>H</u>eader and Footer, or double-click in the header area to view
   the template header and footer.
4. Select the musical note, hold down the Ctrl key, and drag a copy to the left of the
   scale as shown in Figure 3.40. Scale and then rotate the copied note so that it appears
   the same as Figure 3.40.
5. Scroll down to the footer area, select the text and bullets, and change their color to
   Indigo. Type over the placeholder text to place your address details in the footer.
   Close the Header/Footer pane.
6. Turn on Show/Hide ¶, select the paragraph symbol in the body text, and then change
   the font to 11-point Garamond.
7. Press Enter four times and then insert a date code with the automatic update feature
   turned on.
8. Press Enter four times, save **c03sa05, Thank You Letter**, and then close it.
9. Start Microsoft Access.
10. Open the Access **Addresses** file located in your Chapter03 folder. *(Note: You may see
    a dialog box advising you to download a service pack that will protect you from unsafe
    expressions when using Access. You can follow the instructions to download the latest
    service pack, or you can ignore the message and click the Yes button at the bottom of
    the dialog box. If you have the latest service pack you will see another message advising
    you that the file may not be safe if it contains code that was intended to harm your
    computer. Click the Open button to proceed.)*

11. If necessary, click the Tables button, and then click Friends in the Database window that appears.
12. With Friends selected, click Tools, point to Office Links, and then click Merge It with Microsoft Office Word.
13. When the Microsoft Word Mail Merge Wizard dialog box appears, click the *Link your data to an existing Microsoft Word document* option and then click OK.
14. Use the Select Microsoft Word Document file manager dialog box to locate and open **c03sa05, Thank You Letter**.
15. Type the following in the letter body as shown in Figure 3.40. *(Hint: Press Ctrl + End.)*

> Dear *(Note: Do not enter any punctuation after* Dear.*)* (Press Enter twice.)
> Thanks for attending our Christmas party and for the wonderful gift. I really enjoyed seeing you again. (Press Enter twice.)
> I am updating my list of e-mail addresses for future party invitations, and I have discovered that the e-mail address I currently have for you (pasted below) does not seem to work. (Press Enter four times.)
> Please let me know if I should be using another address. (Press Enter twice.)
> Sincerely, (Press Enter four times.)
> John (Press Enter.) *(Note: Type your name here.)*

16. Click the Next: Write your letter link located at the bottom of the Mail Merge task pane.
17. With the insertion point located four lines below the date entry, click the Address block link in the Mail Merge task pane.
18. Choose the *Joshua Randall, Jr.* name format in the *Insert recipient's name in this format* list box. Click OK and then press Enter once after the Address block.
19. Place the insertion point just after *Dear* and the press the spacebar one time.
20. Click the Greeting line link in the Mail Merge task pane. Click the *Greeting Line Format* list box down-pointing arrow and select *(none)*. Select *Josh* in the next list box, and be sure a comma appears in the last list box in that row. Click OK.
21. Place the insertion point in between the *I am updating...* paragraph and the following paragraph, and then click the More items link in the Mail Merge task pane.
22. Make sure the *Database Fields* option is selected, select *EmailAddress*, click the Insert button, and then click Close.
23. Click the Next: Preview your letters link in the Mail Merge task pane.
24. Preview the merged items in your letter. If everything is correct, click the Next: Complete the merge link. If you detect any problems, click the Previous: Write your letter link to return to the previous screen.
25. Once you are satisfied with the letter, select the e-mail address and bold it.
26. Click the Print link in the Mail Merge task pane to print the letter.
27. Save **c03sa05, Thank You Letter** and then close it.
28. Close Access.

FIGURE

3.40 *Assessment 5 Sample Solution*

Just a note to say

Thanks!

June 9, 2004

Dear

Thanks for attending our Christmas party and for the wonderful gift. I really enjoyed seeing you again.

I am updating my list of e-mail addresses for future party invitations, and I have discovered that the e-mail address I currently have for you (pasted below) does not seem to work.

robbo@emcp.net

Please let me know if I should be using another address.

Sincerely,

John

Your Street Address • Your Address • Phone 555.555.0125 • Fax 555.555.0145 • Your E-mail address • Web site address

Assessment 6

Word documents can be imported into Microsoft Publisher, providing you with the convenience of working with Publisher's text box layout and automated design features. Publisher shares many tools with Word, including WordArt, AutoShapes, and Clip Art, but also features exciting design tools such as Color Schemes, Font Schemes, Design Gallery Objects, and much more. Import an existing Word document into Publisher and create an attractive design by completing the following steps:

INTEGRATED

1. Start Publisher.
2. Click <u>F</u>ile on the Menu bar and then <u>N</u>ew.
3. In the New Publication task pane, click *Publications for Print* located under the *New from a design* section.
4. Scroll down the list and click *Import Word Documents*.
5. At the Import Word Documents screen, use the scrollbar to scroll down to the bottom of the design display and click the *Studio Word Document* design.
6. Use the Import Word Document dialog box to locate and open **Gettysburg Address** from your Chapter03 folder. ***(Hint: If a Personal Information dialog box displays, click OK.)***
7. Increase the zoom to *75%*.
8. Remove the *Page 1* text box by clicking its border and then pressing the Delete or Backspace keys.
9. Select the Document Title text at the top of the document and then type The Gettysburg Address.
10. Delete *The Gettysburg Address* title text from the top of the text body.
11. Click the <u>Font Schemes</u> link in the Word Import Options task pane and then scroll down the list to select *Foundry Rockwell Extra Bold*. ***(Hint: The entire font title may not be visible depending on how wide your task pane is sized.)***
12. Select the text in the body of the page and change the font size to 12 points and bold it.
13. Click the <u>Color Schemes</u> link in the task pane and choose *Mahogany*.
14. Select the text in the body of the page and change the font color to the same brown as the border. ***(Hint: When you click the Font Color button you will see the brown in the single row list of color boxes.)***
15. Click <u>I</u>nsert, point to <u>P</u>icture, and then click <u>C</u>lip Art. Type Lincoln in the *Search for* text box and then press Go. Click the picture of Lincoln giving a speech. Alternatively, type the clip art file name (j0149881.wmf) in the *Search for* text box and press Go to find the image. Click the image to insert it into your document.
16. Right-click the image in the document and then click Format Pictu<u>r</u>e. Click the Format Picture dialog box Layout tab and then click the Top and <u>b</u>ottom button in the *Wrapping Style* section. Click the Size tab and change the picture dimensions to 1.38 inches high and 1.82 inches wide.
17. Click the Format Picture dialog box Colors and Lines tab and then click the <u>B</u>orderArt button. Scroll down the *Available Borders* list and select the *Basic... Wide Midline Available Borders* style. Make sure the *Stretch pictures to fit* option is selected and then click the OK button. Change the line weight to *8* and the line color to the same brown as the text and the document border. Click the OK button.
18. Drag the picture so that it is located between the title and the first line of body text, and center it as shown in Figure 3.41.
19. Select the *F* in the first word *(Four)* of the opening paragraph, click F<u>o</u>rmat and then <u>D</u>rop Cap. Click the first drop cap option in the second row and then click OK.
20. Click <u>I</u>nsert and then <u>D</u>esign Gallery Object. Click *Sidebars* in the *Categories* list box, and then in the *Sidebars* list box click the *Capsules Sidebar* design. Click Insert Object to insert the sidebar.
21. Double-click the sidebar border, and use the Format AutoShape dialog box to change the sidebar border to the same brown as the text.
22. Select the text inside the sidebar and change it to the same brown as the rest of the text in the document.
23. Select the sidebar title text and type Gettysburg Facts:.
24. Select the bulleted text and type the following:

> Battle fought July 1-3, 1863. (Press Enter.)
> Over 7,000 soldiers killed. (Press Enter.)

Lincoln gave the address when dedicating burial ground on November 19, 1863.

25. Drag and locate the sidebar as shown in Figure 3.41 and resize it if necessary. *(Hint: You can click the border of the design and then drag it left, right, up, or down on the page to place it exactly where you want it.)*
26. Preview the document and then print it.
27. Use the Save <u>A</u>s command to name the document **c03sa06**, **Publisher**, and then close it.
28. Close Publisher.

F I G U R E

3.41 *Assessment 6 Sample Solution*

The Gettysburg Address

Four score and seven years ago our fathers brought forth on this continent, a new nation, conceived in Liberty, and dedicated to the proposition that all men are created equal.

Now we are engaged in a great civil war, testing whether that nation, or any nation so conceived and so dedicated, can long endure. We are met on a great battlefield of that war. We have come to dedicate a portion of that field, as a final resting place for those who here gave their lives that that nation might live. It is altogether fitting and proper that we should do this.

But, in a larger sense, we can not dedicate—we can not consecrate—we can not hallow—this ground. The brave men, living and dead, who struggled here, have consecrated it, far above our poor power to add or detract. The world will little note, nor long remember what we say here, but it can never forget what they did here. It is for us the living, rather, to be dedicated here to the unfinished work which they who fought here have thus far so nobly advanced. It is rather for us to be here dedicated to the great task remaining before us—that from these honored dead we take increased devotion to that cause for which they gave the last full measure of devotion—that we here highly resolve that these dead shall not have died in vain—that this nation, under God, shall have a new birth of freedom—and that government of the people, by the people, for the people, shall not perish from the earth.

Abraham Lincoln

Gettysburg Facts:

• Battle fought July 1-3, 1863.

• Over 7,000 soldiers killed.

• Lincoln gave address when dedicating burial ground on November 19, 1863.

Assessment 7

Find an example of a letterhead from a business, school, or volunteer organization. Redesign the letterhead using the desktop publishing concepts learned so far. On a separate sheet, type the changes you made and explain why you made those changes. Evaluate your letterhead using the document analysis guide **(Document Analysis Guide.doc)** located in your Chapter03 folder. Name the revised letterhead **c03sa07**. Submit a thumbnail sketch, the original letterhead (or a copy), the revised letterhead, and the document analysis guide.

Design and Create

Creating Personal Documents

PERFORMANCE OBJECTIVES

Upon successful completion of Chapter 4, you will be able to create compact disc face labels, compact disc case covers, calendars, personal address labels, personal stationery and envelopes on odd-sized paper, and certificates.

CHAPTER 04

DESKTOP PUBLISHING TERMS

Bleed	Form field	Placeholder
Crop	Grouping	Stacking
Form	Nudging	Unprintable zone

WORD FEATURES USED

AutoShapes	Header and Footer	Shadow effects
AutoText	Ink mode	Tables
Calendar Wizard	Language bar	Tabs
Drawing canvas	Microsoft Office Online	Text boxes
Drawing Grid	Templates Web	Text fields
Drawing toolbar	page	Text wrapping
Envelopes and Labels	Page Border	Washout
Fill effects	Pictures	Watermark
Form fields	Rotate or flip	WordArt
Group and ungroup	Scribble	Writing Pad

In this chapter, you will produce personal documents using Word's templates and wizards, and create and format your own personal documents. You will use other Word features such as tables, text boxes, and labels to produce compact disc covers, calendars, address labels, personal stationery, and certificates. In addition, you will apply basic desktop publishing concepts of planning document content, maintaining consistency, and achieving balance through pictures, symbols, text, lines, color, and borders.

While you are creating the documents in this chapter, consider how you can apply what you have learned to create other personal documents such as invitations, greeting cards, tickets, bookmarks, recipe cards, bookplates, change-of-address cards, thank-you cards, personal note cards, and even birth announcements. Several sample personal documents are shown Figure 4.1.

FIGURE

4.1 *Sample Personal Documents*

CD Face Label

CD Case Cover

Graduation Invitation

Nutrition Log

Personalized Calendar

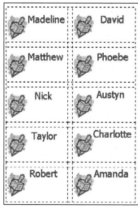
Place Cards

Bookplates

Invitation

Change-of-Address Card

Gift Tags

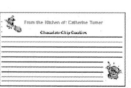
Recipe Card

Personal Note Cards

Creating a Compact Disc Label

Standard diskette labels and compact disc labels are used to catalog the contents of a disk/disc. If you were to purchase a new computer today, you may have the option to purchase a CD-ROM, CD-R, CD-RW, DVD-ROM, and/or Zip drive. Each storage medium is associated with a particular label and/or additional elements to identify the contents. A Zip disk stores about 70 times the capacity of a traditional floppy and looks very similar to a standard floppy disk. Therefore, an Avery standard diskette label measuring 2¾ by 2¾ inches may be customized and used to identify the contents of the disk. The Avery label 8931 includes face, case, and spine definitions, which you can easily customize. With each update to Word, additional product numbers are added to the label definitions that Word can recognize.

The CD-ROM and rewritable CD-RW discs measure approximately 4¾ inches in diameter and may be identified using a label on the disc cover (sometimes called a jewel case). Word includes Avery label definition (#5824) for a CD front and back label measuring 4½ by 4½ inches. However, this label does not fit the case precisely and does not include a spine, which identifies the disc when stored on edge. Word's label feature now includes Avery product numbers 5931 and 8931, which are used for CD case, face, and spines.

In Exercise 1, you will use a CD case template from the Microsoft Office Online Templates Web page and customize it so it will work with a specific label product number that corresponds with the template. Assume you recently purchased a computer with a CD-RW disk drive and as a student in a desktop publishing class, you will prepare a jewel case cover for a CD that will contain your completed documents. Figure 4.2 illustrates several CD case templates from the Microsoft Office Online Templates Web page. As you look over these examples, think of how you would customize any one of them to fit your personal needs.

FIGURE

4.2 *Examples of CD Case Templates from the Microsoft Office Online Templates Web Page*

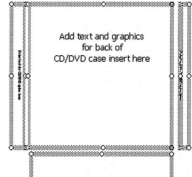

CD Case
(Music)

CD Case
(Music)

CD and DVD case

Working with Placeholders in Templates

A *placeholder* is a reserved area on a page where an object, image, or text is entered later. Templates contain various placeholders (also called *boilerplates*) in the form of text boxes containing formatted sample text or pictures; drawing objects in specific sizes, shapes, and colors; and sample images. The placeholder text or objects may be replaced and customized with text, objects, pictures, and formatting that you choose to use. Generally, you do not delete the selected text, but instead replace it with your text, keeping the formatting in place. The placeholder objects save a great deal of time since they are already sized and formatted to fit properly in the template. Many times the placeholder text will give you tips on how to use the template.

Occasionally, you may need to resize an image and/or *crop* to trim horizontal and vertical edges off the image to fit the placeholder, especially if the desired image originated in a shape other than the placeholder shape. For instance, the image may be rectangular and the placeholder may be square as in Figure 4.3, in which case you may resize the image by dragging a corner sizing handle to fit the parameter of the placeholder. The image may extend into other areas; however, after cropping, resizing, and moving the image, it should fit properly.

FIGURE

4.3   *Resizing and Then Cropping an Image*

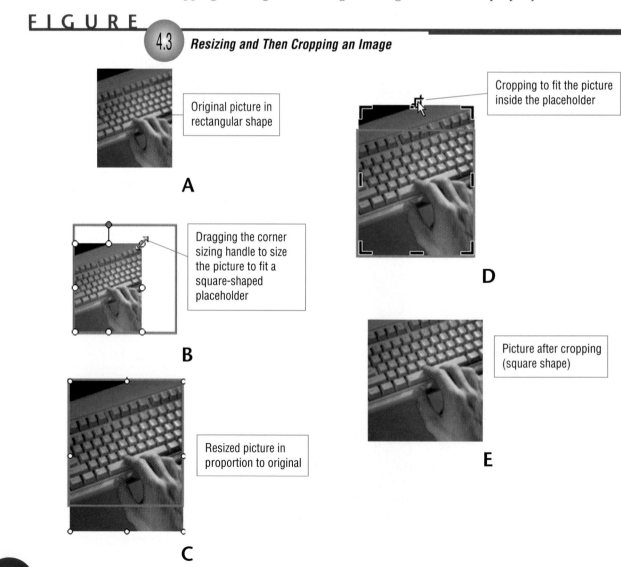

Original picture in rectangular shape

A

Cropping to fit the picture inside the placeholder

D

Dragging the corner sizing handle to size the picture to fit a square-shaped placeholder

B

Picture after cropping (square shape)

Resized picture in proportion to original

E

C

To use the cropping tool, select your image first, and then click the Crop button on the Picture toolbar. Position the cropping tool, which displays as two overlapping right angles, on one of the sizing handles, and then drag. The corner handles enable you to crop from two sides. The center handles cut away part of the picture. As you drag the sizing handles, you see a dotted-line box that represents the picture's new size and shape. The picture adjusts to the size and shape of the box when you release the mouse button. Drag the cropping tool in the reverse direction if you cropped too much off the image. Click the Crop button again to turn off the cropping feature. You can also crop using the Format Picture dialog box by keying specific increments in the Crop from _Left_, _Top_, _Right_, and _Bottom_ text boxes at the Picture tab. Click the Re_s_et button to return to the original picture.

Please turn off the drawing canvas until you are instructed to turn it back on again for some of the exercises. To turn off the drawing canvas, click the check box at the left of _Automatically create drawing canvas when inserting AutoShapes_ at the General tab of the Options dialog box to remove the check. You may also turn off the drawing canvas by pressing Delete before you begin drawing an object.

Crop

DTP POINTERS
Crop to maximize the impact of an image.

**(Before completing computer exercises, delete the Chapter03 folder on your disk. Next, copy the folder from the CD that accompanies this textbook to the Chapter04 folder on your disk and then make Chapter04 the active folder.)**

exercise

Creating a Compact Disc Case Label

1. Create the CD case label in Figure 4.4 using a CD template from the Microsoft Office Online Templates Web page by completing the following steps. (Make sure you are connected to the Internet to complete this exercise.)
   a. At a clear document screen, click _V_iew and then Tas_k_ Pane.
   b. Display the New Document task pane.
   c. Click the Templates on Office Online hyperlink in the _Templates_ section of the New Document task pane.
   d. At the Microsoft Office Online Templates Web page, click the Labels hyperlink located under the Stationery and Labels category hyperlink.
   e. At the Labels Web page, click the CD/DVD and Video Labels hyperlink located near the top of the page.
   f. At the CD/DVD and Video Labels Web page, click the Data back-up CD case inserts hyperlink.
   g. At the Preview Web page, click the Download Now button to download the template into Word.
   h. Customize the front of the CD template by completing the following steps. Press Enter at the end of each line unless directed otherwise. _**(Note: You may replace the course number, semester/quarter and date, college, your name, and so forth, with your own personal information.)**_

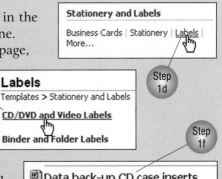

1) Select *Data Back-up* in the Front label, and then using the template font (Verdana) type OFTI 130 (or your course name and number).

2) Select the *Files from July...* text, change the alignment to Align Left, and then type the following:

>   Student Data Files
>   and Exercises
>   Fall Quarter 2005 (press Enter twice)
>   Advanced Word 2003
>   Desktop Publishing (press Enter eight times)
>   Your Name (type your name)
>   Your E-Mail Address (type your e-mail address and then press Enter twice)
>   Your College Name
>   Address
>   City, State ZIP Code

3) Select *OFTI 130* and change the font to 20-point Arial Black in the color Indigo (second color from the right in the first row of the font color palette).

4) Select the *Student Data Files...* text, change the font color to Red (first color from the left in the third row), and add bold.

5) Select the *Advanced Word...* text, change the font color to Indigo, and add bold.

6) Select the *Your Name...* text and change the font color to Indigo.

7) Select the *Your College Name...* text and change the font to 8-point Verdana, bold, color Indigo.

8) Double-click the text box border that contains the above text. At the Format Text Box dialog box, select the Colors and Lines tab.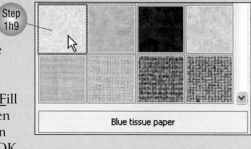

9) Click the down-pointing arrow at the right of *Color* in the *Fill* section, click Fill Effects, select the Texture tab, and then select *Blue tissue paper* (the first pattern from the left in the third row). Click OK.

10) At the Colors and Lines tab, click the down-pointing arrow at the right of *Color* in the *Line* section and select the color Red (the first color from the left in the third row). Click OK. ***(Note: Resize and move the text box if necessary.)***

i. Delete the placeholder picture and then replace it by completing the following steps:

1) Select the default picture and then press Delete. At the New Document task pane, click the down-pointing arrow on the Title bar and then click Clip Art.

2) In the *Search for* text box, type ph02268j.jpg or type CD and then click the Go button. Scroll to find the image in Figure 4.4 and at the right. (Substitute the image if necessary.)

3) Click the image thumbnail once to insert it into the label (it will display behind the label).

4) Select the picture and display the Picture toolbar. Click the Text Wrapping button on the Picture toolbar (fourth from right) and then click In Front of Text.

5) Select the picture and when a four-headed arrow displays, drag the picture to the area where the original picture placeholder displayed. (You will notice that the picture does not fit perfectly into the area.)

6) Position the arrow pointer on the bottom right corner sizing handle and drag the diagonal double-headed arrow outward to increase

Step 1i6

the size of the image until it meets the bottom of the label. (The image will expand into the label text—you must increase the size of the image and then crop the image to fit the placeholder. This method keeps the image in proportion.)

7) Select the image and then click the Crop button on the Picture toolbar.

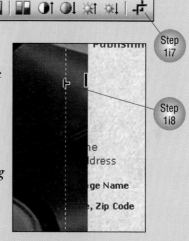

Step 1i7

Step 1i8

8) Position the cropping tool on the middle right sizing handle and drag it inward. Release the left mouse when you are satisfied with the crop. Click the Crop button again to turn off the feature. *(Note: Drag the cropping tool in the reverse direction if you cropped too much off the image.)*

9) Position the image similar to Figure 4.4. *(Hint: Drag to increase or decrease the size of either the text box or the picture to fit inside the underlining rectangular framework. You may want to deselect the Snap objects to grid option by clicking the Draw button on the Drawing toolbar, choosing Grid to open the Drawing Grid dialog box, and then removing the check mark from the Snap objects to grid check box.)*

10) If necessary, resize the picture and/or text box to fit the label size.

j. Format the back and sides of the CD case label by completing the following steps:

1) Select *Data Back-up,* type OFTI 130 (or your course), and then change the alignment to Align Left.

2) Select the *Files from July...* text, type Student Data Files and Exercises, and then change the alignment to Align Left. (Press Enter twice.)

3) Type the list of documents in Figure 4.4.

4) Select *OFTI 130* and change the font to 20-point Arial Black and the color to Indigo.

5) Select the *Student Data...* text, change the font color to Red, and add bold.

6) Select the list of documents and change the font color to Indigo.

7) Add a fill texture and line color to the text box by following steps similar to Steps 1h8 through 1h10.

8) Resize the textured text box to fit inside the underlying rectangle.

k. Format the CD spines by completing the following steps:

1) Select the placeholder text in one of the CD spines and then type OFTI 130: Advanced Word 2003 DTP.

2) Double-click the spine text box to access the Format Text Box dialog box. Choose the Colors and Lines tab, click the down-pointing arrow at the right of *Color* in the *Fill* section, and then click the color Red (first color from the left in the third row). Change the line color to Red. Click OK.

3) Repeat the last two steps to change the text and format the other spine. (Resize the spines if necessary.)

l. Replace the placeholder picture for the back with the same picture used in the front CD case. Follow steps similar to Steps 1i1 through 1i10.

2. View the document in Print Preview.
3. Save the document as a template in your DTP Templates folder and name it **c04ex01, CD Case**.
4. Print and then close **c04ex01, CD Case**.
5. Cut out the front and back of the CD label along the border lines, fold the spines, and then insert each label in the front and back of a CD case.

FIGURE

 Exercise 1

Front

Back and sides

Creating a CD Face Label

In Exercise 2 you will create a CD face label from a CD label template located on the Microsoft Office Online Templates Web page. Buying the right CD for your specific needs can be complicated. You may be asking yourself if you should buy a CD, CD-RW, CD-R, or DVD. A rewritable compact disc (CD-RW) is capable of storing data. The *RW* stands for ReWritable, so data can be saved and resaved on this disc. You must have a CD burner (informal name for a CD Rewriter) on your computer to use this kind of disc. *CD-R* stands for compact disc, recordable and it allows one-time recording of sound files. It is not possible to delete files and then reuse the space. The CD-R disc usually holds 74 minutes or 650 MB of data, although some can hold up to 80 minutes or 700 MB. Audio CDs and CD-ROMS (compact disc, Read Only Memory) are created from copies of the original recordings (which are burned by lasers). These nonrecordable CDs cannot be written or rewritten at a desktop computer. DVDs (digital versatile discs) store much more in the same space as CDs and are used for playing back movies. Photo CD is a process from Kodak that puts film images on a CD as digitally stored images that you can view and work with at your computer. The images look great when printed on special photo-quality paper.

Using a CD Face Label Template

Word includes several CD face label templates from the Microsoft Office Online Templates Web page. Be sure to match the product number (if generic, match the disc label sizes) to the template you are using. Print a hard copy of your disc label before printing on an actual sticky-backed label and hold the sample to your disc to evaluate the fit. When you use the templates, you will be able to format vivid color pictures and text that print to the edge. In desktop publishing, printing to an edge is known as a *bleed*. A bleed may also extend beyond the trim edge, leave no margin, and it may affect one or more sides. Samples of CD label templates from the Microsoft Office Online Templates Web page are shown in Figure 4.5.

Bleed
When an element on a page prints to the edge of the page, extends beyond the trim edge, and leaves no margin.

FIGURE

4.5 *Sample CD Label Templates*

exercise 2

Customizing a CD Face Label from a Template

1. Create the CD face label in Figure 4.6 using a template from the Microsoft Office Online Templates Web page by completing the following steps:
   a. At a clear document screen, click <u>V</u>iew and then Tas<u>k</u> Pane.
   b. Display the New Document task pane.
   c. Click the <u>Templates on Office Online</u> hyperlink in the *Templates* section of the New Document task pane.
   d. At the Microsoft Office Online Templates Web page, click the <u>Labels</u> hyperlink located under the <u>Stationery and Labels</u> category hyperlink.
   e. At the Labels and Inserts Web page, click the <u>CD/DVD and Video Labels</u> hyperlink.
   f. At the CD/DVD and Video Labels Web page, click the <u>CD face labels (works with Avery 5824)</u> hyperlink. (This template also works with the Avery 8931 label.)
   g. At the Preview Web page, click the Download Now button to download the template into Word.
   h. Add a picture to the front of the CD template by completing the following steps:
      1) Select the CD label by clicking the outside rim, and then display the Clip Art task pane.
      2) Type j0148948.jpg or type the keyword beaches in the *Search for* text box and then click Go.
      3) Right-click on the photograph and then click <u>C</u>opy at the shortcut menu.
      4) Display the Drawing toolbar, click the down-pointing arrow at the right of the Fill Color button on the Drawing toolbar, and then click <u>F</u>ill Effects.
      5) At the Fill Effects dialog box, click the Picture tab, and then click the Se<u>l</u>ect Picture button.
      6) At the Select Picture dialog box, right-click in the white area of the dialog box and then click Paste.
      7) Select the photograph and then click In<u>s</u>ert. *(Hint: The file name may differ from the original.)*
      8) At the Picture tab, click OK.
      9) Double-click the rim of the inside circle and change the fill color to White. Click OK.
   i. Format the text on the label by completing the following steps:
      1) Double-click the border of the text box containing the CD title to access the Format Text Box dialog box and change the fill color to No Fill. Click OK.

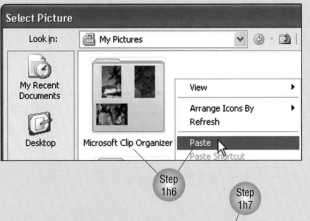

Step 1e

Labels
Templates > Stationery and Labels

CD/DVD and Video Labels

Binder and Folder Labels

Select Picture

Look in: My Pictures

My Recent Documents

Desktop Microsoft Clip Organizer

View ▶
Arrange Icons By ▶
Refresh
Paste
Paste Shortcut

Step 1h6

Step 1h7

My Pictures

Microsoft Clip Organizer vlwjbjb3[1

Dimensions: 379 x 600
Type: JPEG Image
Size: 53.0 KB

2) Select the placeholder text, *CD Title*, and then type Caribbean Cruise Pictures.
3) Select *Date* and then type July 2005.
4) Select *Caribbean Cruise Pictures* and then change the font to 20-point Curlz MT in the color Light Yellow. Click OK.

Step 1i4

Step 1i5

5) Select *July 2005* and change the font to 14-point Curlz MT in the color Light Yellow. (You may need to increase the size of the text box by dragging the bottom middle sizing handle down.)
6) Position the insertion point to the right of *This CD Contains* and type Pictures taken in St. Maarten, St. Thomas, and Nassau.
7) Select the text *This CD Contains: Pictures...* and change the alignment to center. **(Hint: Move the text box if necessary.)**

2. View the document in Print Preview. **Optional:** Format the blank CD label below the label created in this exercise with text and an image of your choosing.
3. Save the document as a template in your DTP Templates folder and name it **c04ex02, CD Label**.
4. Print the label on Avery 8931 or 5824 labels or a similar-sized label and then close **c04ex02, CD Label**.
5. Apply your customized label onto a CD by removing the backing paper from the Label Guide and firmly pressing the label onto the CD.

FIGURE

4.6 *Exercise 2*

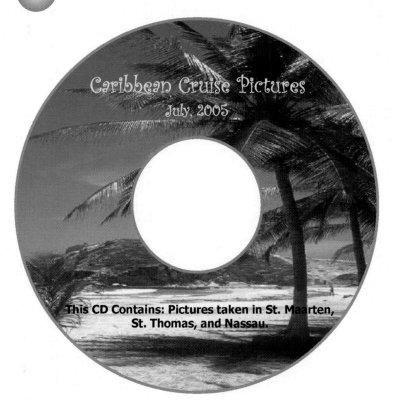

Creating a Personal Calendar

A calendar can be one of the most basic tools of organization in your everyday life. No desk at home or at work is complete without a calendar to schedule appointments, plan activities, and serve as a reminder of important dates and events.

A calendar may also be used as a marketing tool in promoting a service, product, or program. For example, a schedule of upcoming events may be typed on a calendar to serve as a reminder to all of the volunteers working for a charitable organization, or the calendar may be sent to prospective donors to serve as a daily reminder of the organization.

You will customize your own calendar using Word's Calendar Wizard in Exercise 3. In addition, you will find several calendar templates, as shown in Figure 4.7, from the Microsoft Office Online Templates Web page. The Microsoft Office Online Templates Web page also includes templates for calendars and daily/monthly planners created in PowerPoint, Excel, and Publisher. If you want to create your own calendar from scratch without the help of the Calendar Template or Wizard, you may want to start by creating a table.

FIGURE 4.7 *Sample Calendar Templates from the Microsoft Office Online Templates Web Page*

Calendar with Photo

Holiday Calendar

Wall Calendar

Using the Calendar Wizard

The Calendar Wizard helps you create monthly calendars. Three styles of calendars are available: Bo_x_es & borders, B_a_nner, and _J_azzy. See Figure 4.8 for an illustration of the different styles. In addition, other customizing options in the wizard include portrait or landscape orientation, placeholder for a picture, and starting and ending months.

To access the Calendar Wizard, click _F_ile and then _N_ew; or click _V_iew and then Tas_k_ Pane. Choose the New Document task pane and then click the On my computer hyperlink. Select the Other Documents tab and then double-click the _Calendar Wizard_ icon. Proceed with making choices from the prompts built into the wizard. Continue clicking the _N_ext button to advance to the next screen. Click _F_inish when the calendar is complete.

FIGURE

4.8 _Calendar Wizard Template Types_

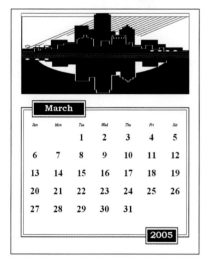

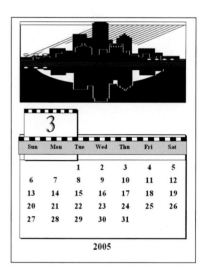

Bo_x_es & Borders   B_a_nner   _J_azzy

Adding, Removing, or Replacing a Picture in a Calendar

The default picture used in the Calendar Wizard is Cityscpe. This picture is in a placeholder, so you can easily replace it with a different image. After using the Calendar Wizard, select the existing picture and then press Delete. To replace the image, click the Other Task Panes button in the task pane Title bar and then click Clip Art, or click _P_icture from the _I_nsert menu and then click the source of your picture—_C_lip Art, _F_rom File, or From _S_canner or Camera. (A photo would look great!)

If you want to add a watermark, complete steps similar to above, but either insert the image in a header or footer or send the image behind the table. You would probably not want to select the option to include a picture through the Calendar Wizard.

> **DTP POINTERS**
> Use scanned photos of family, friends, or pets in your personalized calendar.

Entering Information in a Calendar

To enter information, click where you want to insert the text, and then start typing. To move between different dates in the calendar, press Tab to move forward and press Shift + Tab to move to the previous date. Remember that the calendar template is formatted in a table. Click the Center align button on the Formatting toolbar to center text within a cell. Select rows or columns and apply different styles if you are not satisfied with the default ones, or customize the styles to fit your specific needs. *(Hint: Turn on the Show/Hide ¶ button to view formatting symbols.)*

Adding a Shape to a Calendar

You can automatically create a variety of shapes by using the AutoShapes tools on the Drawing toolbar. The AutoShapes menu contains several categories of shapes. In addition to lines, there are basic shapes, block arrows, flowchart elements, stars and banners, and callouts. One of the star shapes (Explosion 1) is used in Exercise 3 to emphasize and draw attention to an important fact. In addition, red fill was added for impact. Text was added to the shape by selecting the star shape, right-clicking the mouse, and then clicking the Add Text option as shown in Figure 4.9.

To draw an AutoShape, click AutoShapes on the Drawing toolbar, point to a category, and then click the shape you want. Click in the document to add the shape at its default size, or drag it to the size you want. Notice in Figure 4.10 the yellow adjustment handle in the AutoShape form. Many AutoShapes have adjustment handles you can drag to adjust a unique aspect of the shape.

FIGURE

4.9 *Adding Text to an AutoShape in a Calendar*

FIGURE

4.10 *Dragging an Adjustment Handle to Reshape an AutoShape Object*

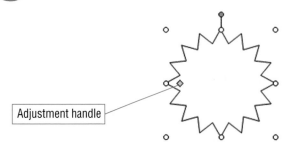

Adjustment handle

Troubleshooting Calendars

If the bottom line of your document does not print, you may have to make adjustments to your document to compensate for the unprintable zone of your particular printer. The **unprintable zone** is an area where text will not print; this area varies with each printer. For instance, if the bottom line of the calendar created in Exercise 3 does not print properly, increase or decrease the top and/or bottom margins, or use a smaller font size, or rewrite some of the text. If the margins cannot be changed, experiment with moving the text up or reducing the length of the document. Another option is to draw a line using the Line tool on the Drawing toolbar.

If you choose to draw a horizontal line to fix the side of a calendar that will not print, you may want to deselect the *Snap objects to grid* option at the Grid feature. To access the Grid controls, click the Draw button on the Drawing toolbar. Choose Grid to open the Drawing Grid dialog box. You can input new values for both the *Horizontal* and *Vertical* spacing. Word automatically aligns objects to this invisible grid, with each square in the grid set to 0.08 inch by 0.08 inch. You can turn off the grid, make the gridlines visible, or even specify where on the page you want the grid to begin. Figure 4.11 illustrates the Drawing Grid dialog box, where you may turn on or off the *Snap objects to grid* option. If you turn off the grid feature, you may move lines closer to other intersecting lines or objects. The Drawing Grid feature will also be used in Chapter 5.

FIGURE

4.11 *Drawing Grid Dialog Box*

Click to add or remove a check mark. This turns on or off the invisible grid. Press the Alt key while dragging or drawing an object to temporarily turn the grid on or off.

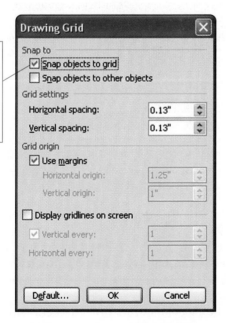

In Exercise 3, assume that a friend of yours owns a small real estate office in your hometown and you occasionally volunteer your time to help with desktop publishing projects. Create a calendar that will be given to prospective homebuyers and sellers.

exercise 3

Customizing a Calendar

1. Use the Calendar Wizard to create a calendar by completing the following steps:
   a. Click File and then New.
   b. Click the <u>On my computer</u> hyperlink at the New Document task pane.
   c. Select the Other Documents tab, select *Document* in the *Create New* section, and then double-click the *Calendar Wizard* icon.
   d. At the Start screen, click Next.
   e. At the Style screen, select the *Banner* style, and then click Next.
   f. At the Direction & Picture screen, select *Portrait*, and then select *Yes* to leave room for a picture. Click Next.
   g. At the Date Range screen, select *February* and *2005* in the *Start Month, End Month,* and *Year* list boxes, and then click Next.

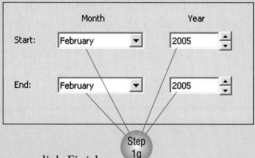

Step 1g

   h. At the Finish screen, click Finish.
   i. If the Office Assistant appears, click the *Add, remove, or replace picture* option. Read the Office Assistant's advice, and then click OK.

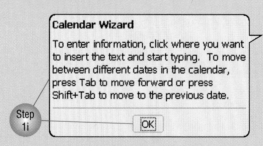

Step 1i

   j. Click the *Enter information into the calendar* option. Read the Office Assistant's advice, and then click OK.
   k. Click the Cancel button to remove the Office Assistant.
2. Save the calendar with Save As and name it **c04ex03, Realty**.
3. Replace the picture in the calendar by completing the following steps:
   a. Display the Drawing toolbar.
   b. Select and then delete the placeholder picture **Cityscpe.wmf**. (You will know the picture has been selected when eight black sizing handles display inside the border of the picture. Be careful not to select the rectangular AutoShape instead of the picture. The AutoShape should remain once the picture has been deleted. If you accidentally remove the rectangle, click the Undo button on the Standard toolbar. Also, make sure the drawing canvas feature has been turned off.)

c. Position the insertion point inside the placeholder.

d. Display the Clip Art task pane, type j0145506.jpg or type the keyword winter in the *Search for* text box, and then click Go. *(Hint: You may use another image if you want.)*

e. Click the image to insert it.

f. If necessary, size by dragging the double-headed arrow at the bottom center of the image upward or downward, and then crop the image from the top and bottom to fit into the placeholder shape as shown in Figure 4.12.

Step 3f

g. Select the placeholder (rectangular shape) and remove the border lines by clicking the down-pointing arrow at the right of the Line Color button on the Drawing toolbar and then clicking No Line.

4. Insert text near calendar dates by completing the following steps: *(Hint: You may want to show the table gridlines or display the cell border lines by clicking F̲ormat, B̲orders and Shading, and then selecting the Gri̲d option in the Setting section.)*

a. Select all of the rows in the calendar (table) except for the first row, which contains the days of the week. (Include the blank cells, too.)

b. Click the down-pointing arrow at the right of the Style button on the Formatting toolbar, and then select *Normal* from the list. (The calendar dates will display in 10 points, allowing space in the cells to add text.)

Step 4b

c. Select all of the rows, including the first row, and click the Center align button on the Formatting toolbar.

d. With all the rows still selected, click F̲ormat and then B̲orders and Shading to open the Borders and Shading dialog box. Click the B̲orders tab, and then click the A̲ll button in the *Setting* section to place a border around all the cells. Click OK. *(Hint: If necessary, resize the right border of the image so that it is in line with the right table border.)*

e. Deselect the rows by clicking anywhere in the calendar.

f. Position the insertion point to the right of *2* and then press Enter.

g. Click I̲nsert and then S̲ymbol.

h. Choose the S̲ymbols tab and change the font to Wingdings.

i. Click the telephone symbol (the ninth symbol from the left in the first row) (Wingdings 40).

j. Click I̲nsert and then Close.

k. Press Enter and then type Call for a free appraisal.

l. Select the telephone symbol and change the font size to 14 points.

m. Position the insertion point to the right of *12* and then press Enter.

n. Type Lincoln's Birthday.

o. Position the insertion point to the right of *14* and then press Enter.

p. Insert the heart symbol located in the Symbol font (the tenth symbol from the left in the ninth row) and then press Enter.

q. Change the font color to Red and then type Valentine's Day.
r. Select the heart symbol and change the font color to Red and the font size to 16 points.
s. Type Presidents' Day on February 18.
t. Type Washington's Birthday on February 22 (change the font size to 9 points).
u. With the Clip Art task pane displayed, type US flag in the *Search for* text box, and then click the Go button. Scroll to find the flag image in Figure 4.12. (Substitute an image, if necessary.) Position the insertion point below *February 24,* insert the image, and resize it to fit into the cell. *(Hint: Type j0384725.jpg in the Search for list box to go directly to the flag image.)*
v. Type Flag Day below the flag image.
w. Type Join Our Tour of Homes at 10 a.m. on February 27.

5. Type the text at the bottom of the calendar in Figure 4.12 by completing the following steps:
a. Select the last row of blank cells, click T̲able, and then click M̲erge Cells.
b. Turn on kerning at 14 points.
c. Type Predicting a Successful Move for You...; press Enter.
d. Type 450 South Ashton ❖ Nashville ❖ TN 37201-5401; then press Enter. (The ❖ symbol is the seventh symbol from the left in the sixth row of the Wingdings *Font* list box—Wingdings 118.)
e. Type Tel (901) 555-1000 ❖ Fax (901) 555-6752 ❖ E-mail Forecast@emcp.net.
f. If necessary, right-click the hyperlink text and then click R̲emove Hyperlink. The e-mail address should remain, but the hyperlink (blue text and underline) should be removed.
g. Select *Predicting...* and change the font to bold 16-point French Script MT. Use the Paragraph dialog box to change the *Before* spacing to 6 points and then click OK.
h. Select the last two lines, *450 South Ashton...* and *Tel 901.555.1000...* and change the font to 10-point Times New Roman if necessary.
i. Select the merged cell by clicking T̲able, Selec̲t, and then Ce̲ll.
j. Click Fo̲rmat, B̲orders and Shading, and then select the S̲hading tab.
k. Click the M̲ore Colors button in the *Fill* section, select the Standard tab, and then select the color blue located second from the left in the top row of the hexagon. Click OK twice.

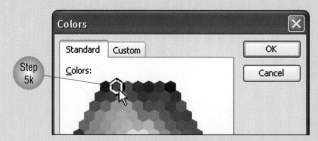

l. Select the text in the cell and change the color to White.
m. Position the insertion point on *February* at the left of the calendar and then click the Center align button on the Formatting toolbar if necessary.

6. Create the AutoShape form at the top of the calendar by completing the following steps:
a. Click the A̲utoShapes button on the Drawing toolbar, point to S̲tars and Banners, and then click the first shape in the first row *(Explosion 1)*. If the drawing canvas displays, press Delete. *(Hint: Consider turning off the drawing canvas feature until instructed otherwise.)*

b. Drag the crosshairs at the top of the calendar and draw a shape in a size similar to Figure 4.12; then release the left mouse button.

c. Select the shape, click the down-pointing arrow at the right of the Fill Color button on the Drawing toolbar, and then select Red.

d. Click the down-pointing arrow at the right of the Line Color button on the Drawing toolbar and then select No Line.

e. With the shape still selected, click the right mouse button, and then select Add Text.

f. Click the Center align button on the Formatting toolbar.

g. Change the font to 12-point Arial Black in White and then type **Forecast Realty is #1!**. *(Hint: You may need to adjust the size of the shape.)*

h. Select the shape, click the Shadow Style button on the Drawing toolbar, and then select Shadow Style 1 (the first style from the left in the first row).

i. Select the *#1!* text and use the Font dialog box to expand the character spacing by 2 points.

7. Create the WordArt text at the top of the picture by completing the following steps:

a. Click Tools and then Options. At the Options dialog box, select the Edit tab, click the down-pointing arrow at the right of *In line with text,* and change the default setting to *In front of text* and then click OK.

b. Click the Insert WordArt button on the Drawing toolbar.

c. At the WordArt Gallery, select the first style from the left in the first row. Click OK.

d. At the Edit WordArt Text dialog box, select 60-point Imprint MT Shadow, bold, and type **Forecast Realty** in the *Text* box. Click OK or press Enter.

e. Select the WordArt text to display the WordArt toolbar and then click the WordArt Shape button. Select the seventh shape from the left in the fifth row *(Cascade Up)*.

Step 7e

f. Click the Format WordArt button on the WordArt toolbar, and change the fill color to the blue color selected in Step 5k. Click OK.

g. Drag the WordArt object to the upper left corner of the calendar. (Make any necessary adjustments so that the document looks similar to Figure 4.12.)

8. Click inside the text box containing *February* and then click the Center align button on the Formatting toolbar.

9. Save the document with the same name, **c04ex03, Realty**.

10. Print and then close **c04ex03, Realty**.

FIGURE

4.12 *Exercise 3*

February	Sun	Mon	Tue	Wed	Thu	Fri	Sat
			1	2 Call for a free appraisal.	3	4	5
	6	7	8	9	10	11	12 Lincoln's Birthday
	13	14 ♥ Valentine's Day	15	16	17	18 President's Day	19
	20	21	22 Washington's Birthday	23	24 Flag Day	25	26
2005	27 Join Our Tour of Homes at 10 a.m.	28					

Predicting a Successful Move for You...
450 South Ashton ❖ Nashville ❖ TN 37201-5401
Tel (901) 555-1000 ❖ Fax (901) 555-6752 ❖ E-mail Forecast@emcp.net

Arranging Drawing Objects to Enhance Personal Documents

See Figure 4.13 for suggestions on enhancing a calendar. A brief explanation of these and other features follows Figure 4.13.

FIGURE

4.13 *Arranging Drawing Objects in a Calendar*

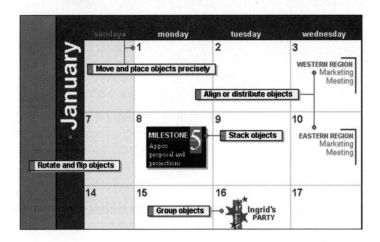

Moving and Placing Objects Precisely

To move a drawing object, click the object and then drag it when the mouse pointer becomes a four-headed arrow, or use the arrow keys on the keyboard. To use the keyboard to move an object, click the object, and then press the arrow key on the keyboard that corresponds to the direction you want to move the object. You will notice that the object moves at a very small increment (1 point) at a time. You are actually *nudging* the object when you use the arrow keys to move it. You may also nudge an object by clicking <u>D</u>raw on the Drawing toolbar and then pointing to <u>N</u>udge. At the Nudge submenu, you may choose to move the object <u>U</u>p, <u>D</u>own, <u>L</u>eft, or <u>R</u>ight as shown in Figure 4.14.

Nudging
To move an object by small increments (points).

FIGURE

4.14 *Using the Nudge Command*

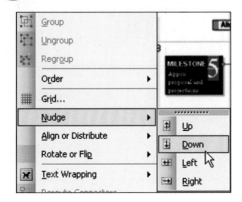

Using the Drawing Canvas to Align Drawing Objects

You will be instructed in future exercises to turn on the drawing canvas. By default this feature is on, but it has been more convenient not to use it in most of the exercises. Word's drawing canvas is an area upon which you can draw multiple shapes such as AutoShapes, text boxes, and lines. Because the shapes are contained within the drawing canvas, they can be moved and resized as a unit. The drawing canvas helps you arrange a drawing in your document. It actually works similarly to the grouping feature in Word. The drawing canvas automatically displays when you create an AutoShape, text box, or any other drawing object from the Drawing toolbar as shown in Figure 4.15. To turn off this feature temporarily, press the Delete key before drawing the object. To turn off this feature permanently, complete the following steps:

1. Click Tools and then Options.
2. At the Options dialog box, select the General tab.
3. Click the check box at the left of *Automatically create drawing canvas when inserting AutoShapes* to remove the check mark. To turn this feature on again, click the check box to insert a check mark, as shown in Figure 4.16.

FIGURE

4.15 *Displaying the Drawing Canvas*

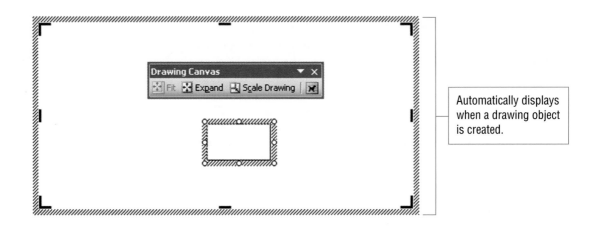

Automatically displays when a drawing object is created.

Click here to turn on or off the drawing canvas.

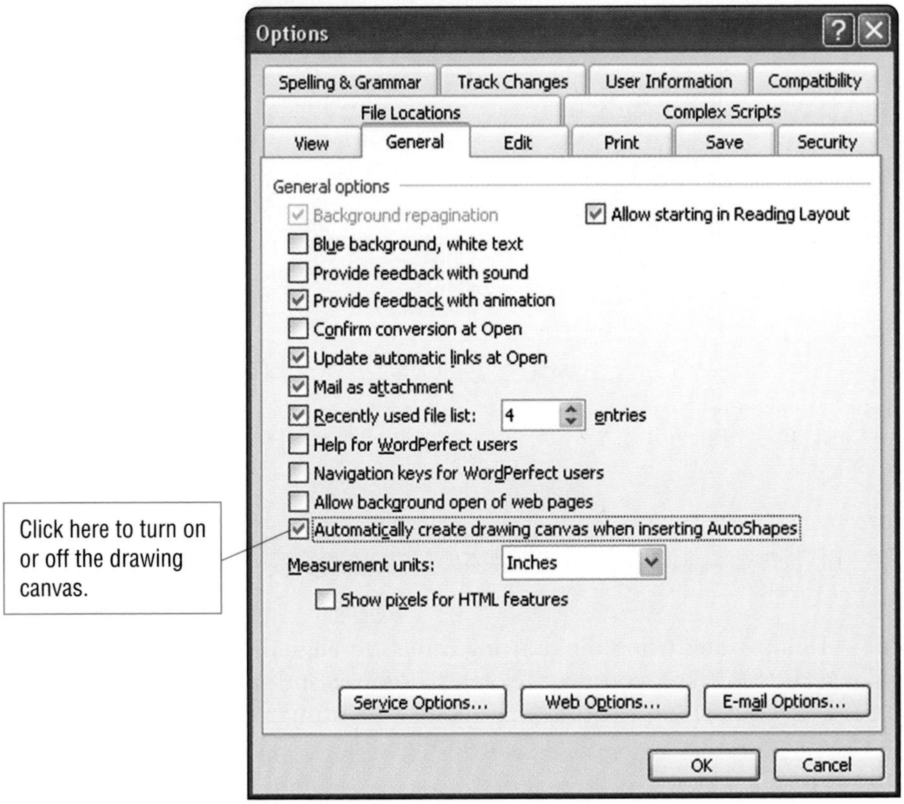

The Drawing Canvas toolbar with the Fit Drawing to Contents button selected is shown in Figure 4.17. Notice that the drawing canvas adjusts to fit all three objects into one tight area. If you change the wrapping style of the drawing canvas to In Front of Text and drag the canvas, all three items will move in unison.

FIGURE

4.17 *Adjusting the Drawing Canvas to Fit the Contents*

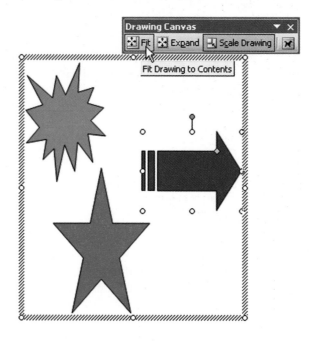

Figure 4.18 illustrates using the drawing canvas to align drawing objects. While holding down the Shift key, you may select each object and then align them by clicking the Draw button on the Drawing toolbar, pointing to Align or Distribute, and then choosing to Align Left, Align Center, Align Right, Align Top, Align Middle, or Align Bottom.

FIGURE

4.18 *Aligning Objects in the Drawing Canvas*

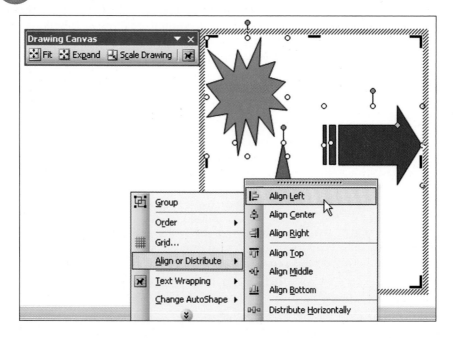

In addition, if you create a drawing in Word, a drawing canvas is placed around it. Click in your document where you want to create your drawing. On the Insert menu, point to Picture, and then click New Drawing.

Resizing AutoShapes to Fit Text

You can specify that text boxes and AutoShapes that contain text will automatically grow or reduce to fit the text they contain by following these steps:

1. Select the text box.
2. Click Text Box at the Format menu.
3. Select the Text Box tab.
4. Click to insert a check mark in the *Resize AutoShape to fit text* check box as shown in Figure 4.19.

FIGURE

4.19 *Resizing AutoShapes or Text Boxes to Fit Text*

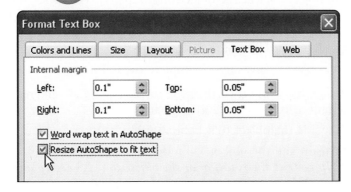

Stacking Objects

When you draw an object on top of another, you create an overlapping stack. Objects automatically stack in individual layers as you add them to a document. You see the *stacking* order when objects overlap. The top object covers a portion of objects beneath it, as discussed in Chapter 2.

Stacking
Drawing an object on top of another.

You may overlap as many drawing objects as you want and then rearrange them in the stack by clicking the Draw button on the Drawing toolbar, pointing to Order, and then selecting one of the options listed, such as Bring to Front, Send to Back, and so on. If you lose an object in a stack that has been grouped together, you can press Tab to cycle forward or Shift + Tab to cycle backward through the objects until it is selected. You may also stack objects inside the drawing canvas. Alternatively, you may group them using the Group option on the Draw menu as explained below.

Grouping Objects

Grouping objects combines the objects as a single unit. To group drawing objects, hold down the Shift key as you click each object, click the Draw button on the Drawing toolbar, and then click Group. Alternatively, you can click the right mouse button, point to Grouping, and then click Group. When objects have been grouped, sizing handles should appear around the new unit, as shown in Figure 4.20, and not around each individual object.

Grouping
Combining objects as a single unit.

4.20 *Grouping Objects*

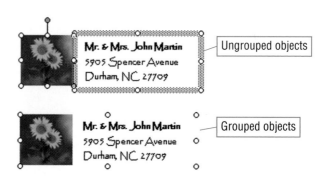

Mr. & Mrs. John Martin
5905 Spencer Avenue
Durham, NC 27709 — Ungrouped objects

Mr. & Mrs. John Martin
5905 Spencer Avenue
Durham, NC 27709 — Grouped objects

Rotating and Flipping Objects

To rotate or flip objects, select the object or grouped objects, click the <u>D</u>raw button on the Drawing toolbar, point to Rotate or Fli<u>p</u>, and then click the option you want. You may also use the rotate handle on the selected object. Generally, you can rotate, align, and distribute pictures in Word.

To rotate an object to any angle, complete the following steps:

1. Select the object and then drag the rotate handle (small green handle) on the object in the direction you want to rotate.
2. Click outside the object to set the rotation.
3. Rotate again and the object will move at the angle determined above. ***(Hint: To restrict the rotation of the object to a 15-degree angle, hold down the Shift key while you drag the rotate handle.)***

Creating Personal Return Address Labels

DTP POINTERS
Use your initials in a fancy font on your personal address labels.

DTP POINTERS
Use seasonal clip art for interest on your labels.

DTP POINTERS
Showing Gridlines from the Table menu helps you position text and graphics in a label.

Return address labels are convenient and cost efficient to use at home as well as at the office. Whether you are paying a huge stack of bills, addressing holiday cards, or volunteering to mail a hundred PTA newsletters, the convenience of having preprinted return and address labels is worth the little time it takes to create them. You can create your own labels using Word's label feature. Word includes a variety of predefined label definitions that coordinate with labels that may be purchased at office supply stores.

When purchasing labels, be careful to select the appropriate labels for your specific printer. Labels are available in sheets for laser and inkjet printers. Carefully follow the directions given with your printer to insert the forms properly into the printer.

Return labels may be created using two different methods—creating labels individually using the label feature and copying them, or creating labels using a data source and Word's merge feature. In Exercise 4, you will create labels that include a picture and you will use the label definition Avery 8167 that results in a label measuring ½ inch by 1¾ inch. You may choose to use larger-sized labels for your own personal return labels, such as ones that measure ¾ inch by 2⁵⁄₁₆ inches. Merging to labels will be discussed in Chapter 7.

exercise 4

Creating Personal Return Address Labels with a Graphic

1. At a clear document screen, create the return address labels in Figure 4.21 by completing the following steps:

   a. Display the Drawing toolbar.

   b. Click Tools, point to Letters and Mailings, and then click Envelopes and Labels.

   c. At the Envelopes and Labels dialog box, choose the Labels tab.

   d. Click the Options button. With *Avery standard* selected in the *Label products* list box, select *5160 - Address* in the *Product number* list box.

   e. Make sure the Printer information is correct for your specific printer and then click OK.

   f. At the Envelopes and Labels dialog box, click the New Document button.

   g. If gridlines of the labels (cells) do not display, click Table and then Show Gridlines.

   h. With the insertion point positioned in the label (cell) located in the upper left corner, click Insert, point to Picture, and then click Clip Art.

   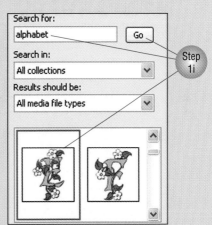

   i. At the Clip Art task pane, type j0244323.wmf or alphabet in the *Search for* text box and then click the Go button or press Enter. Click once on the flower image shown. *(Note: You may substitute a clip art of your choosing.)*

   j. Double-click the picture to open the Format Picture dialog box, click the Layout tab, and then click the In front of text button. Click OK. *(Note: You will have to resize the graphic as shown in Figure 4.21.)*

   k. Click the Text Box button on the Drawing toolbar and drag the crosshairs to create a text box approximately 0.60 inch in height and 1.35 inches in length in the first label.

   l. Create exact settings for the text box by clicking Format and then Text Box. At the Format Text Box dialog box, click the Size tab, and then change the height to 0.60 inch and width to 1.35 inches.

   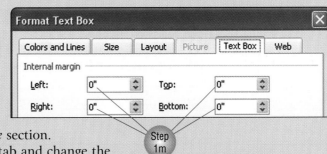

   m. Click the Text Box tab and change the internal margins to 0 inch in each of the margin text boxes.

   n. Click the Layout tab and make sure *In front of text* displays in the *Wrapping style* section.

   o. Select the Colors and Lines tab and change the *Line Color* to *No Line*. Click OK.

   p. With the insertion point positioned in the text box, click the Align Right button on the Formatting toolbar. Change the font to 11-point Agency FB and then type the following (you may substitute your own name and address):

   Mr. & Mrs. John Enter (press Enter)
   55 Pine Island Road (press Enter)
   Myrtle Beach, SC 29572

q. Select *Mr. & Mrs. John Enter* and change the font to 12-point Agency FB in bold and in Green.

r. Group the two text boxes by completing the following steps:
   1) Click the picture, hold down the Shift key, and then click the text box containing the address.
   2) Click the <u>D</u>raw button on the Drawing toolbar.
   3) Click <u>G</u>roup. (Sizing handles should display around the new unit.)

s. Copy the grouped object to the second and third labels in the first row by completing the following steps:
   1) Click the grouped object, hold down the Ctrl key, and then drag a copy to the second label. *(Note: The arrow pointer should display with a + symbol to indicate copying. Release the mouse button and then the Ctrl key; a copy should display in the second label. If the object displays slightly above the label, click the box and drag it down into the label.)*

   2) Drag and drop another copy of the grouped object into the third label.

t. Copy the first row of labels by completing the following steps:
   1) To select the first row, position the insertion point in the selection bar at the left of the first cell (label) in the first row of labels, and then click.

   2) Click <u>E</u>dit and then <u>C</u>opy.
   3) Position the insertion point in the first label in the second row, click <u>E</u>dit, and then <u>P</u>aste Rows.
   4) Continue copying the row of labels by clicking the Paste button or pressing the F4 key. *(Note: Stop at the end of one full page of labels.)*

u. When you have one complete page of labels, select any blank labels that may display on another page, click T<u>a</u>ble, point to <u>D</u>elete, and then click <u>R</u>ows.

2. Use Print Preview to make sure your document will print correctly.

3. Save the document with Save <u>A</u>s and name it **c04ex04, Labels**. *(Hint: If you are concerned about document size, delete the text in all of the labels except the first row and then save the document. You may easily copy the labels when you need more.)*

4. Print, but do not close **c04ex04, Labels**. (If possible, print the labels on an Avery 5160 sheet of labels.)

5. If you want to create the labels in this exercise using the AutoText feature, complete the following steps. If you prefer to stop this exercise, close **c04ex04, Labels**.

   a. Delete all of the labels except for the first label in **c04ex04, Labels**. *(Note: Make sure you have saved this document first.)*

Step 5a

   b. Select the first label, click Insert, point to AutoText, and then click New.
   c. At the Create AutoText dialog box, type Enter. *(Note: This is really a person's name!)* Click OK.

Step 5c

   d. At a clear document screen, click Tools, point to Letters and Mailings, and then click Envelopes and Labels.
   e. At the Envelopes and Labels dialog box, select the Labels tab and then make sure the product number selected is Avery standard 5160.
   f. Position the insertion point in the *Address* text box, type Enter, press F3, and then click New Document. *(Note: It will take a few moments for Word to process the AutoText command to duplicate all of the labels. If you choose a photograph the file size will be huge.)*
   g. View the document in Print Preview.
   h. Make sure you saved **c04ex04, Labels** and then close this document without saving.

FIGURE 4.21 Exercise 4

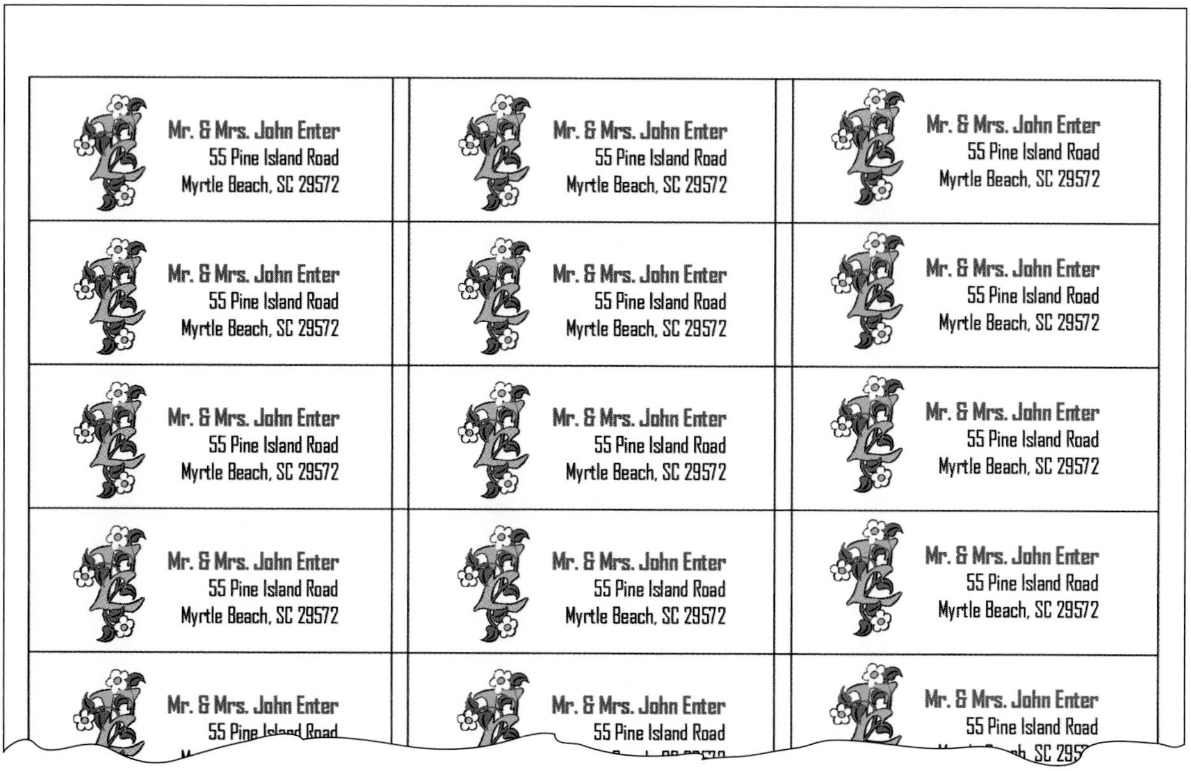

Creating a Certificate

DTP POINTERS
Use high-quality paper in conservative colors for business certificates.

DTP POINTERS
Preprinted papers add interest and professional appearance.

Certificates are generally used to show recognition and promote excellence. Some other suggested uses for certificates include: diplomas, coupons, warranties, special event awards, program completion awards, and special-offer documents.

When printing your certificate, consider using an appropriate choice of high-quality 24 lb. uncoated bond stock or parchment paper in conservative colors, such as natural, cream, off-white, light gray, or any light marbleized color. In addition, consider using preprinted borders, ribbons, seals, and jackets, which are generally available through many mail-order catalogs and office supply stores.

Using Certificate Templates from the Microsoft Office Online Templates Web page

The Microsoft Office Online Templates Web page provides several certificate templates created in either PowerPoint or Word. Certificate templates are available by clicking the <u>*For Teachers*</u> hyperlink in the *Education* category, or you can see a complete list of certificate templates by typing *certificate* in the *Search* text box and then clicking the Go button. Figure 4.22 illustrates two sample certificate templates edited in PowerPoint and in Word.

Company Name

Presents

Employee of the Year Award

To

Employee Name

June 16, 2005

_____

Presenter Title

PowerPoint

Word

Adding a Page Border

Word provides page borders that range from simple to highly ornate. When planning the layout and design of your certificate, choose a border that best complements the content and purpose of your certificate.

You can add a picture border (such as a row of ice cream cones) to any or all sides of each page in a document. To see the different kinds of page borders available, click F_ormat, _Borders and Shading, and then choose the _Page Border tab. You may use one of the standard line borders and select different colors and widths, or click the down-pointing arrow at the right of the _Ar_t list box and choose elaborate designs as shown in Figure 4.23.

F I G U R E

4.23 *Selecting a Page Border*

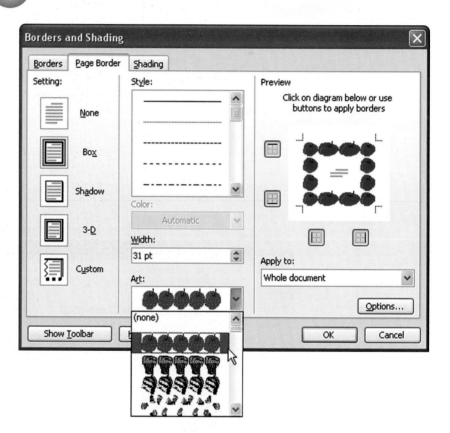

Changing Page Border Margins

Most printers cannot print to the edge of a page, especially at the bottom of the page. If a page border does not print, click the down-pointing arrow at the right of the *Measure from* list box in the Borders and Shading Options dialog box, and select *Text* as shown in Figure 4.24. Also, experiment with changing your document margins.

Click *Text* to position the inside edge of the page border relative to the page margin.

Click *Edge of page* to position the outside edge of the page border relative to the edge of the page.

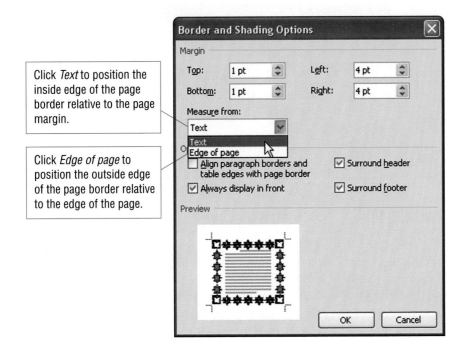

Inserting Text Fields

Whether creating a client survey form for your company's marketing and research department, or creating an award certificate for volunteers at your local hospital, using form fields in your templates saves time and effort. In Word, a *form* is a protected document that includes fields where information is entered. A form document contains *form fields* that are locations in the document where one of three things is performed: text is entered (text field), a check box is turned on or off, or information is selected from a drop-down list. Complete three steps in creating a form document:

1. Design the structure and enter the text that will appear in your document or template.
2. Insert form fields prompting the user to insert information at the keyboard.
3. Save the document as a protected document or template.

In Exercise 5, assume you are a volunteer at Edward Hospital and you have offered to create an award certificate template. In this certificate, you will use the Forms toolbar, as shown in Figure 4.25, and insert basic text fields.

Form

A protected document that includes fields where information is entered.

Form field

Locations in a document where text is entered, a check box is turned on or off, or a drop-down list is accessed.

4.25 *Forms Toolbar*

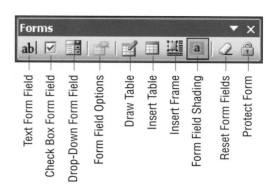

Using Handwriting in Word

DTP POINTERS
Use the Drawing Pad to create a signature that can be moved and edited using the Picture toolbar.

The handwriting interface in Office 2003 allows you to enter handwritten characters into a document using a writing pad and pen (mouse). You can write your name using the handwriting feature, save the signature as an AutoText entry, and then insert the signature into your documents where a signature is preferred.

The handwritten object that you create is a graphic object, not text, so you cannot edit it in the document using text-editing techniques. However, you can format the object using standard formatting methods such as changing the point size, applying bold and italics, and changing the color.

To create handwritten characters, complete the following steps:

EN Icon

1. Access the Language bar by clicking Tools and then Speech. *(Hint: If the Language bar has been minimized, it will display as an icon [EN] on the Windows Taskbar at the bottom of the screen.)* Click the *EN* icon and then click Show the Language bar from the pop-up menu.
2. Click the Handwriting button on the Language bar shown in Figure 4.26, and then click *Writing Pad* from the drop-down list.
3. Click the Ink button in the Writing Pad window to turn on the Ink mode. See Figure 4.27.
4. Write your name on the Writing Pad by pressing the mouse button and dragging. *(Hint: If you pause, the text you have written will be inserted into the document as an embedded Ink object.)*

F I G U R E

4.26 *Language Bar with Handwriting Button Selected*

Writing Pad option is selected.

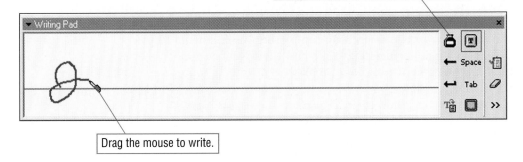

Click the Ink button to turn on Ink mode.

Drag the mouse to write.

Creating an AutoText Signature Entry

After writing your name as instructed previously, complete the following steps to create an AutoText entry:

1. Select your Ink object.
2. Click Insert, point to AutoText, and then click New.
3. At the Create AutoText dialog box, type Signature and then click OK.
4. Type Signature and then press F3 or press Enter anytime you want to insert your signature into a document; or click Insert, point to AutoText, and then click Signature from the *Normal* drop-down list to insert the AutoText entry at the insertion point.

Creating a Signature Using AutoShapes

You can also create a signature in a document by using an AutoShape form. Click the AutoShapes button on the Drawing toolbar, point to Lines, and then click the Scribble button. *(Note: The Scribble button is the last button in the bottom row. Position the mouse pointer on this button and* Scribble *displays after one second in a yellow box.)* The mouse pointer will display as a pen. Write your name by dragging the pen. Save the signature as part of the document.

Using a Scanner to Create a Signature

If you have access to a scanner, write your name on a blank sheet of paper using a thick black ink pen or black marker. Click Insert, Picture, From Scanner or Camera. At the Insert Picture from Scanner or Camera dialog box, make sure the *Print Quality* option is selected and then click Custom Insert. Click the *Black and white picture or text* option and then click Scan. If necessary, crop using the cropping tool on the Picture toolbar to remove any unnecessary white space. With the object selected, change the wrap to In Front of Text. Copy and paste the signature wherever you may want to place it. Size the signature object if necessary and drag to position it appropriately. In addition, you may select the signature object and then save it as an AutoText entry. Type the name you have given to the entry and then press F3 to see the results.

exercise 5

Creating an Award Certificate

1. Create the certificate in Figure 4.28 by completing the following steps:
   a. At a clear document screen, click File and then New.
   b. At the New Document task pane, click the On my computer hyperlink.
   c. At the Templates dialog box, make sure the *Blank Document* icon is selected at the General tab, and then click *Template* in the *Create New* section located at the bottom right corner of the dialog box. Click OK or press Enter.

   Step 1c

   d. Display the Drawing and Picture toolbars.
   e. Select *Landscape* orientation at the Page Setup dialog box, and make sure the top and bottom margins are set at 1 inch and the left and right margins are set at 1.25 inches. Click OK.
   f. Create the page border in Figure 4.28 by completing the following steps:
      1) Click Format and then Borders and Shading.
      2) Select the Page Border tab.

      Step 1f4

      3) Click the down-pointing arrow at the right of the *Art* list box and select the border displayed in Figure 4.28. *(Hint: The border is located about halfway down the list.)*

      Step 1f3

      4) Type **31 pt** in the *Width* text box.
      5) Click the Options button. At the Border and Shading Options dialog box, click the down-pointing arrow at the right of the *Measure from* list box and then select *Text*.
      6) Type **4 pt** in each of the four margin text boxes. Click OK twice.

Step 1f6

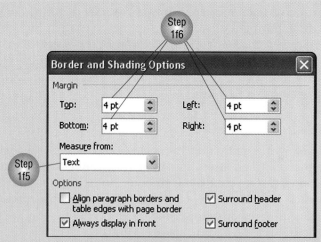

Step 1f5

   g. With the insertion point positioned inside the page border, click Insert, File, and then insert the file **Award** located in your Chapter04 folder.
   h. Select the entire document by pressing Ctrl + A, access the Font dialog box, and then turn on kerning at 14 points. Click OK.
   i. Select the following text and apply the listed formatting:

   Community Service Award   42-point Matura MT Script Capitals
                                                with shadow

Awarded to	14-point Arial bold italic
XXX	24-point Britannic Bold
as an expression of…	12-point Arial
Your commitment of time…	12-point Arial
Presented by	14-point Arial bold italic
Edward Hospital…	22-point Britannic Bold in small caps with spacing expanded by 1.5 points
YYY	14-point Arial bold italic
My Name, Ameeta, Joseph, Laurel…	12-point Arial

j. Change the zoom to *Page Width*.

k. Turn off the drawing grid feature by clicking the <u>D</u>raw button on the Drawing toolbar and then click Gri<u>d</u>. At the Drawing Grid dialog box, remove the check mark from the check box at the left of <u>S</u>nap objects to grid. Click OK.

l. Draw the signature lines in the award by completing the following steps:

1) Turn on the drawing canvas feature by clicking <u>T</u>ools and then <u>O</u>ptions. Choose the General tab and click inside the check box at the left of *Automati<u>c</u>ally create drawing canvas when inserting AutoShapes*. Click OK.

2) Click the Line button on the Drawing toolbar, hold down the Shift key, and then drag the crosshairs inside the drawing canvas and draw a line approximately 3 inches long. *(Note: The drawing canvas may display above or below the signature area and the horizontal line may not appear near the names. If you have difficulty positioning the drawing canvas, turn off this feature.)*

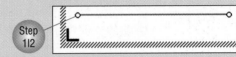
Step 1l2

3) Double-click the border of the drawing canvas to access the Format Drawing Canvas dialog box, choose the Layout tab, and then change the wrapping style to In <u>f</u>ront of text. Click OK.

4) Drag the drawing canvas to the bottom area of the certificate to include the signers' names. *(Note: The horizontal line may not display near the names.)*

5) Drag the line you created in Step 1 above *My Name*, as shown in Figure 4.28. Verify that the line length is 3.25 inches by accessing the Format AutoShape dialog box and choosing the Size tab. Click OK.

6) Select the line, hold down the Ctrl key, and then drag and drop a copy of the line above each of the names.

7) Click the Fit button on the Drawing Canvas toolbar.

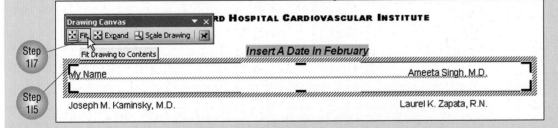
Step 1l7
Step 1l5

m. Align the four lines by completing the following steps:

1) Select the line above *My Name*, hold down the Shift key, and select the line above *Joseph M. Kaminsky, M.D.* **(Hint: Click the E<u>x</u>pand button on the Drawing Canvas toolbar so it will be easier for you to see the lines.)**

2) Click the <u>D</u>raw button on the Drawing toolbar, point to <u>A</u>lign or Distribute, and then click Align <u>L</u>eft.

3) Align the remaining lines by following steps similar to Steps 1m1 and 1m2, but click Align <u>R</u>ight instead of Align <u>L</u>eft.

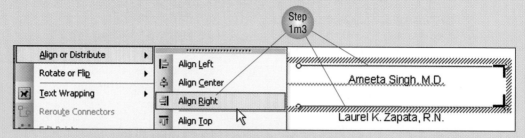

Step 1m3

4) Align the lines horizontally by following steps similar to Steps 1m1 and 1m2. *(Hint: Select a pair of left and right lines, click <u>D</u>raw, point to <u>A</u>lign or Distribute, and then click Align <u>T</u>op.)*

n. Create two text fields to replace *XXX* and *YYY* in the document by completing the following steps:

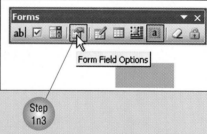

Step 1n2

Text Form Field

XXX

1) Display the Forms toolbar.
2) Select *XXX* and click the Text Form Field button (first button from the left) on the Forms toolbar.
3) Click the Form Field Options button (fourth button from the left) on the Forms toolbar.

Form Field Options

Step 1n3

4) At the Text Form Field Options dialog box, type **Insert Recipient's Name** in the *Default text* text box.
5) Click the down-pointing arrow at the right of the *Text format* list box, click *Title case,* and then click OK or press Enter.
6) Select *YYY* and follow steps similar to Steps 1n3 through 1n5, and then type **Insert a date in February** in the *Default text* text box.

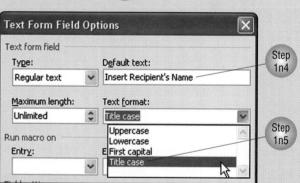

Step 1n4

Step 1n5

o. Create the logo watermark in Figure 4.28 by completing the following steps:

1) Click <u>I</u>nsert, point to Picture, and then click <u>F</u>rom File.
2) At the Insert Picture dialog box, double-click *Edward Cardio Color* in your Chapter04 folder.
3) Select the picture, click the Color button (second from the left) on the Picture toolbar, and then select <u>W</u>ashout.
4) Click the Less Brightness button on the Picture toolbar three times.
5) Click the Text Wrapping button and then click I<u>n</u> Front of Text.
6) Size and position the image similar to Figure 4.28.
7) With the image still selected, click the Text Wrapping button, and then click Behin<u>d</u> Text.

p. Click the Protect Form button (the last button on the Forms toolbar) and then close the Forms toolbar.

2. Save the template with Save <u>A</u>s and name it **(Your name), Award**. (Ask your instructor if you should save the template to the DTP Templates folder.)

3. Close **(Your name), Award**.

4. Click <u>V</u>iew and then Tas<u>k</u> Pane. Click the Home button and at the Getting Started task pane click **(Your name), Award** located under the *Open* section. *(Hint: Alternatively, click <u>F</u>ile and then <u>O</u>pen to locate and open the template.)*

5. Click the first text field and type Grace Chu. Click the next text field and type February 16, 2005.

6. *Optional:* You may choose one of the methods discussed in this chapter to create your signature and add it above the line for *My Name*.

7. Preview and then save the document as **c04ex05, Award**.

8. Print then close **c04ex05, Award**.

F I G U R E

4.28 *Exercise 5*

CHAPTER summary

➤ Fill effects are added to documents for impact and focus.

➤ The Microsoft Office Online Templates Web page, which is accessed from the Templates on Office Online hyperlink located in the New Document task pane, includes numerous templates created in Word, Excel, PowerPoint, and Publisher that may be used for personal documents.

➤ Word provides a Calendar Wizard that guides you through the steps of creating monthly calendars in either portrait (narrow) or landscape (wide) orientation.

➤ A placeholder is a reserved area on a page where an object, image, or text is entered later.

➤ Crop to trim horizontal and vertical edges off an image. Crop to maximize impact from an image.

➤ The unprintable zone is an area where text will not print.

➤ Watermarks, pictures, special characters, shading, and text may be added to a calendar to enhance its appearance and add to its effectiveness. Reducing the shading of a watermark in a calendar improves the readability of the calendar text.

➤ AutoShape objects are added to documents to emphasize important facts. Text and fill may be added to an AutoShape form.

➤ Many AutoShape objects have adjustment handles you can drag to adjust a unique aspect of the shape.

➤ Adjustments may be necessary in the size and position of document elements to compensate for the unprintable zone of a particular printer.

➤ Deselect the *Snap objects to grid* option to easily move an object closer to another object.

➤ You may move objects precisely by pressing an arrow key on the keyboard. This method is called nudging. You may also use the Nudge command on the Drawing toolbar Draw menu.

➤ Objects automatically stack in individual layers as you add them to a document. You see the stacking order when objects overlap—the top object covers a portion of the objects beneath it.

➤ Use the drawing canvas to help you arrange objects in a document.

➤ The drawing canvas may be turned off temporarily by pressing the Delete key before drawing the object.

➤ Grouping objects combines the objects into a single unit.

➤ You can align two or more drawing objects relative to each other by their left, right, top, or bottom edges, or align them horizontally or vertically by their centers.

➤ Selecting a predefined label definition at the Envelopes and Labels dialog box creates personal return labels, shipping labels, address labels, CD labels, place cards, tent cards, and many more useful labels.

➤ Return labels may be duplicated on a sheet of labels by using the AutoText command, copy and paste, or the F4 key to repeat the last command.

➤ A page border can be added to any or all sides of a page.

➤ Form fields are added to documents or templates to allow the user to efficiently insert variable information.

➤ Create a signature by using options on the Language bar and then save the Ink object as an AutoText entry.

➤ Signatures may also be created using the AutoShapes Scribble tool.

➤ Signature objects may also be created by using a scanner to scan your handwritten signature. Once the signature is scanned it may be inserted into a document and then copied and pasted to other locations or documents. This signature may also be saved as an AutoText entry.

COMMANDS review

Command	Mouse/Keyboard
Templates	New Document task pane, <u>On my computer</u> hyperlink
Microsoft Office Online Templates Web page	New Document task pane, <u>Templates on Office Online</u> hyperlink
Margins	File, Page Setup, Margins tab
Portrait/Landscape	File, Page Setup, Margins tab
Paper size	File, Page Setup, Paper tab
Picture	Insert, Picture, Clip Art or From File
File	Insert, File
Grid	Drawing toolbar, Draw, Grid
Text Box	Text Box button on Drawing toolbar; Insert, Text Box
Rotate	Draw, Rotate or Flip
Watermark	View, Header and Footer, Insert, Picture, Clip Art or From File, Color, Washout; or Insert, Picture, Clip Art or From File, Color, Washout, Behind Text
WordArt	Insert, Picture, WordArt; or WordArt button on Drawing toolbar
Group	Drawing toolbar Draw, Group
Ungroup	Drawing toolbar Draw, Ungroup
Nudge	Draw, Nudge, Up, Down, Left, Right; or select object and press arrow keys
AutoText	Insert, AutoText, New
Labels	Tools, Letters and Mailings, Envelopes and Labels
Envelopes	Tools, Letters and Mailings, Envelopes and Labels
Page Border	Format, Borders and Shading, Page Border tab
Align	Drawing toolbar Draw, Align or Distribute
Form fields	View, Toolbars, Forms toolbar
AutoText	Type name, press Enter or F3
Language bar	Tools, Speech
Scribble tool	Drawing toolbar AutoShapes, Lines, Scribble
Scanner	Insert, Picture, From Scanner or Camera

REVIEWING key points

True/False: On a blank sheet of paper, write *True* if the statement is true and *False* if the statement is false.

1. The expanded spacing option at the Font dialog box adjusts the vertical space between lines of text.
2. Modifications made to a calendar template will be reflected in all calendars created with that template from now on.
3. A page border can be added to any or all sides of a page.
4. A watermark created in a header or footer will display on every page of a document.
5. A text field is a form field where the user is prompted to enter text.
6. A watermark image may be inserted into a calendar through a built-in prompt within the Calendar Wizard.
7. Use the F2 key to repeat a command.
8. Objects and text may not be grouped into a single unit.
9. The Shadow option may not be applied to AutoShape objects.

Completion: On a blank sheet of paper, indicate the correct term, command, or number for each item.

1. Turn off the drawing canvas at this dialog box.
2. Hold down this key if you want to select several objects and group the objects.
3. The templates in the Microsoft Office Online Templates Web page include templates that are created and edited in these four office programs.
4. Use this AutoShape option to draw your name.
5. Press this key if you want to disable the drawing canvas temporarily.
6. You can nudge a picture or object by pressing these keys on the keyboard.
7. To position the inside edge of a page border relative to the page margin, select this option at the *Measure from* list box in the Border and Shading Options dialog box.
8. The Crop button is located on this toolbar.
9. Click this button to turn on the Ink mode.
10. Quickly insert a signature that has been saved as this.

APPLYING your skills

Assessment 1

You have volunteered to help your daughter's tennis coach prepare a calendar for the team's activities in June. Figure 4.29 is a sample calendar using a watermark for emphasis—use your own design ideas! Include the following specifications:

- Using the Calendar Wizard, choose a calendar style.
- Select a desired page orientation at the Calendar Wizard.
- Choose to leave room for a picture at the Calendar Wizard if you decide to use a clip art image, photo, or scanned image. Choose not to leave room for a picture if you decide to use a watermark.
- Select June 2005 for the calendar date.
- Use appropriate fonts, font sizes, font styles, and font colors.
- Include the text in Figure 4.29.
- If you wish to add shading to cells in the table structure, click F̲ormat, B̲orders and Shading, and then select the S̲hading tab. Select a color in the Fill palette or select a style and/or color in the *Patterns* section. Make sure *Cell* displays in the *Apply to* list box. Click OK.
- Save the document and name it **c04sa01, Tennis**.
- Print and then close **c04sa01, Tennis**.

F I G U R E

4.29 *Assessment 1 Sample Solution*

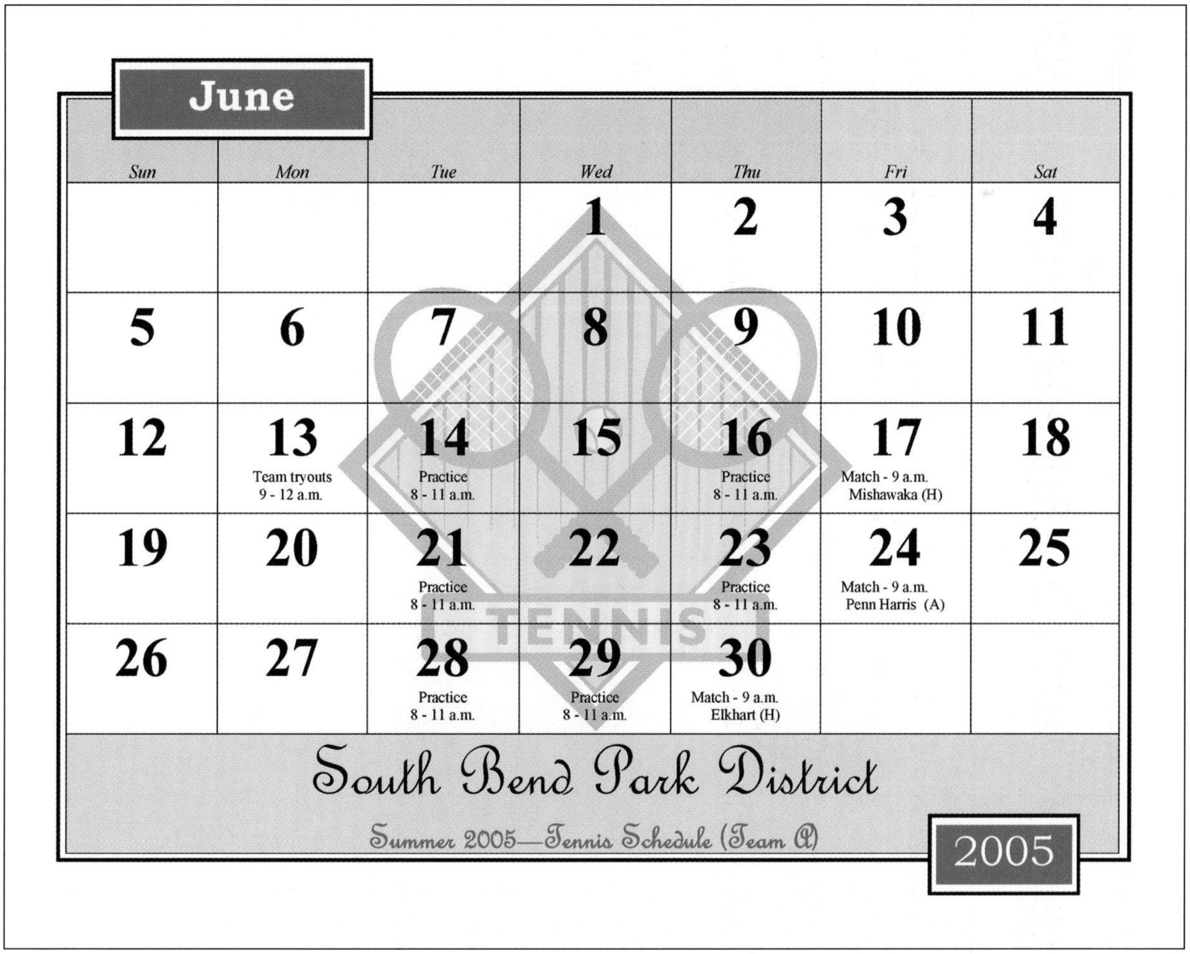

Sun	Mon	Tue	Wed	Thu	Fri	Sat
			1	2	3	4
5	6	7	8	9	10	11
12	13 Team tryouts 9 - 12 a.m.	14 Practice 8 - 11 a.m.	15	16 Practice 8 - 11 a.m.	17 Match - 9 a.m. Mishawaka (H)	18
19	20	21 Practice 8 - 11 a.m.	22	23 Practice 8 - 11 a.m.	24 Match - 9 a.m. Penn Harris (A)	25
26	27	28 Practice 8 - 11 a.m.	29 Practice 8 - 11 a.m.	30 Match - 9 a.m. Elkhart (H)		

June

South Bend Park District

Summer 2005—Tennis Schedule (Team A)

2005

Assessment 2

1. Create the change-of-address postcard in Figure 4.30 by following the specifications in the boxes; however, use your name and address and send the postcard to a friend.
2. Access the Envelopes and Labels feature and choose a postcard definition that measures 4 inches by 6 inches.
3. Insert a clip art image that is similar to the one shown in Figure 4.30. Click Insert, Picture, Clip Art, and then type j0287317.wmf or type the keyword stamp in the *Search for* text box.
4. Use the Papyrus font or a similar font if this one is not available.
5. The triangle-shaped object is a Flowchart AutoShape object.
6. Use AutoShapes in your document to reinforce a consistent color or to draw the reader's eyes through the document.
7. Group any related objects.
8. Save the document as **c04sa02, Address**.
9. Print and then close **c04sa02, Address**.

F I G U R E

4.30 *Assessment 2*

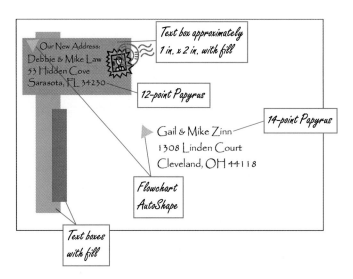

Assessment 3

1. Access a recipe template and a holiday menu template from the Microsoft Office Online Templates Web page in the Diet and Exercise category with the _Healthcare and Wellness_ hyperlink, or the <u>Holiday Occasions</u> hyperlink. Alternatively, type recipe or menu into the _Search_ text box and click the Go button to see a list of recipes or menus. Sample templates for a recipe card and a menu are displayed in Figure 4.31. **_(Hint: Read any directions given on the templates.)_**
2. Customize the recipe card and menu to complement your favorite recipe, special interests, favorite colors, or hobbies.
3. Type a favorite recipe on your card and insert favorite holiday items on your menu.
4. Save the documents as **c04sa03, Recipe** and **c04sa03, Menu**.
5. Print and then distribute enough copies for all of the students in your class and then close **c04sa03, Recipe** and **c04sa03, Menu**.

F I G U R E

4.31 _Assessment 3 Sample Templates_

Assessment 4

1. Create a sheet of personal return or address labels using your name and address. Include a picture of your choice. Use the Avery Standard 5160 Address label definition or another definition of your choosing. Size the picture and address to fit into the label dimensions. You may use the AutoText method or the copy and paste method to produce a sheet of labels.
2. Save the labels as **c04sa04, Labels**.
3. Print and then close **c04sa04, Labels**.

Assessment 5

Create tent cards for a special meeting of your homeowners association. You have five people on the board, but at this time, create just two tent cards for one of the officers with the name printed on both sides. Complete the following steps:

INTEGRATED

1. Click Tools, point to Letters & Mailings, and then click Envelopes and Labels.
2. Select the Labels tab.
3. Click the Options button and then choose *5305 - Tent Card*. Click OK.
4. Click New Document.
5. Click Table on the Menu bar and then click the Show Gridlines option.
6. Locate a house clip art similar to the one shown in Figure 4.32. This clip is j0205456.wmf; you may substitute if necessary.
7. Position the insertion point in the top cell and insert the house clip.
8. Change the wrap of the clip to In Front of Text, and then size and position the image to fit within the cell.
9. Draw a text box to accommodate the text and remove the line color. Type Gail Zinn, President in a thick font in a large font size. Apply a font color that coordinates with the clip art.
10. Group the image and the text box and then while holding down the Ctrl key, drag and drop a copy to the cell shown at the bottom of the label sheet.
11. Save the document as **c04sa5, Tent Card**.
12. Print the tent cards once, flip the label sheet from top to bottom, and then reinsert the label sheet into your printer and print again. The result will be two tent cards, with the name and graphic on each side of the tent cards.
13. Close **c04sa5, Tent Card**.
14. At a clear document screen, type the name of a local building where a homeowners association meeting could be held. When the smart tag appears below the address, click on the hyperlink that will provide you with the directions to the meeting. Print a copy of these directions and then turn this in with your tent cards.

4.32 *Assessment 5 Sample Solution*

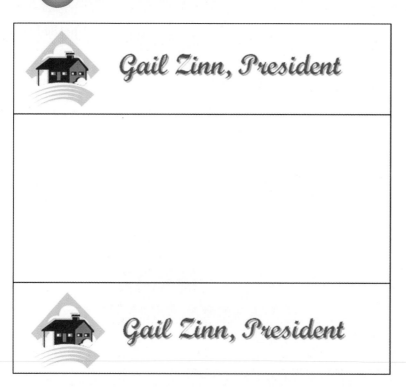

Assessment 6

1. Create a Publisher label template by completing the following steps:

   INTEGRATED

   a. At a clear document screen display the New Document task pane.
   b. Click the <u>Templates on Office Online</u> hyperlink in the *Templates* section.
   c. Type **Label** in the *Search* text box and then click the Go button.
   d. Click the <u>Return Address Labels (works with Avery Label 5160)</u> hyperlink.
   e. At the Preview page, click the Download Now button.
   f. If the Publisher Wizard for this template is not installed on your computer you will see a message informing you of that fact, and asking you if you want to install it now. Click the Yes button to install the wizard. *(Note: Publisher must be installed on your computer for this to work.)*
   g. If the Personal Information dialog box appears, click the Cancel button to close it.
   h. Select the first line of text in the label and type **Malee Pobsayai**.
   i. Use the method described in the previous step to type the following text in the remaining four lines of the label:

      Thanon Phahonyothin
      Soi 66
      Pathum Thani 12130
      THAILAND

2. Format the label by completing the following steps:
   a. Select *Malee Pobsayai*, right-click, point to Change Text, and then click Font.
   b. Change the font size to 12. *(Note: The font used in the label will be highlighted in the Latin text font text box.)*

3. Insert a clip art picture by completing the following steps:
    a. Click Insert, point to Picture, and then click Clip Art.
    b. Type Thailand in the *Search for* text box and then click the Go button.
    c. Locate the image pictured in Figure 4.33 and click once.
    d. Select the image and use one of the corner diagonal two-headed arrows to move the image inward and shrink it to fit the label.
    e. Click File and then Print Preview to preview the sheet of labels you have created.
    f. Click the Print Preview *Printer* icon to print the labels on a sheet of Avery Label 5160 labels or a sheet of plain paper.
4. Save the label sheet as **c04sa06, Publisher Labels**, and then close the document. *(Note: This is a Publisher file and must be opened in Publisher.)*

FIGURE

4.33 *Assessment 6 Sample Solution*

Malee Pobsayai
Thanon Phahonyothin
Soi 66
Pathum Thani 12130
THAILAND

This label is ready to print onto Avery Label #5160.

Assessment 7

1. Find an example of a calendar, certificate, CD case cover, CD face label, award, holiday place cards, vacation travel itinerary, just-moved postcard, personal invitation, or any other type of personal document.
2. Recreate the example, improving it with appropriate font selections and enhancements—a picture, watermark, page border, or special characters. Be sure to apply appropriate desktop design concepts to the layout of your document—draw a thumbnail first!
3. You may recreate the document from scratch or use any of the templates in Word or at the Microsoft Office Online Templates Web page.
4. Save your document as **c04sa07, Redo** and then print and close **c04sa07, Redo**.
5. Attach the original document to your recreated document.

Design and Create

PERFORMANCE Assessments

CREATING BUSINESS AND PERSONAL DOCUMENTS

UNIT01

(Before completing unit assessments, delete the Chapter04 folder on your disk. Next, copy the Unit01 folder from the CD that accompanies this textbook to your disk and then make Unit01 the active folder.)

Assessment one 1

Your employer, First Trust Bank, will be closed July 4 in observance of the national holiday. Please prepare a sign notifying the bank's customers that the bank will not be open and post the sign in the lobby where it can be seen clearly. Complete the following steps:

1. Open **Sign 2** located in your Unit01 folder.
2. Format the sign using appropriate fonts and font sizes.
3. Insert a relevant photo, clip art, or symbol to draw attention to the message. *(Hint: Search for clip art using the keywords* **Fourth of July.**)
4. Save the document as **u01pa01, Sign**.
5. Print and then close **u01pa01, Sign**.

Assessment two 2

1. At a clear document screen, create the letterhead illustrated in Figure U1.1. Use the following list of specifications to help you in the creation process:
   a. Create the letterhead design elements in the header and footer pane.
   b. Complete a search for the keyword *eagle* **(j0290828.wmf)** at the Clip Art task pane.
   c. Insert the image shown in Figure U1.1 and size it similarly to this figure.
   d. Use the second WordArt style in the first row of the WordArt Gallery for the text *Blue Eagle Airlines* in 24-point Arial Black.
   e. Type **On the Wings of Eagles** in 13-point Book Antiqua italics and expand the text by 2.5 points. Change the font color to a color that coordinates with the eagle clip art.

    f. Create the blue dashed arrow extending from the graphic image to the text box containing *On the Wings of Eagles*. **(Hint: Hold down the Shift key as you draw the arrow.)**

    g. Create a text box that contains the address information in 9-point Book Antiqua (substitute a different font if necessary). Type the following data, aligned at right:

> Dallas Love Field
> 22 Mockingbird Lane
> Dallas, TX 75235
> www.emcp.net/beair
> 214.555.6073
> 1.800.555.6033
> 214.555.6077 (Fax)

    h. Create another arrow that extends from *Eagles* to the text box containing the address as shown in Figure U1.1. Use the same arrow style and color used in Step 1f.

2. Save the completed letterhead and name it **u01pa02, Airlines**.
3. Print and then close **u01pa02, Airlines**.
4. Access the Internet and use a search engine to locate the Web site for Dallas Love Field Airport. Once you have located the Web site, print a map of the airport and a one-page information sheet from the Web site's home page. Attach the map and information sheet to your letterhead. Alternatively, you may access a map by clicking the smart tag near the airport's address in your letterhead.

Optional: Create a coordinating envelope using the company name, address, and contact information as in Figure U1.1. Save the envelope as **u01pa02, Envelope**.

On the Wings of Eagles

Dallas Love Field
22 Mockingbird Lane
Dallas, TX 75235
www.emcp.net/beair
214.555.6073
1.800.555.6033
214.555.6077 (Fax)

Figure U1.1 • Assessment 2

Assessment three

1. You work for a company named Design 2000 that specializes in ergonomically designed offices. Your company works hard to create designs that provide maximum worker comfort. Create a sheet of business cards for Design 2000. Include the following information in your business card design:

Slogan	=	Make up a slogan for your company.
Address	=	Type your name, title
		300 Sun Drive
	=	Tucson, AZ 96322
Phone	=	304.555.2344
Fax	=	304.555.2345
Web	=	www.emcp.net/design2000

2. Include the following specifications in your business card design:
   a. Create a thumbnail sketch or sketches of your proposed business card design and layout.
   b. Create an asymmetrical design.
   c. Incorporate appropriate and proportional fonts, font sizes, font colors, and font styles. Consider using the WordArt feature.
   d. Turn on kerning for fonts 14 points and above.
   e. Use tracking (condensing or expanding character spacing) if necessary or to create a special effect.
   f. You may use text boxes, AutoShapes, gradient fills, a graphic image, a watermark, horizontal or vertical ruled lines, special characters, or any other design elements that are appropriate. *(Hint: Borrow a design element from MS Publisher 2003.)*
   g. Use some color if a color printer is available.
   h. Evaluate your design for the concepts of focus, balance, proportion, contrast, directional flow, consistency, and the use of color.
   i. Make sure items of related information are positioned close to each other.
   j. Avoid center alignment; aim for a strong left or right alignment.
3. Save the business card and name it **u01pa03, Design 2000**.
4. Print and then close **u01pa03, Design 2000**.

Optional: Print a copy of the **Document Analysis Guide.doc** located in your Unit01 folder and use it to evaluate your finished document.

Assessment four 4

Create your personal calendar for the month of December (current year) using the Calendar Wizard and including the following specifications (a sample solution is shown in Figure U1.2):

- If you have access to a scanner or digital camera, include a photograph of yourself, a family member, pet, or special scenery. Otherwise, include any appropriate clip art image or photograph from the Clip Organizer or the Web.

- Include on the calendar four noteworthy events, meetings, parties, and so on.

- Include at least two symbols or graphics.

- Experiment with a variety of fonts and font sizes until you achieve the look you want for your calendar.

- Save the calendar and name it **u01pa04, Calendar**.

- Print and then close **u01pa04, Calendar**.

Figure U1.2 • Assessment 4 Sample Solution

Assessment *five*

In this assessment, you will copy an Excel calendar template into Word using the Paste Special command and then customize the calendar as shown in Figure U1.3 by completing the following steps:

1. In Word, click the <u>Templates on Office Online</u> hyperlink at the New Document task pane.
2. At the Microsoft Office Online Templates Web page with *Templates* selected in the *Search* text box, type **calendars** in the *Search* text box and then click Go.
3. Scroll to locate the *2004 calendar with room for notes (1-pg.)* Excel template. Click the template hyperlink and then download the template into Excel.
4. In Excel, select the entire calendar (range A1:AE35) and then click the Copy button.
5. Minimize Excel (keep it open) and maximize Word.
6. In Word, click <u>E</u>dit and then Paste <u>S</u>pecial.
7. At the Paste Special dialog box, make sure the <u>P</u>aste option is selected and then select *Microsoft Office Excel Worksheet Object* in the <u>A</u>s list box. Click OK.
8. Change the page orientation to landscape.
9. Change the top and bottom margins to 0.75 inch. *(Hint: Delete the second page if there is one.)*

10. Double-click the calendar to access the Microsoft Excel toolbars and commands.
11. Select the placeholder text in the title of the note section and type Rental Seasons in Blue.
12. Type BeachTime Rental Seasons in the first row of the note section and format as shown in Figure U1.3.
13. Type the text shown in Figure U1.3 and add a color fill for each of the seasons.
14. Insert BeachTime.bmp located in your Unit01 folder and then drag the image toward the bottom of the note section. *(Note: This grouped WordArt object and clip art image was created in MS Publisher 2003 and saved in the bmp format by right-clicking on the image and then clicking Save as Picture at the shortcut menu.)*
15. Add a coordinating fill color to each of the text boxes containing the dates of each of the months in the calendar. Refer to your season color guide in the note section. *(Hint: Hold down the Shift key as you select multiple text boxes.)*
16. Save the document as u01pa05, Integrated Calendar.
17. Print and then close u01pa05, Integrated Calendar.
18. Close Excel.

Figure U1.3 • Assessment 5

UNIT two

PREPARING PROMOTIONAL DOCUMENTS, WEB PAGES, AND POWERPOINT PRESENTATIONS

Creating Promotional Documents

PERFORMANCE OBJECTIVES

Upon successful completion of Chapter 5, you will be able to produce promotional documents such as flyers and announcements using Word's Tables and Borders toolbar, Picture toolbar, Drawing toolbar, drawing grid, Microsoft Clip Organizer, Microsoft Office Clip Art and Media, Microsoft Office Online Templates, and WordArt along with text boxes, pictures, lines, AutoShapes, 3-D boxes, shadow boxes, and borders.

CHAPTER05

DESKTOP PUBLISHING TERMS

Announcement	Metafiles	Thumbnail sketch
Bitmaps	Nudge	TWAIN
Crop	Pixel	Vector graphics
Fill	Raster graphics	WIA
Flyer	RGB	
HSL	Scale	

WORD FEATURES USED

Align or Distribute	Fill effects	Picture toolbar
AutoShapes	Gradient	Rotate
Character spacing	Group/Ungroup	Scale
Document Imaging	Line color	Scanning
Drawing canvas	Microsoft Clip Organizer	Size
Drawing grid	Microsoft Office Clip	Tables and Borders
Drawing objects	Art and Media	toolbar
Drawing toolbar	Microsoft Office Picture	Text boxes
Embed	Manager	Washout
Fill color	Microsoft Photo Editor	WordArt

In this chapter, you will produce flyers and announcements for advertising products, services, events, and classes using your own design and layout ideas with Word's desktop features. First, you will review basic desktop publishing concepts for planning and designing promotional documents. Next, you will integrate fonts, graphics, borders, and objects into your documents to increase their appeal. Finally, more complex and powerful features such as Microsoft Office Clip Art and Media, Microsoft Clip Organizer, Microsoft Office Online Templates, WordArt, drawing grid, tables, and the tools on the Drawing and Picture toolbars will be used.

Creating Flyers and Announcements

Flyer

Promotional document used to advertise a product or service that is available for a limited amount of time.

Flyers generally advertise a product or service that is available for a limited amount of time. Frequently, you may find flyers stuffed in a grocery bag; attached to a mailbox, door handle, or windshield; placed in a bin near an entrance; or placed on a countertop for customers to carry away. The basic goal of a flyer is to communicate a message at a glance, so the message should be brief and to the point. For the flyer to be effective, the basic layout and design should be free of clutter—without too much text or too many graphics. Use white space generously to set off an image or text and to help promote good directional flow.

Announcement

Promotional document used to inform an audience of an upcoming event.

An *announcement* informs an audience of an upcoming event. An announcement may create interest in an event, but does not necessarily promote a product or service. For instance, you may have received an announcement for course offerings at your local community college or an announcement of an upcoming community event, sporting event, concert, race, contest, raffle, or a new store opening that informs and creates interest, but does not promote the event.

Planning and Designing Promotional Documents

Thumbnail sketch

A rough sketch used in planning layout and design.

As stated in Chapter 1, planning your document is a basic desktop publishing concept that applies to flyers and announcements as well as to other publications. Most important, always prepare a *thumbnail sketch*, which is like thinking on paper, before beginning a project. Clearly define your purpose and assess your target audience. For instance, consider your audience when choosing type sizes—the older your audience, the larger the print might need to be. Besides assessing your needs and your approach, consider your budget as well. Generally, producing flyers and announcements is one of the least expensive means of advertising.

DTP POINTERS

Consider your audience when choosing type sizes.

Successful promotional documents attract the reader's attention and keep it. Consider how you can attract the reader's eyes: by using eye-catching headlines, displaying graphics that create impact, or using color for emphasis or attention. People generally look at the graphics first, then they read the headline, and finally they look at the logo for company identity. The logo may be placed low on the page to anchor the message.

DTP POINTERS

Prepare a thumbnail sketch.

Using a Table for Layout

DTP POINTERS

The upper left corner is usually read first.

Use a thumbnail sketch as a tool to guide you in creating documents. In addition, you may draw a table to block off areas of the page to reflect the layout you have sketched in your thumbnail. Figure 5.1 shows how a table can serve as a framework for an announcement.

5.1 Using a Table to Create an Announcement

First, draw (drag) to create the outer table boundaries.

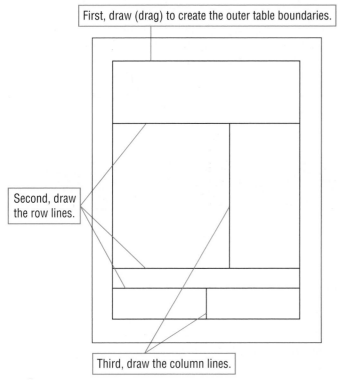

Second, draw the row lines.

Third, draw the column lines.

Tables provide an efficient means for aligning text and objects using options on the Tables and Borders toolbar. These options include Align Top Left, Align Top Center, Align Top Right, Align Center Left, Align Center, Align Center Right, Align Bottom Left, Align Bottom Center, and Align Bottom Right as shown in Figure 5.2. You will learn how to create an announcement in a table in Exercise 1.

To create a table for the announcement in Figure 5.1, complete the following steps:

1. Click the Tables and Borders button located toward the right on the Standard toolbar, or display the Tables and Borders toolbar (see Figure 5.2), and then click the Draw Table button (first button from the left). The arrow pointer will display as a pen.

Draw Table

2. Position the pen in the upper left corner of your screen and then drag from the left corner to the bottom right corner to create a table.

3. Draw lines by clicking and dragging.

4. To erase lines, click the Eraser button on the Tables and Borders toolbar (see Figure 5.2). Drag the eraser along the line you want to erase. Remember to turn off the Eraser when you are done.

Eraser

5. If you do not want borders on your table, click the down-pointing arrow at the right of the Outside Border button on the Tables and Borders toolbar (see Figure 5.2), and then click the No Border option.

Outside Border

6. If you want to change the cell width or length, drag the boundary you want to change. (Position the insertion point on the boundary line you want to change; when the insertion point displays as either two horizontal or two vertical lines with up/down or left/right pointing arrows, drag the line to a new location.)

Table Move Handle

7. By clicking and dragging the *Table Move Handle* icon in the upper left corner of the table, you can move the table to a new location.

FIGURE

5.2 *Tables and Borders Toolbar and the Aligning Palette*

Toolbar Options

Tables and Borders

Draw Table | Eraser | Line Style | Line Weight | Border Color | Outside Border | Shading Color | Insert Table | Merge Cells | Split Cells | Align Top Left | Distribute Rows Evenly | Distribute Columns Evenly | Table AutoFormat | Change Text Direction | Sort Ascending | Sort Descending | AutoSum

Align Top Center

Align Top Left — | — Align Top Right
Align Center Left — | — Align Center Right
Align Bottom Left — | — Align Center
Align Bottom Center — | — Align Bottom Right

DTP POINTERS
Use the
$^1/_3$, $^2/_3$ Rule which states that at least $^1/_3$ of your document should be white space.

DTP POINTERS
White space creates a clean page that is easy to read.

DTP POINTERS
With text-intensive material, vary type sizes and styles. Use various shades of black and white as well as color.

Using Text for Focus

Flyers and announcements provide tremendous opportunities for you to be creative. To grab attention, consider using large graphics, uncommon typefaces, asymmetrical design, and plenty of white space. Use color or white space to emphasize the main message and give the eye a break from too much text—$^1/_3$, $^2/_3$ Rule: $^1/_3$ of the document should be white space, $^2/_3$ of the document may be and/or design objects. Do not use more than three fonts or three colors. An inexpensive alternative is to use colored paper or preprinted paper. Figure 5.3 illustrates a flyer that attracts attention with varying fonts and font attributes.

Once you have finished a document, look at the document from a distance to make sure that the important information is dominant. Also, look through a newspaper or magazine to find ads that grab your attention and prompt you to act. Study the designs and apply what you have learned to your own documents.

FIGURE

5.3   *Sample Flyer (All Text)*

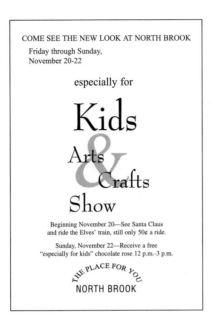

Using Graphics for Emphasis

Graphics can add excitement to and generate enthusiasm for a publication. A well-placed graphic can transform a plain document into a compelling visual document. However, it is effective only if the image relates to the subject of the document. Before selecting a graphic, decide what your theme or text will be. If you are deciding among many graphics, select the simplest. A simple graphic demands more attention and has more impact; too many graphics can cause clutter and confusion.

Use a graphic to aid in directional flow. Also, use a generous amount of white space around a graphic. Use a thumbnail sketch as a tool to help you make decisions on position, size, and design.

Consider using clip art as a basis for your own creations. Combine clip art images with other clip art images, then crop, size, or color different areas of the combined image to create a unique look. Alternatively, you may include photographs in your flyers or announcements. In Office 2003, the clip art collection is accessible through the Clip Art task pane. If you have a version of Office that includes Microsoft Publisher, additional clip art and photo images are available.

Downloading Graphics from the Web

Keep in mind that if you have access to the Internet, you can add to your clip art, photographs, videos, and sound clips collection by downloading images and clips from the Microsoft Office Clip Art and Media Web page or other clip art Web sites. For instance, assume you want to add a frame or border to your document. All you need to do is display the Clip Art task pane, type frame in the *Search for* text box, and then scroll through the selections. If you know the file name, you can type it in the *Search for* text box in the Clip Art task pane. For instance, type

DTP POINTERS
Choose images that relate to the message.

DTP POINTERS
Leave plenty of white space around a graphic.

DTP POINTERS
Do not overuse clip art; use one main visual element per page.

j0242779.wmf in the *Search for* text box and a sun image will display. In addition, if you are connected to the Internet and you then access the Clip Art task pane, the clips that are available online through the Microsoft Web site are now available in the Clip Art task pane.

To download a wide variety of frames, borders, and lines from the Microsoft Office Clip Art and Media Web site, complete the following steps:

1. Display the Clip Art task pane.
2. At the Clip Art task pane, click the <u>Clip art on Office Online</u> hyperlink as shown in Figure 5.4.

FIGURE

5.4 **_Clip art on Office Online_ _Hyperlink at the Clip Art Task Pane_**

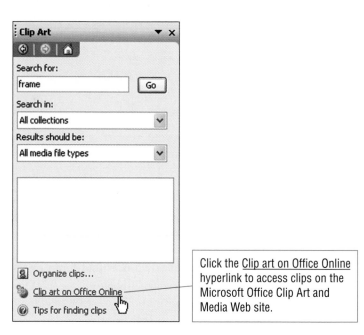

Click the <u>Clip art on Office Online</u> hyperlink to access clips on the Microsoft Office Clip Art and Media Web site.

3. The first screen that displays is the Microsoft Office Clip Art and Media home page as shown in Figure 5.5. Type the desired search topic *(frames)* in the *Search* text box and then click the Go button to execute the search. To limit your search, select the specific types of clip art files (Clip Art, Photographs, Movies, or Sounds) you are looking for by clicking the down-pointing arrow at the right of the *Search* option box.

FIGURE

5.5 *Microsoft Office Clip Art and Media Web Page*

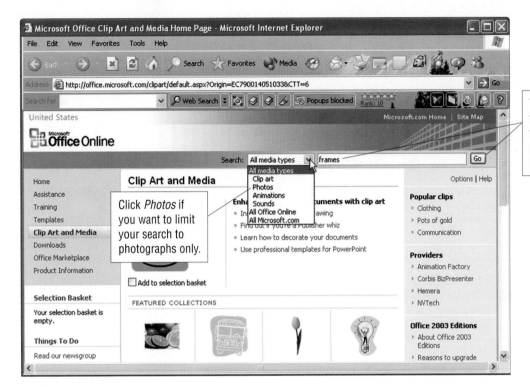

4. Figure 5.6 shows the screen that may display after initiating the search. To download an image, click the check box at the bottom of each image and then click the <u>Download 4 items</u> hyperlink.

FIGURE

5.6 *First Page of Frames*

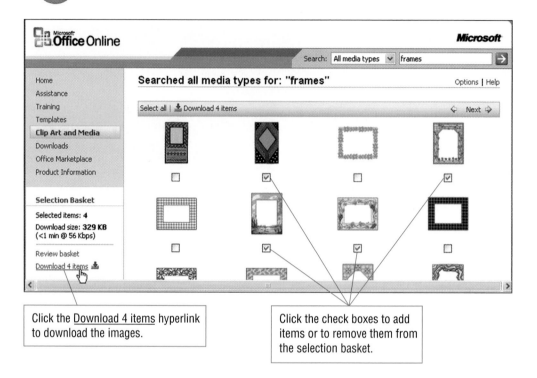

Click the <u>Download 4 items</u> hyperlink to download the images.

Click the check boxes to add items or to remove them from the selection basket.

5. After clicking the <u>Download 4 items</u> hyperlink, the screen shown in Figure 5.7 will display. This screen provides the estimated time for the download, the folder where the files are being sent, and the size of the files. Click the Download Now button to initiate the download.

FIGURE

5.7 *Download Information Screen*

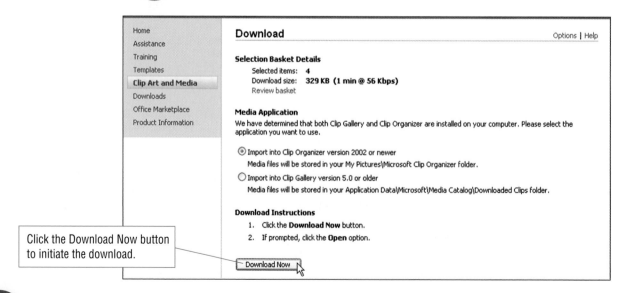

Click the Download Now button to initiate the download.

6. As soon as the downloaded files are copied, the Microsoft Clip Organizer displays. As shown in Figure 5.8, the downloaded frames are stored in subfolder categories such as *Animals, Borders & Frames,* and *Buildings* within the Downloaded Clips folder within My Collections.

F I G U R E

5.8 *Downloading Files to Categories*

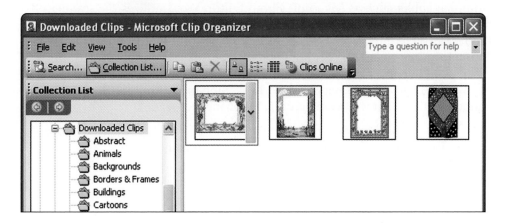

Using the Microsoft Clip Organizer

You can use the Office Clip Organizer to organize, find, preview, and insert pictures, clip art, movies, or sound files into your documents. When you first display the Clip Art task pane, the Add Clips to Organizer dialog box will appear. At the prompt to have Clip Organizer automatically import and catalog all of the media files, click Now. Clicking the Later button postpones the task. Your graphic files are cataloged based on keywords and file types that have been assigned to each image. The keywords provide a means for conducting efficient searches. To review the keywords, captions, and other properties associated with an image, select the image in the Clip Organizer or in the Clip Art task pane, right-click, and then choose Preview/Properties.

The Clip Organizer displays automatically after you download images from the Microsoft Office Clip Art and Media Web site. You can also view the Clip Organizer by clicking the Organize clips hyperlink at the Clip Art task pane. In addition, the Clip Organizer may be accessed by clicking Start, pointing to All Programs, pointing to Microsoft Office Tools, and then clicking Microsoft Clip Organizer. To browse available clips or to organize your clips, click the Collection List button and a list of categories will display as shown in Figure 5.8. Within each category, you may choose options to move, paste, delete, rename, or copy files. When you copy a clip, it is sent to the Office Clipboard. Display the Clipboard task pane and paste the image where you want to use it.

You may also use the *Search* option in the Clip Organizer to locate desired media clip files. The search options are similar to the drop-down list of options at the Clip Art task pane. To help in your searches, Microsoft organizes clip art into three collections that include My Collections, Office Collections, and Web Collections. By default, all three sources (All Collections) are used in a search. When you browse the images to find the one you are looking for, you may see some images that display with a small yellow star in the bottom right corner of the thumbnail picture. The yellow star indicates that the image is an animated graphic. These images are usually formatted in a GIF format (used on the Web) and cannot be ungrouped and edited in Word. In addition, you may have noticed that some pictures display with a globe in the bottom left corner of the thumbnail picture. The globe indicates that the image is located online.

Inserting Clip Art from a Scanner or Digital Camera

TWAIN

A cross-platform interface for acquiring electronic images captured by scanners and digital cameras.

WIA

Acronym for Windows Image Acquisition.

You can insert images directly from a scanner or digital camera without using an additional applet such as Microsoft Photo Editor. Word utilizes the scanner or digital camera drivers that you install, as long as they comply with the *TWAIN* interface or *WIA* interface. TWAIN is a cross-platform interface for acquiring electronic images that have been captured by scanners and digital cameras. Microsoft Office 2003 supports TWAIN version 1.7. Alternatively, your scanner or camera may be WIA (Windows Image Acquisition) compatible. To insert a picture from a scanner or digital camera, complete the following steps:

1. Make sure the scanner or digital camera is properly connected. Place the image in the scanner if you are using a scanner.
2. Position your insertion point in the document where you want the image to display.
3. Click Insert, point to Picture, and then click From Scanner or Camera.
4. Choose the source from the *Device* list box at the Insert Picture from Scanner or Camera dialog box shown in Figure 5.9.

FIGURE

5.9 *Insert Picture from Scanner or Camera Dialog Box*

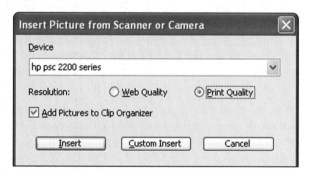

5. Select the desired resolution: *Web Quality* or *Print Quality*, if these options are accessible. If these options are grayed and inaccessible, you may make similar choices through your scanner software.
6. Click Insert and Word captures the image and inserts it in your document. If the Insert button is inaccessible, click the Custom Insert button and proceed with options through your scanner software. By default, Microsoft Clip Organizer automatically catalogs the image(s).
7. You can use any photo editing software that may have come with your scanner or digital camera to edit your images or to save them in a different resolution for use on the Web. Common editing programs include Paint Shop Pro, Adobe Photoshop, Adobe Photo Deluxe, Microsoft Image Composer, Microsoft Photo Editor, and Microsoft Office Picture Manager.

Choosing Scanner Resolution

One of the most common mistakes in scanning is overscanning. Most scanners are capable of scanning up to 1200 dots per inch (dpi) or more, so it may be tempting to scan at the highest resolution. However, if you scan a 5 × 7-inch image at 1200 dpi, the resulting image will take up 140 MB of RAM in memory. Hewlett Packard recommends these settings:

Color/Black & White Photographs:
- 100 dpi scan setting for a 300 dpi printer
- 150 dpi scan setting for a 600 dpi printer
- 300 dpi scan setting for a 1200 dpi printer

Color/Black & White Line Art and Drawing:
- 300 dpi scan setting for a 300 dpi printer
- 500 dpi scan setting for a 600 dpi printer
- 1200 dpi scan setting for a 1200 dpi printer

A 5 × 7-inch scanned photograph will result in these file sizes:
- 300 dpi scanned photo will be approximately 9 MB
- 600 dpi scanned photo will be approximately 36 MB
- 1200 dpi scanned photo will be approximately 144 MB

For photographs, 600 dpi is more resolution than the printer requires and you will not see any noticeable difference in print quality. However, if you are scanning line art and color drawings, you may want to scan at 600 dpi for a sharper picture. Many cameras and scanners produce pictures with resolutions from 300 dpi to 2400 dpi. If you are publishing a Web site, save your photos at 96 dpi. Most computer monitors have a screen resolution of 96 dpi. A photograph with higher or lower resolution may display blurry on a monitor at 96 dpi. A photograph saved at 96 dpi will download 10 times faster than an image saved at 1200 dpi.

If you are printing at a desktop printer, save your photo at the maximum resolution of your printer. In other words, scan your images and save them at the output resolution whether the output is a Web page, where size is linked to download time, or whether your output is a printed copy, in which case you would want to consider cost of ink, quality of paper, and the purpose of the hard copy. If you use a resolution that is much higher than the output device (printer or monitor), the printer or monitor will ignore the excess data. Matching the resolution ensures that the image file is no larger than it needs to be and as a result you waste less disk space and reduce the printing time.

Choosing Scanner and Digital Camera File Formats

The image control for most desktop scanners varies from 300 dpi to 2400 dpi. The optimal setting is often at 600 dpi. When scanning a logo or any other line art save the images as a .tif file or a .gif file if it is being used on a Web page. The logo may also be saved as a .bmp file and edited in any software program that includes the words *paint* or *photo* in its name. Bitmapped graphics use individual pixels of color that can be edited one by one or as a group. A *pixel* is each individual dot or square of color in a picture or bitmapped graphic. An enlarged bitmapped image appears jagged around the edges as shown in Figure 5.10. If the software program has the words *draw* or *illustrate* in its name, it is a ***vector graphics*** program. An

Pixel
Short for picture element, a pixel is each individual dot or square of color in a picture or bitmapped graphic.

Vector graphics
Images made up of mathematically defined lines and curves.

enlarged vector graphic looks smooth around the edges because the shapes are mathematically defined as shown in Figure 5.10 You can size a vector graphic by dragging the sizing handles surrounding the image.

5.10 *Raster (Bitmapped) Image and Vector (Line Art) Image*

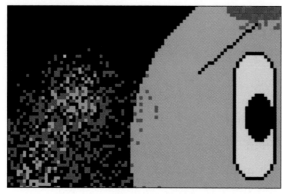

Raster

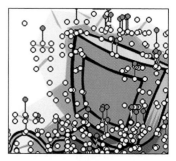

Vector

When scanning photographs, the files may be saved using the following extensions: .tif, .bmp, .gif, or .jpg (.jpeg). The GIF format allows only 256 colors (8-bit), so it may not be as desirable as TIF or JPEG formats where more colors may be selected—12-bit or 24-bit. Typically, JPG or JPEG file formats are used for Web or e-mail purposes, but JPG compression can cause reduced quality. Therefore, instead of saving a photograph as a compressed .jpg file, save it as a .bmp, which will produce a better resolution. Typically scan pictures for e-mail using 75 dpi or 96 dpi resolution and 256 colors, therefore producing a smaller file size for the e-mail attachment. The following guidelines may help you in scanning or using a digital camera:

- The GIF format allows only 256 colors
- 1-bit image is black and white
- 8-bit grayscale image provides 256 shades of gray
- 8-bit color image provides 256 colors
- 24-bit image provides over 16 million colors (called True Color—used for most color photographs)
- Photographs printed on glossy paper scan better than those printed on matte paper
- When scanning text, save in TXT or RTF file formats
- When scanning black/white drawing or logos, save in RTF or WMF file formats
- When scanning color images, save in TIF or BMP formats
- When scanning to a Web page, save in GIF, JPG, HTML (for text or text and image), or PDF file formats
- When using a camera, try to get as close to the subject as possible—enlarging a small image can result in a blurry picture

- The abbreviation *ppi* is pixels per inch (resolution on the screen)
- The abbreviation *dpi* is dots per inch (printed resolution)
- TIFF (or TIF) format is a universally accepted graphic file format (invented for scanning); .tif files are commonly used for exchanging images between application programs and are considered ***raster graphics*** (or bitmapped)
- JPEG is a compressed format for photographs; together with GIF and PNG, the JPEG or JPG is one of the image file formats that is supported by the World Wide Web
- If an image is not a photo and has broad, flat colors, scan for 256 colors

Raster graphics
Images made up of dots of black, white, or another color.

Deleting Images

Delete an image in the Clip Art task pane by right-clicking the image and then clicking <u>D</u>elete from Clip Organizer at the shortcut menu. At the message that displays, click the OK button.

Using Color in Promotional Documents

Color is a powerful tool in communicating information. Choose one or two colors for a document and stick with them to give your page a unified look. Add "spot color" in your document by using color only in specific areas of the page. Also, pick up a color from your graphic and apply it to your text.

Many flyers and announcements are printed on either white or color paper and duplicated on a copy machine to help keep down costs. A color printer or color copier adds to the cost, but can help the appeal of the document. If you are using a color printer, limit the color to small areas so it attracts attention but does not create visual confusion.

As an inexpensive alternative to printing in color, use color paper or specialty papers to help get your message across, as stated in Chapter 1. Specialty papers are predesigned papers used for brochures, letterheads, postcards, business cards, and certificates, and can be purchased through most office supply stores or catalog paper supply companies. Be sure to choose a color that complements your message and/or matches the theme of your document—orange for harvest or fall, green for spring, yellow for summer, or blue for water and sky.

Understanding Desktop Publishing Color Terms

When working in desktop publishing and using Word 2003, you may encounter terms used to explain color. Here is a list of color terms along with definitions:
- *Balance* is the amount of light and dark in a picture.
- *Brightness* or *value* is the amount of light in a color.
- *Contrast* is the amount of gray in a color.
- A *color wheel* is a device used to illustrate color relationships.
- *Complementary colors* are colors directly opposite each other on the color wheel, such as red and green, which are among the most popular color schemes.

- *CYMK* is an acronym for cyan, yellow, magenta, and black. A color printer combines these colors to create different colors.
- *Dither* is a method of combining several different-colored pixels to create new colors.
- *Gradient* is a gradual varying of color.
- *Grayscale* is a range of shades from black to white.
- *Halftone* is a process of taking basic color dots (including black) and combining them to produce many other colors. Your printer driver can use a halftone setting to produce more shades of color.
- *Hue* is a variation of a primary color, such as green-blue.
- *Luminescence* is the brightness of a color, that is, of the amount of black or white added to a color. The larger the luminosity number, the lighter the color.
- *Pixel* is each individual dot or square of color in a picture or bitmapped (or raster) graphic.
- *Resolution* is the number of dots that make up an image on a screen or printer—the higher the resolution, the denser the number of dots and "higher resolution" of the print. There are two types of resolution: spatial and output. Spatial resolution is defined in terms of width and height and is expressed in pixels. Output resolution is defined in terms of the number of dots per inch, or dpi. Typical monitors display images in 96 dpi and inkjet and laser printers print from 150 dpi to 300 dpi. However, some photo-quality printers can print at 600 dpi in black and to 1200 dpi to 2400 dpi in color.
- *Reverse* is a black background and white foreground, or white type against a colored background.
- *RGB* is an acronym for red, green, and blue. Each pixel on your computer monitor is made up of these three colors.
- *Saturation* is the purity of a color. A color is completely pure, or saturated, when it is not diluted with white. Red, for example, has a high saturation.

(Before completing computer exercises, delete the Chapter04 folder on your disk. Next, copy the Chapter05 folder from the CD that accompanies this textbook to your disk and then make Chapter05 the active folder.)

exercise

Creating an Announcement Using a Table

As an employee of Midwest Community College, you are responsible for preparing advertisements for new courses and workshops sponsored by the college. Create the announcement in a table format.

1. At a clear document screen, create the announcement in Figure 5.11 by completing the following steps (you will create a table similar to Figure 5.1):
   a. Change all of the margins to 0.75 inch and change the zoom to *Whole Page*.
   b. Click the Tables and Borders button (ninth button from the right) on the Standard toolbar. The arrow pointer will display as a pen.
   c. Position the pen in the upper left corner, then drag to create the outer boundary lines of a table approximately 1 inch from all edges of the page. The lines should be similar to the illustration at the right. *(Hint: Use your horizontal and vertical ruler bars to guide you.)*
   d. Position the pen approximately 2 inches below the top boundary line of the table and draw a horizontal line by clicking and dragging.
   e. Position the pen approximately 2 inches above the bottom boundary line of the table and draw another horizontal line by clicking and dragging.
   f. Position the pen approximately 0.75 inch below the line created in Step 1e, and then draw another horizontal line by clicking and dragging.

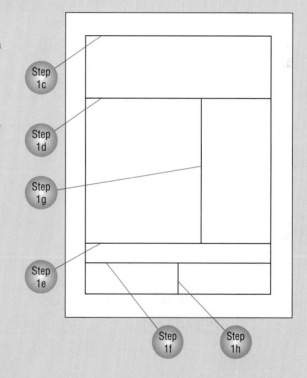

   g. In the center section, position the pen approximately 2.5 inches from the right boundary line and draw a vertical line by clicking and dragging.
   h. In the bottom section, position the pen at the approximate center of the last row, then draw a vertical line by clicking and dragging.
   i. Click the Draw Table button to turn this feature off.
   j. Change the zoom to *Page Width*.
2. Insert the announcement text by completing the following steps:
   a. Position the insertion point in the first cell and insert the **Navigating** file located in your Chapter05 folder. Select the WordArt text and drag it to the center of the cell.

b. Position the insertion point in the first cell of the second row of the table and insert the **Sailing** file located in your Chapter05 folder. Click the down-pointing arrow at the right of the Align Top Left button on the Tables and Borders toolbar and select Align Center Left.

c. Position the insertion point in the second cell in the second row of the table and insert the image shown in Figure 5.11. Click Insert, point to Picture, and then click Clip Art. At the Clip Art task pane, type j0292162.wmf in the *Search for* text box and then click Go. If the sailing picture shown in Figure 5.11 is not available or if you want to find a sailing picture of your own choosing, type sailing and then click Go. Scroll to find the image, click once on the image to insert it, and then size the image similar to Figure 5.11.

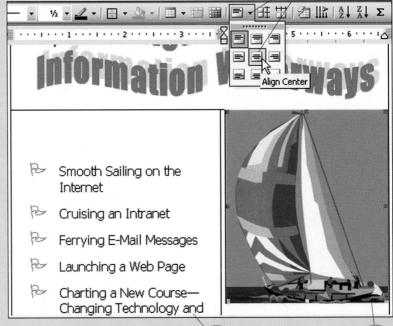

d. With the image selected, center the image by clicking the Align Center button on the Tables and Borders toolbar.

e. Position the insertion point in the cell in the third row of the table, then insert **Trade Fair** located in your Chapter05 folder. Make sure that the text is centered horizontally and vertically in the cell.

f. Position the insertion point in the first cell in the fourth row and insert **Midwest** located in your Chapter05 folder. Align the text at the left and center it vertically.

g. Position the insertion point in the second cell in the fourth row and insert **Register** located in your Chapter05 folder. Align the text at the right and center it vertically.

3. Create the AutoShape object in Figure 5.11 by completing the following steps. *(Hint: Turn off the drawing canvas feature by clicking **Tools**, **Options**, **General tab**, and remove the check mark at the* **Automatically create drawing canvas when inserting AutoShapes** *option.)*

   a. Display the Drawing toolbar.

   b. Click the AutoShapes button on the Drawing toolbar, point to Basic Shapes, and then click the Sun shape in the sixth row.

   c. Drag the crosshairs from the top left of the table and draw the Sun shape similar to Figure 5.11.

   d. Add a gradient fill to the Sun shape by completing the following steps:

      1) Select the Sun shape, click the down-pointing arrow at the right of the Fill Color button on the Drawing toolbar, and then click Fill Effects.

      2) At the Fill Effects dialog box, choose the Gradient tab, and then select *One color*.

      3) Click the down-pointing arrow at the right of the *Color 1* option box and select Gold (the second color from the left in the fourth row).

      4) Move the slider below *Color 1* to the position shown at the right between Dark and Light. In the *Shading styles* section, click *From center* and then click the first variant. Click OK.

      5) With the Sun shape still selected, click the Shadow Style button on the Drawing toolbar, and then select Shadow Style 13 (the first style from the left in the fourth row).

Step 3d3

Step 3d2

Step 3d4

Fill Effects

Gradient | Texture | Pattern | Picture

Colors
- One color
- Two colors
- Preset

Color 1:

Dark   Light

OK

Cancel

Transparency
From: 0 %
To: 0 %

Shading styles
- Horizontal
- Vertical
- Diagonal up
- Diagonal down
- From corner
- From center

Variants

Sample:

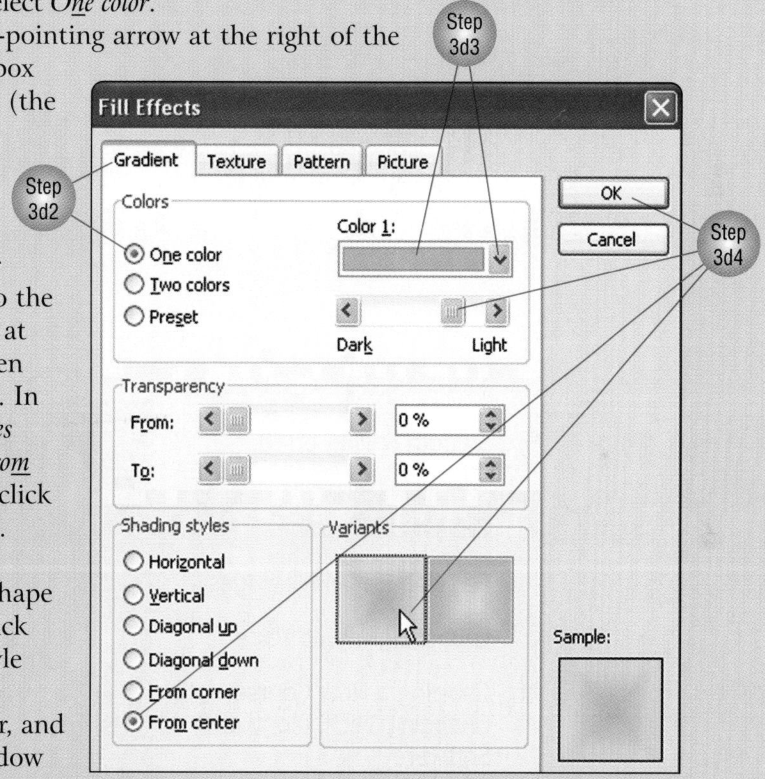

   e. View your announcement at Print Preview. Drag any boundary line in the table if the cells are not sized and positioned as in Figure 5.11. *(Hint: When you click a line in a table, the arrow pointer should display as two vertical bars with two arrows pointing to the left and right or as two horizontal bars pointing to top and bottom; drag to move the line, and then release the left mouse button when you are satisfied with the position.)* If the flyer displays too high or low on the page, change the top and/or bottom margins to help center the flyer vertically on the page. Adjust the position of the autoshape and/or WordArt if necessary. Click the Close button in Print Preview.

4. With the insertion point positioned in the table, click T<u>a</u>ble, point to Sele<u>c</u>t, and then click <u>T</u>able. Click the down-pointing arrow at the right of the Outside Border button on the Tables and Borders toolbar and then select No Border. *(Hint: Light gray gridlines may display if the* Show <u>G</u>ridlines *option is selected at the T<u>a</u>ble menu. These gridlines do not print.)*

5. Save, print, and then close **c05ex01, Sailing**.

FIGURE

5.11 *Exercise 1*

- Smooth Sailing on the Internet
- Cruising an Intranet
- Ferrying E-Mail Messages
- Launching a Web Page
- Charting a New Course— Changing Technology and Software

COMPUTER INFORMATION WORKSHOPS AND TRADE FAIR

MIDWEST COMMUNITY COLLEGE
465 East 86th Street
Indianapolis, IN 46240

Friday, July 22, 2005
8:30 a.m. to 3:30 p.m.
Register by phone: (317) 555-3909
Register online: http://www.emcp.net/mcc

Adding Lines, Borders, and Special Effects to Text, Objects, and Pictures

As discussed in Chapter 3, ruled lines can be used in a document to create a focal point, draw the eye across or down the page, separate columns and sections, or add visual appeal. Borders are generally used to frame text or an image with more than one side. Shading can be added to the background of a table, a paragraph, or selected text, or used as fill in a drawing object. Examples of lines, borders, shading, shadow, and 3-D effects are displayed in Figure 5.12.

FIGURE 5.12 *Sample Lines, Borders, Shading, Shadow, and 3-D Effects*

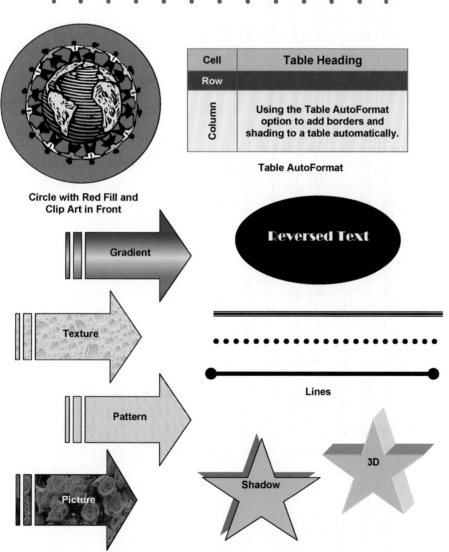

Adding Lines, Borders, and Frames

You can add a border to any or all sides of a table, a paragraph, or selected text in a document. You can add a page border or an art border (such as a row of trees) to any or all sides of each page or section in a document. You can also add borders to text boxes, pictures, and imported pictures using tools on the Drawing toolbar.

Rules and/or borders can be drawn using the Line button or the Rectangle button on the Drawing toolbar, clicking the Border button on the Tables and Borders toolbar or the Formatting toolbar, or using the Borders and Shading dialog box on the Format menu.

In addition, graphic borders are available in Word 2003 and accessed as any other clip art.

Creating Automatic Lines

You can create automatic lines in Word 2003 by using any one of the following methods:

- Type three or more hyphens (-) and then press Enter to create a thin bottom border.
- Type three or more underscores (_) and then press Enter to create a thick bottom border.
- Type three or more equal signs (=) and then press Enter to create a double bottom line.
- Type three or more pound symbols (#) and then press Enter to create a thick/thick/thin bottom border.
- Type three or more tildes (~) and then press Enter to create a wavy bottom border.
- Type three or more asterisks (*) and then press Enter to create a thick dotted bottom border.

Adding Lines and Borders to Tables

All tables default to a single ½-point black solid-line border that prints. To add a line or customized border to a table, display the Tables and Borders toolbar as shown in Figure 5.2. Select the cells where you want the line or border to appear and then click any one or more of the following buttons to customize the line or border: Line Style, Line Weight, Border Color, and/or the Border button. If you prefer drawing the line or border, use the Draw Table button. Alternatively, you can use the Table AutoFormat command to add borders and shading to a table automatically. To add a border to a table, click anywhere in the table. To add borders to specific cells, select only those cells, including the end-of-cell mark.

Adding a Page Border

DTP POINTERS
Use page borders sparingly; they tend to confine space and over decorate a page.

Word provides page borders that range from simple to highly ornate. Choose the art border that best complements the content of your document. Refer to Chapter 4 for additional information on the Page Border option in the Borders and Shading dialog box.

Adding Fill to Design Elements

You can add shading to the background of a table, a paragraph, or selected text. Shading added to drawing objects—including a text box or an AutoShape—is called a *fill*. You can fill drawing objects with solid or gradient (shaded) colors, a pattern, a texture, or a picture.

To add a picture as fill, such as the example in the announcement in Figure 5.15, select the Picture tab at the Fill Effects dialog box and then click the Select Picture button. At the Select Picture dialog box, make sure your desired photo or clip art file displays in the *Look in* option box and then click Insert or press Enter.

Alternatively, you may select a photograph or clip art at the Clip Art task pane, right-click the image, and then click Copy from the shortcut menu sending the image to the Office Clipboard. Proceed with accessing the Fill Effects dialog box, selecting the Picture tab, clicking the Select Picture button, and then pasting the image into the list box at the Select Picture dialog box. Finally, select the file and then click Insert. Numbers, such as ph02829.jpg, identify clip art images in Office 2003. Click the down-pointing arrow at the right of the desired image, click Preview/Properties as shown in Figure 5.13, and then write down the image number if you want to use it later.

F I G U R E

5.13 *Preview/Properties Dialog Box*

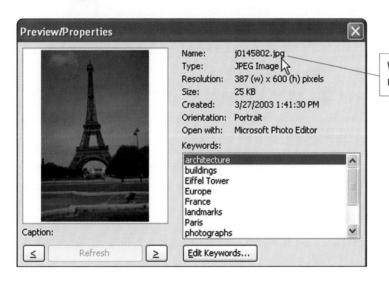

Write down the image number for later use.

Using the Drawing Gridlines

Word's drawing grid is a network of lines that help you align drawing objects, such as AutoShapes. As you drag or draw an object, Word pulls it into alignment with the nearest intersection of gridlines or other objects. By default, gridlines are not visible, but you may choose to display gridlines on the screen at the Drawing Grid dialog box. The horizontal and vertical spacing between the gridlines defaults to 0.13 inch, but you may change this setting. You also have the option to change the starting point or origin for the gridlines from the default 0 (zero) inch to any increments you choose from the margins as shown in Figure 5.14. To override settings for the gridlines temporarily, press the Alt key as you drag or draw an object. In addition, if the *Snap objects to grid* option is enabled, pressing an arrow key to nudge moves the object 1 point at a time.

5.14 *Drawing Grid Dialog Box*

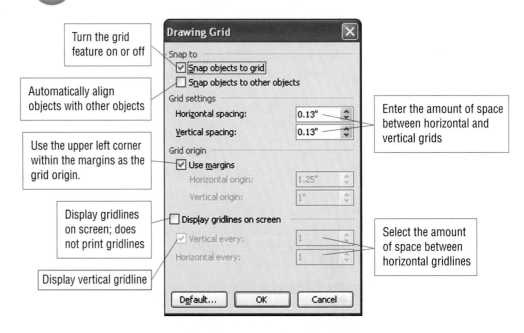

Turn the grid feature on or off

Automatically align objects with other objects

Use the upper left corner within the margins as the grid origin.

Display gridlines on screen; does not print gridlines

Display vertical gridline

Enter the amount of space between horizontal and vertical grids

Select the amount of space between horizontal gridlines

Turning On or Off Snap Objects to Grid

Click inside the *Snap objects to grid* check box at the Drawing Grid dialog box to insert a check mark and turn on this feature. To turn off this feature, remove the check mark. To align objects automatically with other AutoShape objects, click to insert a check mark in the *Snap objects to other objects* check box. Remove the check mark to turn off this feature.

Viewing the Gridlines

To view the gridlines on the screen, complete the following steps:

1. Display the Drawing toolbar.
2. Click Draw and then Grid.
3. At the Drawing Grid dialog box, click the *Display gridlines on screen* option (a check mark should display).

Changing the Spacing between the Drawing Gridlines

To change the spacing between the gridlines, complete the following steps:

1. Display the Drawing toolbar.
2. Click Draw and then Grid.
3. At the Drawing Grid dialog box, enter the spacing you want in the *Horizontal spacing* and *Vertical spacing* text boxes.

Changing the Starting Point for Gridlines

To change the starting point for gridlines, complete the following steps:

1. Display the Drawing toolbar.
2. Click <u>D</u>raw and then Gr<u>i</u>d.
3. At the Drawing Grid dialog box, in the *Horizontal origin* and *Vertical origin* option boxes, specify where you want the horizontal and vertical gridlines to begin, relative to the edges of the page. To use the current margin settings, click the *Use <u>m</u>argins* option.

Creating an Announcement with AutoShapes and Picture Fill and Using the Drawing Grid

Assume you are working part time at the Brighton Health & Fitness Center while attending classes at a local community college. Prepare an announcement promoting a new summer program. The location of the photos may vary; substitute different images if necessary.

1. Create the announcement in Figure 5.15 by completing the following steps:
   a. Open **Health** located in your Chapter05 folder.
   b. Save the document with Save <u>A</u>s and name it **c05ex02, Health**.
   c. Turn on the Show/Hide ¶ feature.
   d. Display the Drawing toolbar.
   e. Select *Healthy choices* point *to healthy lives...*, change the font to 36-point Papyrus in bold, and then select *point* and apply italics. Turn on kerning at 14 points. Remove the fill from this text box.

   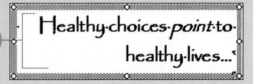

   f. Position the insertion point in the text box below *Healthy choices...* and insert **Cardio** located in your Chapter05 folder.
   g. Select all of the *Cardio* text, right-align the text, and then change the font to 14-point Arial; select *Summer Cardio Mix,* change the point size to 18 points, and apply bold.

   h. Remove the border around the text box containing the *Cardio* text.
   i. Select the text in the text box below *Summer Cardio Mix* and then change the alignment to center. (The text box contains the text *Brighton Health...*)
   j. Select *Brighton Health & Fitness Center* and change the font to 22-point Bauhaus 93 in Green.
   k. Select the address and change the font to 14-point Arial in Green.
   l. Select the text box containing *Brighton...* and change the Fill Color to No Fill and the Line Color to No Line.
   m. Position the insertion point in the text box behind the *Brighton* text, and insert the symbol in Figure 5.15 by completing the following steps:
      1) Click <u>I</u>nsert and then <u>S</u>ymbol.

2) Choose the Symbols tab, select the Webdings font, and then select the **Υ** symbol (Webdings: 134), located seventh from the left in the seventh row. (This symbol is a logo for Brighton.)
3) Click Insert and then Close.
4) Select the symbol and change the point size to 175 points and the color to Gray-25%. Position the text box as shown in Figure 5.15.
5) Change the line color of the text box to No Line.

2. Create an underlining grid to help in aligning the arrow shapes shown in Figure 5.15 by completing the following steps:

   a. Click Draw on the Drawing toolbar and then click Grid.

   b. At the Drawing Grid dialog box make sure a check mark displays in the *Snap objects to grid* check box.

   c. In the *Grid settings* section, type **0.22** in the *Horizontal spacing* and *Vertical spacing* text boxes.

   d. In the *Grid origin* section, make sure a check mark displays in the *Use margins* check box.

   e. Make sure a check mark displays in the *Display gridlines on screen* check box. Also, make sure a check mark displays in the *Vertical every* check box and type **2** in the *Vertical every* and *Horizontal every* text boxes. Click OK.

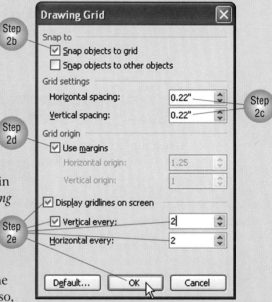

3. Create the arrows by completing the following steps:

   a. Click the AutoShapes button on the Drawing toolbar, point to Block Arrows, and then click the Striped Right Arrow (the first arrow from the left in the fifth row).

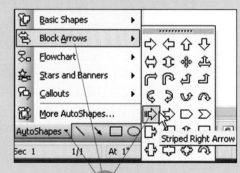

   b. Drag the crosshairs to create an arrow similar to Figure 5.15. Double-click the arrow shape to access the Format AutoShape dialog box. Choose the Size tab and change the *Height* option to *2.64"* and the *Width* option to *3.08"* in the *Size and rotate* section.

   c. Choose the Layout tab and make sure the wrapping style is In front of text and then click OK.

   d. Hold down the Ctrl key as you select the arrow shape and drag a copy below the first shape as shown at the right. The drawing grid will pull your arrow shape to the closest gridline.

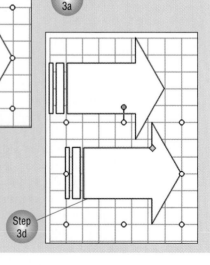

e. Copy another arrow shape below the last one and position it as shown in Figure 5.15.
4. Add the photo picture fill by completing the following steps:
   a. Display the Clip Art task pane.
   b. Click the down-pointing arrow at the *Results should be* option box and then remove the check marks from the different media check boxes except for the *Photographs* check box.

   c. Type **vegetables** in the *Search for* text box and then click Go.
   d. Locate the vegetable photograph **(j0182758.jpg)** shown in Figure 5.15 or a different photograph of your choosing. *(Hint: Remember that you can type the file name, j0182758.jpg, in the* Search for *text box or scroll to find an image you would like to use.)*
   e. Right-click the photograph and then click Copy at the shortcut menu.
   f. Select the first arrow, click the down-pointing arrow at the right of the Fill Color button on the Drawing toolbar, and then click Fill Effects.
   g. At the Fill Effects dialog box, click the Picture tab and then click the Select Picture button.
   h. At the Select Picture dialog box, right-click in the white area of the dialog box and then click Paste.
   i. Select the photograph and then click Insert.
   j. At the Fill Effects dialog box, place a check mark in the *Lock picture aspect ratio* option and then click OK.

   k. Complete steps similar to Steps 4c–4j to insert a fruit photograph in the second AutoShape. *(Hint: The fruit picture in Figure 5.15 is j0144470.jpg.)*
   l. Complete steps similar to Steps 4c–4j to insert an exercise photograph in the third AutoShape. *(Hint: The exercise photograph is j0185177.jpg.)*

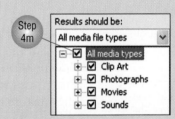

   m. Click the down-pointing arrow at the *Results should be* option box in the Clip Art task pane and add a check mark to the *All media types* check box.
5. View the document in Print Preview and make any necessary adjustments.
6. Remove the check marks from the *Snap objects to grid* and *Display gridlines on screen* options at the Drawing Grid dialog box.
7. Save, print, and then close **c05ex02, Health**.

Healthy choices *point* to healthy lives...

Summer Cardio Mix
One hour of multiple cardiovascular segments
consisting of aerobics, step, circuits,
and interval training; and weight
management training

Begins May 5 and meets for 8 weeks on Monday,
Wednesday, and Friday

Call for information and registration
(317) 555-7200 or online www.emcp.net/brighton

Brighton Health & Fitness Center
440 N. Keystone Avenue
Indianapolis, IN 46201

Matching Colors

RGB
Stands for the colors Red, Green, and Blue.

HSL
Stands for Hue, Saturation, and Luminescence.

To make your document look even more professional, match a color from an image used in your document to your font color as shown in Figure 5.16. To match colors, ungroup the clip art image, select a segment that contains the color you want to use, and then write down the values for Red, Green, and Blue *(RGB)*, or click the down-pointing arrow at the right of the Color model and record the values for Hue, Saturation, and Luminescence *(HSL)*. The RGB and HSL settings are on the Custom tab of the Colors dialog box. Use the same values to color your fonts and/or other drawing objects.

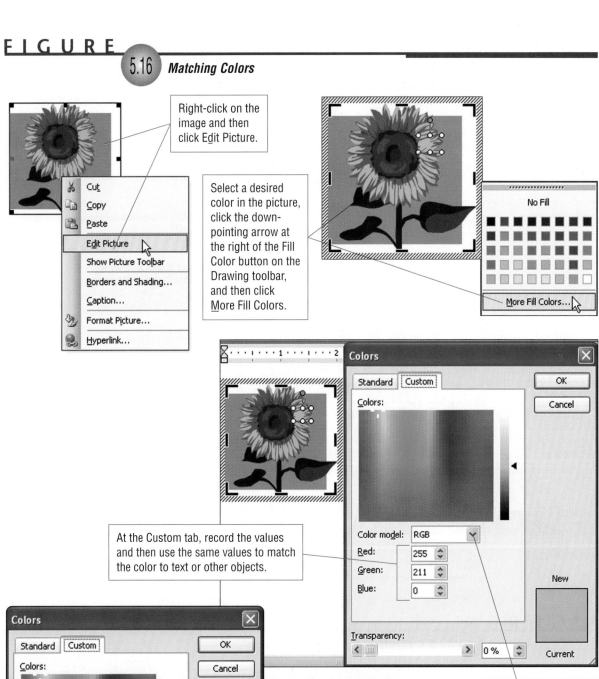

Right-click on the image and then click Edit Picture.

Select a desired color in the picture, click the down-pointing arrow at the right of the Fill Color button on the Drawing toolbar, and then click More Fill Colors.

At the Custom tab, record the values and then use the same values to match the color to text or other objects.

Click the down-pointing arrow to select the *RGB* color model.

Click the down-pointing arrow at the right of the Font Color button on the Drawing toolbar, click More Colors, and then type the same values from the selected area of the picture to apply the color to text.

Adding Special Effects with Shadows and 3-D

Shadow Style

You can add depth to lines, drawing objects, and some pictures by using the Shadow Style button (second button from the right) on the Drawing toolbar. To make adjustments to the shadow effect, click Shadow Settings at the bottom of the Shadow Styles palette, and then click the button that corresponds with your desired effect. Figure 5.17 displays the Shadow Settings toolbar. You can add either a shadow or a 3-D effect to a drawing object, but not both.

FIGURE

5.17 *Shadow Styles Palette and Shadow Settings Toolbar*

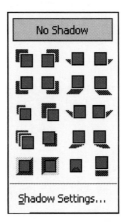

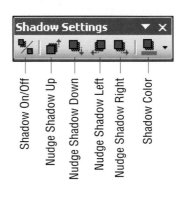

3D Style

You can add a 3-D effect to lines, AutoShapes, and other drawing objects by clicking the 3-D Style button (last button) on the Drawing toolbar. You can modify any of the settings by clicking 3-D Settings, then selecting options to change color, angle, direction, and so on at the 3-D Settings toolbar as shown in Figure 5.18. Experiment with the settings—you will be amazed by the possibilities.

FIGURE

5.18 *3-D Effects and 3-D Settings Toolbar*

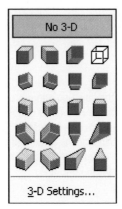

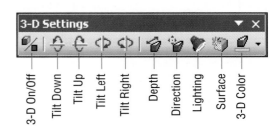

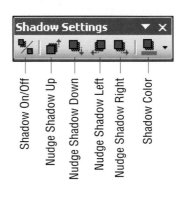

Editing Pictures

The Edit tab of the Options dialog box controls which drawing or image editing program will open when you select an image to be edited. Typically, your choices will be Microsoft Office Word or Microsoft Photo Editor as shown in Figure 5.19.

F I G U R E

5.19 *Choosing a Picture Editor*

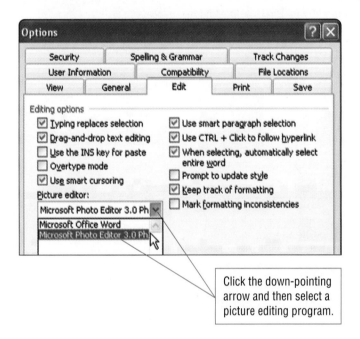

Every edition of Office 2003 also includes an applet called Microsoft Office Picture Manager as shown in Figure 5.20. The Picture Manager is found in the Microsoft Office Tools group on the All Programs menu. It lets you organize collections of image files from disks, shared network folders, and SharePoint Web sites. You can also compress and resize images and perform image-editing tasks, such as removing "red eye" from photographs. In addition, you can convert images to alternative formats (for instance, from Bitmap format to JPEG or GIF format).

5.20 *Microsoft Office Picture Manager*

Click to automatically correct the color balance of a picture or to change the hue and saturation settings.

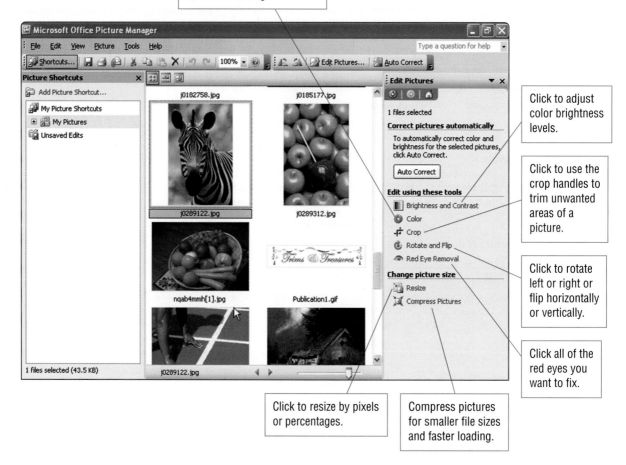

Click to adjust color brightness levels.

Click to use the crop handles to trim unwanted areas of a picture.

Click to rotate left or right or flip horizontally or vertically.

Click all of the red eyes you want to fix.

Click to resize by pixels or percentages.

Compress pictures for smaller file sizes and faster loading.

Editing Pictures Using Microsoft Office Word

Microsoft Office Word is a graphic editor available within Word. After choosing the desired graphic editor at the Options dialog box, you can invoke the editor by selecting the image, right-clicking the mouse, and choosing Edit Picture from the shortcut menu. The object has become ungrouped and you may click on any part of the object and use the buttons on the Drawing toolbar to alter the image. When the picture becomes a drawing object, the drawing canvas automatically surrounds the object as shown in Figure 5.21.

5.21 *Editing a Picture Using the Drawing Toolbar*

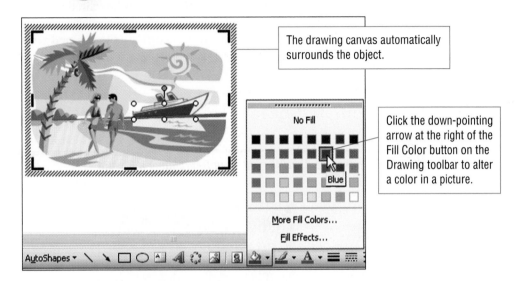

The drawing canvas automatically surrounds the object.

Click the down-pointing arrow at the right of the Fill Color button on the Drawing toolbar to alter a color in a picture.

Editing a Picture Using Microsoft Photo Editor

Word recognizes a wide variety of picture formats dependent on the graphic filters installed with your program. There are two types of pictures: vector and raster images. The main file formats include extensions such as .gif, .jpeg, .bmp, .tif, and .wmf. The GIF file format is normally used on a Web page and you may need to use a graphic editing program such as Microsoft Photo Editor to alter these images. If you have installed Microsoft Photo Editor when you installed Office 2003, you may access it in Word by clicking Insert, Object, and then Microsoft Photo Editor 3.0 Photo as shown in Figure 5.22. At the Microsoft Photo Editor 3.0, you may click File and then Open and select the graphic file you want to alter.

F I G U R E

5.22 *Microsoft Photo Editor*

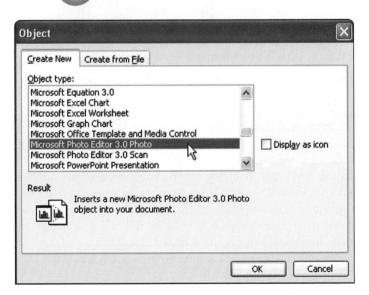

You may also edit a picture by using the Format Picture or Format Object dialog boxes accessed through the Format menu. More than one component of an image can be selected and altered at the same time by holding down the Shift key while clicking to select each component. ***Bitmaps*** can be edited in Microsoft Paint, Microsoft Photo Editor, or Microsoft Program Manager, or the program in which they were created. Most clip art is saved in ***metafiles*** (files named with a .wmf extension) and can be edited in Word using buttons on the Drawing toolbar as shown in Figure 5.23.

FIGURE

5.23 *Ungrouping, Altering, and Then Regrouping a Picture*

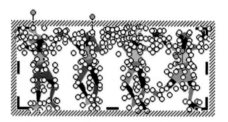

Ungrouping an image

Altering an image

Regrouping an image

Editing a Picture or Text Using Microsoft Office Document Imaging

With Microsoft Office Document Imaging, you can use a scanned document as easily as other Microsoft Office document on your computer. Access this Microsoft Office utility by clicking Start, pointing to All Programs, pointing to Microsoft Office Tools, and then clicking Microsoft Office Document Imaging from the pop-up menu. You should use Microsoft Office Document Imaging when you want to annotate a document and send it to others by e-mail or fax as shown in Figure 5.24, work with text or images contained in scanned documents or faxes, view scanned documents on the screen, or rearrange multiple-page documents.

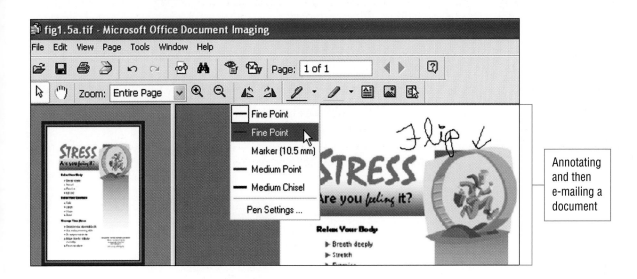

5.24 *Using Microsoft Office Document Imaging*

Annotating and then e-mailing a document

Changing the Way a Picture Displays

The *Insert/paste pictures as* option at the Options dialog box determines how Word inserts pictures relative to the text in your document. Click Tools, Options, and then choose the Edit tab to access the option to change the way a picture displays in Word. You can insert images inline with text, allow images to move with text, or wrap text around, in front of, or behind an image.

Creating a Flyer Using a Graphic Border

In Exercise 3, you will create a flyer using a Word graphic border and insert text inside the border. Compare Figure 5.25 to Figure 5.26. Which flyer attracts your attention and pulls you in to read the text? Of course, Figure 5.26 communicates more effectively because of the relevant graphic border and the varied typefaces, typestyles, and type sizes. How many typefaces can you find in this document? (There are only two typefaces used in this flyer—Brush Script MT and Lucinda Calligraphy.) A graphic border is inserted into a document like any other picture.

FIGURE 5.25 *Flyer Before*

Details by Design
Residential and Commercial Design

Think Spring!

Plan a new look for your home or office—complete
design service available

Space planning and consultation with trained professionals

Call today for an appointment
(614) 555-0898

25 W. Jefferson, Columbus, OH 43201

FIGURE 5.26 *Flyer After*

exercise 3

Creating a Flyer Using a Graphic Border

Assume your neighbor is an interior designer and you have offered to create a flyer advertising her company. Create the flyer in Figure 5.27 by completing the following steps:

1. Open **Graphic Border** located in your Chapter05 folder.
2. Save the document and name it **c05ex03, Border**.
3. Display the Drawing and Picture toolbars.
4. Turn on kerning at 14 points and above.
5. Customize the graphic border by completing the following steps:
   a. Double-click the graphic border and change the *Height* to *8.5"* and the *Width* to *5.97"* at the Format Picture dialog box, and then click OK.
   b. Select the image and then click the Center align button on the Formatting toolbar.
   c. Change the zoom to *Page Width*.
   d. Select the graphic, right-click, and then click E<u>d</u>it Picture at the shortcut menu. (The drawing canvas automatically displays around the image.)
   e. Click to select the large flower, hold down the Shift key, and then click the smaller flower.
   f. Click the down-pointing arrow at the right of the Fill Color button on the Drawing toolbar, select Rose (the first color from the left in the fifth row) or select a color of your choice, and then deselect the flowers.
   g. Change the zoom to *Whole Page*.

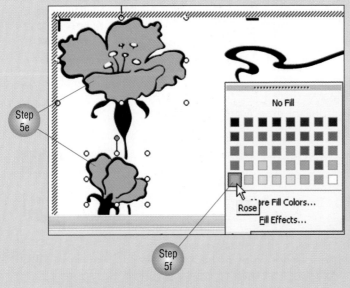

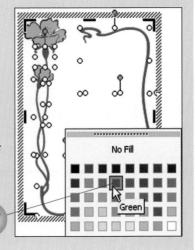

   h. Hold down the Shift key as you select each section of the stem (may involve several selections) and then click the down-pointing arrow at the right of the Fill Color button and select Green (the fourth color from the left in the second row). Also, make sure the Line Color is Green.

i. Click the Select Objects button on the Drawing toolbar. Drag the crosshairs from the top left corner of the image to the bottom right corner, release the mouse, click the <u>D</u>raw button on the Drawing toolbar and then click <u>G</u>roup.

6. Create a text box inside the graphic border by completing the following steps:

a. Click the Text Box button on the Drawing toolbar.

b. Drag the crosshairs inside the graphic border and draw a box near the inside edge of the graphic border.

c. Remove the border around the text box.

d. Position the insertion point inside the text box and type the following text in 12-point Times New Roman and change the zoom to *75%*:

Step 5i

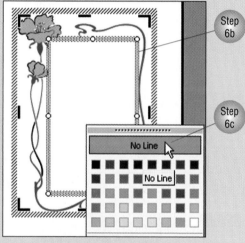

Step 6b

Step 6c

> Details by Design (Press Enter two times—press the backspace key if the AutoFormat feature automatically applies the Heading 1 style.)
>
> Press the Tab key and then type Residential and. (Press Enter.)
>
> Press the Tab key twice and then type Commercial Design. (Press Enter four times.)
>
> Think spring! (Press Enter four times.)
>
> Plan a new look for your home or office—complete design service available. (Use an em dash; press Enter three times.)
>
> We provide space planning and consultation with trained professionals. (Press Enter five times.)
>
> Call today for an appointment. (Press Enter.)
>
> 614.555.0898 (Press Enter.)
>
> 25 W. Jefferson • Columbus, OH • 43201 (Create the bullet symbol by pressing the Num Lock key on the keypad to turn it on, holding down the Alt key, typing 0149 on the keypad, and then turning off the Num Lock key.)

e. Format the company name in WordArt by completing the following steps:

1) Select *Details by Design* and then click the WordArt button on the Drawing toolbar.

2) At the WordArt Gallery, click the style in the fourth row and second from the left and then click OK.

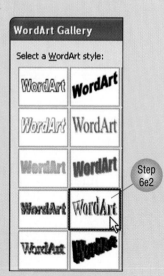

Step 6e2

3) At the Edit WordArt Text dialog box, change the font to 40-point Brush Script MT and then click OK.

4) Select the WordArt, click the Format WordArt button on the WordArt toolbar, choose the Colors and Line tab, click the down-pointing arrow at the right of the *Fill Color* option box, and then click *Fill* Effects.

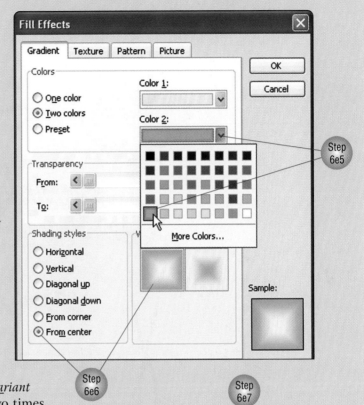

Step 6e5

Step 6e6

Step 6e7

5) At the Fill Effects dialog box, click the down-pointing arrow at the right of the *Color 2* option and then select the Rose color (or a color of your choice).

6) In the *Shading styles* section, click the *From center* option and then click the first option in the *Variant* section. Click OK two times.

7) Click the WordArt Shape button and then click the Chevron Up shape in the first row and fifth shape from the left in the shape palette.

f. Select *Residential and Commercial Design* and then change the font to 14-point Lucida Calligraphy and the font color to Indigo.

g. Position the insertion point before *Think spring!* and press Ctrl + Shift + End to select from the insertion point to the end of the document. Click the Center align button on the Standard toolbar.

h. Select *Think spring!* and then change the font to 22-point Lucida Calligraphy in Green.

i. Select the next two paragraphs and then change the font to 12-point Lucida Calligraphy in Indigo.

j. Select *Call today for an appointment. 614.555.0898* and *25 W. Jefferson • Columbus, OH • 43201* and then change the font to 10-point Lucida Calligraphy in Indigo.

k. Resize the text box if necessary.

7. View the document at Print Preview.

8. Save, print, and then close **c05ex03, Border**.

FIGURE

5.27 *Exercise 3*

Customizing Pictures Using the Picture Toolbar

When you select a picture that you have inserted into a document, the Picture toolbar will appear with tools you can use to crop the picture, add a border to it, or adjust its brightness and contrast, as shown in Figure 5.28. If the Picture toolbar does not appear, right-click the picture and then click Show Picture Toolbar on the shortcut menu.

5.28   *Picture Toolbar*

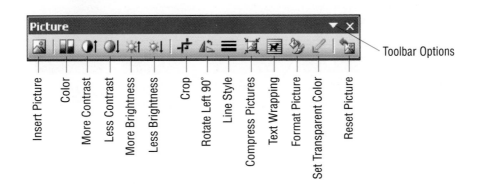

Toolbar Options

Insert Picture
Color
More Contrast
Less Contrast
More Brightness
Less Brightness
Crop
Rotate Left 90°
Line Style
Compress Pictures
Text Wrapping
Format Picture
Set Transparent Color
Reset Picture

Using the Insert Picture Button

To quickly insert a picture into your document, display the Picture toolbar and click the Insert Picture button (first button from the left) on the Picture toolbar.

Insert Picture

Using the Color Button

The Color button provides options to change the color of an image into varying shades of gray, black and white, or <u>W</u>ashout (lightened to create a watermark) as shown in Figure 5.29.

Color

FIGURE

5.29   *Color Options*

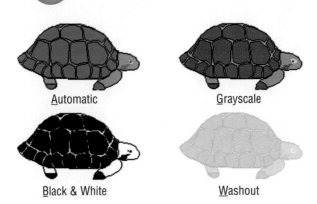

<u>A</u>utomatic   <u>G</u>rayscale

<u>B</u>lack & White   <u>W</u>ashout

Using the Contrast and Brightness Buttons

Less contrast gives a grayer, "flatter" picture; more contrast means more black and white. The Brightness options can darken or brighten a picture as shown in Figure 5.30. In addition, brightness and contrast can be altered at the Format Picture or Format Object dialog boxes. These options are found in the *Image control* section of the Picture or Object tab as slider or percentage settings.

More Contrast   More Brightness

Less Contrast   Less Brightness

5.30 *Contrast and Brightness Settings*

| More Contrast | Less Contrast | More Brightness | Less Brightness |

Crop

Using the Crop Button

Crop

To trim horizontal and vertical edges off a picture.

To *crop* is to trim horizontal and vertical edges off a picture as shown in Figure 5.31. You can crop by using the cropping tool (seventh button from the left) on the Picture toolbar. Photos are usually cropped to focus attention on a particular area of a picture (for instance, a person's face). You can also crop pictures using the Format Picture dialog box by typing specific increments in the *Crop from* text boxes. Click the Re̲set button to return to the original picture.

F I G U R E

5.31 *Scaling and Cropping a Picture*

| Original Picture | Scaled Picture | Cropped Picture |

Scaling or Resizing a Picture or Object

Scale

To increase or decrease the size of an image proportionally or disproportionately.

To *scale* a picture or object is to increase or decrease the size of an image proportionally or disproportionately, as shown in Figure 5.31. To resize a picture or object, move the mouse over a sizing handle until it turns into a two-headed arrow. Drag a corner sizing handle to scale a picture proportionally or drag a side handle to scale a picture disproportionately. Hold down the Ctrl key as you click and drag the mouse over a sizing handle and this will keep the image centered.

In addition, you can scale or size a picture at either the Format Object or Format Picture dialog boxes. If you want your picture to be a specific size, type increments in the *Height* and *Wi̲dth* boxes in the *Size and rotate* section. If you want to scale your picture by percentages, use the options in the *Scale* section, and enter percentages in the *Height* and *Width* text boxes. To scale proportionally, select the *Lock a̲spect ratio* option. To scale in relation to the original size, select the *R̲elative to original picture size* option.

Using the Rotate Left 90° Button

You can use the Rotate Left 90° button to turn an image to the left by 90 degrees. More options to rotate or flip an image are available at the Draw menu accessed at the Drawing toolbar.

Rotate Left 90°

Using the Line Style Button

You can add a border around a picture by clicking the Line Style button on the Picture toolbar as shown in Figure 5.32. You may need to change the text wrapping option before applying a line style to your picture.

Line Style

F I G U R E

5.32   *Adding a Border to a Picture*

Click the Line Style button and then select a line option of your choice.

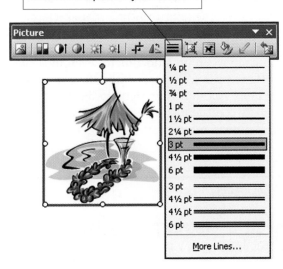

Using the Compress Pictures Button

Since Word may be used as a Web editor, it is becoming more important to control file sizes. You can click the Compress Pictures button on the Picture toolbar to reduce the size of a selected picture or you can choose an option to reduce all pictures in a document. If you choose the *Web/Screen* option as shown in Figure 5.33, Word cuts the image resolution to 96 dpi, which is adequate for a Web page. If you choose *Print*, Word reduces the image resolution to 200 dpi, which is adequate for most desktop printers, but not for high-resolution professional offset printers.

Compress Pictures

If you click the *Compress pictures* check box option, Word compresses the picture similar to applying JPEG compression. As with JPEG compression, this technique reduces the quality of the picture, but usually not too noticeably. If you click the *Delete cropped areas of pictures* option, Word deletes the information associated with the crop and the image becomes smaller, but you can no longer uncrop the picture.

5.33 *Compressing a Picture*

Compresses current selected picture

Compresses all pictures in a document

Compresses to output at 96 dpi

Compresses to output at 200 dpi

Can choose other options to reduce file size, but will not compress

Applies JPEG compression

Discards cropped areas

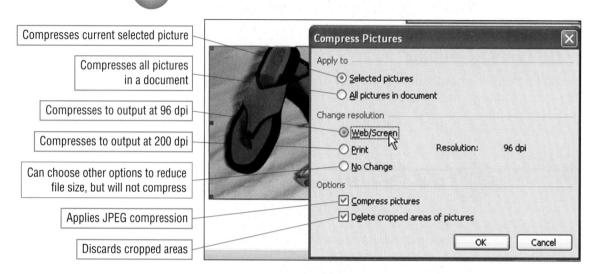

Using the Text Wrapping Button

Text Wrapping

You can place a picture anywhere in a document, even in a margin, and wrap text around it in many different ways. You can shape the text around a picture by editing the wrapping points as shown in Figure 5.34. In addition, you can specify the amount of space between the picture and the text as illustrated and discussed in Chapter 2. *(Hint: To insert sample text, type =rand() and then press Enter.)*

5.34 *Using Wrapping Points*

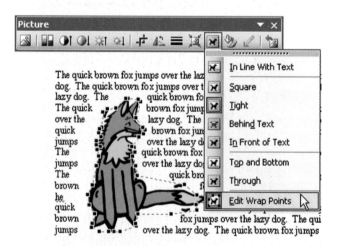

Using the Format Picture Button

Format Picture

To quickly access the Format Picture dialog box, click the Format Picture button (third button from the right) on the Picture toolbar. At the Advanced Layout dialog box, you are able to create precise settings for positioning and wrapping text around images.

Using the Set Transparent Color Button

The Set Transparent Color button on the Picture toolbar offers a tool that can be used to alter colors in bitmap graphics. You can make only one color transparent. When printed, transparent areas will be the same color as the paper they are printed on. In Figure 5.35, an area of the picture was made transparent and another color was added by clicking the Fill Color button on the Drawing toolbar. In an electronic display, such as a Web page or a PowerPoint presentation, transparent areas will be the same color as the background. The area will display in a checkerboard pattern, but will print correctly. To make an area transparent on a .gif or .jpeg picture, you may have to open the file in a graphic editing program such as Microsoft Photo Editor.

Set Transparent Color

Transparent color can also be applied to a picture at the Colors and Lines tab of the Format Picture dialog box. In the *Fill* section, select a fill color, and then drag the transparency slider to lighten the shade of the color you have chosen as shown in Figure 5.36.

FIGURE 5.35 *Using the Set Transparent Color Tool*

1. Original bitmap graphic

Set Transparent Color

2. Click area to become transparent using the Set Transparent Color tool on the Picture toolbar.

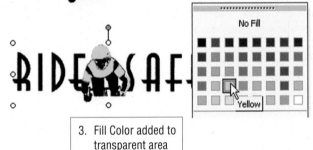

No Fill

Yellow

3. Fill Color added to transparent area

FIGURE 5.36 *Applying Transparent Fill Color*

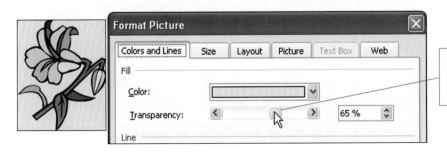

Format Picture

| Colors and Lines | Size | Layout | Picture | Text Box | Web |

Fill

Color:

Transparency: 65 %

Line

Drag the transparency slider left to darken a color and right to lighten a color.

Using the Reset Picture Button

The Reset Picture button returns the picture to its original configuration.

Reset Picture

exercise 4

Creating a Flyer Promoting a Service

As an employee of the Edward Cardiovascular Institute, you will create a flyer promoting a new heart scan service. The flyer will incorporate an asymmetrical design in which the text will align off center. Contrast is achieved by using thick and thin fonts in serif and sans serif designs. Spot color is used to enhance directional flow and reinforce the logo color. In addition, a dark red fill color is added to the clip art image to promote continuity. The clock image in this exercise will be resized, ungrouped, regrouped, and rotated. (Substitute a different image and/or different fonts if necessary.)

1. At a clear document screen, create the flyer in Figure 5.37 by completing the following steps:
    a. Open **Heart Scan** located in your Chapter05 folder.
    b. Select *ANNOUNCING* and change the font to 22-point Tahoma in Dark Red and change the character spacing to Expanded <u>B</u>y 17 points. Turn on kerning.
    c. Select *Ultra Fast* and change the font to 48-point Elephant and expanded by 3 points then turn on kerning. Select *Fast* and apply italics.
    d. Select *Heart Scan* and change the font to 48-point Elephant and expanded by 3 points then turn on kerning.
    e. Select *from the Edward Cardiovascular Institute* and change the font to 22-point. Tahoma bold in Dark Red and turn on kerning. Deselect the text.
2. Save the document with Save <u>A</u>s and name it **c05ex04, Scan**.
3. Insert and then customize a clip art image by completing the following steps:
    a. Display the Clip Art task pane.
    b. Position your insertion point at the top of the page. Type j0287017.wmf or clocks in the *Search for* text box and then click Go.
    c. Scroll until you find the clocks picture shown at the right and in Figure 5.37 (some colors have been changed). Insert the image by clicking on it once. *(Note: Substitute a different image and different fonts if desired.)*

Step 3c

    d. Select the image, change the text wrap to I<u>n</u> Front of Text, and then drag the image to the left and even with the top of the text box containing *from the Edward....*
    e. Double-click the image and change the *He<u>i</u>ght* to 2.75". (The width will adjust automatically in proportion to the height.)
    f. With the image still selected, click <u>D</u>raw on the Drawing toolbar and then click <u>U</u>ngroup. At the prompt asking if you want to convert this picture to a drawing object, click Yes. The drawing canvas will display (even if you turned off the automatic drawing canvas feature). Sizing handles will also display.

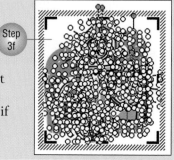

Step 3f

g. Click outside the image, hold down the Shift key, and then click each of the three orange areas in the background of the image. Sizing handles will display around each selected area.

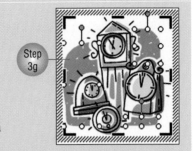

Step 3g

h. With the background areas selected, click the down-pointing arrow at the right of the Fill Color button on the Drawing toolbar and then click Dark Red in the second row. The background color should change from orange to dark red.

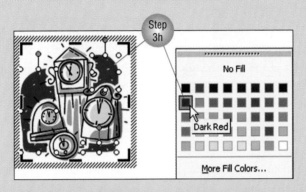

Step 3h

i. Click the sage green color on the clock on the left side of the image, click the down-pointing arrow at the right of the Fill Color button, and then click More Fill Colors.

j. At the Colors dialog box, click the Custom tab, and then write down the settings for RGB. Click OK.

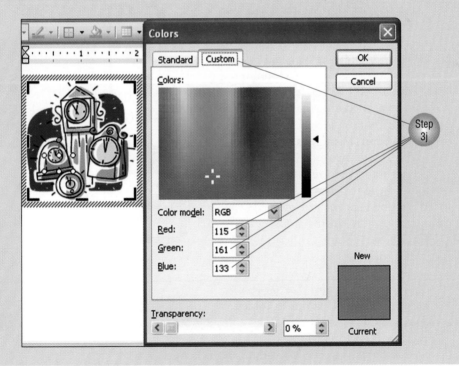

Step 3j

k. Click the Select Objects button on the Drawing toolbar, drag the arrow to create a dashed box around the image (just inside the drawing canvas) beginning at the top left corner and continuing to the bottom right corner, and then release the mouse (an ungrouped image should display). Click the <u>D</u>raw button on the Drawing toolbar and then select <u>G</u>roup. (Only eight sizing handles should display around the entire image.)

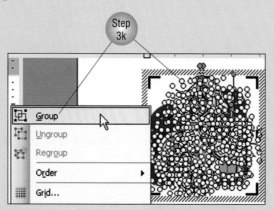

l. Click the green rotating handle on the image and drag it to the left slightly as shown in Figure 5.37.

m. Select the image and position it similarly to Figure 5.37.

4. Format the remaining text by completing the following steps:

a. Select *15 minutes, start to finish…*, change the font to 22-point Tahoma bold, and then change the font color using the settings you recorded in Step 3j. Remove the border around the text box.

b. Select *Take it during your lunch hour…* and change the font to 18-point Tahoma bold. Select *(and be back in time…)* and change the font to 12-point Tahoma bold.

c. Insert **Scan**, located in your Chapter05 folder, in the text box below the text in Step 4b and then remove the border around the text box.

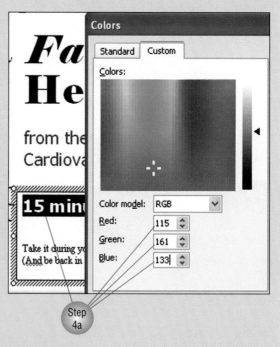

5. Insert the logo shown in Figure 5.37 by completing the following steps:

a. Click <u>I</u>nsert, point to <u>P</u>icture, and then click <u>F</u>rom File.

b. At the Insert Picture dialog box, double-click **Edward Cardio BW** located in your Chapter05 folder.

c. Select the logo, click the Text Wrapping button on the Picture toolbar, and then click I<u>n</u> Front of Text.

d. Size and position the logo similarly to Figure 5.37.

6. View the document in Print Preview and make any necessary adjustments.

7. Save, print, and then close **c05ex04, Scan**.

ANNOUNCING

Ultra *Fast* Heart Scan

from the Edward
Cardiovascular Institute

15 minutes, start to finish...

Take it during your lunch hour...
(and be back in time for your 1 o'clock meeting).

Ultra Fast Heart Scan is the simple, noninvasive
heart test you have heard about—the one that
uses powerful electron beam tomography to
detect coronary artery calcification at an early,
treatable state. It's the only test in the western
suburbs with this technology.

To schedule your appointment,
call Monday–Friday, 8 a.m. to 5 p.m.

1-877-45-HEART

EDWARD
CARDIOVASCULAR INSTITUTE

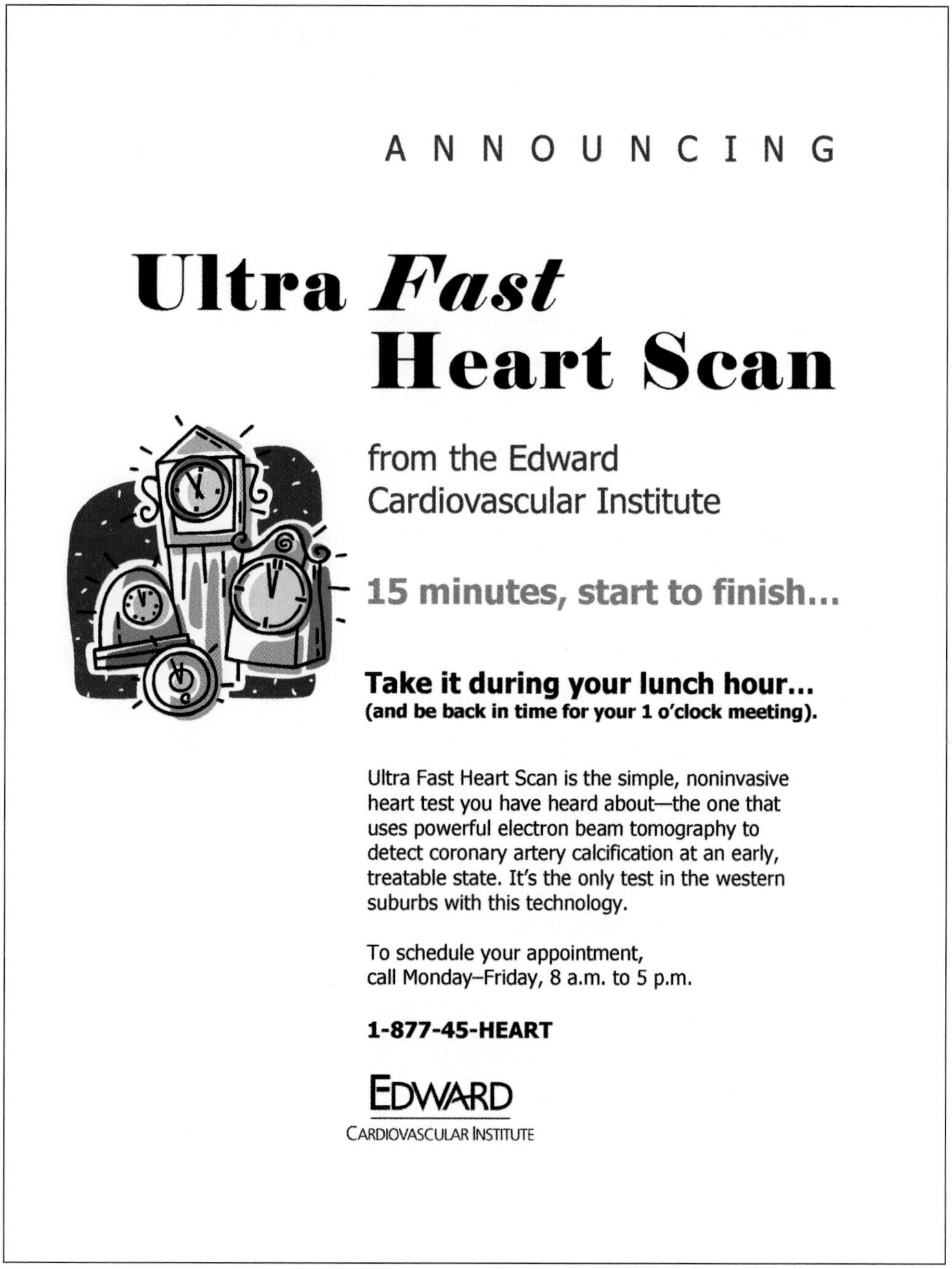

Reviewing the Drawing Toolbar

The Drawing toolbar in Figure 5.38 provides tools you can use to draw, manipulate,
and format all kinds of drawing objects. A brief explanation of each tool follows.
Additional information may be accessed from the Help menu.

5.38 *Drawing Toolbar*

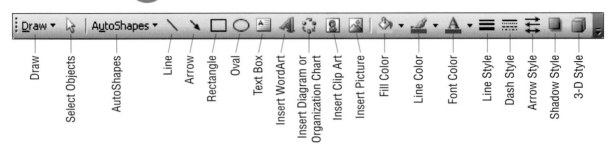

Draw — Select Objects — AutoShapes — Line — Arrow — Rectangle — Oval — Text Box — Insert WordArt — Insert Diagram or Organization Chart — Insert Clip Art — Insert Picture — Fill Color — Line Color — Font Color — Line Style — Dash Style — Arrow Style — Shadow Style — 3-D Style

Using the Draw Button

Draw

The <u>D</u>raw menu has many shape adjustment commands, including grouping, ordering, using a grid, nudging, aligning, distributing, rotating, flipping, editing points, changing shape, and setting AutoShape defaults.

Using the Group, Ungroup, and Regroup Commands

When you group pictures or objects, they function as a single unit. Ungrouping a group releases the individual components from a whole unit. Ungrouping and regrouping the image converts the clip art image into an object, which can be edited using the Drawing tools. See Figure 5.23 for examples of grouping and ungrouping.

Changing the Order of Pictures and Objects

When you create an object on top of another object, you create an overlapping stack. You can rearrange the stacked objects by using the O<u>r</u>der command on the <u>D</u>raw menu. You can also stack groups and then change their stacking order as shown in Figure 5.39.

5.39 *Changing the Stacking Order of Objects*

Bring to Fron<u>t</u>
places a selected object
in front of others.

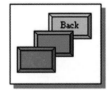

Send to Back
places a selected object
behind others.

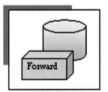

Bring <u>F</u>orward
brings forward a single
object or picture.

Send <u>B</u>ackward
sends a single picture
or object backward.

Bring in Front of Text
brings a picture
in front of text.

Send Be<u>h</u>ind Text
sends a picture
behind text.

Using the Grid Option

The drawing grid is an invisible grid of lines that aligns drawing objects and draws straight lines. It acts as a magnet, attracting your crosshairs as you draw lines at certain increments.

Using the Nudge Option

To *nudge* an object is to move it in small increments. Select the object you want to nudge, click Draw, point to Nudge, and then click the direction you want to nudge the object. You can also nudge an object by selecting it and pressing the arrow keys. Press the arrow keys to nudge an object in one-point increments.

Using the Align or Distribute Command

You can align two or more drawing objects relative to each other by the left, center, right, top, middle, or bottom edges, or distribute them equally horizontally or vertically as shown in Figure 5.40.

F I G U R E

5.40 **Aligning and Distributing Drawing Objects**

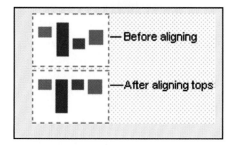
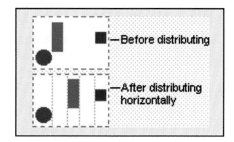

Using the Rotate or Flip Command

You can rotate a drawing object or group of drawing objects 90 degrees to the left or right, or flip a drawing object or group of drawing objects horizontally or vertically as shown in Figure 5.41. Select the object, click Draw, point to Rotate or Flip, and then click the option you want to use. You can also click the Free Rotate tool on the Rotate and Flip drop-down menu.

F I G U R E

5.41 **Rotating and Flipping Pictures**

Free Rotate · Rotate Left 90° · Rotate Right 90° · Flip Horizontal · Flip Vertical

Using the Text Wrapping Command

The Text Wrapping command provides options to change how text will wrap around an object, picture, or text box.

Using Edit Points

The Edit Points command on the Draw menu plots the points of your freehand drawing to enable you to modify it. You can point to any one of the editing points and drag it to a new location, altering the shape of your drawing.

Using the Change AutoShape Command

When you draw an AutoShape object in your document and decide you want to use a different shape, select the object, click Draw, point to Change AutoShape, and then select a different AutoShape. The new shape will automatically replace the old one.

Using the Select Objects Button

Select Objects

The Select Objects button enables the selection of one or more drawing objects as shown in Figure 5.42. You can use the Select Objects button to draw a box around an object or picture to ungroup it, and after selecting a separate component and editing it, you can then group the image again by redrawing the selection box around the object or picture and clicking the Group option from the Draw menu.

The Select Objects command is also helpful in selecting text, objects, or pictures that are positioned in different layers of the document. To select the picture, position the Select Objects pointer over the picture and click to select it; then click the Select Objects button to deselect it when you are finished. In addition, you can select several objects by holding down the Shift key as you select each object.

F I G U R E

5.42 *Selecting Objects Using the Select Objects Button*

The drawing canvas also helps you to arrange drawing objects and pictures and to move them as a unit. By clicking the Fit button on the Drawing Canvas toolbar, you can size the drawing canvas to fit snugly around the drawing objects causing them to move as a single unit as shown in Figure 5.43.

5.43 *Using the Drawing Canvas to Group Objects*

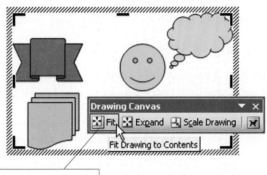

Click the Fit button to size the drawing canvas around the contents.

Using the AutoShapes Button

The AutoShapes button opens a menu of shapes in seven categories as shown in Figure 5.44. Each of the categories offers a variety of shapes. The More AutoShapes category takes you to the Clip Art task pane.

AutoShapes

5.44 *AutoShapes Options*

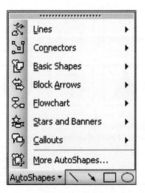

Using the Line, Arrow, Rectangle, and Oval Buttons

You can draw straight lines horizontally, vertically, or at 15-, 30-, 45-, 60-, 75-, or 90-degree angles if you hold down the Shift key as you draw. Use the Arrow button to draw lines with arrowheads. The Shift key will cause the same effects as the Line button. If you hold down the Shift key as you draw a Rectangle shape, you will create a square. If you hold down the Shift key as you draw an Oval shape, you will create an ellipse or a circle.

 Line
 Arrow

 Rectangle
 Oval

Using the Text Box Button

Text Box

Use the Text Box button to create a container for text, pictures, or objects. You can double-click a text box to display the Format Text Box dialog box. Using this dialog box is an efficient way to make several formatting changes at once. Refer to Chapter 3 for additional information concerning text boxes and WordArt.

Using the Insert WordArt Button

Insert WordArt

With WordArt you can pour text into a shape, flip or stretch letters, condense or expand letter spacing, rotate or angle words, or add shading, colors, borders, or shadows to text.

Using the Insert Diagram or Organization Chart Button

Insert Diagram or Organization Chart

You can access the Diagram Gallery by clicking the Insert Diagram or Organization Chart button on the Drawing toolbar. At the Diagram Gallery, shown in Figure 5.45, you can select one of the following diagrams or charts to show relationships to elements: Organization Chart, Cycle Diagram, Radial Diagram, Pyramid Diagram, Venn Diagram, and Target Diagram. On the Diagram toolbar you will find buttons to insert shapes, move shapes backward or forward, change the layout, apply AutoFormat, change the diagram types, and change the text wrap. In addition, flowcharts can be created using a combination of AutoShapes, flowchart shapes, and connectors.

F I G U R E

5.45 *Insert Diagram or Organization Chart Options*

Using the Insert Clip Art Button

Insert Clip Art

This button enables you to access quickly the Insert Clip Art task pane. By default, clip art appears in the text layer. In addition to inserting an image by clicking on the desired image once to insert it, or using an option to copy or insert an image at the drop-down list, you may also drag and drop a clip into a document window.

Using the Insert Picture Button

Insert Picture

The Insert Picture button takes you to the Insert Picture dialog box where you can locate a picture to insert into your document window.

Using the Fill Color Button

The Fill Color option fills a selected object with color, gradient, texture, pattern, or a picture as shown Figure 5.46.

Fill Color

F I G U R E

5.46 *Examples of Fill Effects*

Gradient	Texture	Pattern	Picture
(Preset,	(White	(Solid	(Dove.wmf)
Desert)	Marble)	Diamond)	

Using the Line Color, Font Color, Line Style, Dash Style, and Arrow Style Buttons

The Line Color button colors a selected line (or a line selected around a shape) or sets the default line color if no line is selected. The Font Color button colors the text for selected objects or sets the default if no font color is selected. The Line Style button changes the line width or sets the default if one has not been selected. The Dash Style button provides various types of dashes that can be used on different line styles and arrow styles. The Arrow Style button displays a list of arrowheads that can be added to a line or connector line. See Figure 5.47 for examples created from each of these buttons.

Line Color   Line Style

Font Color   Dash Style

Arrow Style

F I G U R E

5.47 *Examples of Line Colors, Font Colors, Line Styles, Dash Styles, and Arrow Styles*

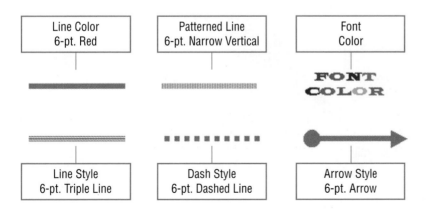

Using the Shadow Style Button

Shadow Style

The Shadow Style button adds a shadow style to a selected object. The Shadow Style button was described in greater detail earlier in the chapter. Refer to Figure 5.17 for the Shadow Styles palette and the Shadow Settings toolbar. See Figure 5.48 for examples of different shadow styles. The effects of the Shadow Style button make the images seem to lift off the page.

F I G U R E

5.48 *Examples of Shadow Styles*

Shadow Style 13
(shadow nudged
up and to the left
using the Shadow
Settings toolbar)

Shadow Style 6
(shadow applied
to an AutoShape
callout)

Shadow Style 10
(shadow color
changed using
the Shadow
Settings toolbar)

Shadow Style 13
(shadow applied
to a picture)

Using the 3-D Style Button

3-D Style

The 3-D Style button applies a three-dimensional effect to a selected object or it sets the default if no object is selected. The 3-D Settings toolbar provides tools to make numerous adjustments to 3-D objects. You can tilt the shape up, down, left, or right to control its perspective. You can add depth, change the lighting source, or change the surface type to add additional effects. You can also change the color of the 3-D effect. See Figure 5.49 for examples of enhanced 3-D objects.

F I G U R E

5.49 *Examples of 3-D Effects*

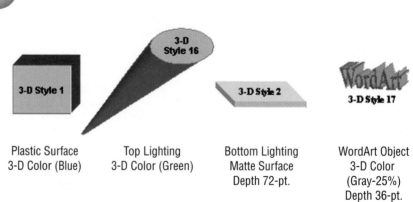

Plastic Surface
3-D Color (Blue)

Top Lighting
3-D Color (Green)

Bottom Lighting
Matte Surface
Depth 72-pt.

WordArt Object
3-D Color
(Gray-25%)
Depth 36-pt.

exercise 5

Creating a Flyer with a Watermark/Original Image

1. At a clear document screen, create the flyer in Figure 5.50 by completing the following steps:

    a. Display the Drawing toolbar.

    b. Display the Clip Art task pane.

    c. Complete a search for a sun graphic (**NA00548_.wmf**) similar to the one used in Figure 5.50 and then insert the image. *(Hint: If you are connected to the Internet when you access the Clip Art task pane, the online clips will display along with the program clips.)*

    d. Select your sun image and make sure the Picture toolbar displays.

    e. With the image selected, change the text wrap to I<u>n</u> Front of Text.

    f. Size the image similarly to Figure 5.50 by dragging one of the corner sizing handles (approximately 4.5 inches).

    g. Click the Copy button on the Standard toolbar. (This places a copy of the image on the Clipboard for use later.)

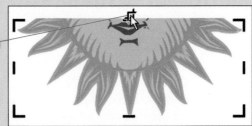

    h. Click the Crop button on the Picture toolbar and then position the cropping tool on the bottom middle sizing handle and drag upward to remove the bottom half of the image as shown in Figure 5.50 and at the right.

    i. Display the Clipboard task pane and insert a copy of the image. *(Hint: Press **Ctrl + C + C** to display the Clipboard task pane.)*

    j. Crop the top section of the image to the point where you cropped the bottom section.

    k. With the image selected, click the Color button on the Picture toolbar and then click <u>W</u>ashout.

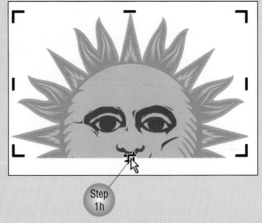

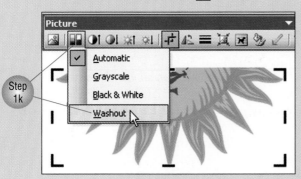

l. Drag the lightened part of the image to the colored part of the image and match the two halves.

Step 1l

m. Select one part of the image, hold down the Shift key, and then select the other part. Click the Draw button on the Drawing toolbar and then click Group.
n. Drag the grouped image to the horizontal center of the page as shown in Figure 5.50.
o. Click the Text Box button on the Drawing toolbar and create a text box that measures approximately 6.75 inches in height and 6.25 inches in width. Position the text box with the top of the text box even with the top of the lightened part of the image.
p. Double-click the text box to access the Format Text Box dialog box. Click the Size tab and make sure the *Height* measures *6.75"* and the *Width* measures *6.25"*.
q. Click the Colors and Lines tab and change the Fill Color to No Fill. Change the Line Color to Orange. Click the down-pointing arrow at the *Dashed* option box and select the third line from the top on the drop-down list. Click the down-pointing arrow at the *Style* option box and select *6 pt*. The *Weight* option box should display at *6 pt*. Click OK.
r. With the insertion point positioned in the text box, insert the **Good Morning** file from your Chapter05 folder.
s. Select the entire document (Ctrl + A) and change the horizontal alignment to Center.
t. Select the title *Good Morning Naperville* and change the font to 40-point Bradley Hand ITC Bold. Position the insertion point before the line beginning *If daytime luncheons,* press Ctrl + Shift + End (to select from the insertion point to the end of the document), and then change the font to 16-point Berlin Sans FB.
u. Select *Tuesday, September 13, 2005* and apply bold.
v. Select *Mergers & Acquisitions—How Do They Impact Our Community?* and apply italics.
2. Insert white space between groups of text as shown in Figure 5.50. *(Hint: Press the Enter key or insert additional spacing before each paragraph at the Paragraph dialog box.)*
3. View the document at Print Preview. Make any necessary adjustments.
4. Save the document and name it **c05ex05, Good Morning**.
5. Print and then close **c05ex05, Good Morning**.

FIGURE

5.50 *Exercise 5*

Good Morning Naperville

If daytime luncheons and meetings don't work for you,
mark your calendar now for the second in a series of
General Membership Breakfast Meetings.

Start your day off with a breakfast full of
networking that will surely get you on the right track.

Tuesday, September 13, 2005
7 a.m.–8:30 a.m.
Holiday Inn Select, 1801 N. Naper Blvd.
Naperville, IL

Topic: *Mergers & Acquisitions—How Do They Impact Our
Community?*
$15 for Members, $20 for Nonmembers

RSVP to the Naperville Area Chamber of Commerce
by Thursday, September 8, 2005
630.555.4141 or napervillechamber@emcp.net

CHAPTER summary

➤ Flyers and announcements are considered among the least expensive means of advertising.

➤ A flyer advertises a product or service that is available for a limited amount of time. An announcement informs an audience of an upcoming event.

➤ When creating headlines for flyers or announcements, select typefaces that match the tone of the document and type sizes that stress important information.

➤ Graphics added to a flyer or announcement can add excitement and generate enthusiasm for the publication. A simple graphic demands more attention and has more impact than a complex one.

➤ Use color in a publication to elicit a particular feeling, emphasize important text, attract attention, organize data, and/or create a pattern in a document. Limit the color to small areas so it attracts attention but does not create visual confusion.

➤ In planning a flyer or announcement, use a table to organize text, graphics, and other design elements on the page.

➤ Borders and lines added to a document aid directional flow, add color, and organize text to produce professional-looking results.

➤ Alter a clip art image by right-clicking on the image and selecting Edit Picture from the shortcut menu that displays or by using tools on the Picture toolbar.

➤ To crop an image is to trim horizontal and vertical edges off a picture.

➤ To scale a picture or object is to increase or decrease the size of an image proportionally or disproportionately.

➤ To nudge an object is to move it in small increments.

➤ The drawing canvas also helps you to arrange drawing objects and pictures and to move them as a single unit.

➤ The Microsoft Program Manager is an Office utility that can compress and resize images and perform image-editing tasks, such as removing "red eye" from photographs.

➤ With Microsoft Office Document Imaging, you can use a scanned document as easily as any other Microsoft Office document on your computer.

➤ Download clip art from the Microsoft Office Clip Art and Media Web page.

➤ The Clip Organizer displays automatically when you download clips from Microsoft Office Clip Art and Media.

➤ If you choose the option to have the Clip Organizer categorize your clips, it will automatically do so when you download clips from the Internet.

➤ When you scan a picture, consider the destination for the picture, the output resolution, and the file format needed.

➤ You may use a table as an underlining structure in page layout.

➤ Use a drawing grid to align objects to gridlines or to other objects.

➤ The *Snap objects to grid* option is on by default.

➤ A raster image is a bitmapped image where pixels of color create the image.

➤ A vector image is one that is created using mathematical equations. Line art and metafile graphics are examples of vector images.

➤ Two common graphic file formats include bitmap and metafile formats.

➤ You cannot ungroup bitmapped graphics.

➤ Metafile graphics can be ungrouped, converted to drawing objects, and then edited by using tools on the Drawing toolbar.

➤ You can ungroup an image, discover the formula for a color used in the image, and then apply the color formula to text.

➤ Images that are used in a Web page can be compressed to reduce the file size.

➤ Pictures and clip art are inserted with the In Line With Text text wrapping style applied.

➤ *RGB* stands for Red, Green, and Blue; *HSL* stands for Hue, Saturation, and Luminescence.

➤ Use WordArt to distort or modify text to create a variety of shapes.

➤ Create your own shapes and images using Word's Drawing toolbar.

➤ Logos may be added to flyers and announcements to reinforce company identity or promote product recognition. The logo may be placed low on the page to anchor the message.

➤ With buttons on the Drawing toolbar, you can add fill color, gradient, pattern, texture, and a picture to an enclosed object; change thickness and color of the line that draws the object; and rotate, align, and change the position of the object.

➤ When objects overlap, use the Bring to Front and Send to Back options from the Order option on the Draw menu. You can also move an object in front of or behind text and position an object in a stack.

➤ Using the Group option on the Draw menu, you can group two or more objects or sections of an object together as a single object. You can also ungroup objects or sections of an object using the Ungroup option.

➤ After you ungroup a picture, the picture becomes an object, and then you can edit it by using options on the Drawing toolbar.

➤ With the drawing grid turned on, an object is pulled into alignment with the nearest intersection of gridlines.

➤ Selected items can be aligned using the Align or Distribute command from the Draw menu.

COMMANDS review

Command	Mouse/Keyboard
AutoShapes	Insert, Picture, AutoShapes; or click the AutoShapes button on Drawing toolbar
Clip Art	Insert, Picture, Clip Art; or click the Insert Clip Art button on the Drawing toolbar
Drawing toolbar	Drawing button on Standard toolbar; right-click toolbar, click Drawing; or click View, Toolbars, Drawing
Microsoft Clip Organizer	Display Clip Art task pane, click Organize clips hyperlink
Microsoft Office Online Templates	Display New Document task pane, click Templates on Office Online hyperlink; or type template name or template category in the *Search online for* text box at the New Document task pane

Picture toolbar	Right-click on Standard toolbar, click Picture; or click View, Toolbars, Picture
Table	Table, Draw Table; or Insert Table button on the Standard toolbar; or click the Draw Table button on the Tables and Borders toolbar
WordArt	Insert, Picture, WordArt; or Insert WordArt button on Drawing toolbar

REVIEWING key points

Matching: On a blank sheet of paper, provide the correct letter or letters that match each definition.

Ⓐ Announcement   Ⓖ Logo   Ⓜ Tables and Borders
Ⓑ Crop   Ⓗ Nudge   toolbar
Ⓒ Drawing toolbar   Ⓘ Picture toolbar   Ⓝ Ungroup
Ⓓ Flyer   Ⓙ Pixel   Ⓞ WordArt
Ⓔ Gradient   Ⓚ Resolution
Ⓕ Group   Ⓛ Scale

1. With this Word feature, you can modify text to create a variety of shapes.
2. A gradual varying of color is called this.
3. Use this method to trim horizontal and vertical edges off a picture.
4. Use this option to select individual components from a whole unit.
5. Each dot in a picture or graphic is called this.
6. Increase or decrease the size of an image using this feature.
7. This term is defined as the number of dots that make up an image on a screen or printer.
8. This type of document communicates or informs an audience of an event.
9. This toolbar includes buttons that are used to create shapes, add fill and effects, access WordArt, add shadows, and apply 3-D effects.
10. This unique design is composed of combinations of letters, words, shapes, or graphics, and serves as an emblem for an organization or a product.
11. This toolbar provides options to rotate text in a table.
12. Use this option to move an object in small increments.

True/False: On a blank sheet of paper, write *True* if the statement is true and *False* if the statement is false.

1. A complex graphic has more impact than a simple graphic.
2. Generally, the upper right side of a document is read first.
3. To display the Drawing toolbar, click Tools, and then Draw.
4. A grouped picture or object functions as a single unit.

5. Bitmap pictures can be converted to drawing objects and customized using tools on the Drawing toolbar.

6. To copy a picture, hold down the Shift key, select the picture, and then drag and drop the picture to another location.

7. To draw a square shape using the Rectangle button on the Drawing toolbar, hold down the Ctrl key as you draw the shape.

8. By default, pictures and clip art are inserted with the In Line With Text text wrapping style applied.

9. Once objects have been grouped, they cannot be ungrouped.

10. If you rotate an AutoShape containing text, the shape rotates but the text does not.

11. Hold down the Shift key and select each object you want to align using the Align or Distribute command from the Draw menu.

12. Text automatically wraps around all sides of a text box.

APPLYING your skills

Assessment 1

Create a flyer promoting the spring session of classes at Midwest College in Oak Park, Illinois. Download the Business Sale Flyer template from the Microsoft Office Online Templates Web page. Substitute the logo placeholder with a college logo you have created in WordArt. Customize the sale flyer to accommodate the text given below. *(Note: Figure 5.51 shows the template document and a sample of the college flyer.)*

1. At the New Document task pane in the *Templates* section, type Business sale flyer in the *Search online for* text box, and then click Go. Click the Business sale flyer (8½ x 11, 3-item) hyperlink, and then click the Download button.
2. Type SUMMER 2005 Midwest in the title text boxes. *(Hint: These boxes are layered. Select each text box, click the Draw button on the Drawing toolbar, and then click the Order option to change the order of the text boxes.)*
3. Type Midwest College, 567 Main Street, Oak Park, IL 60607-5019.
4. Type Dates to Note: Summer Session, June 1 to July 29, Register Online or Call 312.555.0148.
5. Type www.emcp.net/midwest/summer.
6. Type Summer is a chance to: Learn new skills. Complete a prerequisite course. Take one course at a time. Have time to work while taking a class.
7. Insert photographs of college scenes by accessing the Clip Art task pane, typing college in the *Search for* text box, and then clicking the Go button. *(Hint: Click the down-pointing arrow at the Results should be options box, deselect the All media types check box, and then select the Photograph check box. Ungroup the three photograph placeholders in the template before substituting your photos.)*
8. Create a logo for Midwest College using WordArt.
9. Save the document and name it **c05sa01, College**.
10. Print and then close **c05sa01, College**.

5.51 *Assessment 1*

Business Sale Flyer Template
from Microsoft Office Online Templates

Sample Customized College Flyer

Assessment 2

Create the flyer shown in Figure 5.52 by completing the following steps:

You are working in the Dallas office of Universal Packaging Company. Your company is well known for its involvement in environmental issues. On April 22, several Dallas businesses will offer free seminars and distribute flyers, brochures, and so on in an effort to promote public awareness and involvement in Earth Day 2005. Complete the following tasks:

1. Create the document shown in Figure 5.52 with the specifications in a script font.
2. Save the document and name it **c05sa02, Earth**.
3. Print and then close **c05sa02, Earth**.

Assessment 3

Download five frame or border clips from Microsoft Office Clip Art and Media, select one of your favorite frame clip arts, and then create a document with it by completing the following steps. *(Note: You will need access to the Internet to complete this exercise.)*

1. At a clear document screen, display the Clip Art task pane.
2. Make sure you are connected to the Internet and then click the <u>Clip art on Office Online</u> hyperlink at the bottom of the Clip Art task pane.
3. At the Microsoft Office Clip Art and Media home page, type frames or borders in the *Search* text box and then click Go.
4. Evaluate the clips that display at the first screen and click in the check box below the clips that you want to download. Click the Next arrow in the upper right corner to proceed to the next screen where 12 more clips will display. *(Note: You can move forward or backward through the screens by clicking the left- or right-pointing arrows in the upper right corner of the Microsoft Office Clip Art and Media screen. There are hundreds of frame clips to choose from!)*
5. After you have selected five frame clips, click the <u>Download 5 items</u> hyperlink in the *Review basket* area of the *Selection Basket* section.
6. Click the Download Now button at the screen showing the number of clips, file sizes, and estimated download time.

7. At the File Download screen, click Open. Click <u>L</u>ater at the Add Clips to Organizer dialog box.
8. At the Microsoft Clip Organizer, notice that the clips have been added automatically to category subfolders within the Downloaded Clips folder, which displays in the *Collection List* section at the left of the screen. Click the clip art frame you want to use for your document and at the drop-down list, click Copy. ***(Note: You could also insert the clip art from the Clip Art task pane or you could copy and paste from the Clipboard task pane.)***
9. Close the Microsoft Clip Organizer.
10. Close the Microsoft Office Clip Art and Media Web page.
11. Click the Paste button on the Formatting toolbar. ***(Hint: If the Paste button is grayed, display the Clipboard task pane and then copy and paste from there.)***
12. Using your frame clip art, type appropriate text for your document. Suggestions for document text include: flyer announcing the opening of a new office supply store, announcement for a new course offered in the office technology department at your local community college, announcement for an office holiday party, announcement for volunteer help in a local blood drive, or flyer for an office picnic and golfing event. You will probably want to enter your text in a text box.
13. View your document in Print Preview.
14. Save your document and name it **c05sa03, Frame**.
15. Print and then close **c05sa03, Frame**.

Assessment 4

In this assessment, you will integrate a Microsoft Publisher design element into a Word flyer. Assume you have recently completed a desktop publishing class at your local community college, and you are working part time at Steinbock's Art and Frame Shoppe. Create a flyer for Steinbock's promoting their business. Include the following specifications:

1. If you have access to Microsoft Publisher, copy the design element at the top of the flyer in Figure 5.53 by completing the following steps:
   a. Access Microsoft Publisher 2003.
   b. At the Start screen, click the *Design Sets* option in the *New from a design* section of the New Publication task pane.
   c. Click the *Master Sets* option from the *Design Sets* drop-down list.
   d. Select the *Blends* style from the drop-down list.
   e. Double-click the Blends Quick Publication document that displays at the right of the New Publication task pane.
   f. Select the Blends design object at the top of the document and copy it to the Office Clipboard.
   g. Close Microsoft Publisher.
   h. Paste the Blends design object to a clear document screen for your flyer document.
   i. Create the company name and the year the company started in text boxes with No Fill and No Line.
2. Use a photograph, clip art image, or Web free clip art.
3. Create text boxes with gradient fills to complement the Blends design.
4. Include the following text:

   Steinbock's Art and Frame Shoppe
   Founded in 1970
   21 S. Main Street
   Naperville, IL 60540
   (630) 555-0372
   Open daily, 9:30 a.m. to 5:00 p.m. or by appointment

(Closed Sunday)
Fine-quality framing and matting
More than 1,000 frame choices
Limited editions, originals, and reproductions
Design assistance
Enjoy our shoppe and a 20% new neighbor discount on your first order!

5. Save the document and name it **c05sa04, Art**.
6. Print and then close **c05sa04, Art**.

Steinbock's Art and Frame Shoppe

Founded in 1970

- Fine-quality framing and matting
- More than 1,000 frame choices
- Limited editions, originals, and reproductions

- Design assistance
- Enjoy our shoppe and a 20% new neighbor discount on your first order!

- 21 S. Main Street
  Naperville, IL 60540
- (630) 555-0372
- Open daily, 9:30 a.m. to 5:00 p.m. or by appointment
  (Closed Sunday)

Assessment 5

Create a flyer advertising an island rental program for vacation condominiums and embed an Excel table containing information on yearly temperatures. Include the following text and specifications. A sample document has been prepared in Figure 5.54. Use your own design ideas for the flyer.

INTEGRATED

- The name of the rental company is BeachTime Rentals, Inc.
- Prepare a logo with WordArt and possibly a clip art image. Group the design elements.
- Insert an appropriate number of beach scene photographs.
- Include this text: Vacation at the celebrated Lowcountry islands of Kiawah and Seabrook near historic Charlestown, South Carolina. BeachTime Rentals, Inc. offers a variety of unique condos, villas, and homes on Kiawah and on Seabrook. For more information on our short- and/or long-term rental programs, call 843.555.1234 or 1.800.555.4321. Office hours are 9-5 Monday through Friday and 9-6 Saturday seasonally. Visit us online at www.emcp.net/beachtime/rentals
- To embed the Excel table, open Excel and then open **Temperatures** from your Chapter05 folder.
- Select cells A1 through D17 and then copy the table to the Office Clipboard.
- In your Word document, click Edit and then Paste Special.
- At the Paste Special dialog box, make sure the *Paste* option is selected and then select *Microsoft Office Excel Worksheet Object* in the *As* list box. Click OK.
- Close Excel.
- Save the document and name it **c05sa05, Rentals**.
- Print and then close **c05sa05, Rentals**.

FIGURE

5.54 **Assessment 5 Sample Solution**

Island Vacations with

BeachTime Rentals, Inc.

Vacation at the celebrated Lowcountry islands of Kiawah and Seabrook near historic, Charleston, South Carolina. BeachTime Rentals, Inc. offers a variety of unique condos, villas, and homes on Kiawah and on Seabrook.

For more information on our short- and/or long-term rental programs, call 843.555.1234 or 1.800.555.4321. Office hours are 9-5 Monday through Friday and 9-6 Saturday seasonally.

Visit online at www.emcp.net/beachtime/rentals

Temperatures
Average for Charleston, South Carolina

	HIGH	LOW	WATER
January	59	38	52
February	61	42	54
March	67	46	59
April	76	55	67
May	82	62	75
June	86	68	82
July	89	71	84
August	89	71	84
September	84	67	80
October	77	57	73
November	68	47	63
December	61	39	54
Average	**75**	**55**	**69**

Assessment 6

Collect two examples of flyers and/or announcements and evaluate them according to the guidelines presented in the document evaluation checklist. Use any of the flyers and announcements that you started collecting in Chapter 1. Include one example of a flyer or announcement that demonstrates one of these features: poor layout and design; no graphic or one that does not relate to the subject; poor use of fonts, sizes, and styles; or a message that is unclear. Complete the following steps:

1. Open **Document Evaluation Checklist.doc** located in your Chapter05 folder.
2. Print two copies of the form.
3. Complete and attach an evaluation form to each publication.
4. Recreate one of the flyers incorporating your own ideas and formatting. You do not have to reconstruct the poor example. However, the poor example will show the greatest amount of improvement.

Design and Create

5. A few possible suggestions for enhancing your document are to include appropriate fonts, sizes, and styles; reverse text; WordArt; special characters; color paper; color graphics, watermarks, or text; horizontal or vertical lines; and/or borders, shadow, 3-D effects, and so on.

6. Create a thumbnail sketch first.

7. Save your document and name it **c05sa06, Flyer**.

8. Print and then close **c05sa06, Flyer**. Turn in the evaluation forms and examples along with **c05sa06, Flyer**. *(Note: You may want to exhibit this remake in your portfolio.)*

CHAPTER 6

Creating Brochures and Booklets

PERFORMANCE OBJECTIVES

Upon successful completion of Chapter 6, you will be able to create brochures and booklets using a variety of page layouts and design techniques.

CHAPTER06

DESKTOP PUBLISHING TERMS

Book fold	List style	Parallel folds
Character style	Newspaper columns	Reverse text
Drop cap	Normal style	Right-angle folds
Dummy	Panels	Style
Duplex printing	Paragraph style	Table style

WORD FEATURES USED

AutoFormat	Drop caps	Reading Layout view
Book fold	Headers and Footers	Style
Brochure template	Indents	Style Gallery
Bullets and Numbering	Manual duplex	Styles and Formatting
Charts and graphs	Margins	task pane
Columns	Microsoft Office Online	Table
Diagrams and	Templates Web page	Tabs
organization charts	Paper size	Text boxes
Document Maps	Paragraph alignment	2 pages per sheet
Drawing toolbar	Paragraph spacing	

In this chapter, you will be introduced to different methods for creating your own brochures and booklets. You will use text boxes to create a trifold brochure and Word's 2 pages per sheet feature to create a single-fold brochure. In addition, you will use a Microsoft Office Online Templates Web page booklet template along with Word's Book fold feature and then print the booklet pages using Word's manual duplex feature. Purpose, content, paper selection, brochure folds, page layout, design considerations, and desktop publishing concepts will be discussed.

Planning Brochures and Booklets

Clearly defining the purpose of your communication is a very important step in initiating the desktop publishing process. Consequently, defining purpose is as important to the creation of a brochure and a booklet as it is to the creation of any other publication.

Defining the Purpose

The purpose of a brochure or a booklet can be to inform, educate, promote, or sell. Identify the purpose in the following examples:

- A city agency mails brochures to the community explaining a local recycling program.
- A doctor displays brochures on childhood immunizations in the patient waiting room.
- A car salesperson hands out a brochure on a current model to a potential buyer.
- A new management consulting firm sends out brochures introducing its services.
- A professional organization mails booklets to its members listing membership information—addresses, telephone numbers, fax numbers, e-mail addresses, and so on.
- A homeowners association prepares a directory of names, addresses, and services provided by residents (babysitting, pet sitting, garage cleaning, and so on).
- Volunteers for a local theatre prepare a playbill (formatted as a booklet) for distribution during theatrical production.

If you found yourself thinking that some brochures and booklets have more than one purpose, you are correct. As examples, the goals of a brochure on childhood immunizations may be to inform and to educate; the goals of a brochure about a car model may be to inform and promote the sale of the car. Alternatively, the goals of a playbill (booklet) may be to inform an audience of facts about a play, introduce people who are playing the roles, and promote publicity for organizations supporting the community theatre.

In addition, using a brochure or booklet may be another means of establishing your organization's identity and image. Incorporating design elements from your other business documents into the design of your brochure reinforces your image and identity among your readers.

Determining the Content

Before creating the actual layout and design of your brochure or booklet, determine what the content will be. Try to look at the content from a reader's point of view. The content should include the following items:

- A clearly stated description of the topic, product, service, or organization
- A description of the people or company doing the informing, educating, promoting, or selling
- A description of how the reader will benefit from this information, product, service, or organization
- A clear indication of what action you want your audience to take after reading the brochure or booklet
- An easy way for readers to respond to the desired action, such as a fill-in form (addition to a mailing list, contributions form, subscription form) or detachable postcard

Creating Brochures

Before you actually start typing the copy for your brochure there are a number of decisions that need to be made, including determining the size and type of paper that you will use, deciding on the brochure page layout you want, setting the margins for the brochure, and determining the brochure panel widths.

Determining the Size and Type of Paper

Brochures are usually printed on both sides of the page on an assortment of paper stocks. The paper stock may vary in size, weight, color, and texture, and it can also have defined folding lines.

Brochures can be folded in a number of different ways. The manner in which a brochure is folded determines the order in which the panels are set on the page and read by the recipient. The most common brochure fold is called a letter fold. It is also known as a trifold or three-panel brochure. The letter fold and other common folds, as shown in Figure 6.1, are referred to as *parallel folds* because all of the folds run in the same direction. *Right-angle folds* are created by pages that are folded at right angles to each other, such as the folds in a greeting card. Standard-size 8½ by 11-inch (landscape orientation) paper stock can easily accommodate a letter fold, accordion fold, and single fold. Standard legal-size paper that is 8½ by 14 inches can be used to create a brochure with a map fold or a gate fold. Different paper sizes can be used to create variations of these folds. In addition, folds do not always have to create equal panel sizes. Offsetting a fold can produce an interesting effect.

Parallel folds
All folds run in the same direction.

Right-angle folds
Folds created by pages folded at right angles to each other.

FIGURE

6.1 *Brochure Folds*

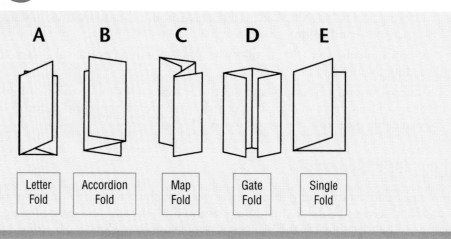

A	B	C	D	E
Letter Fold	Accordion Fold	Map Fold	Gate Fold	Single Fold

The type of paper selected for a brochure affects the total production cost. When selecting the paper stock for a brochure, consider the following cost factors:

- Standard-size brochures, such as a three-panel brochure created from 8½ by 11-inch paper stock or a four-panel brochure created from 8½ by 14-inch paper stock, are easily enclosed in a #10 business envelope.
- Standard-size brochures designed as self-mailers satisfy postal regulations and are, therefore, less costly to mail.
- Nonstandard-size paper stock may be more expensive to purchase and to mail.
- Heavier weight papers are more costly to mail.
- Higher quality paper stocks are more expensive to purchase.
- Color paper is more costly than standard white, ivory, cream, or gray.
- Predesigned paper stock is more expensive than plain paper stock.

Although cost is an important issue when choosing paper stock, you should also take into account how the brochure will be distributed, how often it will be handled, and the image you want to project. If you plan to design the brochure as a self-mailer, take a sample of the paper stock to the post office to see if it meets USPS mailing regulations.

DTP POINTERS
View mailing regulations at www.usps.gov.

If you expect your target audience to keep your brochure for a period of time or to handle it often, plan to purchase a higher quality, heavier paper stock. Similarly, choose a paper within your budget that enhances the image you want to leave in the reader's mind.

If you intend to print the brochure yourself, run a sample of the paper you intend to use through your printer. Some papers are better suited for laser and inkjet printers than others. If you are unsure about what type of paper to purchase, take a master copy of your brochure to a printer for advice on the best type of paper for the situation. You can also take your printed brochure to a print shop and have it folded on commercial folding equipment.

Understanding Brochure Page Layout

A brochure page (defined by the dimensions of the paper stock) is divided into sections called *panels*. At least one fold separates each panel. Folds create distinct sections to place specific blocks of text. For example, a three-panel or letter-fold brochure layout actually has six panels available for text—three panels on one side of the paper and three more panels on the other side. The way a brochure is folded determines the order in which the panels are read by the recipient. The correct placement of text depends on understanding this order. Look how the panels are labeled in the letter-fold page layout illustrated in Figure 6.2. Panels 1, 2, and 3 are located on the inside of the brochure, counting left to right. Panel 4 is the page you see when the cover is opened. Panel 5 is the back of the folded brochure, which may be used for mailing purposes, if desired. Panel 6 is the cover of the brochure. The main content of the brochure is focused in panels 1, 2, and 3.

Panels
Sections separated by folds in a brochure page layout.

FIGURE

6.2 *Letter-Fold Panel Layout*

| PANEL 1 (inside) | PANEL 2 (inside) | PANEL 3 (inside) | PANEL 4 (first flap viewed when cover is opened) | PANEL 5 (back/mailing) | PANEL 6 (cover) |

To avoid confusion about the brochure page layout and the panel reference numbers, create a mockup or *dummy* of your brochure. A dummy is folded in the same manner as the actual brochure and is particularly useful because brochures can be folded in a number of different ways. A dummy can be as simple or as detailed as you would like. If you need only a visual guide to make sure you are placing the correct text in the correct panel, make a simple dummy using the number of columns desired and label each panel as in Figure 6.2. If you need to visualize the placement of text within each panel, the margins, and the white space between columns, make a more detailed dummy that includes very specific margin settings, column width settings, and settings for the spacing between columns.

Dummy
A mockup that is positioned, folded, trimmed, and/or labeled as the actual publication.

A brochure or a dummy can be created using Word's Columns, Table, Text Box, or 2 pages per sheet feature (applicable only to single-fold brochures). For example, for a standard-size three-panel brochure, the actual page size is 8½ by 11 inches positioned in landscape orientation. The page is divided into three columns using the Columns feature or into three columns and one row using the Table feature. Alternatively, three text boxes can be sized and positioned on the page to represent three panels.

Setting Brochure Margins

The left and right margins for a brochure page are usually considerably less than those for standard business documents. Many printers will only allow a minimum of a 0.5 inch left or right side margin (depending on page orientation) because a certain amount of space is needed for the printer to grab the paper and eject it from the printer. If you set margins less than the minimum, Word prompts you with the following message: *One or more margins are set outside the printable area of the page. Choose the Fix button to increase the appropriate margins.* Click Fix to set the margins to the printer's minimum setting. Check the new margin setting at the Margins tab of the Page Setup dialog box. If landscape is the selected paper orientation, the right margin will be the only margin "fixed" by Word because that is the side of the paper the printer grabs to eject the paper from the printer.

When creating a brochure, adjust the opposite side margin to match the margin adjusted by Word. For example, the printer used to create the brochure exercises in this chapter will only allow a minimum of 0.55 inch for the right margin with landscape chosen as the paper orientation. Hence, you are directed to set the left and right margins at 0.55 inch. Alternately, the printer imposes minimum margin settings when portrait is the selected paper orientation. The bottom margin setting is affected the most because it is the last side of the paper to come out of the printer.

If you click Ignore as a response to Word's prompt to "fix" the margins, the program will ignore the printer's minimum requirement and accept whatever margins you have set. However, the printer will not print anything in its defined unprintable area, which will result in text that is cut off. Use Print Preview to view the results of setting margins that are less than the printer's minimum requirements.

Determining Panel Widths

The widths of the panels in most brochures cannot all be equal. If equal panel sizes are used, the margins on some of the panels will appear uneven and the brochure folds will not fall properly in relation to the text. In addition, the thickness of the paper stock affects the amount of space taken up by the fold. To solve this problem, individually size the text boxes for each panel to accommodate the appropriate placement of the text and the folds to achieve the desired result. You will have to experiment somewhat and make adjustments to find the appropriate widths. *(Hint: These suggestions give you a starting point from which to work, but experiment by printing and folding the brochure and then fine-tuning any measurements.)*

To demonstrate several methods of creating pamphlets, Exercise 1 will introduce using column settings, whereas Exercises 2 and 3 will use the Text Box method, Exercise 4 will use the Book Fold feature, and Exercises 5 and 6 will use the 2 pages per sheet method. The trifold brochure template shown in Figure 6.3 uses the Columns feature. Most of the brochure templates accessed through the Templates on Office Online hyperlink at the New Document task pane use text boxes to accommodate the panels in a trifold brochure as shown in Figure 6.4. In addition, a table may be used as the underlining structure of a brochure; however, this method was not used in any of the templates. After each method is introduced, it will be up to you to choose which method is the easiest to use.

6.3 *Using Word's Brochure Template (Formatted in Columns)*

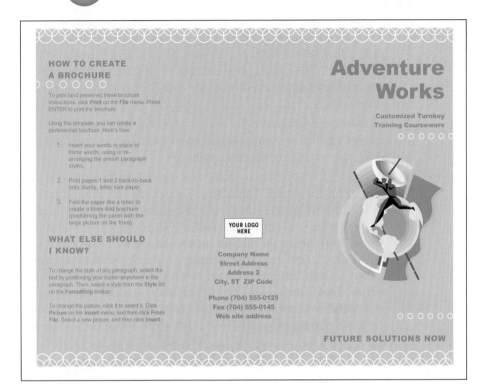

6.4 *Using a Microsoft Office Online Templates Web Page Brochure Template (Formatted in Text Boxes)*

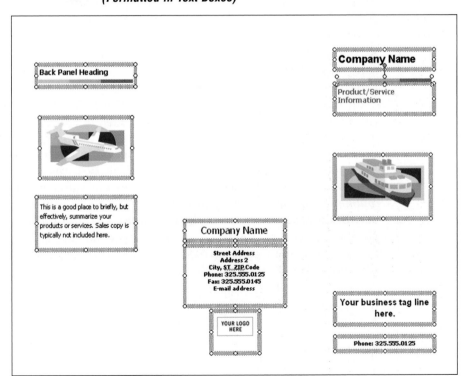

Using panels 1, 2, and 3 of a letter-fold brochure as an example, as shown in Figure 6.5, consider the following suggestions when setting panel widths and the space between columns or text boxes:

1. One way to determine the approximate width of each panel is to fold the brochure paper stock into the desired brochure fold configuration, which, in this example, is a letter-fold brochure. Measure the width of each panel. The width obtained will be approximate because a ruler cannot measure hundredths of an inch, but it will be a good starting point.

2. Establish the left and right margins for the whole page. One-half-inch margin settings, or something close to that, are common. (See the section above on setting brochure margins.)

3. For panel 1, the left margin for the whole brochure page is also the left margin for the panel. Therefore, subtract the left margin setting from the total width of panel 1. From the remaining amount, estimate how much of that space is needed to allow for an appropriate column or text box width for the text and for an appropriate amount of white space on the right side of the panel. For example, if panel 1 measures approximately 3.7 inches and the left page margin is 0.55 inch, subtract 0.55 inch from 3.7 inches. From the 3.15 inches that remain, estimate how much of that space will be occupied by text and how much needs to be allotted for the right margin of panel 1 (i.e., the white space before the fold).

4. For panel 2, use the whole panel width to estimate an appropriate column width or text box width for the text and an appropriate amount of white space on the left and right sides of the panel. The column width in panel 2 will be wider than the widths in panels 1 and 3.

5. For panel 3, the right margin for the whole brochure page is also the right margin for the panel. Therefore, subtract the amount of the right margin setting from the total width of the panel. From the remaining amount, determine an appropriate width for the text and an appropriate amount of white space on the left side of the panel.

6. After establishing text column widths and the amount of white space in between for panels 1, 2, and 3, reverse the measurements for panels 4, 5, and 6. For example, panels 1 and 6 will be the same measurement, panels 2 and 5 will be the same, and panels 3 and 4 will be the same. *(Hint: If you are using the Columns feature, you will need to insert a section break to vary the column formatting on the second page. See the section "Varying Column Formatting within the Same Document" in this chapter for more information. If you are using the Table feature, you will have to create another table for the second page of the brochure reversing the column measurements from panels 1, 2, and 3, and if you are using the Text Box feature, remember to reverse the order as stated above.)*

7. Refer to Figure 6.5 to see that the space between panels is actually divided by the fold, allowing white space on either side of the fold. In other words, the space between columns serves as the margins for two different panels. For example, the space between columns surrounding the first fold in Figure 6.5 provides the white space (or margin) for the right side of panel 1 and the left side of panel 2.

8. Use the suggestions above to create a dummy. Insert random text in every panel and print. *(Hint: To insert random text, **Type** =rand() **and then press Enter**.)* Fold the page as you would the brochure and check the amount of space between columns. Is the text positioned correctly within each panel? If not, adjust the space between columns and/or the column width settings and then print again.

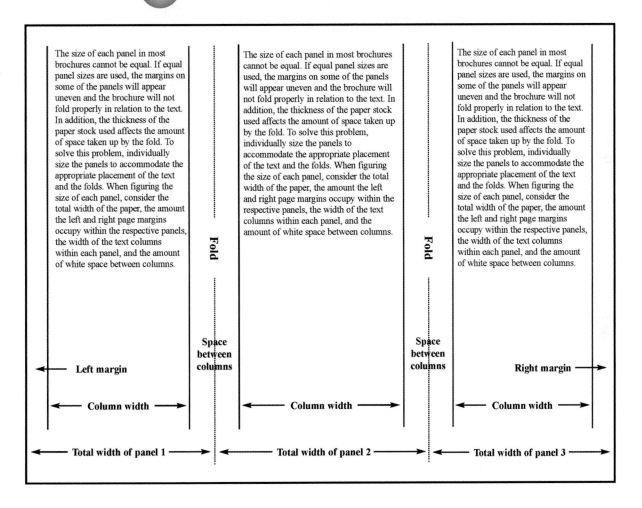

The method used to create the white space between columns depends on the method used to create the columns, as explained in Figure 6.6.

6.6 *Methods Used to Create Spacing between Columns*

Method Used to Create Columns	Method Used to Create Spacing between Columns
Columns feature	At the Columns dialog box in the *Width and spacing* section, adjust the amount in the *Spacing* text box.
Table feature	Create blank columns in between the columns that contain the text for each panel.
Text Box feature	Size and position the text boxes containing the text for each panel, leaving the desired amount of white space between text boxes.
2 pages per sheet feature	Applicable only to single-fold brochures, white space is achieved by adjusting the margin settings.
Book Fold feature	White space is achieved by adjusting the margin settings and the gutter space.

Understanding Newspaper Columns

Newspaper columns
Text flows from the bottom of one column to the top of the next column.

The types of columns created by using the Columns feature are commonly referred to as *newspaper columns*. Newspaper columns are used for text in newspapers, newsletters, brochures, and magazines. Text in these types of columns flows continuously from the bottom of one column to the top of the next column, as shown in Figure 6.7. When the first column on the page is filled with text, the insertion point moves to the top of the next column on the same page, and so on. When the last column on the page is filled with text, the insertion point moves to the beginning of the first column on the next page.

By default, all Word documents are automatically set up in a one-column format. However, a document can include as many columns as there is room for on the page. Word determines how many columns can be included based on the page width, the margin settings, the size of the columns, and the spacing between columns. Column formatting can be assigned to a document before the text is typed or it can be applied to existing text.

FIGURE

6.7 *Newspaper Columns*

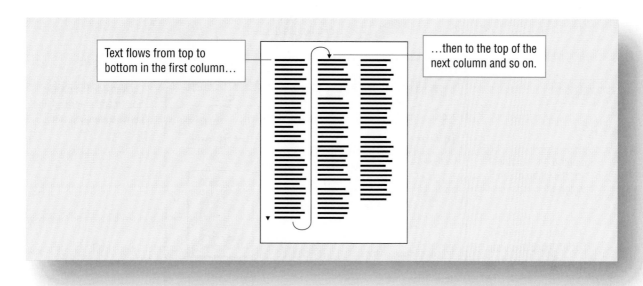

Text flows from top to bottom in the first column...

...then to the top of the next column and so on.

Creating Newspaper Columns of Equal Width

Click the Columns button on the Standard toolbar to easily create newspaper columns of equal width. The view will automatically change to the Print Layout view so you may view the columns side by side.

Columns of equal width can also be created at the Columns dialog box (click F_ormat and then _Columns). By default, the _Equal column width_ option contains a check mark. The number of columns can be specified by selecting _One, T_w_o,_ or _Three_ in the _Presets_ section or by indicating the number in the _Number of columns_ text box in the Columns dialog box as shown in Figure 6.8. By default, columns are separated by 0.5-inch of space. This amount of space can be increased or decreased with the _Spacing_ option in the _Width and spacing_ section.

Columns

DTP POINTERS
Use the Print Layout view to display columns side by side.

6.8 *Columns Dialog Box*

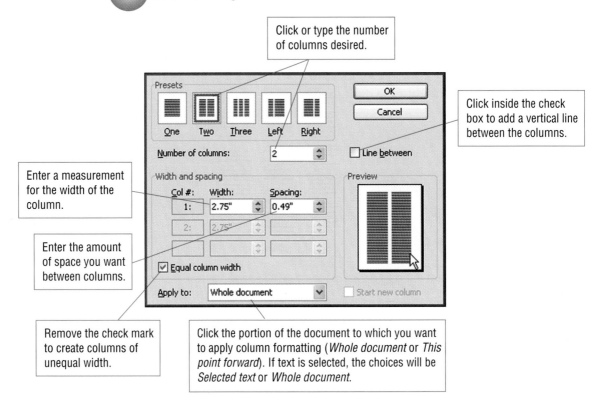

Click or type the number of columns desired.

Click inside the check box to add a vertical line between the columns.

Enter a measurement for the width of the column.

Enter the amount of space you want between columns.

Remove the check mark to create columns of unequal width.

Click the portion of the document to which you want to apply column formatting (*Whole document* or *This point forward*). If text is selected, the choices will be *Selected text* or *Whole document*.

Creating Newspaper Columns of Unequal Width

To create columns of unequal width, display the Columns dialog box, select the number of columns you desire, disable the *Equal column width* option, and then enter the desired column width and spacing between the columns at the corresponding text boxes.

Experiment with changing the width between columns so you can see how the changes affect the text in each panel. For example, in a letter-fold brochure column layout, increasing the space between columns 1 and 2 will cause the text in panel 2 to be shifted to the right, whereas decreasing the space between columns 1 and 2 will cause the text in panel 2 to shift to the left.

DTP POINTERS
Be consistent when varying column widths within a document.

Using the Horizontal Scroll Bar to Adjust Column Settings

Once columns have been created, the width of the columns or the spacing between columns may be changed with the column markers on the horizontal ruler. To do this, make sure the horizontal ruler is displayed (click View and then Ruler). Position the arrow pointer in the middle of the left or right margin column marker on the horizontal ruler until it turns into a double-headed arrow pointing left and right. Hold down the left mouse button, drag the column marker to the left or right to make the column narrower or wider, and then release the mouse button. Hold down the Alt key as you drag the column marker to view exact measurements on the Ruler.

Varying Column Formatting within the Same Document

By default, any column formatting you select is applied to the whole document. If you want to create different numbers or styles of columns within the same document, the document must be divided into sections. For example, if a document contains a title, you may want the title to span the top of all of the columns rather than be included within the column formatting. To span a title across the tops of columns, type and format the title. Position the insertion point at the left margin of the first line of text to be formatted into columns and display the Columns dialog box. Select the desired number of columns, make any necessary column width and spacing changes, and then change the *Apply to* option at the bottom of the Columns dialog box from *Whole document* to *This point forward*.

When *This point forward* is selected, a section break is automatically inserted in your document. Column formatting is applied to text from the location of the insertion point to the end of the document or until other column formatting is encountered.

In addition to the method just described, you can manually insert the section break before accessing the Columns dialog box by choosing Insert and then Break. At the Break dialog box, select *Continuous*, click OK or press Enter, and then access the Columns dialog box.

If text that is formatted into columns is to be followed by text that is not formatted into columns, you must change the column format to one column and select the *This point forward* option. An alternate approach is to insert a section break through the Break dialog box and use the Columns button on the Standard toolbar to create one column.

Specific text in a document can be formatted into columns by first selecting the text and then using the Columns button on the Standard toolbar, or the options from the Columns dialog box.

Removing Column Formatting

To remove column formatting, position the insertion point in the section containing columns and change the column format to one column either by using the Columns button on the Standard toolbar or the Columns dialog box.

Inserting a Column, Page, or Section Break

When formatting text into columns, Word automatically breaks the columns to fit the page. At times, a column may break in an undesirable location or you may want a column to break in a different location. For example, a heading may appear at the bottom of the column, while the text that follows the heading begins at the top of the next column. You can insert a column break into a document to control where columns end and begin on the page.

To insert a column break, position the insertion point where you want the new column to begin and then press Ctrl + Shift + Enter, or click Insert and then Break. At the Break dialog box, click *Column break* and then click OK or press Enter.

If you insert a column break in the last column on a page, the column continues on the next page. If you want any other column on the page that is not the last column to continue on the next page, insert a page break. To do this, press Ctrl + Enter, or click Insert, Break, and then *Page break*.

If you want to "even out" or balance the text in columns, insert a continuous section break at the end of the last column. The text that follows the section break will continue to the top of the next column.

DTP POINTERS
Make sure all column breaks are in appropriate locations.

Moving the Insertion Point within and between Columns

To move the insertion point in a document use the mouse, the Up and Down Arrow keys, or press Alt + Up Arrow or Alt + Down Arrow.

To familiarize yourself with the layout of panels in a letter-fold (or three-panel) brochure, you will create a simple dummy (three even columns with default spacing between the columns) in the following exercise. Measuring the panels and creating unequal column widths is not necessary in this case because you will use the dummy only as a guide to placing text in the correct panels. Remember, you can always make a more detailed dummy if necessary.

(Before completing computer exercises, delete the Chapter05 folder on your disk. Next copy the Chapter06 folder from the CD that accompanies this textbook to your disk and then make Chapter06 the active folder.)

Creating a Dummy of a Three-Panel Brochure Using the Columns Feature

1. At a clear document screen, create a dummy similar to the one illustrated in Figure 6.2 by completing the following steps:
   a. Change to Print Layout view.
   b. Change the paper orientation to landscape at the Page Setup dialog box.
   c. Change to a three-column format by completing the following steps:
      1) Click Format and then Columns.
      2) At the Columns dialog box, change the *Number of columns* to 3, or select *Three* (equal columns) in the *Presets* section of the Columns dialog box.
      3) Make sure the *Equal column width* check box contains a check mark and click OK.

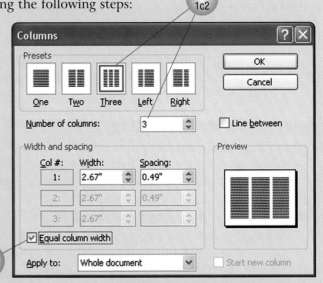

Step 1c2

Step 1c3

   d. Insert the panel labels by completing the following steps:
      1) Change the paragraph alignment to center.
      2) Type PANEL 1, press Enter, and then type (inside) in the first panel (column 1).
      3) Click Insert and then Break.
      4) At the Break dialog box, click *Column break* and then click OK.

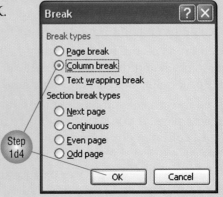

Step 1d4

5) Using Figure 6.2 as a guide, repeat Steps 1d2 through 1d4 until all six panels are labeled. *(Hint: Press Ctrl + Shift + Enter to insert a column break.)*
   e. Print the three-panel brochure dummy by completing the following steps:
      1) Position the insertion point on the first page (panels 1, 2, and 3) by pressing Ctrl + Home.
      2) Click File and then Print.
      3) At the Print dialog box, click *Current page* and then click OK.
      4) Put the first printed page back in the printer so the second page can be printed on the back of the first page. (Experiment with your printer to position the paper correctly.)
      5) Position the insertion point on the second page (panels 4, 5, and 6) and print the current page.
   f. Fold the dummy as you would the real brochure and refer to the panel labels when creating the actual brochure to avoid confusion on the placement of text.
2. Save the dummy brochure to your Chapter06 folder and name it **c06ex01, Dummy**.
3. Close **c06ex01, Dummy**. (Your brochure should look similar to the panel layout illustrated in Figure 6.2.)

You can use a procedure similar to Exercise 1 to create a dummy using a table. Insert a table with five columns and one row—three columns for the panels and two columns for the space between the columns. Label the panels and then print the dummy.

A dummy can also be created with pencil and paper. Take a piece of the paper stock to be used and position it correctly (portrait or landscape). Fold the paper as the brochure will be folded and label each panel as shown in Figure 6.2.

Using Reverse Text as a Design Element

Reverse text usually refers to white text set against a solid background (such as 100% black), as shown in the first example in Figure 6.9. Reversing text is most effective with single words, short phrases such as headings, or special characters set in a large type size. Impact is also achieved by using screens (shading with lighter shades of gray or color) for the background fill. Solid areas of black, white, and varying shades of gray on a page give the visual effect of color, creating a dramatic effect with the use of only one color. In addition, interesting effects are achieved by reversing color text out of a solid, screened, gradient, or textured colored background fill and/or by varying the shape that contains the reverse text. As shown in Figure 6.9, many different variations of reverse type can be created. Keep these examples in mind when you are trying to provide focus, balance, contrast, and directional flow in a document.

Reverse text
White text set against a solid background.

DTP POINTERS
Select Automatic at the Font color palette and the text will automatically change to white when a black fill is added.

FIGURE

6.9 *Reverse Text Examples*

Reverse Text

Shaded Background

60% shading

Text Box

One of the easiest ways to create reverse text is to use the Text Box feature. To create traditional reverse text (solid black background with white text) using a text box, simply create a text box, change the fill to black, change the text color to Automatic or White, and then type the desired text. Or, you can create a reverse text effect using an AutoShape by selecting an AutoShape, adding text, and then adding background fill.

In Exercises 2 and 3, you will have the opportunity to create a letter-fold (or three-panel) brochure using three uneven newspaper columns and other formatting features such as text boxes to create reverse text, color, and bulleted lists. Remember to save often! Creating even a simple brochure involves many steps. Also, view your document frequently to assess the overall layout and design. Adjustments often need to be made that can affect other parts of the document not visible in the document window. The *Page Width* and *Whole Page* options, accessible by clicking the Zoom button on the Standard toolbar, are useful for viewing a brochure layout during the creation process.

DTP POINTERS
Brochures involve many steps, so save often as you work.

Creating Panels 1, 2, and 3 of a Letter-Fold Brochure Using Text Boxes and Reverse Text

1. Keep the dummy created in Exercise 1 on hand to visually guide you in the correct placement of text (or create a new dummy following the directions in Exercise 1).
2. At a clear document screen, create the first three panels of a brochure using text boxes, as shown in Figure 6.10, by completing the following steps:
   a. Change the orientation to landscape and change the top and bottom margins to 0.5 inch and the left and right margins to 0.55 inch. *(Note: Click **Fix** if Word notifies you that one of the margin settings is within your printer's unprintable zone.)*
   b. Make sure the paper size is Letter 8.5 × 11 in.
   c. Turn on automatic kerning for font sizes that are 14 points.
   d. Click the Show/Hide ¶ button.
   e. Click the Text Box button on the Drawing toolbar and draw a text box in the upper left corner that is approximately 1.5 inches square.
   f. Double-click the text box border to access the Format Text Box dialog box. Click the Size tab and change the height and width to 1.3 inches.
   g. Click the Colors and Lines tab, change the fill color to Red, and then change the line color to No Line.
   h. Click the Layout tab and then <u>A</u>dvanced. At the Advanced Layout dialog box, select the Picture Position tab, change the <u>A</u>lignment to *Left* in the *Horizontal* section, the *relative to* option to *Margin*, the *Alignment* to *Top*, and the *relative to* option to *Margin* in the *Vertical* section.
   i. At the same dialog box, select the Text Wrapping tab and change the wrapping style to *Top and bottom*. Click OK twice.
   j. Position the insertion point inside the text box and then type 1.

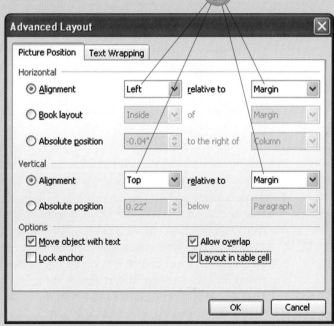

Step 2h

k. Select the number *1* and the paragraph symbol that follows it.
l. Change the font size to 72-point Arial Rounded MT Bold.
m. Change the horizontal alignment to center.
n. Select the text box border and add a shadow effect by clicking the Shadow Style button on the Drawing toolbar and then selecting the third shadow style option in the first row (Shadow Style 3).
o. Copy the text box by holding down the Shift key and the Ctrl key while dragging a copy to the right of the current box. ***(Note: Holding down the Shift key keeps the text box in the same vertical position as the original box.)***
p. Select *1* in the copied box and type *2* in place of it.
q. Double-click the copied text box border and change the fill color to Yellow at the Colors and Lines tab at the Format Text Box dialog box.
r. Click the Layout tab and then Advanced. Click the Picture Position tab, change the *Absolute position* to *4.03"*, and then change the *to the right of* option to *Page* in the *Horizontal* section. The vertical alignment will be the same *(Top relative to Margin)*. Click OK twice.

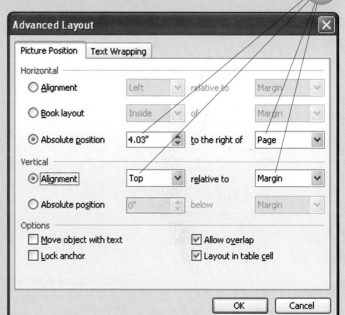

s. Copy the text box again to create a third box, type *3* in place of *2,* and change the fill color to Green. At the Advanced Layout dialog box, change the *Absolute position* to *7.72"* and the *to the right of* option to *Page* in the *Horizontal* section. The vertical alignment will be the same *(Top relative to Margin)*. Click OK twice.
3. Create the text boxes below the numbered text boxes by completing the following steps:
   a. Click the Text Box button on the Drawing toolbar and drag the crosshairs below the number 1 text box. Draw a text box that is approximately 5.75 inches in height by 2.75 inches in width.
   b. Double-click the border of the text box and then click the Size tab. Make sure the *Height* measures *5.8"* and the *Width* measures *2.75"*.
   c. Select the Colors and Lines tab and then change the line color to No Line.
   d. At the Advanced Layout dialog box, click the Picture Position tab and then make sure the *Absolute position* is *0"* and the *to the right of* option is *Margin* in the *Horizontal* section. Make sure the *Absolute position* is *1.6"* and the *below* option is *Margin* in the *Vertical* section. Click OK twice.
   e. Position the insertion point in the text box and click Insert and then File. At the Insert File dialog box, insert **Ride Safe 1** located in your Chapter06 folder.
   f. Save the document and name it **c06ex02, Panels 1,2,3**.
   g. Select *Before entering the street from your driveway or sidewalk:*, change the font size to 20-point Arial Rounded MT Bold, and then turn on italics.

h. Position the insertion point after the colon and then press Enter. *(Hint: a 20-point Enter symbol should display.)*
i. Select the text that starts with *Stop.* and ends with *Listen to be sure no traffic is approaching.* and then change the font size to 20-point Arial Rounded MT Bold.
j. With the text still selected, click F̲ormat and then Bullets and N̲umbering. At the Bullets and Numbering dialog box, select the B̲ulleted tab.
k. Click the first bullet option (the second option from the left in the first row) and then click Cus̲tomize.
l. At the Customize Bulleted List dialog box, click a round bullet in the *Bullet character* section. (If you do not see a round bullet, click C̲haracter and select a round bullet from a font, such as Wingdings, at the Symbol dialog box.)
m. Click the F̲ont button, change the size to 32 points, and then change the font color to Red. Click OK to close the Font dialog box.
n. In the *Bullet position* section, change the *Indent a̲t* to 0". In the *Text position* section, change the *Ta̲b space after* to 0.3" and the I̲ndent at to 0.3".
o. Click OK to close the Customize Bulleted List dialog box.
p. With the bulleted list selected, adjust the spacing between the bulleted items by changing the spacing after the paragraphs to 14 points at the Paragraph dialog box with the I̲ndents and Spacing tab selected.
q. Copy the text box by holding down the Shift key and the Ctrl key while dragging a copy below the text box containing *2*. Double-click the border of the text box to access the Format Text Box dialog box.
r. Click the Size tab and change the *He̲ight* to 5.8" and the *Wid̲th* to 3.0".
s. Click the Layout tab and then A̲dvanced. At the Picture Position tab in the *Horizontal* section, change the *Absolute p̲osition* to 4.03" and the *t̲o the right of* option to *Page*. In the *Vertical* section, change the *Absolute po̲sition* to 1.6" and the *belo̲w* option to *Margin*. Click OK twice.

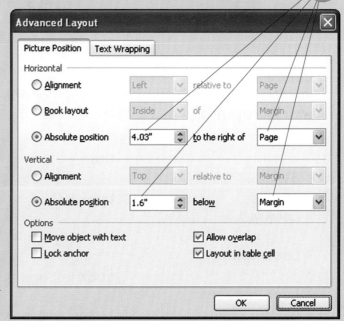

Step 3s

Advanced Layout

Picture Position | Text Wrapping

Horizontal
○ A̲lignment Left relative to Page
○ B̲ook layout Inside of Margin
◉ Absolute p̲osition 4.03" to the right of Page

Vertical
○ Ali̲gnment Top relative to Margin
◉ Absolute po̲sition 1.6" belo̲w Margin

Options
☐ Move object with text   ☑ Allow o̲verlap
☐ Lock anchor   ☑ Layout in table ce̲ll

OK   Cancel

t. Select the text in the box below *2*. Click I̲nsert and then Fi̲le.
u. At the Insert File dialog box, insert **Ride Safe 2** located in your Chapter06 folder.
v. Using the Format Painter, copy the formatting used in the text box below *1* and copy this formatting to the text in the text box below *2*. Change the bullet color to Yellow. *(Hint: You will need to use the Format Painter to copy and apply the formatting for the unbulleted text first and then the bulleted text. Remember to press Enter to create a space after the unbulleted text.)*
w. Drag a copy of the text box below *1* to the area below the text box containing *3*. *(Hint: Hold down the Shift key and the Ctrl key while dragging a copy.)*

x. Double-click the border of the text box to access the Format Text Box dialog box. Click the Layout tab and then click <u>A</u>dvanced. At the picture Position tab in the *Horizontal* section, change the *Absolute position* to *7.72"* and the *<u>t</u>o the right of* option to *Page*. Make sure the *Absolute position* is *1.60"* and the *be<u>l</u>ow* option is *Margin* in the *Vertical* section. Click OK twice.

y. Select the existing text and then insert **Ride Safe 3** located in your Chapter06 folder.

z. Using the Format Painter, copy the formatting to the text box below *3* and change the bullet color to Green.

4. Save the brochure with the same name, **c06ex02, Panels 1,2,3.**

5. Print the first page of this exercise now, or print after completing Exercise 3.

6. Close **c06ex02, Panels 1,2,3.**

FIGURE

 **Exercise 2**

1

Before entering the street from your driveway or sidewalk:

● Stop.

● Look left.

● Look right.

● Look left again.

● Listen to be sure no traffic is approaching.

2

At stop signs, stoplights, or other busy streets:

● Stop.

● Look left.

● Look right.

● Look left again.

● Listen and make sure the street is clear of traffic before crossing.

3

Before turning, changing lanes, or swerving to avoid an obstacle:

● Look back over your shoulder.

● Be sure the road is clear of traffic.

● Signal.

● Look again.

In Exercise 3, you will complete the brochure started in Exercise 2. As in the previous exercise, uneven text boxes will be used to form the panels on the reverse side of the brochure. Refer to your dummy to see that panel 4 is on the reverse side of panel 3, panel 5 is the reverse side of panel 2, and panel 6 is the reverse side of panel 1. Consequently, panel 4 will be the same width as panel 3, panel 5 will be the same width as panel 2, and panel 6 will be the same width as panel 1. As you progress through the exercise, remember to save your document every 10 to 15 minutes.

Creating Panels 4, 5, and 6 of a Letter-Fold Brochure

1. Open **c06ex02, Panels 1,2,3**.
2. Save the document with Save <u>A</u>s and name it **c06ex03, Ride Safe Brochure**.
3. Create panels 4, 5, and 6 of the Ride Safe brochure shown in Figure 6.11 by completing the following steps:
    a. Position the insertion point at the top of the page containing panels 1, 2, and 3 and then press Ctrl + Enter.
    b. Display the Clipboard task pane. *(Hint: Press Ctrl + C + C.)*
    c. Select the red text box in panel 1 that contains *1* and is now located on the second page. Click the Copy button on the Standard toolbar. *(Note: A copy of the red text box should display in the Clipboard task pane at the right of your screen.)*

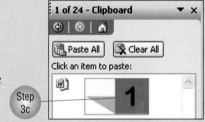

Step 3c

    d. Make sure the insertion point is positioned on the blank page (this will be page 1 of 2) and then press Paste. *(Note: You are now creating panel 4, which is the same size as panel 1.)*
    e. Select *1* and then type *4*.
    f. Select the text box below the *1* on the second page; the box contains the text *Before entering the street...sidewalk*. Copy the text box to the Clipboard task pane.
    g. Position the insertion point at the top of the first page, below *4*, and then click Paste *(Note: You are pasting to panel 4.)*
    h. Double-click the border of the text box to access the Format Text Box dialog box. Click the Size tab and make sure the *H<u>e</u>ight* is *5.8"* and the *Wi<u>d</u>th* is *2.75"*.
    i. Click the Layout tab and then <u>A</u>dvanced. At the Advanced Layout dialog box, click the Picture Position tab and make sure the *Absolute position* is *0"* and the *to the right of* option is *Margin* in the *Horizontal* section and the *Absolute po<u>s</u>ition* is *1.6"* and the *belo<u>w</u>* option is *Margin* in the *Vertical* section. Click OK twice.
    j. Select the text in panel 4 and insert **Ride Safe 4** located in your Chapter06 folder.
    k. Using the Format Painter, copy the formatting from panel 1 to panel 4. (The Red color remains the same.) *(Hint: Remember to press Enter to create a space after the unbulleted text.)*
    l. Select the text box below *2* on the second page and copy the text box to the Clipboard task pane.
    m. Position the insertion point on page 1 and paste the text box from panel 2. *(Note: The text box will display to the right of panel 4, but not in the exact position.)*
    n. Double-click the text box border, click the Size tab, and then change the *H<u>e</u>ight* to *4"* and make sure the *Wi<u>d</u>th* is still *3"*. Click the Layout tab and then <u>A</u>dvanced. Click the Picture Position tab, make sure the *Absolute position* is *4.03"* and the *to the right of* option is *Page* in the *Horizontal* section and the *Absolute po<u>s</u>ition* is *1.6"* and the *belo<u>w</u>* option is *Margin* in the *Vertical* section. Click OK twice.

o. Select the existing text (press Ctrl + A) in the text box in panel 5 and insert **Ride Safe Back** located in your Chapter06 folder.

p. Select the *Ride Safe...we'd like to work with you, too* text and then change the font to 12-point Arial Rounded MT Bold.

q. With the text still selected, create the red paragraph border shown in Figure 6.11 by clicking F<u>o</u>rmat and then <u>B</u>orders and Shading.

r. At the Borders and Shading dialog box, click the <u>B</u>orders tab and then click the *Box* option in the *Setting* section. Select the dashed line fourth from the top in the *Style* list box, change the color to Red, the <u>W</u>idth to *1 pt*, make sure that *Paragraph* displays in the *Apply to* list box, and then click OK.

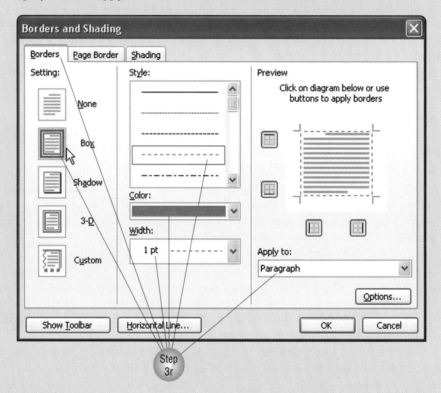

Step 3r

s. Position the insertion point at the left of *We want everyone to RIDE SAFE!* and then press Enter six times.

t. Select *We want everyone to RIDE SAFE!*, change the font to 16-point Arial Rounded MT Bold in Green, add italics, and then change the paragraph alignment to center.

u. Create a text box that measures 0.6 inch in height and 3 inches in width. Position the text box similar to the location of the text located below *We want everyone to RIDE SAFE!* in Figure 6.11, add a Black fill, and then change the font to 14-point Arial Rounded MT Bold in Yellow. Type **Call us today at**, press Enter, type **1-800-555-RIDE**, and then change the paragraph alignment to center.

Call·us·today·at¶
1-800-555-RIDE¶

Step 3u

4. Create the cover (panel 6) for the brochure by completing the following steps:

a. Select the text box in panel 4 and copy it to the Clipboard task pane.

b. Position the insertion point on page 1 (upper left corner) and then click Paste. *(Hint: You will position the text box in the next step.)*

c. Double-click the border of the pasted text box in panel 4, click the Size tab, and then change the *Height* to *7.72"* and the *Width* to *2.72"*.

d. Click the Layout tab and then <u>A</u>dvanced. At the Picture Position tab change the *Absolute position* to *7.72"* and the *to the right of* option to *Page* in the *Horizontal* section and the *Alignment* to *Top* and the *relative to* option to *Margin* in the *Vertical* section. Click OK twice.

e. Select the current text in the text box and then insert the **Ride Safe Front** file located in your Chapter06 folder.

f. Select all of the text and change the font to 12-point Arial Rounded MT Bold and then change the horizontal alignment to center.

g. Position the insertion point at the left of *The Ride Safe Four* and then press Enter once. Select *The Ride Safe Four* and then change the font to 36-point Arial Rounded MT Bold. Change the font colors as shown in Figure 6.11. Select *Safe*, make sure the font color is Yellow, click F<u>o</u>rmat and then <u>B</u>orders and Shading. Select the <u>S</u>hading tab, click Black in the *Fill* section, change the *Apply to* option to *Text*, and then click OK.

h. Position the insertion point at the left of *RIDE SAFE, INC.* and then press Enter twice.

i. Display the Clip Art task pane, type j0342014.jpg or type the keyword stop light in the *Search for* text box, and then click Go. *(Hint: Substitute a similar image if necessary.)* Click the image to insert it.

j. Select the image, change the alignment to center, and then drag a corner sizing handle to increase the size to approximately 2 inches in height and 2.8 inches in width.

k. Position the insertion point at the left of *RIDE SAFE, INC.* and then press Enter five times (or position similar to Figure 6.11).

5. Save the brochure with the same name **c06ex03, Ride Safe Brochure**.

6. Print the first page of the brochure, reinsert the first page back in the printer, and then print the second page on the back of the first page. Refer to the directions for printing in Exercise 1, if necessary.

7. Close **c06ex03, Ride Safe Brochure**.

FIGURE

6.11 *Exercise 3*

4

Every time you go bicycling or in-line skating:

- **Wear an ANSI, ASTM, or Snell certified helmet.**

- **Wear appropriate protective gear!**

Ride Safe is committed to educating children and their parents about bicycle safety and the importance of wearing helmets. In the last year, we have worked with over 1,200 PTAs/PTOs across the country to develop customized bicycle safety programs . . . and we would like to work with you, too.

We want everyone to RIDE SAFE!

Call us today at
1-800-555-RIDE

The Ride Safe Four

RIDE SAFE, INC.
P.O. Box 888
Warrenville, IL 60555
1-800-555-RIDE

Formatting with Styles

Professional-looking documents generally require a great deal of formatting. Formatting within any document that uses a variety of headings, subheadings, and other design elements should remain consistent. Some documents, such as company newsletters, brochures, and manuals, may be created on a regular basis and require consistent formatting within the document as well as from issue to issue. You can save time and keystrokes by using Word's Style feature to store repetitive formatting and to maintain consistent formatting throughout your document.

A *style* is a set of defined formatting instructions saved with a specific name in order to use the formatting instructions over and over. For example, a style may be created for the bulleted text in Figures 6.10 and 6.11 that contains bullet instructions and paragraph spacing instructions. Every time you are ready to format the text to be bulleted, you can quickly apply the specific style and save yourself the time of repeating the same keystrokes for each item. Because formatting instructions are contained within a style, a style may be edited, automatically updating any occurrence of that style within a document. For instance, if you applied a style to

Style
A group of defined formatting instructions that can be applied at one time to a whole document or to various parts of a document.

the bulleted text in all four panels of the brochure that specified an 18-point font size and then changed the font size to 16 points, all you would need to do is edit the formatting instructions in the style and all occurrences of the style would change.

If you export Word files for use in separate desktop publishing programs, most of these programs can recognize Word styles. Microsoft Publisher 2003 can import Word styles directly. Some of the other programs can use optional Word filters.

Understanding the Relationship between Styles and Templates

As previously mentioned, Word bases a new blank document on the Normal template. By default, text that is typed is based on the Normal style. This means that when you start typing text, Word uses the font, font size, line spacing, text alignment, and other formatting instructions assigned to the Normal style, unless you specify other formatting instructions.

When you access a clear document window, *Normal* displays in the *Style* list box located at the left side of the Formatting toolbar. If you click the down-pointing arrow to the right of the *Style* list box, you will see a long list of built-in styles immediately available for your use, as shown in Figure 6.12. The style names are displayed as they would appear if applied to selected text. In addition to these styles, Word provides a large selection of other built-in styles. To view the styles that come with Word in the *Style* list box on the Formatting toolbar, hold down the Shift key and then click the down-pointing arrow on the right side of the *Style* list box.

Normal style
A set of formatting instructions automatically applied to any text that is keyed unless other formatting instructions are specified.

FIGURE

6.12 *Built-in Styles in Word 2003*

Normal ▾ | Times New Roman

Clear Formatting

Heading 1   ¶

Heading 2   ¶

Heading 3   ¶

Normal   ¶

More...

You can also view all available styles by clicking the Styles and Formatting button on the Formatting toolbar and the Styles and Formatting task pane displays, or by choosing Format and then Styles and Formatting. At the Styles and Formatting task pane shown in Figure 6.13, click the down-pointing arrow at the right of the *Show* list box and select *All styles*. Select any style name from the *Pick formatting to apply* list box and a tooltip will display showing a description of the formatting included in that style.

Styles and Formatting

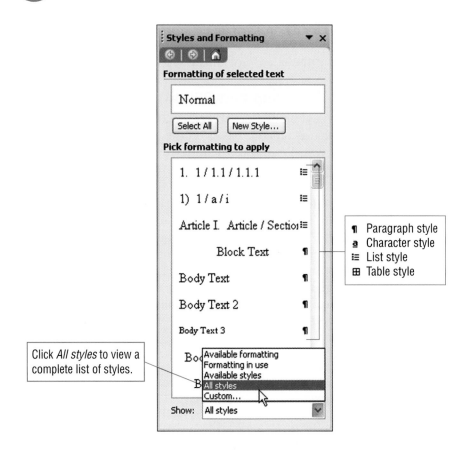

Click *All styles* to view a complete list of styles.

Most of Word's built-in styles are available in any of its template documents. Some of Word's template documents also contain additional styles depending on the type of document being created. If you choose a different template document from the New Document task pane at the <u>On my computer</u> or <u>Templates on Office Online</u> hyperlinks, the *Style* list box on the Formatting toolbar will display the names of styles available for that particular template as shown in Figure 6.14.

FIGURE

6.14 *List of Styles from a Microsoft Office Online Templates Web Page Brochure Template*

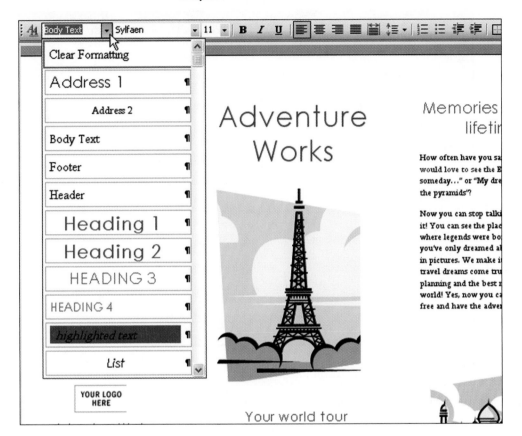

Word contains some styles that are applied automatically to text when you use certain commands. For example, if you use the command to insert page numbers, Word applies a certain style to the page number text. Some other commands for which Word automatically formats text with styles include those for headers, footers, footnotes, endnotes, indexes, and tables of contents.

Using the Style Gallery

As mentioned above, Word provides predesigned styles with other template documents. In addition to the list shown in Figure 6.14, you can also use the Style Gallery dialog box to apply styles from other templates to the current document. This provides you with a large number of predesigned styles for formatting text. To display the Style Gallery dialog box shown in Figure 6.15, click Format and then Theme. At the Theme dialog box, click the Style Gallery button (located at the bottom of the dialog box). In the *Template* list box, select the template that contains styles you want to view or use. When you click OK, styles from the selected template will be copied to your document. To preview how your document will look with the different styles, click *Document* in the *Preview* section. To see a sample document with styles from the selected template, click *Example*. To see a list of the styles used in the selected template, click *Style samples*.

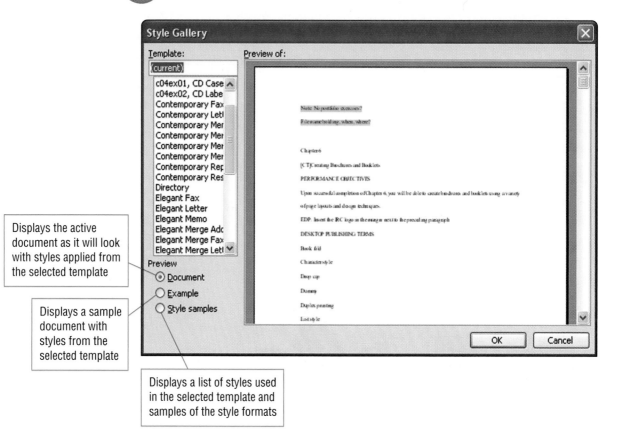

Displays the active document as it will look with styles applied from the selected template

Displays a sample document with styles from the selected template

Displays a list of styles used in the selected template and samples of the style formats

Using AutoFormat

You can use Word's AutoFormat feature, which will automatically apply predesigned styles without your having to select them. With AutoFormat, Word goes through a document paragraph by paragraph and applies appropriate styles. To display the AutoFormat dialog box, click Format and then AutoFormat. You can control the formatting that AutoFormat will apply by clicking the Options button at the AutoFormat dialog box and choosing desired options.

Understanding Word Styles

Paragraph style
A set of formatting instructions that applies to an entire paragraph.

Character style
A set of formatting instructions that applies to selected text only.

Four types of styles exist in Word 2003—paragraph styles, character styles, table styles, and list styles. A *paragraph style* applies formatting instructions to the paragraph that contains the insertion point or to selected text. A paragraph style may include formatting instructions such as text alignment, tab settings, line indents, line spacing, and borders, and can include character formatting.

A *character style* applies formatting to selected text within a paragraph. Character styles include options available at the Font dialog box such as font, font size, and font style (bold, underlining, and italics). Character styles are useful for formatting single characters, technical symbols, special names, or phrases. Characters within a paragraph can have their own style even if a paragraph style is applied to the paragraph as a whole.

A *table style* provides a consistent look to borders, shading, alignment, and fonts that are being used in a table. *List styles* are used to format bulleted or numbered lists.

In the styles list (accessed through the Styles and Formatting task pane or the *Style* list box on the Formatting toolbar), paragraph styles are indicated by a ¶ symbol and character styles by an **a** symbol. List styles are displayed with a bulleted icon at the right of the style, and a foursquare (table) icon indicates table styles, as shown in Figure 6.13.

Table style
Styles including borders, shading, alignment, and fonts used in a table.

List style
Style used to format bulleted or numbered lists.

Creating Styles

If the predesigned styles by Word do not contain the formatting that you desire, you can create your own styles. There are two methods for creating styles. The first method is creating a style by example, and the second method is creating a style using the New Style dialog box.

Creating a Style by Example

A style can be created by formatting text first and then using the Style button on the Formatting toolbar. To do this, position the insertion point in a paragraph of text containing the formatting you wish to include in the style and then click inside the *Style* list box on the Formatting toolbar. With the current style selected in the *Style* list box, type a unique name and then press Enter. The style will be added to the list of styles.

Creating a Style Using the New Style Dialog Box

A style can be created before you use it rather than creating it by example. To do this, use options from the New Style dialog box as shown in Figure 6.16. Click the New Style button in the Styles and Formatting task pane and then type a name for the style and specify what type of style you are creating (paragraph, character, list, table). Click the Format button to select the desired formatting and then click OK.

FIGURE

6.16 **New Style Dialog Box**

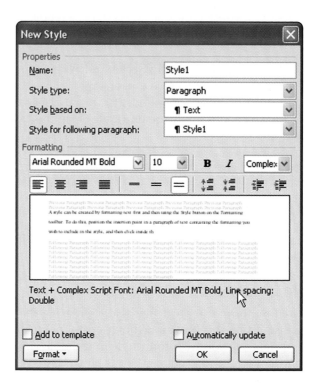

Applying Styles

A style can be applied before you type text, or it can be applied to text in an existing document. The most common methods of applying styles in Word include using the Style button on the Formatting toolbar and the Styles and Formatting task pane. To apply a style to existing text using the Style button on the Formatting toolbar, you would complete the following steps:

1. Position the insertion point in the paragraph to which you want the style applied, or select the text.
2. Click the down-pointing arrow to the right of the Style button on the Formatting toolbar.
3. Click the desired style name in the drop-down list to apply the style to the text in the document.

To apply a style using the Styles and Formatting task pane, display the task pane, and then click the desired style in the *Pick formatting to apply* list box. If you want to apply the same style to different sections of text in a document, such as applying a heading style to all of the headings, apply the style to the first heading, then move the insertion point to each of the remaining headings and press F4, Word's repeat key.

Modifying and Updating an Existing Style

You can modify an existing style by changing the formatting instructions that it contains and then instructing Word to update the style to include the changes. When you modify a style, all text to which that style has been applied is changed accordingly.

To modify a style using the Styles and Formatting task pane, you would complete the following steps:

1. Open the document that contains the style that is to be changed.

2. Click Format and then Styles and Formatting or click the Styles and Formatting button on the Formatting toolbar.

3. At the Styles and Formatting task pane, position the mouse pointer on the style name and then click the down-pointing arrow at the right side of the style name.

4. Click Modify at the drop-down list.

5. At the Modify Style dialog box shown in Figure 6.17, add or delete formatting options by clicking the Format button and then changing the appropriate options.

6. When all changes have been made, click OK to close the Modify Style dialog box.

FIGURE

6.17 *Modify Style Dialog Box*

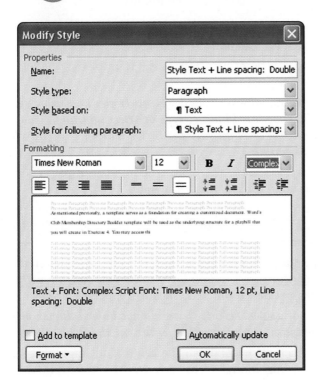

The modified style is available to the current active document. If you would like the modified style to be available in a new document based on the active template (most likely this is the Normal template), click *Add to template* in the Modify Style dialog box to insert a check mark in the check box. For example, if the active template is the Normal template, the modified style is added to that template so that it will be available every time you create a document based on the Normal template.

Removing a Style from Text

If you want to remove a style from text, you can click the Undo button on the Standard toolbar. You can also click Edit and then Undo Style. When a style is removed, the style that was previously applied to the text is applied once again. Word also contains a Clear Formatting style you can use to remove all formatting from selected text. To use this style, position the insertion point in the paragraph of text or select specific text, click the down-pointing arrow at the right side of the Style button on the Formatting toolbar, and then click *Clear Formatting* at the drop-down list.

Using the Microsoft Office Online Templates Web Page Booklet Template

As mentioned previously, a template serves as a foundation for creating a customized document. Word's Club Membership Directory Booklet template will be used as the underlying structure for a playbill that you will create in Exercise 4.

Creating a Folded Booklet

If you are interested in creating a folded booklet from scratch, start at a clear document screen and then complete the following steps:

1. Click File, Page Setup, and then click the Margins tab.
2. Change the page orientation to *Landscape*.
3. Click the down-pointing arrow at the right of the *Multiple pages* list box and then click *Book fold*.
4. Change the margins as desired. *(Hint: If you need more space along the fold to accommodate binding, type or select additional space in the Gutter text box or make sure the inside margin is slightly larger than the outside margin.)*
5. In the *Sheets per booklet* list, select the number of pages you want to include in your booklet (or select *Auto*).
6. Choose any other options in the Page Setup dialog box. *(Note: At the Layout tab you can click the Borders button and place a border around a page or section.)*
7. Add text, graphics, headers or footers, and any other elements to your booklet. *(Hint: Insert section breaks where formatting will vary from one area of the booklet to the next, such as symmetric headers and footers.)*
8. Print on both sides. *(Hint: If you do not have a duplex printer, activate Word's manual duplex printing feature at the Print dialog box.)*
9. Fold the stack of sheets down the center and staple them together in the center using a long-reach stapler.

Printing a Folded Booklet

When you select **Book fold** at the Page Setup dialog box, Word prints two pages on one side of the paper. When you fold the paper, it opens like a book. You would want to use this option when you are creating documents that have more than two pages. For example, in an eight-page booklet, pages 8 and 1 are on the same side of the same sheet; pages 2 and 7 share the same sheet; pages 6 and 3 share the same sheet; and pages 4 and 5 must print on the same sheet as shown in Figure 6.18. It may take some trial and error when working with your printer, so try printing a dummy booklet first.

Book fold
Word feature used to print two pages on one side of the paper.

F I G U R E

6.18 *Pages Arranged for Printing*

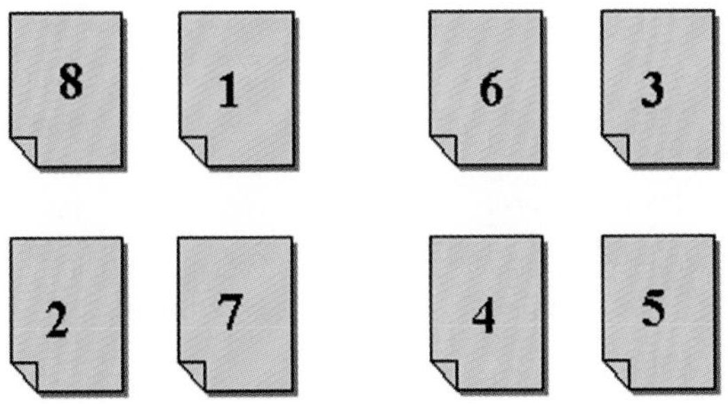

When printing a booklet, be sure to print on both sides of the paper. This is known as **duplex printing**. If you have a duplex printer, be sure to check the printer settings by clicking File, Print, and then Properties.

Duplex printing
Printing on both sides of the paper. Some printers can print in duplex mode.

If you do not have a duplex printer, you can print on both sides by using Word's Manual Duplex feature. To use this feature, click File, Print, and then check the *Manual duplex* check box (in the upper right corner of the Print dialog box). Click OK to print. Word prints the first side of each sheet of paper, and then prompts you to flip the stack of sheets over and reinsert them into your printer for printing on the reverse side. *(Hint: Reinserting the paper correctly may take a few attempts.)*

In addition, you may change the printing order of the booklet pages at the Print tab of the Options dialog box as shown in Figure 6.19. You can choose an option to print either page 1 on the top or bottom of a stack or to print page 2 on the top or bottom of a stack.

6.19 *Duplex Printing Order Options*

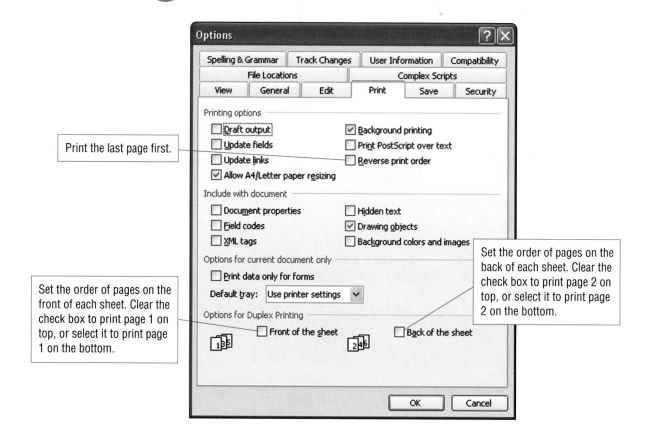

Print the last page first.

Set the order of pages on the front of each sheet. Clear the check box to print page 1 on top, or select it to print page 1 on the bottom.

Set the order of pages on the back of each sheet. Clear the check box to print page 2 on top, or select it to print page 2 on the bottom.

Working with Headers and Footers

A header consists of text or graphics that appear at the top of every page in a section. A footer appears at the bottom of every page. Headers and footers often contain page numbers, chapter titles, company logos, file names, author's name, or dates. At the Page Setup dialog box, click the Layout tab, change the header and footer margins, create a different header or footer for the first page of a document or section, or create one header or footer for even-numbered pages and a different header or footer for odd-numbered pages.

The graphics or text that you insert in a header or footer is automatically left-aligned. To center an item, press Tab; to right-align an item, press Tab twice.

If you have chosen one of the *Multiple pages* options (*Mirror margins, 2 pages per sheet*, or *Book fold*) at the Page Setup dialog box, you may want to include headers and footers that are symmetrical. Figure 6.20 shows a two-page spread with symmetric headers and footers. To turn on this feature, select the *Different odd and even* option in the Layout tab at the Page Setup dialog box.

Figure 6.21 illustrates the Header and Footer toolbar, which you will be using in Exercise 4.

6.20 *Creating Symmetric Headers and Footers*

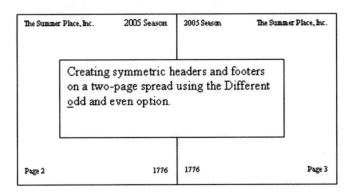

6.21 *Header and Footer Toolbar*

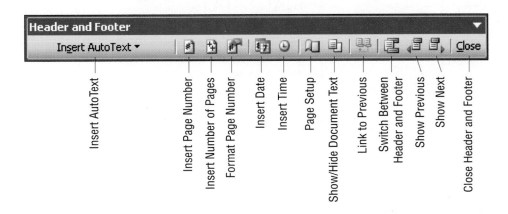

Adding Page Numbering to a Booklet

Page numbering can be added to a booklet and any other document, by clicking Insert and then Page Numbers. This feature inserts page numbering automatically in either a header or a footer, depending on whether you choose to position the number at the top of the page or at the bottom of the page. However, if you are using headers and footers in your booklet, it is simpler to add the numbering by clicking the Insert Page Number button on the Header and Footer toolbar.

Insert Page Number

exercise 4

Creating a Playbill Using a Microsoft Office Online Templates
Web Page Booklet Template

1. Create the playbill shown in Figure 6.22 by completing the following steps:
   a. Open **Membership Directory** from your Chapter06 folder.
   b. Add an additional page to the booklet by pressing Ctrl + End and then pressing Ctrl + Enter. *(Note: Read the Status bar; it should indicate that eight pages are available.)*
2. Save the document and name it **c06ex4, Playbill**.
3. Create the cover for the booklet by completing the following steps:
   a. Press Ctrl + Home and then change all of the margins to 0.75 inch.
   b. Make sure *Book fold* is selected in the *Multiple pages* list box and the orientation is changed to *Landscape*.
   c. Click the Layout tab at the Page Seup dialog box, click the down-pointing arrow at the right of the *Section start* list box, and then click *New page*. In the *Headers and footers* section, click the check box at the left of the *Different odd and even* option to turn this feature on, and then click OK.

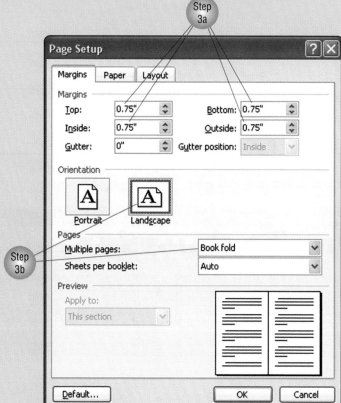

   d. Position the insertion point in the first page, select *Our Organization's Membership Directory,* and then type The Summer Place, Inc. proudly presents.
   e. Select the text *The Summer Place...*, change the font to 18-point Bodoni MT Black, and then change the font color to Black.
   f. Select *proudly presents* and apply italics.
   g. Delete the text *Fall 2004*.
   h. Select the placeholder graphic, display the Clip Art task pane, type ph03348i.jpg or type the keywords usa flag in the *Search for* text box, and then click Go.

i. Click the revolutionary soldiers clip art shown in Figure 6.22. Change the text wrapping style to In Front of Text. Resize the clip so that it is approximately the size as shown in Figure 6.22.

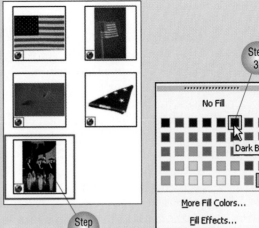

j. Display the Drawing toolbar, click the Insert WordArt button, click the fifth WordArt style from the left in the second row, and then click OK.

k. At the Edit WordArt Text dialog box, change the font to 80-point Book Antiqua bold, type 1776, and then click OK.

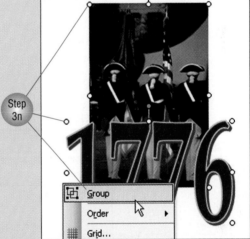

l. Select 1776, click the Format WordArt button on the WordArt toolbar, select the Colors and Lines tab, change the fill color to Dark Blue (sixth color from the left in the first row), and then click OK.

m. Click the Text Wrapping button and change the wrapping style to In Front of Text. Drag the WordArt object below the revolutionary soldiers image as shown in Figure 6.22.

n. Hold down the Shift key and then click the image and the WordArt object, click Draw on the Drawing toolbar, and then click Group.

o. With the grouped image still selected, display the Clipboard task pane and then click the Copy button on the Standard toolbar. (A thumbnail copy of the image should display on the Clipboard task pane.)

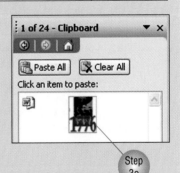

p. Click the Text Box button on the Drawing toolbar and then drag the crosshairs to create a text box approximately 1.25 inches in height by 4.15 inches in width.

q. Position the insertion point inside the text box, change the font to 12-point Bodoni MT Black, change the alignment to center, and then type the following:

> America's Award Winning Musical (press Enter)
> Music and Lyrics by (press Enter)
> SHERMAN EDWARDS (press Enter)
> Book by PETER STONE

r. Remove the border around the text box.

s. Create another text box measuring approximately 0.5 inch in height by 4.75 inches in width, change the font to 18-point Bodoni MT Black and the color to Red, change the alignment to center, and then type June 14–16 and 21–23, 2005 (use en dashes). Remove the border around the text box. Position the text boxes as shown in Figure 6.22.

4. Page 2 of the booklet is blank.
5. Create page 3 of the booklet by completing the following steps:
   a. Position the insertion point in page 3 (see the Status bar). A section break (Odd Page) was created on the second page, so you will need to change the margins again for this section—change all of the margins to 0.75 inch.
   b. Click the Layout tab. Make sure there is a check mark in the check box at the left of the *Different odd and even* option and then click OK.
   c. Click <u>V</u>iew and then <u>H</u>eader and Footer. At the Header and Footer pane, select the placeholder text and delete it and then display the Styles and Formatting task pane.
   d. Make sure *Header* displays in the *Formatting of selected text* box, position the arrow pointer over *Header*, and then click the down-pointing arrow at the right of the text box.
   e. Click <u>M</u>odify at the drop-down menu.
   f. At the Modify Style dialog box, change the font to 9-point Arial. Click the F<u>o</u>rmat button and then click <u>T</u>abs at the drop-down menu.

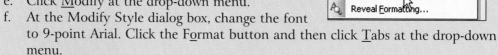

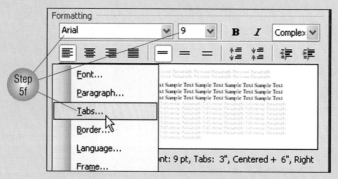

   g. At the Tabs dialog box, click the Clear <u>A</u>ll button to clear the 3-inch and 6-inch tab settings and then set a right tab at 3.75 inches. Click <u>S</u>et and then click OK.
   h. Click F<u>o</u>rmat, <u>P</u>aragraph, and then type **0** in the *Before* and *After* text boxes located in the *Spacing* section. Click OK twice.
   i. In the header pane (Odd Page Header - Section 2), type **2005 Season**, press Tab, and then type **The Summer Place, Inc.**
   j. Click the Switch Between Header and Footer button.
   k. At the footer pane (Odd Page Footer - Section 2), delete the page number in the middle of the pane. Make sure the Styles and Formatting task pane is displayed and the Footer style is active.
   l. Modify the Footer style by clicking the down-pointing arrow at the right of the Footer style displayed in the Styles and Formatting task pane and then clicking <u>M</u>odify.

m. At the Modify Style dialog box, make sure 9-point Arial displays in the *Formatting* section. Click F<u>o</u>rmat and then <u>T</u>abs. At the Tabs dialog box, click Clear <u>A</u>ll and create a right tab at 3.75 inches. Click OK. Click F<u>o</u>rmat, <u>P</u>aragraph, and in the *Spacing* section, make sure *0* displays in the *Be<u>f</u>ore* and *Aft<u>e</u>r* text boxes. Click OK twice.

Tabs ☒

<u>T</u>ab stop position:

3.75"

| 3.75" | | Tab stops to be cleared: |

Alignment
- ○ <u>L</u>eft   ○ <u>C</u>enter   ◉ <u>R</u>ight
- ○ <u>D</u>ecimal   ○ <u>B</u>ar

Step 5m

n. Make sure <u>*Left*</u> alignment is selected, type 1776, press Tab, type Page, press the spacebar once, and then click the Insert Page Number button on the Header and Footer toolbar. Click the Format Page Number button, and type 3 in the *Start <u>at</u>* text box, and then click OK.

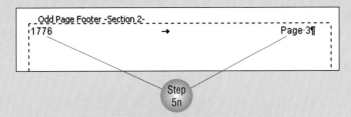

Step 5n

o. Click the Switch Between Header and Footer button.
p. Click the Show Next button on the Header and Footer toolbar.
q. Click the Link to Previous button to turn off this feature.
r. Make sure the Header style displays in the *Style* list box on the Formatting toolbar.
s. Type The Summer Place, Inc., press Tab, and then type 2005 Season.

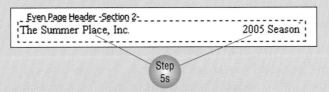

Step 5s

t. Click the Switch Between Header and Footer button.
u. At the Footer pane, make sure the Footer style displays in the *Style* list box. Click the Link to Previous button to turn off this feature, type Page, press the spacebar once, click the Insert Page Number button, press the Tab key, and then type 1776. Click <u>C</u>lose on the Header and Footer toolbar.
v. With the insertion point positioned in page 3 (see Status bar), select the placeholder text, change the alignment to center, change the font to 12-point Bodoni MT Black, and then type the following, pressing Enter after each line:

   The Summer Place, Inc.
   Naperville Community Theatre
   proudly presents

w. Display the Clipboard task pane.
x. Position the insertion point below *proudly presents* and then click the 1776/Flag image in the *Click an item to paste* list box.
y. Size and position the image similar to Figure 6.22.

   z. Click Insert and then File. Insert **Page 3 Playbill** located in your Chapter06 folder. Select the text inside the text box, click Format, Paragraph, select the Indents and Spacing tab, and then type **0** in the *Spacing Before* text box. Click OK. Drag the text box to a position similar to Figure 6.22.

6. Create page 4 of the booklet by completing the following steps:
   a. Position the insertion point in page 4 (see the Status bar).
   b. Select the placeholder text, click Insert, File, and then insert **Page 4 Playbill** located in your Chapter06 folder. *(Hint: You may need to press Enter several times after you insert the text in case text from a subsequent page moves up into the page.)*
   c. Select the text (not the title), click Format, and then Tabs.
   d. At the Tabs dialog box, set a right tab with dot leaders at 3.75 inches. Click Set and then click OK.

7. Create page 5 by completing the following steps:
   a. Position the insertion point on page 5 and then select the placeholder text.
   b. Insert **Page 5 Playbill** located in your Chapter06 folder.

8. Create page 6 by completing the following steps:
   a. Position the insertion point on page 6 and then select the placeholder text and the space above and below the placeholder text.
   b. Insert **Page 6 Playbill** located in your Chapter06 folder.

9. Create page 7 by completing the following steps:
   a. Position the insertion point on page 7 out of 8 (see the Status bar).
   b. Insert **Page 7 Playbill** located in your Chapter06 folder.

10. Remove the header and footer on page 8 by completing the following steps:
   a. Position the insertion point on page 8 out of 8 (see the Status bar).
   b. Click View and then Header and Footer.
   c. Click the Link to Previous button to deactivate this feature.
   d. Delete the header text.
   e. Click the Switch Between Header and Footer button.
   f. Click the Link to Previous button to deactivate this feature.
   g. Delete the footer text and then click Close.

11. Select each object and then position them similar to Figure 6.22. Save the document with the same name **c06ex04, Playbill**.

12. Click File, Print, and then check the *Manual duplex* check box (in the upper right corner of the Print dialog box). Click OK to print. Word prints the first side of each sheet of paper, and then prompts you to flip the stack of sheets over and reinsert them into your printer for printing on the reverse side. *(Hint: Reinserting the paper correctly and printing may take a few attempts.)*

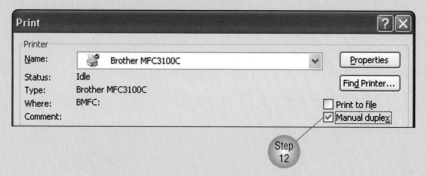

Step 12

13. At the Print dialog box, remove the check mark from the *Manual duplex* check box.
14. Save and close **c06ex04, Playbill**.

FIGURE

6.22 *Exercise 4*

The Summer Place, Inc.
proudly presents

1776

America's Award Winning Musical
Music and Lyrics by
SHERMAN EDWARDS
Book by PETER STONE

June 14–16 and 21–23, 2005

The Summer Place, Inc.   2005 Season

Director's Note

Invariably, a question asked by those who have seen, or read, *1776* is "is it true, did it really happen that way? The answer is "yes." Many elements of this remarkable work are taken directly from historical fact. The weather in Philadelphia was unusually hot and humid, resulting in a bumper crop of horseflies. John Adams was indeed "obnoxious and disliked" the description was his own. Rodney's skin cancer, Franklin's gout, Chase's fetish for food are all true. Rutledge, the youngest member of Congress, was the leading proponent of individual states rights. Washington's dispatches came into Congress via courier and were for a long time ignored by most Congressmen. Of course, bits were deleted and the action has sometimes been rearranged to create a more dramatic progression.

Sherman Edwards, an ex-history teacher, was in love with this period and the people who inhabited it. Happily, he also wrote dozens of top ten songs including *Wonderful, Wonderful, See You in September,* and *Brokenhearted Melody*. His partnership with renowned director Peter Stone led to the winning of the Tony Award for Best Musical, Best Music and Lyrics and the New York Drama Critics Circle Award in 1969, a time when patriotism was at a low ebb in America.

It has been my privilege to work with these talented and dedicated artists for the last two months. It is my hope that whatever questions you may still have at the end of this evening one of the most troublesome will be, "Why didn't I know this?" Without an intimate knowledge of our past, how can we hope to carry our country into a new millennium?

Whether you came for the history lesson or for the entertainment, I think you will not be disappointed. Thank you to the Summer Place Theatre for having the trust and the courage to bring this wonderful material to us.

Jan Mahlstedt, 2005

Page 6   1776

2005 Season   The Summer Place, Inc.

The Summer Place, Inc.
Naperville Community Theatre
proudly presents

1776

Music and Lyrics by
SHERMAN EDWARDS
Book by PETER STONE

Based on a Concept by SHERMAN EDWARDS
Original Production Directed by PETER HUNT
Originally Produced on the Broadway Stage
by Stuart Ostrow

Directed by Jan Mahlstedt
Produced by Bernadette and Roger Budny
Orchestra Direction by Joey Lugay
Vocal Direction by Elizabeth Miller-Wesley
Choreographed by Tracy Brown

1776   Page 3

FIGURE

6.22   *Exercise 4 (continued)*

Are you on our mailing list?

If you wish to be on the Summer Place mailing list, simply fill in this form and return it to the box office, or mail it to the address below.

Name: _____

Address: _____

City: _____

State, Zip: _____

E-Mail Address: _____

The Summer Place, Inc.
P.O. Box 333
Naperville, IL 60566
630.555.1237

The Summer Place, Inc.   2005 Season

The Cast

John Adams .... Steve Arvanites
Abigail Adams .... Lisa Baggott-Miller
Colonel Thomas McKean .... Mike Choate
Leather Apron/Painter .... Josh Culberson
Caesar Rodney .... Patrick Farbo
Stephen Hopkins .... Burke Fry
Andrew McNair .... Craig Gustafson
Robert Livingston .... David Hollander
John Hancock .... Robert Kimmeth
Thomas Jefferson .... Randall Knott
Joseph Hewes .... Garth Lawson
James Wilson .... James Liljegren
Richard Henry Lee .... Daniel Linka
Dr. Josiah Bartlett .... Larry Lipskie
Benjamin Franklin .... Graig Mahlstedt
Rev. J. Witherspoon .... Roger Matson
Charles Thomson .... Daniel Miller
Martha Jefferson .... Eirian Morgan
George Read .... Trevor Morgan
Roger Sherman .... Dan Murphy
Dr. Lyman Hall .... Ned O'Reilly
A Courier .... David Pfenninger
Edward Rutledge .... Steve Tomlitz
Samuel Chase .... Steve Zeidler

Page 4   1776

2005 Season   The Summer Place, Inc.

Act I

May, June, and July 1776

THE CHAMBER OF THE CONTINENTAL CONGRESS
"For God's Sake, John, Sit Down" .... Adams & The Congress
"Piddle, Twiddle" .... Adams
"Till Then" .... Adams & Abigail

THE MALL
"The Lees of Old Virginia" .... Lee, Franklin & Adams

THE CHAMBER
"But Mr. Adams" .... Adams, Franklin, Jefferson, Sherman & .... Livingston

THOMAS JEFFERSON'S PORCH AND HIGH STREET
"Yours, Yours, Yours" .... Adams & Abigail
"He Plays the Violin" .... Martha, Franklin & Adams

THE CHAMBER
"Cool, Cool Considerate Men" ..... Dickinson & The Conservatives
"Momma Look Sharp" .... The Courier

15 Minute Intermission

Act II

A CONGRESSIONAL ANTEROM
"The Egg" .... Franklin, Adams, Jefferson & Congress
THE CHAMBER
"Molasses To Rum" .... Rutledge
"Compliments" .... Abigail

"Is Anybody There?" .... Adams, Franklin, Jefferson & Thomson

1776   Page 5

Copying Individual Styles from Other Documents and Templates

When you work on a document, you may want to use a style that already exists in one of Word's templates or in a document you have created. In Word, the Organizer dialog box, as shown in Figure 6.23, offers options for copying individual styles, in addition to macros, toolbars, and AutoText entries, from an existing document or template to another document or template. For instance, to copy the teal heading style and the violet subheading style from c06ex05, Panels 1,2 (a document you will create in Exercise 5) to a document named Heart Text using the Organizer dialog box, you would complete the following steps:

DTP POINTERS
Styles can help to maintain consistency and reinforce an organization's identity.

1. With the insertion point located in *Heart Text*, click Tools, Templates and Add-Ins, and then click the Organizer button at the Templates tab of the Templates and Add-ins dialog box.

2. At the Organizer dialog box, click the Styles tab. By default, the name of the current document displays above the list box on the left side of the Organizer dialog box and in the *Styles available in* list box, also on the left side of the dialog box. The list box shows a list of the styles available in that particular document. By default, *Normal* will display as the file name on the right side of the dialog box and the list box below will display the styles available in the Normal template.

3. On the right side of the dialog box, click Close File to change the command button to Open File and then click Open File.

4. Select *c06ex05, Panels 1,2* and then click Open or press Enter.

5. In the right list box for c06ex05, Panels 1,2 select *teal heading*, hold down the Ctrl key, and then select *violet subheading*. **(Hint: Both style names should be selected as shown in Figure 6.23.)**

6. Click Copy. (The teal heading and violet subheading styles will now be listed in the *Heart Text* list box on the left side of the dialog box as shown in Figure 6.23.)

7. Click Close.

A document does not have to be open for you to copy styles from one document or template to another. At the Organizer dialog box, you can select a different document name or template for each list box by clicking the Close File (or Close File) command button below either list box to change the command button to an Open File (or Open File) button. Click Open File (or Open File) and select the document or template you want to copy styles to or from.

The Organizer dialog box can be confusing because the Copy button may display arrows pointing to the right, making you think that styles must be copied from the left side to the right side. However, styles can be copied from either side. If you select a style in the list box on the right, the arrows on the Copy button point to the left, as do the labels above each list box (see Figure 6.23).

6.23 *Organizer Dialog Box*

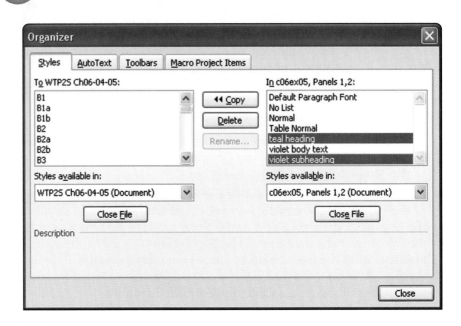

Using Drop Caps as a Design Element

Drop cap

The first letter of the first word in a paragraph formatted in a larger font size and positioned into the beginning of the paragraph.

DTP POINTERS

Use drop caps sparingly.

In publications such as magazines, newsletters, or brochures, a graphics feature called drop caps can be used to enhance the appearance of text. A ***drop cap*** is the first letter of the first word in a paragraph that is set in a larger font size and set into the paragraph. Drop caps identify the beginning of major sections or parts of a document.

Drop caps look best when set in a paragraph containing text set in a proportional font. The drop cap can be set in the same font as the paragraph text or it can be set in a complementary font. For example, a drop cap can be set in a sans serif font while the paragraph text is set in a serif font. A drop cap can be one character or the entire first word of a paragraph. A special character may be used as the first character in a paragraph and then formatted as a drop cap to create an interesting effect. The examples in Figure 6.24 show some of the ways drop caps can be created and formatted. Practice restraint when using this design element or it can be distracting.

A drop cap can be applied only to existing text. To create a drop cap, click Format and then Drop Cap. At the Drop Cap dialog box, select *Dropped* in the *Position* section to create a drop cap positioned into the paragraph with the remaining text wrapping around it; or select *In margin* to create a drop cap that is positioned in the margin to the left of the paragraph. Click Font in the Drop Cap dialog box to select the desired font for the drop cap letter only. Click the *Lines to drop* option to set the number of lines (from 1 to 10 lines) that the drop cap will be vertically positioned into the paragraph. Click *Distance from text* to set the amount of distance the drop cap is positioned in relation to the paragraph text.

6.24 *Drop Cap Examples*

drop cap looks best when set in a paragraph containing text set in a proportional font. The drop cap can be set in the same font as the paragraph text or it can be set in a complementary font. For example, a drop cap can be set in a sans serif font while the paragraph text is set in a serif font. A drop cap can be one character or the entire first word of a paragraph. A special character may be used as the first character in a paragraph and then formatted as a drop cap to create a visually interesting effect. *(The drop cap is set in Curlz MT with a green font color and shadow effect applied; the body text is set in High Tower Text.)*

drop cap looks best when set in a paragraph containing text set in a proportional font. The drop cap can be set in the same font as the paragraph text or it can be set in a complementary font. For example, a drop cap can be set in a sans serif font while the paragraph text is set in a serif font. A drop cap can be one character or the entire first word of a paragraph. A special character may be used as the first character in a paragraph and then formatted as a drop cap to create a visually interesting effect. *(The drop cap is set in Jokerman with a light blue font color; the body text is set in Comic Sans MS.)*

publications such as magazines, newsletters, or brochures, a graphics feature called *drop caps* can be used to enhance the appearance of text. A drop cap is the first letter of the first word in a paragraph that is set in a larger font size and set into the paragraph. Drop caps identify the beginning of major sections or parts of a document. *(The drop cap is set in Mercurius Script MT with a plum font color; the body text is set in Book Antiqua.)*

In publications such as magazines, newsletters, or brochures, a graphics feature called *drop caps* can be used to enhance the appearance of text. A drop cap is the first letter of the first word in a paragraph that is set in a larger font size and set into the paragraph. Drop caps identify the beginning of major sections or parts of a document. *(The drop cap is from the Webdings character set; the body text is set in Verdana.)*

Although text boxes generally have replaced frames in the most recent versions of Word, the drop cap feature still uses a frame to enclose the text. A frame is similar to a text box except that it is inserted in the text layer rather than the drawing layer. You can customize the drop cap letter by selecting the letter within the frame and changing the font color and font style and adding special effects. You can also apply other formatting, such as borders and shading, to the frame itself.

Using Word's 2 Pages Per Sheet Feature

Word 2003 has a feature that makes creating single fold brochures much easier. The 2 pages per sheet feature divides each physical page (not the text) in half as shown in Figure 6.25, so that the printed page can be folded in half and used as a single-fold brochure or several pages can be folded and bound at the fold to create a booklet. Word displays and numbers each half page as a separate page. Any page formatting such as margins, paper size, and orientation can be applied to each half page. Headers and footers, page numbering, and page borders can also be inserted.

To use the 2 pages per sheet feature, click File, Page Setup, and then select the Margins tab. In the *Pages* section of the Margins tab, click the down-pointing arrow at the right of the *Multiple pages* list box and then select *2 pages per sheet* at the drop-down list. In addition, select *Portrait* or *Landscape* in the *Orientation* section.

Enter the desired margin values. When you select the 2 pages per sheet feature, the name of some of the margin boxes will change depending on the page orientation selected. If you select portrait orientation, the *Top* and *Bottom* text box names change to *Outside* and *Inside*. If you select landscape orientation, the *Left* and *Right* margin box names change to *Outside* and *Inside*. Refer to Figure 6.25 to see where the outside and inside margins are located when portrait or landscape is selected.

In Exercise 5, you will create the inside panels of a single-fold brochure using various design and formatting techniques, including 2 pages per sheet, a drop cap, and styles.

F I G U R E

6.25 *2 Pages Per Sheet*

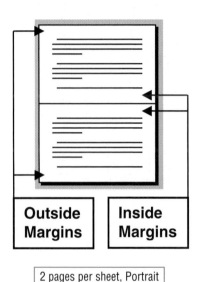

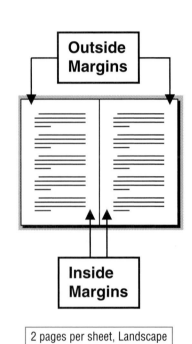

| 2 pages per sheet, Portrait | | 2 pages per sheet, Landscape |

Using Word's Reading Layout View

Reading Layout view is a document view that provides an optimized layout for reading Word documents. In Reading Layout view all toolbars are hidden, with the exception of the Reading Layout and Reviewing toolbars. Because this view is designed to enhance the reading experience, the document display on the screen is not the same as the way the document will appear when it is printed. To display Reading Layout view, click the Read button on the Standard toolbar as shown in Figure 6.26, press Alt + R, click the Reading Layout view button to the left of the horizontal scroll bar, or click View and then Reading Layout. You can edit text in Reading Layout view, and the Reviewing toolbar is displayed so that you can easily add comments or enable the Track Changes feature. Once in Reading Layout view, the Read button changes to the Close button. Clicking the Close button restores the view to the previous view. Alternatively, pressing Esc or Alt + C can be used to close Reading Layout view.

The Reading Layout toolbar shown in Figure 6.27 contains a number of different buttons to facilitate the reading experience. Clicking Document Map displays an outline view of the document. This feature is described in more detail later in this chapter. The Thumbnails button displays a small thumbnail of each page on the left side of the screen. Thumbnails can be clicked to change the current page display. The Find button can be used to search for text within the document, and the Research button displays the Research task pane, which can be used to research reference materials on the Web. The Increase Text Size or Decrease Text Size buttons can be used to change the size of the text displayed in Reading Layout view. Clicking the Actual Page button will display pages as they would appear when printed, while the Allow Multiple Pages button can be used to display two pages at a time.

FIGURE

6.26 *Standard Toolbar Read Button*

FIGURE

6.27 *Reading Layout Toolbar*

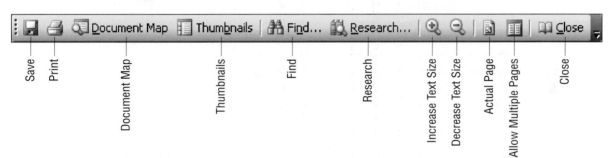

exercise 5

Creating the Inside Panels of a Single-Fold Brochure Using Styles and a Drop Cap

1. Create a dummy for a single-fold brochure by taking a piece of standard-size 8½ by 11-inch paper, holding the long side up, and folding it in half. With a pen or pencil, label the panels on one side of the page as Panel 1 (Inside) and Panel 2 (Inside). Label the panels on the other side as Panel 3 (Back) and Panel 4 (Cover). Refer to the dummy when creating the brochure to ensure that you are typing the appropriate text in the correct location. Save your document periodically as you are working.
2. At a clear document screen, create the inside panels of a single-fold brochure, as shown in Figure 6.28, by completing the following steps:
   a. Set up the 2 pages per sheet feature and change the margins and orientation by completing the following steps:

1) Display the Page Setup dialog box, select the Margins tab, and then select *Landscape* in the *Orientation* section.

2) Click the down-pointing arrow at the right of the *Multiple pages* list box and then click *2 pages per sheet*.

3) Change the top and bottom margins to 0.7 inch and the outside and inside margins to 0.55 inch. Click OK. **(Hint: The outside and inside margin settings were chosen because of the unprintable zone associated with the printer that was used to create and print this brochure. If your printer will not allow you to use these same settings, change your margins accordingly, and then make any necessary adjustments to the settings so that your document basically matches Figure 6.28.)**

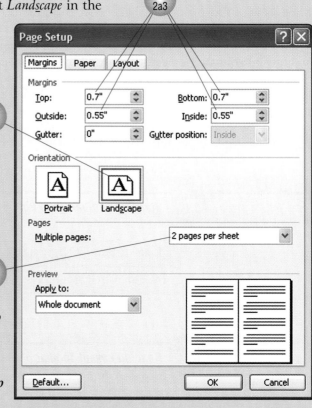

Step 2a3

Step 2a1

Step 2a2

b. Turn on automatic kerning for font sizes 14 points and above.

c. With the insertion point located at the top of the document, insert the **Heart Text** file located in your Chapter06 folder.

d. Format the drop cap paragraph by completing the following steps:

1) Click the Show/Hide ¶ button on the Standard toolbar to display nonprinting symbols.

2) Select the first paragraph and change the font to 16-point Arial Italic and the color to Violet.

3) With the insertion point within the paragraph (the text may still be selected), change the line spacing to 1.5 lines.

4) Make sure the text is deselected and the insertion point is within the same paragraph, click Format, and then **D**rop Cap.

5) At the Drop Cap dialog box, select *Dropped* in the *Position* section.

6) Click the down-pointing arrow at the right of the *Font* list box and select *Impact* as the font.

7) Make sure the *Lines to drop* option displays 3.

8) Change the *Distance from text* option to 0.1″ and then click OK or press Enter.

Step 2d5

Step 2d6

Step 2d7

Step 2d8

9) Make sure the frame around the drop cap is selected (black sizing handles will display), change the font color to Teal, and then turn off italics.

10) Position the insertion point at the end of the same paragraph and then press Enter.

e. Format the first heading and create a style from the formatted heading by completing the following steps:

1) Select *Diabetes: The Latest News* and change the font to 16-point Impact and the color to Teal.

2) Display the Paragraph dialog box and select the Line and Page Breaks tab. In the *Pagination* section, click the check box at the left of *Keep with next* so that the heading will always stay with the paragraph that follows and will not be separated by a column break or a page break and then click OK.

3) Position the insertion point within the heading just formatted (the heading can still be selected). Click the *Style* list box on the Formatting toolbar to select the style name that is currently in the box.

4) Type **teal heading** and then press Enter. (This heading style name will display in the *Style* list box and be added to the list of styles available for this brochure.)

f. Format the first subheading (day, date, name, and title) and create a style by completing the following steps:

1) Select *Tuesday, March 15, 2005* and *Katherine Dwyer, M.D.*

2) Change the font to 12-point Arial Bold Italic and the color to Violet.

3) Display the Paragraph dialog box, select the Line and Page Breaks tab, click the *Keep with next* option to insert a check mark, and then click OK.

Step 2f3

Paragraph

Indents and Spacing | Line and Page Breaks

Pagination
☑ Widow/Orphan control   ☑ Keep with next
☐ Keep lines together   ☐ Page break before

4) Position the insertion point within the subheading just formatted (the subheading can still be selected). Click the *Style* list box on the Formatting toolbar to select the style name that is currently in the box.

5) Type **violet subheading** and then press Enter. This subheading style name displays in the *Style* list box and is added to the list of styles available for this brochure.

g. Format the body text and create a style by completing the following steps:

1) Select the paragraph that begins with *One of the best ways...* and ends with *new medical recommendations.*

2) Change the font to 12-point Arial and the color to Violet.

3) Change the spacing before the paragraph to 6-point and the spacing after to 24-point.

4) Position the insertion point within the paragraph just formatted (the paragraph can still be selected). Click the *Style* list box on the Formatting toolbar to select the style name that is currently in the box.

5) Type **violet body text** and then press Enter. This body text style name displays in the *Style* list box and is added to the list of styles available for this brochure.

h. Position the insertion point within the heading *New Advances in Cardiac Surgery* and apply the teal heading from the *Style* drop-down list on the Formatting toolbar.

i. Select *Tuesday, March 22, 2005* and *Christine Johnson, M.D.* and apply the violet subheading style from the *Style* drop-down list on the Formatting toolbar.

j. Position the insertion point within the paragraph that begins with *Advances in minimally invasive...* and ends with *leads an informative discussion.* and apply the violet body text style from the *Style* drop-down list on the Formatting toolbar.

k. Move the insertion point to the top of the second page (panel 2) and apply the teal heading, the violet subheading, and the violet body text styles to the remaining headings, subheads, and body text (up to but not including *All lectures:...*), as shown in Figure 6.28. *(Note: You can apply the teal heading style to all of the headings by applying the first one, moving the insertion point to each heading, and then pressing F4. Repeat the process for the subheadings and body text.)*

l. Format the lecture information text at the bottom of panel 2 by completing the following steps:

    1) Select from *All lectures:* until the end of the document and then change the font to 12-point Arial and the color to Teal.

    2) Insert tabs to align the lecture information (time and location) as displayed in Figure 6.28.

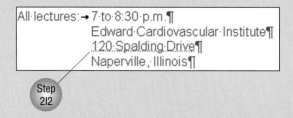

Step
2l2

    3) Position the insertion point to the right of *Naperville, Illinois* and press Enter.

    4) Select the last paragraph and change the font style to italics.

    5) Select *FREE* and change the color to Violet.

    6) Select *(630) 555-4941* and then change the color to Violet.

m. Insert the watermark (heart image) by completing the following steps:

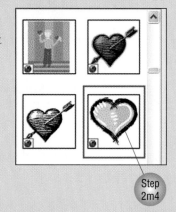

Step
2m4

    1) Move the insertion point to the space below the first paragraph on the first page.

    2) Click the Zoom button on the Standard toolbar and then change the viewing mode to *Whole Page*.

    3) Display the Clip Art task pane, type j0233512.wmf, or type the keyword *heart*.

    4) Scroll through the selections until you find one similar to Figure 6.28 and then insert the image.

    5) Select the heart image, click the Text Wrapping button on the Picture toolbar, and then click In Front of Text. *(Note: You will work with the image on top of the text until all necessary changes are made and then you will send it behind the text.)*

    6) With the image still selected, display the Format Picture dialog box and then select the Size tab. In the *Size and rotate* section, size the image by changing the height to 5.25 inches and the width to 5.33 inches, and then click OK.

    7) Change the color of the heart by completing the following steps:

        a) Right-click the heart image and select Edit Picture from the shortcut menu.

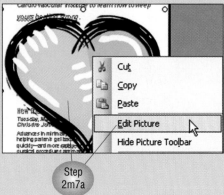

Step
2m7a

b) At the Microsoft Word prompt asking if you want to convert the image into a drawing object, click Yes.

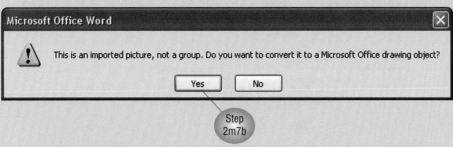

This is an imported picture, not a group. Do you want to convert it to a Microsoft Office drawing object?

Yes   No

Step
2m7b

c) Click the Zoom button on the Standard toolbar and adjust the view to *50%*. Click off the image to deselect heart components.

d) Double-click the right side of the black border that surrounds the heart. At the Format AutoShape dialog box, select the Colors and Lines tab, change the fill color (of the border) to Teal, and then drag the transparency slider to the right or type 70%. Click OK.

e) Double-click the dark pink area of the heart. At the Format AutoShape dialog box, select the Colors and Lines tab, and then add 50% transparency to the existing pink color.

Step
2m7d

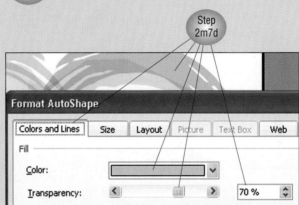

Format AutoShape

Colors and Lines | Size | Layout | Picture | Text Box | Web

Fill

Color:

Transparency: 70 %

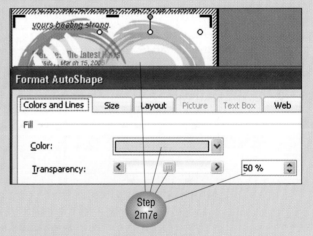

yours beabng strong.

The latest
Mar ch 15, 200

Format AutoShape

Colors and Lines | Size | Layout | Picture | Text Box | Web

Fill

Color:

Transparency: 50 %

Step
2m7e

f) Change the left side of the black border to Teal with 70% transparency and the peach color of the heart to 50% transparency by following steps similar to Steps 2m7d and 2m7e.

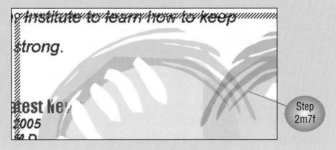

Institute to learn how to keep strong.

est Ne
2005

Step
2m7f

g) Click the Select Objects button on the Drawing toolbar, draw a dashed frame around the ungrouped heart (inside the drawing canvas), click Draw on the Drawing toolbar, and then click Group.

Step
2m7g

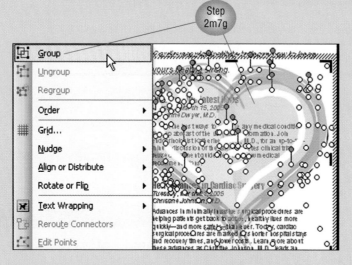

Step
2m8

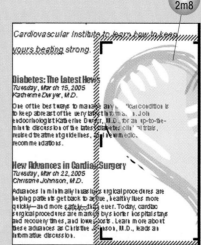

8) Position the image on the right side of the page so that it is approximately half visible. *(Hint: Only half of the image is visible, whether you are viewing your document in Print Layout view or Print Preview, but the remaining half of the image will print on the second page as shown in Figure 6.28.)*

9) With the image still selected (it will display in the drawing canvas), click Format and then Drawing Canvas. At the Format Drawing Canvas dialog box, select the Layout tab, click Advanced, select the Text Wrapping tab, and then click *Behind text*. Click OK twice. *(Hint: If any of the white accent marks on the heart obstruct the readability of the text, select them and add No Fill.)*

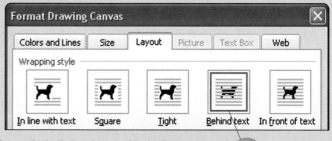

Step
2m9

3. Save panels 1 and 2 of the brochure and name it **c06ex05, Panels 1,2**.
4. Click the Standard toolbar Read button to enable Reading Layout view. Note that the document is easier to read.
5. Click the Increase Text Size button twice to enlarge the text. Click the Decrease Text Size button twice to return to the previous text size.
6. Click the Actual Page button to see how the pages will look when printed. Click the Actual Page button again to return to the previous view.
7. Click the Reading Layout toolbar Close button to return to the previous view.
8. Print and then close **c06ex05, Panels 1,2**. At the Print dialog box, type 1,2 in the *Pages* text box in the *Page range* section. (You may wait until Exercise 6 to print because panels 1 and 2 are printed as part of that exercise.)

FIGURE

6.28 Exercise 5

A fit heart can contribute to a long, healthy life for you and the ones you love. Join experts at the Edward Cardiovascular Institute to learn how to keep yours beating strong.

Diabetes: The Latest News
Tuesday, March 15, 2005
Katherine Dwyer, M.D.

One of the best ways to manage any medical condition is to keep abreast of the very latest information. Join endocrinologist Katherine Dwyer, M.D., for an up-to-the-minute discussion of the latest diabetes clinical trials, revised treatment guidelines, and new medical recommendations.

New Advances in Cardiac Surgery
Tuesday, March 22, 2005
Christine Johnson, M.D.

Advances in minimally invasive surgical procedures are helping patients get back to active, healthy lives more quickly—and more safely—than ever. Today, cardiac surgical procedures are marked by shorter hospital stays and recovery times, and lower costs. Learn more about these advances as Christine Johnson, M.D., leads an informative discussion.

Exercise—Is It the Fountain of Youth?
Tuesday, April 5, 2005
Joan Polak, M.D.

Everyone knows that exercise is good for your heart. Now, learn from a cardiologist exactly why it is good for you and what exercises provide the greatest benefits. Learn the specifics behind the "Just Do It" philosophy from Dr. Joan Polak.

Setting Up a Heart-Healthy Kitchen
Tuesday, April 19, 2005
Kaitlin Anzalone, Registered Dietitian

A great start to beginning a heart-healthy diet is doing a heart-check of your kitchen. Join us for practical tips and suggestions for setting up your kitchen.

Diabetes and Cardiovascular Disease
Tuesday, May 10, 2005
Wilma Schaenfeld, M.D.

During this session, we will discuss the clinical features of heart disease in the diabetic, as well as what you can do to reduce the likelihood of future problems.

All lectures: 7 to 8:30 p.m.
Edward Cardiovascular Institute
120 Spalding Drive
Naperville, Illinois

The talk is FREE, but because space is limited, please register by calling (630) 555-4941.

In Exercise 6, you will create the back and cover (panels 3 and 4) of the heart brochure started in Exercise 5. To make this brochure self-mailing, the back of the brochure will be used for mailing purposes. You will insert return address information and leave the rest of panel 3 blank with the assumption that mailing labels will be used. This exercise involves using the Text Direction feature to create the rotated return address, editing the heart image on the cover to change the fill color, and using text boxes to place text at specific locations on the page.

Creating the Back (Panel 3) and Cover (Panel 4) of a Single-Fold Brochure

1. Open **c06ex05, Panels 1,2**.
2. Save the document with Save <u>A</u>s and name it **c06ex06, Heart Brochure**.
3. Create panels 3 and 4 of the brochure shown in Figure 6.29 by completing the following steps:
   a. Press Ctrl + End to move the insertion point to the end of the document and then press Ctrl + Enter to insert a hard page break.
   b. Create the text box and insert the return address located on the back of the brochure (panel 3) as illustrated in Figure 6.29 by completing the following steps:
      1) With the insertion point positioned on panel 3, click the Text Box button on the Drawing toolbar and draw a text box toward the bottom of the page that is approximately 3.5 inches in height and 1.5 inches in width. (The size and position of the text box will be adjusted later.)
      2) Type the following information:

         EDWARD CARDIOVASCULAR INSTITUTE
         One ECI Plaza
         120 Spalding Drive, Suite 102
         Naperville, IL 60540-9865

      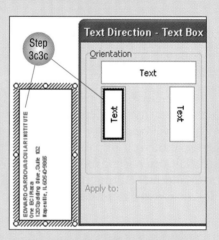

      Step 3b2

   c. Format the return address by completing the following steps:
      1) Select the text just entered and change the font to 10-point Arial and the color to Teal.
      2) Select *EDWARD CARDIOVASCULAR INSTITUTE* and apply bold.
      3) Rotate the position of the text by completing the following steps:
         a) Position the insertion point anywhere within the address.
         b) Click F<u>o</u>rmat and Te<u>x</u>t Direction to display the Text Direction - Text Box dialog box.
         c) In the <u>O</u>rientation section, click the text direction selection that displays text pointing up and matches the direction of the text in Figure 6.29, and then click OK.

         Step 3c3c

         Text Direction - Text Box

         <u>O</u>rientation

         Text

         Text   Text

         Apply to:

   d. Display the Format Text Box dialog box and make the following changes:
      1) Select the Colors and Lines tab, change the line color to Violet, and then change the line weight to 2.25 points.
      2) Select the Size tab and change the height to 2.9 inches and the width to 0.9 inch.
      3) Select the Layout tab and then click <u>A</u>dvanced. At the Advanced Layout dialog box, select the Picture Position tab and change the *Absolute position* to *0.42"* and the *to the right of* option to *Page* in the *Horizontal* section. Change the *Absolute position* to *5.15"* and the *below* option to *Page* in the *Vertical* section.
      4) Select the Text Wrapping tab and change the wrapping style to *Top and bottom*. Click OK twice.

e. Place the insertion point above the text box and double-click to position the insertion point there. *(Hint: The Click and Type feature should insert hard returns.)*

f. Press Ctrl + Enter to insert a hard page break. The text box should remain on panel 3.

g. Create the heart image on the front cover (panel 4) by completing the following steps:

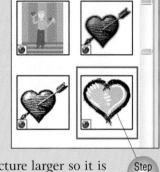

Step
3g3

1) Make sure the insertion point is positioned at the top of the cover page (panel 4).

2) Display the Clip Art task pane and search for clips under the keyword *heart*.

3) Scroll through the selections until you find the heart you used in panels 1 and 2.

4) Click once on the image to insert it into panel 4.

5) Use one of the corner sizing handles and make the picture larger so it is easier to see. You will size the picture more precisely later.

6) Change the color of the black border around the heart image by right-clicking inside the heart image and then click Edit Picture from the shortcut menu. *(Hint: If the prompt appears asking if you want to convert the image into a drawing object, click Yes.)* Click off the image to deselect the heart components. Hold down the Shift key and then click on the left and right black borders that display around the heart. Click the down-pointing arrow at the right of the Fill Color button on the Drawing toolbar and then click Teal. Deselect the image.

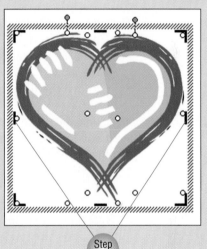

Step
3g6

7) Click the Select Objects button on the Drawing toolbar and draw a dash border around the heart, click Draw, and then Group.

h. Double-click the drawing canvas that surrounds the object. At the Format Drawing Canvas dialog box, select the Size tab and then change the height to 4.0 inches and the width to 4.08 inches (this can be an approximate number).

i. Select the Layout tab and click Advanced. At the Advanced Layout dialog box, select the Text Wrapping tab and then change the wrapping style to *Top and bottom*.

j. Select the Picture Position tab and change the *Alignment* to *Centered* and the *relative to* option to *Margin* in the *Horizontal* section. Change the *Alignment* to *Centered* and the *relative to* option to *Margin* in the *Vertical* section. Click OK twice.

k. Create a text box inside the heart to hold the word *for* by completing the following steps:

1) Click the Text Box button on the Drawing toolbar and draw a text box in the approximate location of the word *for* as shown in Figure 6.29.

2) Change the font to 26-point Impact and the color to Teal and then type **for**.

3) Click the down-pointing arrow at the right of the Fill Color button on the Drawing toolbar and then click No Fill.

4) Click the down-pointing arrow at the right of the Line Color button on the Drawing toolbar and then click No Line.

5) Size the text box with the sizing handles so the text is completely visible, if necessary, and then position the text box with the mouse in the approximate position as displayed in Figure 6.29.

    l. Create a second text box that will contain the word *your* by completing the following steps:

      1) Select the first text box containing *for*, hold down the Ctrl key, and then drag a copy of the text box to the approximate position of the word *your* in Figure 6.29.

      2) Select the word *for* and type your.

      3) Size and position the text box as necessary.

    m. Create a third text box that will contain the word *Heart's* by copying the second text box to the approximate position of the word *Heart's* in Figure 6.29. Select *your*, change the font size to 48-point and the font color to Violet, and type Heart's. Size and position the text box as necessary.

    n. Create a fourth text box that will contain the word *sake* by copying the second text box to the approximate position of the word *sake* in Figure 6.29. Select *your* and type sake. Size and position the text box as necessary.

    o. Check the vertical spacing between the text boxes against Figure 6.29 and adjust accordingly.

    p. Create a fifth text box to hold the text *Spring 2005* by completing the following steps:

      1) Click outside of the heart image to deselect the text boxes.

      2) Click the Text Box button on the Drawing toolbar and draw a text box in the upper left corner of the page. *(Hint: Do not worry about the exact size or position at this time.)*

      3) Change the font to 24-point Impact, the color to Violet, and then type Spring 2005.

      4) Click the down-pointing arrow at the right of the Line Color button on the Drawing toolbar and then click No Line.

      5) Size the text box with the mouse so that the text is visible.

      6) Position the object similar to Figure 6.29.

    q. Create a sixth text box to hold the text *Presented by:* and then insert the Edward Cardiovascular Institute logo by completing the following steps:

      1) Click the Text Box button on the Drawing toolbar and draw a text box below the heart image closer to the bottom of the page. *(Hint: Do not worry about the exact size or position at this time.)*

      2) Change the font to 12-point Impact Italic, the color to Teal, and then type Presented by:.

      3) Size the text box, if necessary, so all of the text is visible.

      4) Click the down-pointing arrow at the right of the Line Color button and click No Line.

      5) Insert the logo as shown in Figure 6.29 by clicking Insert, pointing to Picture, and then clicking From File. *(Hint: Insert the picture outside the text box.)*

      6) Double-click *Edward Cardio BW* located in your Chapter06 folder.

      7) Select the logo, click the Text Wrapping button on the Picture toolbar, and then click In Front of Text.

      8) Size and position the logo similar to Figure 6.29.

      9) Position the text box containing *Presented by:* similar to Figure 6.29.

4. Save the document with the same name **c06ex06, Heart Brochure**.

5. Print both pages of the brochure using both sides of the paper. Print pages 1 and 2 and then print pages 3 and 4. At the Print dialog box, type 1,2 in the *Pages* text box in the *Page range* section and then click OK. Turn the paper over, type 3,4 in the *Pages* text box, and then click OK.

6. Close **c06ex06, Heart Brochure**.

Spring 2005

for
your
Heart's
sake

EDWARD CARDIOVASCULAR INSTITUTE
One ECI Plaza
120 Spalding Drive, Suite 102
Naperville, IL 60540-9865

Presented by:

EDWARD
CARDIOVASCULAR INSTITUTE

Creating Diagrams

Word 2003 makes it easy to insert diagrams into any design project by clicking the Insert Diagram or Organization Chart button on the Drawing toolbar. This opens the Diagram Gallery dialog box, which can be used to select a diagram type as pictured in Figure 6.30. Six diagram formats are available: Organization Chart, Cycle Diagram, Radial Diagram, Pyramid Diagram, Venn Diagram, and Target Diagram. When you click on a diagram type, the name of the diagram and its function are displayed at the bottom of the Diagram Gallery dialog box. Double-clicking a diagram button, or clicking the diagram button once and then clicking OK, inserts the diagram layout at the insertion point in the document you are working on. A diagram-specific toolbar will also appear and can be used to modify the diagram. For example, when working with an Organization Chart diagram, selecting a chart element and then clicking the Insert Shape button on the Organization Chart toolbar allows you to create another chart element. The choices available are dependent on the type of chart element that was selected. For example, if you select the highest chart element in the hierarchy, the choices available are subordinate or assistant as shown in Figure 6.31. Double-clicking a chart element opens the Format AutoShape dialog box, which can be used to format the element.

Diagrams are inserted with all elements contained within a frame. The frame can be resized by selecting it and then using the diagonal resize arrows to shrink or enlarge it. To move a diagram, select it and then use the Text Wrapping button on the diagram's toolbar to select In Front of Text. The diagram can then be moved using the four-headed arrow. To add text to an element click the text and type. The text can be then be formatted just like any other text in the document.

F I G U R E

6.30 *Diagram Gallery Dialog Box*

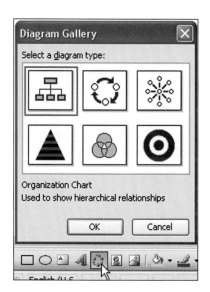

F I G U R E

6.31 *Organization Chart Toolbar*

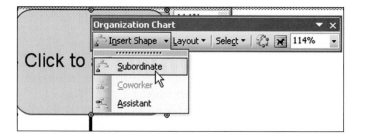

Creating a Chart

Charts and graphs are often an effective method for conveying facts and figures, and when properly used can make it easier for your target audience to understand your message. To insert a chart in a Word document, click Insert and then Object to open the Object dialog box. Click the Create New tab, locate and select *Microsoft Graph Chart* in the *Object type* list box, and then click the OK button. A Column chart and its datasheet will be inserted in the document as shown in Figure 6.32.

To select a different kind of chart, double-click the chart to select it, right-click inside the chart, click Chart Type, and then use the Chart Type dialog box to select a new chart style. To change the data in the data sheet, click a cell and then type over the previous data. You can add new data to empty cells as well. To open a datasheet once it has been closed, double-click the chart, click View, and then click Datasheet.

You can also create a chart using the data in a Word table you have created. Select the table, and then follow the steps for creating a Microsoft Graph Chart outlined in the previous paragraph. A chart and datasheet will be created using the data that was contained in your Word table. The chart and datasheet can then be formatted and modified just like any other chart or datasheet.

FIGURE

6.32 Column Chart and Datasheet

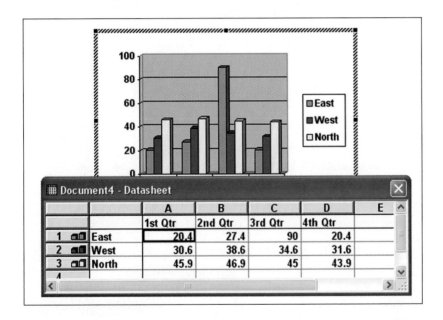

exercise 7

Adding an Organization Chart and a Column Chart to a Brochure

1. Add an organization chart to a brochure by completing the following steps:
   a. At a clear document screen, open the **Business Brochure** file located in your Chapter06 folder.
   b. Click the text in the first panel of the second page to display the text box.

c. Make sure the Drawing toolbar is displayed, position the insertion point at the bottom of the text box, and then click the Insert Diagram or Organization Chart button.

d. Click the Organization Chart button in the Diagram Gallery dialog box and then click OK. *(Hint: The chart will display at the bottom of the page.)*

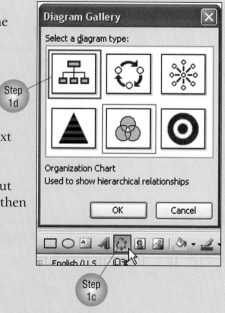

e. Click the diagram chart to select it, click the Text Wrapping button on the Organization Chart toolbar, and then click In Front of Text.

f. Select the top-most chart object, click the Layout button on the Organization Chart toolbar, and then click Right Hanging to change the organization chart style.

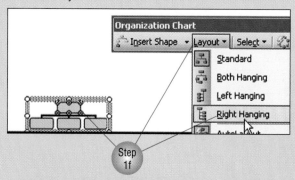

g. With the top-most chart object still selected, click the Insert Shape button on the Organization Chart toolbar and then click Subordinate. Repeat this step two more times to add a total of three subordinate objects to the chart.

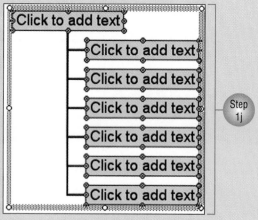

h. If necessary, drag and resize the chart using the middle sizing handles so that it appears in the same size and position as the column chart in Figure 6.33.

i. With the chart objects still selected, click Format and then AutoShape to open the Format AutoShape dialog box. Change the chart object fill color to Light Orange. Click OK. *(Hint: If necessary, hold down the Shift key and select each chart object.)*

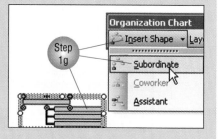

j. With all of the chart objects selected, use the Font dialog box to change the chart object font to 14-point Arial bold.

k. Click inside the first chart object and type Bangkok. Repeat this step to type the remaining city names shown in Figure 6.33. *(Hint: If the names are not centered in the chart object, change the internal margins at the Format AutoShape dialog box.)*

2. Add a column chart to a brochure by completing the following steps:

a. At a clear document screen, open the **Tea Tables** file located in your Chapter06 folder.

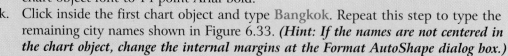

b. Place the insertion point anywhere in the first table, click Table, point to Select, and then click Table to select the table.
c. Click Insert and then Object to open the Object dialog box.
d. Make sure the Create New tab is selected, click *Microsoft Graph Chart* from the *Object type* list box, and then click the OK button to insert a chart and datasheet in the Tea Tables document.

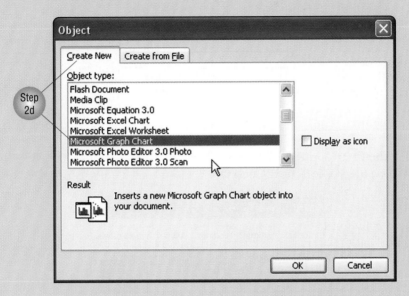

e. In the datasheet, double-click in the cell containing the figure *70* in column A, place the insertion point after *70*, and then type %. Repeat this step to add a percentage symbol after the remaining two figures.
f. Right-click inside the chart grid and then click Clear to remove the gray background from the chart. *(Hint: If you are no longer in the Microsoft Graph Chart feature, double-click the chart to access it again.)*

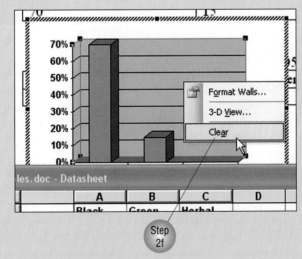

g. With the chart still selected, select one of the chart columns, right-click, and then click Format Data Series. Use the Format Data Series dialog box to change the column color to Light Orange. Click the OK button.

h. With the chart still selected, place the insertion point inside the white space surrounding the chart until you see the Chart Area tooltip. Right-click and then click Chart Options.

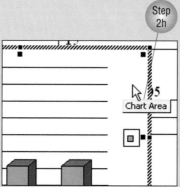

i. Click the Chart Options dialog box Legend tab and remove the check mark from the *Show legend* check box. Click OK.

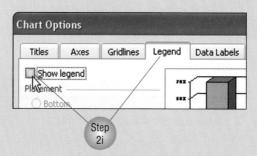

j. With the chart still selected, click Edit and then click Copy Chart.

k. Switch back to the Business Brochure document and then draw a text box inside the text box containing the Rapid Growth text. The text box should be approximately 2 inches in height and 3.25 inches in width.

l. With the insertion point located in the empty text box, click Edit and then click Paste Special. At the Paste Special dialog box, make sure *Microsoft Graph Chart Object* is selected and then click OK.

m. Resize the column chart so that it appears the same as it does in Figure 6.33.

n. Place the insertion point after the last line of text in the Rapid Growth panel, press Enter until the insertion point is just below the table, type 1995, and then center align *1995*.

o. Return to the **Tea Tables** file, select the column chart, and then press the Delete or Backspace key to delete it.

p. Repeat Steps 2b through 2n to create a column chart for the second table. Type 2005 for the year.

3. Close the **Tea Tables** file without saving changes when you are finished.

4. Save the Business Brochure document as **c06ex07, Business Brochure**.

5. Click Preview and then Print to print the brochure. *(Note: Be sure to insert legal-size paper in your printer because this document is formatted at 8½ by 14 inches.)*

6. Save **c06ex07, Business Brochure** and then close it.

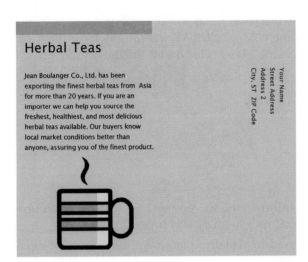

Herbal Teas

Jean Boulanger Co., Ltd. has been exporting the finest herbal teas from Asia for more than 20 years. If you are an importer we can help you source the freshest, healthiest, and most delicious herbal teas available. Our buyers know local market conditions better than anyone, assuring you of the finest product.

Your Name
Street Address
Address 2
City, ST ZIP Code

Jean Boulanger Co., Ltd.
345/57 Sukhumvit Road
Bangkok, Thailand 10110
Phone (555) 555 0125
Fax (555) 555 0145

Jean Boulanger

Exporter of Fine Herbal Teas
jboulanger@emcp.net

JBC

Branch Offices

Jean Boulanger Co., Ltd. has branch offices in Europe, the USA, and Canada. Our trained staff are ready to assist you in identifying and sourcing the finest herbal teas from Asia. We can offer private label assistance and work with you to develop your own blends.

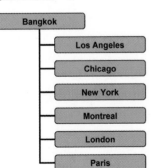

Rapid Growth

The pie charts below show the doubling in growth of herbal tea drinkers from 1995 to 2005. If you are not carrying a full line of herbal teas you are missing a profitable product line.

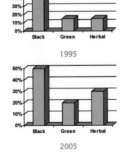

For more information, contact the Jean Boulanger branch nearest you, or visit our Web site: jboulanger@emcp.net. For queries please write: jboulanger@emcp.net

Using a Document Map

A Document Map displays a list of all of the headings used in a document in a pane located to the left of the current document as shown in Figure 6.34. In order for the Document Map tool to work, headings must be formatted using the heading styles (Heading 1 through Heading 9) available in the *Style* list box on the Formatting toolbar. In addition to providing a useful outline view of a document, the Document Map can be used to navigate within a document. Clicking a heading in the Document Map pane moves the insertion point to the heading location in the document. To display the Document Map, click View and then Document Map. Click View and then click Document Map again to turn off the display when the display is active.

CHAPTER summary

➤ Brochures and booklets may be used to inform, educate, promote, or sell. These documents may also be used to establish an organization's identity and image.

➤ A dummy is a mockup of a document used to visualize placement of text and objects to accommodate certain folds.

➤ The manner in which a brochure is folded determines the order in which the panels are set on the page. Folds create distinct sections in which to place blocks of text. The most common brochure fold is called a letter fold.

➤ A dummy can be created to help determine the location of information on the brochure page layout.

➤ Consistent elements are necessary to maintain continuity in a multiple-page brochure.

➤ The easiest method of creating the page layout for a letter-fold brochure is to use text boxes; the easiest method for a booklet is to use the Book fold feature; the easiest method for a single-fold brochure is to use the 2 pages per sheet feature.

➤ Column formatting may be varied within the same document by using section breaks to separate the sections that will be formatted with different column settings.

➤ When you select *Book fold* at the Page Setup dialog box, Word prints two pages on one side of the paper. When you fold the paper, it opens like a book.

➤ When printing a booklet, be sure to print on both sides of the paper. This is known as duplex printing.

➤ A header consists of text or graphics that appear at the top of every page in a section.

➤ A footer appears at the bottom of every page. Headers and footers often contain page numbers, chapter titles, company logos, file names, author's name, or dates.

➤ Reverse text can be created in a document as a design element and usually refers to white text set against a solid black background. Reverse text can also be created with different colors for the text and the background, as well as shading.

➤ The front cover of a brochure sets the mood and tone for the whole brochure. The front cover title must attract attention and let the reader know what the brochure is about.

➤ Repetitive formatting that is used to maintain consistency in a single publication or among a series of documents may be applied to text by using a style.

➤ A style may be edited and any occurrence of the style in the document is automatically updated to reflect the changes.

➤ Click the down-pointing arrow at the right of the Style button on the Formatting toolbar to display a drop-down list of available styles.

➤ Display the Styles and Formatting task pane by clicking the Styles and Formatting button on the Formatting toolbar.

➤ Display all available Word styles by clicking the down-pointing arrow at the right side of the *Show* list box located at the bottom of the Styles and Formatting task pane and then clicking *All Styles* at the drop-down list.

➤ To clear all character and paragraph formatting, select the text, click the down-pointing arrow at the right side of the Style button, and then click *Clear Formatting*; or, click <u>E</u>dit, point to Cle<u>a</u>r, and then click <u>F</u>ormats; or, apply the Normal style.

➤ The Normal style from the Normal template is automatically applied to any text that is typed, unless you specify other formatting instructions.

➤ Word provides four types of styles—character, paragraph, table, and list. A character style applies formatting to selected text only. A paragraph style affects the paragraph that contains the insertion point or selected text. A table style provides a consistent look to borders, shading, alignment, and fonts that are being used in a table. A list style is used to format bulleted or numbered lists.

➤ A drop cap is a design element in which the first letter of the first word in a paragraph is formatted in a larger font size and set into the beginning of the paragraph.

➤ Reading Layout view is a document view that provides an optimized layout for reading Word documents. In Reading Layout view all toolbars are hidden, with the exception of the Reading Layout and Reviewing toolbars.

➤ Charts and graphs are very effective methods for conveying facts and figures. Word lets you choose from a variety of different chart and graph types to find one that is most appropriate for the data that will be displayed by the chart or graph.

➤ Diagrams and organization charts can be used to graphically illustrate organizational heirarchies, or the relationship between various entities.

➤ The Document Map displays a list of all of the headings used in a document in a pane located to the left of the current document. The Document Map can be used to see an outline of a document, and to navigate to header locations within the document. In order for the Document Map tool to work, headings must be formatted using the heading styles available in the *Style* list box on the Formatting toolbar.

COMMANDS review

Command	Mouse/Keyboard
Change margins	<u>F</u>ile, Page Set<u>u</u>p, Margins tab
2 pages per sheet	<u>F</u>ile, Page Set<u>u</u>p, Margins tab, <u>M</u>ultiple pages, *2 pages per sheet*
Book fold	<u>F</u>ile, Page Set<u>u</u>p, Margins tab, <u>M</u>ultiple pages, *Book fold*
Manual duplex printing	<u>F</u>ile, <u>P</u>rint, *Manual duple<u>x</u>*
Columns dialog box	F<u>o</u>rmat, <u>C</u>olumns

Header and Footer	View, Header and Footer
Insert a column break	Insert, Break, *Column break*; or press Ctrl + Shift + Enter
Insert a page break	Insert, Break, *Page break*; or press Ctrl + Enter
Character spacing and kerning	Format, Font, Character Spacing tab
Borders and Shading dialog box	Format, Borders and Shading
Display Drawing toolbar	Drawing button on Standard toolbar; or right-click Standard toolbar, select Drawing; or View, Toolbars, select Drawing
Draw a text box	Text Box button on the Drawing toolbar, click and drag the crosshairs to draw a box
Insert existing text into a text box	Select text, click the Text Box button on the Drawing toolbar
Size a text box	Double-click the text box border, select the Size tab, or drag sizing handles
Position a text box	Double-click the text box border, select the Layout tab, click Advanced, or drag to position
Format Text Box dialog box	Format, Text Box
Drop Cap dialog box	Format, Drop Cap
Styles and Formatting task pane	Format, Styles and Formatting
Font dialog box	Format, Font; or click the *Font* list box, *Font Size* list box, and/or Character formatting buttons on the Formatting toolbar
Reading Layout view	Read button on Standard toolbar
Document Map	View, Document Map; or click Document Map button on Standard toolbar
Chart or graph	Insert, Object, Create New tab, select *Microsoft Graph Chart* in the *Object type* list box
Diagram or organization chart	Insert Diagram or Organization Chart button on Drawing toolbar

REVIEWING key points

Matching: On a blank sheet of paper, provide the correct letter or letters that match each definition.

Ⓐ 2 pages per sheet
Ⓑ All styles
Ⓒ Book fold
Ⓓ Character style
Ⓔ Columns dialog box
Ⓕ Document Map
Ⓖ Drawing toolbar
Ⓗ Drop cap

Ⓘ Dummy
Ⓙ Duplex printing
Ⓚ Gate fold
Ⓛ Header and Footer
Ⓜ Panels
Ⓝ Paragraph dialog box
Ⓞ Parallel folds
Ⓟ Reading Layout view

Ⓠ Reverse text
Ⓡ Link to Previous
Ⓢ Show Next
Ⓣ Style
Ⓤ Styles and Formatting
Ⓥ Table style

1. Folds in a brochure that all run in the same direction are called this.
2. This type of style applies formatting to selected text only.
3. A mockup of a brochure is called this.

4. Click this button on the Header and Footer toolbar to change the formatting for headers or footers in a new section.

5. Use this dialog box to create columns of unequal width.

6. This feature divides a physical page in half and may be used to create single-fold brochures.

7. Text or graphics that appear at either the top or bottom of every page are referred to as this.

8. A set of formatting instructions saved with a name to be used repeatedly on different sections of text is called this.

9. This Word feature prints two pages on one side of the paper so when you fold the paper, it opens like a book.

10. This is the name for the first letter of the first word in a paragraph that is formatted in a larger font size and is set into the paragraph.

11. This is the name for white text set against a black background.

12. This option at the Print dialog box allows you to print the document on both sides of the paper and prompts you to refeed the paper.

13. This Word feature displays an outline view of the headings used in a Word document.

14. This view provides an easy-to-read document display.

15. The Insert Diagram or Organization Chart button is located on this toolbar.

Short Answer: On a blank sheet of paper, provide the correct answer for each question.

1. What is the purpose of creating a dummy before creating a brochure?
2. What is the biggest advantage of using styles?
3. Explain the 2 pages per sheet feature. What does it do? What can it be used for? Explain the difference between choosing portrait or landscape with this feature.
4. How can drop caps and reverse text serve as design elements in a document?
5. What is the purpose of a Document Map?

APPLYING your skills

Assessment 1

You are an involved and supportive member of the Newport Art League. Other members became aware of your desktop publishing skills and asked you to create a promotional brochure for the league. Eager to show off your skills, you volunteer. Your target audience includes the general public, but more specifically artists, aspiring artists, art lovers, and those with a general interest in art. Your audience may also include both adults and children. Your purpose is to let your readers know what the art league has to offer. The content of your brochure will include information on annual art events, classes and workshops, membership, and volunteer opportunities.

In this assessment, you will create the inside panels of the Newport Art League's brochure. In the next assessment, you will create the back panels of the brochure. A sample solution of a complete brochure is provided in Figures 6.34 and 6.35; however, you are to create your own design (using text located in your Chapter06 folder). Include the following specifications in your brochure design:

1. You may create a letter-fold brochure or a single-fold brochure. You may create your brochure layout from scratch using text boxes, columns, or tables. Alternatively, you may use one of the brochure templates included in Word 2003 or on the Microsoft Office Online Templates Web page.
2. Include all of the information contained in the file **Art Text** located in your Chapter06 folder.
3. Create a thumbnail sketch of your design.
4. Create a dummy to guide you in the placement of text.
5. Create styles for the headings, subheadings, and bulleted text. Create any additional styles if appropriate.
6. Use relevant graphics. A large selection of art-related graphics can be viewed by displaying the Clip Organizer and searching for clips with the keyword *art*. Viewing these graphics may serve as an inspiration for the design and color scheme of your brochure.
7. Use a coordinated color scheme. Remember that you can customize text colors to match a color(s) in a clip art image, or you can customize the color(s) of a clip art image to match a specific text color or coordinate colors within another image.
8. For margins, if you are going to create a letter-fold brochure, refer to Exercises 2 and 3. If you are going to create a single-fold brochure, use the 2 pages per sheet feature.
9. Use an appropriate typeface. Make sure all text is legible.
10. Use the Paragraph dialog box to make adjustments to the spacing before and after paragraphs.
11. As you work, evaluate your design for the concepts of focus, balance, proportion, contrast, directional flow, consistency, and color.
12. Save the inside panels of the brochure and name the file **c06sa01, Panels**.
13. Print and then close **c06sa01, Panels**.

6.34 *Assessment 1 Sample Solution*

SUPPORTING FINE ART

Art League Offerings

- Studio and Gallery Open to the Public

- Monthly Lectures and Demonstrations by Professional Artists

- Art Classes, Workshops, & Instruction

- Monthly Exhibits of Juried Fine Art in All Media

- Annual Student Art Show

- Waterfront Art Fair

- Annual Fine Arts Auction

- Annual Christmas Show & Sale

ANNUAL ART EVENTS

Art for the New Millennium

Waterfront Art Fair
Juried Fine Arts Exhibition and Sale
September 13 & 14, 2004

Christmas Show & Sale
Fine Arts & Crafts
Guest Artists
November 28, 2004 thru
January 10, 2005

34th Annual Fine Arts Auction
March 9, 2005

Student Art Show
Award Presentation and Open House
May 11, 2005

Membership

- Participate in all programs

- Exhibit work in the gallery

- Preference for workshops, classes, and demonstrations

CLASSES & WORKSHOPS

Classes

- Watercolors

- Pastels

- Oils

- Drawing and composition

- Framing

Class Schedule

Session I
  September 25–October 27, 2004
Session II
  January 15–February 16, 2005
Session III
  March 18–April 19, 2005

Regular Workshops

- Tuesday evening life drawing workshop at the Gallery, 7 p.m.

- Wednesday workshop at the Gallery, 12–4 p.m. All media.

Assessment 2

In this assessment, you will create the back panels of the brochure created in Assessment 1. Include the following specifications:

1. Open **c06sa01, Panels**. Save the document with Save <u>A</u>s and name it **c06sa02, Art Brochure**.
2. Referring to the dummy created in Assessment 1, create the back panels of the Art League brochure. A sample solution is provided in Figure 6.35.
3. Apply any relevant styles created in Assessment 1.
4. When creating the lines after Name, Address, ZIP, and Phone, set a right tab at the position where the line is to end. When you need to insert a line, turn on underlining, press the Tab key, and then turn off underlining.
5. When creating the ZIP and Phone lines, set a left tab where the ZIP line is to end. Use underline as stated previously.
6. Use the Symbol dialog box to find a check box symbol.
7. Consider using a table to create the two columns of volunteer activities.
8. Make any adjustments to the spacing or positioning of text as you deem necessary.
9. Save the brochure document with the same name **c06sa02, Art Brochure**.

10. Print the first page of the brochure and then print the second page on the back of the first page. Fold your brochure and check the placement of text and images in relation to the folds. Make any adjustments as necessary to produce a professionally finished product.

11. Print a copy of **Document Evaluation Checklist.doc** located in your Chapter06 folder. Using the document evaluation checklist, evaluate your brochure design.

12. Close **c06sa02, Art Brochure**.

6.35 *Assessment 2 Sample Solution*

JOIN THE ART LEAGUE

Membership Application

Name: _____

Address: _____

City: _____ State: _____

ZIP: _____ Phone: _____

Dues are payable June 1 for the year ending May 31.

☐ $5 Junior Membership
(Middle/High School)

☐ $24 Individual Membership

☐ $30 Family Membership

☐ $50 Contributing Membership

☐ $100 Supporting Membership

How would you like to participate in art league activities?

☐ Gallery volunteer   ☐ Committee work

☐ Class instructor ☐ Workshops

☐ Exhibiting   ☐ Board member

Discover the artist in you!

Newport Art League
240 America's Cup Drive
Newport, RI 02040
Phone: 401.555.2730
Fax: 401.555.2732
Internet:
www.emcp.net/Newport

Newport Art League

Studio & Art Gallery

Assessment 3

You are a member of a fund-raising committee for a local charity. Pick a charity, plan an event to raise money, and create a brochure that promotes the charity and advertises the event.

1. Open **Document Evaluation Checklist.doc** located in your Chapter06 folder and print one copy.

2. Use the document evaluation checklist to analyze your brochure and make any additional adjustments if necessary. Label the exercise as **c06sa03, Evaluate**.

3. Attach the completed form to the back of your brochure.

Assessment 4

Create a logo in Publisher, save it in a graphic format, and insert it in a Word document as shown in Figure 6.36 by completing the following steps:

1. Start Publisher.
2. Click *Blank Publications* in the *New from a design* section of the New Publication task pane.
3. Click the *Full Page* design thumbnail.
4. Click Insert and then Design Gallery Object to open the Microsoft Office Publisher Design Gallery. Click the Objects by Category tab.
5. Click *Boxes* in the *Categories* list box.
6. Click the Two Color Boxes design and then click the Insert Object button.
7. Double-click the first blue box in the Two Color Boxes design to open the Format AutoShape dialog box. Click the Colors and Lines tab and change the box color to Orange. Click OK. *(Note: The color of both blue boxes will change to orange automatically.)*
8. Click the Insert WordArt button on the Objects toolbar to open the WordArt Gallery dialog box.
9. Click the second WordArt style in the first row and then click OK to open the Edit WordArt Text dialog box.
10. Change the font size to 24 points, type Jean Boulanger in place of the text *Your Text Here*, and then click OK.
11. Drag and position the WordArt text as shown in Figure 6.36.
12. Click the Select Objects button on the Objects toolbar and then use the Select Objects tool to drag and create a selection box around the Design Gallery Object and WordArt logo you just created.
13. Click the Group Objects box that appears below the selection box to group the Design Gallery Object and the WordArt text.
14. Right-click the grouped logo and then click Save as Picture to save the logo as a .gif file. Use the Save As dialog box file browser to name the file Logo and save it to the Chapter06 folder.
15. In Word, open **c06ex07, Business Brochure** and then use the Save As command to rename the file **c06sa04, Logo** and save it to the Chapter06 folder.
16. Delete the JBC logo in the lower-right portion of the third column on the first page of the brochure.
17. Click Insert, point to Picture, and then click From File to open the Insert Picture dialog box. Use the dialog box File browser to locate and insert the logo picture file you created in Step 14.
18. Drag and resize the logo as shown in Figure 6.36.
19. Print the first page of **c06sa04, Logo**.
20. Save and then close **c06sa04, Logo**. Close Publisher.

6.36 *Assessment 4 Sample Solution*

Assessment 5

Open a Word brochure; customize the brochure using styles, clip art, and WordArt; and then open MS Publisher and copy and paste the Marquee Awning Strip design and an Attention Getter design to the brochure. Include the following specifications:

INTEGRATED

1. Open **Essentials Brochure** in your Chapter06 folder.
2. Save the brochure and name it **c06sa05, Integrated**.
3. Insert appropriate clip art or photographs.
4. Create styles to reinforce consistency and to efficiently format all the headings and text in the brochure. Do not forget to adjust leading, add font color, and apply font attributes.
5. Make sure the brochure text aligns and the folds are correct.
6. Use WordArt to create the heading *Open the Door to Your Career*.
7. Open Publisher.
8. Click the *Blank Publications* option in the *New from a design* section at the New Publication task pane and then click *Full Page*.
9. Click the Design Gallery Object button (last button) on the Objects toolbar.
10. In the *Categories* section of the Objects by Category tab, click Marquee and then click Marquee Awning Stripes. Click the Insert Object button.
11. Select the marquee object and then copy it to the Office clipboard.
12. Paste the marquee object to the top right of the brochure side containing the cover page and then paste a copy to the bottom left of the other side of the brochure.
13. Drag a sizing handle to increase the length of each marquee object as shown in Figure 6.37.
14. Select an Attention Getter design object from MS Publisher and insert it into the brochure.
15. Save the brochure again and then print **c06sa05, Integrated**.

6.37 *Assessment 5 Sample Solution*

COURSE DESCRIPTIONS

OFTI 100—Introduction to Computer Keyboarding

This course includes word processing functions and basic formatting of documents.
(3 lecture hours)

OFTI 101—Computer Keyboarding II

Develop speed and accuracy skills using a computer. Prerequisite: OFTI 100 with a grade level of C or better or keyboarding speed of 25 words per minute.
(4 lecture hours)

OFTI 106—Speed Development Keyboarding

Development of speed and accuracy using a computer keyboard. Prerequisite: OFTI 100 with a grade level of C or better or keyboarding speed of 25 wpm.
(3 lecture hours)

OFTI 127—Beginning Word Processing on a PC

Basic functions using a specific word processing software package which may include insert, delete, cut, paste, find, replace, document formatting, margins, tabs, spell checker, justification, line spacing, footnotes, endnotes, headers, and footers. Prerequisite: Keyboarding skills.
(3 lecture hours)

OFTI 128—Advanced Word Processing on a PC

An advanced word processing course for personal computers. Applications may include tables, charts, graphics, borders, Clip Art, Web pages, columns, forms, outlines, paragraph numbering, styles, sort, select, table of contents, and index. Prerequisites: OFTI 127 or equivalent.
(3 lecture hours)

OFTI 130—Desktop Publishing Using Word 2003

An advanced word processing course designed to integrate the enhanced graphic features used in desktop publishing applications including newsletter, brochures, proposals, manuals, reports, and flyers. Prerequisite: OFTI 128
(3 lecture hours)

OFTI 135—Electronic Presentations for Office Support Staff

Design, prepare, and present effective business presentations utilizing design techniques and current electronic presentation software. Techniques for assessing a business situation and delivering a successful electronic presentation are also included. Prerequisite: Keyboarding skills.
(3 lecture hours)

OFTI 150—Business Correspondence

Basic instruction and practice in developing the vital employment skill of planning, writing, and formatting effective Business spelling, punctuation, and grammar skills will be updated. Prerequisite: OFTI 127 or equivalent.
(4 lecture hours)

OFTI 161—Office 2003 for Support Staff

Beginning Microsoft Office utilizing the basic functions of Windows, Word, Excel, Access, and PowerPoint. software skills. May not be substituted for CIS 108. Prerequisite: Keyboarding skills.
(3 lecture hours)

OFTI 285—Professional Development

A capstone course designed to develop "people skills" essential in the working environment. Topics include human relations, communication skills, professional presence, team building, and stress management. Prerequisite: Keyboarding speed of 45 words per minute or consent of instructor.
(4 lecture hours)

Register Soon!

For more information, contact:

Office Technology Information
at
Midwest College
630.555.7865
midwestcollege@emcp.net
www.emcp.net/midwestcollege

Key Essentials Certificate

- Complete 22 credit hours in one quarter
- All classes taught by experienced OFTI faculty
- Develop effective keyboarding skills
- Learn proper document formatting for business
- Write effective business letters and memos
- Master grammar, punctuation, and spelling
- Understand effective interviewing strategies
- Become familiar with current business software applications (Microsoft Office 2003)

Assessment 6

Visit a business and/or an organization and find examples of brochures and booklets. Places to look include a school or college, chamber of commerce office, travel agency, doctor's office, park district office, hotel lobby, or other publicly accessed location.

1. Select one brochure or booklet that grabs your attention and recreate the brochure or booklet by using any one of the methods you have learned in this chapter. You may use the brochure template in Word or any brochure or booklet templates located on the Microsoft Office Online Templates Web site.
2. Use appropriate graphics from Office 2003 or an online source.
3. Save the document and name **it c06sa06, Brochure**.
4. Print and then close **c06sa06, Brochure**.
5. Prepare a short presentation offering information on how the brochure or booklet was put together.

Creating Specialty Promotional Documents

PERFORMANCE OBJECTIVES

Upon successful completion of Chapter 7, you will be able to create specialty promotional documents such as tickets, subscription forms, gift certificates, postcards, business greeting cards, and invitations.

CHAPTER07

DESKTOP PUBLISHING TERMS

Data source	Mail merge	Merge fields
Field codes	Main document	Record

WORD FEATURES USED

Data source	Microsoft Office Online	Pictures
Forms toolbar	Templates Web	Replicate labels
Labels	page	Tables and Borders
Mail Merge task pane	Page Borders	toolbar
Main document	Page Setup	Tabs

By the time you reach this chapter, you will have accumulated a number of different examples of desktop publishing applications. As you know, studying the work of others is a great way to pick up pointers on layout and design, as well as interesting uses of fonts, color, text, and graphics. There are a number of published sources for useful project ideas, tips, and resources. Also, as mentioned earlier, paper supply companies offer predesigned papers that are frequently available in catalogs; those catalogs may offer many helpful ideas for the layout and design of your documents.

You may have already realized that there are many different approaches to creating documents in Word. You must decide which approach is easiest for you to remember and apply. Mastering a skill takes a lot of practice and experimentation. You may begin thinking of other ways of creating documents that are more efficient or easier to adapt to your setting. Any one of the exercises presented in this chapter can be adapted to just about any personal or business situation. Although this text typically presents one or two different approaches to creating a document, there are usually many other ways to achieve the same results.

Creating Promotional Documents

In addition to flyers and announcements, other promotional documents include tickets, enrollment forms, gift certificates, postcards, bookmarks, name tags, invitations, and business greeting cards. They become promotional documents when a business or organization name is visible or an item or service is mentioned for sale in a document.

Whether creating tickets for a charitable event, discount coupons for a grocery store, bookmarks promoting reading at a public library, or coasters advertising a local restaurant, Word's desktop publishing features combined with a little imagination can produce endless possibilities. Figure 7.1 illustrates other promotional documents created with the same basic design concepts and Word features used in most of the exercises in this chapter.

FIGURE

7.1 *Examples of Promotional Documents Created in Word*

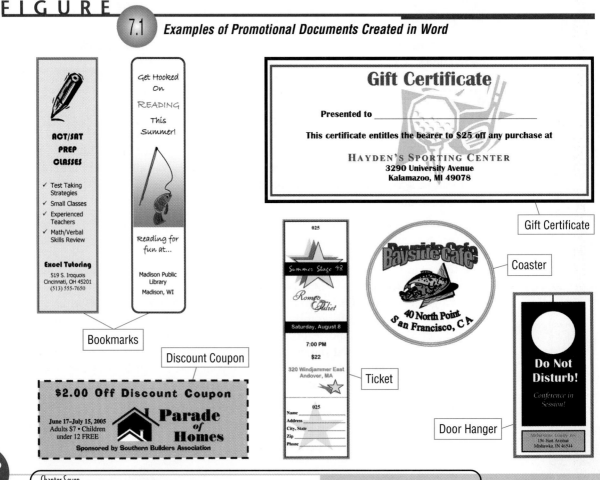

Bookmarks

Discount Coupon

Ticket

Gift Certificate

Coaster

Door Hanger

Web pages on the Internet can also be considered promotional in nature. The vast exposure of the World Wide Web provides endless possibilities for advertising products, services, research, and data that may be presented on a company or corporation Web site. In Chapter 8, you will learn how to design and lay out Web pages.

Creating Tickets Using Microsoft Online

Microsoft Office Online includes a template for creating tickets using text boxes within a rectangular AutoShape as shown in Figure 7.2. A formatted ticket is copied to create eight tickets filling an 8½ × 11-inch sheet of paper. Word's drawing canvas automatically surrounds the eight AutoShape objects, treating them as one organized unit.

The ticket template is accessed by displaying the New Document task pane and then clicking the Templates on Office Online hyperlink. At the Microsoft Office Online page, be sure *Templates* is selected in the *Search* text box, type tickets for an event, and then click Go. Click the Event tickets hyperlink. When the tickets display on the screen, click the Download Now button and the template will appear in a Word document. Save the document, and then it will be available for editing in Word. The tickets shown in Figure 7.2 do not include a stub or automatic numbering. If you are interested in these additional options, you may want to create the tickets from scratch as directed in Exercise 1.

FIGURE

7.2 **Microsoft Office Online Ticket Template**

In addition, for ease in finding templates in the Microsoft Office Online Templates Web site, consider using the search feature at the right of the *Search* text box as shown in Figure 7.3. At the *Search* text box in the upper right side of the Microsoft Office Online home page, type a name for the desired template and then click Go. If this specific template can be found, it will display.

FIGURE

7.3 **Searching for a Template**

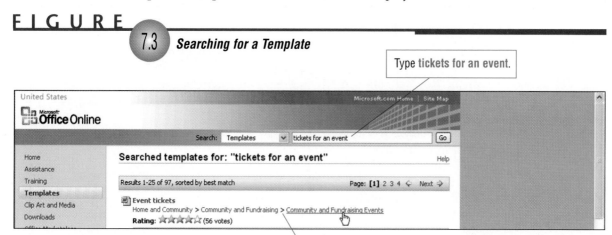

Using Tables to Create Promotional Documents

Tables are useful in desktop publishing because they offer options to format several objects consistently and predictably. Tables can give you precise control over layout. If your document needs to be separated by lines or has several areas that share a common border, tables can be a most efficient choice. However, tables require some planning before you use them in the layout of your document.

In Exercise 1, you will use Word's table feature to format tickets and Word's *AutoNum* field codes to number the tickets and stubs sequentially. You have probably worked with field codes before, although you may have not realized it. For instance, whenever you insert an automatic date, time, or page number, you are inserting *field codes* into your document. In the next exercise, you will insert a specific field code that will enable sequential numbering in tickets and stubs.

Field codes
Command functions in Word that automatically create preformatted results.

As an active volunteer for Charlotte United Charities, you will create raffle ticket codes in your document. In the next exercise, each ticket will need a number printed twice—once on a ticket to serve as a claim ticket and once on a stub to be placed in a raffle. Print the tickets on 65-lb. uncoated cover stock or send a master copy of the ticket without the sequential numbering to a commercial printer to be copied, cut, numbered, and perforated.

(Before completing computer exercises, delete the Chapter06 folder on your disk. Next, copy the Chapter07 folder from the CD that accompanies this textbook to your disk and then make Chapter07 the active folder.)

exercise

Creating Tickets/Stubs with Sequential Numbering

1. At a clear document screen, create a table for the tickets in Figure 7.4 by completing the following steps:
   a. Create a table with two columns and four rows.
   b. Select the entire table, click Table, and then click Table Properties.
   c. At the Table Properties dialog box, select the Row tab, click in the check box at the left of *Specify height*, and then change the setting to 2". At the *Row height is* list box, make sure *At least* displays.

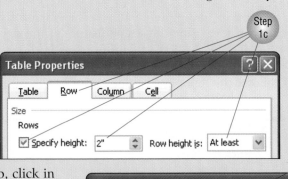

   d. Select the Column tab and type 3.75 inches for the Column 1 *Preferred width*. Click the Next Column button.

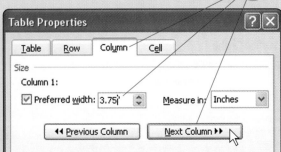

e. At the Column tab type 2.25 inches for the Column 2 *Preferred width*. Click OK or press Enter. *(Hint: You may have to click the **Next Column** button twice to get to the appropriate column.)*

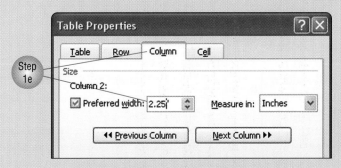

f. Select the first column and change the right cell borderline to a dashed line by completing the following steps:
   1) Click Format and then Borders and Shading.
   2) At the Borders and Shading dialog box, click the Borders tab. Click the down-pointing arrow at the right of the *Apply to* list box and then select *Cell*.
   3) Click the right borderline in the *Preview* box to remove the line, click the third line (dashed line) from the top in the *Style* list box, and then click where the previous line displayed in the *Preview* box. In place of the single line, a dashed line should display. Click OK.

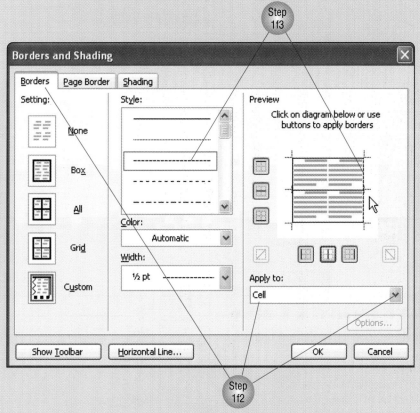

2. Save the document with Save As and name it **c07ex01, Raffle**.

3. Insert the ticket and stub text by completing the following steps:

   a. Position the insertion point in the first cell in the first row and insert **Raffle** located in your Chapter07 folder.

   b. Position the insertion point in the second cell in the first row and insert **Stub** located in your Chapter07 folder.

Step 3a

Step 3b

Dove Award & Raffle
Benefiting Charlotte Unified Charities

Donation: $10 each or 3 for $25
Prizes: 2 round-trip tickets to London; 2 round-trip tickets to Hawaii; $500 shopping spree, and more…
No.

Name _____
Address _____
City _____
State _____
Phone _____
No.

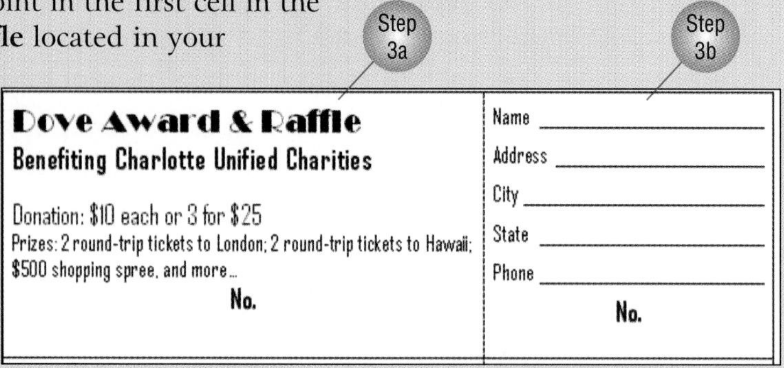

4. Insert the dove image by completing the following steps:

   a. Position the insertion point in the first cell of the first row and insert the dove image shown in Figure 7.4 (substitute a different image if necessary). To find this image, access the Insert Clip Art task pane, type dove or j0238166.wmf in the *Search for* text box, and then press Go. Click once to insert the image.

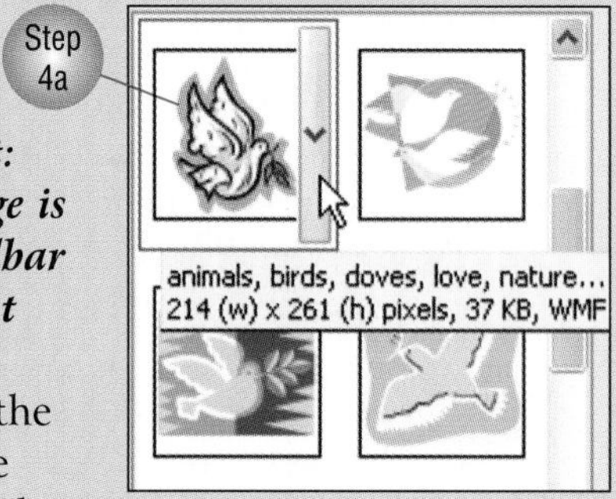

Step 4a

animals, birds, doves, love, nature…
214 (w) x 261 (h) pixels, 37 KB, WMF

   b. Resize the clip art image similar to Figure 7.4. *(Hint: If the Picture toolbar does not display when the image is inserted into the cell, right-click the mouse in the toolbar area and then click Picture at the list of toolbars that displays.)*

   c. Select the dove, click the Text Wrapping button on the Picture toolbar, and then click Tight. Rotate the dove image by clicking Draw, Rotate or Flip, Flip Horizontal.

   d. Position the dove as shown in Figure 7.4.

   e. Hold down the Ctrl key as you drag and drop a copy of the dove to the stub section of the ticket.

   f. Change the dove image in the stub into a watermark by selecting the image, clicking the Color button on the Picture toolbar, and then clicking Washout. *(Hint: Adjust the Contrast and Brightness if necessary.)*

Dove Award & Raffle
Benefiting Charlotte Unified Charities

Donation: $10 each or 3 for $25
Prizes: 2 round-trip tickets to London; 2 round-trip tickets to Hawaii; $500 shopping spree, and more…
No.

Step 4d

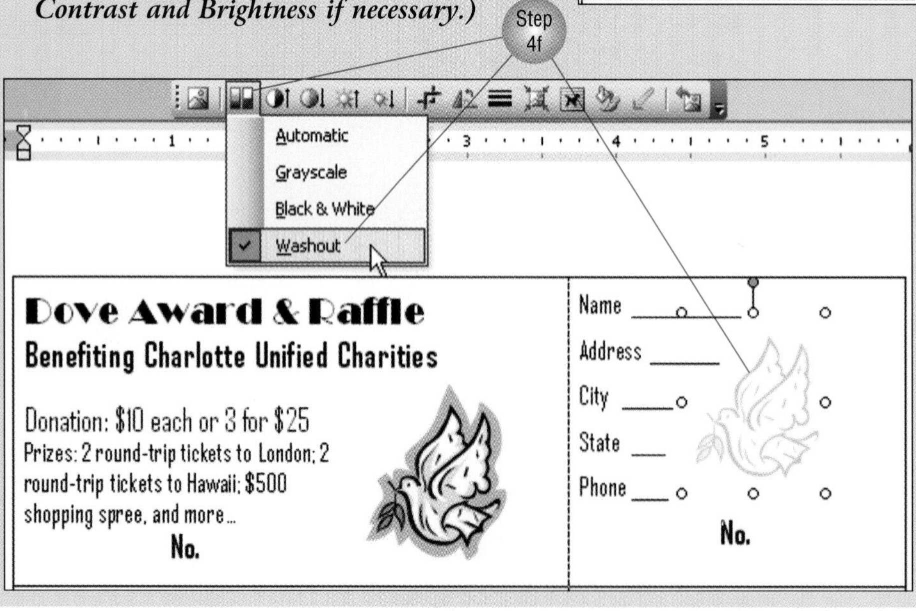

Step 4f

Automatic
Grayscale
Black & White
✓ Washout

Dove Award & Raffle
Benefiting Charlotte Unified Charities

Donation: $10 each or 3 for $25
Prizes: 2 round-trip tickets to London; 2 round-trip tickets to Hawaii; $500 shopping spree, and more…
No.

Name _____
Address _____
City _____
State _____
Phone _____
No.

g. Position the dove as shown in Figure 7.4, click the Text Wrapping button on the Picture toolbar, and then click Behi̱nd Text.

5. Insert the sequential numbering by completing the following steps:
   a. Position the insertion point at the right of *No.* in the first cell in the first row and press the spacebar once.
   b. Click I̱nsert and then F̱ield.
   c. At the Field dialog box, make sure *(All)* displays in the C̱ategories list box.
   d. In the F̱ield names list box, click *AutoNum.* Click OK.

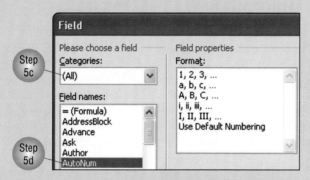

e. Position the insertion point at the right of *No.* in the second cell in the first row (stub), press the spacebar once, and then insert the *AutoNum* field code.
f. Select the first row and copy it to the clipboard.

g. Position your insertion point in the next row and click E̱dit and then P̱aste Rows.
h. Press F4 (repeat command) twice to create a total of four rows of tickets.
i. Delete any empty rows that may appear on the next page.

6. View your tickets in Print Preview.
7. Save the document again as **c07ex01, Raffle**.
8. Print and then close **c07ex01, Raffle**.

FIGURE
7.4 Exercise 1

Dove Award & Raffle
Benefiting Charlotte Unified Charities

Donation: $10 each or 3 for $25
Prizes: 2 round-trip tickets to London; 2
round-trip tickets to Hawaii; $500
shopping spree, and more...
No. 1.

Name _____
Address _____
City _____
State _____
Phone _____
No. 1.

Dove Award & Raffle
Benefiting Charlotte Unified Charities

Donation: $10 each or 3 for $25
Prizes: 2 round-trip tickets to London; 2
round-trip tickets to Hawaii; $500
shopping spree, and more...
No. 2.

Name _____
Address _____
City _____
State _____
Phone _____
No. 2.

Dove Award & Raffle
Benefiting Charlotte Unified Charities

Donation: $10 each or 3 for $25
Prizes: 2 round-trip tickets to London; 2
round-trip tickets to Hawaii; $500
shopping spree, and more...
No. 3.

Name _____
Address _____
City _____
State _____
Phone _____
No. 3.

Dove Award & Raffle
Benefiting Charlotte Unified Charities

Donation: $10 each or 3 for $25
Prizes: 2 round-trip tickets to London; 2
round-trip tickets to Hawaii; $500
shopping spree, and more...
No. 4.

Name _____
Address _____
City _____
State _____
Phone _____
No. 4.

Creating Lines for Typing

There are two methods for creating a line on which you can type. Each of these methods will allow you to successfully place the insertion point on the line and type without typing over the line or pushing it to the right as you type.

The first method requires the use of the underline character and the Tab key for the creation of the line. You will use this method to create the first two lines of the form in Exercise 2. To create a line for typing on by using the Tab and underline keys, set tab settings for the columns of text. Press the Tab key to align the insertion point at the first tab setting. Turn on underlining and press the spacebar once to create a placeholder (you may want to turn on the Show/Hide ¶ feature so you can view the spacebar placeholder). Press the Tab key to create the line. Turn off underlining and press the Enter key to move to the next line or the Tab key to move to the next column. Figure 7.5 shows the tab settings and the use of the underline character and Tab key to create the name and address part of Exercise 2. To be sure it is working, move your insertion point to the position after the spacebar and type some text. The text should appear typed above the line.

FIGURE

7.5 *Use the Underline and Tab Keys to Create Lines*

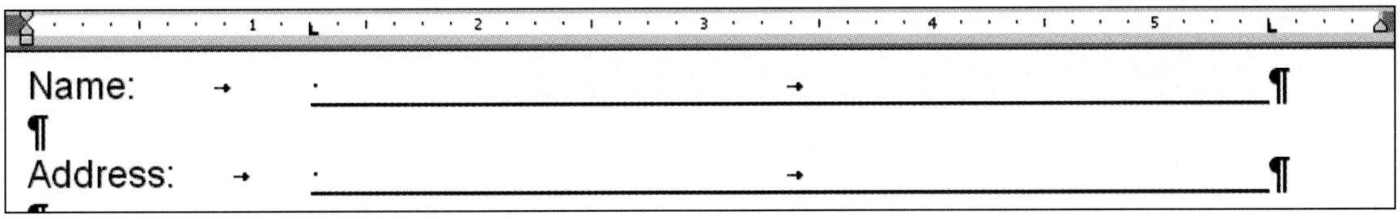

The second method incorporates the use of the Line tool from the Drawing toolbar. When a drawing object is placed within a document, it can be moved around the document by selecting the object and pressing the location (directional) arrows on the keyboard. The object will move in the selected direction along the lines of an invisible grid that exists within each document. Each time an arrow is pressed, the object will move in that direction to the next line of the grid. Often the default spacing between the gridlines of a document is larger than desired for moving an object. In Exercise 2, you will draw lines, adjust the grid settings to support accurate movement of the drawn lines, and position the lines within the form.

To type on the line that was created using the underline and tab method, it is important that the insertion point be placed after the placeholder. If the insertion point is placed on or before the placeholder, the line will be pushed to the right as you type. To type on the line that was created using the Drawing toolbar, simply position the insertion point on the line and type. You may have to use the spacebar to advance the insertion point to the correct position. Remember to align the text on the left for each line.

exercise 2

Creating Lines for Typing

1. At a clear document screen, create the form in Figure 7.6 by completing the following steps:
   a. Change the font to 12-point Arial.
   b. Type the title and heading information as it appears in Figure 7.6.
   c. Position the insertion point at the left margin a double space below *Conference Registration*.
   d. Create a left-aligned tab at 1.25 inches and a second left-aligned tab at 5.5 inches.
   e. Type Name: and then press the Tab key to align the insertion point at the first tab setting. This is where the underline will begin.
   f. Turn on underlining and press the spacebar one time. This creates a placeholder for the starting point of the line.
   g. Press the Tab key. A line is created between the insertion point and the last tab setting.
   h. Turn off underlining.
   i. Press the Enter key twice and type Address:.
   j. Press the Tab key to align the insertion point at the first tab setting.
   k. Turn on underlining and press the spacebar one time to create the placeholder.
   l. Press the Tab key to create the line.
   m. Turn off underlining and press the Enter key twice. The insertion point is positioned at the left margin a double space below the *Address:* line.
2. To create the next three lines of the form, we will use the Line tool from the Drawing toolbar. This method will be used to create the next three lines of the form. The remaining lines of the form can be created using whichever method you feel most comfortable with.
   a. Type City: at the insertion point and press the Enter key twice.
   b. Type Phone: and press the Enter key twice.
   c. Type E-Mail Address:.
   d. Click the Line tool from the Drawing toolbar. The cursor becomes a crossbar.
   e. Position the crossbar to the right of *City:* and visually align it with the left edge of the *Address:* line. This is where the line will begin.
   f. Click and drag the mouse to draw a line for *City:*. *(Hint: Hold down the Shift key as you draw the line. This will guarantee a straight line.)* Once the line is drawn, release the mouse button and the line will be selected.
   g. Press Ctrl + C to copy the line onto the Clipboard.
   h. Press Ctrl + V twice to create two more lines—one for *Phone:* and one for *E-Mail Address:*. The lines are staggered and the last line is selected. *(Note: By copying and pasting the lines, the length of all of the lines is the same.)*
3. Once the lines have been copied and placed within the form, they need to be rearranged and placed in the correct position. To accomplish this, each of the lines must be moved horizontally and vertically into a position that is aligned with the headings.
   a. To decrease the amount of space on the Grid settings, click the Draw button on the Drawing toolbar and then click Grid to display the Drawing Grid dialog box.
   b. Click *Snap objects to grid* if it is not selected. This will ensure that the selected drawing objects will move along the gridlines of the document.

c. Decrease the horizontal and vertical grid settings to 0.013 inch. This will decrease the spacing between the gridlines of the document. As the location (directional) arrows are pressed from the keyboard, the selected drawing object will move the distance set in the grid settings along the gridlines. The smaller the number, the more control you will have over the movement of the selected object.

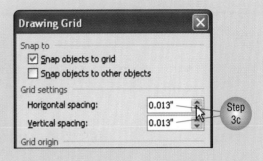
Step 3c

d. Click OK to return to the document

e. To adjust the line drawings, select all three lines. *(Hint: Hold down the Shift key as you select each line drawing.)*

f. Click the Draw button on the Drawing toolbar and then point to Align or Distribute. Click Align Left to align all of the selected lines on the left. On the Ruler, point to the 1.25-inch tab setting. Click and hold down the mouse button on this tab setting. The vertical bar will show. You can use this bar to "eyeball" the horizontal alignment with the lines above.

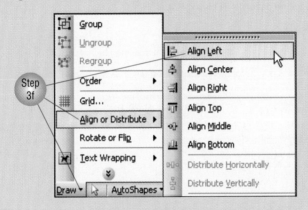
Step 3f

g. The lines are still selected; now they need to be aligned vertically. Click the Draw button on the Drawing toolbar, point to Align or Distribute, and then click Distribute Vertically.

h. Align the lines horizontally (by using the Up Arrow key) with the guide words *City, Phone,* and *E-Mail Address.*

i. Click anywhere within the form to deselect the lines.

4. Create the *ST:* and *ZIP:* lines of the form. Use either method for creating a line you can type on. *(Hint: To use the tab and underline method, set additional left tabs at 3.2", 3.5", 3.8", 4.1", 4.4", and 5.5".)*

5. Complete the remaining items of the form. *(Hint: To use the tab and underline method for the* Check one: *items, set left tabs at 1.25", 1.6", 2.3", and a right tab at 2".)*

6. Save the form as **c07ex02, Lines for Typing**.

7. Print **c07ex02, Lines for Typing**.

8. Complete the form with your name other information. Use a check mark from Insert, Symbols, Wingdings font, for the dollar figure. Save the form as **c07ex02, Lines for Typing Completed**.

9. Print **c07ex02, Lines for Typing Completed**.

BEST SELLERS OF THE WESTERN REGION
March 15, 2006
CONFERENCE REGISTRATION

Name: _____

Address: _____

City: _____ ST: ____ ZIP: _____

Phone: _____

E-Mail Address: _____

Registration deadline – February 23, 2006

Check one:

____	$95	Participant from member institution
____	$90	Participant from non-member institution
____	$100	Institutional Membership Dues

Check must accompany registration
Make checks payable to:
Storyteller Books

Mail registration forms to:
Storyteller Books
123 Main Street
Glen Ellyn, IL 60137

Building the Framework of a Form

One of the beginning steps in creating a form is to determine how the form will be used—hard copy or online. Next, decide what information needs to be included in the form, and if there is an existing Word template that will fit your needs. If a form is to be filled out using Word, the form will consist of areas that contain static information (information that will remain the same each time the form is used) and dynamic information (information that will change each time the form is used).

While designing a Word form, both the static information and special areas called form fields are placed onto the form. The form fields will contain the dynamic information that will be entered by the person who is filling out the form each time the form is used. The static information usually consists of the title, the directions, and the labels that identify the content that is entered into the form field.

Once the form is created with the static information and the form fields, it is saved as a template. As the template is created, it is placed within a predefined area on the computer preserved so that each time it is used to create a new Word document, the information that has been defined within the form is in tact. This practice ensures that the template will be consistent each time it is used.

An example of a form that is saved as a template might be a standardized memo or a fax cover sheet for a company. These forms might contain the company's logo and address and areas where information is to be typed. This practice aids the person who is filling out the form by not requiring them to enter the company address or the field labels. Only the information that is defined within the form field will be typed.

To create a template, click New at the File menu and then click on the On my computer hyperlink in the *Templates* section. At the Templates dialog box, you will select *Template* in the *Create New* section, and then double-click the *Blank Document* icon at the General tab. It is necessary to create the form as a template so that the original remains intact after an employee fills in the form. Information may be typed in the designated fields, a check box may be turned on or off, or information may be selected from a drop-down list.

A table can be very useful when creating a form with form fields. A table can be customized to create a business form such as an invoice or a purchase order.

Adding Interactive Form Fields

The essential commands for creating and editing a form are grouped together on the Forms toolbar as discussed in Chapter 4. The buttons on the Forms toolbar enable you to easily insert a text box, check box, or drop-down list.

Protect Form

Before you make the form available to users, protect it by clicking the Protect Form button on the Forms toolbar. Protection allows users to fill in the form, but prevents them from changing the form's layout. If you want to modify the form, click the Protect Form button on the Forms toolbar to deactivate it. You can also unprotect a document by clicking Tools and then Unprotect Document. Unless you protect a document, users cannot type in a text box, select or clear a check box, or see a down-pointing arrow to display the available options in a drop-down list.

If you save the template in Exercise 3 to your hard drive, you may access it by clicking New at the File menu and then double-clicking the template in the specific tab where you saved it. Otherwise, you may access the template from the DTP Templates folder that you may have created on your hard drive or floppy disk. In either case, if field codes display in the fill-in form fields as shown in Figure 7.7, click Tools, click Options, and then remove the check mark from the *Field codes* check box at the View tab. The *Field shading:* option should display *Always*. The shading will display, but will not print.

7.7 *Completing a Form Document*

1. Your template document form fields should display like this.

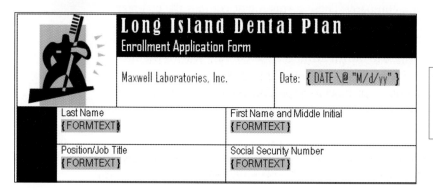

2. If your template document form fields display like this, deactivate the *Field codes* option as shown in 3.

3. Deactivate (remove the check mark from) the *Field codes* option at the View tab of the Options dialog box.

Creating Form Fields with Drop-Down Lists

When creating form fields for a form document, there may be some fields where you want the person entering the information to choose from specific options, rather than typing the data. Figure 7.8 displays the Drop-Down Form Field Options dialog box where you can type the desired options. To display this dialog box, position the insertion point on the drop-down list form field in your document and then click the Form Field Options button on the Forms toolbar.

7.8 **Using the Drop-Down Form Field Options Dialog Box**

Type an item in this text box that you want included in the drop-down list and then click Add.

The item is then added to this list.

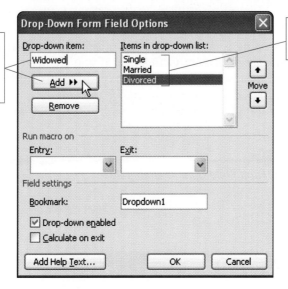

Changing Check Box Form Field Options

Check box form field options can be changed at the Check Box Form Field Options dialog box shown in Figure 7.9. To display this dialog box, position the insertion point on the check box form field in your document and then click the Form Field Options button on the Forms toolbar.

7.9 **Changing Check Box Form Field Options**

Enter the desired check box point size.

If selected, a check mark will automatically display in the check box in your form document.

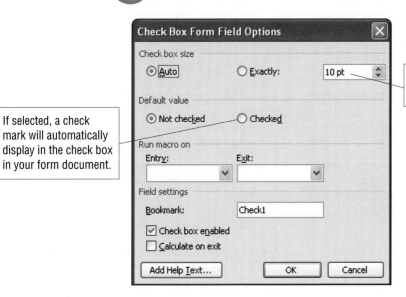

Changing Text Form Field Options

To change options for a text form field, position the insertion point on the text form field you want to change and then click the Form Field Options button on the Forms toolbar. This displays the Text Form Field Options dialog box shown in Figure 7.10. You can change the type of text that is to be inserted in the form field. The default setting is *Regular text*. This option can be changed to *Number, Date, Current date, Current time,* or *Calculation.* If you change the *Type* option, Word will display an error message if the correct type of information (text or numbers) is not entered. In addition, you can change the length option to specify an exact measurement for a form field. The default setting is *Unlimited.*

FIGURE

7.10 *Text Form Field Options Dialog Box*

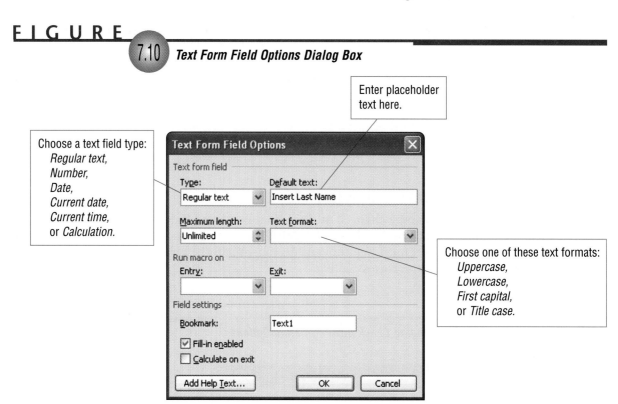

Enter placeholder text here.

Choose a text field type: *Regular text, Number, Date, Current date, Current time,* or *Calculation.*

Choose one of these text formats: *Uppercase, Lowercase, First capital,* or *Title case.*

Whenever you are working in a form template document, press the Tab key to move to the next form field and Shift + Tab to move to a preceding form field. Press the spacebar to insert an *X* in a check box form field, click the down-pointing triangle at the right of the drop-down form field, and then click the desired choice.

As an employee in Human Resources at Maxwell Laboratories, you will create an enrollment application for employees interested in participating in the company's new dental plan. Maxwell employees will access the form via the company intranet, so prepare the form for online completion.

Using Microsoft Office Online Templates

The Microsoft Office Online Templates include numerous predesigned form templates that you may choose to customize to fit your specific needs. Many categories are available. You may choose forms from the following categories:

- Calendars and Planners
- Holidays and Occasions
- Home and Community
- Stationery and Labels

You may customize any one of these forms by adding your company logo or changing fills, shading, and font colors to match the colors in your logo or a favorite clip art. Additionally, you may add field codes to the form so that data can be inserted while using the form online. Figure 7.11 shows form templates accessed through Microsoft Office Online Templates and edited in Word, Excel, and Access.

FIGURE

7.11 Sample Form Templates from the Template Gallery

Detailed invoice template edited in Word

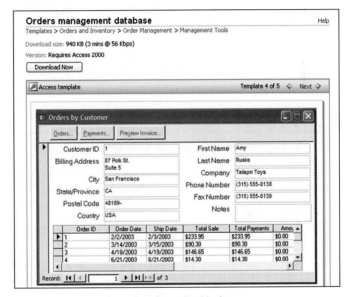

Form template edited in Access

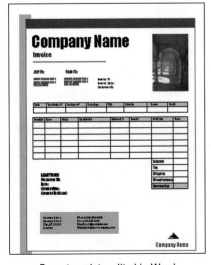

Form template edited in Word

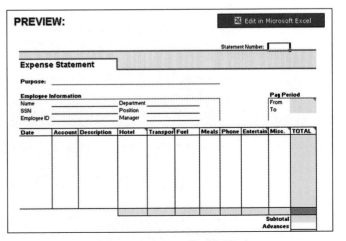

Expense statement edited in Excel

Printing a Form

After the form fields in a form document have been filled in, you may print the form in the normal manner or you may choose to print just the data (not the entire form), or print the form and not the fill-in data.

If you are printing a preprinted form that is inserted in the printer, you will want to print just the data. Word will print the data in the same location on the page as it appears in the form document. To print just the data in a form, click Tools and then Options. At the Options dialog box with the Print tab selected, as shown in Figure 7.12, click *Print data only for forms* in the *Options for current document only* section (this inserts a check mark in the check box), and then click OK. Click the Print button on the Standard toolbar. After printing only the data, complete similar steps to remove the check mark from the *Print data only for forms* check box.

Reset

To print only the form without the data, you would click File and then New, and then click the General Templates hyperlink in the New Document task pane. At the Templates dialog box, double-click the desired template document in the list box. With the form document displayed on the document screen, click the Print button on the Standard toolbar, and then close the document. Additionally, you may click the Reset button on the Forms toolbar and then the current data entered into the fields will be removed and the form fields will display without the data.

FIGURE

7.12 Print Data Only

View	General	Edit	Print	Sa

Printing options

- ☐ Draft output
- ☐ Update fields
- ☐ Update links
- ☑ Allow A4/Letter paper resizing
- ☑ Background printing
- ☐ Print PostScript over text
- ☐ Reverse print order

Include with document

- ☐ Document properties
- ☐ Field codes
- ☐ XML tags
- ☐ Hidden text
- ☑ Drawing objects
- ☐ Background colors and images

Click this option to print the data only for forms.

Options for current document only

- ☑ Print data only for forms

Default tray: Use printer settings ▾

exercise 3

Creating a Form

1. At a clear document screen, create the form in Figure 7.13 by completing the following steps:
   a. Click File and then New.
   b. At the New Document task pane, click the On my computer hyperlink in the *Templates* section.

c. At the Templates dialog box, select the General tab, click *Template* in the *Create New* section, and then double-click *Blank Document*.

d. Insert **Dental** located in your Chapter07 folder. The basic table structure has already been created for you.

e. Save the document and name it **c07ex03, Dental.dot**. (Consult your instructor as to whether you should save the template to the DTP Templates folder you created in Chapter 2 or to the hard drive.)

f. Position the insertion point in the first cell in the first row and insert the dentist image shown in Figure 7.13. Type dentist or j0212489.wmf in the *Search for* text box at the Insert Clip Art task pane.

g. Select the image, size it, and then center it in the cell.

h. Position the insertion point in the top cell to the right of the dentist image. Click Format and then Borders and Shading. At the Borders and Shading dialog box, select the Shading tab and then change the fill to Black (first color in the fourth row of the color palette). Click the down-pointing arrow at the right of the *Apply to* list box and click *Cell*. Click OK.

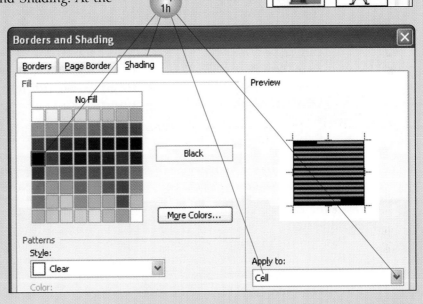

i. Press the spacebar once after *Date:* and insert a date code by clicking Insert and then Date and Time. Select the fourth code from the top and make sure the option to *Update automatically* is selected. (The date command is actually a field code { DATE \ @ "M/d/yy" } ; press Alt + F9 to turn off the field code if necessary.)

j. Position the insertion point in the first column of the table (the text will be rotated). Type Applicant Information and then change the shading of the cell to Black. The text should automatically reverse to White. From the Tables and Borders toolbar, change the alignment to Align Center.

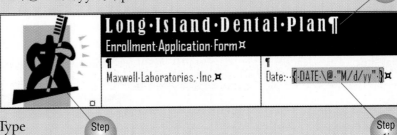

k. Display the Forms toolbar.

2. Insert field codes that will prompt the applicant to fill in information by completing the following steps:
   a. Position the insertion point below *Last Name*, click the Text Form Field button (first button) on the Forms toolbar, and make sure the Form Field Shading button (third button from the right) is active.
   b. Click the Form Field Options button (fourth button from the left) on the Forms toolbar.
   c. At the Text Form Field Options dialog box, make sure *Regular text* displays in the *Type* text box, type **Insert Last Name** in the *Default text* box, and make sure *Unlimited* displays in the *Maximum length* list box. Click OK or press Enter.

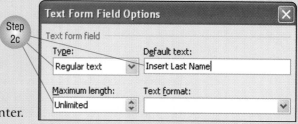

   d. Type the following text in each designated cell by following Steps 2a, 2b, and 2c:

First Name and Middle Initial	**Insert First Name and Middle Initial**
Position/Job Title	**Insert Job Title**
Social Security Number	**Insert Social Security Number**
Street Address	**Insert Street Address**
Date of Birth	**Insert Birth Date**
City, State, ZIP Code	**Insert City, State, ZIP Code**
E-Mail Address	**Insert E-Mail Address**
Home Phone Number	**Insert Area Code + Home Phone #**
Business Phone Number + Ext.	**Insert Area Code + Business Phone #**
Dental Location Number	**Insert Dental Location Number**

3. Create the check boxes for the empty cells, as shown in Figure 7.13, by completing the following steps:
   a. Position the insertion point on the line below *Coverage Type*, click the Check Box Form Field button (second button) on the Forms toolbar, press the spacebar once, and then type **Single**; press Ctrl + Tab, create another check box, press the spacebar once, and then type **Single + 1**; press Ctrl + Tab, insert another check box, press the spacebar once, and then type **Family**.
   b. Position the insertion point below *Gender*, create a check box, press the spacebar once, and then type **Male**; press Ctrl + Tab, create another check box, press the spacebar once, and then type **Female**.
   c. Position the insertion point below *Marital Status* and then create a drop-down list by completing the following steps:
      1) Click the Drop-Down Form Field button (third button) on the Forms toolbar and then click the Form Field Options button (fourth button) on the Forms toolbar.
      2) At the Drop-Down Form Field Options dialog box, type **Single** in the *Drop-down item* text box and then click the *Add* button.
      3) Add *Married, Divorced,* and *Widowed* to the list, following Step 3c2.
      4) Click OK or press Enter.

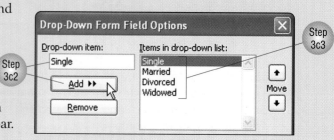

4. Protect the template form by clicking the Protect Form button (last button) on the Forms toolbar.

5. Save the document again with the same name **c07ex03, Dental.dot**.
6. Print and then close **c07ex03, Dental.dot**.
7. Open **c07ex03, Dental.dot**. If you saved **c07ex03, Dental.dot** to your hard drive, you may access this template by clicking <u>F</u>ile, <u>N</u>ew, and then clicking the <u>General Templates</u> hyperlink. Make sure *Document* displays in the *Create New* section of the Templates dialog box in the General Tab. At the Templates dialog box, double-click **c07ex03, Dental.dot**. *(Hint: If field codes display in the fill-in form fields, click <u>T</u>ools, <u>O</u>ptions, and then at the View tab remove the check mark in the <u>F</u>ield codes check box. The <u>F</u>ield shading: option should display* **Always***.)*
8. Press the Tab key to move from one field to the next and type the appropriate information—use your own name, and so on, or make up the information.
9. Click in the appropriate check boxes for the desired responses.
10. Save the document and name it **c07ex03, Dental 2**.
11. Print and then close **c07ex03, Dental 2**.

F I G U R E

7.13 *Exercise 3*

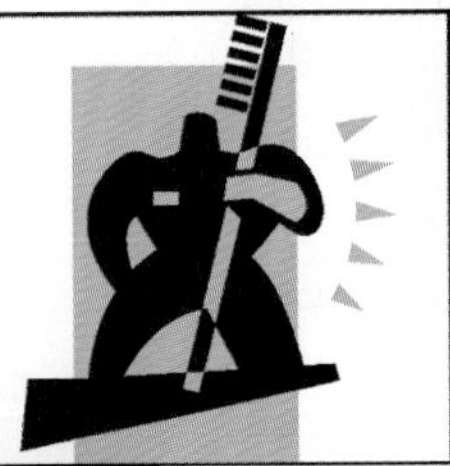

Creating Postcards to Promote Business

If you have a brief message to get across to prospective customers, postcards can be an appropriate means of delivering the message. Postcards are inexpensive to create and use. They can be used as appointment reminders, just-moved notes, return/reply cards, display cards, thank-you cards, or invitations. You can purchase predesigned, printed postcards with attractive borders and color combinations, in differing sizes and weights that meet U.S. Postal Service standards; and you can find blank, prestamped 3.5 by 5.5-inch postcards at any U.S. Postal Service location. Alternatively, you can use the Word Labels feature, which provides a predefined postcard sized at 4 by 6 inches. Two postcards will display on a standard-size sheet of paper when you use Word's postcard label Avery 5389.

Most postcards are created on 100- to 110-lb. uncoated cover stock paper. The paper weight or thickness should be strong enough to hold up in the mail. The front side of the postcard is used for your return address and the recipient's address along with an area reserved for the postage. On the reverse, you can create a headline and use a graphic, photo, or watermark to emphasize the message. You will need to leave room for your message and optional signature.

Figure 7.14 shows a two-postcard template from the Templates on Office Online hyperlink. The postcards include placeholder text that instructs you how to use the template. To locate this template, type **business postcards** in the *Search* text box and then click Go. Click the Postcards (Pacific Northwest design) hyperlink and then click the Download Now button. Two postcards are available per sheet with a front page and a back page. Each postcard may be designed and formatted to include promotional images and text by simply adding an appropriate photo, logo, or clip, along with a promotional statement, that reinforces the identity of the company or promotes a service or product in that organization. In addition, you may customize the postcards for mass mailing by using Word's Mail Merge Wizard.

F I G U R E

7.14 *Postcard Template from Microsoft Office Online*

Creating Postcards Using Word's Labels Feature

1. At a clear document screen, create the two postcards in Figure 7.15 by completing the following steps:
   a. Display the Drawing, Tables and Borders, and Picture toolbars.
   b. Click Tools, Letters and Mailings, and then Envelopes and Labels.
   c. At the Envelopes and Labels dialog box, select the Labels tab and then click the Options button.
   d. At the Labels Option dialog box, select *5389 - Post Card* in the *Product number* list box. Click OK or press Enter.
   e. At the Envelopes and Labels dialog box, click the New Document button.
   f. Click Table and Show Gridlines if the gridlines are not displayed.
   g. Click the Align Top Left button on the Tables and Borders toolbar.

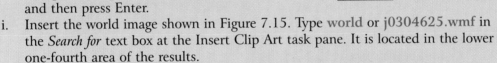

   h. With the insertion point located in the first postcard, press the spacebar once and then press Enter.
   i. Insert the world image shown in Figure 7.15. Type world or j0304625.wmf in the *Search for* text box at the Insert Clip Art task pane. It is located in the lower one-fourth area of the results.

   j. Select the world image and change the text wrap to In Front of Text.
   k. Size and position the image similar to Figure 7.15.
   l. Right-click the picture and select Edit Picture from the shortcut menu.
   m. At the Microsoft Word prompt asking if you want to convert the image to a drawing object, click Yes.

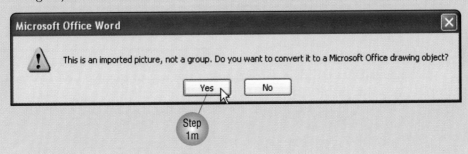

n. Click outside the image once and then double-click the oval shape behind the world image. At the Format AutoShape dialog box, select the Colors and Lines tab, click the down-pointing arrow at the right of the *Fill Color* list box, and then click *More Colors*. At the Colors dialog box, select the Custom tab, and then type this color formula: Red **127**, Green **127**, and Blue **255**. Click OK.

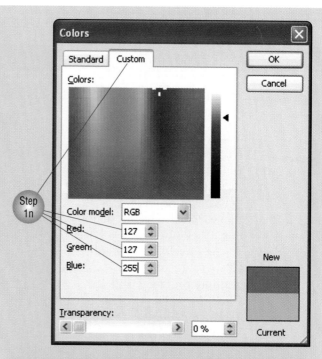

o. At the Colors and Lines tab, click the down-pointing arrow at the right of the *Fill Color* list box and then click *Fill Effects*. Select the Gradient tab, click *One color*, and then drag the slider to the right toward *Light*. In the *Shading styles* section, click the *From center* style, click the variant on the right, and then click OK twice. **(Hint: You many want to group the picture before proceeding with the next step.)**

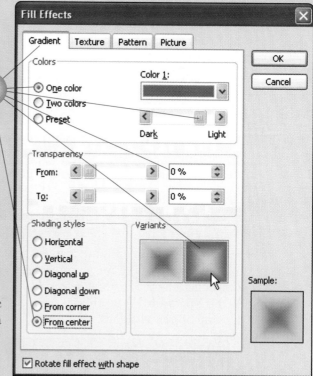

p. Insert the text by completing the following steps:

   1) Click the Text Box button on the Drawing toolbar and drag the crosshairs to draw a box approximately 2.5 inches square. (Verify at the Format Text Box dialog box with the Size tab selected.)

   2) Position the insertion point in the text box and type See the world a little clearer, a little brighter with regular eye examinations.

   3) Select *See the world* and change the font to 24-point Bauhaus 93 in Bright Green. Select the rest of the text and change the font to 24-point Bradley Hand ITC Bold.

   4) Right-align the text and remove the borderline around the text box and change the fill to No Fill.

   5) Position the text box similar to Figure 7.15.

q. Insert the glasses image shown in Figure 7.15. Type glasses or j0300263.wmf in the *Search for* text box at the Insert Clip Art task pane.

r. The glasses are located in the bottom half of the results area. Select the glasses and change the text wrap to I<u>n</u> Front of Text.

s. Size and position the glasses similar to Figure 7.15.

Step 1q

2. Copy the completed postcard to the postcard below by completing the following steps:

a. Position the insertion point in the postcard, select the cell, and then click the Copy button on the Formatting toolbar. *(Hint: The postcard is in a table format.)*

b. Position the insertion point in the second postcard, click <u>E</u>dit, and then click <u>P</u>aste Cells. Delete any additional empty cells.

Step 3

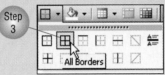

3. Create a single 0.5-point border around the postcards by selecting the entire table and then clicking the All Borders button on the Tables and Borders toolbar.

4. Save the document with Save <u>A</u>s and name it **c07ex04, Postcard**.

5. Print two pages of postcards (four cards in total) and then close **c07ex04, Postcard**.

F I G U R E

7.15 **Exercise 4**

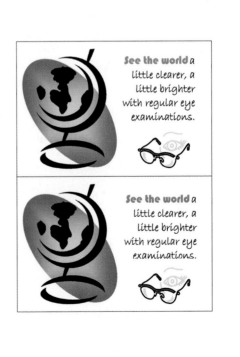

Merging Promotional Documents

Word includes a Mail Merge Wizard you can use to create customized letters, envelopes, labels, directories, e-mail messages, and faxes. The wizard guides you through the merge process and presents six task panes. The six task panes include steps on selecting a document type to executing the final merge in customizing a document. The options in each task pane vary depending on the type of merge you are performing.

Mail merge is the process of combining variable information with standard text to create personalized documents. Generally, a merge takes two documents—the *main document*, which contains standard data such as the text of a form letter or the return address and picture on a postcard, with a *data source*, which contains variable data such as names and addresses. Special codes called *merge fields* in the main document direct Word to collect information from the data source and use it in the main document to create personalized documents. Use these field names if they represent the data you are creating. Variable information in a data source document is saved as a record. A *record* contains all of the information for one unit (for example, a person, family, customer, client, or business). A series of fields makes one record, and a series of records makes a data source document.

Using the Mail Merge Wizard to Merge to a Postcard (Label)

The Mail Merge Wizard can be accessed by clicking Tools, pointing to Letters and Mailings, and then clicking Mail Merge. Figure 7.16 illustrates the Mail Merge task pane and Step 1 of the six steps available. A brief description of each of the six task panes is given below:

Step 1: Identify the type of document (letter, e-mail message, envelope, label, or directory).

Step 2: Specify whether you want to use the current document, start from a template, or start from an existing document.

Step 3: Specify whether you are using an existing list, using an Outlook contact list, or typing a new list.

Step 4: Prepare the main document using items in this task pane.

Step 5: Preview the merged document.

Step 6: Complete the merge and send it to the printer.

Mail merge

The process of combining variable information with standard text to create personalized documents.

Main document

A form that receives the data.

Data source

Contains variable data such as names and addresses.

Merge fields

Special codes in the main document that direct Word to collect information from the data source and use it in the main document to create personalized documents.

Record

Contains all of the information for one unit (person, family, or business).

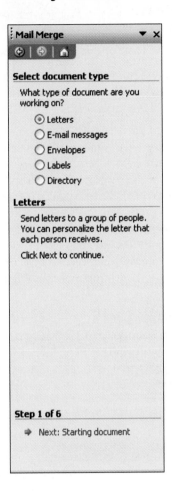

Preparing Labels Using the Mail Merge Wizard

Create mailing labels for records in a data source document in much the same
way that you create envelopes. Use the Mail Merge Wizard to guide you through
the steps for preparing mailing labels. The postcard in Exercise 5 is defined as a
label, which is formatted in a table; therefore, you will use the Tables and Borders
toolbar to make adjustments to the postcard which is merged with a data source
in this exercise.

exercise 5

Creating a Data Source, Main Document, and Merged Postcards

1. At a clear document screen, click <u>T</u>ools, point to Letters and Mailings, and then click <u>M</u>ail Merge.
2. At the first Mail Merge task pane, make sure *Labels* is selected in the *Select document type* section of the task pane, and then click the <u>Next: Starting document</u> hyperlink located toward the bottom of the task pane.
3. At the second Mail Merge task pane, make sure *Change document layout* is selected in the *Select starting document* section of the task pane and then click the <u>Label options</u> hyperlink.
4. At the Label Options dialog box, select *5389 - Post Card* in the *Product number* list box and then click OK. Click the <u>Next: Select recipients</u> hyperlink at the bottom of the task pane.

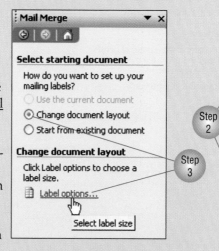

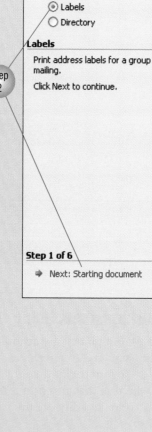

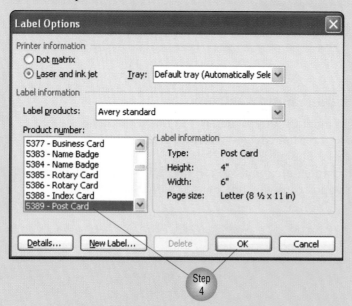

5. At the third Mail Merge task pane, click *Type a new list* in the *Select recipients* section of the task pane. Click the <u>Create</u> hyperlink that displays in the *Type a new list* section.

6. At the New Address List dialog box, the Mail Merge Wizard provides you with a number of predesigned fields. Delete the fields you do not need by completing the following steps:

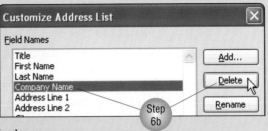

a. Click the Customize button.
b. At the Customize Address List dialog box, click *Company Name* to select it and then click the Delete button.
c. At the message asking if you are sure you want to delete the field, click the Yes button.

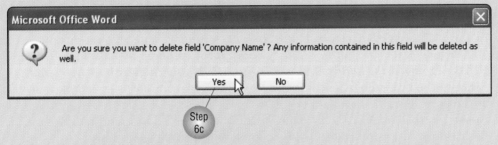

Step 6c

d. Complete steps similar to those in Steps 6b and 6c to delete the following fields:

> *Country*
> *Home Phone*
> *Work Phone*
> *E-mail Address*

e. Click the OK button to close the Customize Address List dialog box.

7. At the New Address List dialog box, enter the information for the first patient shown in Figure 7.17 by completing the following steps:

a. Click in the *Title* text box, type **Mrs.**, and then press the Tab key (press Shift + Tab to move to the previous field).
b. Type **Peggy** and then press Tab.
c. Type **McSherry** and then press Tab.
d. Type **3055 Kinzie Court** and then press Tab twice. *(Hint: Leave* **Address Line 2** *blank.)*
e. Type **Wheaton** and then press Tab.
f. Type **IL** and then press Tab.
g. Type **60187** and then press Tab. *(Hint: This makes the* **New Entry** *button active.)*

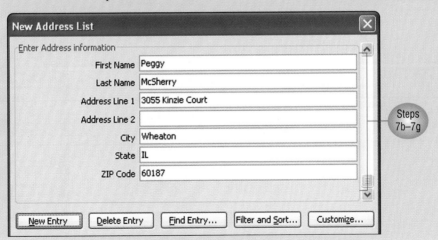

Steps 7b–7g

h. Press Enter and a new blank record form displays in the dialog box.
i. With the insertion point positioned in the *Title* field, complete steps similar to those in Steps 7a through 7h to enter the information for the three other patients shown in Figure 7.17.

8. After entering all of the information for the last patient in Figure 7.17 (Margo Godfrey), click the Close button located in the bottom right corner of the New Address List dialog box.
9. At the Save Address List dialog box, save the data source and name it **Naper Grove Patient List**. *(Hint: Word saves this document as an Access database file with the .mdb extension. By default, Word stores the database file in a new My Data Sources folder created when you installed Word 2003 or Office XP.)*
10. Make sure your data source is saved in the folder you desire and then press Enter or click the <u>S</u>ave button.
11. At the Mail Merge Recipients dialog box, check to make sure all four entries are correct and then click the OK button. *(Hint: Click <u>E</u>dit if you need to make a correction. Click <u>R</u>efresh to reload the data source so the list reflects any changes that were made.)*
12. Move to the next step by clicking the <u>Next: Arrange your labels</u> hyperlink that displays at the bottom of the task pane.
13. At the fourth Mail Merge task pane, create the return address and message on the postcard as shown in Figure 7.18 by completing the following steps:
    a. Display the Tables and Borders toolbar and then click the Align Top Left button (eleventh button from the right). With your insertion point positioned in the upper left corner of the first postcard, press the spacebar once and then press Enter. *(Note: There should be one blank line before you start typing the return address.)*
    b. Type Naper Grove Vision Care in 16-point Arial, small caps, and shadow. Press Enter.
    c. Type in 12-point Arial:

    > 5018 Fairview Avenue
    > Downers Grove, IL 60515

    d. Press Enter twice.
    e. Type Just a friendly reminder! in 16-point Bradley Hand ITC, bold, in this Blue color formula—<u>R</u>ed 127, <u>G</u>reen 127, <u>B</u>lue 255.
    f. Press Enter twice.
    g. Type in 12-point Arial in black:

    > It's time for your eye examination. (Press Enter)
    > Please call our office now for your (Press Enter)
    > appointment (630) 555-3932.

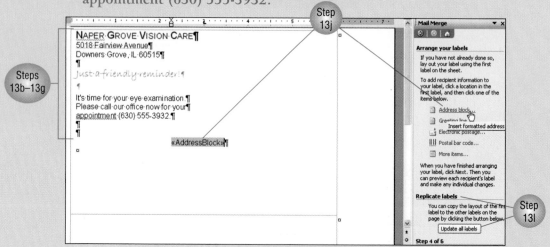

h. Press Enter twice.

i. Click Format, Paragraph, and then change the *Left Indentation* option to *2.25"*. Click OK.

j. At the fourth Mail Merge task pane, click the Address block hyperlink.

k. At the Insert Address Block dialog box, remove the check mark at the left of *Insert company name* and then click OK.

l. In the *Replicate labels* section, click the Update all labels button. *(Note: A copy of **the first postcard should display in the second postcard.**)* If the second postcard text appears too low on the postcard, click the Align Top Left button on the Tables and Borders toolbar.

m. Click the Next: Preview your labels hyperlink.

14. At the fifth Mail Merge task pane, look over the postcards that display in the document window and make sure the information was merged properly. If you want to see the postcards for the other recipients, click the button in the Mail Merge task pane containing the two right-pointing arrows.

15. Click the Next: Complete the merge hyperlink that displays at the bottom of the task pane.

16. At the sixth Mail Merge task pane, click the Print hyperlink in the *Merge* section. Insert **c07ex4, Postcard** (two sheets) into the printer. You will be printing on the reverse side of the postcards.

17. At the Merge to Printer dialog box, make sure *All* is selected and then click OK. Click OK at the Print dialog box.

18. Save the merged postcards in the normal manner and name the document **c07ex05, Merged Doc**.

19. Close **c07ex05, Merged Doc**.

20. *Optional:* If you need additional practice in merging, merge again using the same main document and data source created in this exercise by completing the following steps:

a. Open **c07ex05, Merged Doc**.

b. Click Tools, point to Letters and Mailings, and then click Mail Merge.

c. At the third Mail Merge task pane, which will display first, make sure *Use an existing list* is selected in the *Select recipients* section. Click the Next: Arrange your labels hyperlink.

d. At the fourth Mail Merge task pane, make sure the Address block displays in each postcard (2). Click the Next: Preview your labels hyperlink.

e. In the fifth Mail Merge task pane, preview the labels and then click the Next: Complete the Merge hyperlink.

f. Close the document without saving it.

Step 16

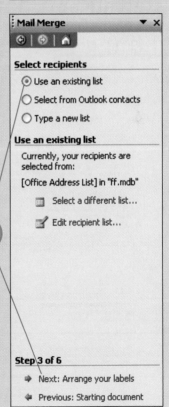

Step 17

Step 20c

7.17 **Information for Data Source Fields**

Title	=	Mrs.		Title	=	Mr.
First Name	=	Peggy		First Name	=	Eric
Last Name	=	McSherry		Last Name	=	Gohlke
Address Line 1	=	3055 Kinzie Court		Address Line 1	=	3090 North Orchard
Address Line 2	=			Address Line 2	=	
City	=	Wheaton		City	=	Downers Grove
State	=	IL		State	=	IL
ZIP Code	=	60187		ZIP Code	=	60515
Title	=	Mrs.		Title	=	Ms.
First Name	=	Kathleen		First Name	=	Margo
Last Name	=	Nixon		Last Name	=	Godfrey
Address Line 1	=	Apt. 14A		Address Line 1	=	Apt. 105B
Address Line 2	=	409 Highland Drive		Address Line 2	=	993 Sandpiper Lane
City	=	Downers Grove		City	=	Westmont
State	=	IL		State	=	IL
ZIP Code	=	60515		ZIP Code	=	60599

7.18 **Exercise 5**

NAPER GROVE VISION CARE
5018 Fairview Avenue
Downers Grove, IL 60515

Just a friendly reminder!

It's time for your eye examination.
Please call our office now for your
appointment (630) 555-3932.

Mrs. Peggy McSherry
3055 Kinzie Court
Wheaton, IL 60187

NAPER GROVE VISION CARE
5018 Fairview Avenue
Downers Grove, IL 60515

Just a friendly reminder!

It's time for your eye examination.
Please call our office now for your
appointment (630) 555-3932.

Mr. Eric Gohlke
3090 North Orchard
Downers Grove, IL 60515

NAPER GROVE VISION CARE
5018 Fairview Avenue
Downers Grove, IL 60515

Just a friendly reminder!

It's time for your eye examination.
Please call our office now for your
appointment (630) 555-3932.

Mrs. Kathleen Nixon
Apt. 14A
409 Highland Drive
Downers Grove, IL 60515

NAPER GROVE VISION CARE
5018 Fairview Avenue
Downers Grove, IL 60515

Just a friendly reminder!

It's time for your eye examination.
Please call our office now for your
appointment (630) 555-3932.

Ms. Margo Godfrey
Apt. 105B
993 Sandpiper Lane
Westmont, IL 60599

Creating Invitations and Cards

You will be using a table and the *2 pages per sheet* option at the Page Setup dialog box to format various cards, such as holiday cards, business or personal invitations, seminar or open house announcements, personal notes, and even birth announcements. Figure 7.19 illustrates the result of dividing a standard-size sheet of paper into four cells using a table, which is then folded to accommodate text and graphics. Each of the four panels (cells) in Figure 7.19 has been identified with a panel number and marked with instructions for rotating text and graphics.

FIGURE

7.19 **Guide for Creating Cards in Portrait Orientation**

Another method produces two invitations or cards on a single sheet of landscaped paper divided into four sections. Using this method, you may type, format, and print the text on one side of a sheet of paper and then reinsert the paper into your printer and print text and/or graphics on the reverse side. The final step is to cut the paper in half and fold the top to meet the bottom as shown in Figure 7.20.

FIGURE
7.20 *Guide for Creating Cards in Landscape Orientation*

Back of card   Cut here   Back of card

———— Fold here ————   ———— Fold here ————
Cover of card   Cover of card

An Evening Out on the Town

An Evening Out on the Town

Top inside of card   Top inside of card

Cut here

———— Fold here ————   ———— Fold here ————

On behalf of **First Bank**,
we would like to cordially invite you to an
"Evening Out on the Town"
Thursday, May 26, 2005

Trattoria 8    *Chicago Theatre*
15 North Dearborn Street   175 North State Street
Chicago, Illinois   Chicago, Illinois

Cocktails: 5:00 p.m.–5:30 p.m.   **Theater: 7:30 p.m.**
Dinner: 5:30 p.m.–7:00 p.m.   ***Phantom of the Opera***

RSVP to Victoria Franz, (302) 555-3456 by April 30, 2005

Bottom inside of card

On behalf of **First Bank**,
we would like to cordially invite you to an
"Evening Out on the Town"
Thursday, May 26, 2005

Trattoria 8   *Chicago Theatre*
15 North Dearborn Street   175 North State Street
Chicago, Illinois   Chicago, Illinois

Cocktails: 5:00 p.m.–5:30 p.m.   **Theater: 7:30 p.m.**
Dinner: 5:30 p.m.–7:00 p.m.   ***Phantom of the Opera***

RSVP to Victoria Franz, (302) 555-3456 by April 30, 2005

Bottom inside of card

As discussed in Chapter 6, Word provides an option to print two half-sheet pages printed in landscape or portrait orientation on the same sheet. A page border may be added to both pages or to just one as shown in Figure 7.23. This option is conducive to creating cards in varying sizes and layouts. Also consider folding a half-sheet in half again and printing on cardstock.

Planning and Designing Cards

In planning and designing your cards, consider focus, balance, consistency, proportion, contrast, and directional flow. Because you are working in a small area, remember to allow plenty of white space around design elements. If you are using a graphic image for focus, be sure that the image relates to the subject of the card. Promote consistency through the use of color, possibly picking out one or two colors from the graphic image used in your card and including the company logo, if one is available, to promote consistency among company documents. Select one or two fonts that match the tone of the document.

Your choice of paper is also important—consider using a heavier weight paper, such as 60- or 65-lb. uncoated cover stock paper. Packaged cardstock such as HP Greeting Card (glossy or matte finish) or HP Premium Inkjet Heavyweight may be used to produce near store-quality cards. Also consider using marbleized paper or parchment paper for invitations and other types of cards.

The envelope size used with the HP Greeting Card paper package measures 5¾ by 8¾ inches. To print a custom-size envelope, type the desired dimensions at the Envelope Size dialog box as shown in Figure 7.21. Refer to your printer documentation to determine the correct way to load envelopes for your specific printer. If you have a long list of recipients, consider creating a master copy of your card and taking it to a commercial printer to have it reproduced and machine folded. For a mass mailing of an invitation or a holiday card, consider creating a data source consisting of names and addresses, and then merging this information onto envelopes or mailing labels.

FIGURE

7.21 *Creating a Custom-Size Envelope*

Using Card Templates

Any card you may create from scratch, with templates from Word, or from the Templates on Office Online hyperlink, may be customized to promote your company's identity or show continuity with other company documents. Figure 7.22

illustrates three card templates that were customized by adding the company's name; text was edited to fit the context of the card. When printing these cards for business purposes, you should use good-quality cardstock with envelopes that match. When printing the envelopes you may want to add a design element from the card to reinforce a complete and professional look. Card templates can be found by using *greeting cards* or *holidays* as the search string.

FIGURE 7.22 *Customized Card Templates from Microsoft Office Online*

Company name added
and text edited

DESKTOP DESIGNS, INC.

*Wishes you
a joyous
holiday
season!*

A

Wishing you
peace, love and
happiness for the
holidays and
always

Desktop
Designs
Inc.

B

Company name added
using WordArt

Company name added

Spring is in the air!
It's the perfect time to visit
the Butterfield
Garden Shop!

Bring this card in for
a 10% discount on
your next purchase.

Spring is in the air!
It's the perfect time to visit
the Butterfield
Garden Shop!

Bring this card in for
a 10% discount on
your next purchase.

Spring is in the air!
It's the perfect time to visit
the Butterfield
Garden Shop!

Bring this card in for
a 10% discount on
your next purchase.

Spring is in the air!
It's the perfect time to visit
the Butterfield
Garden Shop!

Bring this card in for
a 10% discount on
your next purchase.

C

Creating the Cover and Back of a Card

1. At a clear document screen, create the cover and back of the card shown in Figure 7.23 by completing the following steps:
   a. Click File and then Page Setup.
   b. Select the Margins tab at the Page Setup dialog box and select the option *2 pages per sheet* at the *Multiple pages* list box. Click OK.
   c. With the insertion point positioned in the first one-half sheet (page 1), insert a next page section break by clicking Insert, Break, and then *Next page.* Click OK.
   d. Create the border around the two text boxes on page 2 by completing the following steps:
      1) Click Format and then Borders and Shading.
      2) At the Borders and Shading dialog box, select the Page Border tab.
      3) Click the down-pointing arrow at the right of the *Art* list box and select the border shown in the graphic.
      4) Change the border *Color* option to Green and the border *Width* option to 12-point.
      5) Click the down-pointing arrow at the right of the *Apply to* list box and select *This section.* Click the Options button.

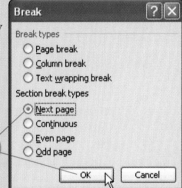

Step 1c

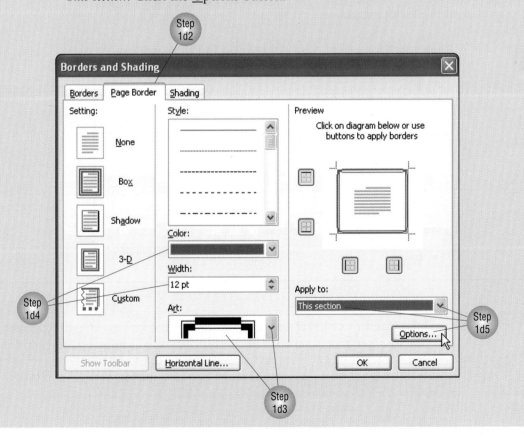

Step 1d2

Step 1d4

Step 1d3

Step 1d5

6) At the Border and Shading Options dialog box, click the down-pointing arrow at the right of the *Measure from* list box and select *Text*.

7) Change the *Top* and *Bottom* margins to *10 pt* and the *Left* and *Right* margins to *2 pt*.

8) Be sure to deselect all of the check boxes in the *Options* section (no check marks). Click OK twice.

e. With the insertion point now positioned in the second one-half sheet (page 2), draw one text box measuring approximately 0.75 inch in height by 2.75 inches in width. Double-click the text box border and verify the measurements at the Format Text Box dialog box at the Size tab.

f. Choose the Layout tab and click the Advanced button.

g. At the Picture Position tab, change the *Absolute position* to *0.65"* and the *to the right of* option to *Page* in the *Horizontal* section.

h. Change the *Absolute position* to *0.4"* and the *below* option to *Page* in the *Vertical* section. Click OK twice.

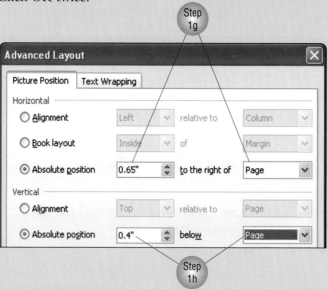

i. Position the insertion point in the text box, change the font to 36-point Bernard MT Condensed in Green with Shadow, and then type **Sharing, Inc.** Center the text within the text box and remove the border around the text box.

j. Create another text box measuring 0.75 inch by 3.75 inches. Verify the setting.

k. Change the *Absolute position* to *4.10"* and the *to the right of* option to *Page* in the *Horizontal* section.

l. Change the *Absolute position* to *4.35"* and the *below* option to *Page* in the *Vertical* section. Click OK twice.

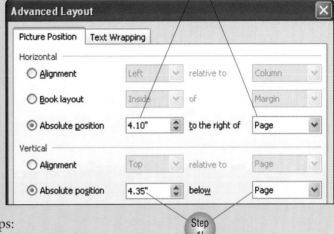

Step 1k

Step 1l

m. Position the insertion point in the text box, change the font to 36-point Bernard MT Condensed in Green, and then type Phonathon 2005. Center the text and remove the border around the text box.

n. Create the photo image in the center of the card by completing the following steps:
1) Insert each of the telephone images shown in Figure 7.23. At the Insert Clip Art task pane, type telephone in the *Search for* text box and then click Go. **(Hint: Most of the photos are located in the bottom half or third of the vertical scroll bar.)**
2) Scroll to find each of the images and then click once on each image to insert it into the document screen. Resize each image to 1.4 inches by 2.1 inches, select each photo, and then change the text wrap to In Front of Text.
3) Align the photos as shown in Figure 7.23. Hold down the Shift key and select each photo. **(Hint: Use the nudge command to move the photos and the Align or Distribute command to align the photos accurately.)** Click the Draw button on the Drawing toolbar and then click Group.
4) Select the combined photo and click *Center* in the *Horizontal alignment* section of the Layout tab at the Format Object dialog box.
5) Position the photo vertically similar to Figure 7.23.

o. Add the design logo to page 1 by completing the following steps:
1) Press Ctrl + Home to position the insertion point in the first page.
2) Click the Insert WordArt button on the Drawing toolbar, select the fourth WordArt style from the left in the first row, and then click OK.
3) Type DTP Designs in the Edit WordArt Text dialog box, change the font to 18-point Arial Black, and then click OK.
4) Select the logo, click Draw on the Drawing toolbar, point to Rotate or Flip, and then click Rotate Right twice (180 degrees).
5) Position the logo similar to Figure 7.23. **(Hint: If the WordArt object is difficult to move, change the wrap to In Front of Text.)**

2. Save the cover and back of the card and name the document **c07ex06, Cover**.
3. Print and then close **c07ex06, Cover**.
4. Open **Sharing** located in your Chapter07 folder.
5. Save this text as the inside document and name it **c07ex06, Inside**.
6. Place the printed cover from Step 3 into your printer. (Be careful to position it correctly so the inside document will print on the reverse side of the cover.)
7. Print and then close **c07ex06, Inside**.
8. Click File and then Page Setup. At the Page Setup dialog box, click the Margins tab, and then click the down-pointing arrow to the right of *Multiple pages* in the *Pages* section and select *Normal*. Click OK.

DTP Designs

Back

Inside

Sharing, Inc.

Phonathon 2005

Cover

It's Phonathon time...

...and we will be calling you! Sharing's annual Phonathon will be held November 9, 10, & 12 from 6 to 9 p.m. Special FAMILY NIGHTS will be held November 17 & 18 for the families of people served by Sharing, Inc.

Phonathon is Sharing's *second largest fundraiser* each year. This year our goal is $75,000! A donation of $25 or more entitles you to become a member of Sharing, Inc.

We serve more than 600 people with disabilities in the Minneapolis area. We appreciate your past support—we look forward to talking with you soon!

Thank you

Inside

Editing Merge Documents Using the Mail Merge Toolbar

The Mail Merge toolbar shown in Figure 7.24 provides buttons for editing a main document and/or a source document. Display this toolbar in the usual manner.

F I G U R E

7.24 *Mail Merge Toolbar*

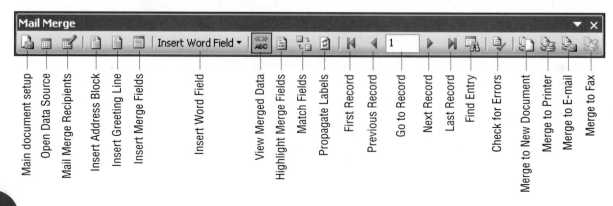

To edit a main document, open the document in the normal manner. You can insert additional fields by clicking the Insert Merge Fields button on the Mail Merge toolbar. At the Insert Merge Field dialog box, click the desired field, click the Insert button, and then click the Close button.

After editing the main document, you can merge it with the associated data source document. Click the Merge to New Document button on the Mail Merge toolbar and the main document is merged with the data source document. You can also merge the documents directly to the printer by clicking the Merge to Printer button. In addition, you have the options to merge to e-mail or to a fax.

Edit a data source document by clicking the Mail Merge Recipients button on the Mail Merge toolbar. At the Mail Merge Recipients dialog box, click the Edit button, and then make the desired edits to the data source records.

If you are creating labels, you can click the Propagate Labels button on the Mail Merge toolbar or click Update all labels in the *Replicate labels* section of the Mail Merge task pane to copy the layout of the first label to the other labels on the page.

Creating Name Badges

An appropriate name badge (tag) shows your name, your title, and the company or organization with which you are affiliated. The individual's name should be easy to read and the most dominant element on the name tag. Remembering a person's name is one of the biggest compliments you can pay to that person. However, if you are in a business where you meet a lot of people, remembering names can be difficult. Name badges can definitely reduce the embarrassment of forgetting someone's name.

An alternative to choosing labels for name badges is to purchase name-tag holders and insert a business card or name badge printed on heavier weight paper inside the holder. The holder is a clear plastic sleeve with a clip or pin on the reverse. Holders are usually available through mail-order paper companies or office supply companies.

exercise 7

Creating Name Badges Using Merge

1. At a clear document screen, create the name badges in Figure 7.25 by completing the following steps:
   a. Display the Drawing toolbar and the Tables and Borders toolbar.
   b. Click Tools, point to Letters and Mailings, and then click Mail Merge Wizard.
   c. At the Mail Merge task pane, click *Labels* in the *Select document type* section. Click the Next: Starting document hyperlink.
   d. At the second Mail Merge task pane, make sure the *Change document layout* option is selected in the *Select starting document* section.
   e. Click the Label options hyperlink in the *Change document layout* section of the task pane.

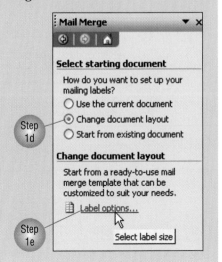

f.   At the Label Options dialog box, make sure *Avery standard* displays in the *Label products* list box. In the *Product number* list box, scroll and then click *5095 - Name Badge*. Click OK.

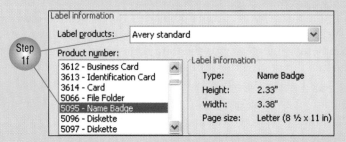

g.   Click the <u>Next: Select recipients</u> hyperlink located toward the bottom of the task pane.
h.   At the third Mail Merge task pane, make sure the *Use an existing list* option is selected in the *Select recipients* section.
i.   Click the <u>Browse</u> hyperlink located in the *Use an existing list* section.
j.   At the Select Data Source dialog box, complete the following steps:
    1) Change the *Look in* option to the drive where your Chapter07 folder is located.
    2) Double-click the Chapter07 folder.
    3) Double-click *Floral Data Source.doc*.
    4) When you confirm that the document has been inserted at the Mail Merge Recipients dialog box, click OK.

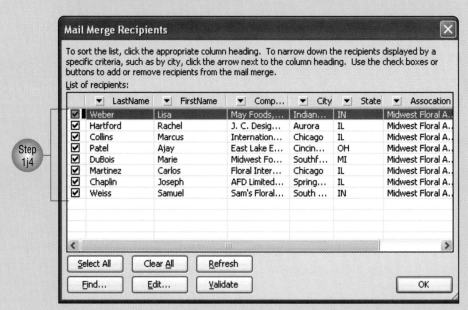

k.   Click the <u>Next: Arrange your labels</u> hyperlink located toward the bottom of the third Mail Merge task pane.
l.   At the fourth Mail Merge task pane, complete the following steps:
    1) Make sure the table gridlines display.
    2) Position the insertion point in the first cell and click the Align Top Left button on the Tables and Borders toolbar.
    3) Position the insertion point on the cell marker below the paragraph symbol in the upper left corner of the first label and change the alignment to Center. *(Hint: Turn on Show/Hide ¶.)*
    4) Turn on kerning at 14 points.

5) Change the font to 16-point Britannic Bold in small caps.
6) Click the <u>More items</u> hyperlink. At the Insert Merge Field dialog box, click *Association* from the *Fields* list box, click <u>I</u>nsert, and then click Close.
7) Press Ctrl + Tab, click <u>I</u>nsert, and then click <u>S</u>ymbol. Select the <u>S</u>ymbols tab and change the <u>F</u>ont to Wingdings. Select the tenth symbol from the left in the eighth row (Wingdings 153). Click <u>I</u>nsert and then Close.
8) Select the symbol and change the color to Teal.
9) Deselect the symbol, change the font to 11-point Britannic Bold in Black, and then press Enter four times.
10) Change the font to 20-point Britannic Bold.
11) Click the <u>More items</u> hyperlink and then click *FirstName*. Click <u>I</u>nsert and then click Close.
12) Press the spacebar once, click the <u>More items</u> hyperlink, and then click *LastName*. Click <u>I</u>nsert and then click Close.
13) Change the font to 11-point Britannic Bold. Press Enter, click the <u>More items</u> hyperlink, insert the *JobTitle* field, click <u>I</u>nsert, and then click Close.
14) Press Enter four times, change the alignment to Align Left, and then insert the *Company* field.
15) Create a right tab at approximately 3.25 inches on the Ruler.
16) Press Ctrl + Tab and insert the *City* and *State* fields separated by a comma and space.
17) Select by dragging from the paragraph symbol above *FirstName* to the paragraph symbol below *JobTitle*, click F<u>o</u>rmat, click <u>B</u>orders and Shading, and then select the <u>S</u>hading tab. Click the Teal color (the fifth color from the left in the fifth row of the color palette). Make sure *Paragraph* displays in the *App<u>l</u>y to* text box and click OK or press Enter.

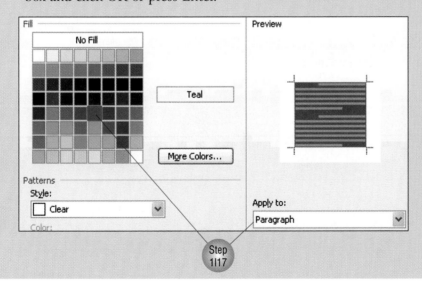

18) Select *FirstName*, *LastName*, and *JobTitle* and change the font color to White.

m. Scroll to the bottom of the fourth task pane and click the Update all labels button. (This adds the formatted field codes to the second and subsequent labels.)

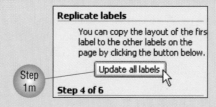

Replicate labels

You can copy the layout of the first label to the other labels on the page by clicking the button below.

[Update all labels]

Step 1m

Step 4 of 6

n. Click the <u>Next: Preview your labels</u> hyperlink at the bottom of the fourth Mail Merge task pane.

MIDWEST·FLORAL·ASSOCIATION

LISA·WEBER
DIRECTOR·OF·FLORAL·MARKETING

MAY·FOODS,·INC. → INDIANAPOLIS,·IN

MIDWEST·FLORAL·ASSOCIATION

RACHEL·HARTFORD
SALES·REPRESENTATIVE

J.·C.·DESIGNS,·INC. → AURORA,·IL

Step 1n

o. At the fifth Mail Merge task pane, view the merged labels, and then click the <u>Next: Complete the merge</u> hyperlink located toward the bottom of the task pane.

p. At the sixth Mail Merge task pane, save the merged labels document in the normal manner and name the document **c07ex07, Nametag**.

2. Print **c07ex07, Nametag**. (Check with your instructor about specific steps for printing labels. You may need to hand feed paper or a sheet of labels into the printer.)

3. Close **c07ex07, Nametag**.

FIGURE

7.25 *Exercise 7*

MIDWEST FLORAL ASSOCIATION

LISA WEBER
DIRECTOR OF FLORAL MARKETING

MAY FOODS, INC.   INDIANAPOLIS, IN

MIDWEST FLORAL ASSOCIATION

RACHEL HARTFORD
SALES REPRESENTATIVE

J. C. DESIGNS, INC.   AURORA, IL

MIDWEST FLORAL ASSOCIATION

MARCUS COLLINS
BUYER

INTERNATIONAL PACKAGING, INC.   CHICAGO, IL

MIDWEST FLORAL ASSOCIATION

AJAY PATEL
REGIONAL MANAGER

EAST LAKE EXPORT   CINCINNATI, OH

MIDWEST FLORAL ASSOCIATION

MARIE DuBOIS
BUYER

MIDWEST FOODS, INC.   SOUTHFIELD, MI

MIDWEST FLORAL ASSOCIATION

CARLOS MARTINEZ
MIDWEST SALES MANAGER

FLORAL INTERNATIONAL   CHICAGO, IL

MIDWEST FLORAL ASSOCIATION

JOSEPH CHAPLIN
RETAIL SALES MANAGER

AFD LIMITED, INC.   SPRINGFIELD, IL

MIDWEST FLORAL ASSOCIATION

SAMUEL WEISS
VICE-PRESIDENT

SAM'S FLORAL SUPPLIES   SOUTH BEND, IN

Using Shipping Labels to Promote Corporate Identity

The Microsoft Office Online Templates Web site includes several shipping labels formatted attractively with business names, logos, and color. Two examples of these labels are shown in Figure 7.26. You can easily adapt these templates to fit your needs by replacing the placeholder text, adding a logo, and changing the colors to reinforce consistency with your other documents. The shipping labels can be accessed by clicking the <u>Labels</u> hyperlink in the *Stationery and Labels* category, or by using *Shipping labels* as the search string.

F I G U R E

7.26 *Shipping Label Templates*

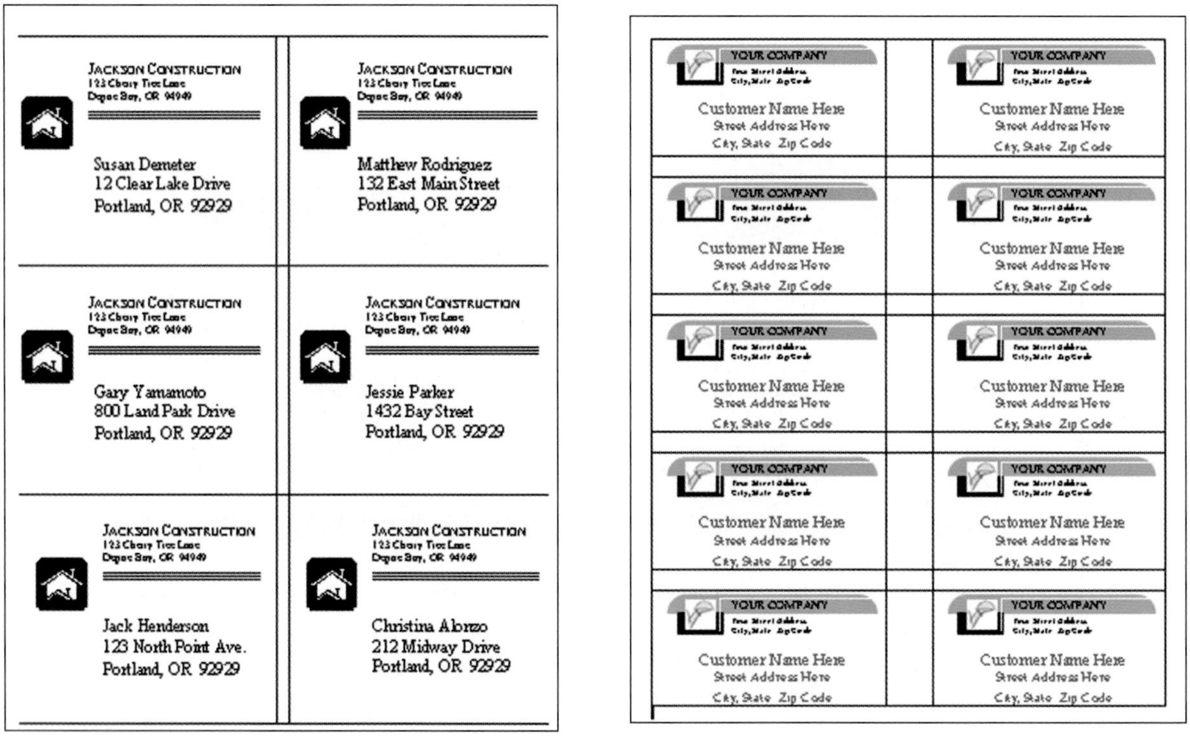

JACKSON CONSTRUCTION 123 Cherry Tree Lane Depoe Bay, OR 94949 Susan Demeter 12 Clear Lake Drive Portland, OR 92929	JACKSON CONSTRUCTION 123 Cherry Tree Lane Depoe Bay, OR 94949 Matthew Rodriguez 132 East Main Street Portland, OR 92929
JACKSON CONSTRUCTION 123 Cherry Tree Lane Depoe Bay, OR 94949 Gary Yamamoto 800 Land Park Drive Portland, OR 92929	JACKSON CONSTRUCTION 123 Cherry Tree Lane Depoe Bay, OR 94949 Jessie Parker 1432 Bay Street Portland, OR 92929
JACKSON CONSTRUCTION 123 Cherry Tree Lane Depoe Bay, OR 94949 Jack Henderson 123 North Point Ave. Portland, OR 92929	JACKSON CONSTRUCTION 123 Cherry Tree Lane Depoe Bay, OR 94949 Christina Alonzo 212 Midway Drive Portland, OR 92929

CHAPTER summary

➤ The Labels feature formats your document so that you can print on designated label sheets.

➤ Field codes are used to format date, time, and page numbers automatically.

➤ When a form template is created and then protected, the text in the template can still be changed. To make changes, you must unprotect the document.

➤ To unprotect a template document, click the Protect Form button on the Forms toolbar to deactivate it.

➤ Mail merge is the process of combining variable information with standard text to create personalized documents.

➤ Word includes a Mail Merge Wizard that you can use to create different documents that include letters, e-mail messages, envelopes, labels, directories, and faxes, all with personalized information.

➤ The Mail Merge Wizard guides you through six steps for merging documents and presents a Mail Merge task pane for each step.

➤ The data source and the main document may be merged to a new document or to the printer.

➤ A data source document and a main document are needed to perform a merge. A data source document contains the variable information. The main document contains the standard text along with identifiers showing where variable information is to be inserted.

➤ A record contains all of the information for one unit (person, family, customer, or client).

➤ You can create your own custom field at the Customize Address List dialog box.

➤ Merge fields are special codes in the main document that direct Word to collect information from the data source and use it in the main document to create personalized documents.

➤ You can edit a main document in the normal manner. Edit a data source document using the Mail Merge Wizard or with buttons on the Mail Merge toolbar.

➤ When editing a main document, insert fields in the document by clicking the Insert Merge Fields button on the Mail Merge toolbar.

➤ You can also use the Mail Merge toolbar to edit a data source document.

➤ The second Mail Merge task pane includes an option to use the current document, to change the document layout, or to start from an existing document.

➤ The third Mail Merge task pane includes an option to select recipients for the merge from an existing list, from an Outlook contact list, or from a new list that you create.

➤ The Address block hyperlink inserts a formatted address field into your main document.

➤ The replicate label feature in the Mail Merge task pane copies the layout of the first label to the other labels on the page. You must click the Update all labels button in the *Replicate labels* section to activate this command.

➤ Any formatting codes you want applied to the merged document should be inserted in the main document.

➤ The More items hyperlink in the *Arrange your labels* section of the fourth step in a merge includes other merge fields.

➤ Use the Rotate or Flip option at the Draw menu on the Drawing toolbar to rotate pictures or objects.

➤ The *2 pages per sheet* option reduces each page to the size of a half-page.

COMMANDS review

Command	Mouse/Keyboard
Insert Table dialog box	Table, Insert, Table
Envelopes and Labels dialog box	Tools, Letters and Mailings, Envelopes and Labels
Field dialog box	Insert, Field
View field codes	Tools, Options, View tab, Field codes; or press Alt + F9

Section break	Insert, Break
Mail Merge Wizard	Tools, Letters and Mailings, Mail Merge
2 pages per sheet	File, Page Setup, *Multiple pages, 2 pages per sheet*

REVIEWING key points

True/False: On a blank sheet of paper, write *True* if the statement is true and *False* if the statement is false.

1. A main document is a document that contains variable information about customers, clients, products, and so forth.
2. A data source document created using the Mail Merge Wizard is created and saved as an Access database file.
3. *FirstName*, *JobTitle*, and *Address1* are examples of field names.
4. Field codes are used to format date, time, and page numbers automatically.
5. The Mail Merge Wizard guides you though five steps to prepare merge documents.
6. When using Word's *2 pages per sheet* option, a border added to one page automatically adds a border to all of the pages in the document.
7. Edit a data source by clicking the Open Data Source button on the Mail Merge toolbar.
8. The Microsoft Office Online Templates Web site includes templates that can be edited in Excel, Word, PowerPoint, or Access.
9. The *2 pages per sheet* option is accessed from the Format menu.
10. Field codes cannot be added to predesigned forms created from templates.

Completion: On a blank sheet of paper, indicate the correct term, symbol, or command for each item.

1. To position a watermark below the text layer, click the Text Wrapping button on the Picture toolbar, and then select this option.
2. The data source and the main document can be merged to a new document or to this.
3. When using the Mail Merge task pane, click this button to replicate or copy the layout of the first label to the other labels.
4. To unprotect a template document, click what button on the Forms toolbar to deactivate it?
5. You can merge the source document to the main document by clicking the Merge to New Document button on which toolbar?
6. To rotate text inside a table, click this button on the Tables and Borders toolbar.
7. To rotate a picture at any degree you desire, click this option at the Rotate or Flip menu.
8. This button on the Forms toolbar controls shading in form fields.
9. Press this to insert a tab code within a table.
10. This contains all of the information for one unit (person, family, customer, or client).

APPLYING your skills

Assessment 1

Gift certificates are excellent promotional documents that can be used for generating further purchases or used as rainchecks, mini-awards, "runner-up" prizes, or warranties. As an employee at Butterfield Gardens, create a gift certificate that may be purchased by customers and used for in-store shopping.

1. At a clear document screen, create a gift certificate similar to Figure 7.27 by completing the following steps. (Type text from Figure 7.27.)
   a. Change all of the margins to 0.65 inch.
   b. Create a table with two columns and one row.
   c. Turn on the table *Show Gridlines* feature.
   d. With the insertion point positioned in the first cell, click Table, Table Properties, and then make the following changes at the Table Properties dialog box:
      1) At the Table tab, select Center Alignment. Click Options, and then change the default cell margins to 0.1 inch.
      2) At the Row tab, type 2.65 inches at the *Specify height* text box and select *Exactly* at the *Row height is* list box.
      3) At the Column tab, type 4.75 inches for the *Preferred width* option for Column 1 and type 2.25 inches for the *Preferred width* option for Column 2.
      4) At the Cell tab, select *Top* in the *Vertical alignment* section.
   e. Add a border around the outside of the table if necessary.
   f. With the insertion point located in the first cell, type **Gift Certificate**. Press Enter twice.
   g. Select *Gift Certificate* and change the font as specified in Figure 7.27.
   h. Set left tabs at 0.5 inch, 1.75 inches, and 4.3 inches.
   i. Type the text in the first cell as shown in Figure 7.27. Press the spacebar once after typing a text label; click the Underline button on the Formatting toolbar and then press Ctrl + Tab to move to the next tab and to create the underline. Turn off the underline feature and then press Enter twice.
   j. Type **Butterfield Gardens** as specified in Figure 7.27. Type the address text as shown in Figure 7.27.
2. Insert a tree image similar to the one shown in Figure 7.27. Type trees or j0280657.wmf in the *Search for* text box at the Insert Clip Art task pane. Size and position the tree image similar to Figure 7.27.
3. Create two more certificates by copying and pasting the table. *(Hint: Insert one hard return between each certificate.)*
4. Save the document and name it **c07sa01, Certificate**.
5. Print and then close **c07sa01, Certificate**.

36-point French Script MT, Blue—
Custom color: <u>R</u>ed 66, <u>G</u>reen 99,
<u>B</u>lue 186

14-point Lucida Calligraphy, Bold,
Shadow, Blue—
Custom color: <u>R</u>ed 66, <u>G</u>reen 99,
<u>B</u>lue 186

12-point Abadi MT Condensed

Gift Certificate

Date _____

This certificate entitles _____

to _____ Dollars $ _____

Presented by _____

Authorized signature _____

Butterfield Gardens
29 W 036 Butterfield Road
Warrenville, IL 60555
(630) 555-1062
http://emcp.net/butterfield

Assessment 2

You are working at Tuscany Realty and have been asked to prepare an announcement for an open house advertising the sale of a custom-built home on a golf course. The announcement is to be prepared as a postcard and mailed to prospective clients and all homeowners in this neighborhood. This promotional document makes the realtor's name visible to any homeowners in the neighborhood who may be thinking of selling their home or buying a new one. The card will be reproduced at a printing company. Create two postcards similar to, but not exactly the same as, the ones shown in Figure 7.28. Choose an image and use complementary colors and fonts for your postcards. Follow the guidelines given below.

1. Create the formatting and text for the postcard by completing the following steps:
   a. Choose the *Avery 5389 - Post Card* definition at the Label Options dialog box.
   b. Click the New <u>D</u>ocument button at the Envelopes and Labels dialog box.
   c. Create the dots in the left top corner and right bottom corner of the postcard by completing the following steps:
      1) Change the alignment in the cell to Align Top Left.
      2) Insert the Wingdings dot symbol. The small dots are also in the Wingdings character set (first symbol from the right in the eighth row ●). (You may substitute a symbol or design of your choosing.)
      3) Use F4, the Repeat key, to save time in duplicating the dots.
   d. The vertical line in the postcard was drawn using the Line button on the Drawing toolbar (be sure to hold down the Shift key as you draw the line).
   e. Create text boxes inside the label (table format) to hold the formatted text.
   f. Type Tuscany Realty in WordArt. Use the Deflate (Bottom) shape (the fourth shape from the left in the fourth row of the shape palette). Select the Wide Latin font and change the font color to match a color in the image or pick a complementary color.
   g. Insert an image of your choosing. **(Hint: *Type* houses *in the* Search for *text box at the* Insert Clip Art *task pane.)***

h. Position and size the image similar to Figure 7.28.
i. Use an appropriate font for the office address, *Open House,* and the message text.
j. Copy the first postcard text to the second postcard.

2. Save the document as **c07sa02, House**.
3. Print and then close **c07sa02, House**.

Optional: Create a data source consisting of four of your friends, neighbors, coworkers, or relatives. Create a main document using your return address, the field codes for the data source, and any graphic or symbol that attracts attention and relates to the subject matter in Assessment 2. Merge the data source to the main document and print the merged document to the reverse side of the postcards created in Assessment 2.

F I G U R E

7.28 *Assessment 2 Sample Solution*

Assessment 3

As an employee at First Bank, one of your responsibilities is to create an invitation for an "Evening Out on the Town" to be sent to several important bank clients. Use Word's table or the *2 pages per sheet* option and create the invitation in either landscape or portrait orientation to produce two on one sheet of paper. If you can find an appropriate template, you may use a template and customize it to include the following specifications:

1. Add graphics, watermarks, lines, borders, symbols, or other enhancements to your document. Use the text below:

    On behalf of First Bank, we cordially invite you to an
    "Evening Out on the Town" Thursday, May 23, 2005.
    Dinner - 5:30 p.m.–7:00 p.m.
    Trattoria 8
    15 North Dearborn Street
    Chicago, Illinois
    Theater - 7:30 p.m.

Phantom of the Opera
Chicago Theatre
175 North State Street
Chicago, Illinois
Please RSVP to Victoria Franz, (302) 555-3456 by May 1, 2005

2. Include the following specifications:

- Consider your audience in creating an appropriate design.
- Prepare a thumbnail sketch.
- Use an appropriate font and vary the type size and typestyle.
- Change the character spacing in at least one occurrence.
- Use horizontal and vertical lines, or an appropriate graphic image, graphic border, or symbols to add interest and impact.
- Use special characters where needed—en or em dashes, bullets, etc.
- Change the leading (spacing between the lines) if necessary.

3. Save the document and name it **c07sa03, Bank**.
4. Print and then close **c07sa03, Bank**.
5. Evaluate your invitation with the document analysis guide located in your Chapter07 folder.

Assessment 4

In this exercise, you will insert an Excel worksheet into a Word form document. Because of Excel's automatic calculating features, you will see that integrating Excel into the Word form makes it easier to make the computations.

INTEGRATED

1. You will complete two of the River Rats Apparel Forms located in the Chapter07 folder, **c07sa04, River Rats Apparel Order Form** in Word. Open **c07sa04, River Rats Apparel Order Form** in Word.
2. Insert the Microsoft Excel sheet with calculations a double space below the e-mail address by completing the following steps:
   a. Click Insert and then Object. At the Create from File tab, click Browse. Locate the Chapter07 folder and double-click *c07sa04, Apparel Order Form.xls*. Click OK. This inserts the Excel worksheet as an object, allowing you to utilize the Excel features while in Word.
   b. Open **c07sa04, Input Data**. You will add this information to **c07sa04, River Rats Apparel Order Form** in Word.
3. Double-click inside the Excel object and you will have Excel's editing features available. Enter the data from **c07sa04, Input Data**.
4. Save the document and name it **c07sa04, Completed Apparel Form**.
5. Print and then close **c07sa04, Completed Apparel Form**.
6. Follow the above procedures to complete the second apparel form.
7. Save the document and name it **c07sa04, Completed Apparel Form 2**.
8. Print and then close **c07sa04, Completed Apparel Form 2**.

River Rats Apparel Order Form

We will place our River Rats apparel order immediately following registration this year to ensure that the swimmers have their items for the summer swim season. Please note: All swimmers registered for summer swim will receive a complimentary team T-shirt.

Name: Barbara Regel

Address: 123 S. Main Street

City: Wheaton   ST: IL   ZIP: 60147

Phone: 555-1447

Child's Name:
(for Sports Bag) Susie

Order forms must be received by May 15 with registration. Please make checks payable to River Rats. If you have any questions, please call Kerry Swimmer at 555-8445 or e-mail at kswimmer@emcp.net.

Item	Size				Quantity	Price	Total
	Small	Medium	Large	X-Large			
Team T-Shirt	1				1	$8	$8
Zip Hoodie Sweatshirt	1	1			2	$24	$48
Micro-Poly Full Zip Jacket					0	$37	$0
Micro-Poly Fully Lined Pants w/zipper on lower leg					0	$30	$0
Cotton Cheer Short	1	1			2	$10	$20
Plaid Flannel PJ Pant					0	$20	$0
Heavy Duty Sports Bag (w/child's name)					0	$32	$0
Total Number of Items Ordered					5		
Total Price							$76

Assessment 5

In this exercise, you will create a scholarship application form using a Word table. You will insert information from an Excel worksheet into the Word table. Because of Excel's automatic calculating features, you will see that integrating Excel into the Word form makes it easier to make the computations.

INTEGRATED

1. Create the scholarship application form shown in Figure 7.30 document A by inserting a table and using the cells as placeholders for the information. Save the document as **c07sa05, Scholarship Application Form.doc**.
2. Start Excel and open **c07sa05, Community Service Hours.xls** from the student data disk Chapter07 folder. Alphabetize the categories by clicking and dragging the "Government" through "Day camp" cells and then clicking the Sort Ascending button on the Standard toolbar. Be sure you have not selected "Other" because this should be listed as the last category. If the Sort Warning dialog box appears, click the Continue with the current selection button and then click Sort.

3. Add borders to the bottom of each fill-in category by positioning your insertion point in cell B2 and then clicking the Borders down-pointing arrow on the Formatting toolbar (to locate the bottom border). Click the Bottom Border button and then click in each cell to add the bottom border. Add the Bottom Double Border to the "Total" cell.

4. Add the AutoSum formula to the right of the "Total" cell by positioning the insertion point in the cell and then clicking the AutoSum button from the Standard toolbar. To add the cell references to the formula, click and drag cells B2 through B8. Release the left mouse button and then click again the AutoSum button.

5. Copy cells A1 through B9 to the Clipboard.

6. Click **c07sa05, Scholarship Application Form.doc** in the Taskbar to open Word. Position the insertion point in the left cell that is a double space below the *Eligibility requirements* paragraph and click Edit, Paste Special, Microsoft Office Excel Worksheet Object, and then click OK.

7. This inserts the Excel worksheet as an object, allowing you to utilize the Excel features while in Word. Double-click in the object and add the numbers shown in Figure 7.30 document B. The "Total" column should automatically recalculate. Click outside the object and you will return to Word's editing functions. Enter the remaining text and symbols as shown in Figure 7.30.

8. Save the document and name it **c07sa05, Scholarship Application Form Completed.doc**.

9. Print and then close **c07sa05, Scholarship Application Form Completed.doc**.

10. Close **c07sa05, Community Service Hours.xls** and then exit Excel.

FIGURE

7.30 *Assessment 5 Sample Solution*

A

B

Assessment 6

1. Create a promotional document of your own design or from an example you have saved or found in the mail, at a store, or from any other source. Use Word's table feature, the *2 pages per sheet* option, or any appropriate template you may find on the Internet. If you are using a sample document, first evaluate the document for good layout and design, a clear and concise message, and proper use of other desktop publishing concepts as outlined in the document analysis guide. Some possible promotional documents include the following examples:

   - Invitation to a new store opening
   - Introduction of a new course at your local community college
   - Invitation to a class reunion
   - Bookmark
   - Name badge including a company or organization name or logo
   - Business greeting card
   - Postcard as a follow-up
   - Postcard used to promote a new business (coffee shop, party planner, attorney's office, computer services)
   - Membership card
   - Ticket with a company or organization name or logo
   - Gift certificate
   - Thank-you card
   - Employee retirement announcement
   - Company party invitation
   - Postcard advertising a sample sale
   - Raffle tickets for a charity
   - Tickets for a play at your community theatre
   - Postcard announcing the opening of a golf course
   - Postcard advertising services at a travel agency

2. Create a copy of the document with any necessary improvements. Try to find unusual, creative documents that were used to promote a business, organization, item, or event.

3. If the sample document was created on odd-size paper, check to see if your printer can accommodate the paper size. You may need to recreate the document on standard-size paper and trim it to size.

4. Save the completed document and name it **c07sa06, Promotional**.

5. Print and then close **c07sa06, Promotional**—attach the original document if one was used.

CHAPTER 8

Creating Web Pages

PERFORMANCE OBJECTIVES

Upon successful completion of Chapter 8, you will be able to create a Web home page with hyperlinks using Word 2003 and apply basic desktop publishing concepts to the layout and design of the Web page.

CHAPTER08

DESKTOP PUBLISHING TERMS

Bookmark	Intranet	World Wide Web
Hypertext Transfer	Marquee	(WWW)
Protocol (HTTP)	Round-trip	WYSIWYG
Hyperlink	Theme	
Internet	Uniform Resource	
Internet Service	Locator (URL)	
Provider (ISP)	Web page	

WORD FEATURES USED

Background color	Heading styles	Sound clips
Blank Web Page	Horizontal lines	Tables
template	Hyperlinks	Templates
Bookmarks	Microsoft Design	Themes
Bullets	Gallery Live	Web Page Preview
Clip art	Microsoft Word Web	Web toolbar
Document Map	site	Web Tools toolbar
Font colors	Objects	WordArt
Forms	Pictures	
Graphics	Scrolling text	

In this chapter, Word is used to create Web pages. Web pages provide promotional information about a company's or organization's products, resources, or services. Increasingly, businesses, organizations, and individuals are accessing the Internet to conduct research, publish product or catalog information, communicate, and market products globally. In addition, companies are using intranets to efficiently share information among employees.

Users access the Internet for several purposes: to communicate using e-mail; to subscribe to news groups; to transfer files; to socialize with other users; and to access virtually any kind of information imaginable.

Web page
A computer file created in HTML and used on the Web.

What is a *Web page*? It is a computer file containing information in the form of text or graphics along with commands in a language called Hypertext Markup Language (HTML). When one of these pages is placed on a server, which is a computer hooked up to the Internet, it receives an address that other users will type to call up the page.

Understanding Internet and Intranet Terminology

Internet
Worldwide network of computers connected together to share information.

World Wide Web (WWW)
A set of standards and protocols used to access information on the Internet.

The *Internet* is a worldwide network of commercial, educational, governmental, and personal computers connected together for the purpose of sharing information. The *World Wide Web (WWW)* is the most commonly used application on the Internet and is a set of standards and protocols used to access information available on the Internet. An *intranet* is an "internal Internet" within an organization that uses the same Web technology and tools as the Internet and is used to share information. Intranets are many times only accessible to the employees within an organization. An intranet may provide employees with online access to reference material, job postings, phone and address lists, company policies and procedures, enrollment in and updates on benefit plans, company newsletters, and other human resource information.

Intranet
An "internal Internet" within an organization that uses Internet technology and tools.

Throughout this chapter, you will simulate creating Web pages for both the Internet and an organization's intranet. These Web pages will be saved as HTML files to a floppy disk or hard drive. You will view each Web page on the Internet Explorer screen.

Using the Web Toolbar

Uniform Resource Locator (URL)
The address used to identify locations on the Internet.

The *Uniform Resource Locator*, referred to as *URL*, is the method used to identify locations on the Internet. It is the address that you type to call up a Web page or site. A typical URL is http://www.microsoft.com. The first part of the URL, *http://*, identifies the protocol. The letters *http* stand for *Hypertext Transfer Protocol*, which is one of the protocols or languages used to transfer data within the World Wide Web. The colon and slashes separate the protocol from the server name. The server name is the second component of the URL. For example, in *http://www.microsoft.com*, the server name is identified as *www.microsoft*. The last part of the URL specifies the domain to which the server belongs—for example, .com refers to "commercial," .edu refers to "educational," .gov stands for "government," and .mil refers to "military."

Hypertext Transfer Protocol (HTTP)
One of the languages used to transfer data within the WWW.

If you know the URL for a specific Web site and would like to visit that site, type the URL in the *Address* text box of the Web toolbar. To display the Web toolbar as shown in Figure 8.1, click View, point to Toolbars, and then click Web. You can also display the Web toolbar by positioning the mouse pointer on a toolbar, clicking the right mouse button, and then clicking Web at the pop-up list.

FIGURE

8.1 Web Toolbar

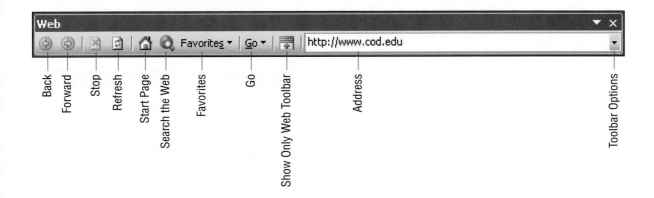

Figure 8.1 Web Toolbar

Before typing a URL in the *Address* text box on the Web toolbar, make sure you are connected to the Internet. Type the URL exactly as written, including any colons (:) or slashes (/).

When you are connected to a URL (Web site address), the home page for the specific URL (Web site) displays. (Web pages are constantly changing. If a particular Web page asked for in an exercise is no longer available, you will need to substitute a different one.) The home page is the starting point for viewing any Web site. At the home page you can "branch off" to other pages within the Web site or jump to other Web sites. You do this with hyperlinks that are embedded in the Web pages. A *hyperlink* is colored and underlined text or a graphic that you click to go to a file, a location in a file, an HTML page on the World Wide Web, or an HTML page on an intranet. Move the mouse pointer on a hyperlink and the mouse pointer becomes a hand. This is one method for determining if something is a hyperlink. Most pages contain a variety of hyperlinks. Using these links, you can zero in on the exact information for which you are searching.

Using the Internet Explorer toolbar, you can jump forward or backward among the documents you have opened and you can add interesting documents you find on the Web to the Favorites folder to return to them later more easily. To do this, display the site, and then click the Favorites button on the toolbar. This causes a side bar to display. To add a favorite site, click the Add button located at the top of the Favorites side bar. Make sure the information in the *Name* text box is correct, and then click OK.

Hyperlink
Text or graphic in a Web page that will connect you to other pages or Web sites in different locations.

FIGURE

8.2   *Understanding Web Pages*

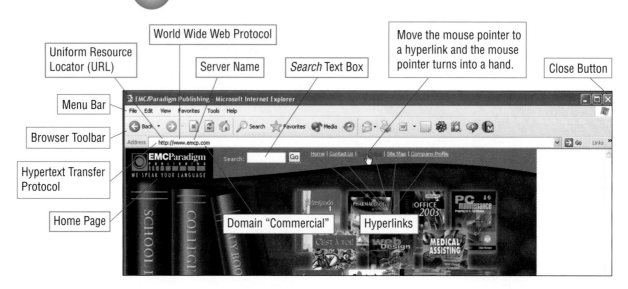

Labels in figure:
Uniform Resource Locator (URL) · World Wide Web Protocol · Server Name · *Search* Text Box · Move the mouse pointer to a hyperlink and the mouse pointer turns into a hand. · Close Button · Menu Bar · Browser Toolbar · Hypertext Transfer Protocol · Home Page · Domain "Commercial" · Hyperlinks

Planning and Designing a Web Page

You can build a Web site yourself, or hire a freelancer or Web access provider. Some advertising consultants develop Web sites for a fee. However, with the help of Word's Blank Web Page template, you can easily create your own Web pages.

Where do you start? Planning is a basic desktop publishing concept that applies to Web pages as well as any other documents created in Word. During the planning stage of your Web page, consider the following Web page design tips:

- Determine the goal of your Web site.
- Identify and focus on your intended audience.
- Review and critique other sites.
- Check your links on a regular basis (sites change often).
- Do not make your audience scroll sideways.
- Do not identify your site as a home page—obviously, it is.
- Do not overuse italics or bold.
- Determine elements to be emphasized and used. Keep the design simple. Use white space effectively.
- Be consistent with hyperlinks so that visitors know where they are, where they came from, and where they can go.
- Create a storyboard (a progression of Web pages or links used to reinforce a theme or goal).
- Do not use annoying animated graphics that do not stop.
- Always check your Web page in a browser for spacing, proportion, readability, line length, etc.
- Make sure your page fits within a standard browser window (640 × 460 pixels).

DTP POINTERS
Look at other Web pages for layout and design ideas.

DTP POINTERS
Keep the background simple.

DTP POINTERS
Use consistency in design elements.

- Do not use large graphics that take forever to download.

- Use clean and clear navigation so it is easy to maneuver within a Web site.

- Maintain a consistent color scheme (consider using predesigned themes in Word).

- Keep the background simple, making sure the text can be seen clearly. Make sure there is enough contrast between the text and background.

- Avoid small text and all caps.

- For bulleted text, avoid using a single bullet. Do not use more than two levels of bullets.

- Use consistent wording in bulleted text.

- Use graphics that relate to the content. Graphics should not distract from the message.

- Keep graphs simple. The most effective graphs are pie charts with three or four slices and column charts with three or four columns.

- Remember that a Web page is the first impression you are giving the world about your product, information, or yourself. A poor Web page can be worse for your business than having none at all.

- Maintain your Web site and keep it current.

Consider using a thumbnail sketch and a storyboard to organize your page layout before actually creating it. Include space for text, photographs, graphics, headlines, divider lines, and so on. Instead of including everything on one huge Web front page, use hyperlinks to other pages.

Remember that the Web site's front door is its home page. This page should contain the elements to achieve the goals an organization (or individual) has set for the Web site. Understand what your goals are before you design the site. Are you creating a Web site on an intranet to share information among employees or a Web page on the Internet to market a product or service? Know your budget before starting. There are things you can do on any budget, but some things (such as videos and animation) may cost more than you can afford.

Some Web designers suggest that you create a nameplate or banner to display a logo and company name in an interesting way. Include your company logo to reinforce your company's identity. The site should also include alternative ways to reach the company such as an address, telephone number, e-mail address, and fax number.

Graphics are probably the simplest way to make your Web page look better. Be sure to choose a graphic that is appropriate to the subject of the page. Animation, video, and scrolling words are eye-catching devices to entice your audience to return to your Web site. They can take a while to load. You may want to avoid using a graphic that takes longer than 15 to 20 seconds to load. Use small graphics that are less than 30 K in size. When in doubt, keep the basic design simple. The main point in designing a Web page is to get the message across! In addition, remember that everything you want to use on your home page must be transferred into computer files. If you want to use a photograph, you must scan the photo to convert it to a graphic file. Format main headings with HTML heading styles so a reader can more quickly browse through a document when using the document map in Word's Outline view.

In Exercise 1, you will take a look at a few Web home pages using URLs. As you view each of the Web sites listed in the exercise, pay attention to the layout

DTP POINTERS
Use a company logo to reinforce company recognition.

DTP POINTERS
Too many graphics or large graphics can slow down your Web page.

and design of each home page. For instance, when viewing http://www.umich.edu, notice the banner. It repeats the blue and maize color scheme used by the school, the watermark of the school emblem reinforces tradition, the circle photo shapes provide variety in design, and the generous amount of white space organizes the text and makes it easy to read. In addition, notice how many of these design elements remain consistent as you view the Academic Units Web site.

(Before completing computer exercises, delete the Chapter07 folder on your disk. Next, copy the Chapter08 folder from the CD that accompanies this textbook to your disk and then make Chapter08 the active folder.)

exercise 1

Viewing Web Site Home Pages for Design and Layout Ideas

1. Make sure you are connected to the Internet.
2. Explore several locations on the World Wide Web from within Word by completing the following steps:
   a. Display the Web toolbar.
   b. Click in the *Address* text box located on the Web toolbar.
   c. Type http://www.umich.edu and then press Enter.
   d. The home page will display similar to the one shown in Figure 8.3. Home pages are frequently updated, so the University of Michigan home page you are viewing may vary slightly from what you see in Figure 8.3. Scroll down the home page, studying the layout.
   e. After viewing the University of Michigan's site, view the Web site for the Chicago Convention and Tourism Bureau. To do this, click the current address located in the *Address* text box, type http://www.chicago.il.org, and then press Enter. Scroll down the home page, studying the layout and design elements.
   f. View the Web site for Eastman Kodak. Type http://kodak.com and then press Enter. (Notice the hyperlinks to send multimedia images, KODAK Picture CD Images and Slideshows, and digital cameras and technology.)
   g. Complete a search for Kodak Picture CD, display the Kodak Picture CD page, and then print the page by clicking the Print button on the Internet Explorer toolbar. (If this page is no longer available, print another page of interest to you.)
3. After printing the Kodak Picture CD page, click File and then Close.

Consistent fonts

Consistent use of color and formatting

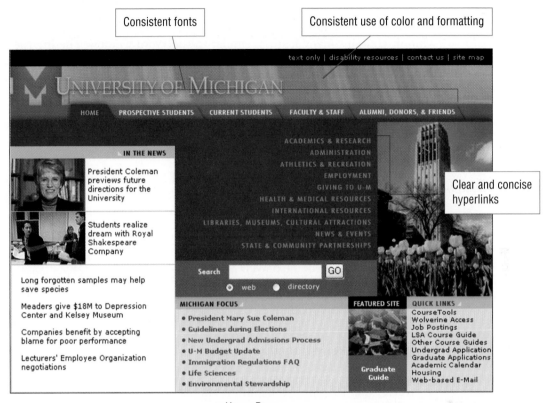

Clear and concise hyperlinks

Home Page

All hyperlinks

Plenty of white space

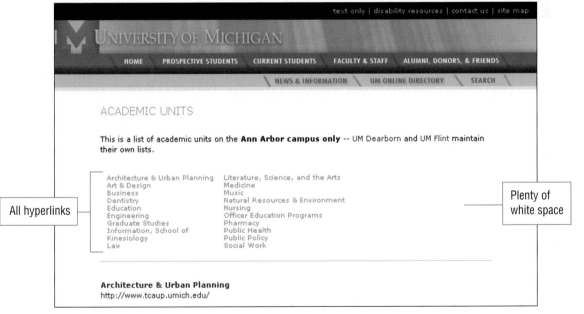

Academic Units Link

Using Internet Explorer

In Exercise 1, you visited the first Web site by typing the URL in the *Address* text box in the Web toolbar. This opened the Internet Explorer program window and also displayed the home page for the Web site. The Internet Explorer program window contains many features similar to the Word window. The Internet Explorer toolbar contains buttons for accessing a variety of commands, which are shown and described in Figure 8.4.

FIGURE

8.4 *Internet Explorer Toolbar Buttons*

Click this button	To do this
 Back	Display previous Web page
 (forward)	Display next Web page
 (stop)	Stop loading a page
 (refresh)	Refresh (update) contents of current page
 (home)	Display the default home page
 Search	Display the Search side bar
 Favorites	Display the Favorites side bar
 Media	Display the WindowsMedia.com site side bar
 (history)	Display the History side bar containing a list of sites visited
 (mail)	Display mail and news options
 (print)	Print the current Web page
 (word)	Display the current Web page in a Word document screen for editing

If you click on a hyperlink in a Web page, you can then click the Back button on the Internet Explorer toolbar to display a previous page or location. If you clicked the Back button and then want to go back to the hyperlink, click the Forward button. By clicking the Back button, you can back your way out of any hyperlinks and return to the default Web home page.

As you visit different Web sites, Internet Explorer keeps track of the sites. Click the History button on the Internet Explorer toolbar. The History side bar displays.

Creating a Web Home Page

Now that you have spent some time viewing several Web site home pages, you may have a few ideas on how to design an appealing home page. The pages were designed using a language called Hypertext Markup Language (HTML). This is a language that Web browsers use to read hypertext documents. In the past, a person needed knowledge of HTML to design a Web page. Now, a Web page can be created in Word with the Web Page template, or a Word document can be converted to HTML. (To convert an existing Word document to a Web page, click File and then Save as Web Page.) Microsoft Office Word, Excel, and PowerPoint include the Save as Web Page option. Word also allows you to save a document in Web Page, Filtered format. This option generates "cleaner" HTML codes than in the previous versions. However, you may not be able to go back to the original Word document; formatting may be lost. Prior versions of Word provided a Web Page Wizard that is no longer available in Word 2003.

Before creating a home page, consider the information you want contained in the home page. Carefully plan the layout of the information and where to position hyperlinks. Good design is a key element to a successful home page.

DTP POINTERS
Choose a design and theme that match the content of your Web page.

FIGURE 8.5   *Web Page Template*

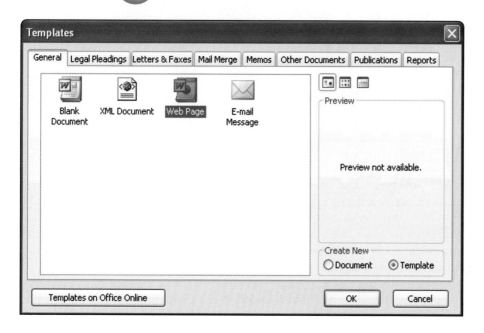

Accessing the Web Page Template

Prior versions of Word provided a Web Page Wizard that is no longer available in Word 2003.

Access the Web Page template by clicking the <u>On my computer</u> hyperlink under the *Templates* category at the New Document task pane. At the Templates dialog box with the General tab selected, double-click the *Web Page* icon. Select a visual theme for your Web page by clicking F<u>o</u>rmat and then T<u>h</u>eme. At the Theme dialog box, choose a coordinated visual theme, as shown in Figure 8.6, and then click OK. You are now ready to begin adding information to your home page.

F I G U R E

8.6 *Web Page Themes*

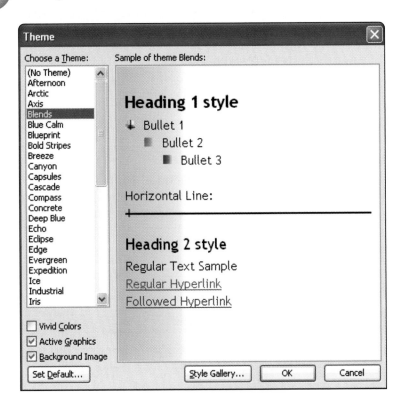

Creating Hyperlinks in a Web Home Page

The Web sites you visited in Exercise 1 included hyperlinks to connect you to other pages or Web sites in different locations. The reader of your document can jump to a location in that document, a different Word document, or a file created in a different program such as an Excel spreadsheet. The destination document or file can be on your hard drive, on your organization's network (intranet), or on the Internet, such as a page on the World Wide Web. You can create hyperlinks from selected text or graphic objects—such as buttons and pictures. By default, the hyperlink text displays in blue and is underlined. When you return to the document after following a hyperlink, the hyperlink text color changes to dark red. You do not have to be on the Internet to use hyperlinks in Word documents.

You can create a hyperlink in your own home page. To do this, select the text you want specified as the hyperlink and then click the Insert Hyperlink button on the Standard toolbar. You can also click Insert and then Hyperlink. At the Insert Hyperlink dialog box shown in Figure 8.7, display a drive, directory, or folder in the Look in text box and then click the OK button.

Insert Hyperlink

8.7 *Insert Hyperlink Dialog Box*

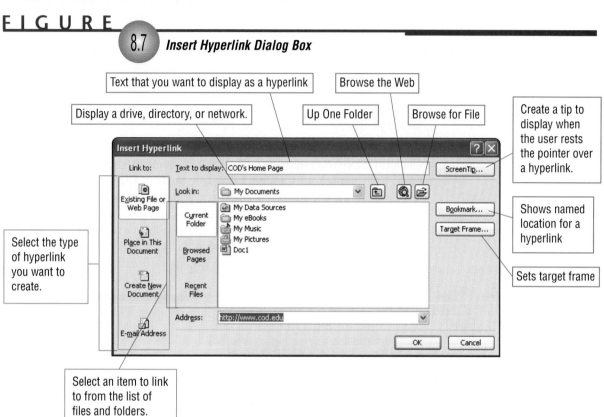

Text that you want to display as a hyperlink

Browse the Web

Display a drive, directory, or network.

Up One Folder

Browse for File

Create a tip to display when the user rests the pointer over a hyperlink.

Select the type of hyperlink you want to create.

Shows named location for a hyperlink

Sets target frame

Select an item to link to from the list of files and folders.

If an e-mail address is typed in the Internet format, yourname@servername.com (it is usually typed at the end of a Web page), Word will automatically create a hyperlink to your default Internet mail program. In addition, you can create hyperlinks to bookmarks in a document, as described below. You can also create a hyperlink from another section in the document to the bookmark or from any other document to the bookmark. Bookmarks are frequently used in Web pages to move the reader quickly from the bottom of a page to the top of a page.

Editing or Deleting a Hyperlink

To edit an existing link, right-click the hyperlink and then choose Edit Hyperlink, Select Hyperlink, Open Hyperlink, Copy Hyperlink, or Remove Hyperlink.

Creating Bookmarks

A ***bookmark*** can be used to move your cursor to another location within the same document. It creates a link within the same page. You must first create a bookmark and then connect it to another location within your page by creating a hyperlink to it. Create a bookmark from the top of a page to a location within the page by completing the following steps:

Bookmark
Link that is used to move your cursor to another location within a document.

1. Insert bookmarks:
   a. Position the insertion point at the location you would like to make a bookmark, or select (highlight) text within your document such as *Top of Page*. The text can also be headings. Click Insert and then Bookmark.
   b. At the Bookmark dialog box shown in Figure 8.8, type a name for your bookmark such as *Top_of_Page*. Bookmark names must begin with a letter and can contain numbers. You cannot include spaces. You can, however, use the underscore character to separate words (i.e., first_heading). Click the Add button.
2. Hyperlink the text at the bottom of your document to your bookmark:
   a. Select the text at the bottom of your page. Do not include the space after the word.
   b. Click the Insert Hyperlink button on the Standard toolbar.
   c. Click the Bookmark button at the Insert Hyperlink dialog box. Click the bookmark name and then click the OK button. Click the OK button to close the dialog box. Consequently, you may click the hyperlink at the bottom of the page and the insertion point will move instantly to the top of the page where you created the bookmark. ***(Hint: If you are not in Web Page Preview, you may test your hyperlink by holding down the Ctrl key and then clicking the hyperlink.)***

FIGURE

8.8 **Bookmark Dialog Box**

Step 1

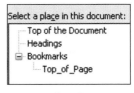

Step 2

Adding Bullets and Lines to a Web Page

DTP POINTERS
Horizontal lines are used to separate sections of a Web page.

Bullets can be added to your document lists by clicking the Bullets button on the Formatting toolbar. You also can change regular bullets to special graphical bullets for your Web page. Select the bulleted list in your document. Click Format and then Bullets and Numbering. Select the Bulleted tab and then click the Customize button. At the Customize Bulleted List dialog box, click Picture. Scroll through the options shown in Figure 8.9, make a choice, and then click OK twice.

FIGURE

8.9 *Picture Bullet Dialog Box*

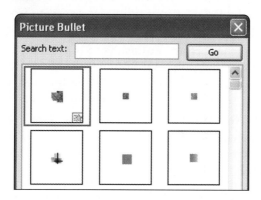

You can use horizontal lines to separate sections of a Web page. Click Format and then Borders and Shading. At the Borders tab, click the Horizontal Line button. At the Horizontal Line dialog box shown in Figure 8.10, scroll and click the desired line type, and then click OK.

FIGURE

8.10 *Horizontal Line Dialog Box*

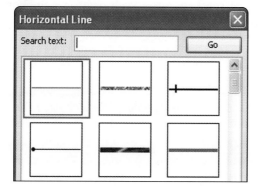

You can also find Web bullets and lines on the Microsoft Office Online Clip Art and Media Web site by clicking the Clip art on Office Online hyperlink at the Clip Art task pane, and then typing Web bullets or Web dividers in the *Search* text box. Some of the items are animated. Also, search the Internet for free Web clips, dividers, bullets, and backgrounds. You may have more success accessing other Web sites by typing the desired URLs in the address text box at your browser (Internet Explorer or Netscape Navigator) rather than at your Internet Service Provider (e.g., America Online).

In this chapter, you will be saving your Web pages onto a floppy disk, CD-RW, or hard drive. For a home page to be available on the Web, however, you must have access to a Web server. Consult your instructor if you are a student. Large businesses usually have their own server and you should contact the Information Systems department of the company to arrange for space on the server to store your HTML documents (Web pages). An option for an individual is to rent space from an *Internet Service Provider (ISP)*, a company that sells access to the Internet. The ISP you use to access the Web will also arrange to store your Web page.

Internet Service Provider (ISP)
Sells access to the Internet.

Saving Web Pages

When you saved your document in earlier versions of Word, the graphical images were saved to your default folder in a subfolder, separate from your HTML document. The images are now saved within the HTML file.

DTP POINTERS
Create a folder to save your Web page.

It is recommended that before you save your document, you create a folder on the disk or hard drive and save your Web page in the folder. When your page is in final form and you are ready to place it on the Internet, you will need to move the folder to the server or "space" you have been given.

To save a regular Word document as a Web page (Word gives it the .mhtml, .htm or .html extensions), click File and then Save as Web Page. At the Save As dialog box, change the *Save in* option to the A drive or the drive where you intend to save your work and then type your file name in the *File name* text box. The *Save as type* text box will display *Single File Web Page* (see Figure 8.11). Click the Save button. Keep in mind that not all formatting will be able to be transferred into Hypertext Markup Language (.htm or .html). However, since the introduction of Word 2000, the majority of the Word commands, interface, and features are basically preserved. Word also provides ***round-trip*** support for HTML. That is, if you save a Word document in HTML, you can later reopen the HTML file and convert it back to a Word document.

Round-trip
Convert an HTML file back to a Word document.

Word documents may also be saved in a Single File Web Page format known as .mhtml or .mht. This format saves all of the components of a Web page including text, sounds, videos, and graphics as an encapsulated HTML file. This file format allows you to send an entire Web page as a single file in an e-mail message or a attachment. The .mhtml format is supported by Internet Explorer 4.0 and later.

FIGURE

8.11 *Save As Dialog Box Displaying Single File Web Page File Type*

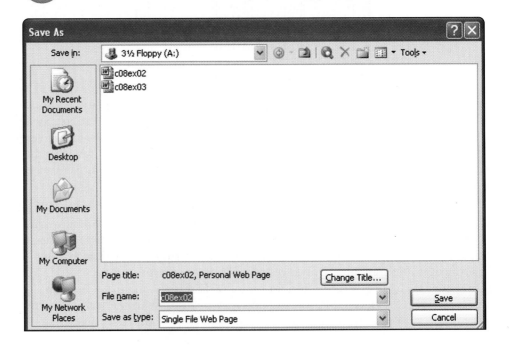

If you know ahead of time that you want to create a Web page, display the New Document task pane, click the <u>On my computer</u> hyperlink in the *Templates* section, click Web Page at the General tab, and then click OK. When you save this document, the document will automatically be saved with an .mhtml extension. An advantage of beginning your page as a Web page is that as you preview your page at your browser, you will know right away what formatting works.

Previewing a Web Page

After creating a Web page or converting a Word document to a Web page, you should preview the page as it will appear on the Internet Explorer screen. To do this, make sure you saved the document and click <u>F</u>ile and then We<u>b</u> Page Preview.

Using Other Office Components in Web Pages

You can create Web pages using each of the applications in Office XP. Excel Web pages may be helpful when you want to use the worksheet's formatting, calculation, and data analysis capabilities, for example, in creating electronic order forms, demographic information, testing or survey information, or a cost comparison. The Save As Web Page dialog box looks similar to Word's Save As dialog box. You will have an option to save the worksheet in HTML or with the XML format, which is a flexible format recommended if the page will be published and if the data is meant to be manipulated or acted on by other programs and scripts. Keep in mind that PowerPoint and Access may also be used in a Web site. All of these Office documents may be customized to reinforce a uniform Web page design by using consistent themes, logos, fonts, colors, and images.

Creating a Personal Web Home Page

1. At a clear document screen, create your personal home page in Word based on the Web Page template by completing the following steps:
   a. Click <u>F</u>ile and then <u>N</u>ew.
   b. Click the <u>On my computer</u> hyperlink in the *Templates* section at the New Document task pane. Click the Web Page icon and then click the OK button.
   c. Click <u>F</u>ile and then Save as Web Page. Create a new folder named *Personal Web Page*. Save the file as **c08ex02, Personal Web Page**. (Word will automatically insert an .mhtml extension.) Click the <u>S</u>ave button. (Save and preview your document often at your browser.)
   d. Insert a clip art image by completing the following steps:
      1) Click <u>I</u>nsert, point to <u>P</u>icture, and then click <u>C</u>lip Art.
      2) At the Clip Art task pane, type computer in the *Search for* text box and then click Go. Scroll to find an image that interests you, and then insert the clip. See Figure 8.12 for a sample document.
      3) Resize the image similar to Figure 8.12 by dragging the corner sizing handles.
      4) Deselect the image, press the spacebar four times, and then press the Enter key twice. Position the insertion point after the four spaces.

e. Display the Drawing toolbar. Click the Insert WordArt button on the Drawing toolbar; choose a WordArt style, font, and font size; and then type your name in the *Text* box at the Edit WordArt dialog box. Click the OK button. Move the WordArt text to the right of the picture image and resize, recolor, and adjust if necessary.

f. Position the insertion point at the end of your document by pressing Ctrl + End.

g. Insert scrolling text by completing the following steps:
   1) Display the Web Tools toolbar.
   2) Click the Scrolling Text button.

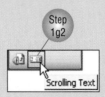

   3) Click the down-pointing arrow at the right of *Background color* and select a color that complements the image that you selected for your page.
   4) Select *Scrolling Text* in the *Type the scrolling text here* text box.
   5) Type a sentence about yourself. Click OK or press the Enter key.
   6) If you prefer to change the font color, select the scrolling text box and then click the down-pointing arrow at the right of the Font Color button on the Formatting toolbar and choose a light color if the background is dark.
   7) Center the scrolling text. To do this, deselect the scrolling text box by clicking to the right of the box. Click the Center align button on the Formatting toolbar. Press the Enter key twice. ***(Hint: Another way to access the Scrolling Text dialog box is to right-click on the scrolling text and then click Properties while at the Word document screen—not in the browser. If the scrolling text is getting annoying, right-click on it and then click Stop.)***

h. Type Experience | Education | Contact and then press Enter. ***(Hint: The | is the shift of the backslash key.)***

i. Position the insertion point on *Experience | Education | Contact,* click the down-pointing arrow at the right of the *Style* list box on the Formatting toolbar, and then click *Heading 3*. Make sure the line is centered horizontally. Press Ctrl + End. You can change the font color if you prefer.

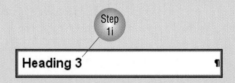

j. Change the alignment to Align Left, apply Heading 2, type Professional Experience, and then press Enter.

k. Click Format, Bullets and Numbering, and then select a bullet. Click OK or press Enter.

l. Type information about your professional experience and press Enter for each item in the list. Press the Enter key twice (the first Enter will add extra white space and the second Enter will turn off the bullets). Change the font if desired.

m. Insert a horizontal line by completing the following steps:
   1) Click Format and then Borders and Shading.

2) Click Horizontal Line at the Borders tab.

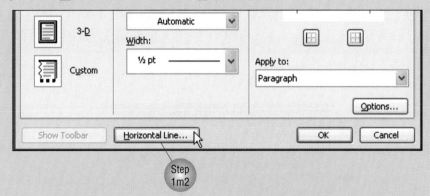

Step
1m2

3) At the Horizontal Line
   dialog box, scroll and select
   the first line option from
   the left in the 15th row.
   *(Hint: You can also type
   bd21318_.gif in the* Search
   text *box.)* Click OK or press
   Enter.

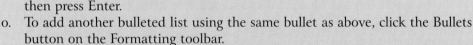

Step
1m3

n. Apply the Heading 2 style, type
   Educational Background, and
   then press Enter.
o. To add another bulleted list using the same bullet as above, click the Bullets
   button on the Formatting toolbar.
p. Type information about your educational background and then press the Enter
   key twice.
q. Insert the same horizontal line as above by selecting it and copying it to the
   Clipboard, pressing Ctrl + End to position the insertion point at the end of the
   document, and then clicking Paste. Press the Enter key.
r. Apply the Heading 2 style, type Contact, and then press the Enter key.
s. To insert symbols, click Insert and then Symbol.
   1) At the Symbols tab, change the Font to *Wingdings*.
   2) Click the phone symbol (the ninth symbol from the left in the first row).
   3) Click Insert and then close the Symbol dialog box. Press the spacebar and type
      your phone number with your area code. Press the Enter key twice.
   4) Insert the mailbox symbol in the Wingdings font (the fourteenth symbol from
      the left in the first row). Press the spacebar and type your mailing address.
      Press the Enter key twice.
   5) Insert the computer symbol in the Wingdings font (the sixth symbol from the
      right in the second row). Type your e-mail address and then press Enter twice.
   6) Enlarge the symbols as desired by selecting the symbol (but not the space)
      individually and clicking the Font Size button on the Formatting toolbar.
      Select a larger font size. While the symbol is still selected, click the down-
      pointing arrow at the right of the Font Color button on the Formatting
      toolbar and select an appropriate color.
t. Insert the same horizontal line as in the sections above as a section divider (use
   copy and paste) and then press Enter.
u. Click the Center align button on the Formatting toolbar and type Top of Page.

v. Insert hyperlinks to employers, colleges, and so on, where appropriate by completing the following steps (Gateway is a sample):

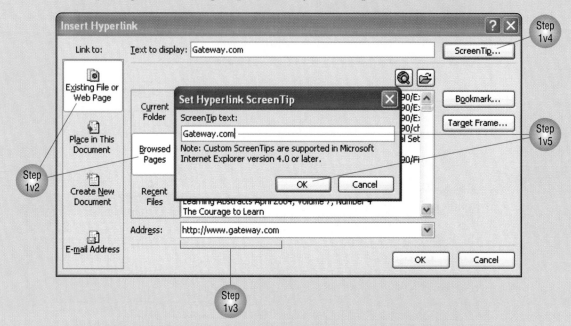

1) Select *Gateway* in the *Professional Experience* section and then click the Insert Hyperlink button on the Standard toolbar.
2) Click E<u>x</u>isting File or Web Page in the *Link to* section of the Insert Hyperlink dialog box and then click <u>B</u>rowsed Pages.
3) Type http://www.gateway.com in the *Address* text box.
4) Click the ScreenTi<u>p</u> button in the upper right corner of the Insert Hyperlink dialog box.
5) Type Gateway.com in the *ScreenTip text* box. Click OK. **(Hint: Test the link by holding down the Ctrl key and clicking the hyperlink.)**
6) Continue creating hyperlinks to employers, colleges, and so forth, by following steps similar to Steps 1v1–1v5.
w. Insert bookmarks to link each section from the top of the page *and* to link the bottom of the page to the top of the page by completing the following steps:

1) Select the image at the top of your page. Click <u>I</u>nsert and then Boo<u>k</u>mark.
2) At the Bookmark dialog box, type Top_of_Page in the *Bookmark name* text box and then click <u>A</u>dd.
3) Position the insertion point anywhere in the text *Professional Experience*. Click <u>I</u>nsert and then Boo<u>k</u>mark.
4) At the Bookmark dialog box, type Experience and then click <u>A</u>dd.
5) Position the insertion point anywhere in the text *Educational Background*. Click <u>I</u>nsert and then Boo<u>k</u>mark.

6) At the Bookmark dialog box, type Education and then click Add.
7) Position the insertion point anywhere in the text *Contact*. Click Insert and then Bookmark.
8) At the Bookmark dialog box, type Contact and then click Add.

x. Hyperlink the bookmarks to the headings at the top and bottom of your page.

1) Select *Experience* at the top of your page (do not include the space after the word) and then click the Insert Hyperlink button on the Standard toolbar.

Step
1x1

2) Click the Bookmark command button at the Insert Hyperlink dialog box.
3) Click on the bookmark name, *Experience*, and then click the OK button. Click the OK button to close the dialog box.

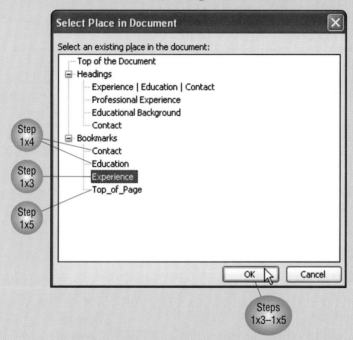

4) Follow the procedure above to hyperlink the bookmarks *Education* and *Contact*.
5) Select the text at the bottom of your document, *Top of Page*, click the Insert Hyperlink button on the Standard toolbar, and then complete the following steps:
   a) Click the Bookmark command button at the Insert Hyperlink dialog box.
   b) Click on the bookmark name, *Top_of_Page*, and then click OK.
   c) Click the OK button to close the dialog box.

2. Save your personal Web page with the same name, **c08ex02, Personal Web Page**.
3. Click File and then Web Page Preview to view your Web page in a browser.
4. If necessary, adjust the top and bottom margins to fit on one page from your browser. (To change margins in a browser, click File, Page Setup, and then type settings in the *Margin* section in the Page Setup dialog box.) Print **c08ex02, Personal Web Page** at the Web Page Preview by clicking the Print button on the Internet Explorer toolbar. Close the browser window when you are finished.
5. Close **c08ex02, Personal Web Page**.

FIGURE

8.12 **Exercise 2**

Your Name Here

Welcome to Your Name Web page. Have a great day!

Experience | Education | Contact

Professional Experience

➤ Assistant Director, 1990-Present. Gateway, 610 Gateway Drive, North Sioux City, SD 57049-2000. Designed and maintained database for the Gateway™ Performance 500 computers.
➤ Intern, 1989-1990. American Cancer Society, Los Angeles, CA. Assisted the Income Development Director and Manager with *Making Strides against Breast Cancer*, a million-dollar fundraiser.

Educational Background

➤ Bachelor of Arts, Communication and Psychology, University of Southern California, Los Angeles, CA 90089. May 1990.
➤ Associate Degree in Applied Science, Office Technology Information, College of DuPage, 425 Fawell Blvd., Glen Ellyn, IL 60137-6599. May 1987.

Contact

☎ Telephone: (605) 555-7867

📠 Snail mail: 633 North State Street, North Sioux City, SD 57049-2000

🖥 E-mail: YourName@xxx.com

Top of Page

Designing a Web Page Using a Table

Working with tables on Web pages is similar to working with tables in Word documents. You can use the Draw Table option to create and modify the structure of the table. Tables are often used as a behind-the-scenes layout tool on Web pages—for instance, to arrange text and graphics. You can add borders, background color, or shading to tables on Web pages by using the Tables and Borders toolbar, or at the Borders and Shading dialog box.

To turn off all of the borders, click inside the table. Click Table and then Table Properties. At the Table tab, click the Borders and Shading button. At the Borders tab, click None. Click the OK button at the Borders and Shading dialog box and then click the OK button on the Table Properties dialog box.

Creating Forms in a Web Page

DTP POINTERS
Users view and complete a Web form in their browser.

You can use Word to create an interactive form that is used on the Web and that provides the viewer options to give input or answer questions. Users view and complete the form in a browser. The completed form is submitted to a database on an HTTP server. Web (HTML) forms use ActiveX controls, which can be created using the Web Tools toolbar (see Figure 8.13). Because forms require additional support files and server support, it is recommended that you work with your network or Web administrator when planning your form. Figure 8.14 describes the form controls that are available on the Web Tools toolbar.

DTP POINTERS
A check box is used when you wish to give the user more than one choice.

F I G U R E

8.13 *Web Tools Toolbar*

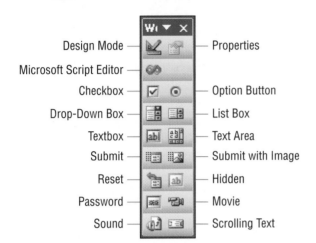

Design Mode — Properties
Microsoft Script Editor —
Checkbox — Option Button
Drop-Down Box — List Box
Textbox — Text Area
Submit — Submit with Image
Reset — Hidden
Password — Movie
Sound — Scrolling Text

DTP POINTERS
An option button is used when you wish to give the user only one choice.

F I G U R E

8.14 *Individual Form Control Button Descriptions*

	Design Mode	Lets you add or modify form controls. You can switch design mode off or on by clicking the Design Mode button on the Web Tools toolbar.
	Properties	Named attributes of control, field, or objects that you set to define one of the object's characteristics, such as size, color, or screen location.
	Microsoft Script Editor	The Microsoft Script Editor window supports viewing HTML for all Office applications that support saving documents in HTML.
	Checkbox	Inserts a check box that can be selected or cleared that is located next to an independent option. Also inserts a check box next to each item in a group of choices that are not mutually exclusive—that is, you can select more than one check box at a time. *Checked:* Determines whether the check box is selected by default.

Continued on next page

Option Button   Inserts an option button next to each item in a group of two or more choices that are mutually exclusive—that is, you can select only one option button at a time. To place text beside this option button, type it on the form.

Checked: Determines whether the option button is selected by default.

HTMLName: The internal name you assign to the control. The name is used to identify the field name when the information is sent to a Web server.

 Drop-Down Box   Inserts a box that displays available choices in a drop-down list box. Enter the items you want to appear in the list box in the DisplayValues property.

DisplayValues: The items to display in the list. Enter all of the items for the list and separate them with semicolons; do not type spaces between the items (for example: Item1;Item2;Item3).

Selected: Defaults to True. Determines whether the first item appears in the box and whether the first item is selected by default.

Size: The size of the font—defaults to l.

Value: The text sent to a Web server for each item in the list. Values are also separated by a semicolon and do not use spaces.

 List Box   Inserts a box that displays available choices in a list format. If the list exceeds the box size, the user can scroll through the list to view additional choices.

 Textbox   Inserts a control in which the user can enter one line of text.

 Text Area   Inserts a control in which the user can enter multiple lines of text.

 Submit   Submits the data that the user filled out. Every form must have one Submit button or one Submit with Image button.

 Submit with Image   Displays a graphic the user clicks to submit data. When you insert this control, the Picture dialog box appears. Select the image you want. When you copy the Web page to a Web server, you must also copy the button image.

 Reset   Resets the form controls to their default settings, and removes data the user has entered into the form.

Continued on next page

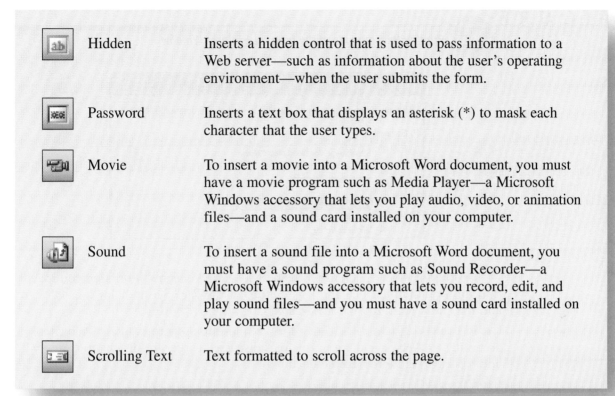

	Hidden	Inserts a hidden control that is used to pass information to a Web server—such as information about the user's operating environment—when the user submits the form.
	Password	Inserts a text box that displays an asterisk (*) to mask each character that the user types.
	Movie	To insert a movie into a Microsoft Word document, you must have a movie program such as Media Player—a Microsoft Windows accessory that lets you play audio, video, or animation files—and a sound card installed on your computer.
	Sound	To insert a sound file into a Microsoft Word document, you must have a sound program such as Sound Recorder—a Microsoft Windows accessory that lets you record, edit, and play sound files—and you must have a sound card installed on your computer.
	Scrolling Text	Text formatted to scroll across the page.

Adding Background Color to a Web Page

You can add background colors and textures to make your document more visually appealing to read online. The backgrounds will be visible on the screen in Word and in your browser (but not in Print Preview from Word). They will not display when the page is printed, unless your browser supports background printing.

DTP POINTERS
Enhance your document with a background.

To enhance your document with a background, point to Background on the Format menu. Click the color you want. Click More Colors for the standard and custom color hues, or Fill Effects to select a gradient, textured, or patterned background. You can also add a picture to the background.

Printing a Background from Your Browser

To print a background or theme in Microsoft Internet Explorer, click Tools, and then Internet Options at the Microsoft Internet Explorer window. At the Advanced tab as shown in Figure 8.15, scroll down to *Printing* and click in the *Print background colors and images* check box to turn on this feature. Click the OK button to close the dialog box. When you print from Explorer, your background and theme colors will print.

DTP POINTERS
Backgrounds can print from your browser.

8.15 *Printing Backgrounds at the Internet Explorer Window*

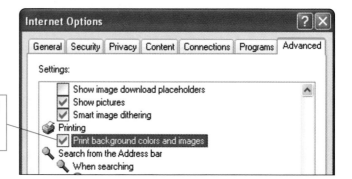

Make sure this option is checked to print the background colors and images.

In other browsers, such as Netscape Navigator version 4.0 or later, you may find this option under File and Page Setup. At the Page Setup dialog box, click to add the check mark to *Print background*. Click the OK button.

In Exercise 3, you will create a form requesting users to evaluate Web sites according to Web page design principles discussed earlier in this chapter. You will add a background effect to the document.

Creating a Web Page Survey Form

1. Create a Web page form as shown in Figure 8.16 using a table and the form control tools by completing the following steps:
   a. Click File and New. At the New Document task pane, click the Web page hyperlink in the *New* section.
   b. Turn on the Web Tools, Tables and Borders, and Drawing toolbars.
   c. Click File and then Save As Web Page. Create a new folder named *Survey Form* on a floppy disk or hard drive and name the document **c08ex03, Web Page Survey Form**. *(Hint: Save your document often.)*

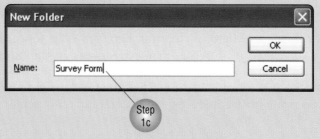

Step
1c

2. Add a background by completing the following steps:
   a. Click Format, point to Background, and then click Fill Effects.

b. At the Texture tab, choose Blue tissue paper (the first texture from the left in the third row) and then click OK.

3. Change the font to 12-point Garamond.

4. Create a table with 3 columns and 12 rows.

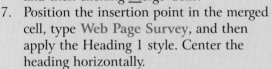

5. Turn off all borders in the table, but display the table gridlines.

6. Merge the cells in the first row by selecting the first row, clicking Table, and then clicking Merge Cells.

7. Position the insertion point in the merged cell, type Web Page Survey, and then apply the Heading 1 style. Center the heading horizontally.

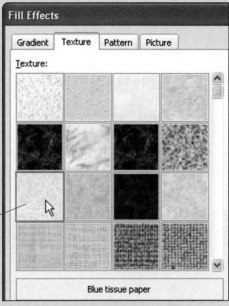

Blue tissue paper

8. Merge the cells in the second row.

9. Click inside the row and type Please complete the following survey so we may encourage professional development of Web pages. Your input is valuable to us; we appreciate your time. Press Enter.

10. Merge the cells in the third row.

11. Click inside the row and type Which Web page will you evaluate?

12. Position the insertion point in the first column of the fourth row and then add a drop-down box by completing the following steps:
    a. Turn on the Design Mode from the Web Tools toolbar by clicking the Design Mode button.
    b. Click the Drop-Down Box button.

    c. Add the choices in the box that you will view and select from your browser by completing the following steps:
       1) While the box is selected, click the Properties button on the Web Tools toolbar.
       2) At the Alphabetic tab, click in the right column beside *Display Values* and type ty.com;coke.com;ual.com. Do not add spaces after the semicolons.
       3) Close the Properties dialog box by clicking the × at the top right corner of the dialog box.
       4) Click to the right of the button and press the Enter key to add white space.

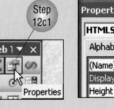

13. Select the fifth row and merge the cells, and then type What is the goal of the Web page?

14. Position the insertion point in the first column of the sixth row and add the first option button by clicking the Option Button button on the Web Tools toolbar.

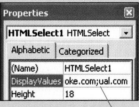

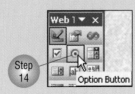

15. Click to the right of the option button, press the spacebar once, and then type Make money.

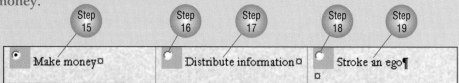

16. Click inside the second column and add the second option button.
17. Click to the right of the option button, press the spacebar once, and then type Distribute information.
18. Click inside the third column and add the third option button.
19. Click to the right of the option button, press the spacebar once, and then type Stroke an ego. Press Enter.
20. When a person is filling out this form in a browser, you will want them to select only one choice from an option button. You also need to decide which choice will be the default choice when the page is opened. We will make the first button the default. To change the option buttons to only allow one choice, each option button must have the same *HTMLName* in the Properties dialog box. To change the default setting, complete the following steps:
    a. Click the first option button to select it.
    b. Click the Properties button on the Web Tools toolbar.
    c. At the Alphabetic tab, click in the right column beside *HTMLName* and then type goal1.
    d. To make this option button the default choice, click in the right column beside the word *Checked* (which shows *False*).
    e. Click the down-pointing arrow and then click *True*.
    f. You can leave the Properties dialog box open.
    g. Select the second option button.
    h. Click inside the Properties dialog box at the right of *HTMLName* and then type goal1. The *Checked* column will say *False*.
    i. Select the third option button.
    j. Click inside the Properties dialog box to the right of *HTMLName* and then type goal1. The *Checked* column will say *False*.
    k. Close the Properties dialog box.
21. Select the seventh row and merge the cells, and then type Who is the intended audience of the Web page?
22. Position the insertion point in the first column of the eighth row and add a check box by completing the following steps:
    a. Click the Checkbox button on the Web Tools toolbar.
    b. Click to the right of the check box that you have inserted, press the spacebar once, and then type 7 years – 15 years (use an en dash).

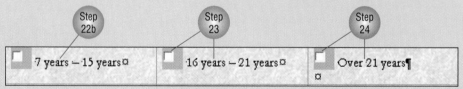

23. Click inside the second column, add a check box, click to the right of the check box, press the spacebar once, and then type 16 years – 21 years.
24. Click inside the third column, add a check box, click to the right of the check box, press the spacebar once, and then type Over 21 years. Press Enter.

25. Select the ninth row and merge the cells.
26. Add a Web Page Divider by completing the following steps:
    a. Click Insert, point to Picture, and then click Clip Art.
    b. At the Clip Art task pane, type **web dividers** in the *Search for* text box and then press Go.
    c. Scroll until you find the colorful divider shown in Figure 8.16, and then click the image once to insert it.

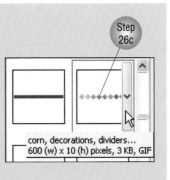

corn, decorations, dividers...
600 (w) x 10 (h) pixels, 3 KB, GIF

Step 26c

27. Position the insertion point in the tenth row, select the first two columns only, and merge the cells.
28. Click inside the cell and change the style to Heading 2, type **Design Elements**, and then press Enter.
29. Type **List a few of the design elements used to draw attention, enhance the message, or encourage you to read further.** *(Hint: If your text style changes to something other than Garamond, select the text and change the font to 12-point Garamond.)* Press Enter.

Text Area

30. Click inside the next column, press Enter twice, and then click the Text Area button on the Web Tools toolbar. Click the Properties button and change the WordWrap to physical by deleting "OFF," typing **physical** in its place, and then close the Properties dialog box.

Step 30

31. Position the insertion point in the next row, select the first two columns only, and merge the cells.
32. Add a text box by completing the following steps:
    a. Click the Textbox button on the Web Tools toolbar, click to the right of the text box, and then press the spacebar once.
    b. Type **Please include your name.**
    c. Press Enter to add space.

Step 32a

Textbox

33. Many times you will want to give the viewer an opportunity to navigate around your page while viewing it from a browser. Create bookmarks and hyperlinks to locations within the page by completing the following steps:
    a. Select the last row and merge the cells.
    b. Click inside the cell and change to Center alignment.
    c. Type **Top of Form | Goal of Home Page | Submit Information.**
    d. Position the insertion point at the top of the page, click Insert, Bookmark, type **top**, and then click Add.
    e. Position the insertion point anywhere in *What is the goal of the Web page?*, click Insert, Bookmark, type **goal**, and then click Add.
    f. Insert hyperlinks by completing the following steps:
        1) Scroll to the bottom of the document and select *Top of Form*. Do not select the space after the word *Form*.
        2) Click the Insert Hyperlink button on the Standard toolbar and then click the Bookmark button.
        3) Click the bookmark *top*. Click OK twice.
        4) Select *Goal of Home Page*. (Do not select the space before or after this text.)
        5) Click the Insert Hyperlink button on the Standard toolbar and then click the Bookmark button.
        6) Click the bookmark *goal*. Click OK twice.
    g. Select *Submit Information* and create a hyperlink to your e-mail address by completing the following steps:
        1) Click the Insert Hyperlink button on the Standard toolbar.

2) In the left frame of the Insert Hyperlink dialog box, click the E-mail Address button.
3) Type your e-mail address or use YourName@emcp.com.
4) Click the OK button to close the dialog box.
34. Exit the Design mode by clicking the Exit Design Mode button.
35. Save your document with the same name, **c08ex03, Web Page Survey Form**.
36. Preview the document in your browser.
37. Print **c08ex03, Web Page Survey Form** from your browser.
38. Complete the form from your browser to be sure the drop-down box, option boxes, check boxes, text area, and text box work and then print again from your browser.
39. Close the browser window and then close **c08ex03, Web Page Survey Form**.

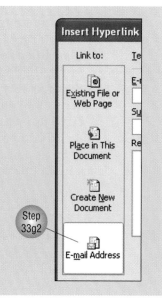

Step 33g2

F I G U R E

8.16 *Exercise 3*

Web Page Survey

Please complete the following survey so we may encourage professional development of Web pages. Your input is valuable to us; we appreciate your time.

Which Web page will you evaluate?
ty.com ▾

What is the goal of the Web page?
◉ Make money   ○ Distribute information   ○ Stroke an ego

Who is the intended audience of the Web page?
☐ 7 years – 15 years   ☑ 16 years – 21 years   ☐ Over 21 years

Design Elements
List a few of the design elements used to draw attention, enhance the message, or encourage you to read further.

Pictures, choice of fonts, color

Student Name   Please include your name.

Top of Form | Goal of Home Page | Submit Information

Turning On or Off Features Not Supported by Web Browsers

Use the Turn On/Off Features Not Supported by Web Browsers option for creating Web pages to be viewed in Microsoft Internet Explorer version 4.0 or later, or Netscape Navigator version 4.0 or later. Click <u>T</u>ools and then <u>O</u>ptions, click the General tab, and then click Web Op<u>t</u>ions. At the Web Options dialog box with the Browsers tab selected, in the <u>O</u>ptions section, select or clear the *Disable features not supported by these browsers* check box. In the *Target Browsers* section, choose your browser and then click OK twice.

Formatting That HTML Will Support

When creating a Web page in Word, you can use many of the same formatting tools you use for Word documents. For instance, you can apply bold, italic, underline, strikethrough, superscript, and subscript formats to selected text.

You can set the colors for hyperlinks and followed hyperlinks for the entire page with the Styles and Formatting task pane in the F<u>o</u>rmat menu. Themes use different hyperlink colors. To change these, you must change the style at the Style dialog box. You can change colors for selected text by clicking the Font Color button on the Formatting toolbar.

You can indent text in 0.5-inch increments by clicking the Increase Indent and Decrease Indent buttons on the Formatting toolbar. In addition, you can change the alignment of text by clicking the Alignment buttons on the Formatting toolbar. A picture can be positioned on a Web page by selecting it first, then clicking an Alignment button. Drawing objects, such as WordArt and AutoShapes, can be inserted into a Web page.

Formatting That HTML Will Not Support

Formatting that is not supported by HTML at this time includes animated text (other than scrolling text), emboss, shadow, engrave, outline, and text effects. Paragraphs will automatically contain space before and after them. In addition, HTML at this time does not support margin changes at the Page Setup dialog box, columns, page borders, headers and footers, footnotes and endnotes, automatic hyphenation, diagonal table borders, comments, outlines, master documents, and cross-references.

Using Word's Standard and Formatting Toolbars with HTML

The Standard and Formatting toolbars are available in Word 2003 when Word is in HTML editing mode. The features that are not available on these toolbars are deselected. To make formatting changes to an HTML document, click the F<u>o</u>rmat option on the Menu bar, and a drop-down menu displays with options for changing the font, adding bullets or numbering, changing case, style, and adding a background or theme. The first button on the Standard toolbar will display as New Web Page instead of New Blank Document.

Word is in HTML editing mode when you open an HTML document, save a document with an .html extension, or choose the Web Page template. When a file is saved in HTML, the basic HTML page structure is in place. Word provides *WYSIWYG (What You See Is What You Get)* support for Web pages with commonly used tags, such as tables, fonts, and background sounds. If you want to view the HTML source code associated with the Web page you have created, click

New Web Page

DTP POINTERS
HTML supports many formatting features in 2003.

WYSIWYG
What You See Is What You Get

View and then HTML Source. At the HTML Source editor you can make changes. To return to the Web page in Word, click File and then Exit. An example of an HTML Source, the Microsoft Script Editor [design] window, is shown in Figure 8.17.

FIGURE

8.17 *An HTML Source, the Microsoft Script Editor [design] Window*

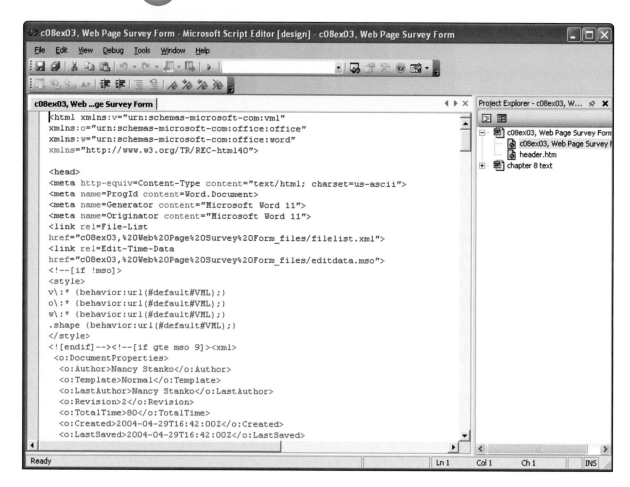

Using Font Colors

Font formats are more limited in HTML pages than in Word documents. At the Font dialog box, you can select from many font colors, which are also available on the Font Color button on the Formatting toolbar. You can also modify the color by going into the HTML source code and replacing the color code with a color you prefer.

Adding Scrolling Text to a Web Page

Marquee
Animated text that travels across the page.

You can enhance your Web page with scrolling text, also known as a *marquee,* which travels across a page. Scrolling text is supported in all versions of Microsoft Internet Explorer 2.0 or later. Some other Web browsers (such as Netscape Navigator) may not support this feature. At the Web Tools toolbar, click the Scrolling Text button. Type the text that you want to scroll in the *Type the scrolling text here* text box as shown in Figure 8.18. Select any other options you want—*Behavior, Direction, Background color, Loop,* or *Speed*—and then click the OK button to add the scrolling text to the page.

DTP POINTERS
Use scrolling text to grab your viewer's attention.

To change the font size and color of scrolling text, select the text box containing the scrolling text and then change the size using the Font Size or Font Color buttons on the Formatting toolbar. To add bold and/or italic, click the corresponding buttons on the Formatting toolbar while the text box is selected.

FIGURE

8.18 *Scrolling Text Dialog Box*

If you want to delete the scrolling text from your Web page, select the text box containing the scrolling text and then press the Delete key.

Using Themes

A theme helps you create professional and well-designed documents. A *theme* is a set of design elements and color schemes. It provides a design for your document by using color, fonts, and graphics. A theme customizes the following elements: background color or graphics, body and heading styles, bullets, horizontal lines, hyperlink colors, and table border colors. You can apply a theme by using the Theme command on the Format menu, as shown earlier in this chapter in Figure 8.6. Select a theme and a sample displays. You may also wish to click the check mark to add *Vivid Colors* and then click the OK button.

Theme
A set of design elements and color schemes.

In Exercise 4, you will create a table for the underlying structure of a form. A theme and an animated .gif are included to quickly create a professional-looking document. When you print the document, the animated .gif will print in a static format.

Creating a Guest Book Form

1. Create a Web page form as shown in Figure 8.19 using a table, the control tools, a theme, and an animated .gif by completing the following steps:
   a. Click File and then New. At the New Document task pane, click the Web page hyperlink in the *New* section.
   b. Turn on the Web Tools, Tables and Borders, and Drawing toolbars.
   c. Click File and then Save As Web Page. Create a new folder named *Guest Book* on a floppy disk or hard drive and name the document **c08ex04, Guest Book Form**. *(Hint: Save your document often.)*
2. Add a theme to your form by completing the following steps:
   a. Click Format and then Theme.
   b. Choose *Rice Paper* and then click OK.

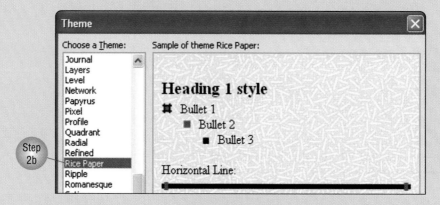

3. Change the font to 22-point Lucida Calligraphy.
4. Type Please Sign My Guest Book and then press Enter.
5. Add an animated .gif by completing the following steps:
   a. Position the insertion point to the left of the word *Please* and click Insert, point to Picture, and then click Clip Art.
   b. At the Clip Art task pane, type writing or j0286670.gif in the *Search for* text box and then click Go.
   c. Scroll until you locate the picture shown in Figure 8.19 and then click once on the image to insert it. *(Note: The images that have a small yellow star displayed in the bottom right corner are animated images.)*

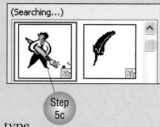

6. Press Ctrl + End, change the font to 12-point Arial, and then type Please sign my guest book. I appreciate your comments. This is my first attempt at a Web page. Press Enter.
7. Change the font style to Heading 1 and type Personal Information. Press Enter.
8. Create a table with 2 columns and 12 rows.
9. Change the first column width to about 2 inches.
10. Change the second column width to about 2.5 inches.
11. Turn off all borders in the table, but display the table gridlines.
12. Create the text in the first column by completing the following steps (at this point, type the text for this column only):

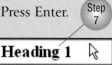

a. Type **First Name**.
b. Position the insertion point in the next row and then type **Last Name**.
c. Position the insertion point in the next row and then type **Street Address**.
d. Continue typing the text in the first column as shown in Figure 8.19 (until the Submit Query button).

13. Insert the Submit Query button by completing the following steps:
a. Position the insertion point in the first column of the eleventh row.
b. Click the Design Mode button on the Web Tools toolbar. (Design mode is now on.)
c. Click the Submit button on the Web Tools toolbar. Click the Properties button. Click to the right of "Submit" in the 'Caption heading. Add a space and type **Query** and then close the Properties dialog box. Press the Enter key to add more space.

Step 13c

14. Insert the Reset button by completing the following steps:
a. Position your insertion point in the second column of the eleventh row.
b. Click the Reset button on the Web Tools toolbar.

15. To add the hyperlink <u>Back to My Home Page</u>, select the last row and complete the following steps:
a. Merge the cells.
b. Center-align the cell.
c. Press Enter and type **Back to My Home Page**.
d. Select *Back to My Home Page*, click the down-pointing arrow at the *Style* list box on the Formatting toolbar, and then click *Hyperlink*.

16. To add the text boxes for the viewers to insert information, complete the following steps (the text boxes may appear short, but they will display correctly in the browser):
a. Position the insertion point in column 2 of row 1.
b. Click the Textbox button on the Web Tools toolbar.
c. Continue adding eight more text boxes in the next seven rows by positioning the insertion point in the cell and clicking the Textbox button on the Web Tools toolbar.

17. Add a text area in the second column of the tenth row. To do this, click the Text Area button on the Web Tools toolbar. Click the Properties button and then delete "OFF" in the *WordWrap* box, type **physical** and then close the Properties dialog box.

18. Save your document again with the same name, **c08ex04, Guest Book Form**.

19. Preview the document in your browser.

20. Print **c08ex04, Guest Book Form** from your browser.

21. Close the browser window and then close **c08ex04, Guest Book Form**.

FIGURE 8.19 Exercise 4

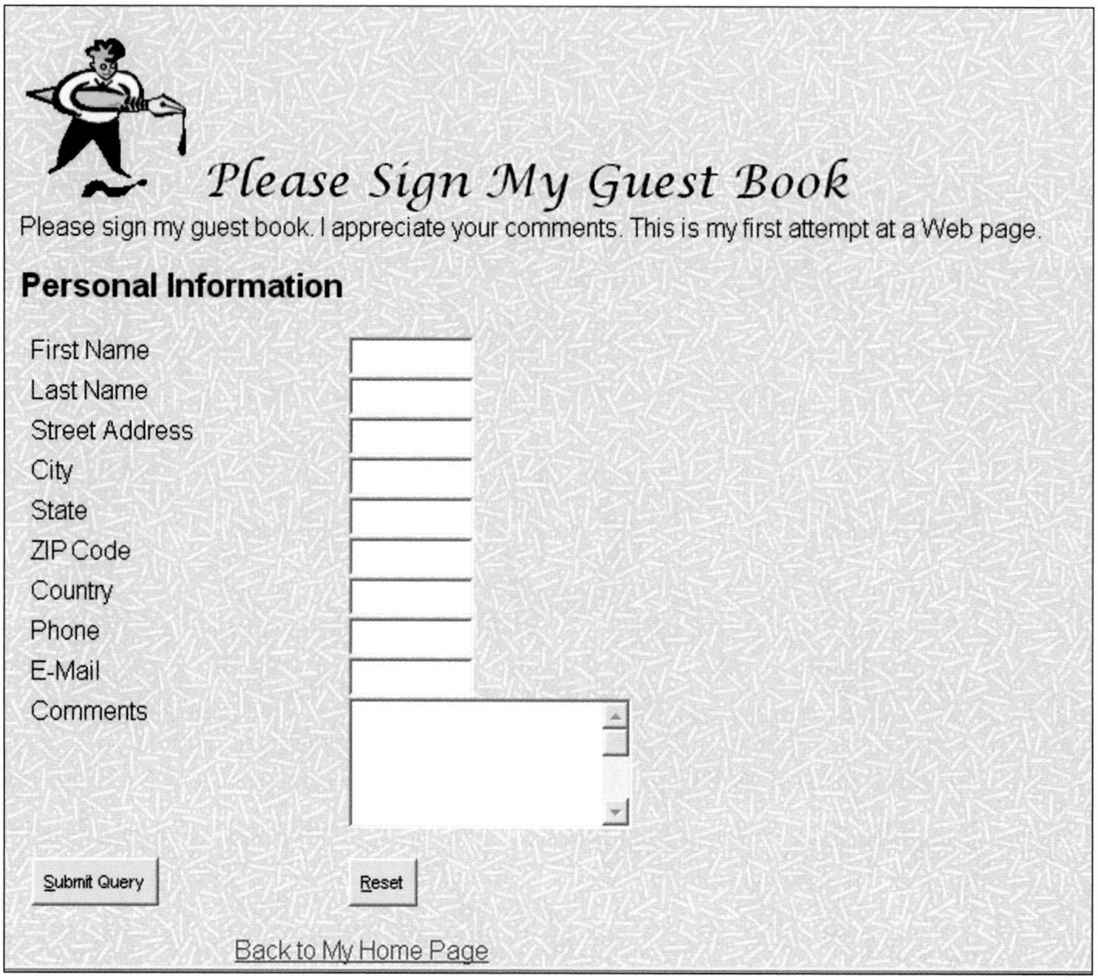

Please Sign My Guest Book
Please sign my guest book. I appreciate your comments. This is my first attempt at a Web page.
Personal Information
First Name
Last Name
Street Address
City
State
ZIP Code
Country
Phone
E-Mail
Comments
Submit Query
Reset
Back to My Home Page

Editing in Web Layout View

DTP POINTERS
The Document Map feature is helpful in jumping between locations in a large document.

Web Layout view enables you to view your document as it might appear online. The Document Map feature is available and it displays to the left of the screen in Web Layout view. Document Map is helpful in jumping between locations in large documents. In order for the Document Map to display the main headings, you must apply HTML heading styles to your heading text.

NaperV and Associates is a large corporation located in Lisle, Illinois. It is sponsoring a conference and has decided to put the conference agenda and evaluation form on its company intranet. In the following exercise, you will create the evaluation form. In the assessments at the end of the chapter, you will work with the agenda.

exercise 5

Creating an Evaluation Form Online

1. Open **NaperV Banner.mhtml** located in your Chapter08 folder.
2. Click <u>F</u>ile and then Save As Web Page. Create a new folder named *Evaluation* on a floppy disk or hard drive and name the document **c08ex05, Evaluation Form**. *(Hint: Make sure the* Save as <u>type</u> *is* Single File Web Page.*)*
3. Click Ctrl + End to move the insertion point below the banner.
4. Display the Web Tools, Tables and Borders, and Drawing toolbars.
5. Press the Center align button on the Formatting toolbar.
6. Check to see that the font is 12-point Arial in the phrase, *"Please tell us what you think....."* *(Hint: The text may not appear centered under the banner.)* Press Enter after the table. You may need to delete some "Enters" in the top part of the document when the document is completed.
7. Create a table by completing the following steps:
   a. Click T<u>a</u>ble, point to <u>I</u>nsert, and then click <u>T</u>able.
   b. At the Insert Table dialog box, create a table with 1 column and 1 row.
   c. In the *AutoFit behavior* section of the Insert Table dialog box, click the <u>A</u>utoFormat button. At the Table AutoFormat dialog box, select the *Table List 1* format in the *Table styles* list box. Click OK twice.

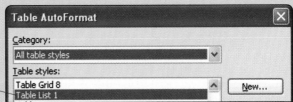

Step 7c

   d. Center the table horizontally by clicking T<u>a</u>ble, Table P<u>r</u>operties, and then *C<u>e</u>nter* in the *Alignment* section of the Table tab. Click OK or press Enter.
   e. Change the font to 9-point Arial bold italic in Dark Red, type 3 Strongly Agree/Excellent, and press the spacebar five times; type 2 Agree/Good, press the spacebar five times; type 1 Disagree/Needs Improvement, press the spacebar five times; and then type NA Not Applicable. (The text may wrap to the next line, but it will display on one line in Web Page Preview.)
8. Deselect the table, click the Align Left button on the Formatting toolbar, and then press Enter twice.
9. Save the document again and view at Web Page Preview.
10. Click the Edit button on the Internet Explorer toolbar to return to Word, and then create another table for the remainder of the document by completing the following steps:
    a. Click T<u>a</u>ble, point to <u>I</u>nsert, and then click <u>T</u>able.
    b. At the Insert Table dialog box, create a table with 3 columns and 20 rows.
    c. In the *AutoFit behavior* section of the Insert Table dialog box, click the <u>A</u>utoFormat button; select the *Table Contemporary* format in the *Table styles* section of the Table AutoFormat dialog box. Click OK twice.

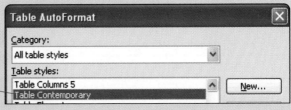

Step 10c

    d. Click T<u>a</u>ble and then Table P<u>r</u>operties.
    e. Select the <u>T</u>able tab and click <u>C</u>enter in the *Alignment* section.

f. Select the Column tab and change the width of column 1 to 0.25 inch, column 2 to 3.25 inches, and column 3 to 2.6 inches. Click OK.

g. Select the entire table and then change the font to 12-point Arial and make sure bold is turned off.

h. Position the insertion point in column 2, row 1, turn on bold, and then type Questions.

i. Press Tab, make sure bold is on, and then type Evaluation.

j. Select column 1 and click the Align Right button on the Formatting toolbar.

k. Select columns 2 and 3 and click the Align Left button on the Formatting toolbar.

l. Position the insertion point in column 1, row 2, and type 1 (without the period and make sure bold is turned off). Press the tab key. Type The conference was interesting, with bold turned off.

m. Continue typing the number of the questions in the first column and the questions in the second column until you reach the heading *Topics*. Refer to Figure 8.20 for the text.

11. After question 5, select the next row and merge the cells.

12. Change the alignment to Align Left, type Topics, and then press Enter.

13. Press Ctrl + Tab to move the insertion point to the default tab.

14. Create the check boxes by completing the following steps:

a. Click the Design Mode button on the Web Tools toolbar.

b. Click the Checkbox button on the Web Tools toolbar.

c. Click to the right of the check box, press the spacebar once, type Getting Organized, and then press Enter.

d. Press Ctrl + Tab and then click the Checkbox button.

e. Click to the right of the check box, press the spacebar once, type How Far Is Too Far?, and then press Enter.

f. Press Ctrl + Tab and then click the Checkbox button.

g. Click to the right of the check box, press the spacebar once, and then type Communicate with Confidence.

15. Continue typing the numbers and questions for 6, 7, and 8. (Refer to Figure 8.20 for the text.)

16. After question 8, select the next row and merge the cells.

17. Change the alignment to Align Left, type Facilities, and then press Tab.

18. Continue typing the numbers and questions for 9–12.

19. After question 12, select the next row and merge the cells.

20. Change the alignment to Align Left, type Additional Comments, and then press Tab.

21. Continue typing the numbers and questions for 13–15. (Refer to Figure 8.20 for the text.)

22. To insert the text areas for questions 13–15, complete the following steps:

a. Position the insertion point in the third column of the seventeenth row (right of question 13) and click the Text Area button on the Web Tools toolbar. *(Hint: If the text area box is too large, resize the box so it looks similar to Figure 8.20.)*

b. Copy and paste the text area box to the eighteenth and nineteenth rows.

| 14 | What other topics are you interested in having presented? | |
| 15 | Comments and suggestions on this conference | |

23. To add the Submit and Reset buttons to the form, complete the following steps:

a. Click inside the second column of the last row.

   b.   Press the Enter key to add extra space.

   c.   Click the Submit button on the Web Tools toolbar. Click the Properties button on the Web Tools toolbar. At the Properties dialog box, click to the right of *Caption*, press the spacebar after *Submit*, and then type **Query**. Close the Properties dialog box.

   d.   Click to the right of the image to get the flashing insertion point, press the spacebar about 10 times, and then click the Reset button on the Web Tools toolbar.

24. You are now ready to create the *Evaluation* column. Complete the following steps:

   a.   Position the insertion point in the third column of the second row.

   b.   Type 3 and then press the spacebar once.

   c.   Click the Option Button button on the Web Tools toolbar.

   d.   Click to the right of the option button and then press the spacebar five times.

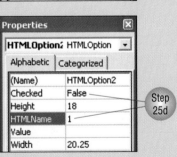

Step 24c

   e.   Type 2 and then press the spacebar.

   f.   Click the Option Button button on the Web Tools toolbar.

   g.   Click to the right of the option button and then press the spacebar five times.

   h.   Type 1 and then press the spacebar.

   i.   Click the Option Button button on the Web Tools toolbar.

   j.   Click to the right of the option button and then press the spacebar five times.

   k.   Type **NA** and then press the spacebar.

   l.   Click the Option Button button on the Web Tools toolbar.

   m. Select the cell containing the four option buttons, click Copy on the Standard toolbar, and then paste this information to the appropriate rows.

25. The option buttons will need to be changed so that the first button in each row is the default. Each row of buttons will have the same HTMLName. Complete the following steps (Design mode must be on):

   a.   Position the insertion point in the first row of option buttons. This is the third column of the second row of the table.

   b.   Click the first option button. With the button selected, click the Properties button on the Web Tools toolbar. In the Alphabetic tab, click to the right of *Checked*. Click on the down-pointing arrow to change to *True*. Click to the right of *HTMLName* and type 1 for the HTMLName.

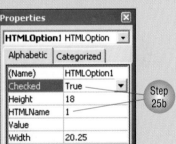

Step 25b

   c.   Click the option button to the right of the *2*.

   d.   At the Properties dialog box, change the HTMLName to *1*. The *Checked* column will indicate *False*. (You do not have to change this.)

   e.   Click the option button to the right of the *1*. At the Properties dialog box, change the HTMLName to *1*. The *Checked* column will indicate *False*. (You do not have to change this.)

   f.   Click the option button at the right of *NA*. At the Properties dialog box, change the HTMLName to *1*. The *Checked* column will indicate *False*. (You do not have to change this.)

Step 25d

   g.   Click the option button to the right of the *3* for the second question. (If the Properties box is not open, click the Properties button.) At the Properties dialog box, change the *Checked* column to *True*. Change the HTMLName to *2*.

   h.   Continue changing the remainder of the rows of option buttons so that the first option button is *True* and each row of option buttons has the same HTMLName. Close the Properties dialog box when you are finished.

i. Click the Design Mode button to turn off this feature.
j. Make sure all border lines have been removed from the table.
26. Save the document again with the same name, **c08ex05, Evaluation Form**.
27. View **c08ex05, Evaluation Form** at Web Page Preview. (Compare the document to Figure 8.20.)
28. Print **c08ex05, Evaluation Form** at Web Page Preview and then close.
29. Close the browser window and then close **c08ex05, Evaluation Form**.

FIGURE

8.20 *Exercise 5*

NaperV and Associates
CONFERENCE: PRIDE AND PROFESSIONALISM
Evaluation Form

Please tell us what you think about the conference. Use the following scale:

3 Strongly Agree/Excellent   2 Agree/Good   1 Disagree/Needs Improvement   NA Not Applicable

	Questions	Evaluation			
1	The conference was interesting	3 ◉	2 ○	1 ○	NA ○
2	The topics and subjects covered were relevant	3 ◉	2 ○	1 ○	NA ○
3	I was energized or stimulated by the conference	3 ◉	2 ○	1 ○	NA ○
4	I would recommend this format for future events	3 ◉	2 ○	1 ○	NA ○
5	Overall quality of the conference	3 ◉	2 ○	1 ○	NA ○

Topics
☐ Getting Organized
☐ How Far Is Too Far?
☐ Communicate with Confidence

6	The presenter was well informed and interesting	3 ◉	2 ○	1 ○	NA ○
7	I am interested in another presentation on this topic with more information	3 ◉	2 ○	1 ○	NA ○
8	Overall quality of the presentation	3 ◉	2 ○	1 ○	NA ○

Facilities

9	The meeting events were well organized	3 ○	2 ○	1 ○	NA ○
10	The facilities were satisfactory	3 ◉	2 ○	1 ○	NA ○
11	The meeting room arrangements were comfortable	3 ◉	2 ○	1 ○	NA ○
12	The quality of the luncheon was good	3 ◉	2 ○	1 ○	NA ○

Additional Comments

13	What was the most useful thing you learned in this conference?	[text box]
14	What other topics are you interested in having presented?	[text box]
15	Comments and suggestions on this conference	[text box]

[Submit Query]   [Reset]

Inserting Graphics and Objects in a Web Page

HTML supports two main graphic file formats: GIF and JPG. However, since Word 2003, you can use many other graphic file formats—such as WMF, TIF, CGM, and BMP—and Word will automatically convert the graphic image to a format suitable for HTML pages when you save the Word document with Save as Web Page.

Resize your image in Word before saving the document as an HTML file. If you have difficulty resizing a particular graphic, you may need to load the image into a graphic-editing program such as Microsoft Word Picture editor or Microsoft Office Picture Manager by clicking Start, pointing to All Programs, pointing to Microsoft Office, pointing to Microsoft Office Tools, and then clicking Microsoft Office Picture Manager. To change to a different editor, click Tools, Options, select the Edit tab, and then select the desired editor in the *Picture editor* list box. To access the Word Picture editor, right-click on the image and select Edit Picture from the shortcut menu and use the tools on the Drawing toolbar to edit the drawing object. You may also invoke an editing program by clicking Insert, Object, and then selecting the editor. However, once the image has been saved in HTML and has been converted to a .gif or .jpeg file, you cannot right-click and then click Edit Picture. You can make changes to the image using the Picture toolbar.

Understanding GIF and JPG File Formats in HTML

When a graphical bullet or line or a clip art image is added to an HTML document, Word 2002 automatically saved the bullet, line, or graphic as a .gif (Graphics Interchange Format, GIF) or .jpg (Joint Picture Experts Group, JPEG) file. The file was saved separately from the document HTML file. However, with Word 2003 you have the option to save a file as a Single File Web Page. The .gif extension is used for clip art and objects, and the .jpg extension is used for photographic pictures.

Downloading More Graphics and Images

Additional images for Web pages are available on the World Wide Web. Display the Insert Clip Art task pane and then click the <u>Clip art on Office Online</u> hyperlink. Type **Web banners** or any other Web graphic search string, click Go, or browse the Clip Art and Media categories. In addition, you can download backgrounds, icons, banners, fonts, and sounds from the Microsoft Web site http://msdn.microsoft.com/downloads, or through your browser you can access a Web search engine and complete a search for free Web design elements.

CHAPTER summary

- ➤ The Internet is a worldwide network of commercial, educational, governmental, and personal computers connected together for the purpose of sharing information.
- ➤ The World Wide Web (WWW) is the most commonly used application on the Internet and is a set of standards and protocols used to access information available on the Internet.
- ➤ An intranet is an "internal Internet" within an organization that uses the same Web technology and tools as the Internet and is also used for sharing information.
- ➤ Word provides the ability to jump to the Internet from the Word document screen.
- ➤ An Internet Service Provider (ISP) sells access to the Internet.
- ➤ The Uniform Resource Locator, referred to as URL, is the method used to identify locations on the Internet.
- ➤ Home pages are the starting point for viewing Web sites. Home pages are also documents that describe a company, school, government, or individual and are created using a language called Hypertext Markup Language (HTML).
- ➤ You can create a home page in Word and then convert it to an HTML document or you can create a Web page using the Web Page template.
- ➤ Plan and design your Web page with a purpose in mind. Review other Web pages on the Internet or an intranet for design ideas.
- ➤ Hyperlinks are colored and underlined text or a graphic that you click to go to a file, a location in a file, an HTML page on the WWW, or an HTML page on an intranet.
- ➤ One method for creating a hyperlink is to select the text and then click the Insert Hyperlink button on the Standard toolbar. At the Insert Hyperlink dialog box, type the URL and then click OK.
- ➤ Bookmarks are created and used to move to another location within a document.
- ➤ Format a Web page with Menu bar options as well as buttons on the toolbars.
- ➤ Lines are added to a Web page through the Clip Art task pane.
- ➤ Preview a Web page document by clicking File and then Web Page Preview.
- ➤ While at the Web Page Preview screen, you can click the Edit button on the browser toolbar to return to Word to edit the Web page.
- ➤ HTML does not support all of the Word formatting features.
- ➤ HTML does not support all graphic formats.
- ➤ Tables can be used to control the layout of a Web page.
- ➤ Forms can be used to collect and present data on a Web page.
- ➤ You can create and use form controls from the Web Tools toolbar.
- ➤ A check box control is used when the user can select more than one choice at once.
- ➤ An option button control is used when the user should select only one option.
- ➤ Many design themes are available to help you create professional and well-designed documents.

COMMANDS review

Command	Mouse/Keyboard
Bookmark	Insert, Bookmark
Display the Web and Web Tools toolbars	Right-click any toolbar and click Web and Web Tools
Display Internet Explorer Search page	Search the Web button on the Web toolbar
Save Word document in HTML format	File, Save as Web Page
Save Excel worksheet in HTML format	File, Save as Web Page
Display a blank Web page	Display the New Document task pane, click Web page hyperlink
Insert graphics	Insert, Picture, and From File or Clip Art; or display the Clip Art task pane
Insert a hyperlink	Insert Hyperlink button on the Standard toolbar; or click Insert, Hyperlink
Preview a Web page	File, Web Page Preview
Edit a hyperlink	Select the hyperlink, right-click, and click Edit Hyperlink
Display lines	Format, Borders and Shading, Horizontal Line
Display Bullets and Numbering dialog box	Format, Bullets and Numbering
Display Scroll Text dialog box	Scrolling Text button on the Web Tools toolbar
Display background color	Format, Background, then select a color or fill effect
Tables	Table, Insert, Table; or click the Draw Table button on the Tables and Borders toolbar
Themes	Format, Themes
Design mode	Design Mode button on the Web Tools toolbar

REVIEWING key points

Completion: On a blank sheet of paper, indicate the correct term, command, or number for each item.

1. List three reasons why users access the Internet.
2. The letters *ISP* stand for this.
3. This is a method used to identify locations on the Internet.
4. This is an "internal Internet" used to share information within an organization.
5. Insert this button control in a form when the user should select only one option.
6. Click this button in the Internet Explorer program window to display the previous page or location.
7. Click this in a home page to link to another page or location.

8. This is used to move to another location within a document.

9. A home page on the Web is created using this language.

10. A home page can be created in Word and then converted to HTML or created with this feature.

11. Click this button on the Standard toolbar to add a hyperlink to selected text.

12. Apply background shading to a Web document by clicking Background at this drop-down menu.

13. This Word feature is used to control the layout of a Web page.

14. This HTML feature displays text like a marquee traveling across the page.

15. Center a graphic horizontally on a Web page by clicking this button on the Formatting toolbar.

16. To create a transparent area in a picture, use this Microsoft graphic editor.

17. Themes are available at this dialog box.

APPLYING your skills

Assessment 1

NaperV and Associates has asked you to create an agenda for the Pride and Professionalism conference to be held in Lisle, Illinois. The agenda will be placed on the intranet of NaperV and Associates, so you must create the agenda as a Web page. Include the following specifications:

1. Create a table so that you will have better control over the layout. Insert a banner at the top of the page. The banner has been created already and is located in your Chapter08 folder as **NaperV Banner2.mhtml**.

2. Use appropriate heading styles, color, and font types and sizes for the heading information.

3. In the sample shown in Figure 8.21 the first column was right-aligned. Right alignment was also used for the second lines in the second column.

4. Be sure to turn off the table lines, but keep the gridlines since they are helpful.

5. An image was added that was changed to a watermark by completing the following steps:
   a. Position the insertion point in the *Getting Organized* cell.
   b. To add the watermark, display the Clip Art task pane, type goal or j0240383.wmf in the *Search for* text box, and then click Go.
   c. Scroll and then insert an appropriate image similar to the image shown in Figure 8.21.
   d. Select the image, click the Color button on the Picture toolbar, and then click Washout.
   e. Select the image, click the Text Wrapping button on the Picture toolbar, and then click Behind Text. *(Hint: If you need to resize or move the image later, click the Select Objects button on the Drawing toolbar and then click on the image to select it.)*
   f. Size and position the image.
   g. Add a background texture by clicking Format, pointing to Background, and then clicking Fill Effects. Select the Texture tab and choose a background.

6. Save your document by clicking File, Save as Web Page, create a folder named *Agenda Web Page,* and then name the Web page **c08sa01, Agenda**.

7. View **c08sa01, Agenda** at Web Page Preview.

8. Print at the browser and then close **c08sa01, Agenda**.

FIGURE

8.21 *Assessment 1 Sample Solution*

NaperV and Associates

Conference Agenda

PRIDE AND PROFESSIONALISM

▶▶ **Wednesday, April 20, 2005** ◀◀

8:30 a.m. - 3:30 p.m.

Holiday Hotel

Room 327
12 East State Street
Lisle, IL 60333

8:30 a.m. - 9:00 a.m.	Continental Breakfast
9:00 a.m. - 9:30 a.m.	**Opening Remarks**
	Gail Lacey, President, NaperV and Associates
9:30 a.m.- 10:30 a.m.	**Getting Organized**
	Speaker: *Janice Bianco*, Author
10:30 a.m. - 11:00 a.m.	Break
11:00 a.m. - 12 noon	**How Far Is Too Far?**
	Speaker: *Cynthia Nielsen*, Human Resources Director
12 noon - 1:45 p.m.	Lunch/Networking
1:45 p.m. - 2:45 p.m.	**Communicate with Confidence**
	Speaker: *Alexander Kemper*, Ph.D.
2:45 p.m. - 3:00 p.m.	Break
3:00 p.m. - 3:30 p.m.	**Closing Remarks, Questions, Answers**
	Gail Lacey, President, NaperV and Associates

Assessment 2

Assume you are working for a travel vacation company named Paradise Vacations that specializes in selling vacation packages to tropical locations. Your company is setting up a Web page to advertise its travel services, which have recently expanded to include travel packages for corporate clients. Figure 8.22 is a sample Web page; use your own design ideas to create Paradise Vacations' Web page using Word's Web page templates or a table. Include the following specifications:

1. Plan what you want to accomplish in this Web page. Do you want to include an introductory paragraph, a table of contents, hyperlinks, a consistent theme, a logo, motion clips, or a navigation bar with hyperlinks to different sections in the Web page or to an e-mail address? View other travel sites on the Web for design ideas.
2. Once you have a basic plan, create a thumbnail sketch of the design and layout of the Web page.
3. Create a folder on a floppy disk or the hard drive and name the folder *Travel Web Page*.
4. Add an appropriate design theme using consistent background, font colors, and design elements.
5. Include at least two graphical elements—pictures, photographs, scanned images, or motion clips.
6. If sound is available, include a sound clip with a tropical overtone.

7. Save your document in MHTML in the Travel Web Page folder and then name it **c08sa02, Travel**. *(Hint: Be sure to save often.)*

8. Include the text in Figure 8.22, although you may rearrange and reword the text if desired.

9. View the Web page frequently in Web Page Preview to arrange the text and design elements properly.

10. Include the following hyperlinks (first try out each of the links to make sure they are operating properly):

> Car Rental—http://www.hertz.com
> Cruises—http://www.cruise.com
> Maps—http://www.mapquest.com
> Hotel Reservations—http://www.marriott.com
> Air Reservations—http://www.ual.com
> Golf—http://www.seasidegolf.com

11. Create a bookmark and hyperlink from the bottom of the page to the top of the page.

12. Save the Web page again with the same name **c08sa02, Travel**.

13. View the document at Web Page Preview, make any necessary adjustments, and test all of the hyperlinks.

14. Close **c08sa02, Travel**.

FIGURE

8.22 *Assessment 2 Sample Solution*

Sunrise Sunset Travel--Sun, Sand, Snorkeling

All About Sunrise Sunset Travel

We are one of the leading travel agencies in the Chicago area specializing in tropical vacation packages and now offering up-to-date travel information via e-mail, in person, and online. Our new Web site, http://www.emcp.net/sunrisesunset, is a one-stop travel site on the Internet providing secure online reservation capabilities for air, car, hotel and vacation reservations, plus access to other travel information.

Fabulous Vacation Destinations

Take a dream vacation to any one of the following locations or talk to one of our travel consultants and we can suggest other locations based on your desires and needs. Contact our corporate travel consultants for all your business needs.

- Florida—Sanibel Island, Miami, Key Biscayne, Orlando
- Hawaii, Maui, Oahu, Kauai
- Mexico—Cancun, Cozumel
- Bahamas & Caribbean—Nassau, Bermuda, Grand Cayman, Jamaica, Virgin Island, St. Croix

Contact Us At...

- 100 West Monroe, Chicago, IL 60601
- (606) 555-2389
- www.emcp.net/sunrisesunset
- E-mail: sunrisesunset@emcp.net

Car Rental   Cruises   Maps

Hotel Reservations   Air Reservations   Golf

Return to Top

Last Updated: December 21, 2005
Copyright © 2005. Sunset Sunrise Travel. All rights reserved.

Assessment 3

You will revise and add Web tools to the form you created in the **c07sa05, Scholarship Application Form** document. Figure 8.23 shows the completed form.

1. Create a folder on a floppy disk or the hard drive and name the folder *Scholarship Web Page*. Open **c08sa03, Scholarship Application Form.doc** from the Chapter08 folder and save it as a Web page in the folder you just created with the name **c08sa03, Scholarship Application Form.mhtml**. Save your document and view it as a Web page often.
2. Select the *Sumi Painting* theme.
3. Change the shading color (Tables and Borders toolbar) of the first row *(Scholarship Application Form)* to Blue. Change the font color to White.
4. Create text boxes as shown in Figure 8.23.
5. Create drop-down boxes for the *State* choices. The *Display Values* in the Properties dialog box should be *CA;FL;HI;IL*.
6. Create option buttons for the Gender choices. Be sure to add the same HTML name to the Properties dialog box.
7. Create check boxes for the *Major Area of Study* choices.
8. Create drop-down boxes for the *H.S. Class Standing* option. The *Display Values* in the Properties dialog box should be *Junior;Senior;Graduate*.
9. Create drop-down boxes for *Intended Student Status*. The *Display Values* in the Properties dialog box should be *Full-time (12 hours or more); 3/4-time (9-11 hours); 1/2-time (6-8 hours)*.
10. Open **c08sa03, Community Service Hours.xls** in Excel. Select cells A1 through D4 and then click Copy on the Standard toolbar. Return to **c08sa03, Scholarship Application Form.mhtml**. Position the insertion point in the empty cell that is below the blank row after the *Eligibility requirements...* paragraph. Click Edit, Paste Special, *HTML Format,* and then click OK.
11. Increase the size of the columns that contain the check marks and add the check mark boxes to these columns.
12. Insert the hyperlink *Kelly Cabana*. Use the e-mail address *cabana@emcp.net.*
13. Insert the Submit Query and Reset buttons.
14. Preview your document as a Web page and fill it out, making sure each of the buttons works. Print the completed form from your browser.
15. Save the document with the same name **c08sa03, Scholarship Application Form.mhtml**, print your document, and then close Word and Excel.

FIGURE

8.23 *Assessment 3 Sample Solution*

Scholarship Application Form

Date: [   ]   SS No.: [   ]

Name: [   ]   [   ]   [   ]
      Last   First   Middle

Address: [   ]
         Number and Street

[   ]   CA ▾   [   ]
City   State   ZIP

Home Phone: [   ]   Male   Female
                               Gender: ○   ○

Major Area of Study
☐ Applied Science   ☐ Education
☐ Arts & Science   ☐ Fine Arts
☐ Business   ☐ Interdisciplinary Studies

H. S. Class Standing   ### Intended Student Status
[Junior ▾]   [Full-time (12 hours or more) ▾]

Eligibility requirements include a minimum of two different types of community service areas that you have completed throughout your 4 years of high school. Click on the category (or categories) that you have completed.

Community Service
Church activity ☐   Government ☐
Day camp ☐   High school ☐
Fund-raising ☐   Homeless shelter ☐

Thank you for your application. Please return to: Kelly Cabana

[Submit Query]   [Reset]

Assessment 4

You will create a registration form to be used on the Web. Figure 8.24 shows the completed form.

INTEGRATED

1. Create a folder on a floppy disk or the hard drive and name the folder *Registration*.
2. Open Word and begin a new Web page and then save the document as **c08sa04, Registration Form.mhtml** (Single File Web Page format). Save the document and view it with Web Page Preview often.
3. Create a table so that you will have better control over the layout of the page. Add color and borders as shown in Figure 8.24, or make other choices.

4. Enter text boxes for the First Name, Middle Initial, and Last Name areas. Change the properties for the text boxes as follows: for the *First Name* text box, set *MaxLength* to 40 and *Width* to 50; for the *Middle Initial* text box, set *MaxLength* to 1 and *Width* to 27; for the *Last Name* text box, set *MaxLength* to 60 and *Width* to 50.
5. Open Excel and then open **c08sa04, Program Information.xls** for the information needed in the drop-down boxes for classes the member is currently enrolled in and for classes the person would like to enroll in. The DisplayValues in the Properties dialog box for the currently enrolled courses should be *Cartooning Class;For the Birds;Personal Safety Awareness;Power Yoga.*
6. The DisplayValues in the Properties dialog box for the classes the member would like to take should be *All Stressed Out?;Entering the Workforce;Starting Your Garden from Seeds;Taking Better Pictures.*
7. Create a drop-down box for *Payment Type* and add the following DisplayValues in the Properties dialing box *American Express;Discover;MasterCard;Visa.*
8. Enter the text boxes for *Credit Card No.* by following these steps. ***(Note: You will insert four text boxes adding "bold" hyphens in between each of the boxes. The changes in the Properties dialog box will limit the number of characters that can be entered into the text form field to 4 and alter the width of the field to accommodate the character limit.)***
   a. Insert the first text box and then click the Properties button and change the *MaxLength* to 4 and the *Width* to 30. Click to the right of the text form box and change the font to bold and then type a hyphen at the insertion point. The combination of the text form field and the hyphen have begun to create a templatelike area that will support the entering of a credit card number. The insertion point is positioned to the right of the hyphen.
   b. Repeat Step 8a1 to place the remaining text boxes and hyphens into the cell. When the cell is complete, there will be four text boxes and three hyphens.
9. Insert the Submit Query and Reset buttons.
10. Preview your document as a Web page and fill it out, making sure each of the buttons works. Print the completed form from your browser.
11. Save the document with the same name, **c08sa04, Registration Form.mhtml**, print the document, and then close Word and Excel.

FIGURE

8.24 **Assessment 4 Sample Solution**

Assessment 5

Create a Web page on a topic of your choosing. Suggested topics include: gardening, a favorite sport or team, community project, volunteer project, hobby, or vacation spot. Look at other Web sites for ideas and layout. Research your topic on the Internet and include at least three hyperlinks. Use appropriate graphics, borders, buttons, dividers, and background. Designate a folder on a floppy disk for your Web files. You may use frames, a blank Web page, or any of the Word Web templates. *Optional:* Include a sound clip if you have sound available on your computer.

CHAPTER 9

Creating Presentations Using PowerPoint

PERFORMANCE OBJECTIVES

Upon successful completion of Chapter 9, you will be able to create onscreen presentations, Web presentations, overhead transparencies, paper printouts, 35mm slides, notes, handouts, and outlines using PowerPoint's AutoContent Wizard and presentation designs. Furthermore, you will be able to integrate a Microsoft Word outline and table, an Excel worksheet, and Microsoft Clip Organizer illustrations into your PowerPoint presentations.

CHAPTER09

DESKTOP PUBLISHING TERMS

Build	Real time	Transition
Effect	Slide indicator	
Published presentation	Storyboard	

WORD AND POWERPOINT FEATURES USED

Animation effects and schemes	Importing from Excel	Outline/Slides pane
AutoContent Wizard	Importing from Word	Package for CD
Background	Media clips	Print Preview
Clip Art task pane	Microsoft Office Online Clip Art and Media	Slide Layout task pane
Clipboard task pane	Microsoft Office Online Templates	Slide Master
Color schemes	New Presentation task pane	Slide Show view
Design templates	Online broadcasts	Slide Sorter view
Diagram Gallery	Online meetings	Slide Transitions task pane
General Templates		Summary slide
Hyperlinks		

Using PowerPoint to Create a Presentation

DTP POINTERS
Creating
presentation
material takes time,
effort, practice, and
patience.

What is a presentation? A presentation communicates information using visual images to convey your message to an audience. Microsoft Office PowerPoint 2003 is a complete graphic presentation program, which allows you to create the following:

- **On-screen presentations.** On-screen presentations are popular because of their many special effects and features. The ability to add animation, movies, sound, and hyperlinks make this form of presentation very attractive and effective. To conduct an on-screen presentation you must have a computer and a compatible projecting device. You may find that an on-screen presentation does not fit on a floppy disk, in which case you may need to store it on a Zip disk or CD-RW disk. PowerPoint has a Projector Wizard that automatically sets and restores screen resolution for the target projection system.

- **Self-running presentations.** Self-running presentations allow the user to set up a presentation to run unattended in a booth or kiosk. A self-running presentation restarts when it is finished and when it has been idle on a manually advanced slide for longer than five minutes.

- **Online meetings.** Online meetings use Microsoft's NetMeeting program with PowerPoint, allowing you to share presentations and exchange information with people at different sites in *real time* as if everyone were in the same room. PowerPoint also includes a Meeting Minder option, which is used to schedule meetings using Microsoft Outlook.

Real time
The actual time in which events take place.

- **Presentation broadcasting.** Presentation broadcasting allows you to broadcast a presentation, including video and audio, over the Web. By using Microsoft Outlook or another e-mail program, you schedule the broadcast. The presentation is saved in HTML and your audience can view the presentation using Microsoft Internet Explorer 4.0 or later.

- **Presentations on the Web.** These presentations are published on the Web. A *published presentation* means a copy of your PowerPoint presentation in HTML format is placed onto the World Wide Web. Because navigation is a critical element, PowerPoint presentations in HTML format include a navigation bar enabling you to advance slides using the Outline pane.

Published presentation
A copy of a presentation in HTML published on the Web.

- **Overhead transparencies.** Overhead transparencies are created by printing the slides as black-and-white or color transparencies. Laser and inkjet printers can print files that you create on transparencies made especially for such printers. At Page Setup make sure you check options to change to Overheads as the medium for which the slides are sized, adjust the dimensions to fit your overheads, as well as specify the orientation.

- **35 mm slides.** PowerPoint allows you to convert the slides to a 35 mm format, and offers a wizard that will send your file to an external service for development.

- **Handouts, Notes Pages, and Outlines.** Handouts, Notes Pages, and Outlines can be printed to assist your audience during a presentation. Handouts are mini versions of the slides with an area for the audience to make notes; notes pages are the speaker's notes; and outlines contain the slide titles and main points of the presentation.

In addition to saving production costs by creating your own presentations, there are other advantages. First, you can maintain control over designing and producing them. Since you can easily make last-minute changes, you can produce a top-quality product right up to the last minute. Second, you have the flexibility of working around your own schedule. Third, creating presentation materials on your own, as with other desktop-published documents, just takes some time, practice, effort, and patience.

Planning the Presentation

The planning process for a presentation is basically the same as for other documents you have created. In the planning stages you must:

- **Establish a purpose.** Do you want to inform, educate, sell, motivate, persuade, or entertain?
- **Evaluate your audience.** Who will listen to and watch your presentation? What is the age range? What are their educational and economic levels? What knowledge do they have of the topic beforehand? What image do you want to project to your audience?
- **Decide on content.** Decide on the content and organization of your message. Do not try to cover too many topics—this may strain the audience's attention or cause confusion. Identify the main point.
- **Determine the medium to be used to convey your message.** To help decide the type of medium to be used, consider such items as topic, equipment availability, location, lighting, audience size, and so on.

Designing the Presentation

When choosing a design for the slides, consider your audience, topic, and method of delivery. You would not want to select a design with bright vibrant colors for an audience of conservative bankers. Nor would you use a design with dark colors or patterns if you plan to photocopy printouts—the contrast of colors and patterns may blur. In addition to design, consider the following items when determining layout:

- **Continuity.** Ensure consistency, avoid redundancy, and use forceful expressions in the design and layout. Repeat specific design elements such as company logos, color, font, and type of bullets used. Consistent elements help to connect one slide to the next and contribute to a cohesive presentation. Some of PowerPoint's design templates coordinate with Microsoft Publisher design sets and Word templates to provide continuation of design across various documents.
- **Color.** Use restraint with color to enhance the message, not detract from it. Colors must look good together. Studies on the psychology of color suggest that certain colors elicit certain feelings in an audience. For example, blue backgrounds promote a conservative approach to the information presented and provide general feelings of calmness, loyalty, and security. Yellow or white text against a dark blue or indigo background is a good combination. Black backgrounds are effective in financial presentations. Black also seems to show directness or forcefulness. Green backgrounds project an image of being direct, social, or intelligent. Green acts to stimulate interaction and is a good choice for use in training and educational presentations. Purple or magenta is appropriate in presentations that tend to entertain or represent less conservative or serious topics.
- **Create an outline.** An outline is a list of headings in the chronological order of the presentation. Follow basic outlining rules such as "Every A needs a B,"

DTP POINTERS
Good presentational skills include attention to message, visuals, and delivery.

DTP POINTERS
Introduce one concept per slide.

DTP POINTERS
If a slide takes more than two or three minutes on a topic, make two or three slides instead.

DTP POINTERS
If a slide takes only a few seconds, consider combining it with another slide.

DTP POINTERS
Consistency is important in maintaining a uniform appearance.

DTP POINTERS
Think about how your audience will respond to the colors in your presentation.

DTP POINTERS
Be consistent when using color to present facts in a presentation.

meaning that you should have at least two supporting points for each main point. You may import outlines created in Word and formatted with heading styles into PowerPoint presentations.

Storyboard
A visual example of the headings in an outline.

- **Create a storyboard.** A *storyboard* is a visual example of the headings in the outline. When creating a storyboard, your information should not exceed what will fit on a 5 × 7-inch index card to avoid filling an entire 8½ × 11-inch sheet of paper. The goal is to limit the amount of information the audience must read so that they can focus on what is being said and visually presented. Write in phrases instead of sentences; you will be less inclined to read from your presentation. Phrases also work well in bulleted format.

- **Use graphics to illustrate your message.** Graphics break up text and stimulate interest in the message. One graphic for every two or three slides is sufficient.

- **Consider the medium.** In addition to careful planning and preparation for your presentation, consider the actual delivery of the presentation. Be sure that the medium you select fits the audience and available equipment.

- **Prepare fully.** Be ready for the unexpected. If you are providing the audience with handouts, know how many you will need. Have a backup plan for equipment failures or if you forget the materials. Bring additional extension cords and power strips. Be prepared for all logical possibilities. You can feel at ease in front of an audience by being fully prepared and practicing the presentation.

Creating Transparencies and Slides

When creating overhead transparencies or slides, consider these guidelines:

DTP POINTERS
Use no more than two fonts per slide—use a sans serif typeface for the title and serif for the body. Serif typefaces are generally used where there is more text.

- **Typeface.** One typeface is fine; use two at the most. Instead of changing typefaces, try varying the type style, such as bold or italics. Legibility is of utmost importance.

- **Type size.** Eighteen points is the minimum. You want everyone in the room to be able to read what you have taken the time to prepare. Choose a thicker font or apply bold to increase the readability of the text.

DTP POINTERS
Keep headings short in transparencies and slides.

- **Headings.** Keep titles short if possible; long headings are harder to read. Kern and track if necessary. Use a sans serif typeface.

- **Organization.** Keep transparencies and slides simple and easy to read. Outline your message to organize ideas and then introduce one main topic or major point per transparency or slide. Each idea or supporting point needs its own line. Limit the number of words per line and the number of lines on a transparency to five or six.

DTP POINTERS
Using ALL CAPS does not leave room for further emphasis.

Giving the Presentation

As the day approaches for you to actually give your presentation, review the following points to make sure you are ready:

- Arrive early to check the equipment and then view the screen from your audience's perspective.

- Be prepared for technical problems—carry extra hard copies of your presentation to use as handouts if the equipment is faulty. Bring an extra power strip, extra bulb, and/or extension cord.

- Have your presentation ready—display the first slide with your name, topic name, and other pertinent information on the screen as your audience enters the room.

- Bring a pointing device, such as a laser pointer.

- Depending on the nature of your presentation, use your imagination to come up with a clever attention-giving device. For instance, if your presentation is on gardening, give each member of your audience an inexpensive package of seeds; if you are presenting information on taking a vacation to Belgium, pass out Belgian chocolates; if your presentation is on a new budget plan, mark one of your handouts with a star and offer a free lunch to the audience member holding that particular handout.

- Practice makes perfect—be sure you are proficient in using the equipment and the software.

- Remain poised and confident.

- Use good volume and speak at a moderate speed.

- Clearly identify each of the points, but do not read them from your slides.

- Do not overentertain your audience—sounds can get annoying, too many graphics distracting, and too many slides boring.

- If your presentation is of a serious nature, do not use unnecessary sound, graphics, or animations. Choose your visual theme and colors carefully.

- Summarize your presentation and ask for questions if appropriate.

- Provide your audience with a handout to take with them—it reinforces follow-up and continued interest.

Creating a PowerPoint Presentation

PowerPoint provides various methods for creating a presentation (see Figure 9.1). To create a presentation, choose one of the following from the New Presentation task pane:

- **Blank presentation.** To begin your presentation at a blank screen, click the Blank presentation hyperlink or press the New button on the Standard toolbar and the Slide Layout task pane will display as shown in Figure 9.2. You start with a single, blank slide in the Title Slide layout.

- **From design template.** A design template includes preformatted layouts, fonts, and colors that blend together to create a consistent look. The Proposal.pot design template is shown in Figure 9.3. You can access the design templates at any time by clicking the Slide Design button on the Formatting Toolbar. This displays the available templates in the Slide Design task pane that displays at the right side of the screen.

- **From AutoContent Wizard.** Creates a new presentation by prompting you for information about content, purpose, style, handouts, and output. You choose from a variety of presentations in specific category groups as shown in Figure 9.4. PowerPoint chooses a background and color scheme based on your responses.

- **From an existing presentation.** Opens an existing presentation so that you can edit or show it. You can also begin by clicking the Open button on the Standard toolbar.

DTP POINTERS
Use the Blank Presentation template if you want complete control over the presentation design.

Slide Design

DTP POINTERS
Keep text parallel; if the first word in a bulleted list ends in *ing*, make sure all of the bulleted items end with *ing*. Example: *Offering, Preparing, Organizing,* and so on.

- **Photo album**. Creates a photo album of pictures from file, disk, scanner, or camera. This is a new feature of 2003.

- **Templates**. At this section of the New Presentation task pane, you may search online for templates by typing in a search string at the *Search online for* text box, and then clicking Go. Access professionally designed templates by clicking the Templates on Office Online hyperlink and you will go to the Microsoft Office Online Web site. To search for templates available on your computer, click the On my computer hyperlink (shown in Figure 9.5). To search for templates available on your Web sites, click the On my Web sites hyperlink.

- **Recently Used Templates**. Shows you the recently used templates on your computer.

FIGURE

9.1 *PowerPoint Window in Normal View*

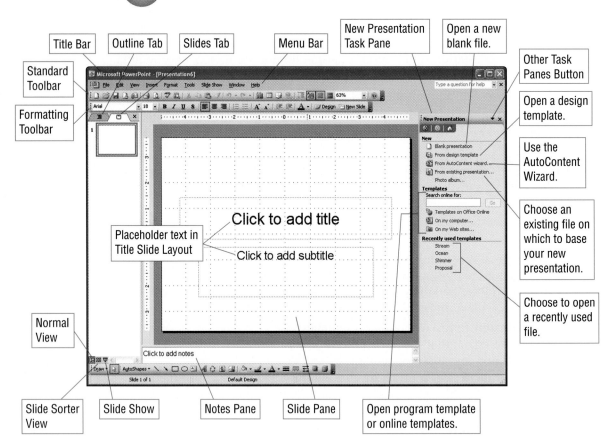

9.2 *Slide Layout Task Pane at a Blank Presentation Window*

Placeholder Text | Title Slide

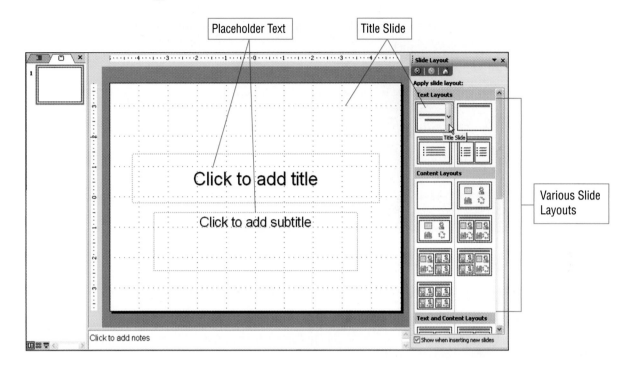

Various Slide Layouts

9.3 *Slide Design Task Pane—Design Templates*

Slide Tab | Title Slide Layout

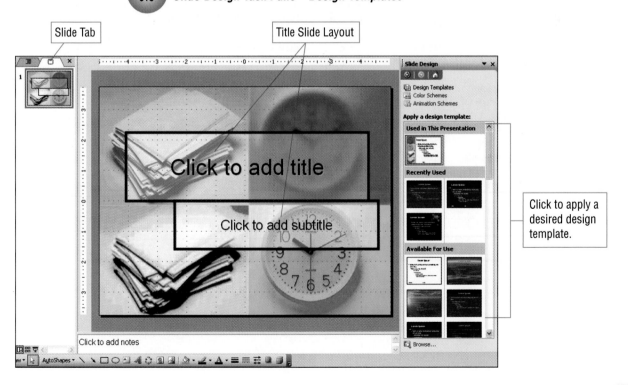

Click to apply a desired design template.

FIGURE 9.4 *AutoContent Wizard*

FIGURE 9.5 *Templates Using the <u>On My Computer</u> Hyperlink with Design Templates Tab Selected*

FIGURE 9.6

Design Templates on Microsoft Office Online

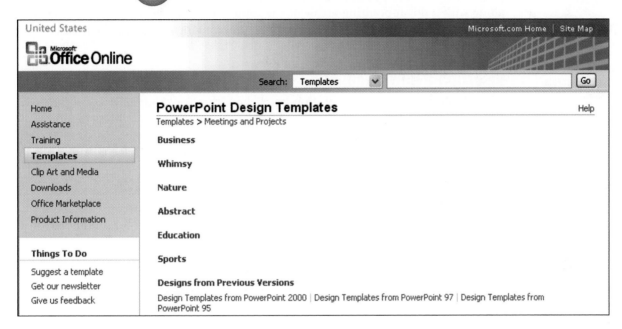

The steps you follow to create a presentation will vary depending on the method you choose, but will probably follow these basic procedures:

1. Open PowerPoint.
2. Choose the desired slide layout.
3. Choose a design template.
4. Type the text for each slide, adding elements as needed.
5. Save the presentation.
6. Run the presentation.
7. Print the presentation as slides, handouts, notes pages, or an outline.
8. Close the presentation.
9. Exit PowerPoint.

Displaying and Maneuvering in Task Panes

As you use various PowerPoint features, a task pane may display at the right side of the screen. A task pane presents features to help you easily identify and use more of the program. The name of the task pane varies depending on the feature. For instance, if you click the Slide Design button on the Formatting toolbar, the Slide Design task pane displays. You can display different task panes by clicking the Other Task Panes button (down-pointing arrow) and then clicking the desired task pane at the drop-down list. You can also control whether a task pane displays by clicking View and then Task Pane. You can close the task pane by clicking the Close button located in the upper right corner of the task pane.

Choosing a Slide Layout

A variety of slide layout options are available at the Slide Layout task pane as shown in Figure 9.2. Besides accessing the layouts from the New Presentation

New Slide

task pane, you may locate the slide layouts by clicking Format and then Slide Layout or clicking the New Slide button on the Formatting toolbar. When you position the mouse pointer on a slide layout, the name of the layout displays along with a down-pointing arrow at the right side of the layout. Click this arrow and a drop-down list displays with options for applying the layout to selected slides, reapplying a layout, or inserting a new slide.

Inserting a New Slide

Create a new slide in a presentation by clicking the New Slide button on the Formatting toolbar. This displays the Slide Layout task pane at the right side of the screen. Click the desired layout in the Slide Layout task pane and then insert the desired data in the slide. The new slide is added after the selected slide.

Understanding PowerPoint's Standard and Formatting Toolbars

Many buttons on PowerPoint's Standard toolbar remain consistent with Word and other Microsoft applications. However, as shown in Figure 9.7, some buttons differ to represent specific PowerPoint features.

F I G U R E

9.7 *Standard Toolbar*

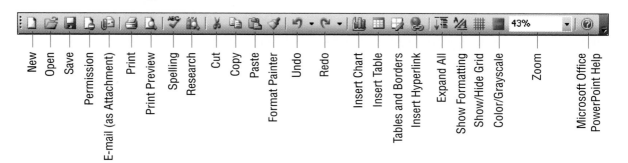

The following buttons on the PowerPoint Standard toolbar activate specific PowerPoint features:

Select this button	*To perform this action*
Research	Display the Research task pane—options to do a Search, All Reference Books Search, get services on Office Marketplace, and Research Options
Print Preview	A new feature since PowerPoint 2002; use to view presentations as they will look in printed form
Insert Chart	Embed a chart in a slide using specified data
Expand All	Expand the Outline pane, displaying all titles and body text for each slide
Show Formatting	Display text formatting in the Outline pane
Show/Hide Grid	Display nonprinting guides that are used to position objects on a slide
Color/Grayscale	Preview presentation in color, grayscale, or pure black and white

PowerPoint's Formatting toolbar (shown in Figure 9.8) includes a variety of options such as changing typeface, typestyle (bold, italics, and underline), and size.

FIGURE

9.8 *Formatting Toolbar*

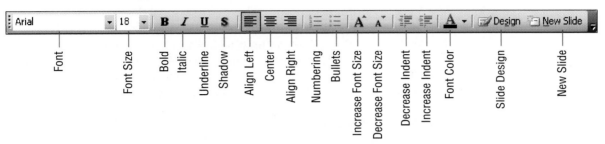

The following buttons on the PowerPoint Formatting toolbar activate specific PowerPoint features:

Select this button	To perform this action
Shadow	Add or remove a shadow to or from selected text
Increase Font Size	Increase font size by approximately 4 to 6 points
Decrease Font Size	Decrease font size by approximately 4 to 6 points
Slide Design	Display the Slide Design task pane
New Slide	Add a new slide to the open presentation or create a new slide

Spell Checking, Saving, and Closing a Presentation

Like Microsoft Office Word 2003, PowerPoint 2003 automatically spell checks text typed into the presentation. In addition, the Save, Save As, and Close features are similar to those in Word.

Spelling

Viewing a Presentation

PowerPoint provides a variety of presentation viewing options. The view can be changed with options from the <u>V</u>iew drop-down menu or with viewing buttons that display on the View bar located at the left side of the horizontal scroll bar, as shown in Figure 9.9.

FIGURE

9.9 *View Bar*

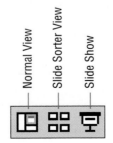

Normal View	This default view displays three panes: outline/slides, slide, and notes.
Slide Sorter View	Displays all slides in the presentation in slide miniatures. You can easily add, move, rearrange, and delete slides.
Slide Show	Used to run a presentation.
Notes Page View	Allows you to add notes to your slides and is actually a subsection of the Normal view. There is only one Notes Page per slide; however, you may use Print Preview to see if all your notes fit on a page. If needed, you may adjust the slide size to fit more notes on the page.

DTP POINTERS
Quickly
and easily
reorganize slides in
Slide Sorter view.

**Previous
Slide**   **Next
Slide**

Slide indicator
The scroll box in the
vertical scroll bar
that is used to
change slides.

In Normal view, change slides by clicking the Previous Slide button or Next Slide button located at the bottom of the vertical scroll bar. You can also change to a different slide by using the mouse pointer on the scroll box (called the elevator) on the vertical scroll bar. To do this, position the arrow pointer on the *slide indicator*, hold down the left mouse button, drag up or down until a box displays with the desired slide number, and then release the mouse button. In addition, you can control which view will be the default by clicking <u>T</u>ools, <u>O</u>ptions, and then clicking the View tab. At the View tab, in the *Default view* section, click the view you are most comfortable using.

Running a Slide Show

Slide Show

Click the Slide Show button on the View bar to start a presentation at the current slide, or click Sli<u>d</u>e Show and then <u>V</u>iew Show. To make sure that you are at the beginning of a slide show, press Ctrl + Home. Several methods for running a slide show are available in PowerPoint. You may run the slide show manually by clicking on each slide, advance slides automatically, or set up a slide show to run continuously. To manually control the movement of the slides, you may use the commands provided in Figure 9.10.

F I G U R E

9.10 *Commands for Controlling a Slide Show*

To do this	Perform this action
Show next slide	Click left mouse; or press one of the following keys: spacebar, N, Right Arrow, Down Arrow, or Page Down
Show previous slide	Click right mouse and then click desired direction; or press one of the following buttons: Backspace, P, Left Arrow, Up Arrow, or Page Up
Show specific slide	Type slide number and then press Enter
Toggle mouse on or off	Type A or equal sign (=)

Continued on next page

Switch to black screen	Type **B** or period (.)
Switch to white screen	Type **W** or comma (,)
End slide show	Press one of the following keys: Esc, hyphen (-), or Ctrl + Break

Using the Slide Show Menu

Once your slide show has begun, you may click the *Slide Show* menu icon that displays in the lower left corner of the slide. Click the icon and a pop-up menu displays as shown in Figure 9.11. Click options on the menu to advance to the next slide or return to the previous one; display the slide titles by using the Go to Slide option; change the screen to black or white; add speaker notes on selected slides; switch programs to turn on the Taskbar; change the pointer to an arrow or pen and choose ink color; erase the pen; access Help; or end the show. If you right-click the middle of the screen while running a slide show, more options will be available.

F I G U R E

9.11 *Slide Show Menu Icon and Pop-Up Menu*

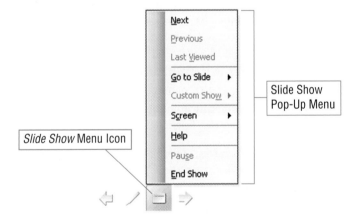

Printing a Presentation

A presentation may be printed in a variety of formats. You may print each slide on a separate piece of paper; print each slide at the top of a page, leaving the bottom of the page for notes; print all or a specific number of slides on a single piece of paper; or print the slide titles and topics in outline form. Use the *Print what* options at the Print dialog box to specify what you want printed, as shown in Figure 9.12. Display the Print dialog box by clicking File and then Print. At the Print dialog box, click the down-pointing arrow at the right of the *Print what* list box, and then click the desired printing format.

DTP POINTERS
Printing a hard copy of your presentation helps reinforce your message.

DTP POINTERS
Prepare backup hard copies in case of technical problems.

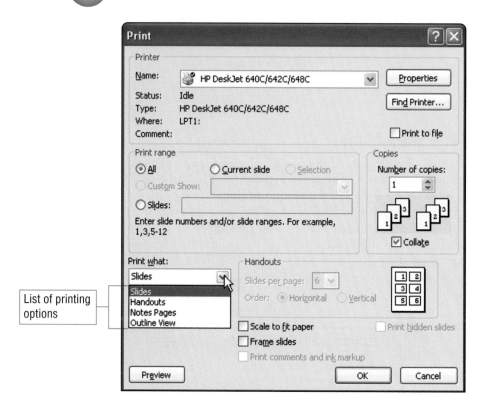

List of printing options

Using Print Preview to View a Presentation

Print Preview

The Print Preview feature may be used to view your slides as they will look when printed. Access this command by clicking File and then Print Preview, or by clicking the Print Preview button on the Formatting toolbar.

(Before completing computer exercises, delete the Chapter08 folder on your disk. Next, copy the Chapter09 folder from the CD that accompanies this textbook to your disk and then make Chapter09 the active folder.)

Creating, Saving, Running, and Printing a Presentation

1. Prepare the slides for a presentation on Microsoft Office 2003 shown in Figure 9.13 by completing the following steps:
   a. At a blank PowerPoint screen, click the New button on the Standard toolbar, and then click the Slide Design button on the Formatting toolbar. *(Hint: The Slide Design task pane should display at the right of the screen.)*

b. Scroll down the list of design templates in the *Apply a design template* list box until the Fireworks template displays. *(Note: The templates are in alphabetical order; the template name will appear when you position the arrow pointer on the template.)*

c. Double-click the Fireworks template. *(Note: This applies the design template to the slide in the Slide pane with the Title Slide layout selected.)*

d. Display slide layout options by clicking Format and then Slide Layout, or by clicking the Other Task Panes button and selecting Slide Layout from the drop-down list.

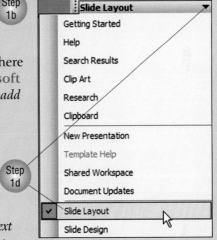

e. At the Title Slide (default first slide), click anywhere in the text *Click to add title* and then type Microsoft Office 2003. Click anywhere in the text *Click to add subtitle* and then type What's New for 2003?

f. Click the New Slide button on the Formatting toolbar.

g. Make sure the Title and Text layout (default layout) has been selected, click anywhere in the text *Click to add title,* and then type Improved Features.

h. Click anywhere in the bulleted text *Click to add text* and then type the following text, pressing the Enter key at the end of each line, except the last item.

- Better collaboration tools
- Extra security options
- Increased use of task panes
- Capability to save "filtered" Web pages, which leaves behind only HTML coding

i. Click the New Slide button on the Formatting toolbar.

j. Complete steps similar to those in Steps 1g through 1i to create the following slides. *(Hint: Press the Increase Indent button on the Formatting toolbar or Tab key to insert the next level of bullets. Press the Decrease Indent button on the Formatting toolbar or Shift + Tab to move the bullet up a level.)*

Slide 3	Title	=	Word 2003
	Bulleted text	=	Increased use of task panes
		=	Research pane in Word
		=	Reading Layout View
	Next level	=	Arranged to fit on the screen
		=	Prints differently than what you see on the screen
		=	Thumbnails pane

Slide 4	Title	=	Outlook 2003
	Bulleted text	=	New Navigation pane replaces Outlook Bar
		=	New Reading pane
		=	Simplified E-mail rules and alerts
		=	New view options
		=	Better privacy protection
		=	New mailbox cleanup
		=	Pictures sent as attachments are automatically compressed
Slide 5	Title	=	PowerPoint 2003 Package for CD Feature
	Bulleted text	=	Add annotations when delivering a presentation
		=	Embed a movie clip and configure it for full-screen playback
		=	Pack and Go has been improved with the Package for CD feature
	Next level	=	Save to a compatible CD burner with Windows XP
		=	PowerPoint Viewer does not need to be included to run the presentations
Slide 6	Title	=	Excel 2003 and Access 2003
	Bulleted text	=	Excel
	Next level	=	List ranges can now be defined
		=	New List and XML toolbars
	Bulleted text	=	Access
	Next level	=	Versions 2002 and 2003 share a common file format
		=	Use Access 2000 format to guarantee compatibility with older versions

   k.   Click in the slide outside the selected area. *(Note: This should deselect the box containing the bulleted text.)*

2. Save the presentation with Save **A**s to your hard drive or to a disk and name it **c09ex01, Office 2003P**. *(Hint: PowerPoint will automatically insert the .ppt extension.)*

3. Change the views by completing the following steps:

   a.   Click the Previous Slide button located at the bottom of the vertical scroll bar until Slide 3 *(Word 2003)* is visible.

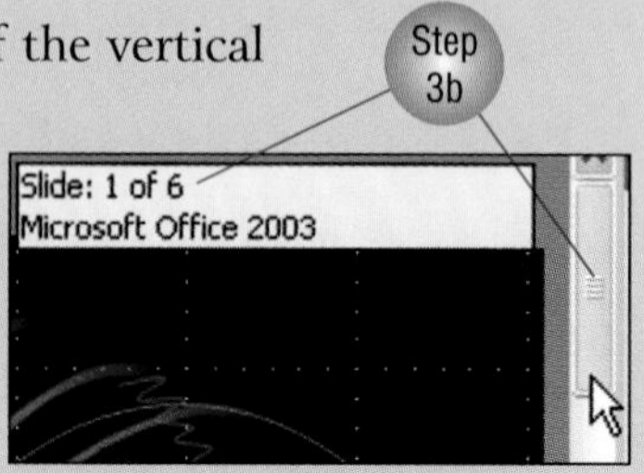

   b.   Position the mouse pointer on the elevator (the scroll box) located on the vertical scroll bar, hold down the left mouse button, drag the elevator to the top until a yellow box displays with Slide 1 and the title of the slide, and then release the mouse button. *(Hint: You may also press Ctrl + Home to get to Slide 1 quickly.)*

Step 3b

Slide: 1 of 6
Microsoft Office 2003

   c.   Change to Notes Page view by clicking **V**iew on the Menu bar and then clicking Notes **P**age at the drop-down list.

d. Scroll to locate Slide 2, click the placeholder text in the notes section of the slide, and then type Use the Clip Art task pane to insert clip art into your presentation. *(Hint: Increase the Zoom to see the text better.)*

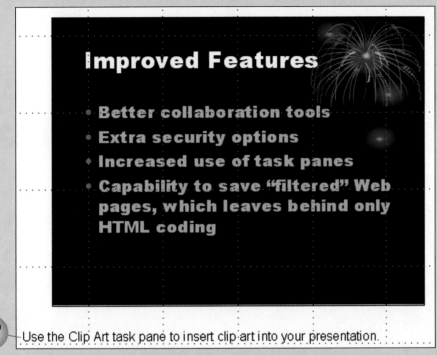

Step 3d —Use the Clip Art task pane to insert clip art into your presentation.

e. Scroll to locate Slide 4, double-click Slide 4 to change the view to Normal, click the placeholder *Click to add notes* in the Notes pane at the bottom of the screen, and then type Of all the Microsoft Office products, Outlook has the most changes in 2003.

f. Change to the Slide Sorter view by clicking the Slide Sorter View button on the View bar.

g. Change to the Normal view by clicking the Normal View button on the View bar.

4. Perform a spelling check on the text in the slides by clicking the Spelling button on the Standard toolbar.

5. Run the presentation by completing the following steps:
   a. Press Ctrl + Home to display Slide 1.
   b. Click the Slide Show button on the View bar.
   c. After viewing Slide 1, click the left mouse button.
   d. Continue viewing slides until the last slide and then click the left mouse button to exit.

6. Run the presentation again and use the pen by completing the following steps:
   a. Make sure Slide 1 displays, click Sli<u>d</u>e Show, and then click <u>V</u>iew Show.
   b. Point to the Slide Show menu pen icon (located in the lower left corner of the slide), and then click the pen. Click <u>B</u>allpoint Pen.

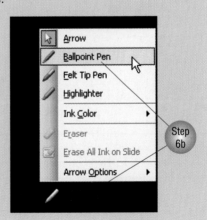

Step 6b

c. Change the pen color by
pointing and clicking on
the Slide Show menu pen
icon. At the pop-up menu,
point to Ink Color and
select Blue (fourth row
under the line and the
sixth from the left). Draw
a circle around *What's New
in 2003?*

d. Draw a line under *Microsoft
Office 2003*.

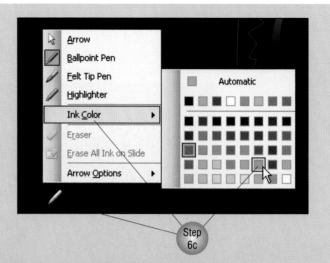

Step
6c

Step
6d

Step
6c

e. Erase the pen markings by clicking the Slide Show menu pen icon and clicking on
Eraser. The pointer is now an eraser. Erase your pen markings.

f. Turn off the eraser by clicking the Slide Show menu pen icon and then clicking Arrow.

g. Turn off the show by right-clicking the screen and then clicking End Show.

7. View the presentation in Print Preview by clicking the Print Preview button on the
Standard toolbar. Click the Close button on the Print Preview toolbar.

8. Print all six slides on one page by completing the following steps:

a. Click File and then Print.

b. At the Print dialog box, click the down-
pointing arrow at the right of
the *Print what* drop-down list
box and select *Handouts*.

c. In the *Handouts* section, make
sure 6 displays in the *Slides per
page* list box.

d. Make sure *Horizontal* is selected in the *Order* section and
then click OK.

9. Save and then close **c09ex01, Office 2003P**.

Microsoft Office 2003

What's New for 2003?

Improved Features

- Better collaboration tools
- Extra security options
- Increased use of task panes
- Capability to save "filtered" Web pages, which leaves behind only HTML coding

Word 2003

- Increased use of task panes
- Research pane in Word
- Reading Layout View
  - Arranged to fit on the screen
  - Prints differently than what you see on the screen
- Thumbnails pane

Outlook 2003

- New Navigation pane replaces Outlook Bar
- New Reading pane
- Simplified E-mail rules and alerts
- New view options
- Better privacy protection
- New mailbox cleanup
- Pictures sent as attachments are automatically compressed

PowerPoint 2003 Package for CD Feature

- Add annotations when delivering a presentation
- Embed a movie clip and configure it for full-screen playback
- Pack and Go has been improved with the Package for CD feature
  - Save to a compatible CD burner with Windows XP
  - PowerPoint Viewer does not need to be included to run the presentations

Excel 2003 and Access 2003

- Excel
  - *List ranges* can now be defined
  - New List and XML toolbars
- Access
  - Versions 2002 and 2003 share a common file format
  - Use Access 2000 format to guarantee compatibility with older versions

Preparing a Presentation in the Outline/Slides View

DTP POINTERS

A presentation displayed in Outline view makes organizing slides easy.

In Exercise 1, you created a presentation using a PowerPoint design template in which you inserted text in each slide. If you are creating a longer presentation with more slides or more text, consider using the Outline/Slides pane with the Outline tab selected as shown in Figure 9.14. Turn on the Outlining toolbar by clicking View, pointing to Toolbars, and then clicking Outlining. Use the Outline feature to organize the topics for the slides without the distractions of colorful designs, clip art, transition effects, or sound. You can create an outline in PowerPoint or import an outline from Microsoft Word.

FIGURE

9.14 *Outline/Slides Pane with the Outline and Slides Tabs Displayed*

Outlining Toolbar

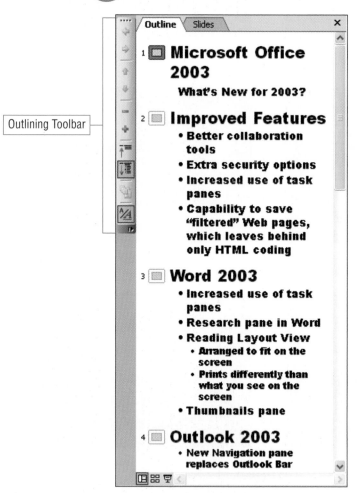

Outline Tab   Slides Tab

Organizing Content

When creating a presentation at the Outline/Slides pane, the slide title appears next to a number followed by an icon. This is the first level of your outline. Body text and bulleted items follow as levels 2 to 5. Navigate up or down with the assistance of the Outlining toolbar located on the left as shown in Figure 9.15.

When using the Outline/Slides pane, click in the pane and then type the text. Press the Tab key or click the Demote button on the Outlining toolbar to move the insertion point to the next tab stop. This move changes the formatting, which is dependent on the design template you are using. Press Shift + Tab or click the Promote button to move the insertion point to the previous tab stop and to change the formatting.

Demote   Promote

F I G U R E

9.15   *Outlining Toolbar*

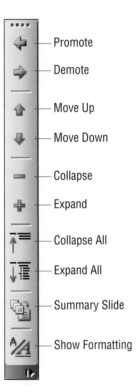

- Promote
- Demote
- Move Up
- Move Down
- Collapse
- Expand
- Collapse All
- Expand All
- Summary Slide
- Show Formatting

Rearranging Slides, Text, and Objects

If you are using the Outline/Slides pane, you may move a slide by collapsing the outline first. Click the Collapse button on the Outlining toolbar, and the title of each slide will display. A gray line below the text represents the rest of the text. Click anywhere in the title of the slide you want to move. Click the Move Down button to move the slide down or click the Move Up button to move the slide up. To expand the outline, click the Expand button on the Outlining toolbar and the levels of the selected slide will display.

Collapse   Expand

Move   Move
Down   Up

You may also rearrange, delete, and add slides in the Slide Sorter view. To move a slide, select the slide and drag it to a new location. To delete a slide, select it and press the Delete key. To add a slide, position the insertion point (vertical line) to the left of the location where you want to add a slide and then click the New Slide button on the Standard toolbar.

Additionally, you may use the mouse to move text with the Outline tab selected. Position the mouse pointer on the slide icon or bullet at the left side of the text

> **DTP POINTERS**
> Press
> Ctrl + Shift + Tab to
> switch between the
> Outline and Slides
> tabs.

until the arrow pointer turns into a four-headed arrow. Hold down the left mouse button, drag the arrow pointer (a thin horizontal line) to the desired location, and then release the mouse button.

With the Cut, Copy, and Paste buttons on the Standard toolbar, you may select text and move it or copy it to another location in the presentation. The Clipboard task pane is available in PowerPoint 2003.

In addition, you may select an entire object box and move it easily in a slide. To do this, click once in the object box to select it and when the arrow pointer becomes a four-headed arrow, you may drag the box to the desired position, and then release the mouse button. To size an object box, select the box and then drag the sizing handles to increase or decrease the size of the box.

DTP POINTERS
Change the size of an object box by dragging a sizing handle.

Importing a Word Outline into PowerPoint

If you have an existing outline created in Word, you can import it into PowerPoint. PowerPoint will create new slides, except the Title Slide, based on the heading levels used in Word. Paragraphs formatted with the Heading 1 style become titles, Heading 2 styles become bulleted text, and so forth. If styles were not used, PowerPoint uses tabs or indents to place the text on slides. To import a Word outline to PowerPoint, click Insert, Slides from Outline, and then at the Insert Outline dialog box, double-click on the file.

Exporting a PowerPoint Presentation into Word

You can also export a PowerPoint presentation to Word. To export a PowerPoint presentation to Word, make sure the file to be exported is open, click File, point to Send To, and then click Microsoft Office Word. The Send To Microsoft Office Word dialog box opens and there are five options to choose from, as shown in Figure 9.16. Select the layout you want to use and then click OK.

FIGURE

9.16 *Send To Microsoft Office Word Dialog Box*

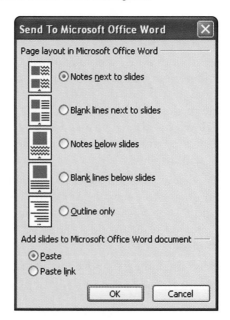

Creating a Summary Slide

You can insert a summary slide at the end of your presentation to recap all of the important points covered in the slides. To create a summary slide, perform the following steps:

1. Display the Outline/Slides pane with the Outline tab selected. Select the desired slides to be included in the Summary Slide by clicking on the first slide and then pressing the Ctrl key while clicking the remaining slides.
2. Click the Summary Slide button on the Outlining toolbar (second button from the bottom). The summary slide will display before the first slide you selected.
3. Change the title of the summary slide and edit and/or delete any bulleted items.
4. Move the summary slide to the location where you want it to display.

Summary Slide

Inserting Headers and Footers in a Presentation

Headers and footers display text, slide or page numbers, and dates you may want at the top or bottom of single slides or all slides. Click View and then Header and Footer to display the Header and Footer dialog box shown in Figure 9.17.

FIGURE

9.17 *Header and Footer Dialog Box*

Displays the current date and time in the Slide footer.

Adds date and time to the Slide footer.

Displays a specific date and time in the Slide footer.

Adds the slide number to the Slide footer.

Displays typed text in the Slide footer.

Does not display footer information on the title slide.

Header and Footer

Slide   Notes and Handouts

Include on slide
☑ Date and time
○ Update automatically
6/12/2004
Language: Calendar type:
English (U.S.)   Western
⦿ Fixed

☐ Slide number
☑ Footer

☐ Don't show on title slide

Apply to All
Apply
Cancel

Preview

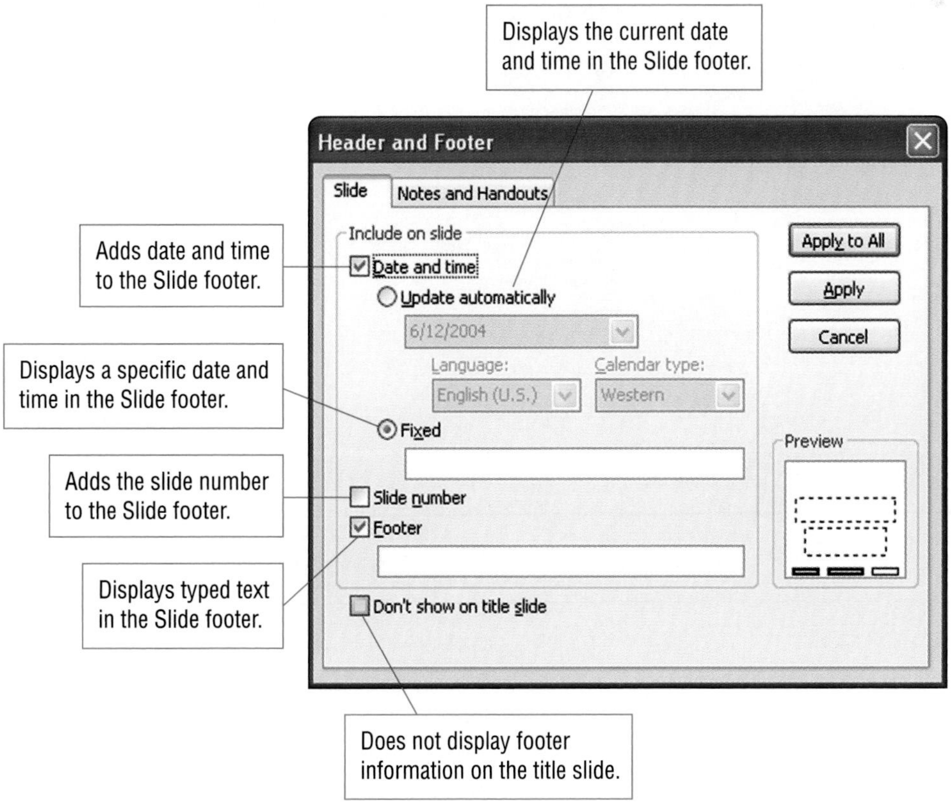

In addition, header and footer information may be typed at the slide master where it may be positioned, sized, and formatted. For instance, to insert information in the Footer area of a slide master, display the Slide Master view, click in the desired section of the slide master, and then type or insert the desired information. When you view your slides in Print Preview, you may make additional changes or delete headers and footers at the same time you are previewing them.

Applying Formatting Using the Slide Master

The Slide Master is a PowerPoint feature that promotes consistency from one slide to the next. Changes made at the Slide Master apply to all slides except the Title Master slide. The title slide differs from the other slides, so a Title Master is available. There is also a slide master for handouts and notes.

Normal View

In Exercise 1, you achieved consistency by using a design template. A more efficient way to change all of the slides at once is to use the Slide Master. The Slide Master screen is shown in Figure 9.18 along with the Title Master screen, which is used for title slides only. Access the Slide Master by clicking View, pointing to Master, and then selecting Slide Master. Alternatively, you may display the Slide Master by positioning the insertion point on the Normal View button in the View bar, holding down the Shift key, and clicking the left mouse button. Make the desired changes and then click the Normal View button (without holding down the Shift key) to exit the Slide Master, or click Close Master View on the Slide Master View toolbar. You may want to insert a company logo or favorite graphic in the Slide Master so the object will display consistently in each slide of the presentation.

If your presentation includes a title slide, make sure you have modified the Slide Master before changing the Title Master. Changes made at the Slide Master will be reflected in the current slide displayed as well as in the remaining slides.

FIGURE
9.18 *Slide Master and Title Master*

Slide Master

Any formatting changes apply to any title slides used in your presentation.

Title Master

In Exercise 2, you will organize your ideas for a new course presentation by using PowerPoint's Outline/Slides pane. In addition, you will make consistent formatting changes by using the Slide Master.

Running a Slide Show Automatically

Slides in a slide show can be advanced automatically after a specific number of seconds. Open a presentation, make sure the first slide is selected, click Slide Show from the Menu bar, and then click Slide Transition (or click View and then Task Pane). At the Slide Transition task pane shown in Figure 9.19, click *Automatically after* (in the *Advance slide* section), and then type the number of seconds. After making changes to the Slide Transition task pane, click the Apply to All Slides button if you want the transition time to affect all slides.

FIGURE

9.19 *Slide Transition Task Pane*

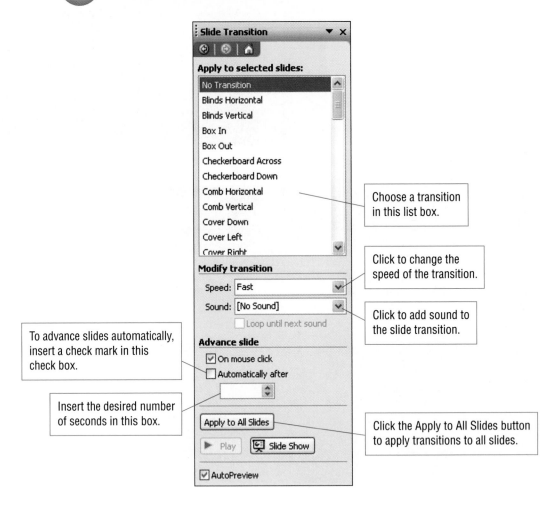

Choose a transition in this list box.

Click to change the speed of the transition.

Click to add sound to the slide transition.

To advance slides automatically, insert a check mark in this check box.

Insert the desired number of seconds in this box.

Click the Apply to All Slides button to apply transitions to all slides.

To run the presentation automatically, be sure Slide 1 is selected. Click the Slide Show button on the View bar. This runs the presentation showing each slide on the screen the specified number of seconds. When a time has been added to a slide (or slides), the time displays at the bottom of the slide (or slides) in Slide Sorter view.

exercise 2

Creating a Presentation at the Outline/Slides Pane and Using the Slide Master

1. Make sure PowerPoint is open and then import an outline created in Word by completing the following steps:
   a. At a blank PowerPoint screen, click the New button on the Standard toolbar.
   b. Click Insert and then Slides from Outline.
   c. At the Insert Outline dialog box, click the down-pointing arrow at the right of the *Look in* list box and then double-click ***Certificate Programs.doc*** located in your Chapter09 folder.
   d. At the Outline/Slides pane, select the Outline tab, click immediately right of the Slide 1 icon, type College of Office Technology, and then press Enter.
   e. Turn on the Outlining toolbar. Click the Demote button on the Outlining toolbar, type Program/Course Outline, press Enter, and then type January 6, 2005.
2. Apply a design template by completing the following steps:
   a. Click the Slide Design button on the Formatting toolbar.
   b. At the Slide Design task pane, scroll down the list of templates and click once on the Proposal.pot template as shown in Figure 9.20.
3. Rearrange and edit the slides by completing the following steps:
   a. Change to Slide Sorter view.
   b. Move Slide 6 *(Professional Development)* before Slide 3 *(Business Correspondence)*. To do this, position the arrow pointer on Slide 6, hold down the left mouse button, drag the arrow pointer (with a square attached) between Slides 2 and 3, and then release the mouse button. A vertical line will display between the two slides.

   Step 3b

   c. Move text from one slide to another by completing the following steps:
      1) Click the Normal View button on the View bar.
      2) At the Outline/Slides pane with the Outline tab selected, select Slide 4 *(Business Correspondence)*.
      3) Select *Flyers* in the bulleted list and then click the Cut button on the Standard toolbar. ***(Hint: Make sure you have deleted the bullet.)***
      4) At the Outline tab, select Slide 5 and paste *Flyers* at the bottom of the list. ***(Hint: Press Enter after Web pages. Delete any extra hard returns.)***
      5) Select *Flyers* and then move it to the top of the list by clicking the Move Up button on the Outlining toolbar four times.

   Step 3c5

4. Create a Summary Slide at the Outline/Slides pane by completing the following steps:
   a. Position the insertion point anywhere in the Outline tab.
   b. Press Ctrl + A to select all of the slides.
   c. Click the Collapse Button on the Outlining toolbar.

   Step 4c

d. Click the Summary Slide button on the Outlining toolbar. *(Hint: The Summary Slide becomes the first slide.)*

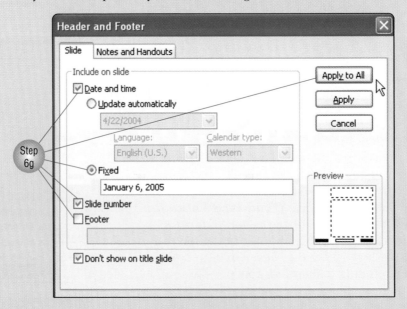

Step 4d

e. Move the Summary Slide to the end of the presentation by selecting it and then clicking the Move Down button on the Outlining toolbar until it is moved below Slide 6.

f. Click the Expand All button.

5. Save the presentation with Save As and name it **c09ex02, College**.

6. Change the formatting at the Master Slide by completing the following steps:

a. Click the Normal View button.

b. Display Slide 2 and then hold down the Shift key while clicking the Normal View button on the View bar.

c. At the Slide Master, click on the text *Click to edit Master title style* and change the font to 40-point Britannic Bold with Shadow. Make sure the alignment is Align Left.

d. Click on the text *Click to edit Master text styles* (this is the first bulleted level) and change the font to 32-point Tahoma with shadow and italic.

e. Select the remaining bulleted levels and change the font to Tahoma (do not change the font sizes).

f. Click View and then Header and Footer.

g. At the Header and Footer dialog box, select the Slide tab and click to insert a check mark at the *Date and time* option and the *Slide number* option. Deselect the Footer option. Select the *Fixed* option and type **January 6, 2005**. Click to insert a check mark in the *Don't Show on title slide* check box. Click Apply to All. Drag the Date Area text box over the Footer Area text box so it is in the middle of the slide. They can overlap since you are not using the Footer Area.

h. Click the Normal View button without the Shift key. (This closes the Slide Master.)

i. Display Slide 1 and hold down the Shift key while clicking the Normal View button.

j. At the Title Master, click on the text *Click to edit Master title style* and change the font to 56-point Britannic Bold, Shadow.

    k.   Click on the text *Click to edit Master subtitle style* and change the font to 32-point Tahoma.

    l.   Close the Title Master.

7. Run the presentation by completing the following steps:

    a.   Click Sli<u>d</u>e Show from the Menu bar and then click Slide <u>T</u>ransition to display the Slide Transition task pane.

    b.   Insert a check mark in the *Automatically after* check box in the *Advance slide* section. Make sure the *On mouse click* option is deselected.

    c.   Insert 3 seconds in the text box below the *Automatically after* option.

    d.   Click the Apply to All Slides button.

    e.   Click the Slide Show button.

8. Save the presentation with the same name **c09ex02, College**.

9. Print the presentation in outline format by displaying the Print dialog box and changing the *Print w̲hat* option to *Outline View*, and then close **c09ex02, College**. (Figure 9.20 displays the presentation as a handout as well—you do not have to print this.)

9.20 **Exercise 2 (Handout, Slides 1–6, and Outline, Slides 1–7)**

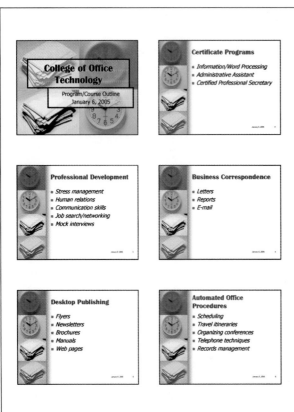

Handout (Slides 1–6)

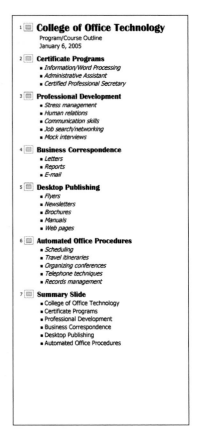

Outline (Slides 1–7)

Applying More than One Design Template to a Presentation

In Exercises 1 and 2, you applied predesigned design templates to each of the presentations you prepared. However, you may apply more than one design template to slides in a presentation. To do this, select the specific slides and then choose the desired design template. If you apply more than one design template to a presentation, multiple slide masters will display in Slide Master view.

Changing Color Schemes

If you are not satisfied with the colors in a design template, you may change the colors at the *Apply a color scheme* section of the Slide Design task pane. A design template includes a color scheme consisting of eight colors. Colors are chosen for the background, text and lines, shadows, title text, fills, accents, and hyperlinks. To change the scheme colors, display the Slide Design task pane, select a desired design template, and then click the <u>Color Schemes</u> hyperlink located toward the top of the Slide Design task pane as shown in Figure 9.21.

FIGURE

9.21 *Slide Design Task Pane with Color Schemes Displayed*

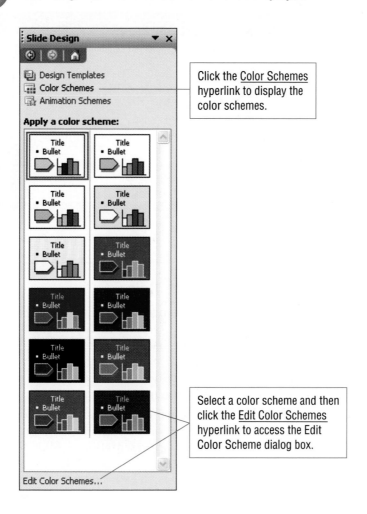

Click the Color Schemes hyperlink to display the color schemes.

Select a color scheme and then click the Edit Color Schemes hyperlink to access the Edit Color Scheme dialog box.

Customizing a Color Scheme

Customize a color scheme by clicking the <u>Edit Color Schemes</u> hyperlink located at the bottom of the pane. The Edit Color Scheme dialog box will display as shown in Figure 9.22. Select the Custom tab and then click on an item in the *Scheme colors* section. Click the Change Color button, choose a desired substitute color, and then click OK.

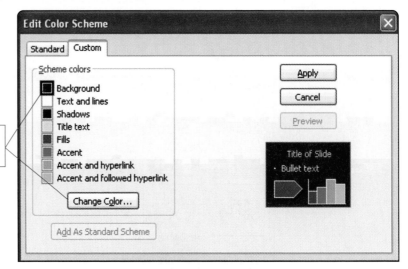

9.22 *Edit Color Scheme Dialog Box*

Select a scheme color and then click the Change Color button.

Changing a Background Color

Background color may be changed at the Edit Color Scheme dialog box or by clicking Format and then Background to display the Background dialog box as shown in Figure 9.23. At the Background dialog box, click the down-pointing arrow at the right of the *Background fill* option box and then click a desired color. Click the Apply button to apply the new background color to a selected slide or click Apply to All to apply the new background color to all slides.

Format Painter

If you change a color scheme for an individual slide and later decide you want to use the same color scheme for another slide, you can use Format Painter to copy the color scheme. Display your presentation in Slide Sorter view and use Format Painter to copy the color scheme from one slide to the next.

9.23 *Background Dialog Box*

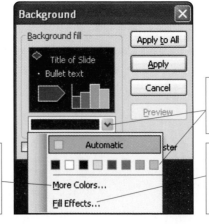

Clicking More Colors displays the Colors dialog box where you can change colors at the Standard and Custom tabs.

Clicking the down-pointing triangle displays this palette of color choices.

Clicking Fill Effects displays the Fill Effects dialog box with Gradient, Texture, Pattern, and Picture tabs.

Adding a Background Picture

A picture background was added to a slide in Figure 9.24 by accessing the Fill Effects dialog box and then choosing the Picture tab. At the Picture tab, click the

Select Picture button and then access the Windows folder where a list of pictures is available. *(Hint: If you cannot find an image listed in the Select Picture dialog box, exit the dialog box, find the clip, and copy it to the Clipboard. Return to the Select Picture dialog box and paste the image in the area below the Look in list box, select the clip, and then click Insert.)*

F I G U R E

9.24 **Choosing a Picture Background**

Choosing a Picture

Using a photograph as a background on a title slide.

Inserting a Picture

Inserting Bullets and Numbers

DTP POINTERS
Use bullets for items that are not sequential.

Many of the design templates will include a Title and Text slide layout containing bullets. Customizing bullets in a slide is similar to customizing bullets in a Word document. You may customize these bullets at the Bullets and Numbering dialog box with the Bulleted tab selected. If the bulleted items in your presentation need to appear in a sequence, select the items and change them to numbers at the Bullets and Numbering dialog box with the Numbered tab selected. At this box, choose the desired numbering style and then click OK.

Adding Objects to Slides

AutoShapes, text boxes, lines, fills, diagrams, charts, and any other objects from the Drawing toolbar may be added to slides in a presentation as they were added and customized in a Word document.

Inserting WordArt in PowerPoint

DTP POINTERS
A logo reinforces a company's identity.

With WordArt, you can apply special effects to text. These special effects become drawing objects, meaning you can use the Drawing toolbar to change the effect. You can add a WordArt object to an individual slide or to several slides using the Slide Master. The advantage of creating WordArt in a slide master is that it will appear automatically on every slide in the presentation (inserting a logo). WordArt is inserted in a PowerPoint slide just as it was inserted into a Word document.

Inserting and Manipulating Images in a Presentation

Insert Clip Art

DTP POINTERS
The basis of communication is people; use photos of faces to make your presentation powerful and effective.

DTP POINTERS
Not every slide needs a picture: insert a picture if it helps make a point.

DTP POINTERS
Insert a graphic in the slide master if you want to add the same graphic to each slide.

To enhance the visual impact of slides in a presentation add clip art, photo images, sound, or drawing objects. Microsoft Office includes a variety of pictures, sounds and motion clips. To insert an image in a presentation, click the Insert Clip Art button on the Drawing toolbar or click Insert, point to Picture, and then click Clip Art. This displays the Clip Art task pane. To insert a sound or motion clip, click Insert, Movies and Sounds, and then select movies and sound from various locations. Also, insert sound, movies, and links to other documents and locations by inserting Action buttons by clicking Slide Show and then Action Buttons.

To view all picture, sound, and media files, make sure no text displays in the *Search for* text box, and then click Go. If you cannot find a particular clip, you may click the Clip art on Office Online hyperlink to access the Clip Art and Media Web site to preview and download additional clips. You may substitute any of the graphic files in the chapter exercises with other appropriate graphics from this site. Remember to consider your audience and the subject of your document in choosing appropriate graphics to enhance your documents.

Another method for inserting graphics, charts, diagrams, and tables is to select a slide layout at the Slide Layout task pane that includes a Content placeholder. A Content placeholder as shown in Figure 9.25 displays with six images including a table, a picture, a chart, a diagram or organization chart, clip art, and a media clip. When you click a Content placeholder, the Select Picture dialog box displays as shown in Figure 9.26. Use the *Search text* box to complete a search for a specific graphic or category of graphics.

9.25 *Content Placeholder*

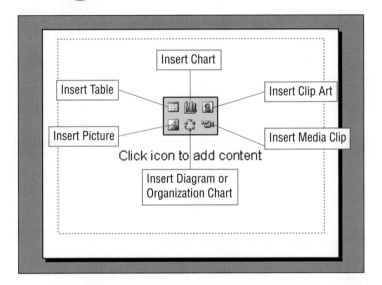

9.26 *Select Picture Dialog Box*

Type search text in the *Search text* box and then click Go.

Recoloring an Image

When you insert a Microsoft Windows Metafile (.wmf file format), you can change the colors in the picture at the Recolor Picture dialog box shown in Figure 9.27. If the picture is a bitmap image (.jpg, .gif, .bmp, or .png file format), you need to edit its colors in an image editing program. To recolor an image, complete the following steps:

Recolor Picture

1. Display the slide in Normal view and select the image you want to recolor.
2. Display the Picture toolbar and then click the Recolor Picture button on the Picture toolbar.
3. At the Recolor Picture dialog box, select the color in the *Original* column that you would like to change, then click the down-pointing arrow to the right of the *New* column and select a new color.
4. Click *P*review to see the color changes.
5. When you are satisfied with the results, click OK.

FIGURE

9.27 *Recoloring an Image*

Select the image and then click the Recolor Picture button on the Picture toolbar.

Choose a new color to replace the original color.

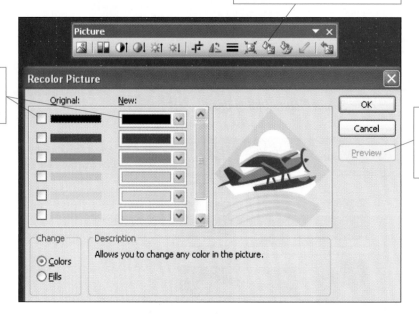

Click the *P*review button to view the new color in the graphic.

Creating Watermarks

Color

Create a watermark in a PowerPoint presentation by clicking the Color button on the Picture toolbar and then clicking Washout. Move the watermark image behind the text by clicking the Draw button on the Drawing toolbar, pointing to Order, and then clicking Send to Back or Send Backward. Use the brightness and contrast buttons on the Picture toolbar to adjust the brightness and intensity of the image. Click the Select Objects button on the Drawing toolbar to help you select an image once it has been sent behind text.

Running a Slide Show

In Exercises 1 and 2 you practiced running a slide show manually by clicking the mouse button at each slide, and automatically by typing a specific increment of time for all of the slides. In Exercise 3, you will practice running the presentation in a continuous loop and ending the loop by pressing the Esc key and then running the presentation with rehearsed times.

Running a Slide Show in a Continuous Loop

In a continuous-loop slide show, all of the slides are viewed over and over again until you stop the show. This feature is especially effective when presenting a new product or service at a trade show or at a new store opening. To run a presentation in PowerPoint in a continuous loop, click Slide Show and then Set Up Show. At the Set Up Show dialog box, click the check box to the left of *Loop continuously until 'Esc'*, as shown in Figure 9.28, and then click OK.

When you are ready to run the presentation, click the Slide Show button on the View bar. When you are ready to end the slide show, press the Esc key on the keyboard. You will then return to Slide Sorter view.

FIGURE

9.28 *Set Up Show Dialog Box*

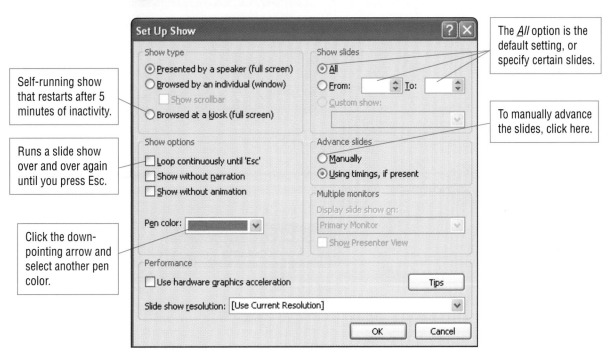

The *All* option is the default setting, or specify certain slides.

Self-running show that restarts after 5 minutes of inactivity.

Runs a slide show over and over again until you press Esc.

Click the down-pointing arrow and select another pen color.

To manually advance the slides, click here.

Setting and Rehearsing Timings for a Presentation

In some presentations, you may want to specify a different amount of time for each slide and then rehearse the presentation to ensure that the time set is appropriate. To rehearse and set a time for each slide, you would complete these steps:

1. Open the presentation.
2. Change to the Slide Sorter view.
3. Click the Rehearse Timings button on the Slide Sorter toolbar, or click Slide Show and then Rehearse Timings. Figure 9.29 displays the Slide Sorter toolbar.
4. The first slide in the presentation displays along with a Rehearsal toolbar that appears in the top left corner of the screen as shown in Figure 9.30. The Rehearsal toolbar shows the time for the current slide and the entire time for the presentation. The timer begins immediately. Click the Next

button when the desired time is displayed; click the Pause button to stop the timer and leave the slide on the screen; or click the Repeat button if you want the time for the current slide to start over.

5. Continue in this manner until the time for all slides in the presentation has been specified.

6. After specifying the time for the last slide, a Microsoft PowerPoint dialog box displays with the total time of the presentation and asks if you want to record the new slide timings. At this dialog box, click Yes to save the new timings.

FIGURE

9.29 *Slide Sorter Toolbar*

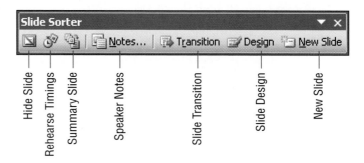

FIGURE

9.30 *Rehearsal Toolbar*

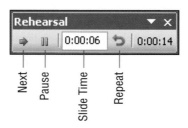

Adding Transitions, Effects, and Sounds

Transition
How one slide is removed from the screen and the next slide is displayed.

If the presentation you are creating will be delivered using an on-screen slide show, the addition of transitions and effects can augment the presentation by providing movement and/or sound between slides. A *transition* is visual movement that affects an entire slide (i.e., a slide dissolving into the next slide).

Effect
Method of displaying movement in individual elements on a slide, such as Fly from Top, Spiral, and Swivel.

In addition, you can add sound to accompany the transition, as well as apply animation effects to individual elements on your slide to create a build. An *effect* also describes movement but refers to the method used to display individual elements on the slide, such as Fly from Top, Spiral, or Swivel. A build is an effective tool in slide shows that helps to keep the audience on track with the major points on each slide. An example of a build is using a bulleted list to display one bullet at a time.

To apply transitions, display the presentation in Slide Sorter view, select the slide(s), click the Transition button on the Slide Sorter toolbar or click Slide Show on the Menu bar, and then click Slide Transition. You may choose transitions, modify transitions, add sound, and specify how the slides will advance at the Slide Transition task pane as shown in Figure 9.19.

exercise 3

Inserting Clip Art, Recoloring Clip Art, and Adding Transitions to a Presentation

1. Open **Cruise.ppt** located in your Chapter09 folder. Save the presentation using Save As and name it **c09ex03, Cruise**.
2. Apply a design template to the presentation by completing the following steps:
   a. Click the Slide Design button on the Formatting toolbar to open the Slide Design task pane.
   b. Scroll down the list of design templates and then click *Shimmer.pot*.
3. Display the first slide in Normal view.
4. Create the three AutoShapes shown in Figure 9.31 by completing the following steps:
   a. Click the AutoShapes button on the Drawing toolbar, point to Basic Shapes, and then click the Diamond shape (last shape from the right in the first row). Drag the crosshairs to create a diamond approximately 2 inches in diameter.
   b. Double-click the diamond shape to open the Format AutoShape dialog box and select the Size tab.
   c. At the Size tab make sure the *Height* option is set to 2 inches and the *Width* option is set to 2.25 inches.
   d. Click the Colors and Lines tab, change the fill to the beige color in the scheme as shown at the right, and then click OK.
   e. Right-click the diamond and then click Add Text at the shortcut menu.
   f. Type St. Thomas in 20-point Arial in Black and in bold.
   g. Copy the diamond to the right two times.
   h. Select the text in the middle diamond and then type St. Maarten.
   i. Select the text in the last diamond and then type Nassau.
   j. Make sure the three diamonds are positioned as shown in Figure 9.31.
   k. Hold down the Shift key and click on each diamond, click the Draw button on the Drawing toolbar, point to Align or Distribute, and then click Align Top. With the diamonds selected, click Draw, Align or Distribute, and then click Distribute Horizontally.
   l. With the diamonds still selected, click Draw and then Group.
5. Create the WordArt object across the top of the diamonds by completing the following steps:
   a. Click the Insert WordArt button on the Drawing toolbar.
   b. Select the fifth WordArt style from the left in the second row and then click OK.
   c. At the Edit WordArt Text dialog box, change the font to 54-point Impact and then type A Caribbean Adventure. Click OK.

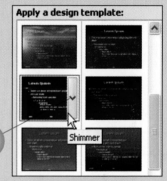

Step 2b

Step 4d

d. Click the WordArt Shape button on the WordArt toolbar and then click the Deflate Bottom shape (the fourth shape from the left in the fourth row).

e. Size and position the object as shown in Figure 9.31.

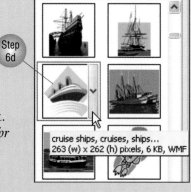

Step 6d

6. Format Slide 2 by completing the following steps:

a. Click Slide 2 at the Slides pane to display Slide 2.

b. Click Insert, point to Picture, and then click Clip Art.

c. At the Clip Art task pane, type **cruise** in the *Search for* text box and then click Go.

d. Scroll to locate the cruise ship used in the logo on Slide 1.

e. Click once on the ship picture **(j0205450.wmf)** to insert it.

f. Reduce the size of the ship logo to approximately 1 inch.

g. Click the Cut button on the Standard toolbar.

h. Hold down the Shift key and click the Normal View button to change to Slide Master view.

i. Paste the ship logo from the clipboard to Slide 2 in Slide Master view.

j. Position the logo similar to Figure 9.31.

k. Select *Click to edit Master title style* and change the font color to the beige color shown at the right.

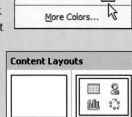

Step 6k

l. Click <u>V</u>iew and then <u>H</u>eader and Footer. Click to add a check mark next to *Slide <u>n</u>umber* and *Don't show on title <u>s</u>lide*. Deselect the <u>D</u>ate and time option and then click Apply to All.

m. Click the <u>C</u>lose Master View button on the Slide Master View toolbar.

n. Click F<u>o</u>rmat and then Slide <u>L</u>ayout.

o. Change the layout of Slide 2 to Title and Content.

p. Click the Insert Diagram or Organization Chart button.

q. At the Diagram Gallery dialog box, click the Organization Chart. Click OK.

Step 6o

r. Click the down-pointing arrow at the right of the Insert Shape button and then click <u>S</u>ubordinate twice (five subordinate shapes should display).

s. Click the <u>L</u>ayout button on the Organization Chart toolbar, click <u>L</u>eft Hanging, and then click Fit <u>T</u>ext on the Organization Chart toolbar.

t. Drag a corner sizing handle to increase the size of the organization chart and position it similar to Figure 9.31.

u. Click to select the placeholder *Click to add text* and then type the following:

> Bring with you:
> Cruise Ticket
> Guest Clearance Form
> Onboard Charge
> Proof of Citizenship
> Immigration Forms

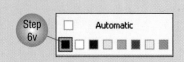

Step 6v

v. Select *Bring with you:* and change the font color to the background color shown at the right.

w. Add a gradient fill to the first box by clicking the down-pointing arrow at the right of the Fill Color button on the Drawing toolbar, clicking Fill Effects, selecting the Gradient tab, clicking *One color*, and then moving the Dark/Light slider to the right. Choose *Horizontal* in the *Shading styles* section. Click OK.

x. Use the Format Painter to change the font color and gradient in each of the chart boxes.

y. Click on Slide 3 from the Slides pane.

7. Format Slide 3 by completing the following steps:

a. Change the slide layout to Title, Text and Clip Art.

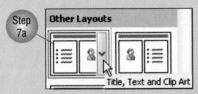

Step 7a

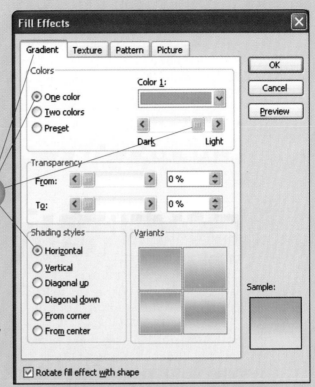

Step 6w

b. Double-click the *Insert Clip Art* icon in the slide layout.

c. At the Select Picture dialog box, type beach in the *Search text* box and then click Go. Double-click on the yellow flippers and mask photo **(j0177934.jpg)** shown at the right.

d. Click on Slide 4 from the Slides pane.

8. Format Slide 4 by completing the following steps:

a. Change the slide layout to Title and Content over Text.

b. Click the *Insert Clip Art* icon in the slide layout.

c. At the Select Picture dialog box, type watch in the *Search text* box and then click Go. Double-click on the watch **(j0208922.wmf)** shown at the right, and then rotate it slightly to the right.

d. Click Insert, point to Picture, and then click Clip Art to insert the other two clips as shown in Figure 9.31. Complete a search for *ring* **(j0283724.gif)** and then *chocolate* **(j0305487.wmf)**. Insert each image, size, and then position each image as shown in Figure 9.31.

e. Click on Slide 5 from the Slides pane.

9. Format Slide 5 by completing the following steps:

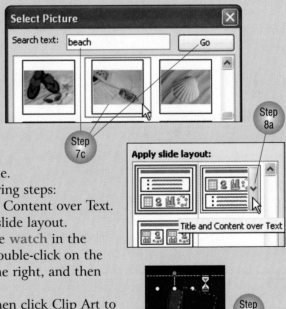

a. Change the slide layout to Title, 2 Content and Text.
b. Click the *Insert Clip Art* icon in the top left placeholder.
c. At the Select Picture dialog box, type beach in the *Search text* box and then click Go. Double-click on the sandals photo (**j0177933.jpg**) shown at the right.
d. Click the *Insert Clip Art* icon in the bottom left placeholder.
e. At the Select Picture dialog box, type fish at the *Search text* box and then click Go. Double-click on the fish photo (**j0262518.jpg**) shown at the right.

Step 9a

Step 9c

Step 9e

f. Click the Next Slide button.
10. Format Slide 6 by completing the following steps:
    a. Change the slide layout to Title and Table.

Step 10a

    b. Double-click the *Table* icon.
    c. At the Insert Table dialog box, change the number of columns to 4 and the number of rows to 9. Click OK.
    d. Adjust the column widths by positioning the insertion point on a borderline of a specific column and when the insertion point displays as a double-pointing arrow with a short vertical line between, click and drag the border line to the left or right to accommodate the text as shown in Figure 9.31. Type the following text, pressing Tab to advance to the next cell or Shift + Tab to go to a previous cell:

		Arrive	Depart
July 8	Ft. Lauderdale		5:00p
July 9	At Sea		
July 10	At Sea		
July 11	St. Maarten	8:00a	6:00p
July 12	St. Thomas	7:00a	5:00p
July 13	At Sea		
July 14	Nassau, Bahamas	11:00a	6:00p
July 15	Ft. Lauderdale	8:30a	

    e. Remove the border lines above and to the left and right of the column headlines *Arrive* and *Depart*. There should not be any top, left, or right border lines for this row.
    f. Merge the cells preceding *Arrive* and *Depart*. **(Hint: If necessary, drag the table to position it as shown in Figure 9.31.)** Right-align the *Arrive* and *Depart* columns.
11. Create Slide 7 using a picture background by completing the following steps:
    a. With the insertion point positioned in Slide 6, click the <u>N</u>ew Slide button.
    b. With the insertion point positioned in Slide 7, change the slide layout to Blank.
    c. Make sure Slide 7 is selected. Change the slide design to the Default Design.pot template by displaying the Slide Design task pane and then clicking the down-pointing arrow at the right of the default template (in the *Available For Use* section). At the pop-up menu, click the option to Apply to <u>S</u>elected Slides.

Step 11c

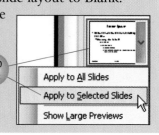

    d. Click F<u>o</u>rmat and then Bac<u>k</u>ground.

e. At the Background dialog box, click the down-pointing arrow at the right of the *Background fill* list box and then click <u>F</u>ill Effects. At the Fill Effects dialog box, select the Picture tab and then click the Select Picture button.

f. At the Select Picture dialog box, insert a tropical image photograph similar to the one shown in Figure 9.31. *(Hint: C:\Program Files\Microsoft Office\media\CntCd1\Photo1\j0177442.)*

g. At the Select Picture dialog box, click In<u>s</u>ert.

h. At the Fill Effects dialog box with the Picture tab selected, click the *Lock picture aspect ratio* option at the bottom of the box (this inserts a check mark) and then click OK.

i. At the Background dialog box, click <u>A</u>pply.

j. Create a WordArt object using the text *Book your cruise today!* Position the WordArt object as shown in Figure 9.31.

12. Recolor the ship in the logo shown on Slide 1 by completing the following steps:

a. Display Slide 1 in Normal view.

b. Click to select the logo at the top and center of Slide 1. Click D<u>r</u>aw and then click <u>U</u>ngroup. Click outside the logo.

c. Click to select the ship (the Picture toolbar should display) and then click the Recolor Picture button on the Picture toolbar.

d. At the Recolor Picture dialog box, click to insert a check mark next to the dark gray color in the *Original* column, click the down-pointing arrow to the right of the current color, and then click <u>M</u>ore Colors.

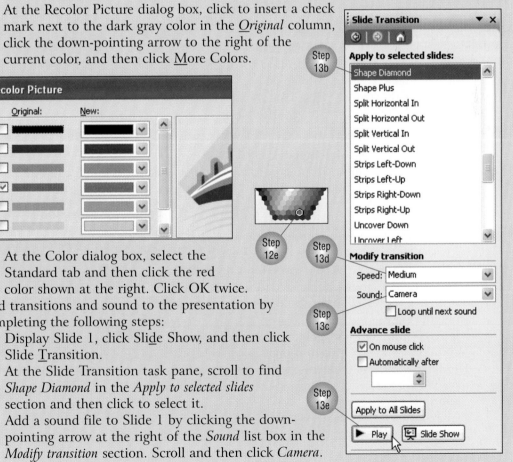

e. At the Color dialog box, select the Standard tab and then click the red color shown at the right. Click OK twice.

13. Add transitions and sound to the presentation by completing the following steps:

a. Display Slide 1, click Sli<u>d</u>e Show, and then click Slide <u>T</u>ransition.

b. At the Slide Transition task pane, scroll to find *Shape Diamond* in the *Apply to selected slides* section and then click to select it.

c. Add a sound file to Slide 1 by clicking the down-pointing arrow at the right of the *Sound* list box in the *Modify transition* section. Scroll and then click *Camera*.

d. Change the speed to *Medium*.

e. Click the Play button at the Slide Transition task pane to preview the sound and the transition.

f. Display Slide 2, scroll to find *Newsflash* in the *Apply to selected slides* section, and then click once to select it. Click Play to preview the transition.

g. Display Slide 3, scroll to find *Wheel Clockwise, 2 Spokes* in the *Apply to selected slides* section, and then click once to select it. Click the Play button to preview the transition.

h. Display Slide 4, then apply the *Box Out* transition.

i. Display Slide 5, then apply the *Comb Vertical* transition.

j. Display Slide 6, then apply the *Split Horizontal Out* transition. In the *Modify transition* section, click the down-pointing arrow at the right of *Sound* and select *Breeze*. Change the speed to *Medium*.

k. Display Slide 7, then apply the *Dissolve* transition and the *Chime* sound. Click Play to preview the transition and sound.

14. Set times for the slides to display during a slide show by completing the following steps:

a. Display the presentation in Slide Sorter view.

b. Click the Rehearse Timings button on the Slide Sorter toolbar.

c. The first slide displays in Slide Show view and the Rehearsal toolbar displays. Wait until the time displayed for the current slide reaches four seconds and then click Next. (If you miss the time, click the Repeat button to reset the clock back to zero for the current slide.)

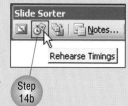

Step 14b

d. Set the times for the remaining slides as follows:

Slide 2 =	6 seconds
Slide 3 =	4 seconds
Slide 4 =	6 seconds
Slide 5 =	4 seconds
Slide 6 =	8 seconds
Slide 7 =	4 seconds

e. After the last slide has displayed, click Yes at the message asking if you want to record the new slide timings.

15. Set up the slide show to run continuously by completing the following steps:

a. Click Slide Show and then select Set Up Show.

b. At the Set Up Show dialog box, click the *Loop continuously until 'Esc'* check box.

c. Click OK to close the Set Up Show dialog box.

16. Click Slide 1 and then click the Slide Show button on the View bar. The slide show will start and run continuously. Watch the presentation until it has started for the second time and then end the show by pressing the Esc key.

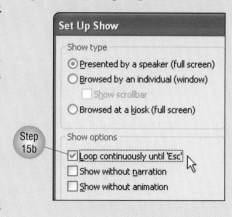

Step 15b

17. Save the presentation again as **c09ex03, Cruise** and then print the presentation as a handout with six slides per page (the presentation will take two sheets of paper with six slides on the first page and one slide on the second).

18. Close **c09ex03, Cruise**.

9.31 *Exercise 3 (Handout—6 slides per page)*

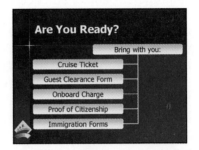

St. Thomas, U.S. Virgin Islands
- 60 miles east of Puerto Rico
- 32 square miles
- Snorkeling, sailing, swimming
- Bargain-shopping bazaar
  - Jewelry, linens, perfume, electronics

St. Maarten
- 144 miles east of St. Thomas
- Dutch side—16 square miles/French side—21 square miles
- Approximately 500 duty-free shops
  - Jewelry, watches, liqueur, Belgian chocolate

Nassau, Bahamas
- 50 miles off coast of Florida
- 21 miles long and 7 miles wide
- Straw market, modern hotels, shops, and restaurants
- White sand beaches

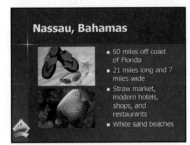

Travel Itinerary

		Arrive	Depart
July 8	Ft. Lauderdale		5:00p
July 9	At Sea		
July 10	At Sea		
July 11	St. Maarten	8:00a	6:00p
July 12	St. Thomas	7:00a	5:00p
July 13	At Sea		
July 14	Nassau, Bahamas	11:00a	6:00p
July 15	Ft. Lauderdale	8:30a	

Adding Animation Effects to a Presentation

DTP POINTERS
To
remove an
animation effect,
click the animation
item in the Custom
Animation task
pane list box, and
then click the
Remove button.

To apply custom animations such as builds, display the presentation in Normal view, select the slide(s), and click Custom Animation at the Slide Show menu or display the Custom Animation task pane as shown in Figure 9.32 where you may add different animated effects for an entrance. In addition, you may choose numerous animation effects for emphasis, when exiting, or for movement according to a path, as shown in Figure 9.33. Figure 9.34 illustrates a build technique where the title appears as the first build entering the slide from the top of the screen and the ship clip art appears as the second build moving from the left upper corner to the bottom right corner following a path that has been drawn by the originator of the presentation.

FIGURE

9.32 *Custom Animation Task Pane with a List of Entrance Effects Displayed*

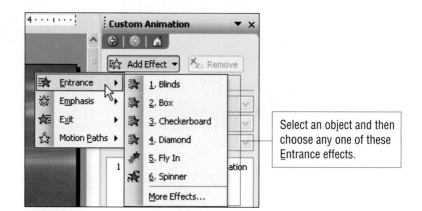

Select an object and then choose any one of these Entrance effects.

9.33 *Adding a Motion Path Custom Animation to a Clip Art Image*

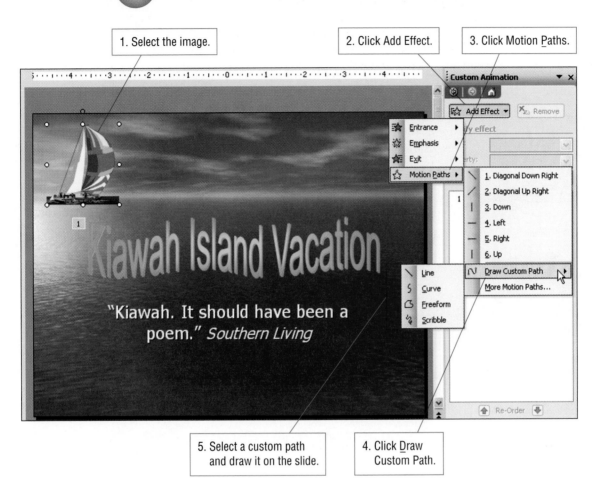

1. Select the image.

2. Click Add Effect.

3. Click Motion Paths.

5. Select a custom path and draw it on the slide.

4. Click Draw Custom Path.

9.34 *Custom Animation—Creating Two Builds*

First Build: Title will fly in.

Path can be locked, unlocked, or reversed.

Click to remove build.

Change speed from very slow to very fast.

List of builds are in order.

Second Build: Ship will follow path from green arrow to red arrow.

To select slides out of sequence, use the Ctrl key in conjunction with the mouse; to select slides in sequence, use the Shift key. Complete Exercise 4 to practice applying these slide enhancements.

Animation effects may be added to a presentation by using various features in PowerPoint. You may access commands from the Slide Show menu, click the Animation Schemes hyperlink at the Slide Design task pane in the *Animation* section, or display the Custom Animation task pane. Some of the animation schemes include *Faded zoom, Unfold, Spin,* and *Boomerang* and exit.

Customizing a Build

Build

A feature that displays information (usually bulleted items) a little at a time.

The preset animation scheme automatically creates a ***build*** with objects on the slide. A build displays important points on a slide one point at a time, and is useful for keeping the audience's attention focused on the point being presented rather than reading ahead.

You can further customize the build in the animation scheme by causing a previous point to dim when the next point is displayed on the slide. To customize an animation scheme, click Slide Show on the Menu bar and then click Custom Animation at the drop-down list. This displays the Custom Animation task pane, as shown in Figure 9.35 and as explained earlier.

To add a dim effect to bulleted items, you would click the object box containing the bulleted text and then click the Add Effect button located toward the top of the Custom Animation task pane. At the drop-down list that displays, point to Entrance, and then click the desired effect in the side menu. This causes a box to display in the Custom Animation task pane list box containing a number, an image or a mouse, and a down-pointing arrow. Click the down-pointing arrow and then click *Effect Options* at the drop-down list. At the dialog box that displays, click the down-pointing arrow at the right of the *After animation* option box and then click the desired color.

DTP POINTERS
Add a build to bulleted items to focus attention on one item at a time.

FIGURE

9.35 *Creating a Build*

Click the left mouse to initiate the build.

Bulleted items appear from bottom of slide.

Level 1 Build

Level 2 Build

Level 3 Build

Using Print Screen

Occasionally, you may want to illustrate a command or feature by showing your audience a picture of what your screen will look like. Displaying the exact screen is an effective way of visually demonstrating a feature. If you would like to capture a picture of your document screen and insert it in a PowerPoint slide as shown in Figure 9.36, you can do so by completing the following steps:

1. Set up your document window exactly as you would like it to look.
2. Press the Print Screen button on your keyboard (top row to the right of the function keys).
3. A copy of the screen is sent to the Clipboard. If you display the Clipboard task pane, you will see a thumbnail of your screen capture.
4. Select a desired slide layout (you may prefer to use the Title Only slide layout).
5. Position the insertion point in the slide and then press the Paste button on the Standard toolbar or click once on the thumbnail in the Clipboard task pane.
6. You may use the buttons on the Picture toolbar to adjust your captured image. If you choose to delete the picture, select it, and then press the Delete key.

FIGURE

9.36 *Using Print Screen*

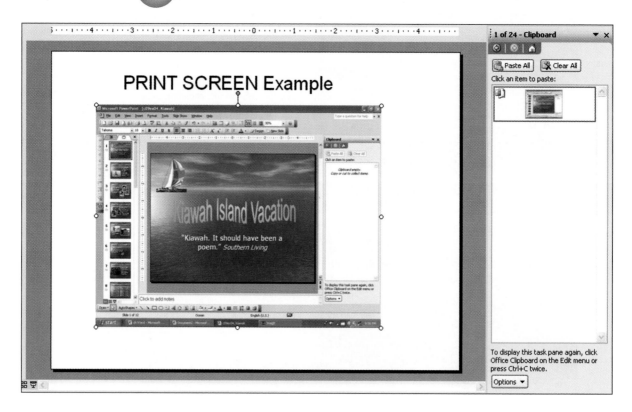

Adding Action Buttons

Action buttons are drawn objects placed on the slide that, when activated, will perform a specific action. For instance, an action button can advance to a specific slide, file, or location on the Web. When inserting action buttons, click the AutoShapes button on the Drawing toolbar, select Action Buttons from the pop-up menu, and then apply the appropriate settings. Or, click Slide Show from the

Menu bar and then click Action Buttons. When the presenter moves the mouse over an action button, the pointer changes to a hand with an index finger, indicating that if you click the mouse some form of action will take place.

Using Hyperlinks

You can enrich your presentation by inserting hyperlinks. A hyperlink can take you to a location within the same document, a different document, or a location on the Web. You can even use hyperlinks to advance to multimedia files, such as sounds or videos. To add a hyperlink, click Insert and then Hyperlink or click the Insert Hyperlink button on the Standard toolbar.

Insert Hyperlink

Adding Media Clips

To achieve a full multimedia effect, you can include media clips (movies and sounds) to your presentation. PowerPoint can play a clip automatically or you can play the clip on demand using the mouse. Use of these features requires your computer system to have a sound card and speakers. Media clips are inserted, resized, moved, and copied in the same way as any other image. To add a movie or sound, click Insert, Movies and Sounds, and then select Movie from Clip Organizer, Movie from File, Sound from Clip Organizer, Sound from File, Play CD Audio Track, or Record Sound.

Inserting a Word Table, Excel Workbook, Animation Effects,
Builds, and Hyperlinks in a PowerPoint Presentation

1. Open **Kiawah.ppt** located in your Chapter09 folder.
2. Save the presentation using Save As and name it **c09ex04, Kiawah**.
3. Apply a design template to the presentation by completing the following steps:
   a. Click the Slide Design button on the Formatting toolbar to open the Slide Design task pane.
   b. Scroll down the list of design templates, and then click *Ocean.pot*.
4. Display Slide 1 in the Slide pane (Normal view). Format Slide 1 by completing the following steps:
   a. Click Slide Show and then click Custom Animation.

Step 3b

b. Select *Kiawah Island Vacation* (white handles should display around the WordArt text) and then at the Custom Animation task pane, click the Add Effect button, point to <u>E</u>ntrance, and then click <u>5</u>. Fly In. *(Hint: The order of the effects may vary.)*

c. Change the *Direction* option to *From Top* and change the *Speed* option to *Fast*. *(Hint: You should now see the first build or item displayed in the list below the Direction and Speed options.)*

d. Select "Kiawah. It should have been a poem." *Southern Living*, click the Add Effect button, point to <u>E</u>ntrance, and then click <u>4</u>. Diamond.

e. Change the *Speed* option to *Medium*. *(Hint: You should now see the second build in the animation list.)*

f. Select the sailboat image, which is to the left of Slide 1, click the Add Effect button, point to Motion <u>P</u>aths, click <u>D</u>raw Custom Path, and then click <u>S</u>cribble.

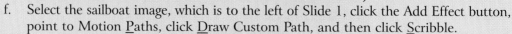

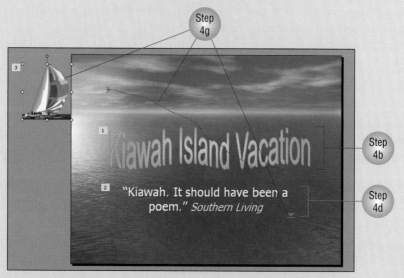

g. Drag the pen pointer from the sailboat to the lower right corner of the slide. Change the speed to *Very Slow*. *(Hint: When you release the mouse, the path will display as a green arrow, a dotted path, and a red arrow. You will also see the third build display in the animation list.)*

h. Click the Play button to preview the build sequence. *(Hint: Practice some of the different effects and motions.)*

i. Click the Next Slide button to display Slide 2.

5. Format Slide 2 by completing the following steps:

a. Select *Why take a vacation on Kiawah?* and then right-click to access Custo<u>m</u> Animation at the shortcut menu. *(Hint: If the shortcut menu does not display, click Sli<u>d</u>e Show and then Custo<u>m</u> Animation.)*

b. With the title selected, click the Add Effect button, point to <u>E</u>ntrance, click <u>M</u>ore Effects, and then click *Spinner* in the *Moderate* category. Click OK.

c. Click the sun image, which is above Slide 2, click the Add Effect button, point to Motion <u>P</u>aths, click <u>D</u>raw Custom Path, and then click <u>L</u>ine.

d. Drag the crosshairs downward from the bottom of the sun to the top of the beach picture.

e. Select the beach picture, click the Add Effect button, point to <u>E</u>ntrance, and then click <u>5</u>. Fly In.

f. Select the bulleted items (white sizing handles will display around the frame surrounding the items).

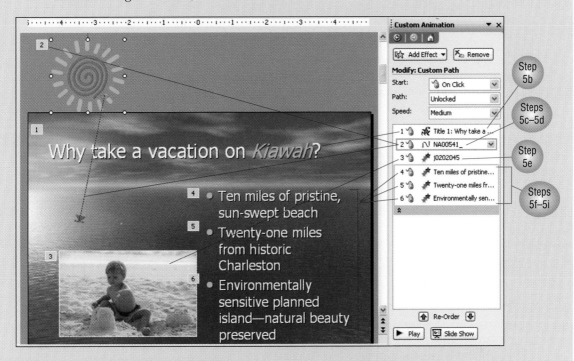

g. Click the Add Effect button, point to <u>E</u>ntrance, and then click <u>5</u>. Fly In. Leave the direction *From Bottom*, but change the speed to *Medium*.

h. Click the down-pointing arrow at the right of the fourth item in the animation list and then click <u>E</u>ffect Options.

i. At the Fly In dialog box, in the *Enhancements* section, click the down-pointing arrow at the right of *<u>A</u>fter animation*. At the drop-down menu, click the last blue color on the palette. Click OK. *(Hint: This will dim the bulleted items to the blue color.)*

j. Click the Next Slide button to display Slide 3.

6. Format Slides 3 and 4 by completing the following steps:

a. Click the Slides tab at the Outline/Slides pane.

b. Click Slide 3 and then hold down the Shift key and click to select Slide 4 at the Slides tab. *(Hint: A dark blue border line will display around each selected slide.)*

c. Click the Slide Design button and then, at the Slide Design task pane, click the <u>Animation Schemes</u> hyperlink.

d. Click the *Faded zoom* option in the *Subtle* section of the *Apply to selected slides* list.

e. Click the Next Slide button to display Slide 5.

7. a. Display the Slide Design task pane and then click the <u>Animation Schemes</u> hyperlink if necessary.

b. With Slide 5 displayed in the Slide pane, click *Ellipse motion* in the *Exciting* category in the *Apply to selected slides* list.

c. Select the picture with the bridge in Slide 5, display the Custom Animation task pane, click the Add Effect button, point to Entrance, and then click 2. Box.

d. Select the picture of a house in Slide 5, and at the Custom Animation task pane, click Add Effect, point to Entrance, and then click 2. Box.

e. Move the fourth and fifth build below the title by clicking the up-pointing arrow at the left of the Re-order option. (The builds should display as shown at the right.)

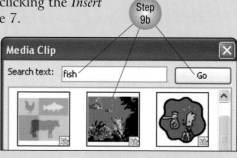

Step 7f

0	○	Title 1: World class …
1	⇗	mso50D24
2	⇗	msoADB6C
3	✳	Island Inn
4	✳	Villas and Cottages
5	✳	Homes

f. Click the Next Slide button to display Slide 6.

8. Format Slide 6 by completing the following steps:

a. With Slide 6 displayed in the Slide pane, apply the *Show in reverse* animation theme in the *Moderate* section of the Slide Design task pane, Animation Schemes.

b. Click the Other Task Panes button and then click the Clip Art task pane.

c. Insert a clip art image from the Microsoft Office Online Clip Art and Media Web site by clicking the <u>Clip art on Office Online</u> hyperlink (make sure you are connected to the Internet).

d. Type magnolia in the *Search* text box and then click Go.

e. Insert a magnolia image by right-clicking an image of your choice and then clicking Copy. Return to your presentation, position the insertion point where the magnolia should be inserted, and then click the Paste button. Click the D<u>r</u>aw button on the Drawing toolbar, click O<u>r</u>der, and click Send <u>B</u>ackward. Size and position the image similar to Figure 9.37.

f. Click the Next Slide button.

9. Format Slide 7 by completing the following steps:

a. Add an animated GIF image to this slide by clicking the *Insert Media Clip* icon in the Content frame of Slide 7.

b. At the Media Clip dialog box, type fish in the *Search text* box, and then click Go. Click the aquarium clip (**j0300492.gif**) shown at the right. Click OK.

c. Size and position the clip as shown in Figure 9.37.

d. Apply the *Pinwheel* animation theme found in the *Exciting* category at the Slide Design task pane, Animation Schemes.

e. Click the Next Slide button.

10. Save the presentation again with the Save button on the Standard toolbar.

11. Copy a Word table into Slide 8 by completing the following steps:

a. Open Microsoft Word.

b. Open **Kiawah Temperature.doc** located in your Chapter09 folder.

c. Position the insertion point inside the table and then click T<u>a</u>ble on the Menu bar, point to Sele<u>c</u>t, and then click <u>T</u>able.

d. Click the Copy button on the Standard toolbar.

e. Close the Word document and then exit Word.

f. Click the button on the Taskbar representing PowerPoint.

g. Make sure Slide 8 displays in the Slide pane.

h. Click the Paste button on the Standard toolbar.

i. Position the table similar to Figure 9.37.

j. Apply the *Faded zoom* animation scheme located in the *Subtle* category at the Slide Design task pane, Animation Schemes to Slide 8.

k.   Click the Next Slide button.
12. Format Slide 9 by completing the following steps:
  a.   Read the instructions within this slide.
  b.   Create hyperlinks from the Web sites given in the slide by completing the
       following steps. (Make sure you are connected to the Internet.)
       1) Select *www.expedia.com* and then click the Insert Hyperlink button on the
           Standard toolbar.
       2) At the Insert Hyperlink dialog box, make sure the E̲xisting File or Web Page
           button is selected in the *Link to* section, *http://www.expedia.com/* displays in the
           Address text box, and the text *www.expedia.com* displays in the T̲ext to display text
           box. Click OK.

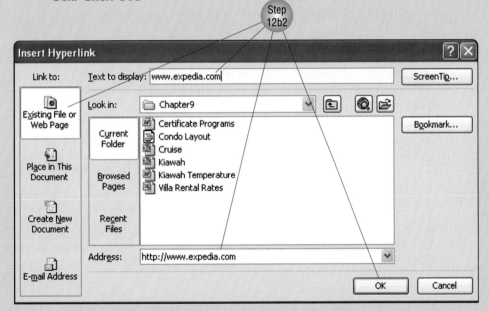

       3) Create hyperlinks for the remaining Web sites given in Slide 9 by following
           the directions in Steps 12b1 and 12b2.
  c.   Find a map on one of the Web sites, right-click on the Web picture, and then click
       Save Picture As from the shortcut menu that displays. Save the map to your
       Chapter09 folder as **Kiawah Map**. Insert the map by pasting or by clicking I̲nsert,
       pointing to P̲icture, and then clicking F̲rom File. Size and position the map as
       necessary.
  d.   Display the Slide Design task pane and apply the *Ellipse* motion found in the *Exciting*
       category of the *Applied to selected slides* list of the Slide Design task pane, Animation
       Schemes.
  e.   Click the Next Slide button.
13. Format Slide 10 by completing the following steps:
  a.   Display Slide 10 in the Slide pane.
  b.   Insert a bitmap image by clicking I̲nsert, pointing to P̲icture, and then clicking
       F̲rom File.
  c.   At the Insert Picture dialog box, locate the **Condo Layout.bmp** file in your
       Chapter09 folder. Click In̲sert.
  d.   Size and position the image as shown in Figure 9.37. *(Hint: Resize the placeholder
       if necessary.)*
  e.   Apply the *Boomerang and exit* animation scheme to Slide 10.
  f.   Click the Next Slide button.

14. Insert an Excel worksheet in Slide 11 by completing the following steps:
    a. Open Microsoft Excel.
    b. Open the worksheet named **Villa Rental Rates.xls** located in your Chapter09 folder.
    c. Copy the workbook to the Clipboard by selecting Columns A and B along with rows 1 through 26 and then clicking the Copy button on the Standard toolbar.
    d. Do not close the Excel workbook or exit Excel.
    e. Click the button on the Taskbar representing PowerPoint.
    f. Display Slide 11 in the Slide pane.
    g. Click Edit and then Paste Special.
    h. In the Paste Special dialog box, make sure *Microsoft Office Excel Worksheet Object* is selected in the <u>A</u>s list box, and then click OK.

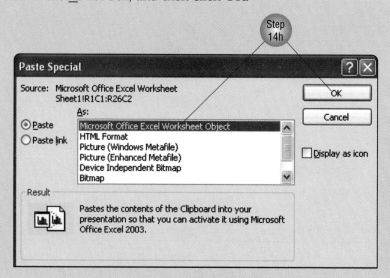

    i. Select the worksheet object, and then click the down-pointing arrow at the right of the Fill Color button on the Drawing toolbar and add a White fill to the worksheet. Reposition the object if necessary to look similar to Figure 9.37.
    j. Display the Slide Design task pane and apply the *Dissolve in* animation scheme in the *Subtle* category of the Slide Design task pane, Animation Schemes.
    k. Close **Villa Rental Rates.xls** and then close Excel.
    l. Click the Next Slide button.
15. Format Slide 12 by applying the *Neutron* animation scheme in the *Exciting* section of the Slide Design – Animation Schemes.
16. Save the presentation again with the same name **c09ex04, Kiawah**.
17. ***Optional:*** Add a sound clip to the entire presentation by completing the following steps:
    a. Display Slide 1 in the Slide pane.
    b. Click <u>I</u>nsert, point to Mo<u>v</u>ies and Sounds, and then click <u>S</u>ound from Clip Organizer, Sound from File, or Play CD Audio Track. Select a sound file of your own choosing.
    c. Display the Custom Animation task pane, click the down-pointing arrow at the right of the sound item, and then click <u>E</u>ffect Options.

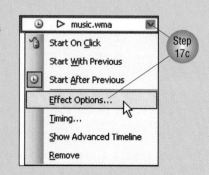

d. At the Play Sound dialog box, click the *From beginning* option in the *Start playing* section and the *After* option in the *Stop playing* section, and then type 12 in the *slides* text box. Click OK.

18. Run the presentation by clicking the Show Slide button on the View bar. *(Hint: The effects, transitions, and animations are advanced by clicking the left mouse button.)*

19. *Optional:* Add Rehearsed Timings to the slides and run the presentation again.

20. Save, print the presentation with six slides per page, and then close **c09ex04, Kiawah**.

F I G U R E

9.37 *Exercise 4 (Handout—6 slides per page)*

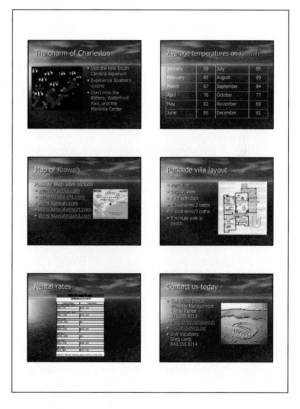

Saving a PowerPoint Presentation as a Web Page

PowerPoint can translate the slides in your presentation to HTML so the presentation can be viewed on the Internet. To do this, open the presentation you want to convert to HTML, click File, and then click Save as Web Page. At the Save As dialog box, the name in the *File name* text box will default to the presentation file name (with the extension .htm). Also, the *Save as type* option defaults to *Single File Web Page*.

When PowerPoint converts the presentation to HTML format, navigation buttons are created for users to navigate through the slides in the Web browser.

If you want to see how the presentation displays in your Web browser, view the presentation in Web Page Preview. To do this, click File, and then click Web Page Preview. If you want to set options for viewing your Web presentation, click File, Save As Web Page, and then click the Publish button. At the Publish as Web Page dialog box, you may choose to present a few slides instead of the entire presentation, select a different browser, alter the navigation controls, and resize graphics to fit the browser window.

Using Pack and Go

The safest way to transport a PowerPoint presentation to another computer to do a slide show is to use PowerPoint's Package for CD. The Package for CD will bundle a presentation onto a file or CD including all of the linked files, fonts used, and the PowerPoint Viewer program in case the destination computer does not have PowerPoint installed on it. To start the process, click File and then Package for CD. Specify whether the presentation will be played automatically (Autorun) when inserted into a Windows computer.

CHAPTER summary

➤ A presentation communicates information using visual images to convey the message to an audience.
➤ When choosing a presentation design for slides, consider the audience, the topic, and the method of delivery.
➤ Selecting a visual medium depends on many factors: the topic, your presentation style, audience size, location, equipment availability, lighting conditions, and so on.
➤ Many buttons on PowerPoint's Standard toolbar remain consistent with Word and other Microsoft applications.
➤ Text in a slide is positioned in an object box. Use the sizing handles to increase and/or decrease the size of the box.
➤ Rearrange slides within a presentation in Slide Sorter view or in Normal view with the Slides tab selected in the Outline/Slides pane.
➤ To see how a presentation will look when printed, display the presentation in Print Preview.
➤ A PowerPoint presentation can be created by using the Blank Presentation screen, design templates, and the AutoContent Wizard.
➤ PowerPoint's AutoContent Wizard provides helpful information on planning and organizing a presentation based on the topic and purpose of the presentation.
➤ Slide layouts contain placeholders where specific text or objects are inserted. Placeholders format a title, bulleted list, clip art, media clip, chart, organizational chart, diagram, table, or object.

- Click the <u>N</u>ew Slide button on the Formatting toolbar to insert a new slide in a presentation.
- If you want changes made to a placeholder to affect all slides in a presentation, make the changes at the Slide Master.
- PowerPoint provides viewing options for presentations that include Normal view, Slide Sorter view, Slide Show, and Notes Page.
- Slides in a slide show can be advanced manually or automatically at specific time intervals, or a slide show can be set up to run continuously.
- Transition refers to what action takes place as one slide is removed from the screen during a presentation and the next slide is displayed.
- Preparing a presentation using the Outline tab in the Outline/Slides pane helps to organize topics for each slide without the distractions of colorful designs, clip art, transitions, or sound. It is a good view to use when brainstorming the creation of a presentation.
- Sound effects and animation create impact in a slide show.
- You can use a pen to mark your slides.
- PowerPoint's build technique displays important points one at a time on a slide.
- If you are creating a long presentation with many slides and text, use the Outline tab in the Outline/Slides pane to organize the topics for the slides.
- You can create an outline in PowerPoint, or import an outline from another program, such as Microsoft Word.
- Create an action button by clicking the A<u>u</u>toShapes button on the Drawing toolbar, pointing to Act<u>i</u>on Buttons, and then clicking the desired category and button. Drag in the slide to create the button.
- If you are not satisfied with a color scheme, you can change the scheme of colors in the background, and add text, lines, shadows, pictures, and so on.
- The background of a presentation should correlate to the visual medium that you are using. You may create a picture background that fills the entire slide.
- You can change the order of your slides in the Slide Sorter view.
- To better organize delivery of your presentation, you can create a summary slide at the beginning or closing of your presentation to highlight the main topics to be discussed.
- A build is an effective way to keep your audiences' attention on the topic under discussion, instead of reading the remainder of the slide.
- Drawing objects include AutoShapes, curves, lines, and WordArt objects and are accessible from the Drawing toolbar.
- Use buttons on the Drawing toolbar to draw a variety of shapes and lines and to apply formatting to a drawn object.
- Format a clip art image with buttons on the Picture toolbar.
- The Microsoft Office Online Clip Art and Media Web site is an online source for a variety of pictures, sounds, and motion clips.
- When you insert movies and sound files to your slides, PowerPoint inserts a small icon on the slide. If you do not want the icon to be noticeable, set the file to play automatically, and then drag the icon off the slide.
- Animation schemes apply a set of animation effects and transitions between slides in your presentation.
- Action buttons are drawn objects placed on the slide that, when activated, will perform a specific action.
- Presentation materials often include handouts for the audience.

➤ In PowerPoint 2003, you can insert predesigned diagrams using tools on the Drawing toolbar. Use the diagrams to illustrate various conceptual information and enliven documents and presentations.

➤ Grids and guides may be used to help position objects on a slide.

➤ Presentations can be printed with each slide on a separate piece of paper; with each slide at the top of a page, leaving room for notes; with all or a specific number of slides on a single piece of paper; or with slide titles and topics in outline form.

➤ Adding tables and charts is an excellent way to show important information about relationships among groups of data.

➤ Sound and/or video effects that will play as the presentation runs can be added. You can configure a sound or video object to play continuously until the slide show is ended.

➤ You can create a custom motion path that lets you control where an object will move.

➤ Microsoft's Package for CD feature allows you to compress your presentation and run it from a computer that does not have PowerPoint loaded on it. It includes a mini-application called PowerPoint Viewer.

COMMANDS review

Command	Mouse/Keyboard
Display Slide Design task pane	Slide Design button on Formatting toolbar
Display Slide Layout task pane	Format and then Slide Layout
Insert a new slide	New Slide button on Formatting toolbar
Display Print dialog box	File and then Print
Close a presentation	File and then Close
Display Open dialog box	Open button on Standard toolbar or click File and then Open
Import Word outline	Insert, Slides from Outline
Export presentation to Word	File, Send To, Microsoft Office Word
Run a presentation	Slide Show button on View bar; or click Slide Show button in Slide Transition task pane; or Slide Show, View Show
Display Slide Transition task pane	Slide Transition button on Slide Sorter toolbar; or Other Task Panes button; or Slide Show, Slide Transition
Begin AutoContent Wizard	From AutoContent wizard hyperlink in the New Presentation task pane
Create summary slide	Select slides to be included, then click Summary Slide button on Slide Sorter toolbar or click Slide Summary button on the Outlining toolbar
Display Outlining toolbar	View, Toolbars, Outlining
Display color scheme options	Color Schemes hyperlink in Slide Design task pane
Display Edit Color Scheme dialog box	Edit Color Schemes hyperlink in Slide Design task pane with color scheme options displayed
Display Background dialog box	Format, Background

Display Bullets and Numbering	Format, Bullets and Numbering dialog box
Display Header and Footer dialog box	View, Header and Footer
Display Insert Clip Art task pane	Insert Clip Art button on Drawing toolbar; or click Insert, Picture, Clip Art
Display Select Picture dialog box	Fill Color on Drawing toolbar, Fill Effects, click Picture tab, Select Picture
Display Recolor Picture dialog box	Recolor Picture button on Picture toolbar
Display Insert Picture dialog box	Insert, Picture, From File
Display animation schemes	Slide Show, Animation Schemes; or click Animation Schemes hyperlink in Slide Design task pane
Display Custom Animation task pane	Slide Show, Custom Animation
Display WordArt Gallery	Insert WordArt button on Drawing toolbar or in Content placeholder; or click Insert, Picture, WordArt
Display Diagram Gallery	Insert Diagram or Organization Chart button on Drawing toolbar or in Content placeholder; or click Insert, Diagram
Display Clipboard task pane	Edit, Office Clipboard; or click Other Task Panes button on task pane, then click Clipboard
Display action buttons	AutoShapes, Action Buttons
Packaging a presentation for use on other computers	File, Package for CD
Save as a Web page	File, Save as Web Page
Preview Web page	File, Web Page Preview
Display Slide Master	Normal View button while holding down Shift key

REVIEWING key points

True/False: On a blank sheet of paper, write *True* if the statement is true and *False* if the statement is false.

1. PowerPoint templates contain placeholders where specific text or objects are inserted.
2. Slide animation refers to how one slide is removed from the screen and replaced with the next slide.
3. Watermarks will not display on slides.
4. If you want changes made to placeholders to affect all slides in a presentation, make the changes at the Slide Master.
5. Click the Draw button on the Drawing toolbar to display a pop-up menu that contains the action button options.
6. At Slide Sorter view, the slide fills the entire screen.
7. A slide layout format may contain a table placeholder.
8. The Recolor Picture button is found on the Drawing toolbar.
9. To run a presentation, click Format and then Slide Show.

10. You can rearrange slides in Slide Sorter view.

11. Copy a slide by holding down the Shift key while dragging the slide.

12. Add a picture background to a slide by clicking the Insert Clip Art button on the Drawing toolbar.

13. Display the Slide Master view by holding the Ctrl key while clicking the Normal View button on the View bar.

14. Click the Esc key to stop a presentation in a continuous loop.

Completion: On a blank sheet of paper, indicate the correct term, symbol, or command for each item.

1. Display this task pane to create builds and animate text and objects for a slide show.

2. Click this view to display several slides on a screen at one time.

3. Use this view to run a presentation.

4. This feature contains formatting that gives each slide in a presentation identical properties.

5. Use this to display important points on a slide one point at a time.

6. With the Outline tab selected at the Outline/Slides pane, click this button on the Outlining toolbar to move the insertion point to the next tab stop.

7. To display the Slide Transition task pane, click this command on the Menu bar, and then click Slide Transition.

8. Insert information you want to appear at the top or bottom of a slide with options from this dialog box.

9. Display additional color schemes for a design template by clicking this hyperlink in the Slide Design task pane.

10. Click Slide Show and then Animation Schemes and preset animation schemes display in this task pane.

APPLYING your skills

Assessment 1

You work for a travel vacation company named Paradise Vacations that specializes in selling vacation package plans to tropical locations. The company is setting up a display booth at a travel trade show. You need to create an electronic slide show to run continuously in your booth. Your target audience is travel consultants who sell vacation package plans to their clients. Your goal is to inform your audience of the travel plan benefits your company can offer to their travel clients, thereby motivating the travel consultants to promote vacation packages when selling travel plans to their clients. Using the text from Figure 9.38, create an on-screen presentation in PowerPoint according to the following specifications:

1. Use a Blank Presentation screen, a design template, the AutoContent Wizard, or a template from the Microsoft Office Online Templates and customize it to complement your presentation. *(Hint: Photographs make dramatic backgrounds.)*
2. Use the text in Figure 9.38 to create your slides. Edit the text to fit your needs.

3. Use several slide layouts to vary the look of your presentation.
4. Apply an appropriate design template.
5. Add any appropriate clip art, animated clips, movies, or photographs.
6. Use a build effect for the bulleted items. You decide on the bullet symbol to be used.
7. Apply transition effects to your slides.
8. Time the slides to change every five seconds.
9. Make the slide show a continuous on-screen presentation.
10. Save the presentation and name it **c09sa01, Paradise**.
11. Run the on-screen presentation for a classmate or your instructor.
12. Print and then close **c09sa01, Paradise**. *(Note: Check with your instructor about printing this presentation. One suggestion is to print six slides per page in black and white to save on paper and printer ink.)*

Optional: Add animation and sound effects to your Paradise presentation.

F I G U R E

9.38 *Paradise Vacations Text*

Paradise Vacations, specializing in tropical vacations, offers more than 35 fabulous vacation destinations. You can select from over 225 hotels, resorts, condos, and villas at some of the most popular destinations in the Caribbean, Mexico, the Bahamas, Bermuda, Florida, and Hawaii. Choose from a range of moderate to luxurious accommodations, including several all-inclusive vacation properties.

Departing from over 50 U.S. cities, Paradise Vacations is one of the nation's leading vacation companies. We offer value, quality, variety, reliability, and superior service. Paradise vacations include roundtrip airfare, hotel accommodations, roundtrip airport-hotel transfers, hotel taxes, hotel service charges and surcharges, and the services of a Paradise representative at your destination.

Your Paradise representative is professionally trained, friendly, and reliable. Your representative will direct you to your airport-hotel transfer, acquaint you with your destination, arrange optional excursions, and answer your questions.

Our own Hotel Rating Guide helps you to select the accommodations that best fit your needs. Ratings are based on property location, cleanliness, amenities, service, and room quality.

We offer a free Price Protection Guarantee. Sometimes the price of a vacation package plan changes. We guarantee that once your balance is paid in full, we will not increase the price of your vacation. In addition, we periodically offer special promotion prices on vacation package plans. If we advertise a discounted price on the exact same vacation you have booked, you will automatically receive the savings.

Travel with Paradise and travel with the best! Contact your travel consultant for vacation packages and ask for Paradise Vacations!

Assessment 2

Use the AutoContent Wizard to create a certificate by completing the following steps: *(Hint: This presentation is also available at the Microsoft Online Templates Web site.)*

1. Display the New Presentation task pane.
2. Click the <u>From AutoContent wizard</u> hyperlink in the *New* section.
3. At the Start screen, click <u>N</u>ext.
4. At the Presentation type screen, click the <u>A</u>ll button.
5. Scroll through the list of presentation types, click *Certificate* from the list, and then click <u>N</u>ext.
6. At the Presentation style screen, click *On-screen presentation*, and then click <u>N</u>ext.
7. At the Presentation options screen, deselect all of the options, and then click <u>N</u>ext.
8. At the Finish screen, click <u>F</u>inish.
9. Choose one of the certificates for customizing.
10. Display either the Certificate of Excellence or the Certificate of Completion in Normal view.
11. At the Outline/Slides pane, select the *company name* placeholder and type the name of your school, select the placeholder *name here* and type your name, select the *Project Name* or *Course Name* placeholder and type your project name or course name and number, and then type your instructor's name and title in the placeholder at the bottom of the form.
12. Delete the unused slides and then save the certificate as a design template and name it **c09sa02, Certificate.pot**.
13. Print the certificate as a slide and then close.

Assessment 3

1. Create a presentation based on the text shown in Figure 9.39. You determine the template and the layout.
2. Insert appropriate transitions, clip art, photographs, backgrounds, and so on.
3. After creating the presentation, save it on the hard drive or a floppy disk and name it **c09sa03, Telephone**.
4. Print and then close **c09sa03, Telephone**. (Check with your instructor about printing this presentation. One suggestion is to print six slides per page.)

F I G U R E

9.39 *Assessment 3*

Slide 1	Title	=	**Telephone Techniques**
	Subtitle		**You have less than 10 seconds to make your first impression!**
Slide 2	Title	=	**Answering Calls**
	Bullets		**Answer on first or second ring**
			Use a pleasant voice
			Identify company and office the caller has reached
			If it is a direct line, identify yourself

Continued on next page

Slide 3	Title	=	Directing the Call
	Bullets		Gather information from the caller
			Handle the request or forward call
			Retrieve information and place call on hold or offer to call back

Slide 4	Title	=	Taking Messages
	Bullets		Use the 3 W's
			Who is to be called back?
			When is the best time to return the call?
			What information is the caller seeking?
			Write clearly and concisely
			Use message form

Slide 5	Title	=	Terminating the Call
	Bullets		Verify information in the message
			Thank caller and ensure follow-up on message
			Give time frame when caller can expect to be called back
			Allow caller to hang up first

Assessment 4

1. Create a presentation based on the text shown in Figure 9.40. You determine the design. After creating the presentation, save it on the hard drive or a floppy disk and name it **c09sa04, The Cellular Connection.ppt**.

INTEGRATED

2. Insert appropriate transitions, clip art, photographs, and backgrounds.
3. Create and type the six slides as shown below.
4. Research historical facts from the Internet for Slide 2. Some suggested Web sites may include the local carriers shown on Slide 4, or complete the search using your favorite search engine.
5. Open **c09sa04, Phone Survey Results.xls** from Microsoft Office Excel. *The Class Survey* on Slide 6 will include the three charts from this worksheet. Each chart is located on a separate sheet.
   a. To add the charts onto Slide 6, be sure your insertion point is located in the *No. of Cell Phones* sheet and then select the *Cell Phone Ownership* chart. Click the Copy button on the Standard toolbar.
   b. Return to **c09sa04, The Cellular Connection.ppt** in PowerPoint by clicking on the file in the Taskbar. Position your insertion point in Slide 6 and paste the chart by clicking Edit, Paste Special, As: Microsoft Office Excel Chart Object, and then click OK. Readjust the chart to fit on the slide.
   c. Click on **c09sa04, Phone Survey Results.xls** in the Taskbar to return to the worksheet. Click on the *Carrier* sheet and select and copy the chart *Local Carrier Usage* to the Clipboard. Follow Steps 5a–5b to place the chart onto Slide 6 using Paste Special.
   d. Copy and use Paste Special to insert the chart *Purpose of Using Phone* located in the *Purpose* sheet in Excel. Close Excel.
6. Print and then close **c09sa04, The Cellular Connection.ppt**. (Check with your instructor about printing this presentation. One suggestion is to print six slides per page.)

9.40 **Assessment 4**

Slide 1	Title	=	**The Cellular Connection**
	Subtitle	=	**Replace** *Add Your Name Here* **with your own name**

Slide 2	Title	=	**Historical Facts**
	Bullets	=	*Add results of your research*

Slide 3	Title	=	**Popular Phones and Functions**
	Bullets	=	**Phones**
	Next Level	=	**Nokia**
		=	**Ericsson**
		=	**Motorola**
		=	**Samsung**
	Bullets	=	**Functions**
	Next Level	=	**Text Messaging**
		=	**Color Screen**
		=	**Digital Camera**
		=	**Speaker Phone**

Slide 4	Title	=	**Local Carriers**
	Bullets	=	**AT&T**
		=	**Cingular**
		=	**Verizon**
		=	**Virgin Mobile**

Slide 5	Title	=	**Contracts**
	Bullets	=	**Monthly Payment**
		=	**Minutes**
		=	**Length**
		=	**Single, Family, or Pre-Pay**
		=	**Rollover Minutes**
		=	**Mobile to Mobile**

Slide 6	Title	=	**Class Survey**
		=	*Add the three charts from the above instructions*

Assessment 5

1. Create a presentation based on the text shown in Figure 9.41. You determine the design. After creating the presentation, save it on the hard drive or a floppy disk and name it **c09sa05, Aging in America.ppt**.

   INTEGRATED

2. Insert appropriate transitions, clip art, photographs, and backgrounds.
3. Create and type the six slides as shown below.

4. The historical facts from Slide 2 have been researched from the Internet and the results have been placed in an Excel worksheet. Open Excel and then open **c09sa05, Aging Population.xls**.
   a. Create the chart by selecting cells A5 through F7 and then clicking the Chart Wizard button from the Standard toolbar. Click the Custom Types tab, select *Column - Area,* and then click the <u>N</u>ext button.
   b. At Step 2 of the Chart Wizard, click the <u>N</u>ext button.
   c. At Step 3, click the Titles tab and then type Aging Population in the *Chart <u>t</u>itle* text box. Type Age Category at the *<u>C</u>ategory (X) axis* and Population in Thousands at the *<u>V</u>alue (Y) axis,* and then click the <u>N</u>ext button.
   d. Click <u>F</u>inish at Step 4 of the Chart Wizard. Resize the chart so that the category axis labels are displayed in full.
5. Copy the chart to the Office Clipboard by clicking on the chart to select it and then clicking the Copy button from the Standard toolbar.
6. Open **c09sa05, Aging in America.ppt** by clicking on the document in the Taskbar. Paste the chart in Slide 2 by clicking <u>E</u>dit, Paste <u>S</u>pecial. At the <u>A</u>s option box, click *Microsoft Office Excel* and then click OK. Readjust the text box and chart to fit on the slide.
7. Close Excel. Print and then close **c09sa05, Aging in America.ppt**. (Check with your instructor about printing this presentation. One suggestion is to print six slides per page.)

FIGURE

9.41 **Assessment 5**

Slide 1	Title	=	**Aging in America**
	Subtitle	=	**New Choices**
			Be sure to add an image
Slide 2	Title	=	**Aging in America**
	Bullets	=	**Fastest growing segment of the population is persons 65 and older**
		=	**The fasted growing group is seniors over 85**
Slide 3	Title	=	**Assisted Living Choices**
	Bullets	=	**What is assisted living?**
	Next Level	=	**Bridge between independent living and 24-hour nursing care**
		=	**Dependable, individualized care in a homelike setting**
		=	**Safe surroundings, delicious food, and a warm and caring staff**
		=	**Ultimate goal is to maximize independence and the dignity of every resident**
Slide 4	Title	=	**Services**
	Bullets	=	**Three meals a day**
		=	**Housekeeping services**

Continued on next page

		=	Transportation
		=	Personal care services
		=	Access to health and medical services
		=	24-hour security and staff availability
		=	Emergency call systems
		=	Health promotion and exercise programs
		=	Medication management
		=	Social and recreational activities
Slide 5	Title	=	Who Pays?
	Bullets	=	Costs vary greatly
		=	Costs are generally less than nursing homes
		=	No Medicare coverage
		=	Long-term-care insurance policies
		=	Most are month-to-month rentals
		=	Some have security deposits or entry fees
		=	Majority are personal finances
Slide 6	Title	=	Assisted Living 2005
		=	*Insert graphics of your choice*

Assessment 6

Create a PowerPoint presentation on a topic of your choosing. Include between 6 to 10 slides. Select a topic that is of interest to you. Possibly research a vacation; a college you would like to attend; a health club; hobby; special-interest group; a gardening project; a new computer, scanner, digital camera, and so forth. Use the Internet to aid in your search for information. Include the following specifications:

1. Be creative and have fun!
2. Select a Blank Presentation screen, the AutoContent Wizard, a design template, or a template from the Microsoft Office Online Templates Web site.
3. Insert at least one hyperlink to the World Wide Web.
4. Use at least one action button.
5. Use a build for your bulleted items.
6. Insert at least one animated graphic or movie.
7. Use consistency in color and design.
8. Use at least one consistent transition in your presentation.
9. Save your presentation to the hard drive or a floppy disk and name it **c09sa06, Creative**.
10. Print the entire presentation as handouts with six slides per page and then close **c09sa06, Creative**.
11. Give your presentation in class and ask your peers to evaluate your presentation and how you presented it. Write a short evaluation on a note card for each presentation and give the cards to the presenter at the end of class. Use the following criteria in evaluating the presentations:
    a. Presenter introduced herself (himself)
    b. Presenter was poised and confident

c. Presenter used equipment properly
d. Presenter did not read the presentation
e. Presenter used clip art appropriately
f. Presenter did not overdecorate (did not use too many bells and whistles)
g. Presenter used appropriate number of words per slide
h. Presenter organized slides in logical order
i. Presenter displayed appropriate choice of background and colors
j. Presenter used correct wording, punctuation, and grammar
k. Presenter gave adequate conclusion

PERFORMANCE
Assessments

PREPARING PROMOTIONAL DOCUMENTS, WEB PAGES, AND POWERPOINT PRESENTATIONS

(Before completing computer exercises, delete the Chapter09 folder on your disk. Next, copy the Unit02 folder from the CD that accompanies this textbook and then make Unit02 the active folder.)

UNIT02

Assume you are working for a well-known certified public accounting firm named Winston & McKenzie, CPA. A relatively new department in your firm, Executive Search Services, offers other companies assistance in searching for individuals to fill executive positions. You have been asked to prepare various presentation materials that will be used to inform other partners (owners), staff members, and clients of the scope of this department.

First, you will create a fact sheet (similar formatting to a flyer) highlighting the services of the Executive Search Services Department and the qualifications of its consultants. Second, you will prepare a self-mailing brochure that lists the services of the Executive Search Services Department, the benefits to the reader, the way to obtain more information, and a mailing label section. You will then create a PowerPoint presentation highlighting the offerings of a local nonprofit organization for which you, as a representative of your company, are an active volunteer. Finally, you will create a Web home page highlighting the services of the Executive Search Services Department.

Think about the audience of an accounting firm in general, and then think more specifically about the audience that might use Executive Search Services. Before you begin, print **Fact Sheet Text.doc**, **W&McK Text1.doc**, **W&McK Text2.doc**, and **W&McK Text3.doc** located in your Unit02 folder. Read the text in these documents to familiarize yourself with the services offered by this company. Include some consistent elements in all of the documents. Use a logo, a graphic image, a special character, text boxes, ruled lines, borders, fill, or color to create unity among the documents. Incorporate design concepts of focus, balance, proportion, contrast, directional flow, color, and appropriate use of white space.

Assessment 1

Using the text in **Fact Sheet Text.doc**, create a fact sheet highlighting the services offered by Winston & McKenzie's Executive Search Services Department according to the following specifications:

1. Create a thumbnail sketch of your proposed page layout and design. You will need to experiment with the layout and design.
2. Create styles for repetitive formatting, such as for bulleted text or headings.
3. Design a simple logo using the Drawing toolbar, WordArt, clip art, or other Word features.
4. Vary the fonts, type sizes, and typestyles to emphasize the relative importance of items.
5. Use bullets to list the services offered. You decide on the character to use as a bullet.
6. You may use any relevant picture, symbols, borders, colors, and so on in your fact sheet. You decide on the position, size, shading, border/fill, spacing, alignment, and so forth.
7. Save the document and name it **u02pa01, Facts**.
8. Print and then close **u02pa01, Facts**.
9. Print a copy of the document evaluation checklist located in your Unit02 folder. Use the checklist to evaluate your fact sheet. Hand in both items.

Assessment 2

Using the text in **W&McK Text1.doc**, **W&McK Text2.doc**, and **W&McK Text3.doc** located in your Unit02 folder, create a double-sided three-panel brochure according to the following specifications. *(Hint: Save periodically as you work through this assessment.)*

1. Create a dummy of the brochure layout so you know exactly which panel will be used for each section of text. Use **W&McK Text1.doc** as the text in panel 1, **W&McK Text2.doc** as the text in panel 2, and **W&McK Text3.doc** as the text in panel 3. (Panel 3 is actually the information request side of a card the reader can send to the company for more information. The mailing address side, which is panel 4, will be created in Step 5.)
2. Prepare a thumbnail sketch of your proposed layout and design.
3. Include the following formatting:
   a. Change the paper orientation to landscape.
   b. Change the top and bottom margins to 0.5 inch, and the left and right margins to 0.55 inch (or as close to this as possible).
   c. Turn on kerning at 14 points.
4. Create the inside panels of the brochure according to the following specifications:
   a. Use the Column feature to divide the page into panels using uneven columns, use text boxes to format the panels, or select a brochure template at the Microsoft Office Online Templates Web site.

b. You decide on appropriate typeface, type size, and typestyle selections that best reflect the mood or tone of this document and the company or business it represents. Insert section breaks to begin each new panel.

c. Create a customized drop cap to be used at the beginning of each paragraph in panel 1. You decide on the color, position, the typeface, the number of lines to drop, and the distance from the text.

d. Create any styles that will save you time and keystrokes, such as styles for headings, body text, and bulleted items.

e. Itemize any lists with bullets. You decide on the bullet symbol, size, color, spacing, and so forth.

f. Use text boxes to specifically position text if necessary or to highlight text in a unique way.

g. Include ruled lines. You decide on the line style, thickness, placement, color, and so on.

5. To make the brochure self-mailing, create the mailing address side of the request for information (created in panel 3) by completing the following steps in panel 4:

a. Insert the mailing address into a text box, then use Word's Text Direction feature to rotate the mailing address 90 degrees. You decide on an appropriate font, type size, and color. Type the following address:

> Winston & McKenzie, CPA
> Executive Search Services
> 4600 North Meridian Street
> Indianapolis, IN 46240

b. Use the mouse to size and position the text box containing the mailing address to an appropriate mailing address position. You can also use the Format Text Box dialog box to position the text box more precisely.

c. Create a vertical dotted line representing a cutting line or perforated line at the right edge of panel 4. Draw the line from the top of the page to the bottom of the page. Pay attention to the placement of this dotted line. If the reader were to cut the reply/request card on this line, are the items on the reverse side of the card (panel 3) placed appropriately? If not, make adjustments.

6. Create the return address on panel 5 by following Steps 5a and 5b to create the return address. Use the same address as in Step 5a. Position the return address text box into an appropriate return address position.

7. Create the cover of the brochure by completing the following steps in panel 6:

a. Type You Can't Afford to Make the Wrong Hiring Decision! as the title of the brochure.

b. Use any appropriate graphic image that is available. A large selection of graphics is available by searching for clips using the keyword *business*. You may also consider creating your own logo on the front cover of the brochure. You decide on the position, size, and border/fill, if any.

c. Decide on an appropriate location and include the company name, address, and the following phone and fax numbers:

> Phone: (317) 555-8900
> Fax: (317) 555-8901

8. Save the brochure and name it **u02pa02, Brochure**.

9. Print and then close **u02pa02, Brochure**.
10. Print a copy of **Document Evaluation Checklist.doc**. Use the checklist to evaluate your brochure. Make any changes, if necessary. Hand in both items.

Optional: To save on mailing costs, you have to send out postcards to prospective clients. Rewrite and shorten the text in **W&McK Text1.doc** so it highlights the pertinent points, but fits onto a 4 × 6-inch postcard. Include the company's name, address, phone, and fax numbers.

Assessment 3

In addition to being an employee at Winston & McKenzie, you represent the company as an active volunteer for the Metropolitan Art League. One of your responsibilities is to create an on-screen presentation highlighting important aspects of the Art League. Create the presentation by completing the following steps:

1. Open **Spotlight.ppt** located in your Unit02 folder.
2. Apply an appropriate presentation design.
3. Use a build effect for bulleted items. You decide on the bullet symbol to be used.
4. Apply transition effects to your slides.
5. Make the slide show a continuous on-screen presentation. You decide the time increments for the slides.
6. Enhance the presentation with varying fonts, font sizes, and colors.
7. Use any appropriate clip art images, symbols, pictures, and so on.
8. Save the presentation and name it **u02pa03, Spotlight.ppt**.
9. Print and then close **u02pa03, Spotlight.ppt**.

Optional: Add an appropriate sound—click Insert, point to Movies and Sounds, and then click Sound from Clip Organizer or Play CD Audio Track.

Assessment 4

Use the text in the brochure in Assessment 2 (the text is also located in your Unit02 folder as **W&McK Text1.doc**, **W&McK Text2.doc**, and **W&McK Text 3.doc**) to create a Web home page for Winston & McKenzie, CPA. The Web page should highlight the services of the Executive Search Services Department. Include the following specifications:

1. Create a thumbnail of the Web home page.
2. Use the Web Page template or create the home page as a Word document and save it in MHTML.
3. Use appropriate graphical bullets.
4. Use a graphic horizontal line—choose an appropriate line style.
5. Enhance the text with bold, italics, and varying fonts, font sizes, and colors.
6. Use a background color or fill effect.
7. Include a graphic or photo. (Consider downloading a clip from the Internet.)
8. Insert two hyperlinks (graphic links or text links).

9. Include an address, phone number, fax number, and an e-mail address.
10. View the Web page in Web Page Preview.
11. Save the document and name it **u02pa04, Web.mhtml**.
12. Print and then close **u02pa04, Web.mhtml**.

Optional: Include scrolling text or sound.

Assessment 5

Using the text in Figure U2.1 you will create an announcement using a PowerPoint design. Open **Office Support Day.ppt** from the Unit02 folder and then save it as **u02pa05, Announcement.ppt**. Revise the presentation by completing the following steps:

1. Change the page setup to portrait. The text for this announcement may be found in the Unit02 folder, **Information for Office Support Day.doc**. Copy this text and image to the Clipboard and then paste it into the PowerPoint file. Revise the formatting and fonts as shown in Figure U2.1.
2. Save the presentation.
3. Print **u02pa05, Announcement.ppt** in the slide format.
4. View the announcement as a Web page by clicking File and then Web Page Preview. Close your browser, PowerPoint, and then Word.

Office Support Celebration

All Classified Staff

Please join us for *coffee and...*

Wednesday, April 27
8:30 – 10:30 a.m.
SBC 3789

We *Appreciate* All You Do!

Sponsored by College of DuPage
Hosted by Business and Technology, Office Technology Information

UNIT three

PREPARING PUBLICATIONS

CHAPTER

10

Creating Basic Elements of a Newsletter

PERFORMANCE OBJECTIVES

Upon successful completion of Chapter 10, you will be able to create newsletters using your own designs based on desktop publishing concepts and Word features such as columns and styles. You will also be able to improve the readability of your newsletters by specifying line spacing, using kerning, adjusting character spacing, and changing alignment.

CHAPTER 10

DESKTOP PUBLISHING TERMS

Byline	Logo	Subtitle
Folio	Nameplate	Tombstoning
Headline	Orphan	Widow
Leading	Subhead	

WORD FEATURES USED

Balanced and unbalanced columns	Clip Art task pane	Styles and Formatting task pane
	Line spacing	
	Newspaper columns	Templates
Character spacing	Paragraph indent	Widow/Orphan control
Column break	Reading Layout view	Windows Paint
Columns	Section break	WordArt
Graphic images	Styles	

Designing a newsletter may appear to be a simple task, but newsletters are more complex than they appear. Newsletters can be the ultimate test of your desktop publishing skills. Remember that your goal is to get the message across. Design is important because it increases the overall appeal of your newsletter, but content is still the most crucial consideration. Whether your purpose for creating a newsletter is to develop better communication within a company or to develop awareness of a product or service, your newsletter must give the appearance of being well planned, orderly, and consistent. In order to establish consistency from one issue of a newsletter to the next, you must plan your document carefully.

Creating Basic Elements of a Newsletter

Successful newsletters contain consistent elements in every issue. Basic newsletter elements divide the newsletter into organized sections to help the reader understand the text, as well as to entice the reader to continue reading. Basic elements usually include the items described in Figure 10.1; Figure 10.2 shows their location on a newsletter page. Additional newsletter enhancements and elements are presented in Chapter 11.

FIGURE

10.1 *Basic Newsletter Elements*

- ***Nameplate:*** The nameplate, or banner, consists of the newsletter's title and is usually located on the front page. Nameplates can include the company logo, a unique typeface, or a graphic image to help create or reinforce an organization's identity. A logo is a distinct graphic symbol representing a company.

- ***Subtitle:*** A subtitle is a short phrase describing the purpose or audience of the newsletter. A subtitle can also be called a *tagline*. The information in the subtitle is usually located below the nameplate near the folio.

- ***Folio:*** A folio is the publication information, including the volume number, issue number, and the current date of the newsletter. The folio usually appears near the nameplate, but it can also be displayed at the bottom or side of a page. In desktop publishing, the term *folio* can also mean page number.

- ***Headlines:*** Headlines are titles to articles and are frequently created to attract the reader's attention. The headline can be set in 22- to 72-point type or larger and is generally typed in a sans serif typeface.

- ***Subheads:*** Subheads, or subheadings, are secondary headings that provide the transition from headlines to body copy. Subheads may also be referred to as *section headings* because they can also break up the text into organized sections. Subheads are usually bolded and sometimes typed in larger type sizes. There may be more space above a subhead than below.

- ***Byline:*** The byline identifies the author of an article.

- ***Body Copy:*** The main part of the newsletter is the body copy or text.

- ***Graphic Image:*** Graphic images are added to newsletters to help stimulate ideas and add interest to the document. They provide visual clues and visual relief from text-intensive copy.

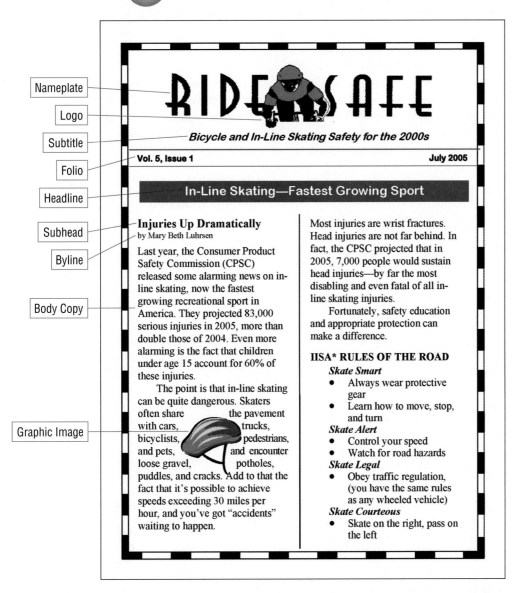

- Nameplate
- Logo
- Subtitle
- Folio
- Headline
- Subhead
- Byline
- Body Copy
- Graphic Image

RIDE SAFE

Bicycle and In-Line Skating Safety for the 2000s

Vol. 5, Issue 1   July 2005

In-Line Skating—Fastest Growing Sport

Injuries Up Dramatically
by Mary Beth Luhrsen

Last year, the Consumer Product Safety Commission (CPSC) released some alarming news on in-line skating, now the fastest growing recreational sport in America. They projected 83,000 serious injuries in 2005, more than double those of 2004. Even more alarming is the fact that children under age 15 account for 60% of these injuries.

The point is that in-line skating can be quite dangerous. Skaters often share the pavement with cars, trucks, bicyclists, pedestrians, and pets, and encounter loose gravel, potholes, puddles, and cracks. Add to that the fact that it's possible to achieve speeds exceeding 30 miles per hour, and you've got "accidents" waiting to happen.

Most injuries are wrist fractures. Head injuries are not far behind. In fact, the CPSC projected that in 2005, 7,000 people would sustain head injuries—by far the most disabling and even fatal of all in-line skating injuries.

Fortunately, safety education and appropriate protection can make a difference.

IISA* RULES OF THE ROAD
Skate Smart
- Always wear protective gear
- Learn how to move, stop, and turn

Skate Alert
- Control your speed
- Watch for road hazards

Skate Legal
- Obey traffic regulation, (you have the same rules as any wheeled vehicle)

Skate Courteous
- Skate on the right, pass on the left

Planning a Newsletter

Before creating a newsletter, consider the target audience and the objective for providing the information. Is the goal of the newsletter to sell, inform, explain, or announce? What is the purpose of the newsletter? Companies and organizations often use newsletters to convey a sense of pride and teamwork among employees or members. When planning a company newsletter, consider the following suggestions:

- If a scanner is available, use pictures of different people from your organization in each issue.
- Provide contributor forms requesting information from employees.
- Keep the focus of the newsletter on issues of interest to the majority of employees.

- Make sure you include articles of interest to varying levels of employment.
- Hand out regular surveys to evaluate newsletter relevancy. If the aim of your newsletter is to promote a product, the focal point may be a graphic image or photograph of the product rather than more general company news. Your aim can also influence the selection of typefaces, type sizes, visual elements, and the placement of elements. Also consider the following questions when planning the newsletter: What is the image you want to project? How often will the newsletter appear? What is your budget? How much time can you devote to its creation? What items are likely to be repeated from issue to issue? And, will your newsletter accommodate ads, photographs, or clip art? After answering these questions, you are ready to begin designing the newsletter.

Designing a Newsletter

Desktop publishing concepts and guidelines discussed in previous chapters provide you with good starting points for your newsletter. These guidelines emphasize the use of consistency, balance, proportion, contrast, white space, focus, directional flow, and color. If you are designing a newsletter for a company or organization, make sure the design coordinates with its design identity by using the same logo, typefaces, type sizes, column arrangements, and color choices that are used in other correspondence.

One of the biggest challenges in creating a newsletter is balancing change with consistency. A newsletter is a document that is typically reproduced on a regular basis, whether monthly, bimonthly, or quarterly. With each issue, new ideas can be presented, new text created, and new graphics or photos used. However, for your newsletter to be effective, each issue must also maintain a consistent appearance. Consistency contributes to your publication's identity and gives your readers a feeling of familiarity.

Consistent newsletter features and elements may include the following: size of margins; column layout; nameplate formatting and location; logos; color; ruled lines; and formatting of headlines, subheads, and body text. Later in the chapter, you will create styles to automate the process of formatting consistent elements.

Focus and balance can be achieved in a newsletter through the design and size of the nameplate, the arrangement of text on the page, the use of graphic images or scanned photographs, or the careful use of lines, borders, and backgrounds. When using graphic images or photos, use restraint and consider the appropriateness of the image. A single, large illustration is usually preferred over many small images scattered throughout the document. Size graphic images or photos according to their relative importance to the content. Headlines and subheads can serve as secondary focal points as well as provide balance to the total document.

White space around a headline creates contrast and attracts the reader's eyes to the headline. Surround text with white space if you want the text to stand out. If you want to draw attention to the nameplate or headline of the newsletter, you may want to choose a bold typestyle and a larger type size. Another option is to use WordArt to emphasize the nameplate title. Use sufficient white space throughout your newsletter to break up gray areas of text and to offer the reader visual relief.

Good directional flow can be achieved by using ruled lines that lead the reader's eyes through the document. Graphic elements, placed strategically throughout a newsletter, can provide a pattern for the reader's eyes to follow.

DTP POINTERS
Many logos are trademarks—before using them, find out whether you need permission.

DTP POINTERS
Look at as many publications as you can to get design ideas.

DTP POINTERS
Newsletter design should be consistent from issue to issue.

DTP POINTERS
Use no more than one or two images per page if possible.

DTP POINTERS
Use repetitive elements such as headers, footers, or headings.

DTP POINTERS
Use three or fewer typefaces.

DTP POINTERS
Use extra wide gutters or margins to counteract dense text.

DTP POINTERS
Use graphic accents with discretion.

In Figure 10.2, focus, balance, contrast, and directional flow were achieved through the placement of graphic images at the top and bottom of the document, the blue shaded text box with reverse text, and bolded headings. If you decide to use color in a newsletter, do so sparingly. Establish focus and directional flow with color to highlight key information or elements in your publication.

Creating a Newsletter Page Layout

Typically, page layout begins with choosing the size and orientation of the paper and determining the margins desired for the newsletter. Next, decisions on the number, length, and width of columns become imperative. Typefaces, type sizes, and typestyles must also be considered, as well as graphic images, ruled lines, and shading and coloring.

Choosing Paper Size and Type

The first considerations in designing a newsletter page layout are the paper size and type. The number of copies needed and the equipment available for creating, printing, and distributing the newsletter can affect this decision. Most newsletters are created on standard 8½ by 11-inch paper, although some are printed on larger sheets such as 8½ by 14 inches. The most economical choice for printing is the standard 8½ by 11-inch paper and it is easier to hold and read, cheaper to mail, and fits easily in standard file folders.

Paper weight is determined by the cost, the quality desired, and the graphics or photographs included. The heavier the stock, the more expensive the paper. In addition, pure white paper is more difficult to read because of glare. If possible, investigate other, more subtle colors. Another option is to purchase predesigned newsletter paper from a paper supply company. These papers come in many colors and designs. Several have different blocks of color created on a page to help separate and organize your text.

Creating Margins for Newsletters

After considering the paper size and type, determine the margins of your newsletter pages. The margin size is linked to the number of columns needed, the formality desired, the visual elements used, the amount of text available, and the type of binding. Keep your margins consistent throughout your newsletter. Listed here are a few generalizations about margins in newsletters:

DTP POINTERS
Be generous with your margins; do not crowd text.

- A wide right margin is considered formal. This approach positions the text at the left side of the page—the side where most readers tend to look first. If the justification is set at full, the newsletter will appear even more formal.

- A wide left margin is less formal. A table of contents or marginal subheads can be placed in the left margin giving the newsletter an airy, open appearance.

- Equal margins tend to create an informal look.

If you plan to create a multiple-paged newsletter with facing pages, you may want to use Word's mirror margin feature, which accommodates wider inside or outside margins. Figures 10.3 and 10.4 illustrate mirror margins in a newsletter. Often the inside margin is wider than the outside margin; however, this may depend on the amount of space the binding takes up. To create facing pages with mirror margins, click File and then Page Setup. At the Page Setup dialog box, select the

DTP POINTERS

Place page numbers on the outside edges when using mirror margins.

Margins tab, click the down-pointing arrow at the right of *Multiple pages* in the *Pages* section, and then click the *Mirror margins* option at the drop-down list. If you plan to include page numbering, position the numbers on the outside edges of each page.

Also, consider increasing the gutter space to accommodate the binding on a multiple-paged newsletter. To add gutter space on facing pages, add the extra space to the inside edges; on regular pages, add space to the left edges. To add gutters, display the Page Setup dialog box with the Margins tab selected, then select or type a gutter width at the *Gutter* option. Gutters do not change the margins, but rather add extra space to the margins. However, gutters make the printing area of your page narrower. Gutter space may be added to the left side of your page, to the left and right sides if the mirrored margin feature is chosen, or to the top of a sheet.

FIGURE

10.3 *Outside Mirror Margins on Facing Pages of a Newsletter*

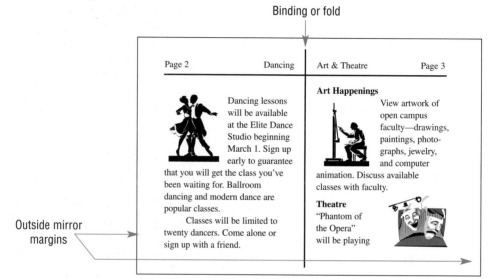

FIGURE

10.4 *Inside Mirror Margins on Facing Pages with Gutter Space*

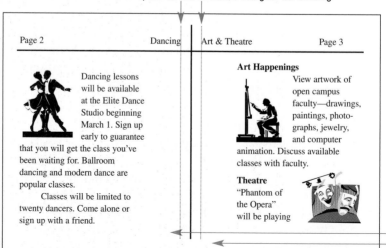

Creating Newspaper Columns for Newsletters

When preparing newsletters, an important consideration is the readability of the document. The line length of text can enhance or detract from the readability of text. Setting the text in columns can make it easier for your audience to read the text. You will use columns to format the newsletter created throughout this chapter; however, keep in mind that you can also use linked text boxes to position text within a newsletter—this method is used in most of the newsletter templates and will be introduced in Chapter 11.

DTP POINTERS
Columns added to newsletters improve readability.

Newspaper columns in a newsletter promote the smooth flow of text and guide the reader's eyes. As discussed earlier, Word's Newspaper Columns feature allows text to flow from column to column in the document. In order to work with columns, Word must be set to Print Layout or Reading Layout view. When the first column on the page is filled with text, the insertion point moves to the top of the next column on the same page in a snaking effect. When the last column on the page is filled, the insertion point moves to the beginning of the first column on the next page.

Newspaper columns can be created using the Columns button on the Standard toolbar or with options from the Columns dialog box. Columns of equal width are created with the Columns button on the Standard toolbar. To create columns of unequal width, use the Columns dialog box as shown in Figure 10.5. Click F̲ormat and then C̲olumns. Generally, typing text first and then formatting the text into newspaper columns is considered faster.

Columns

F I G U R E

10.5 *Columns Dialog Box*

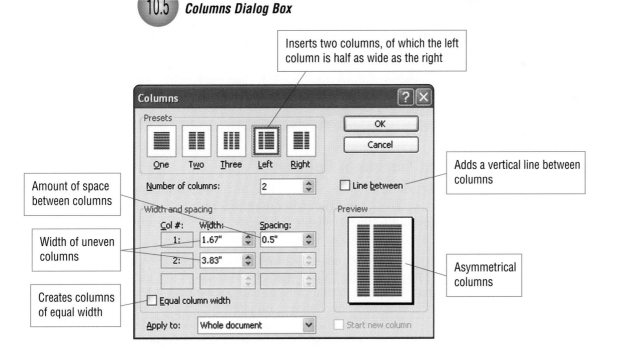

Inserts two columns, of which the left column is half as wide as the right

Amount of space between columns

Width of uneven columns

Creates columns of equal width

Adds a vertical line between columns

Asymmetrical columns

Using Balanced and Unbalanced Columns

Word automatically lines up (balances) the last line of text at the bottom of each column. On the last page of a newsletter, the text is often not balanced between columns. Text in the first column may flow to the bottom of the page, while the text in the second column may end far short of the bottom of the page. Columns can be balanced by inserting a section break at the end of the text by completing the following steps:

1. Position the insertion point at the end of the text in the last column of the section you want to balance.
2. Click Insert and then Break.
3. At the Break dialog box, click Continuous and then click OK.

Figure 10.6 shows the last page of a document containing unbalanced columns and a page where the columns have been balanced. If you want to force a new page to start after the balanced columns, click after the continuous break and then insert a manual page break.

FIGURE

10.6 *Unbalanced and Balanced Columns*

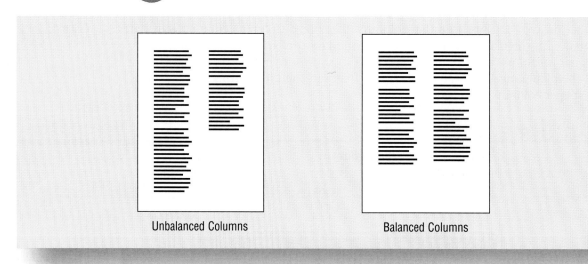

Unbalanced Columns   Balanced Columns

Determining Number of Columns

The number of columns used in newsletters may vary from one column to four or more columns. The size of the paper used, the font and type size selected, the content and amount of text available, and many other design considerations affect this decision.

One-column newsletters are easy to produce because the articles simply follow each other. If you do not have much time to work on your newsletter, this format is the one to use. The one-column format is the simplest to design and work with because it allows you to make changes and additions easily. You will want to use a large type size—usually 12 points—to accommodate the long line length of a one-column design. Be sure to use wide margins with this column layout. Also, keep in mind that an asymmetrically designed page is more interesting to look at than a symmetrical one, as shown in Figure 10.7.

FIGURE

10.7 *Symmetrical and Asymmetrical Designs in Newsletters*

Symmetrical Design

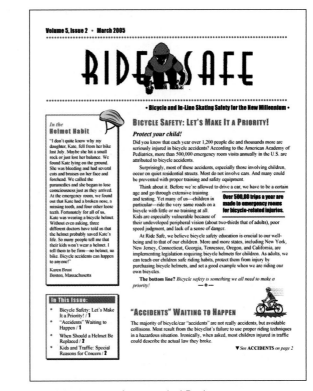

Asymmetrical Design

The two-column newspaper format is the most frequently used selection for newsletters. It gives a formal look, especially if used with justified text. Generally, use type sizes between 10 and 12 points when using a two-column layout. Be careful to avoid *tombstoning*, which occurs when headings display side by side in adjacent columns. Using an asymmetrical design in which one column is wider than the other and adding graphic enhancements will make this classic two-column format more interesting.

A three-column format is successful if you avoid using too much text on the page. This popular format is more flexible for adding interesting design elements. You may use a smaller type size (9 to 11 points) and fit more information on a page. Placing headings, text, or graphics across one, two, or three columns can create a distinctive flow. Often, one column is reserved for a table of contents, marginal subheads, or a masthead (publication information), thus allowing for more white space in the document and more visual interest.

A four-column design gives you even more flexibility than the three-column layout; however, more time may be spent in putting this newsletter layout together. Leaving one column fairly empty with a great deal of white space to offset more text-intensive columns is a visually appealing solution. This format gives you many opportunities to display headings, graphics, and other design elements across one or more columns. You will need to use a small type size for your text—9 to 10 points.

> **Tombstoning**
> When headings display side by side in adjacent columns.

Using Varying Numbers of Columns in a Newsletter

Section breaks can be used to vary the page layout within a single newsletter. For instance, you can use a section break to separate a one-column nameplate from text that can be created in three columns, as shown in Figure 10.8. There are three methods for inserting section breaks in documents. One method uses the Break dialog box. Another method automatically inserts a section break if you select the option *This point forward* in the *Apply to* section of the Columns dialog box. In the third method, select the text first and then apply column formatting. To move the insertion point between columns, use the mouse or press Alt + Up Arrow to move the insertion point to the top of the previous column, or press Alt + Down Arrow to move the insertion point to the top of the next column.

F I G U R E

10.8 *Section Breaks in Newsletters*

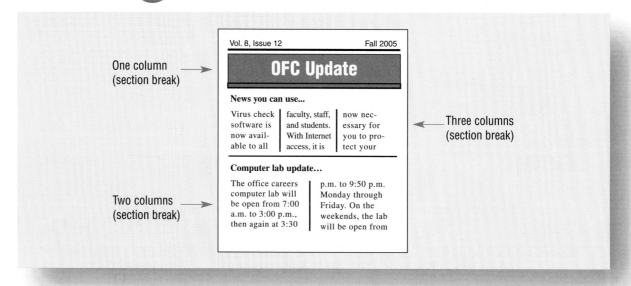

In addition, when formatting text into columns, Word automatically breaks the columns to fit the page. If a column breaks in an undesirable location, you can insert a column break in the document to control where the columns end and begin on the page. To insert a column break, position the insertion point where you want the new column to begin, then press Ctrl + Shift + Enter or click Insert, Break, and then *Column break*.

Changing the Number of Columns

To change the number of columns for an entire newsletter, click Edit, then Select All; to change the number of columns for part of a document, select the affected text only; to change the number of columns in several existing sections, select the multiple sections. After selecting the text you want to change, click Format, Columns, and then enter the number of columns desired. If you want to remove columns in your newsletter, click in the section or select multiple sections you want to change, click Format, Columns, and then click *One* in the *Presets* section.

Changing Column Width

If your newsletter is divided into sections, click in the section you want to change, then drag the column marker on the horizontal ruler. If an adjacent column is hampering your efforts to change a column width, reduce the width of the adjacent column first. If the column widths are equal, all of the columns will change. If the column widths are unequal, only the column you are adjusting changes. To specify exact measurements for column widths, use the Columns dialog box.

Adding Vertical Lines between Columns

Position the insertion point in the section where you want to add a vertical line, click Format, and then Columns. At the Columns dialog box, click to add a check mark in the *Line between* check box and then close the dialog box.

Adding Borders and Horizontal Lines to Newsletter Pages

You can add page borders, paragraph borders, borders around images, borders around text boxes, and horizontal lines between paragraphs to change the appearance of your newsletters. To add a page border, click Format, Borders and Shading, select the Page Border tab, and then select a particular line Style, Color, and Width, or select a predesigned Art border. To create a border around a paragraph of text, select the Borders tab at the Borders and Shading dialog box, and then select a line Style, Color, and Width. Make sure *Paragraph* displays in the *Apply to* list box option. To change a text box border, double-click the text box border, select the Colors and Lines tab, and then select the desired options at the Format Text Box dialog box.

A horizontal line can help separate different articles in a newsletter. Horizontal lines may be created by clicking the Line button on the Drawing toolbar, by clicking the Horizontal Line button at the bottom of the Borders and Shading dialog box to access the Horizontal Line dialog box as shown in Figure 10.9, or by clicking the Border button on the Formatting toolbar and then double-clicking the line to access the Format Horizontal Line dialog box as shown in Figure 10.10.

FIGURE

10.9 *Horizontal Line Dialog Box*

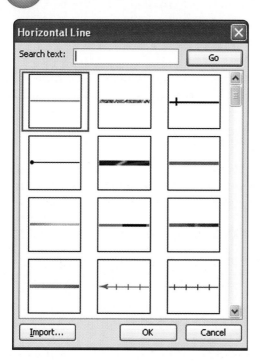

10.10 *Creating Horizontal Lines Using the Border Button on the Formatting Toolbar*

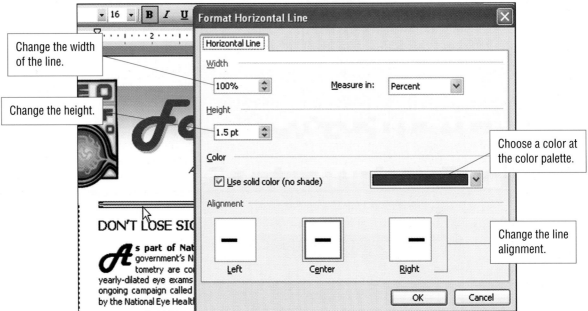

Change the width of the line.

Change the height.

Choose a color at the color palette.

Change the line alignment.

Creating Your Own Newsletter

A thumbnail sketch is an excellent way to experiment with different layouts and designs. Look at the work of others for hints and suggestions on different layouts. Creating a thumbnail is like "thinking" on paper.

Using Styles in Newsletters

Styles are especially valuable for saving time, effort, and keystrokes in creating newsletters. Newsletters are typically one of the most frequently created desktop publishing documents, and they contain elements that must remain consistent from page to page as well as from issue to issue. Styles reinforce consistency in documents by saving repetitive formatting instructions with a name so they can be applied over and over.

In addition to predesigned system styles included in many Word templates or wizards, you have the option to create your own customized styles either based on system styles or created from scratch. Throughout the creation of the newsletter in Figure 10.11, you will use various predesigned system styles and customize them to certain specifications as well as create your own styles based on existing styles. Word includes Paragraph, Character, List, and Table system styles. Click the Styles and Formatting button (first button) on the Formatting toolbar. At the Styles and Formatting task pane, click the down-pointing arrow at the right of the *Show* list box and then select *All styles*. Scroll through the list of styles to view each of the four types of styles; a symbol at the right of each style will indicate the type of style.

Adjusting Leading in Newsletters

While creating newsletters, you may find areas where adjustments should be made to increase or decrease white space between lines. This may occur when creating a nameplate, headline, subhead, or body text. Insufficient *leading*—vertical line spacing measured from the baseline of one line of text to the baseline of the next line of text—makes the text difficult to read; extra leading makes a page look less gray. However, too much leading or too little leading can make it difficult to find the beginning of the next line.

In Word, you can adjust leading by changing the line spacing to 1.0, 1.5, 2.0, 2.5, or 3.0 lines by clicking the *Line Spacing* button on the Formatting toolbar. For other specific increments, click *More* at the *Line Spacing* drop-down list and click *At Least, Exactly,* or *Multiple* at the *Line spacing* list option. Enter the amount of vertical space you want between lines of text in the *At* text box option. In addition, you can access the Paragraph dialog box by clicking F*ormat* from the Menu bar.

Leading can also be added before and/or after paragraphs of text at the Paragraph dialog box by selecting or typing measurement in the *Before* or *After* text boxes in the *Spacing* section. Normal leading in Word is 120% of the type size used. For example, a 10-point type has 12 points of leading. Large type size may require an adjustment from the normal leading. For instance, if a headline contains two lines both typed at 30 points, the space between the two lines may be too wide. Reducing the leading will improve the appearance of the heading. Consider the following guidelines when determining leading:

- Large type requires more leading.
- Longer lines need more leading to make them easier to read.
- Sans serif type requires more leading because it does not have serifs that guide the eyes along the line.
- Use styles to apply line spacing consistently in newsletters.

Reducing the Size of Graphic Files

The logo used in Figure 10.11, which is a graphic file located in your Chapter10 folder (Ridesf1blue.bmp), is a large file at 40.1 KB. To speed up scrolling in your document, you may replace the graphic at the document screen with a picture placeholder. On the Tools menu, click Options, and then click the View tab. To hide pictures, select the *Picture placeholders* check box in the *Show* section. Word displays an outline instead of the picture. If you view the document at Print Preview, the picture will display and it should print properly.

Leading
Vertical line spacing measured from the baseline of one line to the baseline of the next line.

Line Spacing

DTP POINTERS
When line length increases, line spacing (leading) should also increase.

Compress Pictures

Clicking the Compress Pictures button on the Picture toolbar will also reduce the size of the image. For instance, if you selected the Ridesf1blue.bmp file and then clicked the Compress Pictures button, the file would reduce from 40.1 KB to 23.5 KB. However, when compressing a file you may lose some picture quality.

Creating a Folio

Throughout this chapter, you will build the newsletter shown in Figure 10.11. Each exercise involves creating a style for a specific newsletter element. Each exercise builds on the previous one, finally resulting in a completed newsletter with embedded styles and saved as a template to help you create the next issue. Creating a folio for your newsletter will be the first step in building the Ride Safe newsletter. The *folio* will consist of publishing information that will change from issue to issue, such as the volume number, issue number, and date. However, the formatting applied to the folio will remain consistent with each issue. To ensure this consistency, prepare a folio style and apply it to the new information typed into the folio each month. Using this style will reduce time and effort.

Frequently, the folio is preceded or followed by a graphic line that sets the folio information apart from the rest of the nameplate. The folio can appear at the top of the nameplate as in this exercise, although it is more commonly placed below the nameplate. Reverse text can be added for emphasis and interest and text set in italic is often used.

> **Folio**
> A newsletter element consisting of publishing information that will change from issue to issue, such as the volume number, issue number, and date.

FIGURE

10.11   Ride Safe *Newsletter with Elements and Styles Marked*

(Before completing computer exercises, delete the Chapter09 folder on your disk. Next, copy the Chapter10 folder from the CD that accompanies this textbook to your disk and then make Chapter10 the active folder.)

Creating a Folio Style for a Newsletter

1. At a clear document screen, create the folio for the newsletter in Figure 10.11 by completing the following steps:
    a. Change all of the margins to 0.75".
    b. Change to Print Layout view, change the zoom to *75%,* and then click the Show/Hide ¶ button to display nonprinting characters.
    c. Change the font to 13-point Impact, type Volume 5, Issue 1, and then press the spacebar three times.
    d. Insert the bullet symbol (•) in the folio by clicking the Insert and then Symbol.
    e. At the Symbol dialog box, select the Symbols tab, select the *Wingdings 2* font, and then select the eighth symbol from the left in the eighth row (Wingdings 2: 151).
    f. Click Insert and then Close.
    g. Press the spacebar three times, type June 2005, and then press Enter.
    h. Select the line you have just typed and change the *Spacing* option to *Expanded* and the *By* option to 1 point and turn on kerning at 13 points at the Font dialog box. Click OK.
    i. With the text still selected, click Format and then Paragraph.
    j. At the Paragraph dialog box, select the Indents and Spacing tab.
    k. Change the *Left* option in the *Indentation* section to *0.25"* and then in the *Spacing* section change the *After* option to 6 points. Click OK.

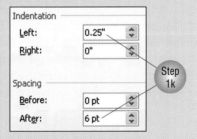

    l. Select the symbol between the issue number and date and change the font color to blue (the third color from the right in the second row in the color palette).
    m. Create a style from existing text by completing the following steps:
        1) Position the insertion point anywhere in the folio text.
        2) Click inside the *Style* list box on the Formatting toolbar to select the current style name.

3) Type **Folio** and then press Enter. (The Folio style is added to the list of styles available in this document.)

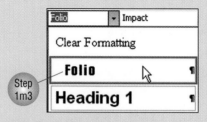

Step 1m3

2. Save the document and name it **c10ex01, Folio**. (You may want to save this exercise and the following *Ride Safe* newsletter exercises under one file name to save disk space.)
3. Close **c10ex01, Folio**. Keep this file open if you are going to work on Exercise 2. *(Note: Print when you are finished with the entire newsletter.)*

DTP POINTERS
Your nameplate should sell the contents of your newsletter.

Nameplate
A newsletter element, also known as a banner, that first captures the reader's eyes and immediately identifies the newsletter.

Logo
A name, symbol, or trademark designed for easy recognition.

DTP POINTERS
Avoid using all caps; small caps are easier to read.

DTP POINTERS
Do not use narrow typefaces in reverse text. Add bold to increase the thickness.

Creating a Nameplate

A *nameplate* or banner is the first thing that captures the reader's eyes; it provides immediate identification of the newsletter. A nameplate is the artwork (graphic, logo, scanned image, or cropped image) and/or type that includes the name of the publication and is usually placed at the top of the first page of a newsletter. The choice of fonts, type sizes, and the designs of the name are important because the reader sees them repeatedly.

The nameplate in Exercise 2 consists of the company's name and a logo bordered by two dotted lines created in the same color as that used in the logo. A *logo* is a name, symbol, or trademark designed for easy recognition. Ride Safe, Inc. uses two different logo designs in most of its publications. The Ride Safe logos may display in several different colors, however, such as blue, red, teal, orange, yellow, or purple. Most nameplates remain unchanged from issue to issue; therefore, saving it as a style is not necessary. But the nameplate should be saved to a newsletter template. Figure 10.12 illustrates several examples of nameplates. Examine them for the use and different location of elements. Looking at the work of others can help you develop your own skills in design and layout.

FIGURE 10.12 **Sample Nameplates**

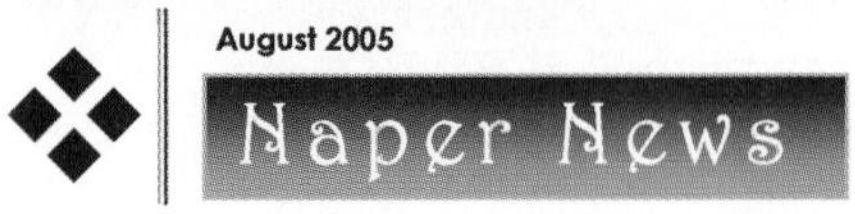

August 2005
Naper News

Nameplate with reversed text, gradient fill, and a symbol

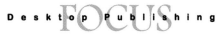

FOCUS
Desktop Publishing
Volume 2 • Issue 5
News & Notes
April • 2005

Nameplate with layered text

July 2005 • Vol. 1, Issue 5
News & Views
for Desktop Publishers

Nameplate with WordArt

Technology Update
Volume 2 • Issue 6
August 2005
Word
News

Nameplate with rotated text, graphic, and reversed text

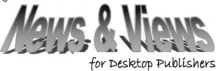

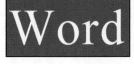

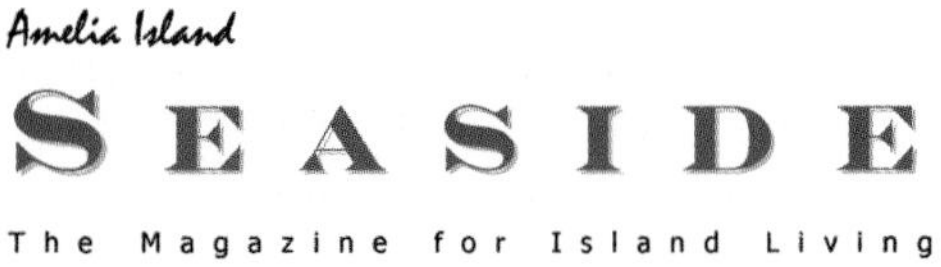

Amelia Island
SEASIDE
The Magazine for Island Living

Nameplate with expanded text

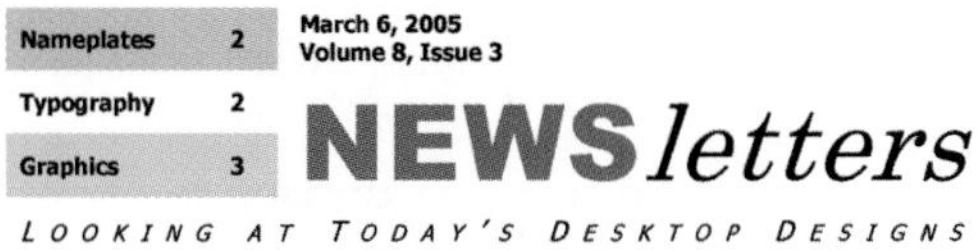

Nameplates 2
Typography 2
Graphics 3
March 6, 2005
Volume 8, Issue 3
NEWSletters
LOOKING AT TODAY'S DESKTOP DESIGNS

Nameplate with a table and serif and sans serif fonts

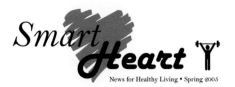

Smart Heart
News for Healthy Living • Spring 2005

Nameplate with a symbol and graphic

Creating a Nameplate for a Newsletter

1. Create the nameplate shown in Figure 10.11 by completing the following steps:
    a. Open **c10ex01, Folio**.
    b. Save the document and name it **c10ex02, Nameplate**.
    c. Format the nameplate by completing the following steps:
       1) Position the insertion point on the paragraph symbol below the folio and make sure *Normal* displays in the *Style* list box on the Formatting toolbar.
       2) Change the font to 13-point Impact in blue.
       3) Click Format, Paragraph, and make sure *0″* displays in the *Left* text box in the *Indentation* section. Click OK.
       4) Click Insert and then Symbol.
       5) At the Symbol dialog box, select the Symbols tab, change the font to Wingdings 2, and then select the eighth bullet symbol from the left in the eighth row (Wingdings 2: 151).
       6) Click Insert and then Close.
       7) Continue pressing the F4 key until you have created an entire row of blue symbols and then press Enter.

Step 1c7

Steps 1d2–1d3

Step 1g

    d. Insert the Ride Safe logo by completing the following steps:
       1) Position the insertion point on the paragraph symbol below the dotted line, click Insert, point to Picture, and then click From File.
       2) Insert **Ridesf1blue** located in your Chapter10 folder. *(Hint: Make sure the graphic text wrap is In Line With Text.)*
       3) Select the image and then click the Center align button on the Formatting toolbar.
       4) Deselect the image, position the insertion point on the paragraph symbol below the image, press Enter, and then change the alignment to Align Left.
    e. Select the blue dotted line (do not select the paragraph symbol at the end of the dotted line).
    f. Click the Copy button on the Standard toolbar.
    g. Position the insertion point on the second paragraph symbol below the logo, click the Paste button on the Standard toolbar, and then press Enter.
2. Save the document again with the same name, **c10ex02, Nameplate**.
3. Close **c10ex02, Nameplate**. *(Note: Print at the end of the entire newsletter.)*

Creating a Subtitle

As the third step in building a newsletter, you will create a subtitle. The text in the subtitle will remain consistent from issue to issue, so creating a style is not necessary. A *subtitle* emphasizes the purpose of the newsletter and identifies the intended audience. It is usually typed in a sans serif typeface in 14 to 24 points, and kerning should be turned on.

exercise 3

Creating a Subtitle in a Newsletter

1. Add a subtitle to the newsletter shown in Figure 10.11 by completing the following steps:
   a. Open **c10ex02, Nameplate**.
   b. Save the document and name it **c10ex03, Subtitle**.
   c. Format the subtitle by completing the following steps:
      1) Position the insertion point on the paragraph symbol below the dotted line and change the font to 13-point Impact italic, making sure the font color displays in black.
      2) Change the *Spacing* option to *Expanded* and the *By* option to 1 point and then turn on kerning at 13 points. Click OK.
      3) Click *Format* and then *Paragraph*.
      4) At the Paragraph dialog box, select the *Indents and Spacing* tab. In the *Spacing* section, change the *Before* option to *0 pt* and the *After* option to *12 pt* and then click the *Tabs* button.
      5) At the Tabs dialog box, type 6.75 in the *Tab stop position* text box, select *Right* in the *Alignment* section, click the *Set* button, and then click OK.

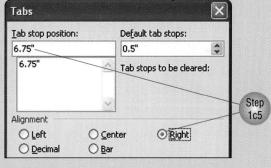

      6) Press Tab and then type Bicycle and In-Line Skating Safety News.
      7) Press the spacebar three times and then click the Italic button on the Formatting toolbar to turn off this feature.
      8) Insert the same bullet symbol used in creating the dotted lines in the nameplate.
      9) Press Enter.
      10) Select the symbol and change the font color to blue.
2. Save the document again with the same name, **c10ex03, Subtitle**.
3. Close **c10ex03, Subtitle**. *(Note: Print at the end of the entire newsletter.)*

Creating a Headline

After completing the folio, nameplate, and subtitle, you will now create a headline in Exercise 4. *Headlines* organize text and help readers decide whether they want to read the article. To set the headline apart from the text, use a larger type size, heavier weight, and a different typeface than the body. When determining a type size for a headline, start with 18 points and increase the size until you find an appropriate one. As a rule, choose a sans serif typeface for a headline; however, this is not a hard-and-fast rule. Because the headline consists of text that will change with each issue of the newsletter, consider creating a style to format the headline.

Headlines of more than one line often improve in readability and appearance if leading is reduced. The leading in a headline should be about the same size as the type used. Using all caps (sparingly) or small caps substantially reduces leading automatically, because capital letters lack descenders. Headlines and subheads should have more space above than below. This indicates that the heading goes with the text that follows rather than the text that precedes the heading.

exercise 4

Creating a Headline Style for a Newsletter

1. Create a headline style for the newsletter in Figure 10.11 by completing the following steps:
   a. Open **c10ex03, Subtitle**.
   b. Save the document and name it **c10ex04, Headline**.
   c. Format the headline in Figure 10.11 by completing the following steps:
      1) Position the insertion point on the paragraph symbol below the subtitle (press Ctrl + End).
      2) Change the font to 24-point Britannic Bold. (Make sure italic is turned off.)
      3) Change the font color to Gray-50% and turn on small caps (Ctrl + Shift + K).
      4) Select the Character Spacing tab at the Font dialog box, change the *Spacing* option to *Expanded* and the *By* option to *1.5 pt*, and make sure kerning is turned on at 13 points. Click OK.
   d. Type **In-Line Skating—Fastest Growing Sport**. (Use an em dash.) Press Enter.
   e. Format the headline by completing the following steps:
      1) Select *In-Line Skating...*, click Format, and then Paragraph.
      2) At the Paragraph dialog box, select the Indents and Spacing tab.
      3) In the *Spacing* section, change the *Before* option to *6 pt* and the *After* option to *18 pt* and then click OK.
   f. Create a style from existing text by completing the following steps:
      1) Position the insertion point anywhere in the headline text.
      2) Click inside the *Style* list box on the Formatting toolbar to select the current style name.
      3) Type **Headline** and then press Enter. (The Headline style is added to the list of styles available in this document.)

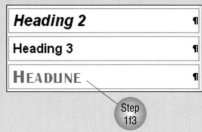

Step 1f3

2. Save the document again with the same name **c10ex04, Headline**.
3. Close **c10ex04, Headline**. *(Note: Print at the end of the entire newsletter.)*

Formatting Body Text in a Newsletter

In Exercise 5, you will format the body text for the newsletter you are building in this chapter. You will change the font and type size, create em spaces for paragraph indentations, and turn on the Columns feature. Before doing so, take a look at some of the formatting options that apply to body text.

Applying the Widow/Orphan Feature

Word's Widow/Orphan control feature is on by default. This feature prevents the first and last lines of paragraphs from being separated across pages. A **widow** is a single line of a paragraph or heading that is pushed to the top of the next page. A single line of text (whether part of a paragraph or heading) appearing by itself at the end of a page is called an **orphan**. This option is located in the Paragraph dialog box at the Line and Page Breaks tab.

Even with this feature on, you should still watch for subheads that are inappropriately separated from text at the end of a column or page. If a heading displays inappropriately, insert a column break. To insert a column break, position the insertion point where you want a new column to begin, then press Ctrl + Shift + Enter, or click Insert, Break, and then Column break.

Aligning Text in Paragraphs in Newsletters

The type of alignment you choose for a newsletter influences the tone of your publication. Text within a paragraph can be aligned in a variety of ways: at both the left and right margins (justified); at the left or right; or on the center of the text body, causing both the left and right margins to be ragged.

 Align Left   Center

 Align Right   Justify

Justified text is common in publications such as textbooks, newspapers, newsletters, and magazines. It is more formal than left-aligned text. For justified text to convey a professional appearance, there must be an appropriate line length. If the line length is too short, the words and/or characters in a paragraph may be widely spaced, causing "rivers" of white space. Remedying this situation requires increasing the line length, changing to a smaller type size, and/or hyphenating long words. Text aligned at the left is the easiest to read. This alignment has become popular with designers for publications of all kinds. Center alignment should be used on small amounts of text.

Indenting Paragraphs with Em Spaces

In typesetting, tabs are generally measured by em spaces rather than inch measurements. An em space is a space as wide as the point size of the type. For example, if the type size is 12 points, an em space is 12 points wide. Usually you will want to indent newsletter text one or two em spaces.

Em space indentations can be created in two ways. One way is to display the Paragraph dialog box with the Indents and Spacing tab selected, and then select or type an inch or point increment at the *Left* or *Right* indentation text boxes (be sure to include *pt* when typing a point increment). Alternatively, you can create an em space at the Tabs dialog box. In Exercise 5, you will change the default tab setting to 0.25 inch to create an em space indentation for each paragraph preceded with a tab code (0.25 inch is approximately 24 points, or 2 em spaces for text typed in 12-point type size). Be sure to use em spaces for any paragraph indentations used in newsletters. Also, use em spaces for spacing around bullets and any other indented text in newsletters.

Generally, the first paragraph after a headline or subhead is not indented even though all remaining paragraphs will have an em space paragraph indentation. In Figure 10.11, notice the paragraph formatting in the newsletter.

Creating a Body Text Style in a Newsletter

1. Create a body text style for the newsletter in Figure 10.11 by completing the following steps:
   a. Open **c10ex04, Headline**.
   b. Save the document and name it **c10ex05, Body**.
   c. Position the insertion point on the paragraph symbol below the headline text. (Make sure the style is Normal.)
   d. Insert **Ride Safe** located in your Chapter10 folder and then delete the paragraph symbol at the end of the document.
   e. Create a section break between the headline and the body text by completing the following steps:
      1) Position the insertion point at the beginning of *Injuries Up Dramatically*.
      2) Click Insert and then Break.
      3) At the Break dialog box, select *Continuous* in the *Section break types* section and then click OK.
   f. Turn on the columns feature by completing the following steps:

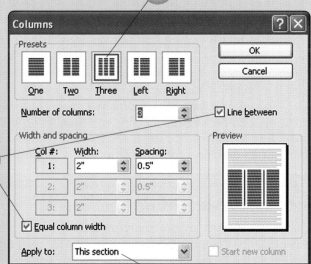

      1) With the insertion point still positioned at the beginning of *Injuries Up Dramatically*, click Format and then Columns.
      2) At the Columns dialog box, select *Three* in the *Presets* section.
      3) Click the *Line between* option (this inserts a line between the columns) and then make sure the *Equal column width* check box is checked.
      4) Make sure *This section* displays in the *Apply to* list box and then click OK.
   g. Format the body text by completing the following steps:
      1) Select all of the text in the three columns beginning with *Injuries Up Dramatically* by pressing Ctrl + Shift + End and then change the font to 11-point Garamond.
      2) With the text still selected, click Format and then Paragraph.
      3) At the Paragraph dialog box, select the Indents and Spacing tab, click the down-pointing arrow at the right of the *Line spacing*

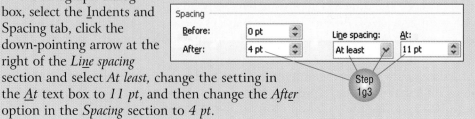

      section and select *At least,* change the setting in the *At* text box to *11 pt*, and then change the *After* option in the *Spacing* section to *4 pt*.

4) To change the paragraph indentions to an em space, click the <u>T</u>abs button at the Paragraph dialog box.

5) At the Tabs dialog box, type **0.25** in the *Tab stop position* text box, make sure *Left* is selected in the *Alignment* section, and then click the <u>S</u>et button.

6) Click OK to close the Tabs dialog box.

h. Create a style to format the body text by completing the following steps:

1) Position the insertion point in one of the paragraphs in the body of the newsletter.

2) Click the Style button on the Formatting toolbar to select the current name, type **RS Body**, and then press Enter. (The RS Body style is added to the list of styles available in this document.)

2. Save the document again with the same name, **c10ex05, Body**.

3. Close **c10ex05, Body**. *(Note: You will print when the newsletter is complete.)*

Creating Subheads for Newsletters

At times, a subhead may appear right after a headline, as is the case with this chapter's newsletter. Refer to Figure 10.11 to view the subheads you will create in this exercise. ***Subheads,*** or ***subheadings,*** organize text and expand on headlines, giving readers more information or clues about the text. In addition, subheads also provide contrast to text-intensive body copy. Marginal subheads are sometimes placed in the left margin or in a narrow column to the left of the body text, providing an airy, open appearance. Subheads can be set in a larger type size, different typeface, or heavier weight than the text. They can be centered, aligned left, or aligned right, and formatted in shaded boxes. In Exercise 6, you will use the Styles and Formatting task pane to create a style based on an existing style. An easy way to access this task pane is to click the Styles and Formatting button on the Formatting toolbar.

Subhead
A newsletter element that organizes text and expands on headlines.

Styles and Formatting

Creating a Subhead Style

1. Create a subhead style for the newsletter in Figure 10.11 by completing the following steps:

a. Open **c10ex05, Body**.

b. Save the document and name it **c10ex06, Subhead**.

c. Create a style to format the subheads in the newsletter in Figure 10.11 based on an existing style by completing the following steps:

1) Select *Injuries Up Dramatically* and then click the down-pointing arrow at the right of the Style button on the Formatting toolbar. Select the Heading 3 style at the Style drop-down list. (This will apply the Heading 3 style to the selected text.)

2) With *Injuries Up Dramatically* still selected, click the Styles and Formatting button on the Formatting toolbar.

3) At the Styles and Formatting task pane, make sure *Heading 3* appears in the *Formatting of selected text* option box. Click the New Style button below *Heading 3*.

Step 1c3

4) At the New Style dialog box, type **Subhead** in the *Name* text box.

5) Make sure *Paragraph* displays in the *Style type* list box.

6) Make sure that *Heading 3* displays in the *Style based on* list box.

7) Make sure *RS Body* displays in the *Style for following paragraph* list box.

8) In the *Formatting* section, change the font to 13-point Britannic Bold. Make sure the Bold option is cleared.

9) Click the Format button in the bottom left corner.

10) Click *Font*, select the Character Spacing tab, click the down-pointing arrow at the right of the *Spacing* list box and choose *Expanded*, and then change the *By* setting to *0.5 pt*. Turn on *Kerning for fonts* and set the *Points and above* option to *13*. Click OK.

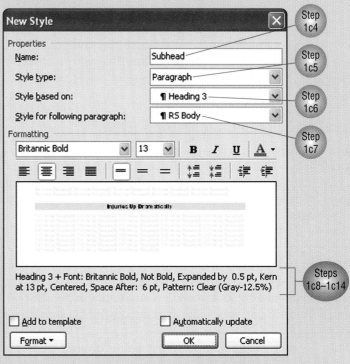

Step 1c4
Step 1c5
Step 1c6
Step 1c7
Steps 1c8–1c14

11) Click the Format button and then *Paragraph*.

12) Select the *Indents* and Spacing tab, change the alignment to *Centered*, change the spacing *Before* setting to *12 pt*, and then change the apacing *After* setting to *6 pt*. Click OK.

13) Click the Format button, click *Border*, and then select the *Shading* tab.

14) Select the fourth fill from the left in the first row of the Fill palette (Gray-12.5%). Make sure *Paragraph* displays in the *Apply to* list box. Click OK.

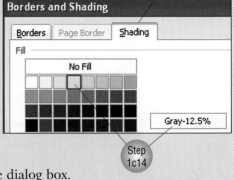

Step 1c13
Step 1c14

15) Click OK or press Enter at the New Style dialog box.

16) Apply the Subhead style by positioning the insertion point on *Injuries Up Dramatically* and then selecting *Subhead* in the *Pick formatting to apply* drop-down list in the Styles and Formatting task pane.

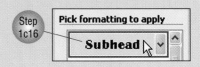

Step 1c16

    17) Position the insertion point on the heading *A Message to Parents*, located in the second column, and then apply the Subhead style. Delete the paragraph symbol before the subheading.

2.   Position the insertion point in the first subhead *Injuries Up Dramatically*, click F̲ormat, and then P̲aragraph. Select the I̲ndents and Spacing tab and then change the spacing *B̲efore* setting to *0 pt*. Click OK or press Enter. (This will eliminate the space before the first subhead at the beginning of the body text. The Subhead style remains unchanged.)

3.   Save the document again with the same name, **c10ex06, Subhead**.

4.   Close **c10ex06, Subhead**. *(Note: You will print when the newsletter is complete.)*

Creating a Byline

The next step in building the newsletter is to create the byline. The **byline** identifies the author of the article and is often typed in italic using the same typeface as the body text. The byline may be the same size as the body typeface, but it may also be set in a type size 1 or 2 points smaller. The byline may appear below the headline or subhead, depending on which is the title of the article, or it may appear as the first line of the body text if it follows a headline or subhead that spans two or more columns. Place the byline at the left margin or right-aligned in a column.

Byline
A newsletter element that identifies the author of the article.

Creating a Byline Style in a Newsletter

1.   Create a byline style for the newsletter in Figure 10.11 by completing the following steps:

   a.   Open **c10ex06, Subhead**.

   b.   Save the document and name it **c10ex07, Byline**.

   c.   Create a style to format the byline in the newsletter in Figure 10.11 by completing the following steps:

      1) Select the byline *by Mary Beth Luhrsen* below the first subhead *Injuries Up Dramatically*.

      2) Change the font to 10-point Garamond italic.

      3) At the Paragraph dialog box in the *Spacing* section, change the *B̲efore* option to *0 pt* and the *A̲fter* option to *6 pt*. Click OK.

   d.   Create a style from existing text by completing the following steps:

      1) Position the insertion point anywhere in the byline text.

      2) Click inside the *Style* list box on the Formatting toolbar to select the current style name.

Step
1d3

      3) Type Byline and then press Enter. (The Byline style is added to the list of styles available in this document.)

Byline	▾	Garamond	▾	10
Byline ⬉				

      4) Apply the Byline style to the byline below *A Message to Parents*.

2.   Save the document again with the same name, **c10ex07, Byline**.

3.   Close **c10ex07, Byline**. *(Note: You will print when the newsletter is complete.)*

Inserting Graphic Images in Newsletters

Clip art added to a newsletter should support or expand points made in the text. Use clip art so that it will give the newsletter the appearance of being well planned, inviting, and consistent. You can modify clip art by ungrouping it using Word as a picture editor or by using Microsoft Photo Editor. Large and relatively inexpensive selections of clip art can be purchased on CD-ROM. In addition, you may want to scan predesigned company logos (with permission) or photographs that relate to the subject of your newsletter.

The image used in the nameplate in Figure 10.11 was scanned professionally and copied to your student files in a file format that was compatible with Word 2003. Because of the bitmap file format in which it was saved, you cannot alter this image in Microsoft Word Picture (you cannot right-click on the image and click Edit Picture). To change the color of the scanned image, you may access Windows Paint or alter the bitmapped image by using the Set Transparent Color tool on the Picture toolbar as shown in Figure 10.13. Bitmap pictures are often saved with a .bmp, .png, .jpg, or .gif extension. Most scanned graphics and photographs are bitmaps. When they are resized, they lose definition, and the individual dots that make up the picture become visible. You can change the way colors look in a bitmap picture by using buttons on the Picture toolbar to adjust brightness and contrast, converting color to black and white or grayscale, or creating the transparent areas. To change specific colors in a bitmap, use a photo-editing program.

FIGURE

10.13 *Using the Set Transparent Color Tool to Change Color in a Bitmapped Image*

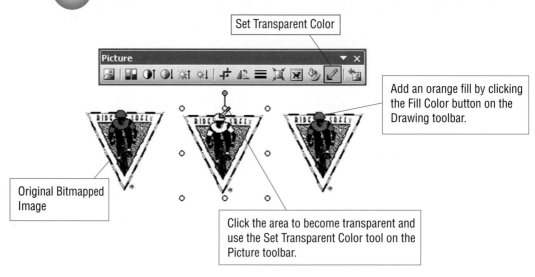

Set Transparent Color

Add an orange fill by clicking the Fill Color button on the Drawing toolbar.

Original Bitmapped Image

Click the area to become transparent and use the Set Transparent Color tool on the Picture toolbar.

You can create a transparent area in most pictures except in animated GIF pictures. GIFs are animated graphic images that are displayed in rapid sequence by some Web browsers to produce an animated effect. GIF images can be edited in GIF editing programs. The Set Transparent Color tool is available for bitmap pictures that do not already have transparency information. If you cannot apply transparency to a bitmap image, the reason may be that the image has been previously altered. The Set Transparent Color tool is also available for some, but not all clip art. Complete the following steps to use the Set Transparent Color tool on a bitmapped graphic:

1. Display the Picture toolbar.
2. Select the bitmapped image.
3. Click the Set Transparent Color button (second from the right) on the Picture toolbar.
4. Position the pointer (appears as a pen) into the area you want to change and then click the left mouse button.
5. Click the down-pointing arrow at the right of the Fill Color button on the Drawing toolbar and select a color.

Optional steps for using Paint are provided at the end of Exercise 8.

Inserting Graphic Images into a Newsletter

1. Insert two graphics in the newsletter shown in Figure 10.11 by completing the following steps:
   a. Open **c10ex07, Byline**.
   b. Save the document and name it **c10ex08, Newsletter**.
   c. Display the Picture toolbar.
   d. Position the insertion point in the second sentence in the second paragraph, near the text *pedestrians, and pets.*
   e. Insert the graphic of a person rollerblading shown in Figure 10.11 by completing the following steps:
      1) Display the Clip Art task pane.
      2) At the *Search for* text box, type j0199061.wmf or, if this image is not available, type skating, and then press Go.
      3) Click once on the image to insert it.
      4) Click the image to select it, click the Text Wrapping button on the Picture toolbar, and then click Tight.
      5) Size and position the image as in Figure 10.11.

   f. Insert the rollerblade graphic shown in Figure 10.11 by completing the following steps:
      1) Position the insertion point near the beginning of the third column.
      2) Display the Clip Art task pane.
      3) At the *Search for* text box, type j0305687.wmf or if this image is not available, type skates, and then click Go.
      4) Click once on the image to insert it.
      5) Change the text wrapping to Tight.
      6) With the image still selected, click the Draw button on the Drawing toolbar, point to Rotate or Flip, and then click Flip Horizontal. *(Note: You always want your graphic to face the text.)*
      7) Size and position the image as in Figure 10.11.

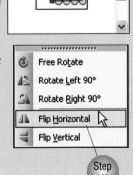

2. View your newsletter in Print Preview.
3. Save the document with the same name, **c10ex08, Newsletter**.
4. Print and then close **c10ex08, Newsletter**.

Accessing the Windows Paint Program to Customize a Graphic

You can customize a graphic by using Windows Paint by completing the following steps:

1. Click the Start button on the Taskbar, point to All Programs, point to Accessories, and then click Paint.
2. At the Paint screen, click File and Open.
3. At the Open dialog box, click the down-pointing arrow at the right of the *Files of type* text box and select *All Files*.
4. Click the down-pointing arrow at the right of the *Look in* list box and select the drive where your graphic is located; then click the Open button.
5. Click View and then click the *Color Box* option to turn it on. (The color palette should display at the bottom of the screen.)
6. Click the Brush tool on the tool palette. Click any color on the color palette to choose a foreground color. Right-click any color on the color palette to choose a background color.
7. Position the insertion point inside the image and then click. Drag the Brush tool to apply the color to the image as shown in Figure 10.14. (The area should display in your chosen foreground color.) If you right-click on a section of an image, the background color will be applied.
8. Save the picture.
9. Click File and then Exit.

FIGURE 10.14 *Using the Paint Program to Customize a Photograph*

Saving the Newsletter as a Template

To save time in creating future issues of your newsletter, save your newsletter as a template. To do this, delete all text, pictures, and objects that will not stay the same for future issues. Likewise, leave the nameplate and all text, pictures, symbols, and so on, that will remain the same (or use the same style) in each issue of your newsletter. For example, to save the *Ride Safe* newsletter in Exercise 8 as a template as shown in Figure 10.15, leave the following items and delete the rest:

- Folio (the month and volume/issue numbers will change, but the titles will remain—use the folio text as placeholder text)
- Nameplate
- Subtitle
- Headline (the headline text will change, but the position and formatting will remain—use the headline text as placeholder text)
- Subheads (the subhead text will change, but the formatting will remain—use the subhead text as placeholder text)
- Byline (the byline text will change, but the position and formatting will remain—use the byline text as placeholder text)
- Body text (the body text will change, but the formatting will remain—leave a paragraph as placeholder text)

Saving a Newsletter as a Template

1. Open **c10ex08, Newsletter** and complete the following steps to save it as a template (see Figure 10.15).
2. Delete all text and newsletter elements that will change with each issue (refer to the bulleted items above).
3. Click <u>F</u>ile and then Save <u>A</u>s.
4. At the Save As dialog box, select *Document Template (*.dot)* at the *Save as <u>t</u>ype* list box, type **Ride Safe Newsletter Template** in the *File <u>n</u>ame* text box, click <u>S</u>ave, and then close the dialog box. *(Note: Consult your instructor if you should save this template to your hard drive or to another drive.)*

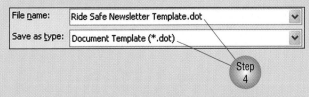

Step 4

5. To use the template, access the New Document task pane and then click the <u>On my computer</u> hyperlink in the *Create New* section. Double-click the *Ride Safe NewsletterTemplate.dot* icon on the General tab at the Templates dialog box.
6. Select and replace text that needs to be updated. Delete any placeholder text when necessary.

Step 5

Ride Safe Newsletter...

Volume 5, Issue 1 • June 2005

Bicycle and In-Line Skating Safety News •

IN-LINE SKATING—FASTEST GROWING SPORT

Injuries Up Dramatically

by Mary Beth Luhrsen

Last year, the Consumer Product Safety Commission (CPSC) released some alarming news on in-line skating, now the fastest growing recreational sport in America. They projected 83,000 serious injuries in 2005, more than double those of 2004. Even more alarming is the fact that children under age 15 account for 60% of these injuries.

CHAPTER summary

➤ Newsletter elements divide the newsletter into organized sections to help the reader understand the text. Basic newsletter elements include a nameplate, subtitle, folio, headline, subhead, byline, and body copy.

➤ Focus and balance can be achieved in a newsletter through the design and size of the nameplate, through the use of graphic images, and through careful use of lines, borders, and backgrounds.

➤ The margin size for a newsletter is linked to the number of columns needed, the formality desired, the visual elements used, and the amount of text available. Keep margins consistent in a newsletter.

➤ The line length of text in a newsletter can enhance or detract from the readability of the text.

➤ Section breaks are used to vary the page layout within a single newsletter.

➤ Setting text in columns may improve the readability of newsletters.

➤ Word's default leading is equal to approximately 120% of the type size used.

➤ Headlines and subheads should have more leading above than below.

➤ Word automatically lines up (balances) the last line of text at the bottom of each column.

➤ The last page of columns can be balanced by inserting a continuous section break at the end of the text.

➤ Set tabs in a typeset document by em spaces rather than inch measurements.

➤ An em space is a space as wide as the point size of the type.

➤ A challenge in creating a newsletter is determining how to balance change with consistency. Styles assist in maintaining consistency in recurring elements.

➤ When formatting instructions contained within a style are changed, all of the text to which the style has been applied is automatically updated.

➤ Styles are created for a particular document and are saved with the document.

➤ A style can be applied using the Style drop-down list on the Formatting toolbar or the Styles and Formatting task pane.

➤ Clip art added to a newsletter should support or expand points made in the text. Use clip art so that it will give the newsletter the appearance of being well planned, inviting, and consistent.

➤ You can make areas of a bitmapped image transparent by using the Set Transparent Color button on the Picture toolbar.

➤ Customize your graphic by using the Windows Paint program.

➤ To establish consistency from one issue to the next and to save time, you can save your newsletter as a template.

COMMANDS review

Commands	Mouse/Keyboard
Clip Art task pane	Insert, Picture, Clip Art
Columns	Format, Columns; or click the Columns button on the Standard toolbar
Character Spacing	Format, Font, Character Spacing tab
Insert a column break	Insert, Break, *Column break*; or press Ctrl + Shift + Enter
Insert a section break	Insert, Break, then *Next page, Continuous, Even page,* or *Odd page*
Insert Picture dialog box	Insert, Picture, From File
Insert symbols	Insert, Symbol, Symbols tab
Kerning	Format, Font, Character Spacing tab
Leading	Format, Paragraph, Indents and Spacing tab, *Before* and *After*
Styles	Styles and Formatting button on Formatting toolbar; Style button on Formatting toolbar; or View, Task Pane, Other Task Panes button, Styles and Formatting
Styles and Formatting task pane	Styles and Formatting button on the Formatting toolbar; or View, Task Pane, Other Task Panes button, Styles and Formatting
Templates	New Document task pane, On my computer hyperlink or Templates on Office Online hyperlink
Widow/Orphan	Format, Paragraph, Line and Page Breaks tab, *Widow/Orphan control*
Windows Paint	Start, All Programs, Accessories, Paint

REVIEWING key points

True/False: On a blank sheet of paper, write *True* if the statement is true and write *False* if the statement is false.

1. A folio provides information that describes the purpose of the newsletter and/or the intended audience of the newsletter.
2. Column formatting affects the entire document unless your document is divided into sections.
3. Columns are separated by a default setting of 0.25 inch of space.
4. If one column is longer than another, you can balance the text within the columns by inserting a text wrapping break.
5. A bitmapped image can be edited using the buttons on the Drawing toolbar.
6. An em space indentation can be created at the Tabs dialog box and typed in a point or inch increment.
7. Extra leading can make a page look less gray.
8. If a headline contains two lines both typed in 36 points, the default spacing between the two lines (leading) should be increased to improve readability.

9. One advantage of using styles in formatting a newsletter is that when formatting within a style is changed, the text to which it has been applied changes also.

10. Once a style has been created, the only way to change the style is to rename it and create it again.

Completion: On a blank sheet of paper, indicate the correct term, command, or number for each item.

1. Insert this (or these) into a document to control where columns end and begin on a page.

2. A set of formatting instructions that is saved with a name and can be used over and over is called this.

3. This feature prevents the first and last lines of paragraphs from being separated across pages.

4. This newsletter element identifies the author of an article.

5. If you create a multiple-paged newsletter with facing pages, you may want to use this margin feature to accommodate wider inside or outside margins.

6. This Word feature marks the end of a section and stores the section's formatting.

7. This newsletter element may include a logo, a unique typeface, or a graphic image to help create or reinforce an organization's identity.

8. This newsletter element includes a short phrase describing the purpose or audience of the newsletter.

APPLYING your skills

Assessment 1

1. Design and create two nameplates (including subtitle, folio, graphics, and/or logo) for two newsletters for organizations, schools, or a homeowners association to which you belong (real or fictional). Prepare thumbnail sketches of your designs and attach them to the back of your nameplates. Prepare one nameplate using an asymmetrical design. Also, include a graphic image, scanned image, WordArt, or special character symbol in at least one of the nameplates.

2. Save the documents and name them **c10sa01a, Nameplate** and **c10sa01b, Nameplate**.

3. Print and then **close c10sa01a, Nameplate** and **c10sa01b, Nameplate**.

Assessment 2

Besides taking classes, you also work part time creating desktop published documents for several offices and stores in your hometown. Naper Grove Vision Care recently hired you to design and produce its quarterly newsletter, which is distributed to patients in its offices in Naperville and Downers Grove. Figure 10.16 is provided as a sample newsletter. Create a newsletter using your own design ideas and knowledge of newsletter concepts and Word features presented in Chapter 10. *(Hint: Type j028685.wmf or eyes at the Search for text box at the Clip Art task pane to find an appropriate graphic.)* Include the following specifications:

1. Prepare a thumbnail sketch of your design.
2. Create an attention-getting nameplate.
3. Use a sans serif font in an appropriate size for the heading for the newsletter.

4. Open **Focal Point** located in your Chapter10 folder.
5. Use either a symmetrical or asymmetrical design.
6. Consider using a graphic from the Internet.
7. *Optional:* Include an inspirational, popular, or thought-provoking quotation at the end of your newsletter. There may be books of popular quotations at your public library, school library, or on the Internet (use a search engine and search for *quotes*).
8. Save your newsletter and name it **c10sa02, Eyes**.
9. Print and then close **c10sa02, Eyes**. (Attach your thumbnail sketch.)

FIGURE

10.16 *Assessment 2 Sample Solution*

Focal Point

An informative newsletter from Drs. Sims, Depukat, Giancola, and Kampschroeder
Fall 2005

NAPER GROVE VISION CARE
29 S. Webster, Suite 200
Naperville, IL 60540
(630) 555-3511

5018 Fairview Avenue
Downers Grove, IL 60515
(630) 555-3268

DON'T LOSE SIGHT OF DIABETIC EYE DISEASE

*A*s part of **National Diabetes Month in November,** the Federal government's National Eye Institute and the American Academy of Optometry are continuing their efforts to focus upon the importance of yearly-dilated eye exams for people with diabetes. These efforts are part of an ongoing campaign called "Don't Lose Sight of Diabetic Eye Disease," sponsored by the National Eye Health Education Program Partnership.

During their lifetime nearly half of the nation's estimated 16 million people with diabetes will develop some degree of diabetic retinopathy, the most common form of diabetic eye disease. Diabetic retinopathy damages the tiny blood vessels in the retina, the light-sensitive tissue that lines the back of the eye. As many as 25,000 people annually go blind from the disorder, making it a leading cause of blindness among working-age Americans. Diabetic eye disease can be detected through a dilated eye examination, which is recommended at least once a year. If discovered in time, severe vision loss or blindness can be prevented.

For more information or to learn more about diabetic eye disease, call our office or write: National Eye Health Education Program, 2020 Vision Place, Bethesda, MD 20892-3655.

LASER VISION CORRECTION NEWS

*O*f all the **Refractive Surgery options available currently,** the two most common and most successful are PRK (Photo Refractive Keratectomy) and Lasik (Laser Assisted In-Situ Keratomileusis). PRK is a refractive surgery that attempts to surgically correct myopia (nearsightedness) at the corneal plane by laser removal of corneal tissue. PRK has been performed since 1992 and is gaining worldwide acceptance.

Lasik is a laser procedure, which can reshape the surface of the eye in order to reduce the amount of refractive error and is most advantageous for patients who have moderate to high levels of myopia. Documentation and research is available to substantiate the effectiveness of Lasik.

Our doctors will gladly meet with you to discuss laser vision options and answer any questions you may have. If you are a candidate for laser surgery, we will refer you to a prominent surgeon for the procedure and co-manage all postoperative care with you and the surgeon.

Assessment 3

Open and then print a copy of **Butterfield Gardens** located in your Chapter10 folder. Assume you received this newsletter in the mail as a marketing device. The newsletter looks relatively neat and organized, but with closer inspection, you notice there are a few errors in spelling, formatting, and layout and design. Recreate the newsletter according to the following specifications, using your own ideas for an interesting newsletter layout and design:

1. Prepare a thumbnail sketch of your design.
2. Recreate the nameplate or create a nameplate (logo, subtitle, folio) of your own for this company; consider using WordArt in your nameplate design. *(Hint: The Butterfield Gardens logo is located in your Chapter10 folder.)*
3. Create a different layout and design for the newsletter using newspaper columns. Use more than one column in an asymmetrical design or consider using a template from Microsoft Publisher 2003 or from the Microsoft Office Online Templates Web site.
4. Correct all spelling and formatting errors. *(Hint: There are several errors in the data file.)*
5. Use any graphics or scanned images that seem appropriate.
6. Consider using a graphic or photo from the Internet.
7. Use any newsletter elements and enhancements that will improve the effectiveness and appeal of this newsletter. *(Hint: Remember to kern character pairs and condense or expand characters.)*
8. Save your publication and name it **c10sa03, Butterfield**.
9. Print and then close **c10sa03, Butterfield**. Attach the thumbnail sketch to the back of the newsletter.

Assessment 4

In this assessment you will open a Word document and then use the Mail Merge Wizard to merge an Access database. You **INTEGRATED** will print two copies of the Naper Grove newsletter created in Assessment 2 and then print the document in Figure 10.17 on the back of the newsletter after merging a data source to the address section of the page. To create the merge, complete the following steps:

1. Print two copies of the Naper Grove newsletter, **c10sa02, Eyes**.
2. Open **NG Address Main** from your Chapter10 folder.
3. Click <u>T</u>ools, point to <u>L</u>etters and Mailings, and then click <u>M</u>ail Merge.
4. At the first wizard step at the Mail Merge task pane, make sure *Letters* is selected in the *Select document type* section and then click the <u>Next: Starting document</u> hyperlink located toward the bottom of the task pane.
5. At the second wizard step, make sure *Use the current document* is selected in the *Select starting document* section and then click the <u>Next: Select recipients</u> hyperlink.
6. At the third wizard step, click *Use an existing list* in the *Select recipients* section, and then click the <u>Browse</u> hyperlink in the *Use an existing list* section. Select the Access database named **Naper Grove Patients** located in your Chapter10 folder.
7. At the Mail Merge Recipients dialog box, make sure all of the records are selected (a check box should display next to each row) and then click OK.
8. Click the <u>Next: Write your letter</u> hyperlink located toward the bottom of the Mail Merge task pane.
9. Position your insertion point inside the text box that displays at the right of the clip art at the bottom of the page and then click the <u>Address block</u> hyperlink.
10. At the Insert Address Block dialog box, make sure the address elements include *First name, Last name, Address, City, State Zip*, and then click OK.
11. At the fourth wizard step, click the <u>Next: Preview your letters</u> hyperlink.
12. At the fifth wizard step, click the <u>Next: Complete the merge</u> hyperlink.

13. At the sixth wizard step, click the <u>Edit individual letters</u> hyperlink located in the *Merge* section.
14. At the Merge to New Document dialog box, make sure <u>All</u> is selected and then click OK.
15. Save the merged letters and name the document **c10sa04, NG Addresses**.
16. Print the first and last merged letter to the back of each of the two copies of **c10sa02, Eyes**.
17. At the sixth wizard step, save the edited main document with the same name **(NG Address Main)**.
18. Close **NG Address Main**.
19. Close **c10sa04, NG Addresses** and then fold each newsletter with the address displaying on the outside—ready to mail.

F I G U R E

10.17 *Assessment 4 Sample Solution*

Fold Here

Fold Here

Naper Grove Vision Care
5018 Fairview Avenue
Downers Grove, IL 60515

Jansen Dell
1489 Belmont Avenue
Apt. #2
Downers Grove, IL 60616

Assessment 5

In this assessment, you will edit a photograph in Windows Paint and then insert the image into the Ride Safe newsletter you created in Exercises 1 through 8 as shown in Figure 10.18. Complete the following steps:

INTEGRATED

1. Open **c10ex08, Newsletter**.
2. Change the column layout of the newsletter by completing the following steps:
    a. Position the insertion point in the first paragraph, click F*o*rmat, and then C*o*lumns.
    b. At the Columns dialog box, select *L*eft in the *Presets* section.
    c. Deselect the check box at the *Line between* option to remove the vertical lines between the columns. Click OK.
3. Change the color of the dotted borders in the nameplate by selecting each line of dots, clicking the down-pointing arrow at the right of the Font Color button, and then selecting the Indigo color.
4. Select the Ride Safe logo and make sure the Picture toolbar displays.
5. Click the Set Transparent Color button on the Picture toolbar and click on the helmet of the cyclist in the logo.
6. After the cyclist's hat and shirt becomes transparent, click the down-pointing arrow at the right of the Fill Color button on the Drawing toolbar and select the Indigo color.
7. Display the Clip Art task pane, type j0316846.jpg (or **skates**, if the photograph is not available) in the *Search for* text box, and then click Go.
8. Delete the rollerblade clip art and insert the photograph found in Step 7.
9. Select the photograph and then click the Compress Pictures button on the Picture toolbar. Click A*p*ply at the optimization prompt.
10. Type j0316846.jpg (or **helmet**) at the *Search for* text box at the Clip Art task pane.
11. Right-click on the photograph found in Step 10 and then click C*o*py at the shortcut menu.
12. Use Windows Paint to customize the photograph found in Step 10 by completing the following steps:
    a. Click Start, point to All Programs, point to Accessories, and then click Paint.
    b. Click File and then Open at the Paint menu.
    c. At the Open dialog box, right-click in the white area of the My Pictures folder and then click Paste.
    d. Select the photograph and then click Open.
    e. Click the lime green color at the color palette at the bottom of the screen.
    f. Click the Brush tool on the tools palette at the left of the screen.
    g. Drag the crosshairs to draw four lines on the helmet as shown in Figure 10.18.
    h. Click File, Save As, type **Altered helmet** in the *File name* text box, and make sure *My Pictures* displays in the *Save in* list box, and then click Save.
    i. Close the Paint program.
    j. Delete the skater clip art in the newsletter and then insert **Altered helmet**.
13. Crop, resize, and then position the images as shown in Figure 10.18.
14. Save the newsletter and name it **c10sa05, Altered Newsletter**.
15. Print and then close **c10sa05, Altered Newsletter**.

10.18 *Assessment 5 Sample Solution*

Volume 5, Issue 1 • June 2005

RIDE SAFE

Bicycle and In-Line Skating Safety News •

IN-LINE SKATING—FASTEST GROWING SPORT

Injuries Up Dramatically

by Mary Beth Luhrsen

Last year, the Consumer Product Safety Commission (CPSC) released some alarming news on in-line skating, now the fastest growing recreational sport in America. They projected 83,000 serious injuries in 2005, more than double those of 2004. Even more alarming is the fact that children under age 15 account for 60% of these injuries.

The point is that in-line skating can be quite dangerous. Skaters often share the pavement with cars, trucks, bicyclists, pedestrians, and pets and

encounter loose gravel, potholes, puddles, and cracks. Add to that the fact that it is possible to achieve speeds exceeding 30 miles per hour, and you've got "accidents" waiting to happen.

Most injuries are wrist fractures, followed by elbows or lower arm fractures. Head injuries are not far behind. In fact, the CPSC projected that in 2002, 7,000 people would sustain head injuries—by far the most potentially disabling and even fatal of all in-line skating injuries.

Fortunately, safety education and appropriate protection can make a difference. The International In-Line Skating Association (IISA) recommends helmets be certified to the ANSI, ASTM, or Snell bicycle helmet safety standards. Remember to think "Safety on Wheels" in 2005.

A Message to Parents

by Mary Beth and Dane Luhrsen

For the past four years, Ride Safe has been committed to promoting safe bicycling and bicycle helmets. We started with our own four children (ages 2–8), who didn't want to wear helmets because their friends didn't wear them. We thought if we could offer "cool" looking helmets to a group of children, we could diminish this negative peer pressure. Our strategy worked, and the Ride Safe program has already convinced 300,000 people at over 2,500 schools to wear bicycle helmets.

In 1999, we expanded our program to include educational materials and protective gear for another very popular sport—in-line skating. Our new **Safety on Wheels**™ program includes safety gear made by Skating—In Line, "the choice of champions."

We hope you will play an active role in your children's "Safety on Wheels" and give serious consideration to purchasing protective equipment for your entire family. If you have any questions about Ride Safe products and services, please call us at 800-555-RIDE.

Assessment 6

1. Bring to class an example of a newsletter you have collected, received in the mail, picked up at a local business, or received from an organization of which you are a member. Use **Document Evaluation Checklist.doc** located in your Chapter10 folder to evaluate the newsletter. Revise this newsletter using a completely different layout and design. Incorporate your own ideas and use graphics or scanned images if available. Remember to use consistent elements throughout the document. Create your own styles or use the system styles included in Word to aid in formatting your document. *(Hint: Remember there are Paragraph, Character, Table, and List program styles available. Click All styles from the Show drop-down list at the bottom of the Styles and Formatting task pane.)* You may use a newsletter template at the Microsoft Office Online Templates Web page. Type newsletters in the *Search* text box to quickly locate the newsletter templates. Be sure to read the placeholder text—it may provide you with some valuable advice on formatting your newsletter. You may want to include this revision in your portfolio along with the original.
2. Save your publication and name it **c10sa06, Newsletter**.
3. Print and then close **c10sa06, Newsletter**. Attach the document evaluation checklist and the original document to the back of your revised version.
4. *Optional:* Draw a thumbnail sketch of a different nameplate for this publication. Include the folio and subtitle in the sketch. Add specifications as to which typeface, colors, clip art, and so on should be used in this design.

CHAPTER 11

Incorporating Newsletter Design Elements

PERFORMANCE OBJECTIVES

Upon successful completion of Chapter 11, you will be able to define and create design elements such as a header/footer, table of contents, masthead, sidebar, pull quote, kicker, end sign, jump line, caption, and color, and incorporate them into newsletters.

CHAPTER 11

DESKTOP PUBLISHING TERMS

Caption	Kicker	Sidebar
Copyfitting	Masthead	Spot color
End sign	Pull quote	Table of contents
Header/Footer	Scanner	
Jump line	Screening	

WORD FEATURES USED

Borders and Shading	Microsoft Office Online	Print 2 pages per sheet
Character spacing	Templates	Reading Layout view
Color	Newspaper columns	Styles
Headers/Footers	Paragraph spacing	Symbols
Line spacing	Picture	Text boxes
Linking text boxes	Picture editor	

Chapter 10 introduced you to the basic elements of a newsletter. Additional elements can be used to enhance the visual impact of a newsletter and to provide the reader with clues to the newsletter content. Newsletter-enhancing elements such as a table of contents, headers/footers, masthead, pull quotes, kickers, sidebars, captions, ruled lines, jump lines, graphics, illustrations, photos, and end signs are discussed in this chapter.

Adding Visually Enhancing Elements to a Newsletter

The most effective newsletters contain an appealing blend of text and visual elements. As illustrated in Figure 11.1, visual elements such as a table of contents, pull quote, kicker, and sidebar can be used as focal points to tempt the intended audience into reading more than just the nameplate. Visual elements such as headings, subheads, tables of contents, headers/footers, ruled lines, jump lines, and end signs can be used to indicate the directional flow of information in the document. Visual elements such as headings, subheads, headers/footers, pull quotes, sidebars, and page borders can be used to provide balance, proportion, and contrast in a newsletter. All of these elements, if used in a consistent format and manner, can create unity within a single newsletter and among different issues of a newsletter.

Formatting a Newsletter Using Columns, Text Boxes, and Tables

The majority of newsletters are formatted in a two- or three-column page layout. As discussed in Chapter 10, columns may be equal in width, providing a symmetrical design, or they may be unequal in width, providing an asymmetrical design. There are three ways to create the appearance of columns in a newsletter page layout—newspaper columns, text boxes, or tables. Your challenge is to determine which method will work best to achieve the desired results in your newsletter.

Using the Columns feature may seem like an obvious choice, especially when creating newsletters similar to those displayed and created in Chapter 10. However, placing text within text boxes or tables allows you to more easily change the position or shape (height and width) of an article, as is so often required when trying to copyfit text in a newsletter. For example, in the newsletter in Figure 11.1, a text box with a shadow border was used to create the sidebar; a table with a top border was used to create the table of contents. The second column was created by placing each article within a separate table. The dark blue line was drawn using the Line button on the Drawing toolbar to act as a visual separator between the two articles (tables). In this case, tables were the preferred method because of the graphic and pull quote that were contained in the articles. In a table, text will wrap around a graphic or text box, whereas text will not wrap around these elements if the original text is also contained within a text box. As compared to text boxes, however, tables are not as easy to position and may produce unpredictable results when inserting text boxes within the table.

As another example, look at Figure 11.6. To accommodate the "Bicycle Safety" article (on page 1) and the text wrapping around the pull quote, the Columns feature was used to format the page into two uneven columns. All of the remaining articles and features are contained in text boxes. When using any of these methods to format a newsletter, pay special attention to the alignment of these elements in relation to the columns you are trying to create visually.

11.1 *Visually Enhancing Elements in a Newsletter*

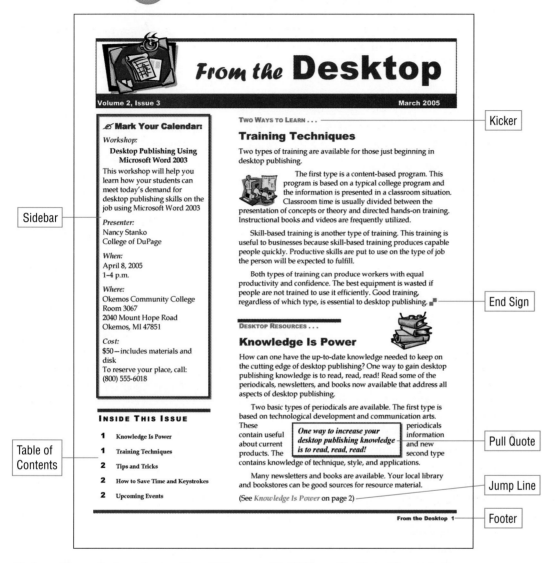

Using Templates from the Microsoft Office Online Templates Web Page

The Microsoft Office Online Templates Web page includes at least five newsletter templates, but this number may vary since templates are occasionally added to the collection. Figure 11.2 illustrates a list of templates available to you when you type newsletters in the *Search online for* text box in the *Templates* section of the New Document task pane and when you click the <u>Templates on Office Online</u> hyperlink in the *Templates* section of the New Document task pane and type newsletters Word in the *Search* text box on the Microsoft Office Online Templates Web page. If you preview the templates in Word, you will find that all of them were created using linked text boxes. The text box method is efficient when you need to make adjustments for *copyfitting* an entire page or document. The size of each text box can be increased or decreased to fit more or less text and the location of the boxes can be easily changed by dragging them to accommodate other elements in the newsletter.

Copyfitting
Fitting varying amounts of text or typographical enhancements into a fixed amount of space.

FIGURE

Newsletter Templates at the New Document Task Pane and at the Microsoft Office Online Templates Web Page

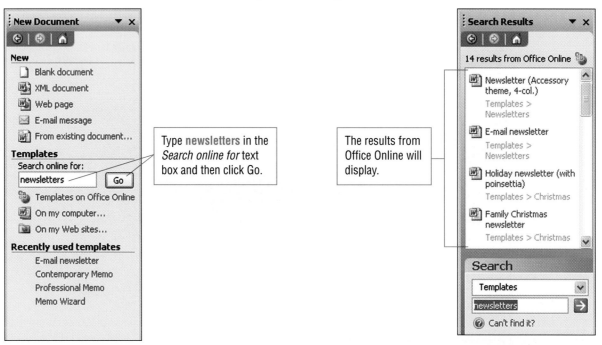

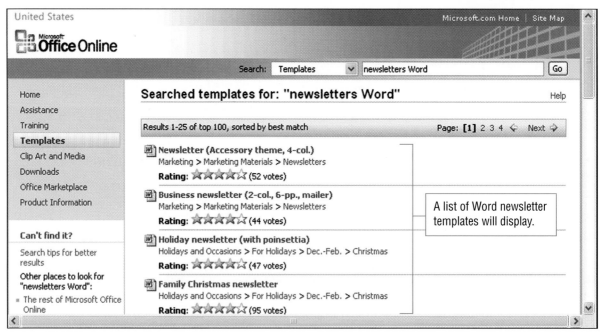

The newsletter templates illustrated in Figure 11.2 are formatted using styles that reinforce consistency within the newsletter. In addition, the basic design and colors used in each newsletter stay consistent from page to page. As you can see in Figure 11.3 each newsletter includes many predesigned design elements such as banners, table of contents, pull quotes, picture captions, headers and footers, sidebars, and a placeholder for the recipient's address.

11.3 *Viewing Design Elements in Word Newsletter Templates*

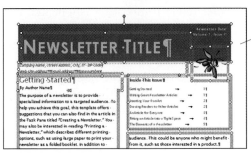

Business Newsletter

Business newsletter created in text boxes, in a 2-column layout, with 6 pages and a mailer

E-mail newsletter created in a table; use Web Layout view when creating this newsletter

Business E-Mail Newsletter

Business E-Mail Newsletter

Business e-mail newsletter created in a 2-column table, uneven layout with a narrow column on the left with background color and a wide column on the right with no background color, with hyperlinks

Holiday newsletter created in text boxes in a 2-column layout with a dots theme; includes a header, pull quote, and 6 pages

Holiday Newsletter with Poinsettia

Newsletter Template with Simple Theme

Newsletter template using text boxes

Newsletter template wizard using text boxes in a 2-column layout

Newsletter Wizard—Requires 2002 or Later

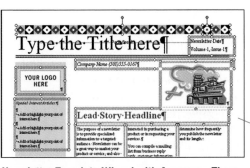

Newsletter Template Wizard with Accessory Theme

Newsletter template wizard using text boxes in a 4-column layout with 4 pages

Creating Headers and Footers

Header

Text repeated at the top of every page.

Header

Text repeated at the top of every page.

Footer

Text repeated at the bottom of every page.

Headers and/or footers are commonly used in newsletters, manuscripts, textbooks, reports, and other publications. The term *header* refers to text that is repeated at the top of every page. Alternately, the term *footer* refers to text that repeats at the bottom of every page. In Figure 11.1, a horizontal, dark blue ruled line, the name of the newsletter, and the page number are included in a footer at the bottom of the page. In a newsletter, information such as a page number, the name of the newsletter, the issue or date of the newsletter, and the name of the organization producing the newsletter are often included in a header or footer, as illustrated in the header and footer examples in Figure 11.4.

F I G U R E

11.4 *Examples of Headers and Footers*

TRAINING NEWS

Header Example

FINANCIAL SPOTLIGHT   NOVEMBER 2005

Header Example

·· *Winners wear helmets!*

Header Example

Footer Example

Page 2   **Fly with Sunshine Air**

Footer Example

Community News   **3**

Footer Example

3

DTP POINTERS

Use a header or footer to reinforce company or organizational identity.

Since a header or footer is commonly repeated on every page starting with the second page, it provides the perfect place to reinforce the identity of a company or organization. For example, including the company or organization name, a very small version of the nameplate, or a logo in a header or footer can increase a reader's awareness of your identity. In Figure 11.4, the *Ride Safe* header (the third header example) includes both the company logo and slogan, while the *Community News* footer includes the newsletter name and the page number.

Headers or footers, consistently formatted, help to establish unity among the pages of a newsletter, as well as among different issues of a newsletter. In addition, they serve as landmarks for the reader, adding to the directional flow of the document.

Horizontal ruled lines are frequently placed in headers or footers. These serve as a visually contrasting element that clearly identifies the top or bottom of each page. Different effects can be achieved by varying the weight (thickness) of the line, the number of lines, and the arrangement of the lines.

To create a header or footer, click <u>V</u>iew and then click <u>H</u>eader and Footer. Type the desired header text in the header pane. If you are creating a footer, click the Switch Between Header and Footer button on the Header and Footer toolbar, then type the desired footer text in the footer pane. Click <u>C</u>lose on the Header and Footer toolbar.

When you access the Header and Footer feature, Word automatically changes the viewing mode to Print Layout view, and your document text is dimmed in the background. After you insert text in the header and/or footer panes and then click <u>C</u>lose on the Header and Footer toolbar, the document text is displayed in black and the header and/or footer is dimmed. If the Normal viewing mode was selected before the header and/or footer was created, you are returned to the Normal viewing mode. In Normal view, a header or footer does not display on the screen. Change to Print Layout or Reading Layout viewing mode to view the header or footer text dimmed in the background, or use Print Preview to view how a header and/or footer will print. Figure 11.5 shows the *Ride Safe* newsletter in Reading Layout view. Notice the header and footer on the second page; even though the header and footer text displays dimmed, you can still read the text and it should print properly. Reading Layout view optimizes reading text and increases legibility.

DTP POINTERS
Consistent formatting of a header/footer helps to establish unity in a publication.

FIGURE 11.5 *Viewing a Newsletter in Reading Layout View*

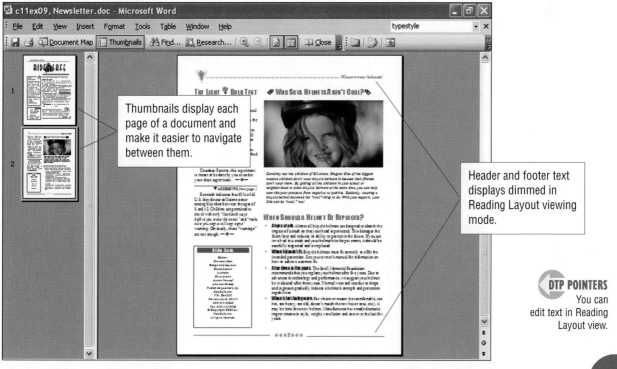

Thumbnails display each page of a document and make it easier to navigate between them.

Header and footer text displays dimmed in Reading Layout viewing mode.

DTP POINTERS
You can edit text in Reading Layout view.

Placing Headers/Footers on Different Pages

By default, Word will insert a header and/or footer on every page in the document. You can create different headers and footers in a document. For example, you can do the following:

- Create a unique header or footer on the first page.
- Omit a header or footer on the first page.
- Create different headers or footers for odd and even pages.
- Create different headers or footers for sections in a document.

Switch Between Header and Footer

Page Setup

Show Next

A different header or footer can be created on the first page of a document. To do this, position the insertion point anywhere in the first page, choose <u>V</u>iew, and then click <u>H</u>eader and Footer. (If you are creating a footer, click the Switch Between Header and Footer button.) Click the Page Setup button on the Header and Footer toolbar. Make sure the Layout tab is selected, choose the *Different first page* option, and then click OK or press Enter. The header/footer pane will be labeled *First Page Header (or Footer)*. Type the desired text for the first page header or footer, then click the Show Next button on the Header and Footer toolbar to open another header or footer pane labeled *Header (or Footer)*. Type the text for the header or footer that will print on all but the first page, then choose <u>C</u>lose at the Header and Footer toolbar. You can follow similar steps to omit a header or footer on the first page. Simply do not type any text when the first header or footer pane is opened.

The ability to place different headers and footers on odd and even pages is useful when numbering pages in a multiple-paged newsletter. Odd page numbers can be placed on the right side of the page and even page numbers can be placed on the left side of the page. For example, in a four-page newsletter, a footer can be created that includes right-aligned page numbering that will appear on the odd pages only. Alternately, another footer can be created that contains left-aligned page numbering that will appear on even pages only.

To create a different header and/or footer on odd and even pages, choose <u>V</u>iew, then <u>H</u>eader and Footer. (If you are creating a footer, click the Switch Between Header and Footer button.) Click the Page Setup button on the Header and Footer toolbar and then select the Layout tab. Make sure there is no check mark in the *Different first page* option. Choose the *Different <u>o</u>dd and even* option and then choose OK or press Enter. The header/footer pane will be labeled *Odd Page Header (or Footer)*. Type the desired text at the header or footer pane. Click the Show Next button on the Header and Footer toolbar. At the next header/footer pane, labeled *Even Page Header (or Footer),* type the desired text, and then click the <u>C</u>lose button on the Header and Footer toolbar.

Using Spot Color

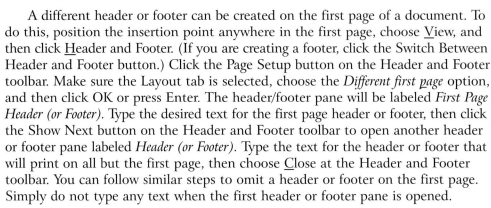

Spot color

Using another color in addition to black as an accent color in a publication.

Spot color refers to using one other color, in addition to black, as an accent color in a publication. Using spot color can make a black-and-white publication more appealing. If you have a color printer, you can see the results of using a second color immediately. You can then take the newsletter to be professionally printed on high-quality paper. Using color always adds to the cost of a publication, so be sure to price this out in the planning stages of your document. The more colors used in a publication, the more expensive it is to produce.

Spot color can be applied to such elements as graphic lines, graphic images, borders, background fill, headings, special characters, and end signs. If your logo or organizational seal contains a particular color, use that color as a unifying element throughout your publication. You can also apply spot color to the background in a reverse text box or to a drop cap. Variations of a spot color can be obtained by *screening*, or producing a lighter shade of the same color. Just as an all black-and-white page may have a gray look to it, using too much spot color can change the whole "color" of the document, defeating the purpose of using spot color for emphasis, contrast, and/or directional flow. Refer to the two newsletter samples in Figure 11.6 to see how spot color can add to the visual appeal of a publication.

Screening
Decreasing the intensity of a color to produce a lighter shade.

FIGURE

11.6 *Newsletter with and without Spot Color*

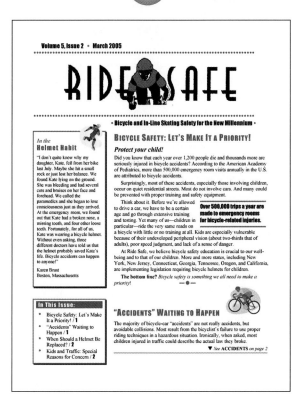

With spot color

Without spot color

In Exercises 1 through 9, you will build a two-page newsletter, as shown in Figure 11.21, adding visual enhancements as you proceed. In addition, you will use copyfitting techniques and add spot color to the newsletter throughout the range of exercises. First, in Exercise 1, you will create a header and footer that will begin on the second page of the newsletter. You will also create a blank different first page header/footer so that the header and footer text will not print on the first page.

(Before completing computer exercises, delete the Chapter10 folder on your disk. Next, copy the Chapter11 folder from the CD that accompanies this textbook to your disk and then make Chapter11 the active folder.)

Creating a Header and Footer in a Newsletter

1. Add a header and footer to the beginning stages of a newsletter, as shown on the second page of the *Ride Safe* newsletter in Figure 11.7, by completing the following steps:
    a. Open **Newsletter Banner** located in your Chapter11 folder.
    b. Save the document with Save As and name it **c11ex01, Header&Footer**.
    c. Change the zoom to *75%* and turn on the display of nonprinting characters.
    d. Select the month and year in the folio and type the current month and year.
    e. Select one of the dotted lines in the banner, display the Clipboard task pane by pressing Ctrl + C twice, and then click the Copy button on the Standard toolbar. (This line will be pasted in the header later.)
    f. Create two uneven columns using the Columns feature by completing the following steps (these columns are being set up for some steps in future exercises and to avoid some potential problems):
        1) Press Ctrl + End to position the insertion point below the newsletter banner, click Format, and then Columns.
        2) At the Columns dialog box, select *Left* in the *Presets* section, change the *Spacing* between the columns to *0.4"*, and then select *This point forward* in the *Apply to* list box.

        > Columns
        >
        > Presets: One, Two, Three, Left, Right
        >
        > Number of columns: 2   ☐ Line between
        >
        > Width and spacing
        > Col #: Width: Spacing:
        > 1:   2.07"   0.4"
        > 2:   4.73"
        >
        > ☐ Equal column width
        >
        > Apply to: This point forward   ☐ Start new column
        >
        > OK   Cancel
        >
        > Preview
        >
        > *Step 1f2*

        3) Click OK.
        4) Click Insert, Break, and then select *Column break*. Click OK. (Or press Ctrl + Shift + Enter.)
        5) With the insertion point at the top of the second column, repeat the previous step to insert one more column break. This will produce a second page, which is necessary to produce the header and footer.
    g. Press Ctrl + Home to position the insertion point at the beginning of the document.
    h. Create a different first page header/footer by completing the following steps:
        1) Click View and then Header and Footer.
        2) Click the Page Setup button on the Header and Footer toolbar, make sure the Layout tab is selected, and then click the *Different first page* check box.

        > *Step 1h2*
        >
        > Headers and footers
        > ☐ Different odd and even
        > ☑ Different first page

        3) Click OK. The header pane should display *First Page Header – Section 1*.

4) Leave the header pane blank so header/footer text will not print on the first page.

i. Create the header for the rest of the newsletter by completing the following steps:

1) Click the Show Next button on the Header and Footer toolbar. The header pane should be labeled *Header – Section 2*.

2) With the insertion point in the header pane, click Insert, point to Picture, and then click From File.

3) At the Insert Picture dialog box, change the *Look in* list box to display the location of your student data files and then double-click **Ridesf2teal** located in your Chapter11 folder.

4) Format the picture by completing the following steps:

   a) Select the image, select Format, and then click Picture.

   b) At the Format Picture dialog box, select the Size tab and change the *Height* and *Width* options in the *Scale* section to *35 %*.

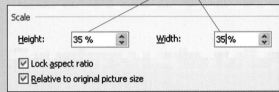

Step 1i4b

   c) Click OK or press Enter.

   d) Click once to the right of the image to deselect it.

5) Click the Text Box button on the Drawing toolbar and draw a text box to the right of the Ride Safe logo that will accommodate the dotted line and slogan shown on page 2 of the newsletter in Figure 11.7.

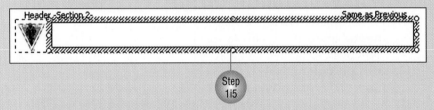

Step 1i5

6) Double-click the text box border to display the Format Text Box dialog box and make the following changes:

   a) Select the Colors and Lines tab and change the *Fill Color* option to No Fill and the *Line Color* option to No Line.

   b) Select the Size tab and then change the *Height* option to *0.3"* and the *Width* option to *6.8"*.

   c) Select the Layout tab and then click the Advanced button. Change the horizontal *Absolute position* option to *1.1"* and the *to the right of* option to *Page*, and change the vertical *Absolute position* option to *0.7"* and the *below* option to *Page*.

   d) Click OK to close the Advanced Layout dialog box.

   e) Click the Text Box tab and change the *Left* and *Right* margins in the *Internal margin* section to *0"*.

Step 1i6e

   f) Click OK or press Enter.

7) Insert the dotted line and slogan by completing the following steps:

   a) Click once inside the text box to position the insertion point.

b) Display the Clipboard task pane and click once on the dotted line item to insert it inside the text box. The line length will be adjusted in the following steps.

c) Position the insertion point in the middle of the dotted line, then press Delete until the paragraph symbol displays at the end of the dotted line within the text box. Continue pressing the Delete key until there is approximately enough space at the end of the line to type the slogan within the text box.

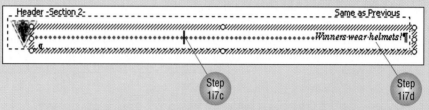

Step 1i7c

Step 1i7d

d) Position the insertion point at the end of the dotted line, then type **Winners wear helmets!** (If some of the text disappears, delete more of the dotted line until the entire slogan is visible.)

8) Select the slogan, display the Font dialog box, and then make the following changes:

a) Click the Fo_n_t tab and change the font to 12-point Times New Roman Bold Italic and the color to Black.

b) Click the Cha_r_acter Spacing tab, click the down-pointing arrow in the _Position_ list box, and select _Raised_. Make sure _3 pt_ displays in the _By_ text box. (This raises the slogan to be in alignment with the dotted line.)

| Spacing: | Normal ⌄ | B_y_: | ⌄ |
| Position: | Raised ⌄ | B_y_: | 3 pt ⌄ |

Step 1i8b

c) Click OK or press Enter.

d) If the slogan wraps to the next line, delete more of the dotted line until the slogan fits in the text box. If you delete more than necessary, click the Undo button on the Standard toolbar. If the slogan does not extend to the right margin, select a section of the line, and copy and paste it to the existing line.

j. Create the footer that will begin on the second page by completing the following steps:

1) Click the Switch Between Header and Footer button on the Header and Footer toolbar to switch to the footer pane.

2) Insert the round bullets by completing the following steps:

a) Click the Center alignment button on the Formatting toolbar.

b) Click Insert, _S_ymbol, and then make sure the _S_ymbols tab is selected.

c) Change the _Font_ option to Wingdings 2 and select the ninth bullet from the left in the eighth row (Wingdings 2: 152).

d) Click _I_nsert six times to insert six bullets and then click Close.

e) Select the six bullets and then change the font to 11-point Impact and the color to Teal.

f) Insert a space between each bullet, with the exception of inserting two spaces between the third and fourth bullets.

Step 1j2c

3) Insert and format automatic page numbering by completing the following steps:

a) Position the insertion point between the two spaces following the third bullet.

b) Click the Insert Page Number button on the Header and Footer toolbar to automatically insert a page number.

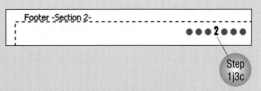

c) Select the page number and change the font to 14-point Impact.

4) Click the Page Setup button on the Header and Footer toolbar and select the Layout tab. In the *From edge* area of the *Headers and footers* section, change the distance from the bottom edge of the page in the *Footer* text box to *0.6"*. (Within the existing bottom margin setting, the footer may be partially cut off when printed, making this adjustment necessary. Increase this distance if the footer is only partially visible when viewing the document in Print Preview.) Click OK or press Enter.

5) Insert the horizontal lines on each side of the bullets by completing the following steps:

   a) Display the Drawing toolbar and then click the Line button on the Drawing toolbar.

   b) Hold down the Shift key and draw a line to the left of the three bullets that is the same approximate length and in the same approximate location as shown in Figure 11.7 (second page).

6) Double-click the horizontal line and make the following changes at the Format AutoShape dialog box:

   a) Select the Colors and Lines tab and change the setting in the line *Weight* text box to *2 pt*.

   b) Select the Size tab and change the line setting in the *Width* text box in the *Size and rotate* section to *2.9"*.

   c) Select the Layout tab and then click the *Advanced* button. At the Advanced Layout dialog box, select the Picture Position tab and then change the *Alignment* option in the *Horizontal* section to *Left* and the *relative to* option to *Margin*. Change the *Absolute position* option in the *Vertical* section to *10.3"* and the *below* option to *Page*.

   d) Click OK two times.

7) Select the line, hold down the Ctrl key and the Shift key, and then drag a copy of the line and position it to the right of the page number. Make sure the lines align properly.

8) Click *C*lose on the Header and Footer toolbar.

k. View the newsletter in Print Preview. Make sure no header or footer text displays on page 1 and the header and footer text correctly displays on page 2.

2. Save **c11ex01, Header&Footer**.

3. Position the insertion point on page 2 to print the page displaying the header and footer. Display the Print dialog box and select *Current page* in the *Page range* section. Click OK or press Enter.

4. Close **c11ex01, Header&Footer**.

FIGURE

11.7 *Exercise 1*

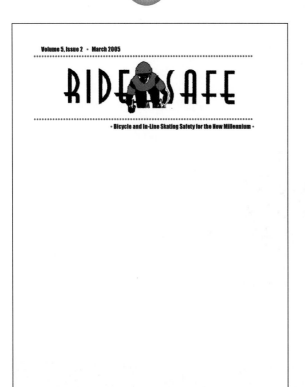

Page 1   Page 2

    Look at a hard copy of c11ex01, Header&Footer, and notice how the triangular logo in the header repeats the image of the bicyclist in the nameplate. In addition, the dotted line in the header on page 2 is consistent in style and color with the dotted lines located within the nameplate on page 1. The typeface used for the slogan is the same typeface that will be used for the body text. The footer repeats the round bullet symbols found in the nameplate, the header, and the end signs, which will later be used within the body copy to indicate the end of an article. As you can see, headers and footers can provide a visual connection between the separate pages in a multiple-paged publication.

Creating Sidebars in a Newsletter

Sidebar

Information or a related story set off from the body text in a graphics box.

A *sidebar* is a block of information or a related story that is set off from the body text in some type of a graphics box. In Figure 11.1, a sidebar is included in the first column. A sidebar can also include a photograph or a graphic image along with the text. Frequently, the sidebar contains a shaded or screened background. A screened (lighter) version of the main color used in a newsletter can serve as the background screen. The sidebar can be set in any position relative to the body text. In Word, sidebars can easily be created by creating a text box and inserting text. View the sample sidebars in Figure 11.8.

FIGURE

In Exercise 2, you will create a sidebar using a text box and then position the text box at the left margin to set up the boundaries for the first column. The newsletter page layout will include two columns based on an underlying three-column grid. In later exercises, you will add more visually enhancing elements to the same newsletter.

exercise 2

Inserting a Sidebar in a Newsletter

1. Insert a sidebar (containing the "In the Helmet Habit" feature) in the newsletter from Exercise 1, as shown in Figure 11.9, by completing the following steps:

    a. Open **c11ex01, Header&Footer**.
    b. Save the document with Save <u>A</u>s and name it **c11ex02, Sidebar**.
    c. Change the zoom to *75%* and then turn on the display of nonprinting characters.
    d. Turn on kerning at 14 points.
    e. Position the insertion point to the left of the first column break in the first column on page 1.
    f. Click the Text Box button on the Drawing toolbar and draw a text box that is approximately the same size and in the same position as the sidebar (see "In the Helmet Habit") shown in Figure 11.9.
    g. Make sure the insertion point is positioned within the text box and then insert **Helmet Habit Text** located in your Chapter11 folder. Do not be concerned if all of the text is not visible at this point.

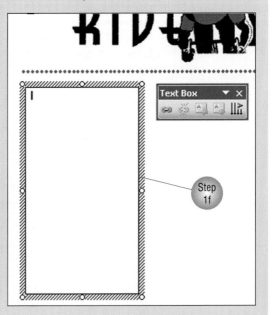

h. Make sure the font size of the sidebar text is 10 points. If not, click the text box border and then change the font size to 10 points.

i. Double-click the text box border and make the following changes at the Format Text Box dialog box:

1) Select the Colors and Lines tab and change the *Color* option in the *Line* section to Teal and the *Weight* option in the *Line* section to *1.5 pt*.

2) Select the Size tab and change the *Height* option in the *Size and rotate* section to *4.6"* and the *Width* option to *2.2"*.

3) Select the Layout tab and click the Advanced button. At the Advanced Layout dialog box, select the Picture Position tab and change the *Alignment* option in the *Horizontal* section to *Left* and

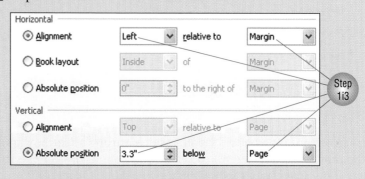

Step 1i3

the *relative to* option to *Margin*. In the *Vertical* section, change the *Absolute position* option to *3.3"* and the *below* option to *Page*.

4) Click OK twice.

j. Add a shadow to the text box border by completing the following steps:

1) With the text box still selected, click the Shadow Style button on the Drawing toolbar, and then click the downpointing arrow at the right of the Shadow Settings button at the bottom of the palette.

2) Change the shadow color to Black using the down-pointing arrow at the right of the Shadow Color button on the Shadow Settings toolbar. The shadow will automatically be added to the text box border.

Step 1j2

3) Close the Shadow Settings toolbar.

k. Format the title of the sidebar text by completing the following steps:

1) Change the zoom to *100%*.

2) Position the insertion point at the beginning of the title *In the Helmet Habit* and then press Enter.

3) Select *In the* and then change the font to 12-point Times New Roman Bold Italic and the color to Teal.

4) Position the insertion point after *In the,* delete the space, and then press Enter.

5) Select *Helmet Habit* and make the following changes:

a) Change the font to 14-point Impact and the color to Teal and then expand the character spacing by 1.2 points.

b) Position the insertion point within *In the,* display the Paragraph dialog box, and then change the *Line spacing* option to *Exactly* and the *At* option to *10 pt*.

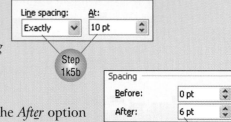

Step 1k5b

Step 1k5c

c) Position the insertion point within the words *Helmet Habit* and change the *After* option in the *Spacing* section to *6 pt*.

l. For use in future issues, create styles for the sidebar heading by completing the following steps:

1) Position the insertion point within *In the* and click inside the *Style* list box on the Formatting toolbar.
2) Type **Sidebar Heading-1** and press Enter.
3) Position the insertion point anywhere within *Helmet Habit,* then follow the preceding two steps and name this style **Sidebar Heading-2**.

m. Position the insertion point after *...anyone!"* in the last line of the article text, press Delete to eliminate the extra hard return, and change the spacing *After* paragraph option to *6 pt*.

n. Insert the skater image by completing the following steps:
1) Deselect the text box and make sure your insertion point is not located in the text box containing the sidebar text.
2) Display the Clip Art task pane box and then type **j0199061.wmf** in the *Search for* text box or type the keyword **skating** and then click Go. *(Hint: Substitute the clip art if necessary or desired.)*
3) Click the image to place a copy of the image in your newsletter. Do not be concerned if parts of your newsletter move out of place. Adjustments will be made in the next step.

o. Format the skater image by completing the following steps:
1) Select the skater image, click the Text Wrapping button on the Picture toolbar, and then click the In Front of Text option.

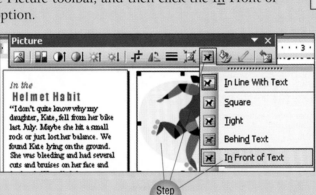

2) Use the corner sizing handles and reduce the size of the image so that it is similar to the skater image shown in Figure 11.9.
3) Click and drag the image so that it is overlapping the upper right corner of the sidebar text box as shown in Figure 11.9.

2. Save **c11ex02, Sidebar**.

3. Print the first page only and then **close c11ex02, Sidebar**. *(Hint: This newsletter continues to build throughout the remaining chapter exercises. Saving each exercise as a separate document takes up a tremendous amount of disk space. As an alternative, open c11ex02, Sidebar, save the document with Save **A**s, and name the document c11newsletter. Continue completing the remaining exercises and save each exercise with the same name, c11newsletter, as you progress through the exercises. Consult with your instructor about this recommendation.)*

FIGURE

11.9 *Exercise 2, Page 1*

Volume 5, Issue 2 • March 2005

RIDE SAFE

• Bicycle and In-Line Skating Safety for the New Millennium •

In the
Helmet Habit

"I don't quite know why my daughter, Kate, fell from her bike last July. Maybe she hit a small rock or just lost her balance. We found Kate lying on the ground. She was bleeding and had several cuts and bruises on her face and forehead. We called the paramedics and she began to lose consciousness just as they arrived. At the emergency room, we found out that Kate had a broken nose, a missing tooth, and four other loose teeth. Fortunately, for all of us, Kate was wearing a bicycle helmet. Without even asking, three different doctors have told us that the helmet probably saved Kate's life. Bicycle accidents can happen to anyone!"

Karen Brust
Boston, Massachusetts

Creating a Newsletter Table of Contents

Table of contents
A list of articles and features and their page numbers.

A table of contents is optional in a one- or two-page newsletter. However, in multiple-paged newsletters, a table of contents is an important and necessary element. A *table of contents* lists the names of articles and features in the newsletter, along with their page numbers. The information in the table of contents greatly influences whether the reader moves beyond the front page. Consequently, the table of contents needs to stand out from the surrounding information. It must also be legible and easy to follow.

A table of contents is usually located on the front page of a newsletter. It is often placed in the lower left or right corner of the page. It can, however, be placed closer to the top of the page on either side or even within an asymmetrically designed nameplate. If a newsletter is designed to be a self-mailer, the table of contents can be placed in the mailing section so the reader is invited into the newsletter before it is even opened.

The table of contents in Figure 11.1 is located in the lower left corner. The dark blue top border and the bold title and numbers make the table of contents easily identifiable while adding visual interest to the page. The table of contents, along with the shadow box above it, also adds weight to the left side of the page and balance to the page as a whole.

There are many ways to format a table of contents to make it easy to find and visually interesting. As illustrated in Figure 11.10, a table of contents can easily be made by inserting text in a text box and then adding various borders, screened backgrounds, fonts, graphics, lines, reverse text, and special characters. You can also use paragraph borders and shading to highlight text in a table of contents.

FIGURE

11.10 *Examples of Tables of Contents*

Inside! 📖

Strong Performance on
  Standardized Tests   2
National Merit Scholars
  Named   2
District Reaffirms Long-
  Range Plans   3
Districtwide Cleaning
  Service Contract   4
Volunteers Needed   4
Board of Education   4

In This Issue:

Who's Using Desktop
Publishing?/1

From the Director's
Desk/1

Academic News/2

Administrative News/3

In the Future/4

Training News/4

Inside This Issue:
▲ Fitness and Family Fun 2
▲ Runner's Training Program 3
▲ Fitness and Pregnancy 3
▲ Fitness and Weight Control 4

IN THIS ISSUE:
➤ Announcing PC Help Version 4.0—
  Coming Soon! (**Page 1**)
➤ From the Editor's Desk (**Page 2**)
➤ The Technical Advisor (**Page 2**)

exercise 3

Inserting a Table of Contents in a Newsletter

1. Add a table of contents, as shown in Figure 11.11, to the newsletter from Exercise 2 by completing the following steps:
   a. Open **c11ex02, Sidebar**.
   b. Save the document with Save <u>A</u>s and name it **c11ex03, Table of Contents**.

c. Change the zoom to *75%* and turn on the display of nonprinting characters.
d. Insert the table of contents text in a text box by completing the following steps:
  1) Draw a text box that is approximately the same size and in the same position as the table of contents text box shown in Figure 11.11.
  2) Position the insertion point within the text box and insert the file **Table of Contents Text** located in your Chapter11 folder.
e. Double-click the text box border and make the following changes at the Format Text Box dialog box:

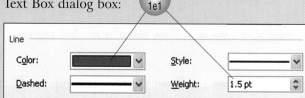

  1) Select the Colors and Lines tab, change the line *Color* option to Teal, and then change the line *Weight* option to *1.5 pt*.
  2) Select the Size tab, change the *Height* option to *1.9"*, and change the *Width* option to *2.2"*.
  3) Select the Layout tab and click the <u>A</u>dvanced button. At the Advanced Layout dialog box, select the Picture Position tab, and then change the *Alignment* option in the *Horizontal* section to *Left* and the *relative to* option to *Margin*. In the *Vertical* section, change the *Absolute position* option to *7.62"* and the *below* option to *Margin*.
  4) Click OK twice.
f. Add a black shadow border to the text box by using the Shadow Style button on the Drawing toolbar. Follow the same steps to create the shadow as listed in Exercise 2, Steps 1j1–1j3.

g. Format the table of contents title by completing the following steps:
  1) Change the zoom to *100%*.
  2) Position the insertion point to the left of *In This Issue:* and then press the spacebar once.
  3) Select *In This Issue:* and make the following changes at the Font dialog box:
    a) Click the Fo<u>n</u>t tab and change the font to 12-point Impact.
    b) Click the Character Spacing tab and change the *Spacing* option to *Expanded* and the *By* option to *1.2 pt*.
    c) Click OK or press Enter.
  4) Position the insertion point to the right of the colon in the title, display the Paragraph dialog box, and then change the spacing *After* the paragraph to 8 points. Click OK or press Enter.
  5) Position the insertion point anywhere within the title, then create the shaded background by completing the following steps:
    a) Click Format, <u>B</u>orders and Shading, and then select the <u>S</u>hading tab.
    b) Select Teal (the fifth color from the left in the fifth row of the *Fill* section).
    c) Click OK or press Enter.

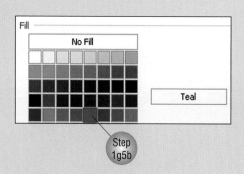

  6) Select *In This Issue:* and change the text color to white.

h. For use in future issues, create a style from the formatted title by completing the following steps:
   1) Position the insertion point within *In This Issue:* and then click inside the *Style* list box on the Formatting toolbar.
   2) Type ToC Heading and then press Enter.
i. Format the bulleted text in the table of contents by completing the following steps:
   1) Select the remaining text below the title and change the font to 11-point Times New Roman. ***(Hint: Do not be concerned if some of the text is not visible at this point.)***
   2) With the text still selected, display the Paragraph dialog box, and then make the following changes:
      a) Change the spacing *After* the paragraph to *2 pt*.
      b) Change the *Line Spacing* option to *Exactly* and the *At* option to *12 pt*.
      c) Click OK to close the Paragraph dialog box.
   3) With the text still selected, add a bullet to each article name by completing the following steps:
      a) Select Format, Bullets and Numbering and then select the Bulleted tab.
      b) Click the first bulleted selection and then click Customize.
      c) At the Customize Bulleted List dialog box, click Font, then change the font size to 14 points and the color to Teal.
      d) Click OK or press Enter.
      e) Click the Character button and change the *Font* option to Wingdings. Select the last (round) bullet from the left in the eighth row (Wingdings: 159). Click OK to close the Symbol dialog box.

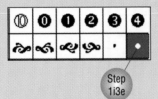

Step
1i3e

      f) Change the *Indent at* option in the *Bullet position* section to 0″. In the *Text position* section, change the *Tab space after* option to 0.3″ and the *Indent at* option to 0.3″.
      g) Click OK or press Enter to close the Customize Bulleted List dialog box.
   4) Select each page number and change the font to Impact.
j. For use in future issues, create a style for the bulleted items in the table of contents by completing the following steps:
   1) Position the insertion point anywhere within the first bulleted item.
   2) Click once in the *Style* list box on the Formatting toolbar to select the current style name.
   3) Type ToC Bullets as the new style name and press Enter.
2. Save **c11ex03, Table of Contents** (or save as **c11newsletter** as suggested in Exercise 2, Step 3).
3. Print the first page only and then close **c11ex03, Table of Contents**. ***(Hint: You may want to wait and print the whole newsletter when it is completed in Exercise 9.)***

Volume 5, Issue 2 • March 2005

RIDE SAFE

• **Bicycle and In-Line Skating Safety for the New Millennium** •

In the
Helmet Habit

"I don't quite know why my daughter, Kate, fell from her bike last July. Maybe she hit a small rock or just lost her balance. We found Kate lying on the ground. She was bleeding and had several cuts and bruises on her face and forehead. We called the paramedics and she began to lose consciousness just as they arrived. At the emergency room, we found out that Kate had a broken nose, a missing tooth, and four other loose teeth. Fortunately for all of us, Kate was wearing a bicycle helmet. Without even asking, three different doctors have told us that the helmet probably saved Kate's life. Bicycle accidents can happen to anyone!"

Karen Brust
Boston, Massachusetts

In This Issue:

- Bicycle Safety: Let's Make It a Priority! / **1**
- "Accidents" Waiting to Happen / **1**
- When Should a Helmet Be Replaced? / **2**
- Kids and Traffic: Special Reasons for Concern / **2**

Pull quote
A short, direct phrase, statement, or important point formatted to stand out from the rest of the body copy.

Creating Pull Quotes

A pull quote, as illustrated in Figure 11.12, acts as a focal point, helps to break up lengthy blocks of text, and provides visual contrast. A *pull quote* (also called a *pullout* or *callout*) is a direct phrase, summarizing statement, or important point associated with the body copy of a newsletter. Using pull quotes is an excellent way to draw readers into an article.

Effective pull quotes are interesting, brief, and formatted to stand out from the rest of the body copy. Keep in mind the following tips when creating pull quotes for a newsletter:

- Include relevant and interesting text in a pull quote. Edit any direct quotes so they will not be taken out of context when read individually as a pull quote.
- Keep pull quotes brief—approximately 10 to 15 words and never longer than a few lines.
- Choose a font or font style that contrasts with the font used for the article text.
- Increase the type size.
- Vary the typestyle by bolding and/or italicizing the pull quote text.
- Set off the pull quote from the rest of the body text with ruled lines or a graphics box.
- Use at least one element in your pull quote design that establishes a visual connection with the rest of your newsletter.
- Be consistent. Use the same format for other pull quotes throughout the newsletter and throughout future issues of the same newsletter.

The pull quotes displayed in Figure 11.12 show some different ways that pull quote formatting can be customized to attract the reader's attention. The rectangular pull quote examples were created using text boxes. The oval and round rectangle were created using AutoShapes. Various background fills were used including solid fill, textured fill, and gradient fill. Additional effects such as borders, shadows, and 3-D were also used. These pull quote examples are only a small representation of the many ways that pull quotes can be customized.

DTP POINTERS
Pull quotes should be brief and interesting, and stand out from the rest of the text.

FIGURE

11.12 *Examples of Various Pull Quote Formats*

In design, function dictates form . . .

In design, function dictates form . . .

In design, function dictates form . . .

In design, function dictates form . . .

In design, function dictates form . . .

IN DESIGN, FUNCTION DICTATES FORM . . .

DTP POINTERS
Create styles for repetitive formatting.

In Exercise 4, you will insert the first newsletter article, format the article heading and article text, and create a pull quote. Since these particular elements may be repeated throughout the newsletter, you will then create styles for these elements.

Creating Styles and a Pull Quote in a Newsletter

1. Insert and format the first article, create a pull quote, and create styles, as shown in Figure 11.13, by completing the following steps:
   a. Open **c11ex03, Table of Contents**.
   b. Save the document with Save <u>A</u>s and name it **c11ex04, Pull Quote**.
   c. Change the zoom to *75%* and turn on the display of nonprinting characters.
   d. Position the insertion point to the left of the column break in the second column and then insert **Bicycle Safety Text** located in your Chapter11 folder.
   e. Select the article heading *Bicycle Safety: Let's Make It a Priority!* and make the following changes:
      1) Change the font to 18-point Impact, change the color to Teal, and apply S<u>m</u>all caps (Ctrl + Shift + K).
      2) Expand the character spacing by 1.2 points.
      3) Change the spacing after the paragraph to 6 points.
   f. Create a style for future article headings by completing the following steps:
      1) Make sure the insertion point is positioned within the article heading.
      2) Click once in the *Style* list box located on the Formatting toolbar to select the current style name.
      3) Type Article Head as the new style name and press Enter.
   g. Format the article text by completing the following steps:
      1) Position the insertion point at the beginning of the line *Did you know...* and select all of the article text.
      2) Change the font to 11-point Times New Roman.
      3) Display the Paragraph dialog box and make the following changes:
         a) At the <u>I</u>ndents and Spacing tab, change the spacing *A<u>f</u>ter* the paragraph to *3 pt.*
         b) In the *Indentation* section, click the down-pointing arrow to the right of the *Special* option and select *First line*, and then change the *By* option to *0.2"* to indent the first line of each paragraph.

> **Step 1g3b**

Indentation				
<u>L</u>eft:	5"		<u>S</u>pecial:	B<u>y</u>:
<u>R</u>ight:	0"		First line	0.2"

Spacing				
<u>B</u>efore:	0 pt		Li<u>n</u>e spacing:	<u>A</u>t:
Af<u>t</u>er:	3 pt		Single	

> **Step 1g3a**

   c) Click OK or press Enter.
   h. Create a style for the article text by completing the following steps:
      1) With the article text still selected, click once in the *Style* list box located on the Formatting toolbar to select the current style name.
      2) Type Article Text as the style name and press Enter.

i. Create a style for the first paragraph of the article that eliminates the first line indentation by completing the following steps:
   1) Position the insertion point within the first paragraph of article text.
   2) Display the Paragraph dialog box, make sure the Indents and Spacing tab is selected, then change the *Special* option to *(none)* in the *Indentation* section.

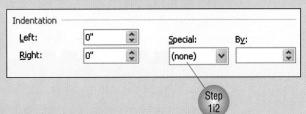

   3) Click OK or press Enter.
   4) Click once in the *Style* list box on the Formatting toolbar to select the current style name.
   5) Type **1st Paragraph** as the style name and then press Enter.
j. Insert and format a text box to hold the pull quote by completing the following steps:
   1) Click the Text Box button on the Drawing toolbar and then draw a text box that is approximately the same size and in the same location as the pull quote shown in Figure 11.13.
   2) Double-click the text box border and make the following changes at the Format Text Box dialog box:
      a) Select the Colors and Lines tab and change the line *Color* option to No Line.
      b) Select the Size tab and then change the *Height* option to *0.78"* and the *Width* option to *2.01"*.
      c) Select the Layout tab, change the *Wrapping style* option to *Tight*, and then click the *Advanced* button.

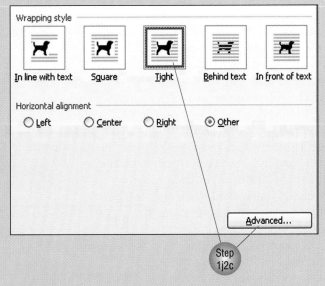

      d) At the Advanced Layout dialog box, select the Picture Position tab and then change the *Absolute position* option in the *Horizontal* section to *5.75"* and the *to the right of* option to *Page*. Change the *Absolute position* option in the *Vertical* section to *5.36"* and the *below* option to *Page* and click OK.
      e) Select the Text Box tab, and then change the *Left, Right, Top,* and *Bottom* margins in the *Internal margin* section to *0"*.
      f) Click OK.

k. Insert and format the pull quote text by completing the following steps:
  1) Click once in the text box to position the insertion point.
  2) Type Over 500,000 trips a year are made to emergency rooms for bicycle-related injuries.
  3) Select the text just entered and change the font to 12-point Impact.
l. Add the top and bottom borders to the pull quote text by completing the following steps:
  1) With the insertion point positioned within the pull quote text, display the Borders and Shading dialog box and then select the Borders tab.

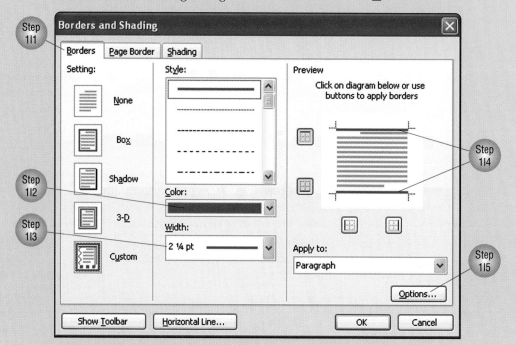

  2) Change the border color to Teal.
  3) Change the border line _Width_ option to 2¼ points.
  4) In the _Preview_ section, click the top and bottom of the diagram to insert borders in these areas; the left and right sides of the diagram should be borderless.
  5) Click the Options button to display the Border and Shading Options dialog box.
  6) Adjust the distance from the top border to the text to 2 points and then click OK.
  7) Click OK again to close the Borders and Shading dialog box.
m. Create a style for the pull quote by completing the following steps:
  1) With the insertion point located within the pull quote text, click once in the _Style_ list box on the Formatting toolbar to select the current style name.
  2) Type Pull Quote as the new style name and press Enter.
n. In the last paragraph, select and bold _The bottom line?_ Then select and italicize the last sentence, _Bicycle safety is something we all need to make a priority!_

2. Save **c11ex04, Pull Quote** (or save as **c11newsletter** as suggested in Exercise 2, Step 3).
3. Print the first page only and then close **c11ex04, Pull Quote**. _(Hint: You may want to wait and print the whole newsletter when it is completed in Exercise 9.)_

FIGURE

11.13 *Exercise 4, Page 1*

Volume 5, Issue 2 • March 2005

RIDE SAFE

• Bicycle and In-Line Skating Safety for the New Millennium •

In the
Helmet Habit

"I don't quite know why my daughter, Kate, fell from her bike last July. Maybe she hit a small rock or just lost her balance. We found Kate lying on the ground. She was bleeding and had several cuts and bruises on her face and forehead. We called the paramedics and she began to lose consciousness just as they arrived. At the emergency room, we found out that Kate had a broken nose, a missing tooth, and four other loose teeth. Fortunately, for all of us, Kate was wearing a bicycle helmet. Without even asking, three different doctors have told us that the helmet probably saved Kate's life. Bicycle accidents can happen to anyone!"

Karen Brust
Boston, Massachusetts

BICYCLE SAFETY: LET'S MAKE IT A PRIORITY!

Did you know that each year over 1,200 people die and thousands more are seriously injured in bicycle accidents? According to the American Academy of Pediatrics, more than 500,000 emergency room visits annually in the U.S. are attributed to bicycle accidents.

Surprisingly, most of these accidents, especially those involving children, occur on quiet residential streets. Most do not involve cars. And many could be prevented with proper training and safety equipment.

Think about it. Before we're allowed to drive a car, we have to be a certain age and go through extensive training and testing. Yet many of us—children in particular—ride the very same roads on a bicycle with little or no training at all. Kids are especially vulnerable because of their undeveloped peripheral vision (about two-thirds that of adults), poor speed judgment, and lack of a sense of danger.

Over 500,000 trips a year are made to emergency rooms for bicycle-related injuries.

At Ride Safe, we believe bicycle safety education is crucial to our well-being and to that of our children. More and more states, including New York, New Jersey, Connecticut, Georgia, Tennessee, Oregon, and California, are implementing legislation requiring bicycle helmets for children.

The bottom line? *Bicycle safety is something we all need to make a priority!*

In This Issue:

Creating Kickers and End Signs

Additional elements, such as kickers and end signs, can also be used in a newsletter. A *kicker* is a brief sentence or phrase that is a lead-in to an article. Generally, it is set in a size smaller than the headline but larger than the body text. It is often stylistically distinct from both the headline and the body text. Kickers can be placed above or below the headline or article heading. In Figure 11.1, a kicker is placed above the first article heading and serves as a lead-in to the first article.

Kicker
A lead-in phrase or sentence that precedes the beginning of an article.

End sign

A symbol or special character indicating the end of an article.

Symbols or special characters used to indicate the end of a section of text, such as the end of an article, are known as ***end signs***. In Figure 11.1, an end sign follows the last paragraph in the first article. The end sign is the same color as the accent color in the newsletter to contribute to the unified appearance of this newsletter. The end sign in the *Ride Safe* newsletter, shown in Figure 11.14, mimics the dots in the nameplate and the footer and the colors coordinate with the newsletter's color scheme. Appropriate special characters or combinations of these characters—such as ❖, ❀, •, ◈, ▶, ☌, ✗, ▪, and ☧, from the Wingdings and Webdings font selections—may be used as end signs.

In Exercise 5, you will add a kicker and an end sign to the *Ride Safe* newsletter from Exercise 4.

exercise 5

Creating a Kicker and an End Sign in a Newsletter

1. Insert the kicker and end sign shown in Figure 11.14 to the newsletter from Exercise 4 by completing the following steps:
   a. Open **c11ex04, Pull Quote**.
   b. Save the document with Save <u>A</u>s and name it **c11ex05, End Sign**.
   c. Change the zoom to *75%* and turn on the display of nonprinting characters.
   d. Create the kicker by completing the following steps:
      1) Position the insertion point at the beginning of the first paragraph below the article heading.
      2) Type Protect your child! and then press Enter.
      3) Select *Protect your child!* and change the font to 14-point Times New Roman Bold Italic.
   e. Create a style for the kicker formatting by completing the following steps:
      1) Position the insertion point anywhere within the kicker.
      2) Click once in the *Style* list box on the Formatting toolbar to select the current style name.
      3) Type Kicker and press Enter.
   f. Create the end sign by completing the following steps:
      1) Position the insertion point at the end of the first article and press the Tab type three times. *(Hint: Make sure italic formatting is turned off.)*
      2) Display the Symbol dialog box and select the S<u>p</u>ecial Characters tab.
      3) Double-click the *Em Dash* selection and then select the <u>S</u>ymbols tab.

      Symbol

      | <u>S</u>ymbols | Special Characters |

      <u>F</u>ont: Wingdings 2

      Step 1f4

      4) Change the *Font* option to Wingdings 2 and double-click the ninth (round) bullet from the left in the eighth row (Wingdings 2: 152).
      5) Click the Special Characters tab again, double-click the *Em Dash* selection, and then click Close.
      6) Insert one space on each side of the bullet.

7) Select the end sign and change the font to 11-point Impact. Select the round bullet and change the color to Teal.

2. Save **c11ex05, End Sign** (or save as **c11newsletter** as suggested in Exercise 2, Step 3).

3. Print the first page only and then close **c11ex05, End Sign**. *(Hint: You may want to wait and print the whole newsletter when it is completed in Exercise 9.)*

F I G U R E

11.14 *Exercise 5, Page 1*

Volume 5, Issue 2 • March 2005

• **Bicycle and In-Line Skating Safety for the New Millennium** •

BICYCLE SAFETY: LET'S MAKE IT A PRIORITY!

Protect your child!

Did you know that each year over 1,200 people die and thousands more are seriously injured in bicycle accidents? According to the American Academy of Pediatrics, more than 500,000 emergency room visits annually in the U.S. are attributed to bicycle accidents.

Surprisingly, most of these accidents, especially those involving children, occur on quiet residential streets. Most do not involve cars. And many could be prevented with proper training and safety equipment.

Think about it. Before we're allowed to drive a car, we have to be a certain age and go through extensive training and testing. Yet many of us—children in particular—ride the very same roads on a bicycle with little or no training at all. Kids are especially vulnerable because of their undeveloped peripheral vision (about two-thirds that of adults), poor speed judgment, and lack of a sense of danger.

Over 500,000 trips a year are made to emergency rooms for bicycle-related injuries.

At Ride Safe, we believe bicycle safety education is crucial to our well-being and to that of our children. More and more states, including New York, New Jersey, Connecticut, Georgia, Tennessee, Oregon, and California, are implementing legislation requiring bicycle helmets for children.

The bottom line? *Bicycle safety is something we all need to make a priority!*
— ● —

In the
Helmet Habit

"I don't quite know why my daughter, Kate, fell from her bike last July. Maybe she hit a small rock or just lost her balance. We found Kate lying on the ground. She was bleeding and had several cuts and bruises on her face and forehead. We called the paramedics and she began to lose consciousness just as they arrived. At the emergency room, we found out that Kate had a broken nose, a missing tooth, and four other loose teeth. Fortunately for all of us, Kate was wearing a bicycle helmet. Without even asking, three different doctors have told us that the helmet probably saved Kate's life. Bicycle accidents can happen to anyone!"

Karen Brust
Boston, Massachusetts

In This Issue:

- Bicycle Safety: Let's Make It a Priority! / **1**
- "Accidents" Waiting to Happen / **1**
- When Should a Helmet Be Replaced? / **2**
- Kids and Traffic: Special Reasons for Concern / **2**

Using Linked Text Boxes in Newsletters

Newsletters routinely contain articles that start on one page and are continued onto another page. Word's text box linking feature makes it easier to create articles that are continued on subsequent pages. This feature allows text to flow from one text box to another even if the text boxes are not adjacent or on the same page. Any text box can be linked with any other text box. You need at least two text boxes to create a link; however, any number of text boxes can be used to create a chain of linked text boxes. For example, if your article starts on page 1, is continued on page 2, and then finishes on page 4, you can create a chain of three linked text boxes that will contain the article text. When the first text box is filled, the text automatically flows into the second text box, and then into the third text box in the chain. This is especially useful in editing and positioning an article that is continued on another page. If you add or delete text in one of the text boxes, the remaining text in the article in the other text boxes adjusts to the change also. Furthermore, you can establish more than one chain of linked text boxes in a document. For example, you can create a chain of linked text boxes for an article that begins on page 1, and then continues on pages 3 and 4. In the same newsletter, you can create another chain of linked text boxes for another article that begins on page 2 and then continues on page 4.

Creating the Link

To link text boxes, you must first create two or more text boxes. For example, if you have an article that begins on page 1 and is to be continued on page 2 of a newsletter, create a text box on page 1 and then create another text box on page 2. Size the text boxes to fit appropriately within the allotted column width, and then position the text boxes as desired. If necessary, additional size and position adjustments can be made after the text is added to the text boxes. To create a link between the two text boxes, complete these steps:

1. Click the text box that is to be the first text box in the chain of linked text boxes.
2. If the Text Box toolbar does not automatically display, right-click anywhere within the Standard toolbar and select Text Box, or click View, Toolbars, and then select Text Box.
3. Click the Create Text Box Link button on the Text Box toolbar as displayed in Figure 11.15. The mouse will display as a small upright pitcher. (You can also right-click on the text box and then click Create a Text Box Link from the shortcut menu.)
4. Position the pitcher in the text box to be linked as shown in Figure 11.15. The pitcher appears tipped with letters spilling out of it when it is over a text box that can receive the link. Click once to complete the link.
5. To create a link from the second text box to a third text box, click the second text box, and then repeat Steps 3 and 4 above. Repeat these steps to add more links to the chain.

11.15 *Linking Text Boxes Using the Text Box Toolbar*

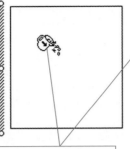
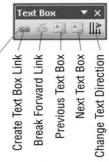

Create Text Box Link
Break Forward Link
Previous Text Box
Next Text Box
Change Text Direction

Click the Create Text Box Link button to create a link to another box where text will flow from one text box to another.

Moving between Linked Text Boxes

You can use the Next Text Box and the Previous Text Box buttons on the Text Box toolbar, as displayed in Figure 11.15, to move between linked text boxes. If you select a text box that is at the beginning of a chain of linked text boxes, the Next Text Box button is active and the Previous Text Box button is dimmed. If you select a text box that is at the end of a chain of linked text boxes, only the Previous Text Box button is active. If you select a text box that is in the middle of a chain of linked text boxes, both the Next Text Box and the Previous Text Box buttons will be available. If one or both of these buttons are active, you know that the currently selected text box is linked to another text box. If neither of these buttons is active, then the currently selected text box is not linked to any other text box.

Creating Jump Lines

Featuring the beginning of several articles on the front page of a newsletter increases the chances of attracting readers. Also, some articles may just be too lengthy to fit on one page. You must, therefore, provide a way for your readers to know where to find the remainder of an article. A *jump line* in a newsletter is used to indicate that an article or feature continues on another page.

As an aid in the directional flow of information in a document, a jump line must be distinguishable from surrounding text so the reader can easily find it. A jump line is commonly set in small italic type, approximately two points smaller than the body copy type. As an option, jump lines can also be enclosed in parentheses.

Jump line
Text telling the reader that an article continues on another page or is being continued from another page.

Creating Linked Text Boxes and a Jump Line in a Newsletter

1. Add an article and a jump line to the newsletter from Exercise 5, as shown in Figure 11.16, by completing the following steps:
   a. Open **c11ex05, End Sign**. Save the document with Save <u>A</u>s and name it **c11ex06, Jump Line**.
   b. Change the zoom to *75%* and turn on the display of nonprinting characters.
   c. Insert text boxes to hold the second article on page 1, which will be continued on page 2, by completing the following steps:
      1) Scroll to the bottom of page 1.
      2) Click the Text Box button on the Drawing toolbar and then draw a text box below the column break to hold the beginning of the second article. Adjustments will be made to the size and position of the text box in future steps.
      3) Scroll to the top of the first column on page 2, click the Text Box button again, and draw a second text box to hold the remaining article text. Using the horizontal ruler as a guide, limit the width of the text box to the column width. Adjustments will be made to the size and position of this text box in an upcoming exercise.
   d. Create a link between the two text boxes so that text will automatically flow from one text box to another by completing the following steps:
      1) Select the first text box and click the Create Text Box Link button on the Text Box toolbar. If the toolbar is not displayed, right-click anywhere within the Standard toolbar, then select Text Box from the list of toolbars.
      2) Position the mouse, which now displays as an upright pitcher, in the second text box until it displays as a pouring pitcher, and then click once to complete the link.
   e. Double-click the border of the first text box in the link (at the bottom of page 1, second column) and make the following changes at the Format Text Box dialog box:
      1) Click the Colors and Lines tab and change the line color to No Line.
      2) Select the Size tab, change the *Height* option of the text box to *1.6"*, and change the *Wi<u>d</u>th* option to *4.7"*.
      3) Select the Layout tab and click the <u>A</u>dvanced button. At the Advanced Layout dialog box, select the Picture Position tab, and then change the *Absolute position* option in the *Horizontal* section to *3.11"* and the *<u>t</u>o the right of* option to *Page*. Change the *Absolute po<u>s</u>ition* option in the *Vertical* section to *8.5"* and the *belo<u>w</u>* option to *Page*.
      4) Click OK to return to the Format Text Box dialog box.
      5) Click the Text Box tab, change the *Left, Right, Top,* and *Bottom* margins in the *Internal margin* section to *0"*, and then click OK.
   f. Click once inside the first text box to position the insertion point and insert the file **Accident Text** located in your Chapter11 folder.

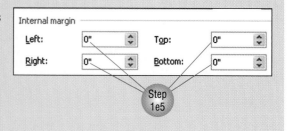

g. Check the text box on page 2 and make sure the remaining article text is visible. If not, use the sizing handles to enlarge the box.

h. Format the title of the second article by completing the following steps:
   1) Position the insertion point anywhere within the title *"Accidents" Waiting to Happen*.
   2) Click the down-pointing arrow at the right of the *Style* list box located on the Formatting toolbar and select Article Head from the drop-down list.

Step
1h2

> **ARTICLE HEAD** ¶

i. Format the article text by completing the following steps:
   1) Position the insertion point at the beginning of the line *The majority of bicycle-car "accidents"...*, hold down the Shift key, and press Ctrl + End to select all of the article text in both text boxes. ***(Note: The text in the second text box will not be highlighted even though it is really selected.)***
   2) Click the down-pointing arrow to the right of the *Style* list box located on the Formatting toolbar and select the Article Text style from the drop-down list.
   3) Position the insertion point anywhere within the first paragraph and apply the 1st Paragraph style from the *Style* list box on the Formatting toolbar.

j. Insert and format the jump line by completing the following steps:
   1) Position the insertion point at the end of the first paragraph and press Enter once.
   2) Change the paragraph alignment to right.
   3) Access the Symbol dialog box, change the font to Wingdings 3, insert the second (triangle) symbol from the left in the sixth row (Wingdings 3: 113), and then click Close.
   4) Press the spacebar once, type See ACCIDENTS on page 2, and then press Enter. If the beginning of the second paragraph is still visible below the jump line, press Enter again to force this text to appear at the beginning of the linked text box on page 2.
   5) Select *See* and apply italics.
   6) Select *ACCIDENTS* and apply bold.
   7) Select *on page 2* and apply italics.
   8) Select the entire jump line and change the font to 10-point Times New Roman.
   9) Make sure the *After* option in the *Spacing* section is set to 3 points.

k. Create an AutoText entry out of the formatted jump line by completing the following steps (an AutoText entry is created here instead of a style because the jump line contains mixed formatting and text that can be used in other jump lines):
   1) Select the entire jump line, including the triangle symbol.
   2) Click Insert, point to AutoText, and then click New.
   3) At the Create AutoText dialog box, type jump line as the AutoText entry name.
   4) Click OK or press Enter.

l. Insert the image of the man riding a bicycle by completing the following steps:
   1) Position the insertion point to the left of the column break.
   2) Display the Clip Art task pane, type j0281077.wmf in the *Search for* text box, and then click Go. (If this clip art image is not available, type the keyword biker in the *Search for* text box, and then choose a different image.)
   3) Insert the image shown in Figure 11.16 or a similar one.
   4) Select the image, click the Text Wrapping button on the Picture toolbar, and then click In Front of Text.

m. Format the image by completing the following steps:
   1) Right-click the image and click Format Picture.
   2) At the Format Picture dialog box, select the Size tab and change the *Height* to *1"* and the *Width* to *1.3"*. Click OK.
   3) Use the mouse to move the image into the same approximate position as displayed in Figure 11.16.

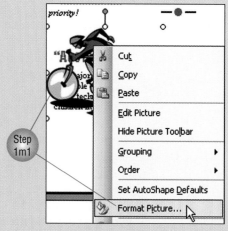

Step 1m1

n. Change the color of the helmet and the shirt on the cyclist image by completing the following steps:
   1) Right-click the image and then click Edit Picture from the shortcut menu.
   2) At the prompt asking if you want the image to be converted into a drawing object, click Yes.

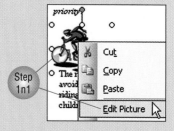

Step 1n1

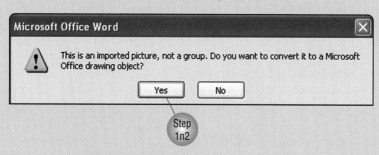

Step 1n2

Step 1n4

Step 1n5

   3) Click the down-pointing arrow at the right of the Zoom button on the Standard toolbar and then select *100%*.
   4) When the image displays with all of the sizing handles, deselect the image, click to select the helmet, and then hold down the Shift key and select the different segments of the shirt.
   5) Click the down-pointing arrow at the right of the Fill Color button on the Drawing toolbar, and then click Teal (the fifth color from the left in the second row).
   6) Click the border around the image, click the Draw button on the Drawing toolbar, and then click Ungroup.
   7) When all of the sizing handles display in the image, click Draw, and then Group.

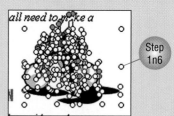

Step 1n6

2. Save **c11ex06, Jump Line**.
3. Print the first page only and then close **c11ex06, Jump Line**. *(Hint: You may want to wait and print the whole newsletter when it is completed in Exercise 9.)*

Volume 5, Issue 2 • March 2005

RIDE SAFE

• Bicycle and In-Line Skating Safety for the New Millennium •

In the
Helmet Habit

"I don't quite know why my daughter, Kate, fell from her bike last July. Maybe she hit a small rock or just lost her balance. We found Kate lying on the ground. She was bleeding and had several cuts and bruises on her face and forehead. We called the paramedics and she began to lose consciousness just as they arrived. At the emergency room, we found out that Kate had a broken nose, a missing tooth, and four other loose teeth. Fortunately, for all of us, Kate was wearing a bicycle helmet. Without even asking, three different doctors have told us that the helmet probably saved Kate's life. Bicycle accidents can happen to anyone!"

Karen Brust
Boston, Massachusetts

In This Issue:

* Bicycle Safety: Let's Make It a Priority! / **1**
* "Accidents" Waiting to Happen / **1**
* When Should a Helmet Be Replaced? / **2**
* Kids and Traffic: Special Reasons for Concern / **2**

BICYCLE SAFETY: LET'S MAKE IT A PRIORITY!

Protect your child!

Did you know that each year over 1,200 people die and thousands more are seriously injured in bicycle accidents? According to the American Academy of Pediatrics, more than 500,000 emergency room visits annually in the U.S. are attributed to bicycle accidents.

Surprisingly, most of these accidents, especially those involving children, occur on quiet residential streets. Most do not involve cars. And many could be prevented with proper training and safety equipment.

Think about it. Before we're allowed to drive a car, we have to be a certain age and go through extensive training and testing. Yet many of us—children in particular—ride the very same roads on

Over 500,000 trips a year are made to emergency rooms for bicycle-related injuries.

a bicycle with little or no training at all. Kids are especially vulnerable because of their undeveloped peripheral vision (about two-thirds that of adults), poor speed judgment, and lack of a sense of danger.

At Ride Safe, we believe bicycle safety education is crucial to our well-being and to that of our children. More and more states, including New York, New Jersey, Connecticut, Georgia, Tennessee, Oregon, and California, are implementing legislation requiring bicycle helmets for children.

The bottom line? *Bicycle safety is something we all need to make a priority*!
— ● —

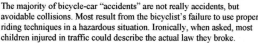

"ACCIDENTS" WAITING TO HAPPEN

The majority of bicycle-car "accidents" are not really accidents, but avoidable collisions. Most result from the bicyclist's failure to use proper riding techniques in a hazardous situation. Ironically, when asked, most children injured in traffic could describe the actual law they broke.

▼ *See* **ACCIDENTS** *on page 2*

Using Scanned Images in a Newsletter

Noncomputer-generated images, such as photographs, illustrations, and diagrams, can be included in a newsletter through the use of a scanner and compatible scanner software. A *scanner* and its associated software convert a photograph, drawing, or text into a compatible digital file format that can be retrieved into a program such

Scanner
Equipment that converts a photograph, drawing, or text into a compatible digital file format that can be retrieved into specific programs.

as Word. You may also use a digital camera and compatible digital camera software to convert photographs into compatible file formats that may be inserted into Word. See Chapter 5 for a brief discussion of this process.

One very important factor to keep in mind is that you must get permission to use artwork, photos, or illustrations before you can legally scan them into a document. This includes artwork from the Web, even though you do not see the traditional copyright symbol. You may type the keywords free graphics or free clip art in a Web search engine to find an extremely large selection of graphics that you are free to use. When you purchase clip art and stock photography, you generally buy the right to use it and even modify it, but you may not resell the images themselves as hard copy or computer images. When purchasing these items, read the copyright information provided in the front of the accompanying documentation.

If you want to include a photograph in a newsletter and a scanner is not available, you can insert a placeholder, such as a text box, in your newsletter. You can then print your newsletter, paste a photograph into the area reserved by the text box, and have a commercial printer duplicate your newsletter.

When trying to determine if your photographs should be scanned professionally, keep the following two points in mind:

- If you do not need high-quality output, using images scanned from a desk model scanner is acceptable.
- If you need high-quality output, use a service bureau to have your photos professionally scanned into your newsletter.

Using Captions

Think of all of the times you pick up a newspaper, newsletter, or magazine. How often do you look at a photograph and immediately read the accompanying explanation? Many graphic images can stand on their own; however, most photographs, illustrations, and charts need to be explained to the reader. Remember that your reader's eyes are automatically drawn to images or elements that stand out on the page. Adding an explanation to your image or photo quickly gives your reader an idea of what is going on, as shown in Figure 11.17. It may even entice your reader to read the corresponding article. Accompanying descriptions or explanations of graphic images, illustrations, or photographs are referred to as *captions*.

Caption

An accompanying description or explanation of a graphic image, illustration, or photograph.

Captions should explain their associated images while at the same time establish a connection to the body copy. Make the caption text different from the body text by bolding and decreasing the type size slightly. Legibility is still the key. Keep captions as short as possible and consistent throughout your document.

Elements, such as a Word picture, Word table, Excel worksheet, PowerPoint presentation, PowerPoint slide or graph, and so on, can be labeled and numbered using Word's Caption feature. (See Word Help or a Word reference manual for more information on this feature.) This type of captioning is very useful when creating detailed reports or publications such as a year-end financial statement, technical instructional manual, or research analysis. If elements do not have to be numbered, such as photographs in a newsletter, the easiest way to create a caption is to position the insertion point below the element, and then type and format the desired caption.

11.17 *Caption Examples*

July 4ᵗʰ Balloon Launch

Leave the selling to us!

Do you need a technological checkup? See our new course offerings on page 3.

The Eiffel Tower

exercise 7

Inserting a Picture Placeholder and Caption in a Newsletter

1. Add a placeholder for a photograph and caption text to the second page of the newsletter from Exercise 6, as shown in Figure 11.18, by completing the following steps:
   a. Open **c11ex06, Jump Line**.
   b. Save the document with Save <u>A</u>s and name it **c11ex07, Picture**.
   c. Change the zoom to *75%* and then turn on the display of nonprinting characters.
   d. Insert a text box that will contain the title by completing the following steps:
      1) Press Ctrl + End to position the insertion point at the top of page 2.
      2) Click the Text Box button on the Drawing toolbar and then draw a text box at the top of the second column that is approximately 0.5 inch by 4.5 inches. *(Note: You may have to resize the linked text box in the first column on the second page.)*
   e. Double-click the text box border and make the following changes at the Format Text Box dialog box:

1) Click the Colors and Lines tab and then change the line color to No Line.
2) Click the Size tab and change the *Height* of the text box to *0.5"* and the *Width* to *4.5"*.
3) Select the Layout tab and click the <u>A</u>dvanced button. At the Advanced Layout dialog box, select the Picture Position tab, and then in the *Horizontal* section, change the *Absolute position* option to *3.3"* and the *to the right* option to *Page*. In the *Vertical* section, change the *Absolute position* option to *1.15"* and the *below* option to *Page*.

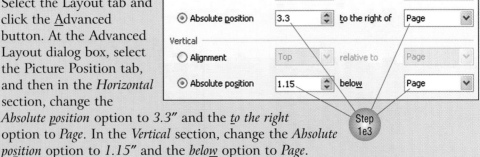

Step 1e3

4) Click OK twice.

f. If the text box in column 1 and the text box just inserted in column 2 overlap each other, reduce the width of the text box in the first column so that it is approximately the same width as the column width. Use the horizontal ruler as a guide.

g. Insert and format the title by completing the following steps:
1) Click once in the text box to position the insertion point.
2) Type ☞**Who Says Helmets Aren't Cool?**☜ (insert the arrow symbols from the Wingdings font, the tenth and eleventh symbols from the left in the eleventh row—Wingdings: 201 and 202).
3) Position the insertion point within the title just typed and then apply the Article Head style.
4) Select each of the arrow symbols, change the color to black, and then apply bold.

h. Insert a text box that contains the picture placeholder text by clicking the Text Box button on the Drawing toolbar and then drawing a text box that is approximately 2.5 inches in height by 4.5 inches in width.

i. Double-click the text box border and make the following changes at the Format Text Box dialog box:
1) Click the Colors and Lines tab, then change the *Color* option in the *Line* section to Teal and the <u>W</u>eight option in the *Line* section to 1.5 points.
2) Click the Size tab, in the *Size and rotate* section, change the *Height* option of the text box to *2.5"* and the *Width* option to *4.5"*.
3) Select the Layout tab and then click the <u>A</u>dvanced button. At the Advanced Layout dialog box, select the Picture Position tab, and then change the horizontal *Absolute position* option to *3.3"* and the *to the right* option to *Page*. Change the vertical *Absolute position* option to *1.65"* and the *below* option to *Page*. Click OK.

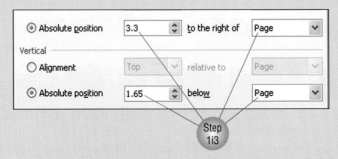

Step 1i3

4) Select the Text Box tab and change the *Left*, *Right*, *Top*, and *Bottom* margins in the *Internal margin* section to *0"*.

5) Click OK to close the Format Text Box dialog box.
j. Insert the placeholder text by completing the following steps:
   1) Click once inside the text box to position the insertion point.
   2) Press Enter seven times and change the alignment to center.
   3) Type Insert picture of children from Silverton, Oregon here.
k. Insert a caption below the picture placeholder by completing the following steps:
   1) Click the picture placeholder text box to select it.
   2) With the text box selected, click Insert, point to Reference, and then click Caption.
   3) At the Caption dialog box, make sure *Below selected item* displays in the *Position* list box and then accept all the default settings by clicking OK.

   4) Drag the caption text box directly below the picture placeholder.
   5) With the insertion point inside the caption text box, select *Figure 1*, and then insert the file **Picture Text** located in your Chapter11 folder.
   6) Select the text just inserted and change the font to 10.5-point Times New Roman, bold, and italic.
2. Save **c11ex07, Picture**.
3. Position the insertion point on page 2. Print page 2 only and close **c11ex07, Picture**. *(Hint: You may want to wait and print the whole newsletter when it is completed in Exercise 9.)*

FIGURE

11.18 *Exercise 7, Page 2*

....●*Winners wear helmets!*

Research indicates that 60% of all U.S. bicycle-car collisions occur among bicyclists between the ages of 8 and 12. Children are permitted to travel with only *"look both ways before you cross the street"* and *"make sure you stop at all stop signs"* warning. Obviously, these "warnings" are not enough.

☞WHO SAYS HELMETS AREN'T COOL?☜

Insert picture of children from Silverton, Oregon here.

Certainly not the children of Silverton, Oregon! One of the biggest reasons children don't wear bicycle helmets is because their friends don't wear them. By getting all the children in your school or neighborhood to order bicycle helmets at the same time, you can help turn this peer pressure from negative to positive. Suddenly, wearing a bicycle helmet becomes the "cool" thing to do. With your support, your kids can be "cool," too!

●●●2●●●

Creating a Newsletter Masthead

Masthead
A list of persons contributing to the production of a newsletter and other general publication information.

The *masthead* is a newsletter element that contains the newsletter's publication information. A masthead (see Figure 11.19) usually contains the following items:

- company or organization (producing the newsletter) name and address
- newsletter's publication schedule, such as weekly, monthly, or biannually

- names of those contributing to the production of the newsletter, such as editor, authors, and graphic designers
- copyright information

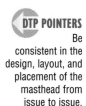

The masthead may also contain a small logo, seal, or other graphic identifier. Although a masthead is commonly located on the back page of a newsletter, you will sometimes find it on the first page. Wherever you decide to place the masthead, be consistent from issue to issue in the masthead's design, layout, and location.

DTP POINTERS
Be consistent in the design, layout, and placement of the masthead from issue to issue.

FIGURE 11.19 ***Examples of Masthead Designs***

From the □□□ Desktop

Editor: **Martha Ridoux**
Design and Layout:
Grace Shevick
Contributing Authors:
Jonathan Dwyer
Nancy Shipley
Christine Johnson
Published Monthly by:
DTP Training, Inc.
4550 North Wabash St.
Chicago, IL 60155
312 555-6840
Fax: 312 555-9366
http://www.emcp.net/dtp
©Copyright 2005 by:
DTP Training, Inc.
All rights reserved.

From the □□□ Desktop

Editor:
Martha Ridoux
Design and Layout:
Grace Shevick
Authors:
Jonathan Dwyer
Nancy Shipley
Christine Johnson
Published Monthly by:
DTP Training, Inc.
4550 North Wabash St.
Chicago, IL 60155
312 555-6840
Fax: 312 555-9366
http://www.emcp.net/dtp
©Copyright 2005 by:
DTP Training, Inc.
All rights reserved.

exercise 8

Creating a Newsletter Masthead

1. Add a masthead to the second page of the newsletter from Exercise 7, as shown in Figure 11.20, by completing the following steps:
   a. Open **c11ex07, Picture**.
   b. Save the document with Save As and name it **c11ex08, Masthead**.
   c. Change the zoom viewing mode to *Whole Page* and turn on the display of nonprinting characters.
   d. Insert a text box to hold the masthead text by completing the following steps:
      1) Click the Text Box button on the Drawing toolbar.
      2) Position the crosshairs toward the bottom half of the first column on page 2 and draw a text box of the approximate size and location as shown in Figure 11.20.

e. Double-click the text box border and make the following changes at the Format Text Box dialog box:
   1) Select the Colors and Lines tab, change the line color to Teal, and change the line weight to 1.5 points.
   2) Select the Size tab, change the height of the text box to 3 inches, and change the width to 2.2 inches.
   3) Select the Layout tab and click the <u>A</u>dvanced button. At the Advanced Layout dialog box, select the Picture Position tab and change the *<u>A</u>lignment* option in the *Horizontal* section to *Left* and the *<u>r</u>elative to* option to *Margin*. Change the *Absolute po<u>s</u>ition* option in the *Vertical* section to *7"* and the *belo<u>w</u>* option to *Page*.

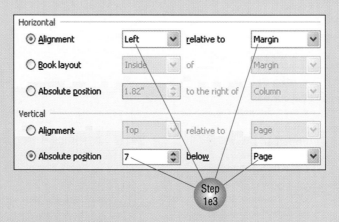

Step
1e3

   4) Click OK twice.
f. Change the zoom to *100%*.
g. Click once inside the text box to position the insertion point and then insert the file **Masthead Text** located in your Chapter11 folder. *(Note: All of the text will be visible after formatting is completed in the following steps.)*
h. Format the masthead title by completing the following steps:
   1) Position the insertion point within *Ride Safe* and apply the ToC Heading style from the *Style* list box on the Formatting toolbar.
   2) Change the alignment to center.
   3) Change the spacing after the paragraph to 6 points.
i. Format the remaining masthead text by completing the following steps:
   1) Select the remaining masthead text and change the alignment to center. *(Hint: Hold down the Shift key and press Ctrl + End to select the remaining text in the text box, even if some of the text is not completely visible.)*
   2) With the text still selected, change the font to 9-point Times New Roman.
   3) Bold the following: *Editor:, Design and Layout:, Authors:, Published quarterly by:, and © Copyright 2005 by:*.
   4) Apply italics to the remaining text that was not bolded.
   5) Select all of the masthead text, except for the heading, and change the *Li<u>n</u>e spacing* option to *Exactly* and the *<u>A</u>t* option to *10 pt* at the Paragraph dialog box.
2. Save **c11ex08, Masthead**.
3. Print page 2 only and then close **c11ex08, Masthead**. *(Hint: You may want to wait and print the whole newsletter when it is completed in Exercise 9.)*

FIGURE

11.20 *Exercise 8, Page 2*

Winners wear helmets!

Research indicates that 60% of all U.S. bicycle-car collisions occur among bicyclists between the ages of 8 and 12. Children are permitted to travel with only *"look both ways before you cross the street"* and *"make sure you stop at all stop signs"* warning. Obviously, these "warnings" are not enough.

☞ WHO SAYS HELMETS AREN'T COOL? ☜

Certainly not the children of Silverton, Oregon! One of the biggest reasons children don't wear bicycle helmets is because their friends don't wear them. By getting all the children in your school or neighborhood to order bicycle helmets at the same time, you can help turn this peer pressure from negative to positive. Suddenly, wearing a bicycle helmet becomes the "cool" thing to do. With your support, your kids can be "cool," too!

Ride Safe

Editor:
Brandon Keith
Design and Layout:
Cassie Lizbeth
Authors:
Chris Urban
Justine Youssef
Amanda Knicker
Published quarterly by:
Ride Safe, Inc.
P.O. Box 888
Warrenville, IL 60555
800-555-RIDE
Fax: 630-555-9068
© Copyright 2005 by:
Ride Safe, Inc.
All rights reserved.

● ● ● **2** ● ● ●

Using Additional Enhancements for Starting Paragraphs

In Chapter 6, you learned about the Drop Cap feature. This design element is often used to indicate the beginning paragraph of a new article. Other types of paragraph enhancements can also be included in a newsletter. The following is a short list of paragraph enhancements—you may think of many more:

- Set the first few words of the beginning paragraph in all caps.
- Set the first line of the beginning paragraph in all caps.
- Set the first word of the beginning paragraph in small caps.
- Set the first line of the beginning paragraph in color.
- Use a larger type size with more leading in the first line of the beginning paragraph.

Understanding Copyfitting

Publications such as magazines and newsletters contain information that varies from issue to issue. Though there is structure in how the articles or stories are laid out on the page (such as the unequal two-column format in the *Ride Safe* newsletter), there may be times when more or less text is needed to fill the page. Making varying amounts of text or typographical enhancements fit in a fixed amount of space is referred to as ***copyfitting***. Many copyfitting techniques have been used in the exercises throughout this textbook. Some copyfitting suggestions include the following:

To create more space:
- Reduce the margins.
- Change the alignment.
- Change the typeface, typestyle, or size, but limit body type size to a minimum of 9 points, preferably 10 or 11 points.
- Reduce the spacing before and after paragraphs (or hard returns) to reduce the spacing around the nameplate, headlines, subheads, frames, or text boxes.
- Reduce the spacing between paragraphs.
- Turn on hyphenation.
- Condense the spacing between characters.
- Reduce the leading (line spacing) in the body copy.
- Remove a sidebar, pull quote, kicker, or end sign.
- Edit the text, including rewriting and eliminating sections.

To fill extra space:
- Increase the margins.
- Change the alignment.
- Change font size, but limit body type size to a maximum of 12 points.
- Increase the spacing between paragraphs.
- Adjust the character spacing.
- Increase the leading (line spacing) in the body copy.
- Increase the spacing around the nameplate, headlines, subheads, text boxes, or graphic images.
- Add a sidebar, pull quote, kicker, end sign, graphic lines, clip art, photo, etc.
- Add text.

Be consistent when making any copyfitting adjustments. For example, if you increase the white space after a headline, increase the white space after all headlines. Alternatively, if you decrease the type size of the body copy in an article, decrease the point size of all body copy in all articles. Adjustments are less noticeable when done uniformly. Also, adjustments often can be very small. For instance, rather than reducing type size by a whole point, try reducing it 0.25 or 0.5 point. In addition, Word includes a Shrink to Fit feature that automatically "shrinks" the contents of the last page in a document so that they will fit on the previous page if there is only a small amount of text on the last page. To access this copyfitting feature, click the Print Preview button on the Standard toolbar (or click File and then Print Preview), then click the Shrink to Fit button (seventh button from the left) on the Print Preview toolbar. Word will automatically reduce the point size in order to fit the text on the previous page. Carefully check your document after using the Shrink to Fit feature, as the results are not always desirable.

In the *Ride Safe* newsletter created in the previous exercises, adjustments were made to the typeface, type size, typestyle, spacing above and below the article headings, spacing between paragraphs, spacing within the paragraphs (leading), and size and position of text boxes.

In the next exercise, you will position the linked text box and add two more articles to the second page of the *Ride Safe* newsletter. You will also apply styles and insert a clip art image. These articles are selected and adjusted to "fit" into the remaining space.

Shrink to Fit

exercise 9

Adding Articles, Applying Styles, and Using Copyfitting Techniques

1. Add two articles and complete the "continued" article on the second page of the newsletter from Exercise 8, as shown in Figure 11.21, by completing the following steps (make your own minor adjustments if necessary to fit the articles in their respective locations):
    a. Open **c11ex08, Masthead**.
    b. Save the document with Save As and name it **c11ex09, Newsletter**.
    c. Change the zoom to *Whole Page* and turn on the display of nonprinting characters.
    d. To make room for the article "The Light Bulb Test" at the beginning of page 2, click and drag the linked text box located on page 2 that contains the remaining text from the "Accidents" article to the open space in the second column. This text box will be formatted in future steps.
    e. Position the insertion point at the top of page 2 and then click the Text Box button on the Drawing toolbar. Draw a text box to hold "The Light Bulb Test" that is approximately the same size and in the same location as shown in Figure 11.21.
    f. Double-click the text box border and make the following changes at the Format Text Box dialog box:
        1) Click the Colors and Lines tab and change the line color to No Line.
        2) Click the Size tab, change the *Height* to 3.65", and change the *Width* to 2.4".

3) Select the Layout tab and click the <u>A</u>dvanced button. At the Advanced Layout dialog box, select the Picture Position tab, and then change the *Alignment* option in the *Horizontal* section to *Left* and the *relative* option to *Margin*. Change the *Absolute po<u>s</u>ition* option in the *Vertical* section to *1.1"* and the *belo<u>w</u>* option to *Page*.

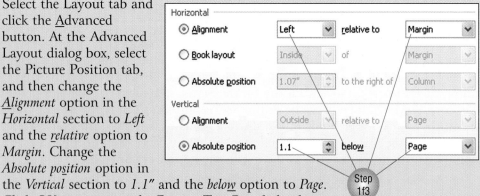

Step 1f3

4) Click OK to return to the Format Text Box dialog box.
5) Click the Text Box tab, and then change the <u>L</u>eft, <u>R</u>ight, <u>T</u>op, and <u>B</u>ottom margins in the *Internal margin* section to *0"*.
6) Click OK or press Enter.
g. Change the zoom to *100%*.
h. Click once inside the text box to position the insertion point and insert the file **Light Bulb Text** located in your Chapter11 folder.
i. Position the insertion point within the heading *The Light Bulb Test* and apply the Article Head style.
j. Insert the light bulb image by completing the following steps:
1) Position the insertion point between *Light* and *Bulb* in the heading and press the spacebar one time.
2) Turn on the drawing canvas by clicking <u>T</u>ools and then <u>O</u>ptions. Select the General tab and then click to add a check mark next to the *Automati<u>c</u>ally create drawing canvas when inserting AutoShapes* option. Click OK.
3) Make sure the insertion point is positioned between the two spaces and display the Clip Art task pane.
4) At the Clip Art task pane, search for the light bulb clip by typing **j0233518.wmf** or, if this clip art image is not available, type the keywords *light bulb* in the *Search for* text box and select a similar image.
5) Insert the light bulb image, which will be quite large, and it will appear that your article text has disappeared. This will be corrected in the next step.

Step 1j4

k. Click the light bulb image to select it (black sizing handles should appear), and then use one of the corner sizing handles to size the light bulb image so that it resembles the image shown in Figure 11.21. Make sure the light bulb is small enough so that your article heading fits on one line and the article text fits within the text box.

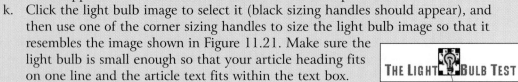

Step 1k

l. Position the insertion point within the first paragraph and apply the 1st Paragraph style.
m. Position the insertion point within the second paragraph and apply the Article Text style.
n. Create the end sign at the end of the article by completing the following steps:
1) On page 1, select the end sign at the end of the first article.
2) Click the Copy button on the Standard toolbar.

3) Position the insertion point at the end of the article "The Light Bulb Test," press the spacebar three times, and then click the Paste button on the Standard toolbar.

Caution: Parents, this experiment is meant to be done by you or under your close supervision. —●—

Step 1n3

o. Double-click the border of the linked text box that contains the remaining text from the "Accidents" article and make the following changes at the Format Text Box dialog box:

1) Click the Colors and Lines tab and change the line color to No Line.
2) Click the Size tab, change the height of the text box to 2 inches, and change the width to 2.4 inches.
3) Select the Layout tab and click the Advanced button. At the Advanced Layout dialog box, select the Picture Position tab, and then change the *Alignment* option in the *Horizontal* section to *Left* and change the *relative to* option to *Margin*. Change the *Absolute position* option in the *Vertical* section to 4.78″ and the *below* option to *Page*.

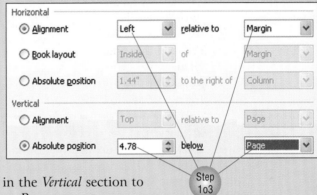

Step 1o3

4) Click OK to return to the Format Text Box dialog box.
5) Click the Text Box tab, and then change the *Left, Right, Top,* and *Bottom* margins in the *Internal margin* section to *0″*.
6) Click OK or press Enter.

p. Insert and format the "continued" jump line at the beginning of the text in the linked text box by completing the following steps:

1) Position the insertion point at the beginning of the text in the linked text box.
2) Click Insert, point to AutoText, and then click AutoText. Select *jump line* from the AutoText entry list box at the AutoText tab located in the AutoCorrect dialog box and then click Insert.
3) Delete the word *See*.
4) Select the word *on* and type from.
5) Select the number *2* and type 1.

▼ACCIDENTS *from page 1*

Step 1p5

q. Insert the line above the jump line by completing the following steps:

1) With the insertion point still within the jump line, display the Borders and Shading dialog box, and make sure the Borders tab is selected.
2) Make sure the border color is Teal, change the border line width to 1 point, and then click the top of the diagram in the *Preview* section to insert a top border. Make sure no borders display on the remaining sides of the diagram. Click OK.

r. Copy and paste the end sign from the article "The Light Bulb Test" to the end of this article. (Drag the masthead text box downward slightly if necessary.)

s. Save **c11ex09, Newsletter**.

t. Insert an article in the remaining space in the second column by completing the following steps:

1) Click the Text Box button on the Drawing toolbar and draw a text box to hold the article "When Should a Helmet Be Replaced?" that is approximately the same size and in the same location as shown in Figure 11.21.

2) Double-click the border of the text box and make the following changes at the Format Text Box dialog box:
   a) Select the Colors and Lines tab and change line color to No Line.
   b) Select the Size tab and then change the height of the text box to 4.1 inches and the width to 4.5 inches.
   c) Select the Layout tab and click the Advanced button. At the Advanced Layout dialog box, select the Picture Position tab, then change the *Absolute position* option in the *Horizontal* section to

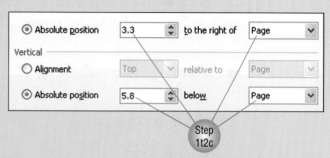

Step 1t2c

   3.3″ and the *to the right of* option to *Page*. Change the *Absolute position* option in the *Vertical* section to *5.8″* and the *below* option to *Page*.
   d) Click OK to return to the Format Text Box dialog box.
   e) Select the Text Box tab, and then change the *Left*, *Right*, *Top*, and *Bottom* margins in the *Internal margin* section to *0″*. Click OK.
u. Click once inside the text box to position the insertion point and insert the file **Replace Helmet Text** located in your Chapter11 folder.
v. Apply styles to the article text just inserted by completing the following steps:
   1) Position the insertion point within the title *When Should a Helmet Be Replaced?*, and then apply the Article Head style.
   2) Select all of the paragraph text and apply the 1st Paragraph style.
w. Insert the bullet and emphasize the text at the beginning of each paragraph by completing the following steps:
   1) Select the article text if necessary.
   2) Click Format, Bullets and Numbering, and then select the Bulleted tab.
   3) Select the first bulleted example and click Customize.
   4) In the *Bullet character* section, click Font, change the font size to 11 points and the bullet color to Teal, and then click OK.
   5) Click Character, change the Font to Wingdings, and then select the first

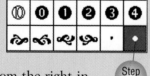

Step 1w5

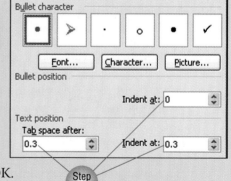

   (round) bullet from the right in the eighth row (Wingdings: 159). Click OK.
   6) In the *Bullet position* section, change the *Indent at* option to *0″*. In the *Text position* section, change the *Tab space after* to *0.3″* and the *Indent at* position to *0.3″*. Click OK.

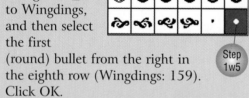

Step 1w6

   7) Select the phrase *After a crash.* and change the font to 11-point Impact.
   8) Repeat Step 7 to format the three remaining phrases at the beginning of each bulleted item. (A style could be created for this formatting, if desired; otherwise, use the Format Painter.)

x. Replace the picture placeholder above the article "When Should a Helmet Be Replaced?" with a similar photograph of children or a child (**j0227794.jpg**) as shown in Figure 11.21. Make any necessary adjustments to the photograph (such as cropping) or to the placeholder text box. You may need to delete the placeholder text box to change the Picture Text Wrapping option to In Front of Text. *(Note: You may type children in the Search for text box at the Clip Art task pane to locate a photo. In addition, if the teal border displays around the picture, select the text box and remove it.)*

y. Scroll through the newsletter and make any copyfitting adjustments that may be necessary.

2. Save **c11ex09, Newsletter**.

3. Print both pages of the *Ride Safe* newsletter and then close **c11ex09, Newsletter**.

4. Print both pages again, but print them on one sheet of paper by completing the following steps:

a. Click <u>F</u>ile and then <u>P</u>rint.

b. At the Print dialog box, click the down-pointing arrow at the right of the *Pages per sheet* option in the *Zoom* section (bottom right corner), and then select *2 pages* at the drop-down list.

c. Click OK. (Make sure the first page prints on the left side of the paper and the second page prints on the right side of the paper—click <u>T</u>ools and then <u>O</u>ptions, select the Print tab, and then clear the check mark in the check box next to the *Reverse print order* option. Click OK.)

Step 4b

Zoom

Pages per sheet: 2 pages

Scale to paper size: No Scaling

FIGURE

11.21 *Exercise 9, Pages 1 and 2*

Saving Your Newsletter as a Template

DTP POINTERS
Saving a newsletter as a template saves time and keystrokes in the creation of future issues.

To save time when creating future issues of your newsletter, save it as a template document. To save it as a template, delete all text, text boxes, pictures, objects, and so on, that will not stay the same for future issues. Likewise, leave all text, pictures, symbols, text boxes, headers and footers, and so on that will remain the same in each issue of your newsletter. All styles created for the newsletter will remain with the template. For example, to save the *Ride Safe* newsletter as a template, leave the following items and delete the rest:

- Folio
- Nameplate
- Headers and footers
- Sidebar with the title because this will be a feature article every month; delete the sidebar article text only
- Table of contents and heading; delete the table of contents text only
- Masthead
- Remaining text boxes: delete the articles within each text box (the text boxes will most likely need to be reformatted each time you create a new issue of your newsletter; however, they serve as a basic framework for future issues)

Once you have deleted the text and elements that will change every month, add placeholder text if desired, and then save the newsletter with Save As. At the Save As dialog box, click the down-pointing arrow at the right of the *Save as type* list box and select *Document Template* as the file type. Double-click the template folder in which you want to save your newsletter template (consult your instructor as to where to save your template—to your hard drive or to the DTP Templates folder), type a name for your newsletter template, and then click Save. See Figure 11.22 for an example of how the *Ride Safe* newsletter might look if saved as a template.

F I G U R E

11.22 *Sample Newsletter Template*

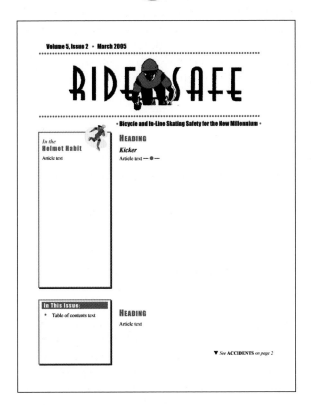

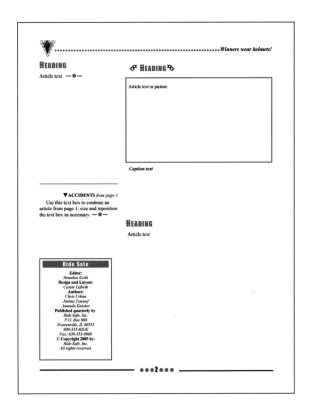

Sending a Newsletter as an E-Mail Attachment

Imagine that you are the owner of a small business and you would like to inform your customers of your new products, upcoming sales or special promotions, and articles that may be of interest to them. You are thinking of preparing a monthly newsletter; however, you do not want the added expense of duplicating the newsletter and the cost of postage necessary to send the document. In addition, you do not have a Web site for your business so the prospect of posting the newsletter is not viable. You would like to send the newsletter to your customers via e-mail; however, you cannot be certain that all of your customers will have access to Microsoft Word. What can you do to ensure that your customers can read the newsletter when it is sent to them as an e-mail attachment?

If your newsletter is a one-page document, you could scan it and save it with a .pdf extension and send it as an e-mail attachment. The recipient of the e-mail will need to download Adobe Acrobat Reader® from the Internet and then open the attachment. Adobe Acrobat Reader is presently available free of charge at this Web site (www.adobe.com). However, keep in mind that this offer may not be available in the future. If you have created a lengthly newsletter, you may want to use Adobe Writer® software to save your document in PDF format and then e-mail it to your customers.

PDF (Portable Document Format) files are created using Adobe Acrobat software—more information on the software is available at the Adobe Web site.

Acrobat software can convert documents created in Word, Excel, or PowerPoint to PDF files and then they can be viewed and printed using Adobe Acrobat Reader. The PDF file format captures all of the elements of a printed document as an electronic image that you can view, print, and forward.

CHAPTER summary

➤ Elements can be added to a newsletter to enhance the visual impact, including table of contents, headers and/or footers, masthead, pull quotes, kickers, sidebars, captions, ruled lines, jump lines, page borders, and end signs.

➤ Use spot color—a color in addition to black—in a newsletter as an accent to such features as graphic lines, graphic images, borders, backgrounds, headings, and end signs.

➤ Headers and footers are commonly used in newsletters. Headers/footers can be placed on specific pages, only odd pages, or only even pages and can include page numbering, a slogan, a logo, or a horizontal ruled line.

➤ A sidebar is set off from the body text in a text box and can include a photograph or graphic image along with text.

➤ In multiple-paged newsletters, a table of contents is an important element and is generally located on the front page in the lower left or right corner.

➤ A pull quote acts as a focal point, helps to break up lengthy blocks of text, and provides visual contrast.

➤ A masthead is a repeating element that usually contains the company address, newsletter publication schedule, names of those contributing to the production, and copyright information. It is generally located on the back page of a newsletter.

➤ A kicker is typically set in a smaller type size than the headline but larger than the body text and is placed above or below the headline or article heading.

➤ Symbols or special characters used to indicate the end of a section of text are called end signs.

➤ In a newsletter, a jump line indicates a continuation of an article or feature on another page and enables the newsletter to feature the beginning of several articles on the front page.

➤ Graphic images, illustrations, charts, diagrams, and photographs can add focus, balance, proportion, contrast, directional flow, and consistency to a newsletter.

➤ Noncomputer-generated images such as photographs and illustrations can be scanned and inserted in a newsletter.

➤ Captions can be added to images to establish a connection to the body copy. Bold caption text and set it in a smaller point size to make it different from the body text.

➤ Copyfitting refers to making varying amounts of text or typographical enhancements fit in a fixed amount of space.

➤ Newsletters may be formatted in columns, tables, or text boxes.

➤ To continue an article created on one page of a newsletter to another page, use linked text boxes and jump lines.

➤ Newsletters may be saved in HTML, added to a Web page, and then viewed in Web Page Preview.

- A newsletter may be saved and then sent as an e-mail attachment. If the recipient does not have Word, the newsletter may be saved in PDF file format, then opened and viewed by using Adobe Acrobat.
- A multiple-paged document may be viewed in Reading Layout viewing mode.
- Newsletters are often saved as templates to save time when creating future issues of the newsletter.
- Multiple pages can be printed on a single sheet of paper by selecting the *Pages per sheet* option in the *Zoom* section of the Print dialog box.
- All styles created for the newsletter remain with the newsletter template.

COMMANDS review

Command	Mouse/Keyboard
Borders and Shading dialog box	Format, Borders and Shading
Bullets and Numbering dialog box	Format, Bullets and Numbering
Clip Art task pane	View, Task Pane, Other Task Panes, Clip Art task pane; Insert, Picture, Clip Art; or Insert Clip Art button on Drawing toolbar
Columns	Format, Columns; or Columns button on Standard toolbar
Display Drawing toolbar	Drawing button on Standard toolbar; or right-click on the Standard toolbar, select Drawing; or View, Toolbars, Drawing
Draw a text box	Text Box button on the Drawing toolbar; or Insert, Text Box
Edit Picture	Right-click on picture, click Edit Picture at shortcut menu
Format Object dialog box	Select object, Format, Object
Format Picture dialog box	Select picture, Format, Picture
Format Text Box dialog box	Select text box, Format, Text Box
Headers and footers	View, Header and Footer, click Switch Between Header and Footer button to display header or footer pane
Insert a column break	Insert, Break, *Column break;* or press Ctrl + Shift + Enter
Insert a text box around selected text	Select text, click Text Box button on Drawing toolbar
Insert File dialog box	Insert, File
Insert Picture dialog box	Insert, point to Picture, click From File
Insert special characters	Insert, Symbol, select Special Characters tab
Kerning	Format, Font, Character Spacing tab, *Kerning for fonts,* enter specific amount of *Points and above* to be kerned
Link text boxes	Select text box, click Create Text Box Link button on Text Box toolbar; or right-click on selected box, click Create Text Box Link, click inside other text box
Paragraph spacing	Format, Paragraph

Styles	Format, Styles and Formatting; or click View, Task Pane, Other Task Panes, Styles and Formatting; or click Styles and Formatting button on Formatting toolbar; or click the *Style* list box on Formatting toolbar and click More
Tracking	Format, Font, Character Spacing tab, *Spacing, Expanded* or *Condensed* or *Normal*, enter point value in *By* text box

REVIEWING key points

Matching: On a blank sheet of paper, provide the correct letter or letters that match each definition.

Ⓐ Caption
Ⓑ Copyfitting
Ⓒ End sign
Ⓓ Footer
Ⓔ Header
Ⓕ Jump line

Ⓖ Kicker
Ⓗ Masthead
Ⓘ Pull quote
Ⓙ Scanner
Ⓚ Sidebar
Ⓛ Spot color

1. A repeating element that can add consistency among newsletter issues and that contains the company address, newsletter publication schedule, names of those contributing to the production of the newsletter, and copyright information is called this.
2. This feature describes or explains a graphic image, illustration, or photograph.
3. Text that is repeated at the top of every page is referred to as this.
4. A block of information or a related story that is set off from the body text in a graphic box is called this.
5. This is the term for a color in a newsletter, other than black, used as an accent.
6. This is the term for a brief direct phrase, summarizing statement, or important point associated with the body copy of a newsletter.
7. A symbol or special character used to indicate the end of a section of text is called this.
8. This feature is used to indicate that an article or feature continues on another page.
9. A brief sentence or phrase that is a lead-in to an article is referred to as this.
10. This device converts a photograph, drawing, or text into a compatible digital file format.

Short Answer: On a blank sheet of paper, provide the correct answer for each question.

1. List at least three tips to consider when creating a pull quote.
2. Why is it important to have some knowledge of graphic file formats?
3. List at least four copyfitting ideas to create more space in a document.
4. What is the purpose of linking text boxes, and why is this feature advantageous to use in a newsletter?
5. List at least three paragraph enhancements that can be included in a newsletter.

APPLYING your skills

Assessment 1

Find two newsletters from two different sources. Review the newsletters for the items listed below. Label those items that you find in each newsletter, scan the newsletter with the items labeled, and send it to your instructor as an e-mail attachment. (Consult your instructor if a scanner or e-mail is not available.)

Caption	Jump line	Spot color
End sign	Kicker	Subheads
Folio	Masthead	Subtitle
Footer	Nameplate	Table of contents
Header	Pull quote	
Headlines	Sidebar	

Optional: Write a summary explaining which of the two newsletters is the most appealing, and why.

Assessment 2

In this assessment, you are to redesign the first page of a newsletter located in your Chapter11 folder. Two pages of text are provided. You only need to redesign the first page, but you may use any of the text on the second page for copyfitting purposes.

1. Redesign a basic newsletter named **Redesign Text** located in your Chapter11 folder according to the following specifications. (You may edit or reduce some of the text.)
   a. Create a new nameplate, subtitle, and folio. Experiment with thumbnail sketches.
   b. Create the body of the newsletter using an asymmetrical column layout.
   c. Include the following:

      Header and footer
      Table of contents
      Sidebar
      Pull quote
      Graphic with caption
      Spot color (or varying shades of gray)

   d. Use a kicker, end signs, jump line, clip art, or a text box placeholder for a photo for visual effect or copyfitting.
   e. Use tracking (character spacing), leading (line spacing), paragraph spacing before and after, text boxes, and so forth to set the body copy attractively on the page.
2. Save the new newsletter and name it **c11sa02, Newsletter**.
3. Print and then close **c11sa02, Newsletter**.
4. In class, edit each other's newsletters by completing the following steps:
   a. Independently choose an editor's name for yourself and do not share it with the rest of the class. (This is your chance to be famous!)
   b. Your instructor will collect all of the newsletters and randomly distribute a newsletter to each class participant.

 c. Sign your individual editor's "name" on the back of the newsletter and make editorial comments addressing such items as target audience, visual appeal, overall layout and design, font selection, graphic image selection, focus, balance, proportion, contrast, directional flow, consistency, and use of color.

 d. Rotate the newsletters so that you have an opportunity to write editor's comments on the back of each newsletter, identified by your individual editor's name only.

 e. Review the editors' comments on the back of your own newsletter, and revise your newsletter keeping your editorial staff's comments in mind.

5. Save and name the revised version of your newsletter **c11sa02, Revised**.

6. Print **c11sa02, Revised**.

7. Evaluate your revised newsletter with the document evaluation checklist (**Document Evaluation Checklist.doc**) located in your Chapter11 folder.

Assessment 3

Assume that you are an employee of Ride Safe, Inc., and are responsible for creating the company newsletter. You have already completed an issue of this newsletter in **c11ex09**, and now you have to create the next issue using articles that other employees have submitted to you. Using text (articles) from your student data files and the *Ride Safe* newsletter already created, create the next issue of the *Ride Safe* newsletter according to the following specifications:

1. Print **RideSafe Issue 3 Text** located in your Chapter11 folder.

2. Review the printout of possible articles to be used for the second issue of your newsletter. Decide what articles you would like to include. Save the rest for possible fillers.

3. Make a thumbnail sketch of a possible layout and design. You can open **c11ex09, Newsletter** and use the framework of that newsletter to create this second issue. Be consistent in column layout and design elements used. Include the following items:

> Caption
> End sign
> Masthead
> Picture
> Pull quote
> Sidebar
> Spot color

4. For the masthead, use your instructor's name as the editor and your name for the design and layout.

5. Create a style for the article headings.

6. You decide on the order and placement of articles. Use bullets, bold, italics, reverse text, and so on, if appropriate to the design and layout of this new issue of your newsletter.

7. Make any copyfitting adjustments as necessary.

8. Save the document and name it **c11sa03, Ride Safe Issue 3**.

9. Print and then close **c11sa03, Ride Safe Issue 3**.

10. Evaluate your newsletter with the document evaluation checklist.

Optional: Rewrite and redesign all of the article heads to be more clever, interesting, and eye-catching.

Assessment 4

In this assessment you will open **Butterfield Gardens** in your Chapter11 folder and add a second page to the newsletter. You may use the Internet to find interesting articles about gardening. Include the following specifications:

I N T E G R A T E D

- You may select a Word or Publisher newsletter template or you may design this newsletter from scratch. You may use Word's column feature and/or incorporate linked text boxes. You may also borrow design elements from Publisher and copy and paste them into your newsletter. Be creative and remember to use plenty of white space. Use the Butterfield logo provided in the Chapter11 folder. *(Hint: You may add a color background to this logo by selecting the logo, clicking the Set Transparency Color button on the Picture toolbar, clicking the down-pointing arrow at the right of the Fill Color button on the Drawing toolbar, and then selecting a color, gradient, or pattern.)*

- Insert several appropriate photographs or clip art images to enhance your document.

- The newsletter must be at least two pages in length.

- You may use the Internet to find interesting articles about gardening. Use a search engine to aid you in your search. Example: Type gardening in the *Search* text box at Google.com.

- The **Butterfield Gardens** file contains proofreading errors and formatting inconsistencies. Correct all of the errors and create styles to aid in reinforcing consistency.

- Save your document and name it **c11sa04, Butterfield Integrated**.

- Print your newsletter back-to-back and then close **c11sa04, Butterfield Integrated**.

Assessment 5

Open **c11ex09, Newsletter**, which you created in Exercises 1 through 9 in Chapter 11, and then format and embed a table created in Excel as shown in Figure 11.23. Include the following specifications:

I N T E G R A T E D

1. Save **c11ex09, Newsletter** with Save <u>A</u>s and name it **c11sa05, RS Integrated**.
2. Minimize Word and then Open Excel 2003.
3. At the Excel screen, open **Ride Safe Products** located in your Chapter11 folder.
4. Enhance the Excel table by completing the following steps:
   a. Select cell A1 containing *Ride Safe Products* – 2005 (a thick black border should display around the cell), click F<u>o</u>rmat, <u>C</u>ells, choose the Patterns tab, and then select the Teal color.
   b. Select the Border tab, select the sixth line style in the right column in the *Line Style* list option, select Orange in the <u>C</u>olor option box, and then click to add the border at the bottom of the preview diagram.
   c. Choose the Font tab and then change the font to 22-point Forte and the color to White. Click OK.
   d. Select cells A2:C2 and change the font to 11-point Impact in Orange. *(Hint: You may use Font, Font Size, and Font Color buttons on the Formatting toolbar.)*
   e. Select cells A3:C11 and change the font to 10-point Franklin Gothic Book.
   f. Select cell A13 and complete the following steps:
      1) Click F<u>o</u>rmat, point to <u>R</u>ow, click H<u>e</u>ight, and then type 28 at the Row Height dialog box.

2) Click Format, point to Cells, select the Font tab, and then change the font to 8-point Franklin Gothic Book Italic.

3) Select the Alignment tab, change the horizontal alignment to *Center*, and then click to place a check mark beside <u>*Wrap text*</u> in the *Text control* section. Click OK to close the Format Cells dialog box.

g. Select cells C3:C11, click F<u>o</u>rmat, Cells, choose the Number tab, and then select *Currency* in the <u>*Category*</u> option box. Click OK.

h. Select cells A1:C13 and apply the same thick orange border as in Step 4b.

i. Save the Excel spreadsheet as **Ride Safe Products Formatted**.

5. Copy **Ride Safe Products Formatted** to the Clipboard.

6. Minimize Excel and maximize Word.

7. Delete the last article in **c11ex09, Newsletter**.

8. Draw a text box similar in size to the text box that contained the article in Step 7 and change the line color to No Line.

9. With the insertion point located inside the text box, click <u>E</u>dit and then Paste Special. Click the *Microsoft Office Excel Worksheet* option in the Paste Special dialog box and then click OK. Adjust the size and position of the text box if necessary.

10. Save, print, and then close **c11sa05, RS Integrated**.

11. Close **Ride Safe Products Formatted** and then close Excel.

F I G U R E

11.23 *Assessment 5 Sample Solution*

Assessment 6

The newsletter **News2001-2.pdf** has been saved in the PDF file format and is located in your Chapter11 folder. Open this file using Adobe Acrobat Reader® software, which is currently free on the Internet (www.adobe.com) and print any two pages of the newsletter. (Consult your instructor as to whether you may download this software.) If the Adobe Acrobat Reader software is not available to you, complete the creative activity given below. After printing the newsletter, recreate the newsletter using your own design ideas. Save the document as **c11sa06, Recreated**.

With a partner, find a poor example of a newsletter and redesign the first page, including the nameplate. Use a different layout and design and incorporate copyfitting techniques to produce a newsletter that entices people to actually read your publication. Rewrite the text copy to make it more interesting. Recreate, save the document and name it **c11sa06, Newsletter**, and then close it. In class, break up into small groups of four to six students and present the before and after versions of your newsletter. Give a brief explanation of the changes made, problems encountered, and solutions found. Vote on the most creative copy and the most creative design separately.

Alternatively, open **c11ex09, Newsletter**, save it in HTML, and view it on the Web Page Preview screen. Discuss with your class how the newsletter looks in the browser. Did all of the document formatting and text attributes convert? If not, how could you fix the page so that it will display properly on the Web?

Introducing Microsoft Publisher 2003

PERFORMANCE OBJECTIVES

Upon successful completion of Chapter 12, you will be able to use Publisher to create professional-looking desktop documents such as a flyer, a trifold brochure, and a newsletter using Publisher's powerful, yet easy-to-use templates. You will also understand when it is best to use Word and when to use Publisher to create such documents. In addition, you will apply desktop publishing design concepts to your documents.

DESKTOP PUBLISHING TERMS

Layout guides	Ruler guides	Story
Master page	Smart objects	

PUBLISHER FEATURES USED

AutoFit Text	Layout guides	Rotate or flip
Catalog merge	Master page	Ruler guides
Clipboard task pane	Microsoft Publisher	Save as Picture
Color schemes	Design Gallery	Smart objects
Commercial printing	New Publication task	Snap To
Connected text boxes	pane	Templates
Continued notice	Objects toolbar	Text overflow
Design sets	Pack and Go Wizard	Ungroup
Font schemes	Page numbers	Watermarks
Graphics Manager	Picture Frame	
Group	Publication designs	

Microsoft Publisher 2003 is a complete, easy-to-use desktop publishing program designed for small business users and individuals who want to create their own high-quality, professional-looking marketing materials and other business documents without the assistance of professional designers. Publisher consists of thousands of customizable templates, design sets, flexible page layout guides, high-quality printing options (commercial printing), and a full range of desktop publishing tools. In addition, Publisher offers a consistent user interface, menus, toolbars, and task panes to provide easy transitioning and integration from one Office component to the next. Publisher 2003 includes other Word and Office features such as headers and footers, Office Clipboard, AutoRecover, multiple documents, Print Preview, a thesaurus, WordArt, AutoShapes, and customizable toolbars.

New features in Publisher 2003 include the Catalog Merge feature, which lets you create product catalogs and similar publications using data from a range of data sources. Publisher also has improved its capability to transform one publication into a variety of different formats. You can convert a newsletter into a Web page or you can convert the design of the Web page into the body of an e-mail message. The simplest way to create a Web page in Publisher is to use the new Easy Web Site Builder and to add additional pages by choosing pages from Publisher's extensive list of prebuilt pages to expand the site. A new baseline guide lets you line up text more accurately. Publisher has also improved typography and layout features to enable you to create multiple master pages in a publication. New formatting options include widow and orphan control and the ability to keep lines together. The Graphic Manager feature allows you to convert an embedded image to a linked image and vice versa. The Duplicate Page feature will insert a duplicate of your page immediately after the selected page.

Knowing When to Use Publisher, Word, or FrontPage

If you are comfortable using Word to create professional-looking documents, use Word. Throughout Chapters 1 through 11, you have become familiar with many Word desktop publishing features, which make Word more than just a basic word processing program. Word's numerous templates, both within the program and online, are similar to the types that Publisher contains. However, you may consider using Publisher if your publications require commercial printing. Publisher offers full support for commercial printing, including four-color separation, spot color processing, and automatic trapping for printing on an offset or digital press. Pantone Solid (spot colors) and Pantone Process colors are available to Publisher users who want to precisely match Pantone colors to colors used in business. However, you can work with Word from inside Publisher to edit a Publisher story or you can pick a design set in Publisher and import a Word document.

Also, consider using Publisher if your document layouts need to be especially precise or complex. Publisher includes easy-to-use layout guides, ruler guides, baseline guides, and Snap To options to align objects to ruler marks, guides, or other objects. Publisher includes more than 8,500 template options for common business publications and powerful design tasks, including color schemes, font schemes, and predesigned layouts and publication designs. Additional templates are available at the Microsoft Office Online templates Web page, which is accessed at http://office.microsoft.com/templates. These online templates are organized with other Office templates in various categories so you can quickly access all of the Publisher templates by typing the keyword Publisher in the *Search* text box.

Use Publisher to create Web pages that are visually coordinated with your print publications. Limit the size of your Publisher-created Web pages to around 10 pages. Use Microsoft FrontPage for sites that exceed 10 pages, are frequently updated, and are interactive with forms and search engines. You can adapt a Web page started in Publisher and then finished in FrontPage.

DTP POINTERS
Use Publisher if your publication requires commercial printing.

DTP POINTERS
Publisher offers full support for commercial printing, including color separation and spot color processing.

DTP POINTERS
A commercial printer must have the same version of Publisher to use the files without possible reformatting.

DTP POINTERS
Adobe Writer™ is required to save Publisher files in PDF file format.

Applying Design Concepts

Whether or not you create documents in Publisher using templates, you should understand and apply good design principles. You will still need to make critical choices as to the type of publication that best conveys your message, which color scheme reinforces the feel of your document, who is your target audience, or which design elements enrich the message and promote readability. Therefore, careful planning and organizing of content and design elements is as necessary using Publisher as it is using Word to create professional-looking documents. Keep the overall look of your publication simple and use plenty of white space. Reinforce consistency by using design sets in Publisher and using styles for consistent spacing, fonts, alignment, repetition, color, and decorative elements such as borders, drop caps, initial caps, and so on. Figure 12.1 shows how easy it is to create consistency among your business documents by selecting one of the design set templates. There are approximately 50 design sets.

Create interest in your publication by using strong contrast, alignment, and focus. Achieve balance and proportion and establish smooth directional flow in a document by organizing and positioning elements in such a way that the reader's eyes scan through the text and find particular words or images that you wish to emphasize. As discussed earlier, color may create focus; however, it is also a powerful tool in communicating a message and portraying an image. The colors you choose should reflect the nature of the business you represent.

FIGURE 12.1   Selecting the Accent Box Design Set

Start a publication by choosing *Design Sets*.

Select a master set for a uniform look for all of your business publications.

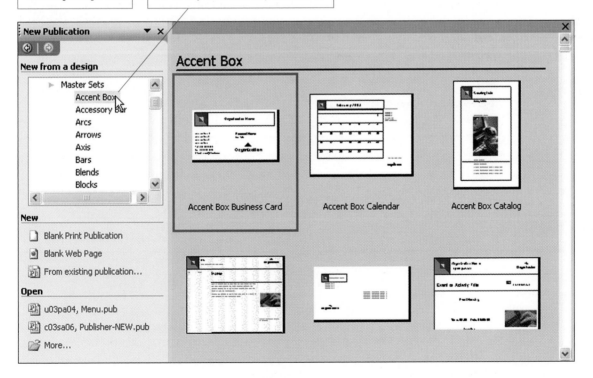

Exploring the Publisher Window

To start Publisher, click the Start button, point to All Programs, point to Microsoft Office, and then click Microsoft Office Publisher 2003. When you first start Publisher, on the left side of the screen you will see the task pane, which includes the following options: *Publications for Print, Web Sites and E-mail, Design Sets,* or *Blank Publications* as shown in Figure 12.2. Depending on which task pane you have accessed, you may see a blank document or a list of publication templates. As shown in Figure 12.3, you may click the Other Task Panes button at the right of the existing task pane title (New Publication) to choose from 16 other task panes.

FIGURE

12.2 *Publisher Start Screen and New Publication Task Pane*

Click to begin your publication with a template.

Click to create a Web site or to send your publication via e-mail.

Click to choose a uniform look for several publications.

Click to start your publication from scratch.

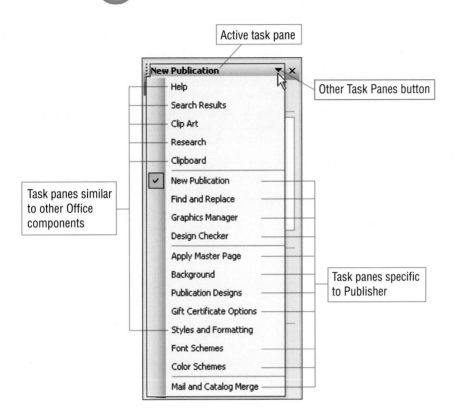

Notice in Figure 12.4 that the Publisher user interface shares many features with the other programs in the Microsoft Office 2003 suite, including the Menu bar, toolbars (by default, Publisher displays the Standard, Formatting, Connect Text Boxes, and Objects toolbars), task panes, Status bar, sizing buttons (minimize, maximize, restore, and close), scroll arrows, rulers, and the Online Help tool.

FIGURE 12.4 *Microsoft Publisher Window and Objects Toolbar*

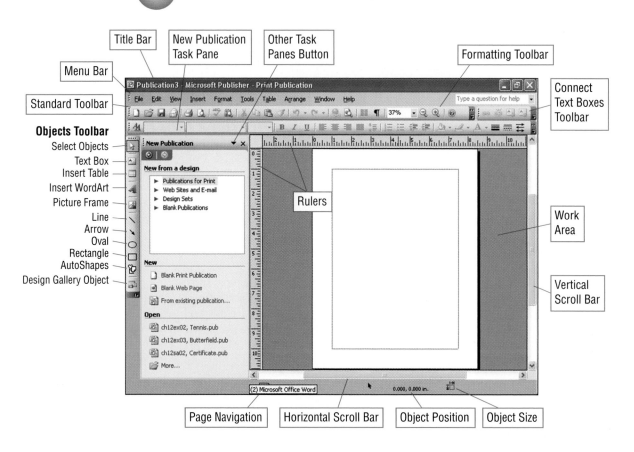

Creating a New Publication

One of the first steps in preparing a publication in Publisher is to display the New Publication task pane. In Publisher 2003, this task pane automatically displays when you open Publisher. If the *Task Pane* option has been deselected at the View menu, you can turn it back on by clicking View and then Task Pane, clicking File and then New, or, if a different task pane is active, clicking the Other Task Panes button and then selecting *New Publication* from the drop-down list. From this task pane, you may choose to start your publication based on any one of the templates displayed at the drop-down list under the *Publications for Print* option as shown in Figure 12.5. The templates are located in various categories or subcategories and display as thumbnails at the right of the task pane. Alternatively, you may choose the *Web Sites and E-mail* option which provides templates for creating Web pages or for converting publications to e-mail newsletters, letters, and so on as shown in Figure 12.6. The *Design Sets* option, as shown in Figure 12.1, displays templates used for creating publications with a consistent design. You may also choose to begin your publication at a blank full page or use one of the blank templates shown in the *Blank Publications* list as shown in Figure 12.7.

12.5 *Publications for Print with Quick Publications Displayed*

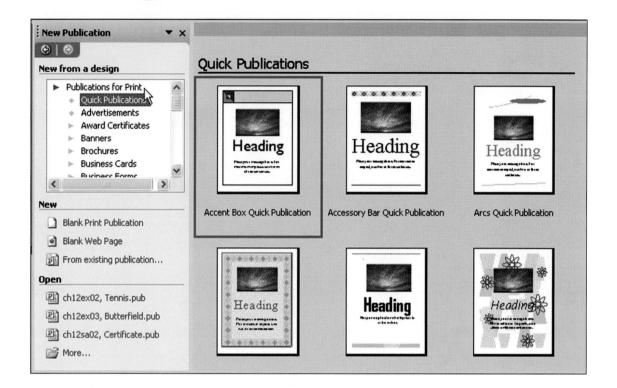

12.6 *Web Sites and E-mail with the Easy Web Site Builder Displayed*

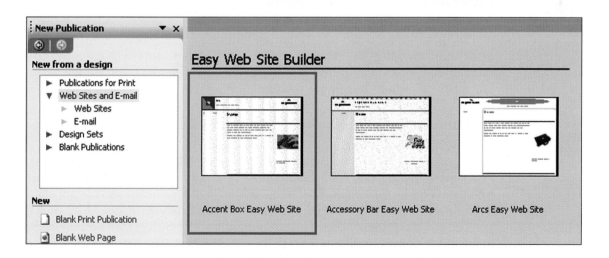

FIGURE

12.7 *Blank Publications with Blank Templates Displayed*

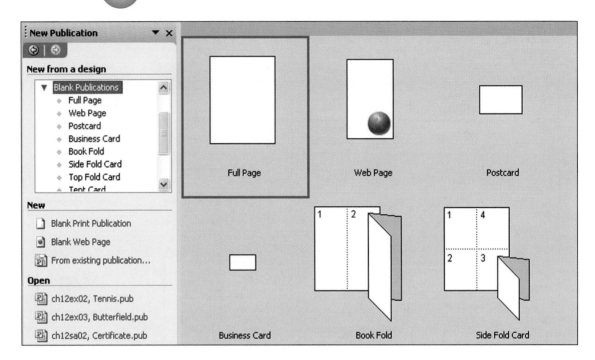

In Publisher, unlike Word, you must place all objects such as text, graphics, pictures, WordArt, and AutoShapes inside a frame before you can use them in your publication. When using Word, you simply begin typing your text at a blank document screen in a linear manner. However, with Publisher, text is considered an object and it must be placed in a text box.

Creating a Personal Information Set

After you select a template, you will be prompted to fill in a personal information set. The data will automatically display in your publication when you use a template containing these fields. Changes made in one field synchronize changes to other similar fields. Consult your instructor on whether you should complete the personal information set in a classroom situation.

DTP POINTERS
Complete the personal information set to save time and energy in formatting a publication.

Working with Color Schemes and Font Schemes

To avoid a "canned" design for your publications, you may want to customize your publication to reflect colors used in your company logo or fonts preferred by your department. By default, Publisher applies color schemes to blank publications as well as wizard-based templates. The predefined color schemes include six colors in addition to the default colors for hyperlinks, and they are accessed by clicking Format and then Color Schemes or clicking the Color Schemes hyperlink at the designated template task pane.

To customize a color scheme, complete the following steps:

1. Click Format and then Color Schemes.
2. Click the Custom color scheme hyperlink at the bottom of the task pane as shown in Figure 12.8.

3. At the Color Schemes dialog box, select the Custom tab and then select the color/colors you want to use from the six drop-down palettes as shown in Figure 12.9.

4. Click Save Scheme and then type a name for the custom scheme.

F I G U R E

12.8 **Color Schemes Task Pane**

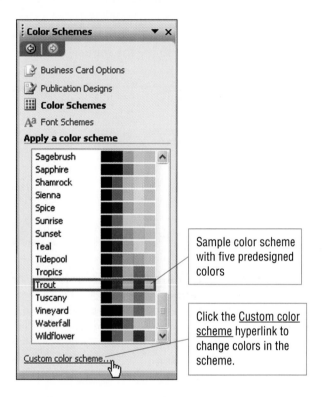

Sample color scheme with five predesigned colors

Click the Custom color scheme hyperlink to change colors in the scheme.

F I G U R E

12.9 **Selecting a Color to Customize a Color Scheme**

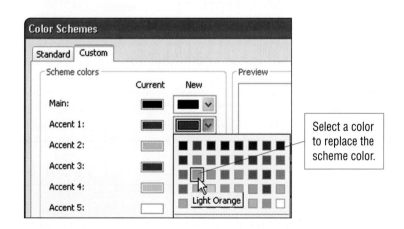

Select a color to replace the scheme color.

Font schemes make it quick and easy to pick fonts that look good together. To change all of the fonts in your publication, you may apply a new font scheme by completing the following steps:

1. Click the Font Schemes hyperlink in the task pane of your open publication.
2. Point to a scheme in the font schemes list box to view a ScreenTip that lists the scheme's fonts as shown in Figure 12.10.
3. Click the down-pointing arrow at the right of the font scheme box for options to insert, modify, or delete the selected font scheme.
4. Click the Font Scheme Options hyperlink at the bottom of the task pane to further customize the font scheme.

FIGURE

12.10 *Applying a Font Scheme*

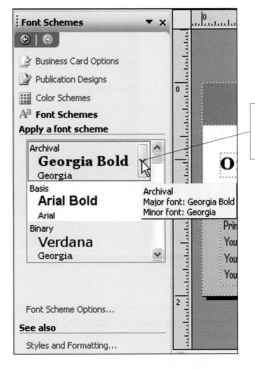

Choose a major font and a minor font combination for your publication.

Working with Layout Guides and Ruler Guides

Layout guides
Layout guides create a grid that is used to arrange text, pictures, and other objects.

The *layout guides* create a framework or grid for text boxes, columns, graphics, headings, and other objects used in a publication. Click Arrange and then Layout Guides to display the Layout Guides dialog box. At this dialog box, you can set margins for your publication; the grid lines, which are column and row guides; and the baseline guides to which lines of text can be aligned to provide a uniform appearance. Layout guides are created at the master page and they display as blue nonprinting dotted lines as shown in Figure 12.11.

Master page
The background layer in Publisher. Elements on this page appear on every page.

Every page in a publication has a foreground and background layer. The foreground is where you insert text and design objects. The background layer is known as the *master page*. Any objects placed in the master page will appear on every page, which makes it a good place to insert headers and footers, page numbers, and logos. The layout guides and ruler guides are created at the master page. To specify how you want a page to be laid out, complete the following steps:

1. Click Arrange and then Layout Guides.
2. At the Layout Guides dialog box, enter settings for margins, columns, rows, and baselines.
3. To create mirrored layouts, select the Margin Guides tab, click the *Two-page master* option, and then click OK.
4. To move a layout guide, click View and then Master Page or press Ctrl + M.

Ruler guides display as green dotted lines and are created at the master page as shown in Figure 12.11. Ruler guides are useful when you want to align several objects or position an object at an exact location on the page. Click Arrange, point to Ruler Guides, and then click Add Horizontal Ruler Guide, Add Vertical Ruler Guide, Format Ruler Guides, or Clear All Ruler Guides. Hold down the Shift key and then drag the Adjust handle from the rulers to create a new position for the guide.

Ruler guides

Ruler guides are useful to measure or align objects.

FIGURE

12.11 *Layout Guides (Margin, Grid, and Baseline) and Ruler Guides (Vertical and Horizontal) for a Brochure*

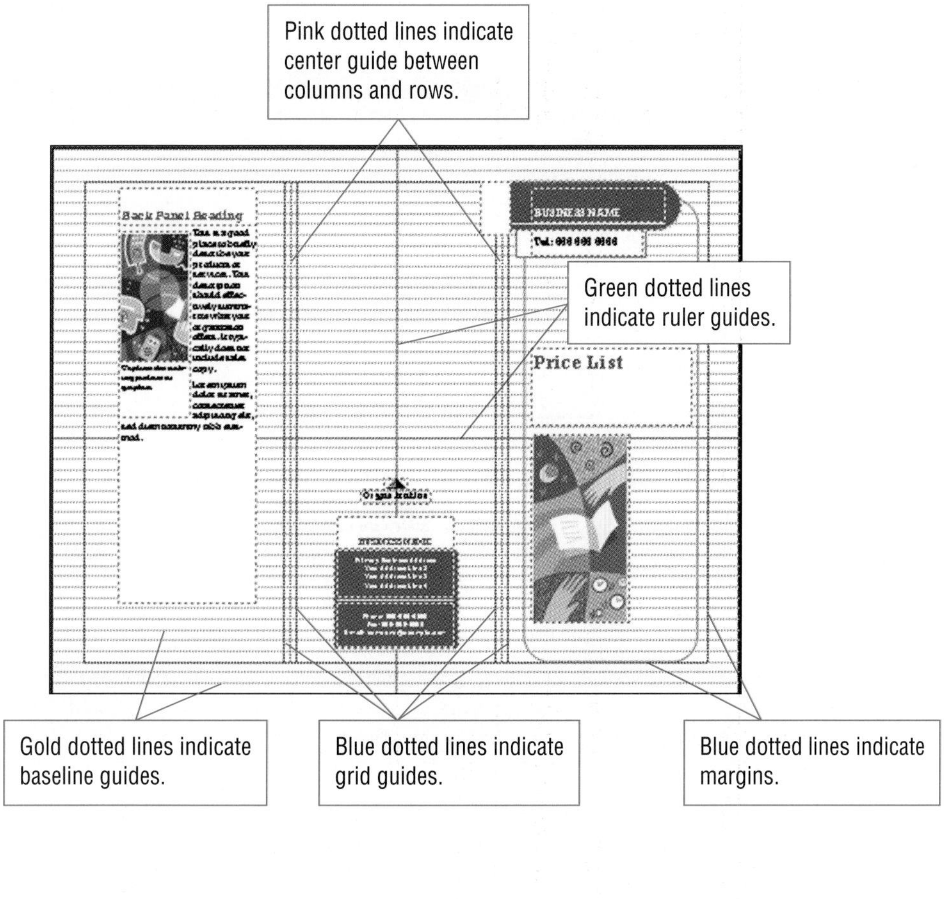

Pink dotted lines indicate center guide between columns and rows.

Green dotted lines indicate ruler guides.

Gold dotted lines indicate baseline guides.

Blue dotted lines indicate grid guides.

Blue dotted lines indicate margins.

The Snap To commands make objects on a page align with the rulers, guides, or other objects. When you move an object near another object, ruler, or guide, you will feel the object being pulled to the nearest guide. The Snap To commands are accessed by clicking Arrange and then pointing to Snap.

Using the Microsoft Publisher Design Gallery

Smart objects
Design objects that have a wizard associated with them.

Design Gallery
Object

The Microsoft Publisher Design Gallery contains a wide variety of predesigned objects to enhance your document, including logos, headlines, calendars, pull quotes, and attention-getters as shown in Figure 12.12. These objects are called *smart objects*, which are design objects that have a template wizard associated with them. To insert a Design Gallery object into your publication, click Insert and then Design Gallery Object, or click the Design Gallery Object button on the Objects toolbar. Select the category of design you want to use, and when you have made your choice, click Insert Object. If you want to select an object based on a specific design style, click the Objects by Design tab.

F I G U R E

12.12 *Using the Microsoft Publisher Design Gallery*

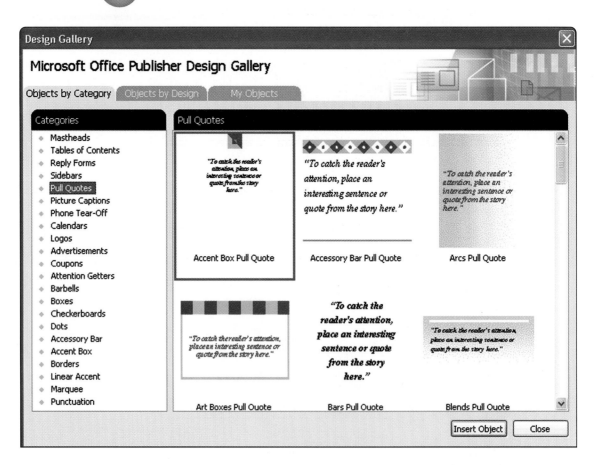

Chapter Twelve

Using AutoFit Text

The AutoFit Text feature automatically resizes text so that the text will fit into the allotted amount of space. To turn on the AutoFit feature, click Format, point to AutoFit Text, and then select Do Not Autofit, Best Fit, or Shrink Text On Overflow. Do Not Autofit turns off the feature. Best Fit reduces or enlarges the text to fill the text box. Shrink Text On Overflow reduces the text to fit into the text box, but does not increase the font size to fit the text box.

(Before completing computer exercises, delete the Chapter11 folder on your disk. Next, copy the Chapter12 folder from the CD that accompanies this textbook to your disk and then make Chapter12 the active folder.)

exercise 1

Creating a Flyer Using a Flyer Template

1. Open Publisher.
2. At the Start screen, click the *Publications for Print* option in the *New from a design* section of the New Publication task pane.
3. Scroll to locate *Flyers*.
4. Click *Flyers* and then click *Informational*.
5. Scroll vertically until the Eclipse Informational Flyer template displays and then click once on this template thumbnail. *(Hint: Publisher builds the publication and opens a task pane with options to change the color scheme, font scheme, and publication design. If the Personal Information dialog box displays, ask your instructor whether you should ignore it.)*

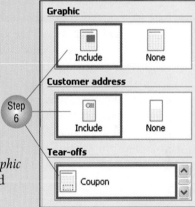

6. At the Flyer Options task pane, click *Include* in the *Graphic* section, click *Include* in the *Customer address* section, and then click *Coupon* in the *Tear-offs* section.
7. Save the flyer and name it **c12ex01, Music**.
8. Click the <u>Color Schemes</u> hyperlink at the Flyer Options task pane.
9. Click the *Waterfall* color scheme.

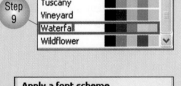

10. Click the <u>Font Schemes</u> hyperlink at the Color Scheme task pane.
11. Click once on the *Streamline* font scheme, which includes the Bodoni MT Condensed and TW Cen MT Bold fonts.
12. Press the F9 key or click the Zoom In button on the Standard toolbar to zoom to 100%.

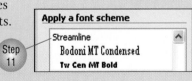

13. Select the placeholder text *Business Name* and then type Michael Costanza.
14. With the insertion point located in the text box containing *Product/Service Information*, click Format, point to AutoFit Text, and then click Best Fit.
15. Select the placeholder text *Product/Service Information*, turn on bold, type Forever Music, press Enter, and then type Teaching Studio.

16. Change the leading between *Forever Music* and *Teaching Studio* by completing the following steps:
    a. Select *Forever Music Teaching Studio*.
    b. Click F<u>o</u>rmat and then <u>P</u>aragraph.
    c. At the Paragraph dialog box, type **.80 sp** in the *Between lines* text box in the *Line spacing* section and then click OK.
17. Add a gradient fill to the text frame containing *Forever Music...* by completing the following steps:
    a. With the text box selected, click F<u>o</u>rmat and then Te<u>x</u>t Box.
    b. At the Format Text Box dialog box, select the Colors and Lines tab, click the down-pointing arrow at the right of the <u>C</u>olor list box in the *Fill* section, and then click <u>F</u>ill Effects.
    c. At the Fill Effects dialog box, select the Gradient tab.
    d. In the *Colors* section, select O<u>n</u>e color, click the down-pointing arrow at the right of the *Color 1* list box, and then click the Accent 2 (Teal) color.

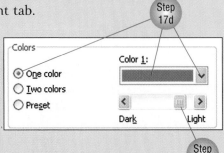

Step
17d

    e. Drag the slider toward Light as shown at the right.
    f. In the *Shading styles* section, select Hori<u>z</u>ontal, click the first option in the V<u>a</u>riants section, and then click OK twice.

Step
17e

18. Select the placeholder text *Place text here that introduces...*, click <u>I</u>nsert, and Te<u>x</u>t File, and then select the **Lessons.doc** file located in your Chapter12 folder.
19. Press Ctrl + A to select all of the text in the text box and then apply the Body Text style by clicking the down-pointing arrow at the right of the Style list box on the Formatting toolbar and then clicking Body Text.
20. Click F<u>o</u>rmat, point to AutoFit Te<u>x</u>t, and then click <u>B</u>est Fit.
21. To avoid hyphenating *orchestra*, click <u>T</u>ools, point to <u>L</u>anguage, click <u>H</u>yphenation, remove the check mark next to *Automatically hyphenate this story*, and then click OK.
22. Select the tagline placeholder text, type **May your home forever be filled with love and music.**, select *forever* and *music,* and then apply the Accent 2 font color (Teal) and small caps. *(Hint: You will need to apply the formatting changes to each word separately.)*
23. Delete the telephone number placeholder by right-clicking on the text box and then clicking <u>D</u>elete Object from the shortcut menu.
24. Select *Organization* in the logo and then type **Forever Music**.
25. Customize the logo by completing the following steps:
    a. Select the logo and then click the Wizard button to start the Logo Wizard.
    b. At the Logo Designs task pane and in the *Apply a design* section click the *Open Oval* design.
    c. Click the <u>Logo Options</u> hyperlink near the top of the task pane and then click *None* in the *Graphic* section.

Step
25a

26. *Michael Costanza* should automatically display in the text box below the logo—since you typed *Michael Costanza* in another text box formatted with the Organization Name style, the personal information set automatically inserts the organization name text. If the name is later changed in one box, click once in the other text box containing the name to propagate the personal information set.
27. Select the text box containing the primary business address, press Ctrl + A to select all of the placeholder text, and then type the following:

Forever Music Teaching Studio
1234 Third Street
Bloomington, IN 47406

28. Select the text box containing the telephone numbers, press Ctrl + A to select the placeholder text, and then type the following. *(Hint: Press Tab after each colon.)*

> *Phone:*   812.555.9843
> *Fax:*   812.555.9845
> *E-mail:*   forevermusic@emcp.net

29. Type the following text in place of the coupon placeholder text:

> *Name of Item or Service:*   Guitar Lesson
> *00% Off*   One Free Lesson
> *Business Name*   Forever Music Teaching Studio
> *Describe your location…*   Downtown Bloomington
> *Tel: 555-555-5555*   Tel: 812.555.9853

30. Click the Wizard button below the expiration date.
31. At the Coupon Designs task pane, view the *Coupon Designs* options, and then click the <u>Coupon Options</u> hyperlink and view the options provided (do not make any changes).
32. Select the expiration date placeholder text and type 01/01/06.
33. Save the flyer with the same name **c12ex01, Music**. *(Hint: If a prompt appears asking if you want to save the modified logo to the Personal Information Set, click No.)*
34. Insert a graphic by completing the following steps:
    a. Double-click the computer image in the coupon. This displays the Clip Art task pane.
    b. At the Clip Art task pane, type j0238805.wmf or type the keyword guitar in the *Search for* text box, and then click Go. Click once to insert the image.

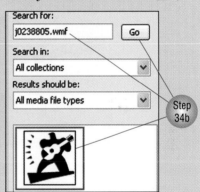

35. Double-click an outside border line of the coupon to access the Format AutoShape dialog box, change the fill color to Accent 2 (Teal), and then click OK.
36. Insert a graphic in place of the sky picture by completing the following steps:
    a. Double-click the sky picture in the middle of the flyer.
    b. At the Clip Art task pane, type j0281073.wmf or type the keyword piano in the *Search for* text box, and then click Go. Click once to insert the image; the image should be similar to Figure 12.13.
    c. If necessary, ungroup the image and the AutoShape box to size and position the image similar to Figure 12.13. *(Hint: If the graphic overlaps another text box, remove the fill from the text box.)*

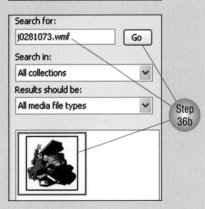

37. Click page 2 on the Page Navigation control on the Status bar. *(Hint: This will move your insertion point to the second page.)*
38. Notice that Publisher automatically inserted the return address information from the information provided on page 1. Replace the mailing address information with your name, your street address, city, state, and ZIP. *(Hint: Delete the text box with the number in it.)*

39. Save **c12ex01, Music**.
40. Print the first page of the flyer and then reinsert the flyer into your printer and print the address information on the back of the flyer.
41. Close **c12ex01, Music**.

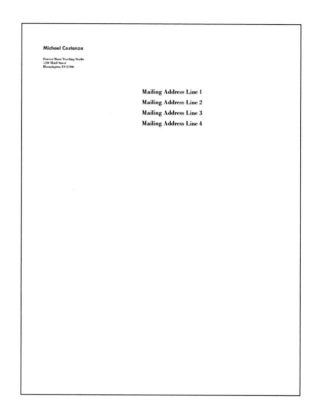

Creating a Logo from Scratch

In advertising, a logo (or logotype) is a special design used as a trademark for a company or product. A logo can help a business make a big impression since a logo embellishes the company name and reinforces company identification. Create simple, but distinctive logos in Publisher with WordArt effects, drawn objects, clip art, and wise use of color and fonts. When grouping an appropriate clip art with the name of the company, look for a special visual relationship between the two elements.

DTP POINTERS
Keep your logo design simple.

Many Publisher features can be used to position objects precisely. Such features include the Size and Position toolbar, <u>L</u>ayout Guides, Ruler Gui<u>d</u>es, <u>A</u>lign or Distribute, <u>S</u>nap, <u>N</u>udge, Rotate or Fli<u>p</u>, <u>E</u>dit Points, and <u>G</u>roup. Most of these features are found on the A<u>r</u>range menu.

When finished, the logo can be used for standard business documents, such as a letterhead or business form, and for promotional items, such as a shopping bag or company give-aways including pens, t-shirts, caps, mouse pads, and more.

Saving a Logo in Publisher

One of the most useful features in Publisher 2003 is the new Save as Picture option. You may group objects together and save the entire selection as a picture. With this feature, you may create mastheads, logos, and other designs and save them in a file format for use on Web pages or print, and reuse them within other publications.

To use the Save as Picture feature, complete the following steps:

1. Select your objects and group them together.
2. Right-click on the grouped object and then choose <u>S</u>ave as Picture from the shortcut menu.
3. Choose a desired file format in the *Save as type* list box at the Save As dialog box.

Creating a Trifold Brochure Using a Publisher Template

1. Open Publisher and then display the New Publication task pane.
2. At the Start screen, click the *Publications for Print* option in the *New from a design* section of the New Publication task pane.
3. Scroll down and then click *Brochures*.
4. Sroll down vertically until the Watermark Informational Brochure template displays and then click once on this template thumbnail. Click Cancel at the Personal Information dialog box.

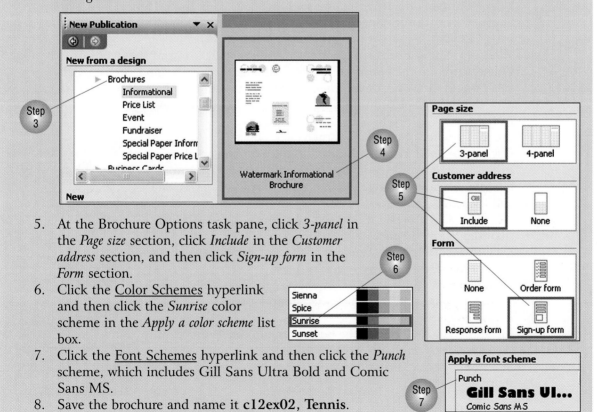

5. At the Brochure Options task pane, click *3-panel* in the *Page size* section, click *Include* in the *Customer address* section, and then click *Sign-up form* in the *Form* section.
6. Click the <u>Color Schemes</u> hyperlink and then click the *Sunrise* color scheme in the *Apply a color scheme* list box.
7. Click the <u>Font Schemes</u> hyperlink and then click the *Punch* scheme, which includes Gill Sans Ultra Bold and Comic Sans MS.
8. Save the brochure and name it **c12ex02, Tennis**.

9. With the first page displayed, format the cover (far right panel) by completing the following steps:

Step 9d

a. Select the product/service information placeholder text and then type 2005 Summer Tennis Camp.

b. With the text box containing *2005 Summer Tennis Camp* selected, click Format, AutoFit Text, and then Best Fit.

c. Double-click the swim image in the middle of the cover panel. This displays the Clip Art task pane.

d. Type j0090189.wmf or type the keyword tennis in the *Search for* text box and then click Go.

e. Click once on the image to insert it and then size and position the image as shown in Figure 12.14.

f. Select the business name placeholder text, type Court Sports, change the font color to Accent 1 (Red), and then change the font size to 18 points.

g. Select the tagline placeholder text and then type Make time for tennis. *(Hint: Press F9 or click the Zoom In button to increase the zoom of this page.)*

h. Select *Make time for tennis.* and change the font size to 12 points.

i. Select the telephone placeholder text and then type Tel: 517.555.8711.

10. Create the Court Sports logo by completing the following steps:

a. Click to the right of the scroll box on the horizontal scroll bar to view more of the work area (dark gray area). Click the Rectangle button on the Objects toolbar. Drag the crosshairs into the work area and create a rectangle approximately 0.375 inch in height and 0.675 inch in width. *(Hint: Verify the size at the Format AutoShape dialog box.)*

Step 10a

b. Click to select the rectangle shape, click the Line/Border Style button on the Formatting toolbar, and then click the Thick/Thin line at 4½ pt (twelfth line style from the top of the drop-down list).

c. With the rectangle selected, click the down-pointing arrow at the right of the Line Color button on the Formatting toolbar and apply the Accent 1 (Red).

d. Click the Insert WordArt button on the Objects toolbar. At the WordArt Gallery, click the fifth shape from the left in the second row and then click OK.

e. At the Edit WordArt Text dialog box, type Court Sports, change the font size to 14 points, and then click OK.

f. Click the Format WordArt button on the WordArt toolbar.

g. At the Format WordArt dialog box, change the fill color to the Accent 2 (Yellow), change the line color to the Accent 1 (Red), and then click OK.

Triangle Up

h. Click the WordArt Shape button and then click the third shape from the left in the first row (Triangle Up).

Step 10h

i. Drag the WordArt object on top of the rectangle image as shown at the right. *(Hint: Nudge if needed.)*

Step 10i

j. Hold down the Shift key, click the rectangle shape, click the WordArt shape, and then click the Group Objects button below the shapes.

k. Move the grouped logo to the bottom right corner of the cover panel as shown in Figure 12.14.

l. Save the logo as a picture by completing the following steps:

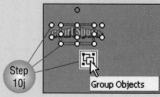

Step 10j

Group Objects

1) Click to select the grouped logo.
2) Right-click the logo and then click <u>S</u>ave as Picture.
3) At the Save As dialog box, type Court Sports in the *File name* text box, select *Tag Image File Format (*.tif)* in the *Save as type* list box, select your Chapter12 folder at the *Save in* list box, and then click <u>S</u>ave.

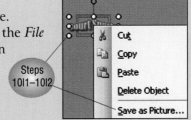

Steps 10l1–10l2

11. Format the address (middle) panel by completing the following steps:
   a. Delete the text box containing the company name placeholder by right-clicking on the object and then clicking <u>D</u>elete Object from the shortcut menu.
   b. Select the Court Sport logo in the first panel and while holding down the Ctrl key, drag and drop a copy of the logo above the return address in panel 2.
   c. Using the Free Rotate tool, rotate the logo and then position it as shown in Figure 12.14.

Step 11c

   d. Select the return address placeholder and then type the following:

   Nick Borm
   55 East Mt. Hope Avenue
   Lansing, MI 48901

   e. Change the return address alignment to Align Left.
   f. Type your name, street address, city, state, and ZIP in place of the mailing address placeholder text.
12. Format the back panel (left panel) by completing the following steps:
   a. Click the back panel heading placeholder text and type Head Instructor, press Enter, and then type Nick Borm.
   b. Click the body placeholder text and then insert **Back Panel Text** located in your Chapter12 folder.
   c. Select the first paragraph and apply the Body Text style.
   d. Select the remaining paragraphs and apply the List Bullet style.
   e. Add a texture fill by completing the following steps:
      1) Double-click the text box.
      2) At the Format Text Box dialog box, select the Colors and Lines tab.

Step 12h

      3) Click the down-pointing arrow at the right of *Color* in the *Fill* section and then click <u>F</u>ill Effects.

      4) At the Fill Effects dialog box, select the Texture tab and then click the first texture in the first row (Newsprint). Click OK twice.
      5) Resize the text box similar to Figure 12.14.
   f. Select and then delete the swimmer image and the caption at the bottom of the panel.
   g. Display the Clip Art task pane.
   h. Type j0202183.jpg or type the keyword tennis in the *Search for* text box and then click Go. Click the image once to insert it.
   i. Size and position the tennis image as shown in Figure 12.14.
13. Save the brochure with the same name **c12ex02, Tennis**.
14. Close **c12ex02, Tennis**.

FIGURE
12.14 Exercise 2

Head Instructor
Nick Borm

Nick Borm has been an instructor
at Court Sports for the past
twelve years.

- Holder of 6 USTA (United
  States Tennis Association)
  National Tournaments
- Finalist in 10 additional
  USTA National Tournaments
- Holder of 10 National Public
  Parks Tennis Titles
- #1 National Ranking in Men's
  Doubles in 2004, 2003, 2001

Nick Borm
55 East Mt. Hope Avenue
Lansing, MI 48901

Your Name
Your Address
Your City, State ZIP

2005
Summer
Tennis Camp

Court Sports

Make time for tennis.

Tel: 517.555.8711

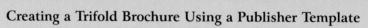

exercise 3

Portfolio

Creating a Trifold Brochure Using a Publisher Template

1. Open **c12ex02, Tennis**.
2. Format the left panel on page 2 by completing the following steps:
   a. Click page 2 on the Page Navigation control on the Status bar.
   b. Click the main inside heading placeholder text and then type Tennis for adults and juniors.
   c. With the text box containing *Tennis for adults and juniors* selected, click Format, AutoFit Text, and then Best Fit.
   d. Click the body placeholder text to select it and then insert **Panel 1 Text** located in your Chapter12 folder and change the font size to 10 points.
   e. Select and then delete the ski image.
   f. Drag the tennis image with the blue circular background toward the bottom of the panel as shown in Figure 12.15.

   g.   Select the caption placeholder text and then type Get into shape and have fun at the same time!

3. Format the middle inside panel by completing the following steps:
   a.   Click the secondary heading placeholder at the top of the panel and then type General Information.
   b.   Select the placeholder text and then insert **Panel 2 Top** located in your Chapter12 folder.
   c.   Click the secondary heading placeholder and then type Summer Tournament.
   d.   Select the placeholder text and then insert **Panel 2 Bottom** located in your Chapter12 folder.
   e.   Drag the text box down so it is positioned similar to Figure 12.15.

4. Format the panel at the right by completing the following steps:
   a.   Click the placeholder text *Sign-Up Form Title* and then type July Tennis Camp Registration. *(Hint: Press F9 to increase the zoom.)*
   b.   Replace all of the placeholder text in the top section of the form with the text given below:

Step 4a

Step 4b

July Tennis Camp Registration

Sign up for: July Tennis Camp	Time	Price
☐ Adult Group Lessons M W	6 p.m.	$75
☐ Adult Group Lessons T TH	7 p.m.	$75
☐ Junior Group Lessons M W	9 a.m.	$75
☐ Junior Group Lessons T TH	11 a.m.	$75
☐ Junior Group Lessons M W F	1 p.m.	$100
☐ Summer Tournament (August 6)	8 a.m.	$45

Sign up for: July Tennis Camp	Time	Price
Adult Group Lessons M W	6 p.m.	$75
Adult Group Lessons T TH	7 p.m.	$75
Junior Group Lessons M W	9 a.m.	$75
Junior Group Lessons T TH	11 a.m.	$75
Junior Group Lessons M W F	1 p.m.	$100
Summer Tournament (August 2 & 3)	8 a.m.	$45

   c.   Right-click in the text box containing the business name placeholder (Court Sports) in the shaded box at the bottom of the panel and then click <u>D</u>elete Object.
   d.   Click <u>I</u>nsert, <u>P</u>icture, <u>F</u>rom File, and then locate and insert the **Court Sports.tif** file in your Chapter12 folder or click the Picture Frame button on the Objects toolbar. Position the logo as shown in Figure 12.15.
   e.   Make sure the following text displays in the primary business address text box:

Step 4d

Step 4e

       Nick Borm
       55 East Mt. Hope Avenue
       Lansing, MI 48901

   f.   Edit the phone, fax, and e-mail placeholder text as follows:

       Phone: 517.555.8711
       Fax: 517.555.8712
       E-mail: courtsports@emcp.net

5. Use Print Preview to view your brochure.
6. Save the brochure as **c12ex03, Tennis**.
7. Print both pages of the brochure using both sides of the paper.
8. Close **c12ex03, Tennis**.

FIGURE

12.15 *Exercise 3*

**Head Instructor
Nick Borm**

Nick Borm has been an instructor at Court Sports for the past twelve years.

- Holder of 6 USTA (united States Tennis Association) National Tournaments
- Finalist in 10 additional USTA National Tournaments
- Holder of 10 National Public Parks Tennis Titles
- #1 National Ranking in Men's Doubles in 2004, 2003, 2001.

Nick Borm
55 East Mt. Hope Avenue
Lansing, MI 48901

Your Name
Your Address
Your City, State Zip

2005
Summer
Tennis Camp

Court Sports

Make time for tennis.

Tel: 517.555.8711

Tennis for adults and juniors

Court Sports is proud to offer one of the best tennis programs in Michigan. Our facility includes eight Har-Tru clay tennis courts for outdoor play and eight indoor Plexipave courts.

Our pro shop is one of the best in the Midwest, and we offer a wide range of activities including:

- adult group lessons
- junior group lessons
- private lessons
- leagues
- traveling teams
- clinics
- special events
- tournaments

Get into shape and have fun at the same time!

General Information

- Bring your own racket
- Outdoor classes canceled due to rain will be made up at a later date during the summer program
- Lessons are open to members and non-members
- No refunds once sessions begin
- Private lessons are available upon request
- Prices will be prorated for the week of July 3rd

If you have any questions, call Nick Borm at 517.555.8711 ext. 25.

Summer Tournament

Court Sports Summer Tennis Tournament is open to members only. Our tournament is a great way to practice competing in a friendly, social environment. Our summer tournament is scheduled for August 2 & 3.

July Tennis Camp Registration

Sign up for: July Tennis Camp	Time	Price
☐ Adult Group Lessons M W	6 p.m.	$75
☐ Adult Group Lessons T TH	7 p.m.	$75
☐ Junior Group Lessons M W	9 a.m.	$75
☐ Junior Group Lessons T TH	11 a.m.	$75
☐ Junior Group Lessons M W F	1 p.m.	$100
☐ Summer Tournament (August 6)	8 a.m.	$45

Subtotal: _____
Tax: _____
Total: _____

Name _____
Address _____
_____
_____
_____

Method of Payment

- ☐ Check
- ☐ Bill Me
- ☐ Visa
- ☐ MasterCard
- ☐ American Express

Credit Card # _____ Exp. date _____
Signature _____

Nick Borm
55 East Mt. Hope Avenue
Lansing, MI 48901

Phone: 517.555.8711
Fax: 517.555.8712
E-mail: courtsports@emcp.net

Working with Text in Overflow

If you have inserted or typed more text than what your text box can hold, Publisher displays a message asking if you want Publisher to flow the text automatically or if you want to connect the text boxes yourself. If Publisher flows the text automatically, it will create text boxes as needed and then flow the text into the text boxes. However, if you decide to connect the text boxes yourself, the Text in Overflow indicator will display at the bottom of your text box as shown in Figure 12.16.

Text in Overflow

FIGURE

12.16 *Text in Overflow*

To accommodate the overflow text, you could click Format, point to AutoFit Text, and then click Best Fit or Shrink Text On Overflow; or, you could resize the text box, or create another text box and connect the text boxes.

Using Connected Text Boxes

Text boxes are generally used in creating newsletters and many other publications in Publisher. Layout guides may be set up in a column format and then used to assist in sizing and positioning the text boxes for consistent-looking columns. For text to flow from one text box to the next, you must use the connected text box feature. Publisher 2003 refers to connected text boxes in a series as a *story*. To create a chain of connected text boxes, complete the following steps:

1. Create as many text boxes as you think you may need.
2. Select the first text box in the series. By default the Connect Text Boxes toolbar displays at the right of the Standard toolbar. (See Figure 12.17 for the Connect Text Boxes toolbar.)
3. Click the Create Text Box Link button on the Connect Text Boxes toolbar. The pointer becomes an upright pitcher when you move it over the page.
4. Position the pointer (pitcher) over an empty text box and the pitcher tilts, as shown in Figure 12.18.
5. Click the empty text box to make the connection to the original text box.

Text boxes that are connected will display the Go to Next Text Box and Go to Previous Text Box buttons in the corner of each box. To help a reader follow a story that may begin on one page and continue to another page, you may want to add a Continued notice at the bottom of the text box informing the reader where to find the rest of the story.

Story
Connected text boxes in a series.

DTP POINTERS
Connected text boxes reinforce continuity and consistency.

Go to Next Text Box

Go to Previous Text Box

FIGURE

12.17 *Connect Text Boxes Toolbar*

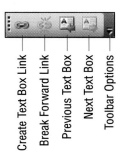

Create Text Box Link
Break Forward Link
Previous Text Box
Next Text Box
Toolbar Options

FIGURE

12.18 *"Pouring" Text into a Connected Text Box*

Adding a Continued Notice

When you connect text boxes, text that does not fit into the first text box flows into the next connected text box. A chain of connected text boxes can span numerous pages. To add a Continued notice to a text box, complete the following steps:

1. Select the text box where you want to place a Continued notice and click Format and then Text Box.
2. At the Format Text Box dialog box, click the Text Box tab.
3. Under the *Text autofitting* section, click to add a check mark in the *Include "Continued on page..."* check box, or click the *Include "Continued from page..."* check box to add a check mark, and then click OK.

Using Master Pages

As explained in earlier versions of Publisher, the master page is a page that exists below the foreground or text layer. Design objects placed on a master page will appear on every page of your publication. For instance, if you place a watermark on a master page of a three-page publication, the watermark will display on all three pages. Typically, a page numbering code will be inserted in a master page so that all of the pages in the publication will be numbered consecutively. However, in Publisher 2003 you may use multiple master pages in a single publication. This allows you to create different master pages for different aspects of a publication.

To view a master page(s), click View, Master Page, or press Ctrl + M. To create a master page, open the Edit Master Pages task pane, click the New Master Page button, and give the page a name (the default name is Master A). You can also create a two-page master, which is used when you create a publication that displays in a two-page spread. A two-page master allows you to put page numbering on the left for an even page and on the right for an odd page. To apply master pages, you must be working with pages in your publication. To apply the master pages, click the Apply to Page Range button on the Apply Master Page task pane. Select the master page to apply and then choose the page(s) to apply it to.

Inserting Page Numbering

Page numbering may be added to a publication in the foreground layer or in the Master Page layer. To insert page numbers, click Insert, Page Numbers, and then select options to position the number in the current text box, in a header, or in a footer. Next, select Left, Center, or Right alignment. For a two-page spread, you would choose Inside, Center, or Outside. Finally, click the check box to *Show page number on first page* or remove the check mark if you do not want numbering on the first page. If you are using more than one master page, you will want to place page numbering on each master page, whether it is a single page or a two-page spread. You can also set up headers and footers on a master page and insert the page numbering code, date, and time within them. The Add On the Master Page option enables you to add headers and footers to the entire publication or to a single page. To insert a header or footer, click View and then Header and Footer.

To apply a master page layout to a publication, you must have your publication open, click Format and then Apply Master Page as shown in Figure 12.19.

F I G U R E

12.19 *Apply Master Page Task Pane*

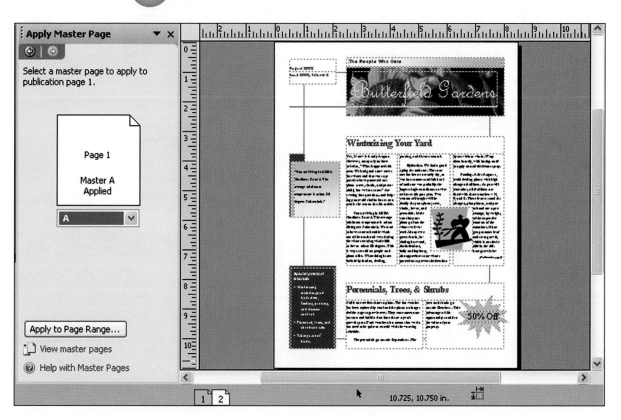

Creating a Watermark

You may create a watermark in the master page and subsequently it will display on every page of your publication. Otherwise, you may insert an image in the foreground layer, click the Color button on the Picture toolbar, click <u>W</u>ashout, click A<u>r</u>range, point to O<u>r</u>der, and then click Send <u>B</u>ackward. If the watermark does not display, you may have to change the text box fill to No Fill.

exercise 4

Creating a Newsletter from a Publisher Template

1. Display the New Publication task pane.
2. Click *Publications for Print* in the *New from a design* section.
3. Click the *Newsletters* category in the list box, scroll down vertically until the Summer Newsletter template displays, and then click once on this template thumbnail. *(Hint: Ask your instructor if you should complete the Personal Information; otherwise, click Cancel at the Personal Information dialog box.)*

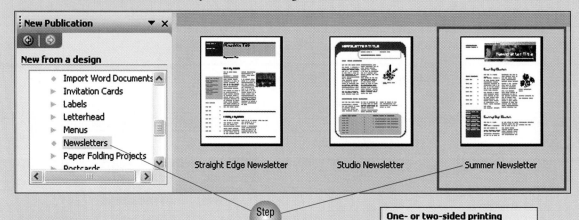

4. At the Newsletter Options task pane, click *1* in the *One- or two-sided printing* section, and then click *None* in the *Customer address* section.
5. Click the <u>Page Content</u> hyperlink and then click *1* in the *Columns* section and view the changes in the document window. Click *2* in the *Columns* section and view the changes; click *3* in the *Columns* section and view the changes; and then click *Mixed* in the *Columns* section. This is the column layout you will use. *(Hint: The down-pointing arrow to the right of each column icon allows you to choose whether to apply the formatting to one page or all pages.)*
6. Click the <u>Color Schemes</u> hyperlink, click the *Ivy* color scheme in the *Apply a color scheme* list box, and then click the <u>Custom color scheme</u> hyperlink at the bottom of the task pane.

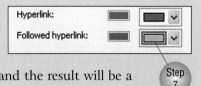

Step
7

7. At the Color Schemes dialog box, select the Custom tab and then click the down-pointing arrow at the right of the *Followed hyperlink* option. Click the gold color (the second color from the left in the fourth row) and then click OK. The gold color will replace the previous color and the result will be a custom scheme.

8. Click the <u>Font Schemes</u> hyperlink and then click the *Fusion* scheme, which includes French Script MT and Calisto MT.

9. Save the brochure and name it **c12ex04, Butterfield**.

10. Delete two pages of the newsletter by completing the following steps:
    a. Click page 2 on the Page Navigation control on the Status bar, click <u>E</u>dit, and then click Delete P<u>a</u>ge.
    b. Click the new page 2 icon and delete that page.

11. With the first page displayed, press F9, click the newsletter date placeholder, and then type **August 2005**.

12. Click the volume and issue placeholder and then type Issue 2003, Volume 2.

13. Click the business name placeholder and then type The people who care.

14. Click the newsletter title placeholder and then type Butterfield Gardens.

15. Click the lead story headline placeholder and then type Winterizing Your Yard.

16. The article text you will insert will not fit into the connected text boxes on page 1; therefore, you will need to continue your story on page 2. To do this, complete the following steps:
    a. Click page 2 on the Page Navigation control on the Status bar.
    b. Select the text box to the right of *The people who care.* near the top of the page, change the zoom to a percentage that allows you to clearly see the text, and then drag the bottom center resizing handle downward to the horizontal line above the back page story headline placeholder to increase the height of the text box. Drag the top middle sizing handle upward to the blue layout guide (margin guide). ***(Hint: You will feel the resizing handle snap to the layout guide as you approach it.)***
    c. Click the page 1 icon on the Status bar and then click to select the third connected text box (contains the flower graphic) under the heading *Winterizing Your Yard*. ***(Hint: When you click to select a specific connected text box, you will see <u>Go to Previous Text Box</u> or <u>Go to Next Text Box</u> hyperlinks at the top or at the bottom of the selected text box. Use these hyperlinks to move between the connected text frames.)***

Step
16c   Step
16d

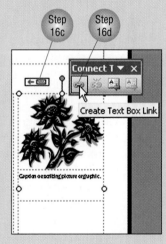

    d. Click the Create Text Box Link button on the Connect Text Boxes toolbar. The arrow pointer will display as a pitcher.
    e. Click page 2 on the Page Navigation control on the Status bar, position the pouring pitcher into the text box at the top of the page and to the right of *The people who care.*, and then click once. The text box should now be linked to the text boxes on the first page. ***(Hint: The* Go to Previous Text Box *icon should display at the top of this box.)***

Step
16e

    f. Click the Go to Previous Text Box button at the top of the connected text box on page 2.

g. Position your insertion point in the first connected text box under *Winterizing Your Yard* and insert the **Winterizing** text file located in your Chapter12 folder.

h. With the insertion point positioned anywhere in the article, press Ctrl + A.

i. Apply the Body Text 3 style by clicking the down-pointing arrow at the right of the Style list box on the Formatting toolbar and then clicking once on the Body Text 3 style to apply this style to the selected text.

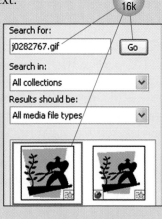

Step
16k

j. Double-click the flower graphic and caption displaying in the "Winterizing Your Yard" article to display the Clip Art task pane.

k. At the Clip Art task pane type j0282767.gif in the *Search for* text box or type gardening to find a gardening graphic of your choosing and then click Go. Click once on the image to insert it.

l. Click the Ungroup Objects button at the bottom of the caption box and graphic.

m. Right-click the caption text box only and then click Delete Object from the shortcut menu.

n. Size and position the image as shown in Figure 12.20.

o. Add a jump line from "Winterizing Your Yard" article on page 1 to the rest of the article on page 2 by completing the following steps:

   1) Right-click the third connected text on page 1 of the winterizing article and then click Format Text Box at the shortcut menu.

   2) At the Format Text Box dialog box, select the Text Box tab.

   3) Click to add a check mark in the check box next to *Include "Continued on page..."* and then click OK.

   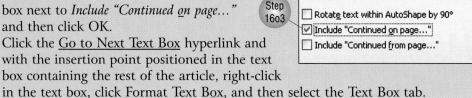

   Step
   16o3

   4) Click the Go to Next Text Box hyperlink and with the insertion point positioned in the text box containing the rest of the article, right-click in the text box, click Format Text Box, and then select the Text Box tab.

   5) Click to add a check mark in the check box next to *Include "Continued from page..."* and then click OK.

   Step
   16o5

   6) Click the Go to Previous Text Box and Go to Next Text Box hyperlinks to view the jump lines.

17. Create a pull quote to the left of the "Winterizing Your Yard" article by completing the following steps:

a. Right-click the table of contents on page 1 and then click Delete Object.

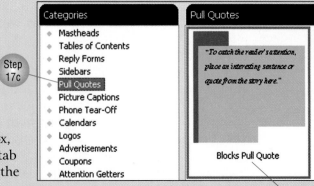

Step
17c

b. Click the Design Gallery Object button on the Objects toolbar.

c. At the Design Gallery dialog box, select the Objects by Category tab and then click *Pull Quotes* from the *Categories* list box.

d. Scroll and then click the *Blocks Pull Quote* object from the *Pull Quotes* section. Click Insert Object.

Step
17d

e. Select the pull quote object, click the down-pointing arrow at the right of the Fill Color button on the Formatting toolbar, and then click <u>F</u>ill Effects.

f. At the Fill Effects dialog box, select the Gradient tab, click the *O<u>n</u>e color* option, click the down-pointing arrow to the right of *Color <u>1</u>*, and then click the gold color in the color scheme (second from right).

g. Drag the slider toward Light as shown at the right and then click OK.

h. Size and position the pull quote similar to Figure 12.20.

i. Select the first two sentences in the second paragraph of the "Winterizing Your Yard" article and then click the Copy button on the Standard toolbar.

j. Select the pull quote placeholder text and then click the Paste button. Center the text vertically and then insert quotation marks around the quote. *(**Hint: Center the text vertically by double-clicking the border of the pull quote, selecting the Text Box tab, and then selecting** Middle **in the** <u>V</u>ertical alignment **drop-down list.**)*

18. Format the sidebar object located below the pull quote object by completing the following steps:
    a. Select the bulleted text.
    b. Type the following:

    Winterizing includes good hydration, feeding, pruning, and disease control.
    Perennials, trees, and shrubs on sale.
    Taking care of birds.

19. Select the secondary story headline placeholder and then type Perennials, Trees, & Shrubs.

20. Select the story text placeholder text and then insert the **Sale** text file located in your Chapter12 folder.

21. Press Ctrl + A to select the entire article and then apply the Body Text 3 style.

22. Insert an attention-getting object by completing the following steps:
    a. Click the Design Gallery Object button on the Objects toolbar.
    b. At the Design Gallery dialog box, select the Objects by Category tab and then click *Attention Getters* in the *Categories* list box.
    c. Scroll and then click the *Explosion Attention Getter* object shown at the right. Click Insert Object.
    d. Click the outside border lines of the shape to select the entire shape, click the down-pointing arrow at the right of the Fill Color button on the Formatting toolbar, and then click the gold color in the scheme (second from the right).

Explosion Attention Getter

    e. Click to select the placeholder text inside the shape, type 50% Off, and then change the font color to Black.
    f. Size and then position the shape similar to Figure 12.20.

23. Save the newsletter with the same name **c12ex04, Butterfield**.

24. Close **c12ex04, Butterfield**.

FIGURE

12.20 *Exercise 4*

August 2005
Issue 2003, Volume 2

The people who care.

Butterfield Gardens

Winterizing Your Yard

Yes, I know it is only August. However, many of you have asked us, "What happened this year. We had good snow cover last winter and that was supposed to have protected our plants (trees, shrubs, and perennials), but we lost some." Answering that question...and helping you avoid similar losses next year is the reason for this article.

You are living in USDA Hardiness Zone 5. The average minimum temperature is minus 20 degrees Fahrenheit. We tend to have some miserable winds out of the north and west during the winter creating wind chills as low as minus 80 degrees. This is very stressful on people and plants alike. Winterizing issues include hydration, feeding,

pruning, and disease control.

Hydration. We had a god spring for moisture. The summer has been extremely dry, as was last summer and fall. Lack of moisture was probably the largest single contributor to winter losses this past year. Two seasons of drought will be deadly for your plants; trees, shrubs, lawns, and perennials. Make sure that your plants go into the winter well watered. May evergreen shrubs, including boxwood, rhododendron, holly

and bayberry, also appreciate some winter protection to prevent desiccation by our vicious winds. Wrap them loosely, with burlap and/or apply an anti-desiccant spray.

Feeding. After August 1, avoid feeding plants with high nitrogen fertilizers. As you will remember, all fertilizers are listed with three numbers – N, P, and K. These letters stand for nitrogen, phosphorus, and potash and are a percentage, by weight, of the respective contents of

(Continued on page 2)

> "You are living in USDA Hardiness Zone 5. The average minimum temperature is minus 20 degrees Fahrenheit."

Special points of interest:

- Winterizing includes good hydration, feeding, pruning, and disease control.
- Perennials, trees, and shrubs on sale.
- Taking care of birds.

Perennials, Trees, & Shrubs

Fall is an excellent time to plant. The hot weather has been replaced by cool and the plants no longer feel the urge to grow leaves. They can concentrate on roots and build a firm base for next year's growth spurt. Cool weather also means that we do not need to be quite as careful with the watering schedule.

The perennials go on sale September 1. The trees

and shrubs go on sale October 1. Take advantage of this opportunity to add to the value of your property.

50% Off

Creating a Newsletter from a Publisher Template

1. Open **ch12ex04, Butterfield** and save it as **ch12ex05, Butterfield**.
2. Click page 2 on the Page Navigation control on the Status bar, select the address placeholder text at the top left of the page, and then type the following:

   Primary Business Address:
   Butterfield Gardens
   29 W 036 Butterfield Road
   Warrenville, IL 60555

   Phone: 630.555.1062
   Fax: 630.555.1072
   E-mail: butterfieldgardens@emcp.net

3. Edit the text box containing the Web address by selecting the example Web address placeholder text and then typing www.emcp.net/butterfieldgardens. *(Hint: Retype* **We're on the Web!** *and resize the text box if necessary.)*
4. Right-click on the tagline text box and then click Delete Object from the shortcut menu.
5. Right-click on the logo object and then click Delete Object.
6. Insert a logo by completing the following steps:
   a. Click the Picture Frame button on the Objects toolbar.
   b. Click the Picture from File option, and then drag the crosshairs to create a picture frame. The size is not important.
   c. At the Insert Picture dialog box, locate your Chapter12 folder and then insert **Bglogo.tif**.
   d. Size and position the logo similar to Figure 12.21.
7. Format the back story on page 2 by completing the following steps:
   a. Click to select the back page story headline placeholder text and then type Fine Feathered Friends.
   b. Double-click the corn graphic to access the Clip Art task pane.
   c. At the Clip Art task pane, type j0180524.jpg or type the keyword birds in the *Search for* text box and then click Go. Insert the image and then close the task pane.

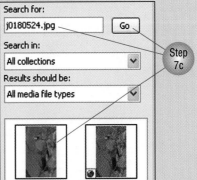

   d. Size and then position the image as shown in Figure 12.21.
   e. Rotate the bird picture so that the bird faces the article text by clicking the down-pointing arrow at the right of the Free Rotate button on the Standard toolbar.
   f. Click Flip Horizontal from the drop-down list.
   g. Select the caption placeholder text and then type Stop at Butterfield Gardens and see our selection of feeders, birdbaths, heaters, and quality bird food. If necessary, ungroup the caption and drag the middle sizing handle to make the caption larger to hold all of the text.

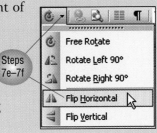

h. Add a fill color to the caption box by clicking the down-pointing arrow at the right of the Fill Color button on the Formatting toolbar and then clicking the Accent 3 color in the color scheme.

8. With the insertion point positioned in the first connected text box below *Fine Feathered Friends*, insert the **Birds** text file located in your Chapter12 folder.

9. Select the text in the "Fine Feathered Friends" article and apply the Body Text 3 style.

10. Add a watermark to the text box on page 2 that contains the winterizing text by completing the following steps:

a. Click the Picture Frame button on the Objects toolbar and then click the Clip Art option from the drop-down list. *(Note: Since you do not want to add the watermark to both pages, you will not want to create the watermark in the master page screen.)*

b. At the Clip Art task pane, type j0197570.wmf or type the keyword bugs in the *Search for* text box and then click Go. Insert the image.

c. Select the bug picture and make sure the Picture toolbar displays.

d. With the image selected, click the Color button on the Picture toolbar and then click <u>W</u>ashout.

e. Size and position the watermark as shown in Figure 12.21.

f. With the image still selected, click A<u>r</u>range, point to O<u>r</u>der, and then click Send <u>B</u>ackward.

g. If the image does not show through, select the text box containing the winterizing article and then change the fill to No Fill.

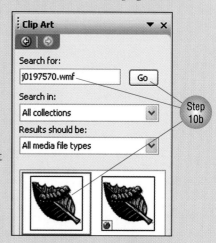

Step 10b

11. Add a page number to page 2 in a master page by completing the following steps:

a. Display page 1 and click <u>V</u>iew and then <u>M</u>aster Page.

b. At the Edit Master Pages task pane, click the New Master Page button at the bottom of the task pane.

Step 11c

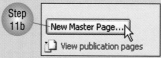

Step 11b

c. At the New Master Page dialog box, make sure the *Page ID* option displays *B* and the *Description* option displays *Master Page B* and then click OK.

d. Two master pages will display in the Edit Master Page task pane. Make sure Master Page B is selected.

Step 11d

e. Click page 2 (B) on the Page Navigation control on the Status bar to make sure your insertion point is located in page 2. With a blank Master Page B displaying to the right of the Edit Master Pages task pane, click <u>V</u>iew and then <u>H</u>eader and Footer.

f. Click the Show Header/Footer button on the Header and Footer toolbar. *(Hint: Clicking the Show Header/Footer button will move you between the Header [top] and Footer [bottom] of the Master Page.)*

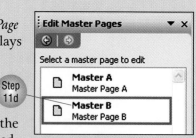

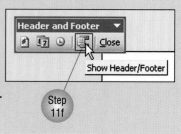

Step 11f

g. At the Footer pane, press Tab twice, type Page, press the spacebar once, and then click the Insert Page Number button on the Header and Footer toolbar. *(Hint: The # symbol represents a page number code.)*

h. Click the Close button on the Header and Footer toolbar.

i. Click the <u>View publication pages</u> hyperlink at the bottom of the Edit Master Pages task pane. The Apply Master Page task pane should display.

Step 11i

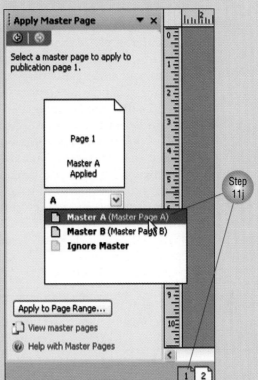

Step 11j

j. Click the page 1 navigation icon on the Status bar and then make sure Master A displays in the Apply Master Page task pane.

k. Click the Apply to Page Range button, make sure *Master A (Master Page A)* displays in the *Select a master page* section, and then select the *Current page(s)* option. Click OK.

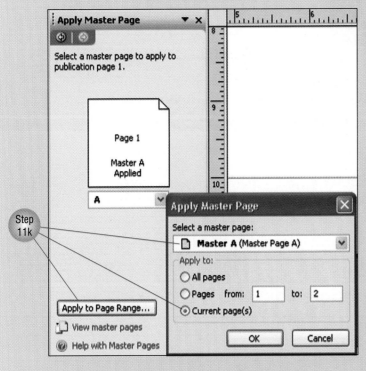

Step 11k

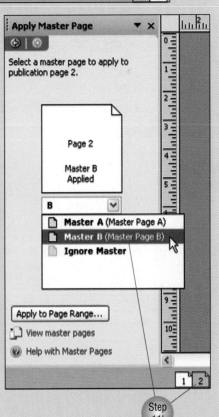

Step 11l

l. Click page 2 on the Page Navigation control on the Status bar and then make sure Master B displays in the Apply Master Page task pane.

m. Click the Apply to Page Range button, make sure *Master B (Master Page B)* displays in the *Select a master page* section, and then select the *Current page(s)* option. Click OK.

n. Close the Apply Master Page task pane.

o. Click the page 1 navigation icon to view page 1—no page number should display. Click page 2 on the Page Navigation control to view page 2—*Page 2* should display. If *Page 2* does not display in the lower right corner of page 2, click to select the last text box on the page and change the fill color to No Fill.

12. Save the newsletter with the same name **c12ex05, Butterfield**.

13. View the document in Print Preview and make any necessary adjustments.

14. Print both pages of the newsletter using both sides of the paper.

15. Close **c12ex05, Butterfield**.

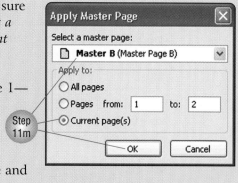

FIGURE

12.21 *Exercise 5*

Using Mail Merge

You can use mail merge to combine records from a data source with a Publisher publication to create multiple copies of the publication that are individually customized as shown in the Mail and Catalog Merge task pane in Figure 12.22. Mail merge can be used to create form letters or to add name and address information to bulk mailings. You can also use mail merge to personalize other kinds of publications such as postcards, envelopes, labels, and more. When you complete a mail merge, each record in a data source becomes a unique publication.

Using Publisher's Catalog Merge

You can use Publisher 2003's new catalog merge feature as shown in Figure 12.22 to combine records from a data source with a catalog merge template to create merged pages for a single publication that displays one or more records per page. Catalog merge can be used to create catalogs, directories, photo albums, or other publications. When you complete a catalog merge, the records in your data source are merged to a single publication. After you create and save a catalog merge template, you can use it again, whenever you change or update your data source, to create merged pages for new publications.

F I G U R E

12.22 *Mail and Catalog Merge Task Pane*

Converting a Publisher Publication to a Web Publication

You can convert a print publication to a Web publication, and vice versa. However, if you used a wizard to create your original publication, you will not be able to use the options available in that wizard in your Web publication. Also, certain Publisher features are not available in Web mode.

To convert a print publication to a Web publication, complete the following steps:

1. Open the print publication you want to convert to a Web publication.
2. Click File and then Convert to Web Publication.
3. Follow the instructions in the Convert to Web Publication Wizard.

Using the Pack and Go Wizard

To package your publication for printing, use the Pack and Go Wizard. The Pack and Go Wizard makes it easy for you to prepare your work for reproduction by a commercial printer. You may choose to use a commercial printer if you need a large number of copies; if the copies need to be folded, bound, or stapled; or if you need your publication to be embossed, foil stamped, or die cut. To use the Pack and Go Wizard, click File, point to Pack and Go, and then click Take to a Commercial Printing Service. Follow the steps in the wizard to complete the process. The file Unpack.exe is created along with the packed files. The Unpack.exe file is used to unpack your files.

CHAPTER summary

➤ Microsoft Publisher 2003 is a complete easy-to-use desktop publishing program designed for small business users and individuals who want to create their own high-quality, professional-looking marketing materials and other business documents without the assistance of professional designers.

➤ Use Publisher if your publications require commercial printing. Publisher offers full support for commercial printing, including four-color separation and spot color processing.

➤ Use Publisher if your document layouts need to be especially precise or complex. Publisher includes easy-to-use layout guides, ruler guides, and Snap To options to align objects to ruler marks, guides, or other objects.

➤ Reinforce consistency by using design sets in Publisher and using styles for spacing, fonts, alignment, repetition, color, and decorative elements such as borders, drop caps, initial caps, and so on.

➤ In Publisher, unlike Word, you must place all objects such as text, graphics, pictures, WordArt, and AutoShapes inside a frame before you can use them in your publication.

➤ When you use a template wizard, the personal information set automatically inserts data stored on its page to placeholder text containing its fields.

➤ By default, Publisher applies color schemes to blank publications as well as wizard-based templates.

- Font schemes make it quick and easy to pick fonts that look good together. To change all of the fonts in your publication, you may apply a new font scheme.

- Every page in a publication has a foreground and background layer. The foreground is where you insert text and design objects. The background layer is known as the master page.

- Any objects placed on the master page will appear on every page.

- The layout guides create a framework or grid for margins, text boxes, columns, graphics, headings, and other objects used in a publication.

- Baseline guides are guides to which lines of text can be aligned to provide a uniform appearance between columns of text.

- Ruler guides display as green dotted lines and are created at the master page. Ruler guides are useful when you want to align several objects or position an object at an exact location on the page.

- The Snap To commands make objects on a page align with the rulers, guides, or other objects.

- The Microsoft Publisher Design Gallery contains a wide variety of predesigned objects to enhance your document, including logos, headlines, calendars, pull quotes, and attention-getters.

- Smart objects are design objects that have a template wizard associated with them.

- The AutoFit Text feature automatically resizes text so that the text will fit into the allotted amount of space.

- One of the most useful features in Publisher 2003 is the new Save as Picture option. You may group objects together and save the entire selection as a picture.

- When you connect text boxes, text that does not fit into the first text box flows into the next connected text box.

- Publisher 2003 refers to connected text boxes in a series as a story.

- To help a reader follow a story that may begin on one page and continue to another page, you may want to add a Continued notice at the bottom of the text box informing the reader where to find the rest of the story and a Continued from notice at the top of the next text box.

- Page numbering may be added to a publication in the foreground layer or in the master page layer.

- You can create headers and footers with automatic page numbers, current date and time display, and any text.

- You may create a watermark in the master page and subsequently it will display on every page of your publication.

- You can use mail merge to combine records from a data source with a Publisher publication to create multiple copies of the publication that are individually customized as shown in the Mail and Catalog Merge task pane.

- You can use Publisher 2003's new catalog merge feature to combine records from a data source with a catalog merge template to create merged pages for a single publication that displays one or more records per page.

- Convert a print publication to a Web page by clicking the Convert to Web Publication option on the File menu.

- Publisher includes a Pack and Go Wizard for packing your publication for reproduction by a commercial printer.

COMMANDS review

Command	Mouse/Keyboard
New Publication task pane	File, New
Color schemes	*Color Schemes* hyperlink at Publication Designs task pane; or click Format, Color Schemes
Font schemes	*Font Schemes* hyperlink at Publication Designs task pane; or click Format, Font Schemes
AutoFit Text	Format, AutoFit Text, and then select Do Not Autofit, Best Fit, or Shrink Text On Overflow
Line spacing	Format, Paragraph, Indents and Spacing tab, Line spacing
Layout guides	Arrange, Layout Guides
Ruler guides	Arrange, Ruler Guides
Snap To	Arrange, Snap
Nudge	Arrange, Nudge; or press arrow keys
Rotate or flip	Arrange, Rotate or Flip
Group, ungroup, regroup	Arrange, then select Group, Ungroup, or Regroup; or press Ctrl + Shift + G
Send Backward	Arrange, Order, Send Backward
Boundaries and guides	View, Boundaries and Guides
Connect text boxes	Select text box, click Create Text Box Link button on Connect Text Boxes toolbar
Continued notice	Right-click text box, click Format Text Box, click Text Box tab, then click *Include "Continued on page…"* or *Include "Continued from page…"*
Page numbers	Insert, Page Numbers
Personal information set	Insert, Personal Information; or click Edit, Personal Information
Master page	View, Master Page; or press Ctrl + M
Apply Master Page	Format, Apply Master Page
Header and footer	View, Header and Footer
Microsoft Publisher Design Gallery	Insert, Design Gallery Object; or Design Gallery Object button on Objects toolbar
Pack and Go Wizard	File, Pack and Go
Print Preview	File, Print Preview; or click Print Preview button on Standard toolbar
Save as Picture	Right-click Picture, click Save as Picture
Delete page	Edit, Delete Page
Delete object	Edit, Delete Object
Watermark	Select picture, click Color button on Picture toolbar, click Washout, Arrange, Order, Send Backward
Text file	Insert, Text File

Mail and Catalog Merge	View, Task Pane, Other Task Panes, Mail and Catalog Merge
Commercial printing	Tools, Commercial Printing Tools
Convert to Web Publication	File, Convert to Web Publication
Web Page Preview	File, Web Page Preview; or click Web Page Preview button on Standard toolbar

REVIEWING key points

Completion: On a blank sheet of paper, indicate the correct term, command, or number for each item.

1. This is another name for the background layer in Publisher.
2. Create consistency among your business documents by selecting one of these templates.
3. These guides are used to adjust margins, grids (columns and rows), and baselines.
4. Use this feature to group objects together and save the entire selection as a picture.
5. These design objects have a template wizard associated with them.
6. This feature makes it quick and easy to pick fonts that look good together.
7. This feature automatically resizes text so that the text will fit into an allotted amount of space.
8. Use this feature to access a wide variety of predesigned objects to enhance your document, including logos, headlines, calendars, pull quotes, and attention-getters.
9. Publisher includes this wizard for packing your publication for reproduction by a commercial printer.
10. To automatically insert stored data to placeholder text containing its fields, use this Publisher function.

APPLYING your skills

Assessment 1

1. As a realtor in Cincinnati, you are eager to inform neighbors, friends, and prospective clients of a new marketing technique where clients may view a panoramic video of a home by visiting your company Web site. Create a postcard promoting a virtual home tour and include the following specifications:
   - Use an appropriate postcard template wizard.
   - Create multiple copies on a sheet.
   - Choose a font scheme.

- Choose a color scheme.
- Include a logo, graphic, or picture.
- Use the AutoFit Text feature in at least one text box.
- Include the following information:

  Virtual Home Tour
  Call me for information on having a customized 360° Panoramic
  Video of your home placed on the Internet for buyers to view!
  One Northbrook Lane
  Columbus, OH 43204
  Sarah Fuhs
  Phone: 513.555.3489
  Fax: 513.555.3488
  www.emcp.net/pleasantvl

2. Save your publication and name it **c12sa01**, **Virtual**.
3. Print and then close.

Assessment 2

1. Create a gift certificate for Butterfield Gardens and include the following specifications:

   - Refer to Figure 12.21 for facts about Butterfield Gardens such as address, phone number, fax number, and e-mail address.
   - Insert a certificate number, expiration date, and redemption value.
   - Create multiple copies on a sheet.
   - Choose a color scheme that complements the newsletter created in Exercises 4 and 5.
   - Choose a font scheme that is interesting and appropriate for the document.
   - Include one graphic image, picture, and/or the Butterfield logo.

2. Save your publication and name it **c12sa02**, **Certificate**.
3. Print and then close.

Assessment 3

In this assessment, you will open a Publisher flyer and convert it to a Web publication and then create a hyperlink to an Excel spreadsheet by completing the following steps:

1. Open **c12ex01**, **Music**.
2. Save the document as **c12sa03**, **Integrated Web**.
3. Delete the design objects on page 2 (the page should be blank) and then return to page 1.
4. Click File and then Convert to Web Publication. Accept the wizard defaults and then click Finish.
5. Open Excel and then open **Schedule of Lessons.xls** located in your Chapter12 folder.
6. Select cells A1:F14 and then click Copy.
7. Make page 2 active and click Edit and then Paste Special. At the Paste Special dialog box, click the *Microsoft Office Excel Worksheet Object* option and then click OK.
8. Move the table below the navigation bar and center it horizontally.
9. Click File, Page Setup, and then select the Layout tab. Click *Web page* in the *Publication type* section and *Standard* in the *Page size* section and then click OK.

10. Select the placeholder text in the green navigation bar, type Home Page, and then change the font color to Accent 1. Select the placeholder text in the blue navigation bar and type Schedule of Lessons. Change the font colors on the page 1 navigation bar if necessary. Click the Save button. *(Hint: In Publisher, you can hold down the Ctrl key and click on the navigation to move between the pages.)*
11. Click the Web Page Preview button on the Standard toolbar. Click the navigation bar to move between the pages. Click <u>F</u>ile and then Close to return to Publisher.
12. Print and then close **c12sa03, Integrated Web**.
13. Close Excel.

Assessment 4

In this assessment, you will use Publisher's Mail and Catalog Merge task pane to merge data to the postcard created in Assessment 1. You will edit the Access database and use the filter feature to select only the addresses in Columbus, OH. Complete the following instructions:

1. Open **c12sa01, Virtual**.
2. Click page 2 in the Page Navigation control on the Status bar.
3. Display the Mail and Catalog Merge task pane.
4. Select the *Mail Merge* option and then click the <u>Next: Select data source</u> hyperlink.
5. Make sure the *Use an existing list* option is selected in the *Select data source* section and then click the <u>Browse</u> hyperlink.
6. Select **Ohio List.mdb** (Access file) located in your Chapter12 folder.
7. Click the <u>E</u>dit button at the Mail Merge Recipients dialog box.
8. Click the Filter and <u>S</u>ort button at the Office Address List dialog box.
9. At the Filter and Sort dialog box, select the <u>F</u>ilter Records tab, click the down-pointing arrow at the right of the *Field* list box, and then click *ZIP Code*. The *Comparison* list box should display *Equal to*. Type 43204 in the *Compare to* text box. Click the OK button to close the Filter and Sort dialog box, click the Close button at the Office Address List dialog box, and then click the OK button to close the Mail Merge Recipients dialog box.
10. Click the <u>Next: Create your publication</u> hyperlink.
11. Select the Primary Business address in the return address section and type the address given on the message side of the postcard. Select the Mailing Address and then change the line spacing by removing the *9 pt* measurement in the *After paragraphs* text box at the Paragraph dialog box.
12. Click the <u>Address block</u> hyperlink and accept all of the defaults.
13. Click the <u>Next: Preview your publication</u> hyperlink. View each recipient (4).
14. Click the <u>Next: Complete the merge</u> hyperlink.
15. Click the <u>Print</u> hyperlink and make multiple copies.
16. Click the <u>Create new publication</u> hyperlink.
17. Save your merged postcards and name them **c12sa04, Integrated**.

Assessment 5

1. Find a flyer at your college announcing a new class, promoting a club, informing students of a study abroad program, and so forth, and recreate the flyer in Publisher. Choose one of Publisher's flyer template wizards and customize the template to fit your needs. Your flyer should include the following:

    - School or department logo
    - At least one graphic or picture

- Appropriate color scheme
- Interesting fonts
- A Microsoft Publisher Design Gallery object

2. Save the publication and name it **c12sa05, Flyer.**
3. Print and then close **c12sa05, Flyer**.

PERFORMANCE Assessments

PREPARING PUBLICATIONS

(Before completing unit assessments, delete the Chapter12 folder on your disk. Next, copy the Unit03 folder from the CD that accompanies this textbook and then make Unit03 the active folder.)

UNIT 03

Assessment 1

Create a one-page newsletter by completing the following instructions. This newsletter may be a holiday, personal, or family newsletter that you would like to duplicate and mail to your friends or relatives. Write four or five short paragraphs describing the highlights of this year and your expectations for next year. You may include items about your accomplishments, awards, talents, skills, hobbies, or any vacations you may have taken. Use the Thesaurus and Spelling features to assist you. Also, be sure to create your own styles, use any appropriate built-in styles, or use the Format Painter to assist you in repetitive formatting.

1. Create a thumbnail sketch of your newsletter.
2. Incorporate the following in your newsletter:
   - Use appropriate typefaces and type sizes for all of the elements in your newsletter.
   - Use em spaces for any indented text.
   - The nameplate should include your last name (e.g., Smith Family Newsletter).
   - Create a subtitle.
   - Create a folio.
   - Use appropriate column numbers and widths; use connected text boxes; or use a newsletter template.
   - Apply the desktop publishing concepts of focus, balance, proportion, contrast, directional flow, and consistency to your newsletter design and layout.
   - Use kerning and character spacing.
   - Use appropriate leading (paragraph spacing) before and after the headline and all subheads.
   - Use a graphic, symbol, WordArt object, clip art, or a scanned picture. (A photograph would add a nice personal touch!)
   - Be creative.

3. Save the newsletter and name it **u03pa01, Newsletter**.
4. After completing **u03pa01, Newsletter**, print and exchange newsletters in the classroom and evaluate them using the document evaluation checklist **(Document Evaluation Checklist.doc)** located in your Unit03 folder. Write any additional comments or suggestions, discussing weaknesses and strengths, on the bottom of the second page of the evaluation form.

Optional: Write and create a newsletter about the program in your major area of study. Research your program and include course descriptions, course learning objectives, certificate and degree options, prerequisites, and so on. Relate your program's course of study to current trends in business.

Assessment **two** 2

In this assessment, you will create a two-page newsletter.

1. Open **Redesign Text** located in your Unit03 folder.
2. Save the document with Save <u>A</u>s and name it **u03pa02, Disclosures**.
3. Redesign both pages of the newsletter and include the following elements and techniques:

   - Nameplate
   - Folio
   - Heading and subhead styles
   - Header and footer
   - Table of contents
   - Sidebar
   - Pull quote
   - Graphic image with caption
   - Spot color
   - A kicker, end signs, jump lines, and/or graphic images if desired or needed for copyfitting.
   - Tracking, leading, paragraph spacing, and so on to set the body copy attractively on the page.
   - Any design elements necessary to achieve consistency and unity between the two pages.

4. When completed, save the document again with the same name, **u03pa02, Disclosures**.
5. Print and then close **u03pa02, Disclosures**. (Ask your instructor about printing each page separately or printing the pages back to back.)
6. Evaluate your own work using the document evaluation checklist **(Document Evaluation Checklist.doc)** located in your Unit03 folder. Revise your document if any areas need improvement.

Assessment three 3

1. Create a cover for your portfolio with the following specifications:
   - Create a thumbnail sketch of your cover.
   - Use at least one graphic element such as WordArt, a watermark, ruled lines, a graphic image, or a scanned image.
   - Consider balance, focus, contrast, directional flow, and proportion when creating the cover.
2. Save the completed cover and name it **u03pa03, Cover**.
3. Print and then close **u03pa03, Cover**.

Optional: Create another cover for your portfolio. Assume you are applying for a government position or for a job in a comedy gallery and try to convey a tone that is appropriate to your purpose.

Assessment four 4

In this assessment you will open **Focal Point** in your Unit03 folder and create a two-page newsletter. You may use the Internet to find interesting articles about vision. Include the following specifications:

- You may select a Word or Publisher newsletter template or you may design this newsletter from scratch. You may use Word's column feature and/or incorporate linked text boxes. You may also borrow design elements from Publisher and copy and paste them into your newsletter. Be creative and remember to use plenty of white space. Create a company logo. *(Hint: You may add a color background to this logo by selecting the logo, clicking the Set Transparency Color button on the Picture toolbar, clicking the Fill Color button on the Drawing toolbar, and then selecting a color, gradient, or pattern.)*
- Insert several appropriate photographs or clip art images to enhance your document.
- The newsletter must be at least two pages in length.
- You may use the Internet to find interesting articles about vision. Use a search engine to aid you in your search, for example type vision in the *Search* text box at Google.com.
- Correct all errors and create styles to aid in reinforcing consistency.
- Save your document and name it **u03sa04, Focal Integrated**.
- Print your newsletter back-to-back and then close **u03sa04, Focal Integrated**.

Index